AMERICAN COLORS are raised over Ara Saki, southernmost point of Okinawa, by men of Company G, 2d Battalion, 22d Marines, symbolizing the end of organized resistance in the III Amphibious Corps zone of action.

OKINAWA:

VICTORY IN THE PACIFIC

Major Chas. S. Nichols, Jr., USMC

Henry I. Shaw, Jr.

HISTORICAL BRANCH
G-3 DIVISION
HEADQUARTERS
U. S. MARINE CORPS

1955

Marine Corps Monographs
In This Series

The Defense of Wake
The Battle for Tarawa
Marines at Midway
Bougainville and the Northern Solomons
The Guadalcanal Campaign
The Assault on Peleliu
Saipan: The Beginning of the End
The Seizure of Tinian
Marine Aviation in the Philippines
The Campaign on New Britain
Marines in the Central Solomons
The Recapture of Guam
The Marshalls: Increasing the Tempo
Iwo Jima: Amphibious Epic

For sale by the Superintendent of Documents, U. S. Government Printing Office
Washington 25, D. C.

5978

COVER PICTURE: Marines hurdle a stone wall as they drive
inland from the Hagushi Beaches on L–Day at Okinawa

Foreword

The Okinawa Operation was in many ways the most difficult of the Pacific War. Conceived, launched, and supported at long range, it required meticulous detail in both planning and execution. Bad weather, defenses which employed the rugged terrain with great skill and cunning, and a well-trained, resolute defense force combined to give the enemy an advantage that was overcome only by courage, ingenuity, and endurance of the highest order.

As Commanding General of the Sixth Marine Division, I was privileged to take part in this operation. I saw the many obstacles that had to be overcome, and was impressed each day with the great qualities of those who overcame them. This excellent account of that bitter struggle recalls those stirring days and testifies to the military virtues of the American people. It is a vital chapter in the history of our nation.

LEMUEL C. SHEPHERD, Jr.,
GENERAL, U. S. MARINE CORPS,
COMMANDANT OF THE MARINE CORPS.

Preface

OKINAWA: VICTORY IN THE PACIFIC is the fifteenth in a series of operational monographs prepared by the Historical Branch, G–3 Division, Headquarters U. S. Marine Corps, designed to give the military student and casual reader an accurate and detailed account of the operations in which Marines participated during World War II. These monographs are now being integrated into a final Operational History of the Marine Corps in World War II.

With Marines fighting directly beside Army units as a major component of the Tenth Army, Army activities are treated herein with sufficient detail to reflect the Marines' contribution to the overall mission.

Many officers and men who participated in this campaign have contributed to the preparation of this monograph by generously answering specific inquiries, commenting on preliminary drafts, or submitting to interview. Grateful acknowledgment is made herewith. Additionally, appreciation is extended to Lieutenant Colonel Philips D. Carlton and Lieutenant Colonel James R. Stockman, who prepared tentative histories of the Marine divisions at Okinawa which were distributed to key participants shortly after the war. The circulation of these accounts, dealing principally with small unit actions, elicited most helpful comment. Special recognition is extended to the Office of Naval History, Naval Records and Library, and Office of the Chief of Military History, Department of the Army—in particular Dr. Philip A. Crowl of the Pacific Section. Maps included herein were prepared by the Reproduction Section, Marine Corps Schools, Quantico, Virginia. Official Marine Corps photographs have been used to illustrate this monograph unless otherwise noted.

T. A. WORNHAM
BRIGADIER GENERAL, U. S. MARINE CORPS
ASSISTANT CHIEF OF STAFF, G–3

Contents

Page

Foreword. V

Preface. VI

Chapter I.   Background. 1
Strategic Situation, *p.* 1
Historical Notes, *p.* 3
Okinawa and the Okinawans, *p.* 6

Chapter II.   Planning ICEBERG. 12
Strategic Concepts, *p.* 12
Command Relationships, *p.* 17
Intelligence, *p.* 19
Tactical Planning, *p.* 22
Logistical Planning, *p.* 27

Chapter III. Preparations for the Assault. 30
Training and Rehearsing, *p.* 30
Mounting and Staging for the Assault, *p.* 34
Preliminary Covering Strikes, *p.* 36
Seizure of Kerama Retto, *p.* 38
Prelanding Operations, *p.* 43

Chapter IV.   Japanese Defensive Preparations. 48
The Thirty-second Army, *p.* 49
Strengthening the Defenses, *p.* 53
Reinforcing the Army, *p.* 56
Prelanding Dispositions, *p.* 59

Chapter V.   Seizure of the Beachhead. 63
L-Day, *p.* 63
Severing the Island, *p.* 69
Meeting the Enemy, *p.* 77
Logistical Progress, *p.* 80
Kamikaze, *p.* 82

Chapter VI.   Action in the North. 87
Securing the Eastern Islands, *p.* 87
6th Marine Division Advances, *p.* 90
Battle for Motobu Peninsula, *p.* 96

Page

Marines' "Guerrilla War," *p.* 104
Capture of Ie Shima, *p.* 111

Chapter VII. Developing the Shuri Defenses. 119
Penetrating the Outpost Line, *p.* 119
Build-up in the South, *p.* 124
Attack of 19 April, *p.* 126
Assaulting the Second Defense Ring, *p.* 131
1st Marine Division Joins the XXIV Corps, *p.* 134

Chapter VIII. IIIAC Enters the Lists. 142
Japanese Counterattack, *p.* 142
The Battle Lines Are Drawn, *p.* 151
Tenth Army Attacks, *p.* 160
Logistical Progress, *p.* 172

Chapter IX.   Reduction of the Shuri Bastion. 176
Sugar Loaf Hill, *p.* 176
Wana Draw, *p.* 185
Shuri Heights and Conical Hill, *p.* 192
Struggle in the Rain, *p.* 196
Japanese Withdrawal, *p.* 207

Chapter X.   Ushijima's Last Stand. 210
Breakout to the South, *p.* 210
The Capture of Oroku Peninsula, *p.* 217
Kunishi Ridge, *p.* 228
Iheya-Aguni Operation, *p.* 243
Yaeju Dake-Yuza Dake, *p.* 244
End of Organized Resistance, *p.* 249

Chapter XI.   Campaign Summary. 258
The Clean-up Drive, *p.* 258
The Tenth Army's Air Force, *p.* 261
Island Command Activities, *p.* 266
Tactical Evaluation, *p.* 269
Key to Conquest, *p.* 273

Page
Appendices. **276**
    I. Bibliography, *p.* 276
   II. Chronology, *p.* 281
  III. Command and Staff List of
       Marine Units on Okinawa, *p.* 284
  IV. III Amphibious Corps Task
       Organization, *p.* 298

Page
    V. Japanese Order of Battle, *p.* 302
   VI. Marine Casualties, *p.* 305
  VII. Marine and Naval Corpsmen
       Medal of Honor Winners, *p.* 309
 VIII. Navy Unit Commendations, *v.* 313
Index **316**

VIII

CHAPTER I

Background

They had come from the vast reaches of the Pacific, these men who stood offshore at Okinawa before dawn of 1945's Easter Sunday.

The impersonal summons of strategy had gathered them from the coconut groves and kunai plains of the Solomons, the coral islands of the Marshalls, the cane fields of the Marianas, and the jungles of the Philippines. They rode with the Pacific's largest fleet—a proud fleet which had taught the Japanese that it controlled the ocean.

A British armada guarded their south flank. To the north an American carrier task force stood poised to intercept attacks from the Imperial homeland less than 400 miles away.

The big guns of the fleet off the landing beaches scorched the haze of morning nautical twilight, and as the gunfire shifted inland more than 100 aircraft began their final runs above the beaches. The landing craft churned shoreward on a front nearly eight miles wide.

Ahead of the men in those tractors was a battle; behind them, a war. But also behind them, even if few considered it in that moment, was a finely geared combat machine precision tooled by days, months, and years of planning.

STRATEGIC SITUATION[1]

The basic strategic concept governing the offensive stages of the war with Japan was approved by President Roosevelt and Prime Minister Churchill during the Cairo Conference at the close of 1943. This concept envisioned an advance across the vast expanse of

the Pacific along two principal axes of operations. The forces commanded by General Douglas MacArthur were to advance along the north coast of New Guinea to the Philippines; and Admiral Chester W. Nimitz would direct a converging drive through the Central Pacific to the core of the Japanese defenses. Accomplishment of this broad plan entailed a series of concurrent and mutually supporting amphibious attacks directed toward the Luzon-Formosa-China triangle. As required, the major combatant elements of the Pacific Fleet would cover the specific operations within both strategic commands and contain the Japanese fleet.

Implementation of this strategy resulted in an advance toward the heart of the Japanese Empire that surged forward with constantly increasing acceleration throughout the entire year of 1944. The year opened with a landing in New Guinea at Saidor. In February deep thrusts into the Central Marshalls collapsed the outer shell of Empire defenses. On the southern flank, by the end of March a permanent breach in the Bismarck Archipelago barrier had been secured and airfields and harbors seized in the Admiralty Islands. The drive up

[1] Unless otherwise noted the material in this section is derived from *The War Reports of General of the Army George C. Marshall, General of the Army H. H. Arnold, and Fleet Admiral Ernest J. King*, (Philadelphia, 1945), hereinafter cited as *War Reports;* USSBS(Pac), NavAnalysis Div, *The Campaigns of the Pacific War*, (Washington, 1946), hereinafter cited as *Campaigns.*

the New Guinea coast began the following month with landings at Hollandia and Aitape. By midsummer Central Pacific forces were consolidating their hard-won footholds in the Southern Marianas after driving the entering wedge into the inner ring of Japanese island positions. At the end of July, by a series of leapfrogging envelopments, Southwest Pacific forces had advanced hundreds of miles along the northern coast of New Guinea, isolating thousands of enemy soldiers beyond hope of further effective employment. (See Map 1, Map Section.)

MacArthur's troops occupied Morotai in September, preparatory to attacking Mindanao. Simultaneously, Nimitz' forces linked the two lines of advance by the seizure of airfield sites and a fleet anchorage in the Western Carolines. Denial of the airfields to the Japanese secured the eastern flank of the Philippine assault while possession of the anchorage, at Ulithi, was vital to both the Philippine campaign and the movement north to Japan.

When the customary covering strikes by Admiral William F. Halsey's fast carrier forces, preliminary to the Morotai and Western Carolines operations, uncovered surprisingly weak resistance in the Central Philippines the line of advance through the Southwest Pacific veered northward. Halsey, ever aware of "the necessity of being alert for symptoms of enemy weakness and of being ready to exploit them," recommended cancellation of certain scheduled operations and an early return to the Philippines in the Leyte-Samar area.[2] Consequently, on the day that Peleliu was stormed and Morotai occupied, the Joint Chiefs of Staff made the significant decision to bypass Mindanao, cancel contemplated operations in the Carolines against Yap, and land on Leyte on 20 October.

A sound strategy implemented by careful planning, prompt exploitation of enemy weaknesses, and willingness to take calculated risks had paid high dividends throughout the year. The once formidable advance bases at Truk and Rabaul were rendered innocuous without direct assault. In conjunction with the campaigns in the Marianas and the Philippines the Japanese

fleet was brought to battle and decisively defeated. The relentless depredations of American submarines added constantly to the heavy toll of enemy merchant shipping. By the end of 1944 the sea power of Japan was virtually eliminated, and the spoiling attacks of B-29's were carrying the war to the heart of the Japanese homeland. The Allies had advanced 3,000 miles and established a strategic line 1,300 miles from Japan proper, cutting the enemy communications with their resources to the south.

Early in 1945, as Japanese strength ebbed, United States forces at long last gained a position from which a major assault could be launched against the enemy center of resistance. Luzon was invaded and the eastern strategic flank was advanced to within 750 miles of Tokyo by the capture of Iwo Jima.

By March 1945 the Pacific War had progressed far beyond all expectations of 12 months before, and with good reason Fleet Admiral Ernest J. King noted with pride the accomplishments of the preceding year in his second official report to the Secretary of the Navy. He cautioned, however, against complacency and warned of "a long, tough and laborious road ahead." [3] For as Admiral Raymond A. Spruance later said, "We were looking ahead to a prolonged operation at Okinawa, which was only 325 miles from Southern Kyushu." [4]

Okinawa was the central link in a chain of islands, the Nansei Shoto, which extended in an arc from the Japanese home island of Kyushu to the Japanese-held island of Formosa. Thus anchored on these two enemy bastions, the Nansei Shoto formed an effective barrier screening the East China Sea from the North Pacific. Okinawa was a vital communication center linking Japan and its holdings to the southwest. Largest and most populous island of the archipelago, it was suitable for the development of a large number of airfields and extensive base facilities. In addition to a small harbor, it possessed the only two substantial Japanese fleet anchorages south of Kyushu.

---

[2] FAdm W. F. Halsey and LCdr J. Bryan, III, *Admiral Halsey's Story*, (New York, 1947), 199.

[3] *War Reports*, 649.

[4] Adm R. A. Spruance, "The Victory in the Pacific," *Royal United Service Institution Journal*, November 1946, 552.

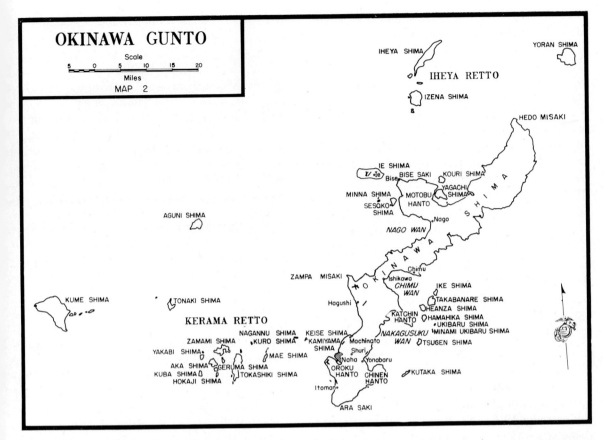

OKINAWA GUNTO

Scale

5   0   5   10   15   20

Miles

MAP 2

Okinawa, then, was a significant strategic objective. Its capture would secure command of the East China Sea and consequently open the approaches to the Yellow Sea and the Straits of Tsushima. Finally, it would provide a base for future operations against the Japanese homeland or the China coast.

HISTORICAL NOTES [5]

By the irony of fate and geographical misfortune, Okinawa occupies a unique position in the history of the rise and fall of the Japanese Empire. It was the scene of the final battle of the war that destroyed the Empire of Japan; and for the same basic reason (its position in relation to China and Japan), the island figured prominently in the operations that unleashed the forces of Japanese imperial expansion— Commodore Matthew C. Perry's expedition of nearly a century before.

The Perry voyage culminated 50 years of growing American interests in the Far East. Specifically, these interests involved trade with China and attempts to open the ports of Japan. At the beginning of the nineteenth century, the fur trade of the Pacific Northwest had provided the impetus for the promotion of trade with China; and, coincident with the decline of the fur trade in the 1820's, the rapid rise of the whaling industry in the North Pacific stimulated a desire for "ports of refuge and supply" [6] in Japan. Finally, in the second half of the 1840's, the extension of the boundaries of the United States to the Pacific coast, accompanied by an influx of settlers to that region, spurred the expansion of American Far Eastern relations to a climax. Consequently, in 1852,

---

[5] Unless otherwise noted the material in this section is derived from F. L. Hawks, *United States Japan Expedition by Com M. C. Perry*, 3 vols, (Washington, 1856), hereinafter cited as *Perry Narrative;* USAFPOA G–2 Study of Okinawa Gunto, n. d., hereinafter cited as *USAFPOA Study;* MIS, WD, Survey of the Nansei Shoto and the Nanpo Shoto, 15Feb43, hereinafter cited as *WD Survey.*

[6] *Perry Narrative*, I, 85.

Commodore Perry was commissioned to negotiate a commercial treaty with Japan.

Fully cognizant of the difficulties involved, Perry laid his plans accordingly. Although confident of ultimate success, relatively recent experience with the reluctant Japanese cast doubt in his mind "as to any immediate success in bringing that strange government to any practicable negotiation." [7] He therefore deemed it "necessary that the squadron should establish places of rendezvous at one or two of the islands south of Japan, having a good harbor and possessing facilities for obtaining water and supplies." [8] These islands, Perry continued, in further delineation of his plans, "called the Lew Chew group are said to be dependencies of Japan, as conquered by that power centuries ago; but their actual sovereignty is disputed by the government of China." [9]

This vague and anomalous status of the Ryukyus [10] in respect to China and Japan was one of long standing. It persisted for 250 years preceding Commodore Perry's arrival at Okinawa in 1853, and it continued in varying degrees another 40 years after his final departure the following year. Nevertheless, by direct negotiations with the local authorities, Perry established the proposed base at Okinawa preliminary to entering Japan.

The first foreigners to come into contact with the Okinawans were the Chinese, who initiated a series of forays into the Ryukyus in the sixth or seventh century. These raids continued in-

SHURI CASTLE is shown in prewar view from a captured Japanese tourist postcard. (Navy Photograph)

termittently for hundreds of years, but the Chinese never established firm military domination. However, when a Chinese envoy demanded tribute, shortly after the accession of the Ming Dynasty in 1368, the Okinawan king promptly complied and acknowledged himself a Chinese subject.

Amicable relations existed between Japan and the Ryukyus from very early times, but the Japanese apparently obtained a certain amount of jurisdiction over the islands in the mid-fifteenth century. Positive Japanese control was established in 1609 when the Okinawan king refused to contribute men and supplies to Hideoshi's Korean Campaigns. In reprisal, the Prince of Satsuma overran the country, devastated the land, captured the king, and exacted tribute. Henceforth, the Ryukyuan kingdom maintained a dubious semi-independent status, assenting to the dual suzerainty of China and Japan, and paying tribute to both.

The emergence of Japan as a modern power followed close on the heels of Commodore Perry's successful negotiations, and each stage of her meteoric rise from fuedalism was accompanied by a corresponding decline of Okinawan independence. When the Mikado was restored to dominant authority in 1867 the powers of the feudal lords passed to the imperial government, and the Satsumas were forced to relinquish their control of the Ryukyus to the Foreign Office. The Japanese feudal system was

---

[7] *Ibid.* The American unarmed ship *Morrison* was fired on when private interests attempted to open Japan in 1837. The precursor of the Perry Mission, under Como J. Biddle, failed even to begin negotiations in 1846, although the Japanese did provision Biddle's small squadron of two ships. C. Yanaga, *Japan Since Perry*, (New York, 1949), 16–17.

[8] *Perry Narrative*, I, 85.

[9] *Ibid.*

[10] "A Chinese envoy, Shukan, named the islands Loochoo [Lew Chew or Liuchiu] (or Ryuku in Japanese) as the islands resembled 'floating globes' or in another translation 'precious stone balls.'" *USAFPOA Study*, 1. Presumably the Japanese name Ryuku or Ryukyu stems from their inability to pronounce the letter "L". Throughout this monograph the more common spelling "Ryukyu" has been used.

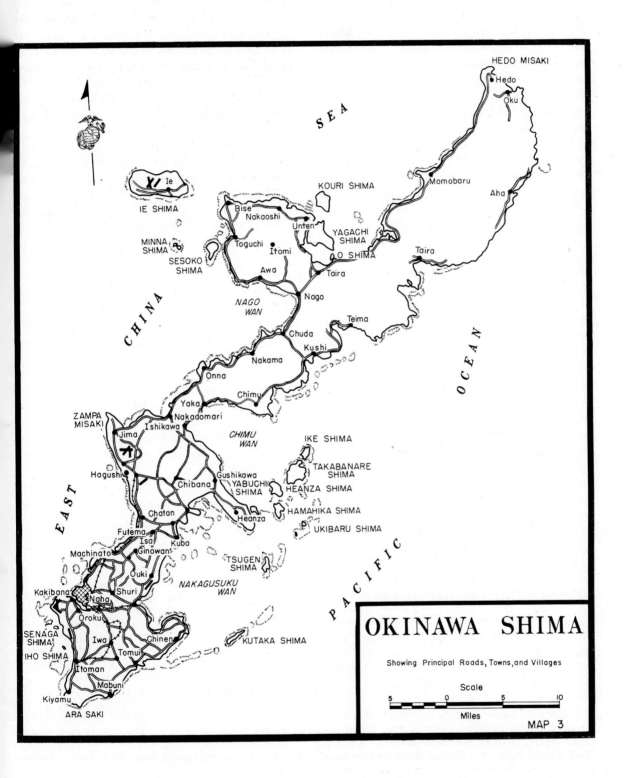

HEDO MISAKI
Hedo
Oku

SEA

Momobaru

Aha

KOURI SHIMA

Ie
IE SHIMA
Bise
Nakaoshi
Unten
YAGACHI
SHIMA
Taira
MINNA
SHIMA
Toguchi
Itomi
O SHIMA
Taira
SESOKO
SHIMA
Awa
Taira
Nago
CHINA
NAGO
WAN
Teima
Chuda
Kushi
Nakama
Onna
Chimu
Yaka
Nakadomari
IKE SHIMA
ZAMPA
MISAKI
Ishikawa
CHIMU
WAN
TAKABANARE
SHIMA
Jima
HEANZA SHIMA
Hagushi
Gushikawa
YABUCHI
SHIMA
HAMAHIKA SHIMA
Chibana
Heanza
EAST
Chatan
UKIBARU SHIMA
Futema
Isa
Kuba
Machinato
Ginowan
TSUGEN
SHIMA
Ouki
NAKAGUSUKU
WAN
Kakibana
Shuri
Naha
Oroku
SENAGA
Iwa
Chinen
KUTAKA SHIMA
SHIMA
Tomui
IHO SHIMA
Itoman
Mabuni
Kiyamu
ARA SAKI

OCEAN

PACIFIC

OKINAWA SHIMA

Showing Principal Roads, Towns, and Villages

Scale

5   0   5   10

Miles

MAP 3

abolished in 1871, and shortly thereafter the Okinawan king (although permitted to retain his regal title) was installed in a residence in Tokyo as a Marquis of Japan. Three years later the islands were transferred from the jurisdiction of the Minister for Foreign Affairs to that of the Home Minister, and further payment of tribute to China by the Okinawans was forbidden.

Despite this virtually complete political integration of Japan and the Ryukyus, China still maintained adamant claims to suzerainty over the islands. The Okinawans themselves protested to the utmost the idea of single sovereignty, and complained of being "heartlessly disowned by father China."[11] Indeed, even though the Okinawan king was deposed and replaced by a Japanese governor when the islands were incorporated into Japan proper as the prefecture of Okinawa in 1879, vestiges of the old tributary relationship still remained. Not until Japan resorted to the sword in the Sino-Japanese War of 1894 was the last tenuous connection with China severed.

From 1879 onwards, through education, conscription, and careful supervision of local government, the Japanese conducted a comprehensive program aimed toward complete amalgamation of the Okinawans. The political status of Okinawa prefecture was equalized with the northern prefectures in 1920 by the establishment of a prefectural assembly and Okinawan representation in the Japanese Diet. In 1943, the domestic structure of Japan was reorganized, and Okinawa was combined with seven other prefectures into the District of Kyushu.

OKINAWA AND THE OKINAWANS[12]

The Ryukyu Retto, which comprises most of the Nansei Shoto, includes five major island groups: the Osumi, Tokara, Amami, Okinawa, and Sakishima Guntos. Okinawa Shima occu-

pies the central position in the Okinawa Gunto. The principal satellites surrounding the main island are: Kerama Retto, Kume Shima, Aguni Shima, and Ie Shima to the west; Iheya Retto and Yoron Shima in the north; and a chain of small islands, called the Eastern Islands by the Americans, running roughly parallel to the east coast of southern Okinawa.[13] (See Map 2)

The island of Okinawa is some 60 miles in length, oriented generally northeast to southwest, and of variable width. In the north the Motobu Peninsula, jutting out into the East China Sea, extends the island to its maximum breadth of 18 miles. Similarly, the Katchin Peninsula, stretching out toward the Pacific, widens the island to 15 miles just south of the Ishikawa Isthmus. This isthmus, only two miles wide and the narrowest part of the island, separates Okinawa into two sharply contrasting regions.

The northern portion, constituting two-thirds of the island's area, is mountainous, heavily wooded, and rimmed with dissected terraces.[14] Blanketed with a dense growth of live oak and conifers, climbing vines and underbrush, the highlands of the north rise to jagged peaks of 1,000–1,500 feet which extend the entire length of the region. Normally, the terraces bordering the spinous mountains terminate at the coast in sheer cliffs.

The shallow topsoil of the interior of northern Okinawa, principally clay or sandy loam, is well drained by numerous small, swift streams. With few exceptions, it is trafficable

---

[11] *Ibid.*, 3.

[12] Unless otherwise noted the material in this section is derived from CinCPac-CinCPOA Bull 161–44, Okinawa Gunto, 15Nov44, hereinafter cited as *CinCPOA Bull 161–44;* EngrSect, FMFPac, Engineer Intelligence Information, Okinawa Shima, n.d.; *WD Survey; USAFPOA Study.* The terrain description presented furnishes a general picture of Okinawa at the time of

the American landings before the giant earth-moving machinery of the engineers and Seabees substantially altered its appearance. Detailed studies of various sections of the island that figured prominently in the operation will be embodied in the narrative.

[13] Free translation of Japanese geographical terms, regarding which there is no hard and fast rule, yields *Shoto*—various islands or group of islands; *Gunto*— a group of islands; and *Shima* or *Jima*—an island. A glance at a map will show that there has been no norm followed in the distribution of these names. In this monograph wherever there has been a question regarding the proper name to use, the term in most common usage has been adopted.

[14] The term "dissected terrace" refers to an area which was once essentially flat, but which has been so cut up by erosion that the high portions between ravines are the only remnants of the former flatland.

TYPICAL PATCHWORK TERRAIN of central Okinawa with its small fields, walled houses, and scattered woods appears in this pre-invasion aerial photograph. (Navy Photograph)

under all conditions, a military boon largely cancelled out by the paucity of roads, which were mainly along the coast. Furthermore, the rugged topography of the country, aggravated by the lush vegetation, precludes cross-country movement.

Excluding a limited area just south of Ishikawa Isthmus which resembles northern Okinawa, the southern third of the island is for the most part rolling, lightly wooded country broken by precipitous scarps and ravines. Four-fifths of the land is arable, and the valleys, hills, and plateaus are intensely cultivated. The hills rarely exceed 500 feet in elevation, and the few streams flowing through them are narrow and shallow. While Okinawan streams

are easily bridged or forded, they are frequently rendered significant obstacles by steep, thickly forested embankments and flash floods. (See Map 4)

The densely populated south [15] contained an intricate network of roads, but only one, the broad stone-paved highway connecting the cities of Naha and Shuri, could support two lanes of traffic. Although the narrow, arterial routes were surfaced with coral, other thoroughfares were no more than cart trails. Because of the drainage and soil conditions of the region, these

---

[15] An area about four times as large as Guam, Okinawa was inhabited by twenty times as many people, three-quarters of whom were located in the southern third of the island.

LYRE-SHAPED Okinawan tomb of the type that studded the hillsides of the island. Many of these tombs were converted into strongpoints by Japanese defenders.

primitive roads were for the most part impassable during prolonged wet weather. In the Naha-Shuri area the road net was augmented by approximately 30 miles of narrow-gauge railway. A trans-island line ran from Naha to Yonabaru by way of Kobakura and Kokuba, while branch lines linked Kobakura with Kadena and Kokuba with Itoman. In some places the track of this rail system was laid below the surface of the ground in cuts deep enough to conceal a man walking upright. (See Map 3)

Okinawa lies between 26° 03' and 26° 52' north latitude and 127° 41' and 128° 41' east longitude, and its climate is characterized by moderate temperatures throughout the year. Minimum temperatures are above 40°, with a mean maximum in July of 89°. Relative humidity, however, is high in all months, winter humidity averaging only 10% less than that prevailing in the summer.[16] The year-round humidity is highest in the early morning hours and lowest in the early afternoon.

Annual precipitation is heavy and erratic, and a day's downpour frequently equals a month's average. In general, the heaviest rains occur from May through September. An average of almost two typhoons a month pass through the area in the season from May to

---

[16] The summer humidity range is 72%–90%; the winter range is 65%–80%.

November. For the remainder of the year the normal typhoon track lies well to the east of Okinawa.

In 1940 Okinawa had a population of nearly half a million. Within this community most of the higher officials, businessmen, and urban "white collar" class were main-island Japanese. The rural element, who formed the broad base of the social structure, comprised the bulk of the native populace.

On small farms, averaging little more than an acre and a half, the Okinawans cultivated three principal crops. Half the arable land produced sweet potatoes, the staple food of both men and animals. Second in acreage to the sweet potato, sugar cane constituted the principal commercial crop. Rice, the third of the group, was grown in the low alluvial coastal regions, but the yield fell far below local requirements.

Individually sheltered by stone walls or bamboo windbreaks, the small, thatched, clay farmhouses were customarily clustered in villages around an open market place. The size of these villages ranged from less than 100 to more than 1,000 inhabitants. The towns (Itoman and Nago) were substantially outsize villages with several modern business and government buildings. In the cities (Naha and Shuri) many of the public buildings were of stone or concrete construction, and the one-story wooden dwellings were surrounded by stone walls. Shuri had been the ancient capital of the Ryukyus and the citadel of its kings still stood on a high hill on its outskirts. Naha, with a population of more than 60,000, was the commercial and communications center of the Ryukyus, as well as the seat of the prefectural government.

The elected prefectural assembly acted as a gubernatorial advisory body, but the governor could accept or ignore as he saw fit any advice tendered. He could also disapprove any legislative act; and he answered for his actions only to the Home Minister, on whose recommendation he was appointed. Local assemblies also were elected in the cities, towns, and townships, the latter composed of groups of rural settlements. These local assemblies selected a mayor for towns and townships. In

DRESS and physical appearance of typical Okinawan natives is shown is this photograph taken shortly after the Tenth Army landing.

the cities a council was elected. The local administrative units were directly under the governor, and their acts were subject to his veto. Both assemblies and councils could be dissolved by the Home Minister.

Although the Japanese educational system reduced the language barrier to some extent,[17] it failed to apply to the native population more than a thin veneer of Japanese culture. Generations of direct Chinese influence stamped the Okinawans with national characteristics that could not be removed by half a dozen decades of formal education.[18] The natives retained their own culture, religion, and form of ancestor worship. The outstanding material manifestations of their particular customs were the lyre-shaped tombs which thickly studded the countryside. Despite marked physical resemblance and common ethnological origins,[19] the Japanese and Okinawans remained essen-

---

[17] Although the Japanese and Okinawan languages are derived from the same archaic tongue, they are mutually unintelligible.

[18] At the time of the Manchu conquest of China, in the mid-seventeenth century, a number of nonconformist Chinese families fled to Okinawa. These emigres and their descendants generally became the schoolmasters of the country. *Perry Narrative*, I, 223.

[19] Both Japanese and Okinawans stem from branches of the Ainu aborigines; however, there is a greater infusion of Mongoloid and Maylayan blood in the Okinawans.

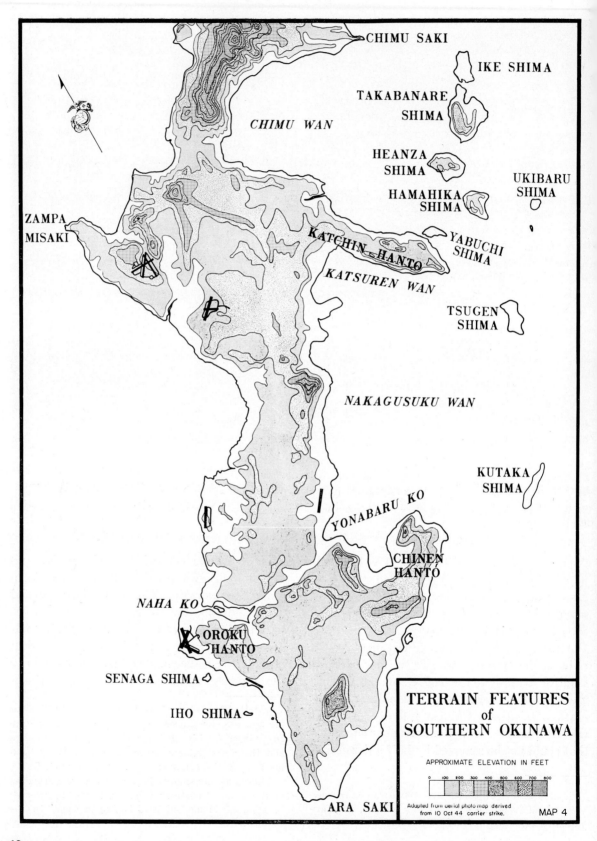

CHIMU SAKI

IKE SHIMA

TAKABANARE
SHIMA

CHIMU WAN

HEANZA
SHIMA

UKIBARU
SHIMA

HAMAHIKA
SHIMA

ZAMPA
MISAKI

KATCHIN HANTO

YABUCHI
SHIMA

KATSUREN WAN

TSUGEN
SHIMA

NAKAGUSUKU WAN

KUTAKA
SHIMA

YONABARU KO

CHINEN
HANTO

NAHA KO

OROKU
HANTO

SENAGA SHIMA

IHO SHIMA

ARA SAKI

TERRAIN FEATURES
of
SOUTHERN OKINAWA

APPROXIMATE ELEVATION IN FEET

| 0 | 100 | 200 | 300 | 400 | 500 | 600 | 700 | 800 |

Adapted from aerial photo map derived
from 10 Oct 44 carrier strike.

MAP 4

ially foreign to each other.[20] From the native islanders standpoint, there was a deep feeling of resentment because of the social, political, and economic discrimination that existed in favor of the Japanese.[21]

The tacit assumption by the Japanese of the Ryukyuans' inferior status did not prevent the imposition of one obligation of citizenship—military service. The periodic calls of various age groups into the ranks affected natives of Okinawa and the rest of the Ryukyus as well as those of Honshu and Kyushu. A reservoir of experienced reservists, who had completed their active service in the armed forces of the Empire, was available for recall. Captured Japanese orders, organization tables, and military proclamations indicate that many of these reservists were integrated into regular Japanese units assigned to the defense of the Nansei Shoto.[22]

Except for regular drafts of men leaving for service and the unwelcome news of those who had died for the Emperor, the early stages of the war touched the rustic life of the islands very little. The situation of the garrison on Okinawa typified the state of readiness of all the major islands of the group.

The Nakagusuku Wan Fortress Artillery Unit, whose formidable title disguised its actual lack of strength, arrived on the island in 1941. Numbering less than 600 men, organized into a headquarters and three batteries with six 75mm and two 12cm guns, the unit furnished inadequate protection to the anchorage for which it was named. For three years this organization, together with a few lightly-armed guard companies, a skeletal naval base force, and a minimum of airfield maintenance personnel, constituted the entire garrison of Okinawa Gunto.[23]

The importance of the Nansei Shoto to the defensive cordon surrounding Japan proper was heightened in early 1944 by the clear implication of the converging Allied pincers in the Southwest and Central Pacific. On 1 April 1944, Imperial General Headquarters set up the Thirty-second Army, with headquarters on Okinawa, to control the defense of the island chain.[24] The months immediately following saw substantial reinforcements, ground, naval, and air, flow into the Thirty-second Army area. In preparation for "a show-down battle . . . for the preservation of national unity when the enemy advances to the Nansei Shoto," the Japanese began to dig themselves into the naturally strong defensive terrain.[25]

Planners on both sides realized that the topographical characteristics of the islands, especially Okinawa with its wide and deep area for the deployment of troops, projected a battle on a scale as yet unseen in the Pacific. In the coming engagement the Japanese counted on concentrating "the combined force of land, sea, and air power . . . for the destruction of the enemy." [26]

---

[20] A Japanese superior private, who landed on Okinawa in late 1944, after a visit to Shuri noted in his diary, that "the houses and customs here resemble those of China and remind one of a Chinese town." CinCPac-CinCPOA Bull 147–45, Translations and Interrogations No 32, 16Jun45, Diary of Superior Pvt, 272d IIB, 43–49.

[21] As the war progressed, this feeling apparently rose very near to the surface. In November 1944, a Japanese soldier recorded that "the natives bear ill feeling toward military personnel, and as the days go by, their feelings appear in their actions. This has become a very unpleasant place to live." CinCPac-CinCPOA Bull 161–45, Translations and Interrogations No 34, 27Jun45, Diary of Signalman, 5th Sea Raiding Base Hq, 51–53.

[22] Tenth Army G–2, Combat Intelligence Collecting Agency Subsection Translations Nos 4–308, 17Apr–4Jul45, hereinafter cited as CICAS Trans. See especially CICAS Trans No 83, Standards for the Establishment of Nansei Shoto Garrison Plans, 1Jan45.

[23] Tenth Army G–2 Intelligence Monograph, August 1945, Part I, Sect B, 10; Part I, Sect D, Chap 1, 3, hereinafter cited as IntelMono.

[24] Ibid., Part I, Sect B, 8.

[25] Tenth Army G–2 Weekly Summary No 1, 28May45, Annex B, 32d Army Ord #82, 19Jul44.

[26] Ibid., 32d Army Instructions, 6Aug44.

CHAPTER II

Planning Iceberg

The fundamental principle underlying all operations of war—to project superior combat power, successively, upon the decisive points of a theater of war—is simplicity itself. The difficulty lies in recognizing these points and selecting the most favorable lines of operations. A different state of policy, strategy, and relative strength requires continual re-evaluation and revision of strategical estimates and plans. Thus, strategical plans must be kept up to date during the course of a campaign; but the extent of the field of strategy, plus the breadth of experience and knowledge of those charged with its formulation, provide ample room for honest differences of opinion. Consequently, the views of General MacArthur relative to the conduct of the war with the Japanese were often at variance with the thinking of Admiral King concerning Pacific strategy.

STRATEGIC CONCEPTS

In the early stages of the strategic offensive in the Pacific, General MacArthur, determined to return to the Philippines, doubted the necessity of capturing the Marianas and generally opposed the Central Pacific approach. From Admiral King's viewpoint occupation of the Marianas was essential, the need to recapture the entire Philippine archipelago was questionable, and a drive through the Central Pacific toward the China coast, probably by way of Formosa, should constitute the main effort.[1]

These conflicting concepts were partially resolved by the Joint Chiefs of Staff on 12 March 1944. Admiral Nimitz was directed to land in the southern Marianas on 15 June, and attack the Palaus on 15 September 1944. General MacArthur's instructions were to capture Hollandia in April and contemplated eventual occupation of Mindanao on 15 November. The long-range strategy outlined in the directive also required CinCPOA [2] to prepare plans for an assault on Formosa early in 1945, while CinCSWPA was charged with the preparation of plans for the recapture of Luzon "should such operation prove necessary prior to the move on Formosa." [3]

---

[1] FAdm E. J. King and Cdr W. M. Whitehill, *Fleet Admiral King: A Naval Record*, (New York, 1952), 537, 566, hereinafter cited as *King Naval Record*. For a detailed discussion of the development of strategic plans culminating in the decision to seize the southern Marianas see Maj C. W. Hoffman, *Saipan: The Beginning of the End*, MC Historical Monograph, (Washington, 1950), 17ff, hereinafter cited as *Saipan*.

[2] Adm Nimitz as senior naval officer in the Pacific was in command of all ships in the Pacific Fleet (CinCPac). At the same time, he and Gen MacArthur divided American command of Pacific areas. Nimitz exercised control of all Army, Navy, and Marine forces in the South, Central, and North Pacific, jointly titled Pacific Ocean Areas, as CinCPOA. MacArthur had the same role in the Southwest Pacific (CinCSWPA). CinCSoWesPac is the abbreviation of MacArthur's title used in most naval documents; however, CinCSWPA appears in JCS documents and will be used throughout this monograph.

[3] JCS 713/4, 12Mar44.

YONTAN AIRFIELD, strategic objective in IIIAC zone of action, photographed on 4 April. (Army Photograph)

As the summer of 1944 drew near, the strategy of the war against Germany had crystallized, and the Anglo-American armies in the United Kingdom were poised for the decisive cross-channel attack to "enter the continent of Europe and . . . undertake operations aimed at the heart of Germany and the destruction of her armed forces." [4] Pacific strategy still was fluid. Early in May 1944, during the lull preceding the landings in France and the Marianas, Admiral King met with Admirals Nimitz and Halsey in San Francisco to consider probable operations in the Pacific subsequent to the latter campaign.

In the discussions during this conference of the top naval command, opening sea communications with China and securing air bases in the Western Pacific were primary considerations. [5] A strong Japanese drive on Chungking was in progress at the moment, which indicated a pos-

sibility that Japan might attempt to force a separate peace with China. [6] Consequently, Admiral Nimitz advanced the view that establishment of positions on the China coast, in order to supply and equip the Chinese and exploit their manpower potential, appeared essential. It was envisaged that operations along the coast would progress northward as far as Shanghai, with a view to gaining river and rail access to the interior. [7]

In mid-June, when the lodgment in Europe had been successfully effected and concurrent with the initial landings on Saipan, the Combined Chiefs of Staff turned their attention to operations in the Pacific following the campaign in the Marianas. The possibility of bypassing the Philippines and Palaus and attacking Formosa before it could be substantially reinforced was considered. The fundamental factors involved in the selection of Formosa as

---

[4] *War Reports*, 178.
[5] *King Naval Record*, 542.

[6] *War Reports*, 218.
[7] *King Naval Record*, 541–542.

a major objective were its value as a base for very long-range (VLR) bombers, and the necessity of occupying that island in order to get supplies into China. The criterion governing the Combined Chiefs' interchange of views was the importance of doing the unexpected. Hence, the concept of avoiding Formosa and moving directly to Kyushu, in the interests of gaining strategic surprise, was presented for study.[8]

While the Joint Staff planners studied the various possibilities for accelerating the Pacific war, including a direct invasion of Japan proper without reference to Formosa, the Joint Chiefs set up a tentative schedule of operations for planning purposes. Based on the hypothesis that all operations preliminary to the Formosan campaign, which were contemplated in the directive of 12 March 1944, had been consummated, an over-all concept of operations subsequent to the capture of Formosa was projected. It envisaged advances into the Bonins and the Ryukyus, in concert with a continuing operation along the southeast coast of China northward from Amoy. These operations were to begin about 1 April 1945 and the positions gained in these areas consolidated by the end of September, preparatory to assaults on Kyushu and the Tokyo Plain which were to be undertaken before the close of the year.[9]

When President Roosevelt visited Pearl Harbor in the latter part of July 1944 to confer with Admiral Nimitz and General MacArthur, the decisive campaign for the southern Marianas was drawing to a close, but the next major move toward defeat of Japan still was unresolved. Consequently, at this meeting the two theater commanders presented their differing views to the Commander in Chief for decision.

MacArthur contended that a major attack against the Japanese in territory north of Luzon should not be attempted until the Philippines had been occupied. Moreover, he was of the opinion that, except for landing craft and naval support, the resources already available to him were sufficient to recapture the Philippines.

The Navy plan developed by Nimitz proposed "by-passing the Philippines and attacking Formosa."[10] However, during the discussions, the naval commander agreed that future developments might indicate a need to occupy Luzon, although at the time he felt that other areas in the archipelago offered equal advantages and could be taken at less cost. Admiral Nimitz believed his forces were sufficient for either the Luzon or Formosa operations, and the area of disagreement was finally narrowed down to the desirability of retaking the Manila area.[11]

A tentative course of action evolved by the Joint Chiefs of Staff in September contemplated the following schedule of operations: Talaud, 15 October 1944; Mindanao, 15 November 1944; Leyte-Suriago Area, 20 December 1944; and either the invasion of the Formosa-Amoy Area on 1 March 1945 or Luzon on 20 February 1945. In the event the Formosa operation materialized, it was anticipated that the subsequent schedule would include the Bonins in April and the Ryukyus in May. Operations along the China coast during the period of March to June were proposed, with the invasion of Japan proper to begin in October.[12]

Shortly after this tentative plan was promulgated, Lieutenant General Millard F. Harmon, Commanding General, Army Air Forces, Pacific Ocean Areas (CGAAFPOA), submitted a plan to Admiral Nimitz proposing that the Formosa operation be abandoned in favor of the Bonins and Ryukyus. It envisaged the capture of Iwo Jima by 1 January 1945 and the reconquest of Luzon by 1 June 1945. Concurrent with the operations of Southwest Pacific forces on Luzon, Pacific Ocean Areas troops were to seize Okinawa and Amami-O-Shima in the Ryukyus. Kyushu would be invaded in September.

---

[8] *Ibid.*, 552.

[9] JCS 924, 30Jun44.

[10] FAdm W. D. Leahy, *I Was There*, (New York, 1950), 250, hereinafter cited as *Leahy*. Presumably, "bypassing the Philippines" did not preclude the Mindanao operation, inasmuch as the purpose for which that island was to be occupied, as set forth in the JCS directive then in effect, was to obtain air bases to support an attack on Formosa; either direct or by way of Luzon. JCS 713/4, 12Mar44.

[11] *Leahy*, 250–251.

[12] CCS 417/8, 9Sept44.

Although offered as an alternative in the event that Campaign Plan CAUSEWAY (Formosa) should not be implemented, the compelling arguments with which General Harmon supported the proposed change of strategy clearly indicated that the concept of bypassing Formosa was not only practicable but also desirable. The burden of the theater air commander's discussion was a comparison of the relative utility of Formosa and the Marianas for the conduct of air operations against Japan.

General Harmon noted that the distances from Formosa and the Marianas to Japan were approximately equal, but the geographical situation of Formosa produced inherent disadvantages militating against its usefulness as a base for long-range air operations. The plans then current provided for only partial occupation of the island—the southwestern portion. Inasmuch as the prevailing winds were from the north, heavily loaded B–29's taking off would be exposed to hostile antiaircraft-fire when most vulnerable. Along the entire route to targets on Honshu, through the Ryukyuan chain and across Kyushu, the flights could be easily tracked and intercepted. These obstacles would be avoided in making strikes from the Marianas, especially after the capture of Iwo Jima and the establishment of bases there for fighter escorts. Finally, more favorable flying weather prevailed between the Marianas and Honshu.

Surveys of the Marianas indicated potential bases for 24 B–29 groups. Construction of these facilities promised a task of considerable magnitude, but comparable development of Formosa entailed an even greater undertaking. Besides the formidable task of developing the area, logistic support of Formosa would be considerably more complicated and its initial occupation costly and time consuming.

From the standpoint of over-all strategy, General Harmon believed that the capture and use of Luzon was essential, and that engaging in major operations on Formosa would decelerate the momentum of the advance against the Japanese Empire. Air operations from Luzon could neutralize Formosa and effectively cut enemy communications to South China and Malaya.[13]

When invasion of the Palaus brought Central Pacific forces up on the northern flank of the Southwest Pacific theater and closed this gap in the front, strategy in the Pacific began to crystallize rapidly. The single moot question remaining from the Commander in Chief's conference with the two theater commanders was resolved by the tactically bold and strategically brilliant decision to begin the Philippine invasion at Leyte rather than Mindanao.[14]

This momentous decision, accompanied by a firm directive to enter the Central Philippines two months earlier than had been tentatively planned, gave occasion for immediate re-examination of the objectives of the Formosa operation in the light of the changed situation.

Formosa had been selected as an objective for the purposes of bombing Japanese industry; opening sea and air communications to the China Coast, while denying the same to the enemy between the Empire and the resources to the south; supporting a further advance into China; and maintaining "unremitting military pressure against Japan."[15]

Over and above the questionable worth of Formosa as a base from which VLR bombers could be launched against the enemy homeland, the acquisition of the anchorage facilities of Leyte suggested the possibility of an advance northward, without securing intermediate positions on the China Coast. Occupation of Iwo Jima and Okinawa would be accomplished as

[13] CGAAFPOA Ltr to CinCPOA (no file or serial number), 11Sept44.

[14] *Leahy*, 251. Seizure of Leyte would breach the barrier screening the South China Sea and protecting the Japanese lines of communication to South China and Malaya. It would dislocate this strategic front of the enemy by separating his principal forces garrisoned on Mindanao and Luzon. In order to re-establish a continuous front, the Japanese would be obliged to bring their fleet into action and expose it to destruction. Decisive defeat of the hostile fleet would enable American forces to roll up the flanks created by the penetration under their own terms and defeat the main forces of the enemy in detail. MajGen J. F. C. Fuller, *The Second World War*, (New York, 1949), 373–374.

[15] CinCPOA Ltr to ComFifthFlt, ComGenTen, and ComPhibsPac, serial 00013, 16Sept44.

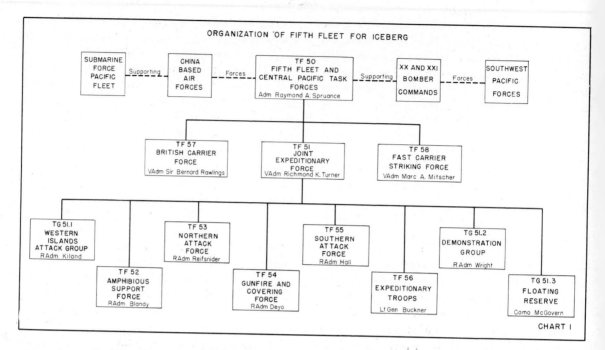

ORGANIZATION OF FIFTH FLEET FOR ICEBERG

SUBMARINE FORCE PACIFIC FLEET	—Supporting—	CHINA BASED AIR FORCES

CHINA BASED AIR FORCES —Forces— TF 50 FIFTH FLEET AND CENTRAL PACIFIC TASK FORCES (Adm Raymond A. Spruance) —Supporting— XX AND XXI BOMBER COMMANDS —Forces— SOUTHWEST PACIFIC FORCES

TF 57 BRITISH CARRIER FORCE (VAdm Sir Bernard Rawlings)

TF 51 JOINT EXPEDITIONARY FORCE (VAdm Richmond K. Turner)

TF 58 FAST CARRIER STRIKING FORCE (VAdm Marc A. Mitscher)

TG 51.1 WESTERN ISLANDS ATTACK GROUP (RAdm Kiland)

TF 52 AMPHIBIOUS SUPPORT FORCE (RAdm Blandy)

TF 53 NORTHERN ATTACK FORCE (RAdm Reifsnider)

TF 54 GUNFIRE AND COVERING FORCE (RAdm Deyo)

TF 55 SOUTHERN ATTACK FORCE (RAdm Hall)

TF 56 EXPEDITIONARY TROOPS (Lt Gen Buckner)

TG 51.2 DEMONSTRATION GROUP (RAdm Wright)

TG 51.3 FLOATING RESERVE (Como McGovern)

CHART I

soon as practicable after CAUSEWAY. The necessity of opening communications to the coast of China was nullified further by the success of recent Japanese offensives against the Chinese. This implied the ineffectiveness of China's forces and rendered doubtful the expediency of attempting to support a Chinese land campaign.

In view of a possible reorientation of strategy which would shift the direction of advance northwards toward Japan, Admiral Nimitz directed the principal CAUSEWAY commanders, Admiral Raymond A. Spruance, Vice Admiral Richmond K. Turner, and Lieutenant General Simon B. Buckner, Jr., to recommend suitable physical objectives in the Formosa-Amoy-Pescadores areas for the CAUSEWAY Operation. Guiding considerations were the number of naval and air bases which should be established and the number of major troop units required.[16] Ten days later General Buckner replied that sufficient troops were not available and CAUSEWAY was not feasible.[17] Within hours of Buckner's reply Lieutenant General Robert C. Richardson, Jr., Commanding General, United States Army Forces Pacific

Ocean Areas (CGAFPOA), who had also been invited to express his views, forwarded his remarks indicating that operations in the Formosa area were also undesirable.

General Richardson reiterated General Harmon's objections to Formosa as a B–29 base and agreed that possession of Luzon negated the need for occupying Formosa. From the ground forces point of view, an advance along the coast of China would contribute very little toward the prosecution of the war. Since the seizure of Formosa was for the purpose of supporting a further advance into China, he concluded that the capture of Formosa was unnecessary. On the other hand, the facilities which would be gained by possession of Luzon, together with the bases which it would be possible to obtain in the Ryukyus and the Bonins offered "unusual advantages for the rapid advance on the final objective, and prosecution of the war."[18]

Admiral Spruance, who also favored the capture of Iwo Jima and Okinawa rather than Formosa, has described his part in the formulation of the strategy of the Okinawa operation as follows:

When Admirals King and Nimitz visited Saipan about 12 July 1944—shortly after the end of organized

---

[16] Ibid.

[17] USAFMidPac, History of the G–5 Sect, 7Dec41–2Sept45, 176.

[18] ComGenPOA Ltr to CinCPOA, serial 00013, 27Sept44.

esistance—Admiral King asked me for my ideas on my next operation. At this time the Philippines campaign had not yet been definitely decided upon, but I expected to be relieved by Admiral Halsey after the completion of the Marianas operation, which still involved the capture of Guam and Tinian. My reply to Admiral King was that I would like to take Okinawa.

Before I arrived back in Pearl Harbor in the *Indianapolis* about 4 September 1944, I gave considerable thought to the question of the next operation for the Fifth Fleet. I came to the conclusion that Okinawa was the proper objective, but that Iwo Jima would have to be captured first. On reporting to Admiral Nimitz, he informed me that my next operation would be Amoy and Formosa. I then recommended that we take first Iwo Jima and then Okinawa instead, but was told that the decision had already been made for Formosa, and that, as soon as I was ready, I should fly to California for about two weeks' leave.

Shortly before I was due to return to Pearl Harbor, I received orders to delay and to attend the CominCh-CinCPac conference in San Francisco about 28 September. It was at this conference that Admiral Nimitz recommended to Admiral King the substitution of Iwo Jima and Okinawa for Amoy and Formosa. This change was necessary because General Buckner had said he did not have enough service troops for an objective as large as Formosa, but he could handle Okinawa. The Marines had said they could take Iwo Jima. The paper submitting Admiral Nimitz' recommendations for the change was, I believe, prepared by his War Plans Officer, Captain Forrest Sherman. It was the clear and logical presentation needed to overcome Admiral King's strong belief in the value of Formosa.[19]

Thus, by 1 October 1944 Admiral Nimitz had conferred with Admiral King and apprised him of the views of his senior commanders in the Pacific. On the basis of this consultation, King proposed a course of future action in the Pacific to the Joint Chiefs of Staff.[20] Whereupon the Joint Chiefs directed General MacArthur to seize and occupy Luzon on 20 December 1944 and Admiral Nimitz to effect a landing on Iwo Jima 20 January 1945. These were to be followed by Operation ICEBERG, the Okinawa campaign, on 1 March 1945.[21] The date for the Okinawa landing, however, depended on securing Iwo Jima in time to release fire support units and close air support for Okinawa; prompt release of supporting naval forces and assault shipping from Luzon; and whether preliminary strikes against the Ryukyus, Formosa, and the Empire promised indisputable control of the sea and air in the objective area.[22]

CAUSEWAY was held in abeyance as a strategic objective for possible future implementation.[23] The fundamental command and organization concepts which had been devised for that operation were retained for employment at Okinawa.[24]

COMMAND RELATIONSHIPS[25]

The command relationships, which had hitherto been prescribed in the Central Pacific for the seizure of small land areas far removed from Japan required modification for the Okinawa campaign. The amphibious operations which had carried Admiral Nimitz' forces across the Pacific had required relatively few ground forces,[26] but now the establishment of one or more positions in the Ryukyus called for the employment of a field army. Proximity of the objective to the Japanese homeland and major enemy bases presaged a prolonged period of active combat.

Admiral Spruance, Commander Fifth Fleet, was designated as the implementing commander of the operation, under the strategic direction of Admiral Nimitz, Commander in Chief,

[19] Adm R. A. Spruance Ltr to CMC, 28Sept54.

[20] E. J. King Memo for JCS, 2Oct44. Concerning Adm Nimitz' own position during the "dispatch debate" anent the decision to bypass Luzon in favor of Formosa, the impression gained by the Chief of Staff of Tenth Army was that "Nimitz was holding out for Formosa instead of Luzon because the Joint Chiefs of Staff had directed him to plan the operation and be ready to execute it at a specified time. There was nothing personal in Nimitz' position; he was simply doing what he had been told to do." MajGen E. D. Post Ltr to CMC, 5Oct54.

[21] JCS 713/19, 3Oct44.

[22] CinCPOA Joint Staff Study—ICEBERG, 25Oct44, 1, hereinafter cited as *ICEBERG Study.*

[23] JCS 713/19, 30Oct44.

[24] Tenth Army AR, Ryukyus, 26Mar–30Jun45, 3Sept45, Chap 3, 3, hereinafter cited as *Tenth Army AR.*

[25] Unless otherwise noted the material in this section is derived from CinCPOA OpPlan 14–44, 21Nov44, Annex F; Tenth Army Tentative OpPlan 1–45, 6Jan45, Annexes 1 and 12.

[26] At Iwo Jima the ratio of naval personnel afloat to ground forces employed ashore was almost four to one. *War Reports*, 648.

LIEUTENANT GENERAL SIMON B. BUCKNER, Commanding General, Expeditionary Troops (Tenth Army), in the Okinawa operation. General Buckner was killed in action just prior to the successful ending of the campaign. (Army Photograph)

Pacific Ocean Areas.[27] Command of the Joint Expeditionary Force devolved upon Admiral Turner, Commander, Amphibious Forces Pacific Fleet. General Buckner, Commanding General, Tenth Army was assigned the status of Commanding General, Expeditionary Troops for the amphibious phase of the operation. (See Chart 1)

The principal units included in the Joint Expeditionary Force (TF 51) were: the Amphibious Support Force (TF 52), Rear Admiral William H. P. Blandy; the Gunfire and Covering Force (TF 54), Rear Admiral Morton L. Deyo; the Northern Attack Force (TF 53), Rear Admiral Lawrence F. Reifsnider; and the Southern Attack Force (TF 55), Rear Admiral John L. Hall, Jr.

Within the amphibious forces, major element of the Expeditionary Troops (TF 56) wer allotted as follows: III Amphibious Corp (IIIAC), Major General Roy S. Geiger, as th landing force of the Northern Attack Force and XXIV Corps, Major General John R Hodge, as the landing force of the Southern Attack Force. In addition, the 77th Infantry Division (Major General Andrew D. Bruce) and the 2d Marine Division (Major General Thomas E. Watson) were assigned as the landing forces of the Western Islands Attack Group under Rear Admiral Ingolf N. Kiland, and the Demonstration Group of Rear Admiral Jerauld Wright, respectively. (See Chart 2)

Land-based air support for the operation was to be furnished by Tactical Air Force (TAF), Tenth Army under Major General Francis P. Mulcahy, whose initial squadrons were to be mainly elements of his own 2d Marine Aircraft Wing. The 27th Infantry Division (Major General George W. Griner, Jr.) composed General Buckner's floating reserve, and the 81st Infantry Division (Major General Paul Mueller) was designated area reserve under Admiral Nimitz.

Initial planning anticipated that the ships of the Amphibious Support Force and the Gunfire and Covering Force would assemble at and sortie from Ulithi. Following the departure of these task forces from the fleet anchorage, original plans contemplated that the commander of the Gunfire and Covering Force would be responsible for the movement and approach to the target and act as Senior Officer Present Afloat (SOPA) upon arrival in the objective area, while responsibility for the execution of all operations at the objective would devolve upon Commander, Amphibious Support Force.[28] Unless delegated to a task fleet commander, the responsibility for the sea areas to the north and west of the forward

---

[27] In addition to over-all command of all Central Pacific Task Forces, Admiral Spruance also exercised direct command of the Covering Forces and Special Groups (TF 50), which included the Fast Carrier Force (TF 58) and the British Carrier Force (TF 57).

[28] CTF 52 AR, Okinawa Gunto, 21Mar–20Apr45, 1 May 45, Part II, Sect A, 1–2, hereinafter cited as CTF 52 AR. VAdm Oldendorf, who was expected to command the Gunfire and Support Force, was injured shortly before the operation and RAdm Deyo was designated to command that task force. Whereupon RAdm Blandy, commanding the Amphibious Support Force, acted as SOPA in the objective area.

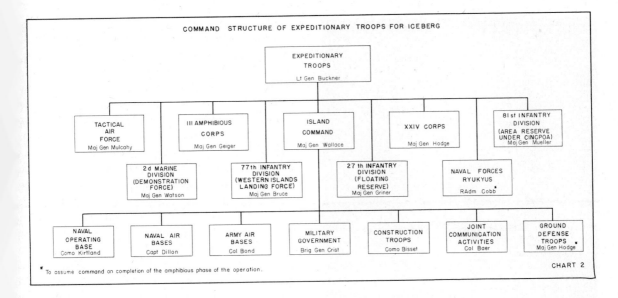

COMMAND STRUCTURE OF EXPEDITIONARY TROOPS FOR ICEBERG

EXPEDITIONARY TROOPS
Lt Gen Buckner

TACTICAL AIR FORCE
Maj Gen Mulcahy

III AMPHIBIOUS CORPS
Maj Gen Geiger

ISLAND COMMAND
Maj Gen Wallace

XXIV CORPS
Maj Gen Hodge

81st INFANTRY DIVISION (AREA RESERVE UNDER CINCPOA)
Maj Gen Mueller

2d MARINE DIVISION (DEMONSTRATION FORCE)
Maj Gen Watson

77th INFANTRY DIVISION (WESTERN ISLANDS LANDING FORCE)
Maj Gen Bruce

27th INFANTRY DIVISION (FLOATING RESERVE)
Maj Gen Griner

NAVAL FORCES RYUKYUS
RAdm Cobb

NAVAL OPERATING BASE
Como Kirtland

NAVAL AIR BASES
Capt Dillon

ARMY AIR BASES
Col Bond

MILITARY GOVERNMENT
Brig Gen Crist

CONSTRUCTION TROOPS
Como Bisset

JOINT COMMUNICATION ACTIVITIES
Col Baer

GROUND DEFENSE TROOPS
Maj Gen Hodge *

* To assume command on completion of the amphibious phase of the operation.

CHART 2

zone of the Central Pacific Area rested with CinCPOA.

Upon completion of the amphibious operations at each objective and when directed by Commander, Fifth Fleet, the Commanding General, Tenth Army would assume command of all forces ashore. Thenceforth the latter would be responsible to the former for the development and defense of captured positions. Directives promulgated by Headquarters, Pacific Ocean Areas, would govern the organization and administration of the area and defense forces under the Commanding General, Tenth Army.

As the campaign progressed, and when warranted by the situation, Admiral Nimitz would relieve Admiral Spruance of responsibility for the development and defense of the Ryukyus, and assign that function to General Buckner. The Commanding General, Tenth Army would then be directly responsible to CinCPOA for the island positions and surrounding waters within a radius of 25 miles.

Plans for the garrison phase contemplated three principal implementing commanders for General Buckner in the development and defense of the captured bases: A general officer of the Army Ground Forces assigned as Island Commander, Okinawa; [29] a flag officer of the Navy in command of the local naval defense forces; and a general officer of the Marine Corps in command of a joint air task force

designated Tactical Air Force, Ryukyus. Strategic air forces and naval search squadrons based in the Ryukyus would operate normally under the control of CGAAFPOA and the Commander, Fifth Fleet respectively.

Long-range planning envisaged direct liaison between the Commanding General, Tenth Army and the strategic command of the Pacific Ocean Areas in the preparation of plans for operations subsequent to the Okinawa campaign. During the planning for ICEBERG, however, the Tenth Army Commander was authorized to deal directly with the Commander, Amphibious Forces Pacific Fleet, who would command the Joint Expeditionary Force.

INTELLIGENCE

In order to establish a firm planning base and ensure a common frame of reference within which each Expeditionary Troops staff section could confer with its naval counterpart, Tenth Army intelligence was closely coordinated with that of the Pacific Fleet's Amphibious Force. For the most part, the intelligence produced throughout the planning of ICEBERG was derived from detailed studies of aerial photographs, interpreted and evaluated in conjunc-

---

[29] In addition to the Okinawa garrison force, Island Command, Okinawa, also included the Ie Shima garrison, and the Naval Operating Base and Naval Air Base at Okinawa.

19

MAJOR GENERAL ROY S. GEIGER, Commanding General, III Amphibious Corps at Okinawa.

tion with enemy information collected by other regular intelligence agencies.

But when photographs were needed to initiate planning, the nearest Allied base was some 1,200 miles from the objective area, reducing the agencies capable of performing photographic missions to B–29's and carrier air. Beyond this initial handicap, the hazy weather common to the Ryukyus restricted the effectiveness of the B–29 missions, and reconnaissance by carrier planes was of necessity contingent upon the scheduling of carrier strikes. These difficulties were compounded further by the vast area to be photographed.[30]

The initial mapping mission was flown by B–29's on 29 September 1944. It covered all of Okinawa and its outlying islands to a limited degree. However, about half the area covered, chiefly in the northern portion of the main island, was obscured by cloud cover.[31] Because

of inadequate photographic coverage, the original map unfortunately included a considerable amount of "unknown" area. Subsequently, these blank spaces were filled in with contouring taken from captured Japanese maps; but the final map, based on aerial photography, was not completed and issued until midway through the campaign.[32]

The scale of the basic planning map was 1:25,000, from which 1:10,000 maps of the initial zones of action were prepared for the benefit of the lower units. Small-scale maps were produced for use as road maps and in traffic circulation planning.[33]

Rubber relief maps of 1:10,000 scale were issued to III Amphibious Corps by Tenth Army in sufficient quantity for distribution down to assault battalions. In addition, plaster terrain models of the Corps zone of action were prepared by the III Amphibious Corps relief mapping section in conjunction with those of the 1st and 6th Marine Divisions. These models were to a scale of 1:5,000, constructed with a 2:1 vertical exaggeration to facilitate the briefing of commanders and troops for prospective operations over unusual terrain against intricate defenses.[34] Final distribution of these reliefs was made after embarkation, at which time the 1st Marine Division also issued some 600 copies of a special 1:5,000 map of the landing beaches.[35]

Large-scale vertical and oblique photographs, covering 90 per cent of the Okinawa Gunto and suitable for detailed study, were acquired during the fast carrier strike of 10 October 1944. Thenceforth partial coverage

---

[30] *Tenth Army AR*, Chap 11, Sect II, 3.

[31] CTF 51 General AR, Capture of Okinawa Gunto, Phases I and II, 17Feb–17May45, 25Jul45, Part V, Sect A, 8, hereinafter cited as *CTF 51 AR*.

[32] ". . . the absence of an adequate one over twenty-five thousand map during the planning phase, and even during the early phases of the operation, served greatly to influence everything the landing force did. It was often a critical impediment. As a matter of fact, the area in which the 6th Division operated as early as L-plus 4 had large blank segments on the map." CMC Memo to G–3, 18Jan55, hereinafter cited as *CMC Memo*.

[33] *Tenth Army AR*, Chap 11, Sect II, 4–5.

[34] IIIAC AR, Ryukyus Operation, Phases I and II, 1Jul45, 9, hereinafter cited as *IIIAC AR*.

[35] 1st MarDiv SAR, Nansei Shoto Operation, 1Apr–30Jun45, 10Jul45, Part III, IntelAnnex, 1–10, hereinafter cited as *1st MarDiv SAR*.

.vas obtained at least once a month [36] until the week immediately preceding the main landing, during which reconnaissances were flown daily by photographic planes based on escort carriers (CVE).[37] Although many enemy installations were concealed eventually by effective camouflage, they were easily located by reference to early photographs. Careful study of successive sorties enabled photo interpreters to determine displacement of defense positions and changes in their relative strength [38] and to compile a preliminary Japanese battery list which was disseminated to all artillery units within the III Amphibious Corps.[39]

The initial intelligence estimate set enemy strength in the Okinawa Gunto at 48,600. Of this number, two first line infantry divisions and a tank regiment were believed to constitute both the hard core and the major portion of the garrison.[40] The over-all estimate presented by G–2, Tenth Army in early January 1945 assumed that the enemy could reasonably reinforce the Okinawa garrison to 66,000 by the target date, this figure to include two and a half infantry divisions. If the enemy exerted his maximum reinforcement capability, it was calculated that the defense forces could be increased to 87,000 men, with four infantry divisions constituting the principal combat elements.

Enemy troop dispositions, studied in the light of Japanese tactical doctrine as it had evolved throughout the course of the war, indicated that they would most likely organize the southern third of the island for a defense in depth and withhold the bulk of their troops in mobile reserve. Besides conforming to current enemy combat principles, this course of action was also potentially more dangerous to the assaulting forces than the alternative of a determined defense at the water's edge.[41]

By 1 February 1945 the enemy situation on Okinawa appeared to be roughly analogous to that which had obtained on Guam, where a single battalion composed the entire garrison of the northern sector. Photographic interpretation revealed evidence that the force on Okinawa comprised two infantry divisions and an independent mixed brigade, reinforced by service and supporting units to bring the estimated strength to 56,000–58,000 troops. In the main these forces were concentrated to the south in the XXIV Corps area. Apparently two infantry regiments—some six or seven thousand men who could conceivably be augmented to a total force of almost 15,000 by local auxiliary troops—were located in the Marine zone of action.

While counterattacks by the small garrison in the north against the left flank of the corps were considered likely, the most violent enemy reaction was expected to materialize from the south in the XXIV Corps zone, where it was surmised that a mobile reserve of considerable size would be maintained. It was anticipated that the enemy would commit this reserve to a counteroffensive as soon as he had clarified the dispositions of the landing force.[42]

Information available in mid-February indicated that a full division had been withdrawn from Okinawa, and the estimated Japanese strength there was revised downward to 37,500–39,500 men. Consideration of this over-all reduction in strength, together with indications that the enemy was concentrating in the Nakagasuku Wan area, led to a presumption that no more than one infantry regiment would be available to the enemy for deployment in the III Corps zone and the total number of Japanese in the sector would not exceed 10,000.[43]

A month later the strength of the Okinawa garrison was reassessed upward to 64,000. The Japanese had apparently been reinforced by an

---

[36] CTF 51 AR, Part V, Sect A, 8.
[37] Tenth Army AR, Chap 11, Sect II, 7.
[38] CTF 51 AR, Part V, Sect A, 8.
[39] IIIAC Arty AR, Phase I, Nansei Shoto, 1Apr–30Jun45, 25Jul45, 7, hereinafter cited as IIIAC Arty AR.
[40] ICEBERG Study, 8. This early study recognized that the population of upwards of 300,000 located in southern Okinawa provided a potential source of militia, homeguards, and guerrillas as an additional serious threat to the attackers.

[41] Tenth Army Tentative OpPlan 1–45, 6Jan45, Annex 3, 11.
[42] IIIAC OpPlan 1–45, 1Feb45, Annex A, Appendix I, 1–2.
[43] Ibid., Supplement I to Appendix I.

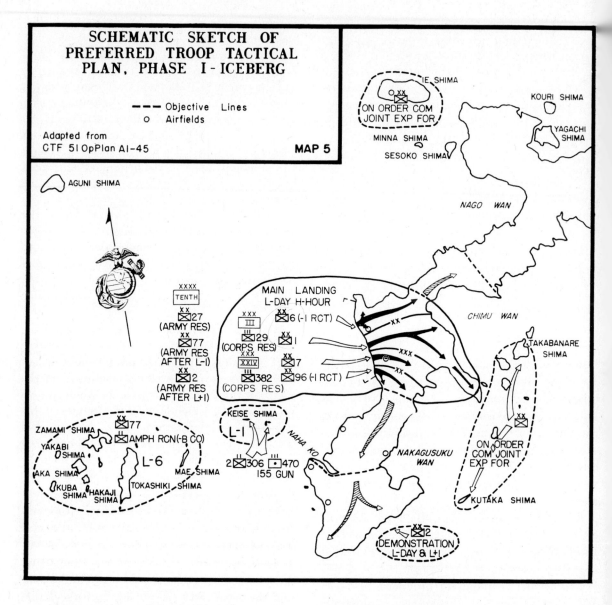

SCHEMATIC SKETCH OF PREFERRED TROOP TACTICAL PLAN, PHASE I - ICEBERG

- - - Objective Lines
○ Airfields

Adapted from
CTF 51 OpPlan A1-45

MAP 5

TACTICAL PLANNING

understrength infantry division and miscellaneous units, amounting to about 20,000 troops. An additional four to six thousand men were believed to have been lifted by subsequent shipping arriving in March. If the March arrivals were the advance elements of another division, it seemed reasonable to expect that the landing force would be opposed by at least 75,000 men on the target date—L Day. By the time the leading naval units had sortied for the target, the garrison in the III Amphibious Corps zone was estimated at 16,000 of which the principal enemy strength was believed to be embodied in two reinforced infantry regiments.[44]

TACTICAL PLANNING

Despite the fluctuating enemy order of battle and the cogent arguments questioning the feasibility of the preferred landing plan, the scheme of maneuver initially deemed the most acceptable withstood the test of continued reevaluation and remained virtually unchanged. After being subjected to critical examination over an extended period, the scheme of maneuver executed in the spring of 1945 was essentially the preferred plan of the fall of 1944.

---

[44] *Ibid.*, Supplement II to Appendix I.

The earliest planning was based on the assumption that carrier attacks on Japan, long-range air operations from the Marianas, and the seizure of Iwo Jima would force a concentration of enemy air strength in the heart of the Empire. It could be expected that the Japanese would react violently to an invasion of the Ryukyus by subjecting the expeditionary forces to heavy aerial attacks staged through Kyushu and Formosa. The scheme of maneuver was therefore "designed to gain early use of sufficient airdrome capacity on Okinawa, together with unloading facilities adequate to support its development, to maintain positive control of the air in the area."[45]

The guiding conception of operations in the Ryukyus was that of a campaign conducted in three major stages. Because it was the most susceptible to the construction of airfields and the development of port facilities, seizure of the southern portion of Okinawa and the neighboring small islands was to constitute the first phase; Ie Shima and the remainder of Okinawa would be secured during the second; and the positions thus gained would be exploited in the final phase by the capture of additional bases in the archipelago.[46] However, eventual tactical developments reversed the sequence of the first two phases and later logistical considerations negated the reasons for the third.[47]

After a searching study of all beaches in southern Okinawa, the west coast beaches lying to the north and south of Hagushi appeared to be the most practicable landing area. Moreover, an initial landing in this area promised a most significant advantage: the early capture and development of the Yontan and Kadena airfields lying directly behind the Hagushi beaches. Accordingly, a plan which committed the assault divisions to the western beaches was prepared and recommended as the most favorable course of action. This scheme also provided for the pre-L Day seizure of Keise Shima where artillery could be emplaced to augment the fires of naval guns supporting the main landing. (See Map 5)

This concept was presented to the combined naval and landing force staffs on 1 November 1944, at which time Admiral Turner presented his views. He held that the adjacent islands should be neutralized and an anchorage secured near Okinawa for the logistic support of the fleet. Because of the unfavorable weather prevailing in March, the admiral was apprehensive of an attempted landing in the west during that season and requested that the possibilities of a landing on the east coast be explored.[48]

After general discussion of the problem, it was agreed that a landing on the western beaches on 1 March would involve considerable risk, and that the landing should be made on the east coast or the western landings should be delayed at least 30 days. After a re-examination of the possible courses of action, the Hagushi landing was again recommended and on 6 November the initial estimates and overlays were forwarded to all major headquarters to initiate planning.

Still dubious as to the practicality of landing and supporting the planned assault force of four divisions over the Hagushi beaches, Admiral Turner withheld final approval. Another detailed study was made on 9 November which supported the original recommendation. This time, Admiral Turner accepted the plan, provided that both Kerama Retto and Keise Shima were captured prior to a landing on Okinawa. With minor exceptions, General Buckner concurred in the modifications. Within a month, because of difficulties in maintaining shipping schedules as well as potential unfavorable

---

[45] *ICEBERG Study*, 3.

[46] *Ibid.*, 4. The original estimate contemplated the occupation of Okino Daito, Kume, Miyako, Kikai, and Tokuno Shima. Later intelligence indicated that only Miyako and Kikai would be susceptible to extensive base development. For planning purposes, only these two islands were retained as objectives for Phase III after 28Feb45: Miyako for B-29's and Kikai for an advanced fighter base. *Ibid.*, 2SFeb45 Change, 87.

[47] Occupation of positions in the Okinawa Gunto revealed a greater capacity for base facilities than aerial reconnaissance had indicated, and Phase III was cancelled late in April. *Tenth Army AR*, Chap 1, 4; Chap 11, Sect IV, 25.

[48] From October to March strong northerly winds, with a mean velocity of 17–19 mph, prevail in the Ryukyus; gales are most frequent in this period. In April the wind varies from south to east and is generally moderate in strength, averaging 11 mph, and marking the beginning of the summer monsoon. *USAFPOA Study*, Sect XX, 1.

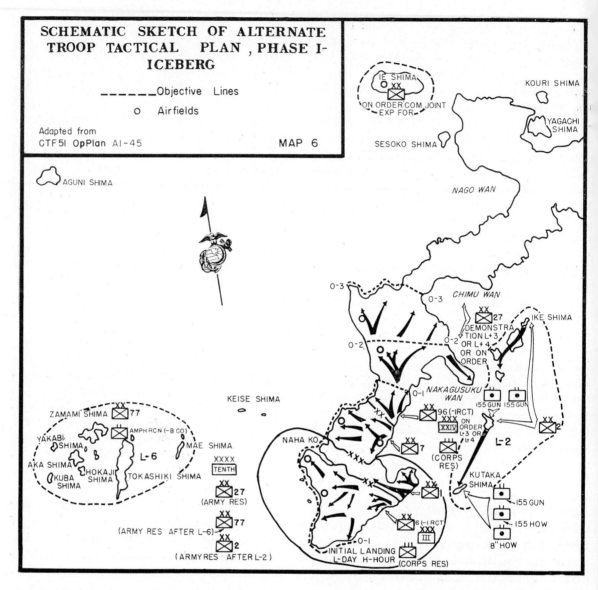

SCHEMATIC SKETCH OF ALTERNATE TROOP TACTICAL PLAN, PHASE I-ICEBERG

— — — — Objective Lines

O Airfields

Adapted from CTF 51 OpPlan A1-45

MAP 6

weather, the target date (L-Day) was successively deferred to 15 March and finally 1 April 1945.[49]

[49] *Tenth Army AR*, Chap 3, 8–10. "The deferment of target date to 1 April was the most fortunate from the logistic angle. Under CinCPOA procedures all maintenance supplies for Okinawa were to be shipped from the West Coast to the control point at Ulithi (3d and subsequent echelons were staged through Eniwetok) for call forward as required. Requisitions for these supplies had to be in the hands of West Coast supply agencies 60 days prior to sailing date of the shipment. Due to the sailing time required, requisitions for the first maintenance shipment to support a 1 March target date had to be on the West Coast by 20 November. With no firm tactical plan until after the conference

When it was first decided to use the Kerama Retto as a protected anchorage for rearming and refueling the bombardment ships, only amphibious raids to destroy enemy coastal guns were considered. A subsequent proposal by

with Admiral Turner on 9 November and lacking a firm troop basis, the determination of supply requirements had to be based on very rough estimates. The 30-day delay in target date enabled supply agencies to make a more careful estimate of the supply requirements of the assault force. This delay also enabled critical supplies and augmentation personnel, required for the assault, to be shipped to mounting points of the divisions (some had to be shipped by air) prior to the mounting date." BrigGen D. H. Blakelock Ltr to CMC, 30Oct54. hereinafter cited as *Blakelock*.

Admiral Turner to establish a permanent seaplane base and a small boat pool in the Keramas resulted in plans to secure each of these islands. Further studies in relation to the capture of the Keramas and Keise Shima indicated it was a task for a division, and the 2d Marine Division was initially designated as the landing force.

As planning progressed and an early commitment of the 2d Division in support of operations on Okinawa was foreseen, the 77th Infantry Division was selected for the Kerama-Keise operation and the 2d Division tentatively assigned to implement Turner's idea of a feint landing off southeastern Okinawa.[50] In response to a request for the release of an area reserve division to replace the 77th Division, the 27th Infantry Division was designated Expeditionary Troops floating reserve and the 81st Division assigned as an area reserve division.[51]

The alternate plan adopted for the operation made no change in the assigned mission of the 77th Division to seize the Kerama Retto preliminary to landing on Okinawa, but it committed the main effort to the east coast beaches. It further provided for the capture of the Eastern Islands by the 2d Marine Division 48 hours in advance of the principal landings so that corps artillery could be emplaced to support both corps in the assault on Okinawa. The III Amphibious Corps would land on L-Day across the Minatoga beaches (against which the preferred plan called for demonstrations by the 2d Marine Division) and gain contact at Yonabaru with the XXIV Corps, which would probably land on L-plus 2. Both corps were to advance across the island as rapidly as possible and capture the airfields in their assigned zones of action. Feints against the Chimu Wan area were contemplated on L-plus 3 or 4. The plan also provided for the capture of Ie Shima and the commitment of Army reserves to either of the corps zones or on the northern flank of the XXIV Corps.[52] (See Map 6)

A tentative operation plan was issued by Tenth Army on 6 January 1945,[53] with instructions that it would be placed in effect on order of Commanding General, Tenth Army. This was done on 11 March 1945, concurrent with the briefing of Fifth Fleet units which had been actively engaged against the enemy at Iwo Jima and had had little time to prepare for the Okinawa operation.[54]

The operation order directed XXIV Corps to land with two divisions abreast on the beaches south of Hagushi; 96th Division (Major General James L. Bradley) on the right, less one regiment in corps reserve; 7th Division (Major General Archibald V. Arnold) on the left with one regiment in division reserve but under the operational control of Commanding General, XXIV Corps. On order of the Commanding General, 77th Division, one field artillery group of XXIV Corps Artillery was to be landed on Keise Shima prior to L-Day to support the attack on Okinawa. The group would revert to control of Commanding General, XXIV Corps upon his arrival in the objective area. The remainder of XXIV Corps Artillery (Brigadier General Josef R. Sheetz) would land on corps order and support the corps attack with long-range interdiction, counterbattery, and harassing fires.[55]

Simultaneously, the III Amphibious Corps was to land with two divisions abreast on the beaches north of Hagushi and move rapidly inland, coordinating its advance with XXIV Corps. The 1st Marine Division (Major General Pedro A. del Valle) was to assist the 6th Marine Division (Major General Lemuel C. Shepherd, Jr.) in the capture of Yontan airfield by quickly seizing the high ground northeast of China; thereafter, it was to continue the

[50] *Tenth Army AR*, Chap 3, 11–12. Early planning anticipated that the 2d MarDiv would come out of army reserve, pass through the 1st MarDiv, and take the Katchin Peninsula to the southeast of the 1st MarDiv zone. *1st MarDiv SAR*, Part III, OpAnnex, 1–2.

[51] *Tenth Army AR*, Chap 3, 11–12.

[52] Tenth Army Tentative OpPlan 1–45, 6Jan45, Annex 18, 2–4.

[53] The Tenth Army Logistics Plan was published at the same time as the Tentative Operation Plan, but much of the information contained therein had been disseminated previously to lower echelons by dispatch and memorandum. This procedure considerably eased the difficulty involved in the solution of logistical problems. *Blakelock*.

[54] *Tenth Army AR*, Chap 3, 17.

[55] XXIV Corps FldOrd 45, 4–8.

attack, making the main effort on the right to maintain contact with XXIV Corps and assist its advance.[56] The 1st Marine Division scheme of maneuver placed the 5th and 7th Marines in assault with the 5th Marines on the right. The 1st Marines remained in division reserve.[57]

The 6th Marine Division, less the 29th Marines, would land on the left of the 1st Marine Division. The 4th Marines, less the 2d Battalion in division reserve, would be on the right and the 22d Marines on the left. The division was charged with the initial mission of capturing Yontan airfield and protecting the northern flank of the Tenth Army.[58] The 29th Marines in corps reserve, in addition to being prepared to land on designated beaches, would stand ready to revert one battalion landing team (BLT) to the 6th Marine Division on order. IIIAC Artillery was to land on corps order to support the attack, and once ashore to coordinate field artillery, air support, and naval gunfire in the Marines' area.[59]

For the initial phase of the operation, following the landing, the objective area consisted of that part of the island lying south of a general line across the Ishikawa Isthmus running through Chimu and including the Eastern Islands. To isolate the objective, the isthmus was to be seized quickly by IIIAC in order to block enemy reinforcement from the north. At the same time XXIV Corps was to secure a general east-west line through Kuba Saki to seal off the Japanese in the south. After the capture and occupation of central Okinawa, the attack would continue to the south to secure the remainder of the objective.

---

[56] IIIAC OpPlan 1–45, 1Feb45, Change 1, 4–5.

[57] *1st MarDiv SAR*, Part III, OpAnnex, 1–2.

[58] IIIAC OpPlan 1–45, 1Feb45, Change 1, 5–6.

[59] *Ibid.* Under the over-all command of BrigGen D. R. Nimmer, IIIAC Arty was originally formed for combat in two groups: one under Col J. A. Bemis consisting of HqBtry of IIIAC Arty, 6th 155mm HowBn, 8th 155mm Gun Bn, and 9th 155mm Gun Bn; and the other, commanded by LtCol C. Burton, Jr., composed the HqBtry of the 2d ProvFAGrp, 1st 155mm HowBn, 3d 155mm HowBn, and 7th 155mm Gun Bn. The Bemis group was to be in general support of 1st MarDiv, while the 2d ProvFAGrp was to be in general support of 6th MarDiv. *IIIAC Arty AR*, 7–8.

Upon the completion of Phase I, the second phase was to be executed when directed by General Buckner with troops locally available. This involved the seizure of Ie Shima and the rest of Okinawa. It was contemplated that Motobu Peninsula in the north of the island would be secured by means of a combined shore-to-shore amphibious and land assault, followed by a shore-to-shore attack against Ie Shima. The capture of the rest of northern Okinawa would bring the end of Phase II.[60]

Although many of the supporting naval units assigned to ICEBERG had been given little respite between operations, the fact that they had participated in the capture of Iwo Jima simplified planning to a certain extent. Command and communication arrangements of TF 51 were tested and proven at Iwo Jima and modified as required by the peculiar circumstances of operations at Okinawa.

The particular difficulties expected at Okinawa involved several new factors. For the first time in the Pacific, four divisions were to land abreast on a front of almost 10,000 yards. This extended beach frontage, coupled with the offshore navigational hazards, limited the density of fire which could be provided by the support ships. In addition, a considerable number of coastal guns had to be destroyed before ships could close to a range from which they could deliver the most effective fire against enemy defenses opposing the landing. A large portion of the selected beaches were backed by extensive sea walls, which it would be necessary to breach in order to provide exits for combat vehicles. Detailed knowledge of the Japanese defensive dispositions in relation to the beaches was lacking, and the enemy possessed the capability of moving major units within a few hours to contest any attempted landing, unless continuous interdiction was maintained on a large number of roads.[61]

Naval gunfire officers of the 1st and 6th Marine Divisions, III Amphibious Corps, and the Northern Attack Force established early liaison. Priority naval gunfire targets were

---

[60] *ICEBERG Study*, 11–12.

[61] *CTF 51 AR*, Part V, Sect C, 1–2.

selected by the divisions and submitted to III Corps,[62] a representative of which participated in preparing the initial ships' gunfire support plan during the early part of the Iwo Jima operation.

Circumstances prevented the inclusion of a schedule of fires with this preliminary plan, but the delay in disseminating this information was not without certain advantages. It permitted the use of the latest intelligence; and issuance of the NGF schedule in a separate supplement provided gunnery officers with a more convenient reference than had been the case when the gunfire annex was part of a bulky operation plan. No specific ships were assigned on the schedules. Instead, types and numbers were designated for particular missions and individual ships possessing the requisite capabilities were subsequently assigned these numbers for the actual performance of the task.[63]

The original draft of the air plan was prepared in the Hawaiian area in early November and the final plan formulated on board Admiral Turner's flagship en route to Iwo Jima. Personnel of the fast carriers and most of the escort carriers were briefed at Ulithi between 10–15 March, and the remainder of the CVE men at Leyte on 19 March.[64] For the most part, air support of the landing force at the target devolved upon escort carriers, until such time as airfields were uncovered and developed, when increased responsibility would be assumed by Major General Mulcahy's Tactical Air Force of Tenth Army.[65]

LOGISTICAL PLANNING [66]

While judgment and a certain amount of imagination are needed to perceive where and when forces should be committed, a great deal of knowledge and much hard work are necessary to determine how they are to be moved to the objective area and whether they can be maintained after they are there. Consequently, detailed planning for both naval gunfire and logistic support commenced as soon as the Commanding General, Tenth Army verbally approved a tentative tactical plan.[67]

Implementation of the tactical plan demanded logistical competence in the fullest and most literal sense of the term.[68] It required arrangements for the procurement and delivery of initial supplies and equipment to the assault units dispersed throughout the Pacific at Leyte, Espiritu Santo, Guadalcanal, the Russells, Saipan, Eniwetok, and Oahu. An elaborate base development plan produced a second logistical mission which was related to, yet separate from, supporting the assault on Okinawa. Accomplishment of this task entailed scheduling of shipping for the garrison troops with their equipment and construction materials from New Caledonia, Leyte, the Marianas, Oahu, and the west coast of the continental United States. A continuous replenishment of essential materials and equipment involved maintaining a supply line more than 6,000 miles long—26 days steaming time from the West Coast. Besides the great distances from mounting points and sources of supply to the objective, logistical plans were governed by the capacity of the beaches and the availability of shipping.

The Hagushi beaches were adequate to handle the tonnage required to maintain the assault echelon of two corps and their supporting troops; but very little margin remained to support the base development plan. This plan contemplated the seizure and development of two airfields in the first five days of the assault and two more within another 15 days. Additional construction projects included repair of the port of Naha, installation of an advance fleet base at Nakagusuku Wan, and development of Okinawa as a rehabilitation area and a mounting point for future operations. Unloading the necessary materials for these undertakings depended for the most part on the capture of additional beaches.

[62] 6th MarDiv SAR, Phases I and II, Okinawa Operation, 30Apr45, Part III, 4–5, hereinafter cited as *6th MarDiv SAR, Ph I&II.*

[63] *CTF 51 AR*, Part V, Sect C, 2–3.

[64] *Ibid.*, Part V, Sect E, 2.

[65] *ICEBERG Study*, 14–15.

[66] Unless otherwise noted the material in this section is derived from *Tenth Army AR.*

[67] *IIIAC AR*, 7.

[68] The term logistics is derived from the Greek *logistikos*, meaning "skilled in calculations."

The available shipping provided the basis for the assignment of tonnage to assault units; but the estimated capacity of beach and port unloading facilities determined the allocation to elements of the garrison force. Pending the establishment of a firm troop list, a tentative allotment of shipping, based on the experience of previous operations, was made to lift three reinforced Marine divisions, three reinforced Army infantry divisions, a Marine amphibious corps headquarters and corps troops, and an Army corps headquarters and corps troops. The tonnage thus allocated was deducted from the total shipping available. The remainder established the basis for the assignment of Tenth Army support troops, including naval, air, and airfield construction units.

Early in January it became apparent that insufficient shipping had been assigned to accomplish the tactical mission, support early base development, and accommodate the necessary air units. The deficiency in transport for engineer troops needed for early airfield, road, and water front construction was partially overcome by preparations for immediate return of the assault LST's to Saipan to load eight naval construction battalions. Similarly, arrangements were made to shuttle LST's to Leyte to lift equipment of the XXIV Corps that could not be carried in the assault shipping.[69] Closely co-ordinated shipping schedules made available vessels which were also to be used in the landings on Luzon and Iwo Jima. Based on the premise that the 2d Marine Division would not be committed at once and III Amphibious Corps could afford a delay, the tonnage requirements of that corps were substantially reduced to provide additional space for army troops. Because of the limited prospects for beaching on the coral-bound island, landing ships were loaded to the limit of their established trim and sailing characteristics. The over-all lift was increased also to some extent by new construction.

The peculiar requirements of the Okinawa operation led to a revision of the task organization of assault shipping. The transport group which had formerly sufficed to lift a division with appropriate attachments consisted of three transport divisions totalling 12 APA's and three AKA's. In order to accommodate a proportionate share of corps and army troops the transport squadron (transron) was set up. This organization also comprised three transport divisions, but the divisions were increased from three to five APA's and from one to two AKA's.

One hospital transport (APH)[70] accompanied each transron making the initial assault. Of the six hospital ships assigned for the operation one was to be on station with the Western Islands Attack Force on L-minus 5, two with the Northern Attack Force, and one with the Southern Attack Force on L-plus 1. The remaining two were scheduled to arrive in the objective area on L-plus 5.

In order to control the evacuation of casualties from the beach, four hospital landing ships (LST(H)) were assigned to each of the attack forces assaulting the western beaches of Okinawa. The medical officer assigned to each LST(H) as Evacuation Control Officer was responsible for the screening and proper distribution of casualties in accordance with three major classifications of wounded. Seriously wounded men requiring more than two months hospitalization would normally be evacuated in hospital ships; those requiring treatment for more than two weeks but less than two months would be avacuated in transports during the initial assault phase; and those who could be returned to duty within two weeks would be retained at the objective afloat until such time as medical facilities were established ashore.

The LST(H)'s would remain on station until relieved by the Attack Force Commander, and the Evacuation Control Officers then would move ashore and assign casualties directly to the ships. Responsibility for medical service ashore, including air evacuation when airfields were established, rested with Commanding General, Expeditionary Troops.[71]

Aside from certain supplies and equipment specified by Tenth Army to accompany troops,

[69] Blakelock.

[70] This vessel is not to be confused with the hospital ship (AH), which is unarmed and protected by the Geneva Convention.

[71] CTF 51 OpPlan A1-45, 16Feb45, Annex N, 1-4.

the decision as to what equipment should be carried lay with the corps and lower units, limited only by the shipping assigned. At division level logistical planning was predicated on the premises that the landing beaches would be heavily defended, and the advance inland stubbornly contested. Consequently, only "hot cargo" [72] (certain amounts of high priority supplies) were to be landed on L-Day. With operations on a relatively large land mass over a poor road net in prospect, the decision was made to use all available shipping space to transport organic division motor vehicles to the target.

Logistical planning for the 1st Marine Divi-

sion was simplified by the fact that that unit was concentrated with its supply source in the Russell Islands.[73] The 6th Division, however, experienced difficulties because of the distance of the division from its supply agencies. The 6th Division supply agency on Guadalcanal was was only a transfer installation, not a stocking agency, the source of supply being located in the Russells, which was in turn under the 2d Field Service Command on Guadalcanal. Cumbersome administrative procedures through the several service commands in the area caused many delays in the delivery of equipment and supplies. As in the past, equipment and supplies arrived after the transports had been loaded; but the divisions embarked with no major shortages which effected combat efficiency.[74]

---

[72] This cargo included one unit of fire for all weapons, rations and water for one day, sufficient fuel for the operation of tracked vehicles, fortification and demolition material, and necessary signal and medical supplies. *1st MarDiv SAR*, Part III, SupAnnex, 1–2.

[73] *Ibid.*
[74] *Ibid; 6th MarDiv SAR, Ph I&II*, Part III, 5–9.

Preparations for the Assault

CHAPTER III

TRAINING AND REHEARSING[1]

Because of the vast distances separating Tenth Army Headquarters and its subordinate commands, General Buckner charged corps and division commanders with the responsibility for supervising unit training. At Schofield Barracks on Oahu. army section promulgated training directives for appropriate echelons of Expeditionary Troops. In order to maintain maximum efficiency FMFPac (Fleet Marine Force, Pacific) continued to supervise the training of Marine units, basing its actions, however, on the Tenth Army directives. Monthly status of training reports were submitted by all units, enabling ICEBERG planners to evaluate combat readiness. In the latter part of January 1945, General Buckner, accompanied by his principal staff officers, personally checked the state of readiness of the scattered elements of his command during a series of flying visits to each division and corps headquarters.[2]

The shortage of service and support troops that had been a definite factor in postponing the Formosa-South China operations continued to plague Tenth Army during the training period. Many units, assigned in the operation plans to reinforce corps and divisions for the assault and to augment Island Command during the base development period, had primary missions intimately connected with the build-up for the operation. It was impossible, without seriously disrupting logistical time schedules, to release many of these vital troops for attachment to assault units for training. A strong effort was made, though, to meet individual training goals such as weapons qualification and adequate physical conditioning.[3] If the

---

[1] Unless otherwise noted the material in this section is derived from *Tenth Army AR;* TAF, Tenth Army AR, Phase I, Nansei Shoto, 8Dec44–30Jun45, 12Jul45, hereinafter cited as *TAF AR; IIIAC AR; IIIAC Arty AR;* XXIV Corps AR, Ryukyus, 1Apr–30Jun45, n. d., hereinafter cited as *XXIV Corps AR;* XXIV Corps Arty AR, 31Mar–30Jun45, n. d., hereinafter cited as *XXIV Corps Arty AR; 1st MarDiv SAR;* 2d MarDiv AR, Nansei Shoto, Phase I, 15Apr45, hereinafter cited as *2d MarDiv AR; 6th MarDiv SAR, Ph I&II;* 7th InfDiv AR, Ryukyus Campaign, 30Jul45, hereinafter cited as *7th InfDiv AR;* 27th InfDiv OpRpt, Phase I, Nansei Shoto, 1Jan–30Jun45, 19Jul45, hereinafter cited as *27th InfDiv OpRpt;* 77th InfDiv OpRpt, Phase I, (in 3 parts: Kerama Retto and Keise Shima; Ie Shima; Okinawa), n. d., hereinafter cited as *77th InfDiv OpRpt* and appropriate part; 96th InfDiv AR, Ryukyus Campaign, 28Jul45, hereinafter cited as *96th InfDiv AR.*

[2] "This personal visit by General Buckner and his staff did much to weld the far flung units of the Tenth Army into a unified whole." *Blakelock.*

[3] In addition to normal accomplishment of all subjects in individual training programs, Tenth Army required personnel staging in the Hawaiian area to complete: (1) a minimum of one week's jungle training; (2) three days to one week of amphibious training; (3) qualification with individual and familiariza-

final status of training report revealed deficiencies, extensive shipboard training programs were instituted.

Although all the major assault units of Tenth Army were combat experienced, each needed intensive training to absorb replacements and maintain a high level of fighting efficiency. Army and Marine units in the South Pacific and the 2d Marine Division on Saipan completed planned training programs. Units of XXIV Corps, however, committed in battle on Leyte until 25 December 1944 and then engaged in further extensive combat operations [4] were not released for ICEBERG until February, a scant month before embarkation.

The few elements of XXIV Corps that were available during January found themselves helping to load out units scheduled for the Luzon operation.[5] The chronic shortage of service troops within Leyte's base command, charged with processing supplies for Luzon and Okinawa, necessitated large labor drafts from infantry divisions as soon as they were released from mopping-up. This fact, coupled with the need for servicing, crating, and loading organic equipment, precluded any major training program. As one division reported, "deterioration of the physical and mental condition of combat personnel after 110 days of continuous contact with the enemy made it plain that rigorous field training in the wet and muddy terrain would prove more detrimental than beneficial."[6]

However, XXIV Corps did ensure that the special problem presented by the sea walls behind the beaches at Okinawa was covered in intensive breaching and scaling training of infantry-engineer assault units. Within the divisions, in the short time available, emphasis was placed on tank-infantry training. This was especially true with the replacements received just prior to mounting out who had little or no experience in combined arms tactics. The 96th Infantry Division was fortunate in that it received many replacements during the mopping-up stages on Leyte. These men had an opportunity to take an "active part in combat and reconnaissance patrols, gaining valuable battle indoctrination through physical contact and skirmishes with small isolated groups of Japanese."[7]

From an over-all viewpoint, the necessity for conducting both combat rehabilitation and preparation during February 1945 severely curtailed the scope of XXIV Corps training for ICEBERG. The record of the corps on Okinawa, therefore, is an effective testimony of the battle readiness, despite substantial handicaps, of its veteran units.

The training picture for Tenth Army troops in the South Pacific and Marianas was substantially brighter. The last elements of the 27th Infantry Division, assigned the role of floating reserve, arrived on Espiritu Santo from Saipan late in October 1944. In common with the divisions that staged and trained in the torrid and inhospitable Solomons, the 27th regarded its base in the New Hebrides as a "hellhole," ill suited by climate and topography for rehabilitation or effective training.[8] Once word was received, however, that the division was earmarked for ICEBERG, an intensive training program was undertaken with the idea of readying the unit for a prolonged combat operation by 30 January 1945. From 23 October when the program started, the training progressed from individual schooling through

tion with organizational weapons; (4) physical conditioning; and (5) combat swimming qualification. IsCom AR, Okinawa, 13Dec44–30Jun45, 30Jun45, Chap 4, Sect 0, 1, hereinafter cited as *IsCom AR.*

[4] According to the G–3 of XXIV Corps the period following the official declaration of the end of organized resistance "was not regarded at that time as 'mopping up'" and was, in fact, "a continuation of bitter fighting marked by repeated Japanese attempts at reinforcement on an extensive scale." Col J. W. Guerard Ltr to CMC, 9Sept54.

[5] "Approximately 700 troops" of the 77th InfDiv, scheduled to make the first assault in the operation, "actually accompanied other unit's shipping to Luzon, acting as ships' platoons and returning to the division just prior to loading for ICEBERG." *77th InfDiv OpRpt, Kerama Retto and Keise Shima,* 19.

[6] *7th InfDiv AR,* 28.

[7] *96th InfDiv AR,* Chap V, 1.

[8] Capt E. G. Love, *The 27th Infantry Division In World War II,* (Washington, 1949), 521, hereinafter cited as *27th InfDiv History.*

MARINES OF IIIAC disembarking from an LVT during maneuvers at Guadalcanal.

radar and antiaircraftmen from disbanded AAA units) to ensure optimum firing efficiency.[9] The delay in the return from Peleliu of the 3d 155mm Howitzer and 8th 155mm Gun Battalions until 15 November and 10 December respectively, further complicated the training problem. The observation squadron assigned to corps—VMO-7—did not arrive prior to mounting out and joined later at the target. Despite these very real problems, which affected division artillery regiments in a similar manner,[10] corps artillery considered all its embarked units combat ready, although "both individual and unit proficiency were not up to the standards that could have been obtained under more favorable circumstances." [11]

Between 11 and 13 January, all Marine artillery in the Solomons assigned to ICEBERG conducted a combined firing problem on Guadalcanal, simulating as near as possible the conditions at the target.[12] Guadalcanal was also

small unit, company, and battalion exercises, to two weeks of RCT (Regimental Combat Team) maneuvers. During this period 2,700 replacements were absorbed. Special emphasis was laid on training for night operations, which paid off in substantial gains of Japanese territory on Okinawa.

Training schedules of IIIAC units were just as thorough as those for the 27th Division. The limited areas available for large unit problems, however, especially in the Russells and on Saipan, curtailed the effectiveness of some portions of the planned program. During the training period, each Marine command absorbed large numbers of replacements, but IIIAC Artillery's replacement problem was the most pressing. Cadres were withdrawn from existing units to form the 6th 155mm Howitzer Battalion and Headquarters Battery of the 2d Provisional Field Artillery Group during October–November 1944. Five hundred veterans, mostly NCO's, were rotated to the states in late November. Among the replacements received, experienced field artillerymen were at a premium.

Therefore, concurrently with practice for the coming operation, Brigadier General David I. Nimmer's battalions were forced to conduct extensive training (retraining in the case of

---

[9] Approximately 10% of corps artillery's strength joined after active unit training had ceased in February. Seventy-eight communication and 92 field artillerymen joined after embarkation.

[10] In commenting on the complexities of the division artillery personnel situation during the training period, the CO of the 11th Mar stated that "the heavy casualties suffered at Peleliu plus the rotation without immediate replacement of all officers and men with 30 months' service in the Pacific after that battle posed a severe problem. Only one battalion commander remained of the four who went to Peleliu. There were only eight field officers in the regiment including myself and the NGF officer. Fourteen captains with 24 months' Pacific service were allowed a month's leave plus travel time in the United States, and they left Pavuvu at the end of November and were not available for the training maneuver at first. I recall that the 4th Battalion (LtCol L. F. Chapman, Jr.) had only 18 officers present including himself. He had no captains whatever. The other battalions and RHQ were in very similar shape. The 3d Battalion had to be completely reorganized due to heavy casualties on Peleliu and was the only one with two field officers. But it had only about 20 officers of all ranks present." MajGen W. S. Brown Ltr to CMC, 10Oct54, hereinafter cited as *Brown.*

[11] *IIIAC Arty AR,* 10.

[12] After the arrival of the 11th Mar on Guadalcanal on 15Dec44, both division artillery regiments trained with IIIAC Arty for seven straight weeks with only one break—Christmas day. Proper conduct of fire was stressed with battalions displacing, registering,

the site of most of the combined arms training and field maneuvers of IIIAC. The 1st Marine Division's RCT's were rotated from their base at Pavuvu Island in the Russells to the larger island as their training cycle reached the large unit stage. However, the press of time limited each regiment to little more than two weeks intensive combined arms training prior to the final rehearsal. The division's home, rat-infested Pavuvu, was so small "that eventually units were forced to skirmish down company streets" and so unpopular that a universal sigh of relief went up when the transports pulled away from its palm-shrouded shores for the last time.[13] In one aspect of training the 1st Division faced a new problem, for it was "the first time it was landing as an integral part of a much larger landing force, and matters of coordination and control not met in previous campaigns had to be considered."[14]

The 6th Marine Division, although it had not as yet operated as a unit in combat, was composed of veteran troops. Division Headquarters, substantially the same as that of the 1st Provisional Marine Brigade which had operated under IIIAC at Guam, and most men of the 4th and 22d Marines as well as substantial portions of the 15th and 29th Marines, had at least one campaign under their belts.[15] Since it was based on Guadalcanal, the 6th Division was better off than the 1st in the matter of training room. The presence of corps troops and large supply installations did crowd the bivouac area, but kunai grass plains and tangled reaches of jungle bordering the unit tent camps were available for a rugged training and conditioning program. A full schedule, stretching from fire team to regimental combined arms problems, culminated in a eight-day division exercise in January. Anticipating the nature of the division's employment on Okinawa, General Shepherd stressed efficient execution of large unit maneuvers, swift movements, and rapid redeployment of troops.

The remaining major element of IIIAC, the 2d Marine Division, effectively integrated its training with mopping-up operations on Saipan. Over 8,000 replacements absorbed during the training period gained valuable experience routing Japanese holdouts. Eventually, the extensive development of Saipan as a supply center and air base crowded the division out of its training grounds until there was no room for battalion problems or artillery impact areas. In fact, lack of suitable beaches confined the division's final rehearsals to simulated landings. Because of the indefinite nature of its employment, the division had to select an arbitrary landing scheme of two RCT's abreast as the rehearsal pattern. Bad weather prevented LVT launchings on two days, neither air nor NGF support was available, and finally, on the last day of the exercises (19 March), only the naval portion of TG 51.2 (Demonstration Group) was able to participate in the demonstration rehearsal. Taken altogether, the accomplishments of the rehearsal period of the 2d Division were not up to the standard met by other elements of Expeditionary Troops.

The other relatively isolated division of Tenth Army, the 27th, conducted its rehearsals

---

and firing several times a day "to overcome the improvised jungle methods theretofore used by the divisions in previous campaigns." *Brown.*

[13] One of the many tragicomic stories told of this island's effect on its reluctant inhabitants is related in the division's history, about "the man who ran out of his tent at dusk and began to pound his fists against a coconut tree, sobbing angrily, 'I hate you, goddamit, I hate you.' 'Hit it once for me,' came a cry from a nearby tent, the only comment that was made then or later by the man's buddies." G. J. McMillan, *The Old Breed,* (Washington, 1949), 231, hereinafter cited as *The Old Breed.* For the story of Pavuvu's selection as a training base and conditions on the island see Maj F. O. Hough, *The Assault on Peleliu*, MC Historical Monograph, (Washington, 1950), 25–29, hereinafter cited as *Peleliu.*

[14] *1st MarDiv SAR*, Chap IV, 2. For the story of the division's other campaigns in the Pacific see: Maj J. L. Zimmerman, *The Guadalcanal Campaign*, MC Historical Monograph, (Washington, 1949); LtCol F. O. Hough and Maj J. A. Crown, *The Campaign on New Britain*, MC Historical Monograph, (Washington, 1953), *Peleliu.*

[15] For the story of the combat action of the 6th MarDiv's components see: Maj O. R. Lodge, *The Recapture of Guam*, MC Historical Monograph, (Washington, 1954); LtCol J. A. Crown and LtCol R. D. Heinl, *The Marshalls: Increasing the Tempo*, MC Historical Monograph, (Washington, 1954); *Saipan.*

from 20–25 March at Espiritu Santo while loading of its transron was being accomplished. Faced as was the 2d Marine Division with a multiplicity of possible roles at Okinawa, the 27th Infantry Division also concentrated on a hypothetical landing maneuver. Although the available LVT's had been allotted to assault divisions, General Griner's unit substituted landing boats for tractors and practiced transshipment of troops and reef transfer during simulated landings.

Both Tenth Army corps were able to conduct satisfactory landing rehearsals, putting ashore all assault troops. Although no reef existed off the Cape Esperance-Doma Cove beaches on Guadalcanal, IIIAC established a transfer line 200 yards offshore in an attempt to duplicate landing conditions at the target. Throughout the six-day rehearsal period, 2–7 March, naval officers of Rear Admiral Lawrence F. Reifsnider's Northern Attack Force placed emphasis on control of assault waves and training of communication elements at all echelons of command. Limited NGF and air support were available during the exercises to approximate the tremendous volume of fire to be delivered on the Hagushi beaches. On 6 March, after two preliminary landings and a critique, the entire assault echelon of IIIAC was landed. Advanced elements of corps and division command posts set up ashore, and token unloadings of equipment were made. The reserve regiments, 1st Marines for the 1st Division and 29th Marines for IIIAC, formed boat waves and exercised off the beaches, landing themselves on 7 March.

Across the Pacific in Leyte Gulf XXIV Corps conducted rehearsals from 14–19 March. The 77th Infantry Division, scheduled to make the initial assault, practiced separately in landings on islands in Hinunangan Bay that closely resembled Kerama Retto. Although adverse weather conditions on 14 March considerably retarded planned exercises, the nature of the 77th's mission, independent battalion operations, permitted landings to go ahead despite schedule interruptions. When heavy swells and rain continued on 15 March, the division was forced to cancel portions of a planned rehearsal for the capture of Ie Shima. With clear weather, the division reserve (307th Infantry) was able to practice its landings on 16 March. General Bruce considered that the rehearsals were successful since "all elements scheduled for a specific mission satisfactorily executed a close approximation of their mission."[16] On the other hand, the Western Islands Attack Group Commander, Admiral Kiland, felt that "considering the complexity of the operation and the relative inexperience of naval personnel involved, the curtailment of these exercises by weather conditions made the training provided entirely inadequate."[17]

The weather was not a factor in the landings of the 7th and 96th Divisions on 17 and 19 March. A corps landing was made on both days with unit critiques held on 18 March to help iron out difficulties discovered in the first exercise. After the full-scale landing on the 19th during which NGF and air support were simulated, another critique was held for units involved and points of error noted for correction. On 21 March, on board USS *Teton*, flagship of Admiral Hall, a meeting of all major Army and Navy commanders was held to evaluate the whole rehearsal and ensure coordination during the actual landing. Admiral Turner and General Buckner were present at this critique-briefing which raised the curtain on the final preparatory stages for ICEBERG.

MOUNTING AND STAGING FOR THE ASSAULT[18]

Each attack force of the Joint Expeditionary Force was organized differently for loading, movement, and unloading at the target. The three transrons (nine transport divisions) of Admiral Hall's Southern Attack Force were divided into eleven transport divisions. Assigned to the two temporary divisions were the

[16] 77th InfDiv OpRpt, Kerama Retto and Keise Shima, 20.

[17] CTG 51.1 AR, Capture of Okinawa Gunto, Phases 1 and 2, 9Mar–2Apr45, 26May45, Chap II, 2, hereinafter cited as CTG 51.1 AR.

[18] Unless otherwise noted the material in this section is derived from CTF 51 AR; Tenth Army AR; TAF AR; IIIAC AR; XXIV Corps AR; 1st MarDiv SAR; 2d MarDiv AR; 6th MarDiv SAR, Ph I&II; 7th InfDiv AR; 27th InfDiv OpRpt; 77th InfDiv OpRpt, Kerama Retto and Keise Shima; 96th InfDiv AR.

IIIAC EQUIPMENT slated for the Okinawa operation is loaded on transports and landing ships in the Solomons.

ships slated to lift XXIV Corps troops and those which loaded Tenth Army and Island Command forces at Oahu. Separate provisional units to carry IIIAC troops were not formed within Admiral Reifsnider's Northern Attack Force. Ships from Transrons 12 and 18 which loaded Tenth Army support troops accompanying III Corps reported to parent organizations when they reached the Solomons. The ease of control during movement and increased efficiency during loading and unloading phases of Admiral Hall's temporary reorganization led General Geiger to request formation of a similar corps shipping group for future IIIAC operations.

The proximity of Leyte Gulf to Okinawa allowed XXIV Corps both to mount and stage in that area for the operation. The relative closeness of Saipan, Tinian, and Guam to the target also allowed units on those islands to complete both these phases of assault preparation in the Marianas. Since the normal duties of most of the scattered squadrons of the Tac-

tical Air Force constituted their combat training, the main problem facing air units was the coordinated loading of ground and flight echelons. Local area commanders supervised the mounting out of the air groups, whose planes and pilots proceeded to the target on board escort carriers, while ground crews accompanied assault and first echelon shipping. The funnel through which some of these air units and most of the remaining elements of Expeditionary Troops eventually poured was the immense anchorage at Ulithi Atoll.

IIIAC made the 1st and 6th Divisions responsible for the loading and embarkation of their respective organic and attached units, while the corps itself supervised loading of corps troops. Units in the first reinforcing echelon, due at the target immediately following the assault, were loaded under control of local naval area commanders. Although some vessels were partially loaded prior to the rehearsal period, all required additional time off the beaches of Guadalcanal and the Russells to take on vital cargo.

35

When the Northern Tractor Flotilla got under way for Ulithi on 12 March, its landing ships carried full loads of amphibious vehicles, tanks, artillery, and combat equipment. Corps wanted to avoid exposing assault troops to the crowded conditions imposed by the limited berthing space available on LST's and LSM's for as long a period as possible. To avoid the debilitating effects of prolonged shipboard confinement, many of these men were embarked on the faster attack transports (APA's) for movement to Ulithi. Three days after the tractor flotilla departed, APA's and AKA's (cargo ships, attack) of the transport groups, now fully loaded with men and equipment left the Solomons for the staging area.

Both elements of TF 53 arrived at Ulithi on 21 March, and the transfer of APA-borne assault troops to landing ships took place the following day. Within the confines of the vast anchorage lay a substantial portion of the greatest amphibious fleet ever assembled in the Pacific. During their stay at Ulithi some of the embarked troops were put ashore on the tiny islets of the atoll to take part in a limited program of physical conditioning and recreation. The best cure for boredom, however, was the fascinating sight of the constantly shifting fleet which changed in makeup from day to day as some ships departed for preliminary strikes and bombardment and others arrived with the scattered elements of Expeditionary Troops. The shooting war remained close at hand, even at Ulithi, with Japanese snooper planes causing nightly alerts and the battered carriers of TF 58 limping into the anchorage in mute testimony to the fury of enemy suicide air attacks.[19] On 25 March, the tractor flotilla sortied from the anchorage bound for Okinawa, and two days later the remainder of the assault echelon steamed toward the target.

On these same dates, 25 and 27 March, the tractor and transport echelons of the Demonstration Group left Saipan. The 2d Marine Division had been aided in its loading operations by the fact that Transron 15, which carried it to Okinawa, had passed through Saipan

en route to Iwo Jima. With accurate table of ship's characteristics available, unit TQM's (Transport Quartermasters) were able to plan the most efficient utilization of cargo and personnel space.[20] The commanding general, Major General Thomas E. Watson, in addition to the responsibility for loading his reinforced division, was given the duty of coordinating all assault and first echelon shipping in the Marianas and at Roi in the Marshalls.[21]

Since the XXIV Corps had no intermediate staging area, it departed for the target directly from Leyte. The 77th Division, which was to lead the way with the assault on Kerama Retto, completed loading its landing ships on 18 March and transports on 20 March, each echelon leaving for the target the following day.[22] Under the supervision of General Hodge's staff, which handled the details of ship spotting, each division conducted its own loading. The Southern Tractor Flotilla departed Leyte the morning of 24 March, and the transport groups followed in three days. By the evening of 27 March all assault elements of Tenth Army were at sea converging on Okinawa.

PRELIMINARY COVERING STRIKES[23]

A Japanese replacement, confiding to his diary on 3 January 1945 that "seeing enemy planes for the first time since coming to Okinawa somehow or other gave me the feeling of being in a combat zone," [24] may have made one

---

[19] BrigGen E. W. Snedeker Ltr to CMC, 18Oct54, hereinafter cited as *Snedeker*.

[20] Ship characteristics furnished by FMFPac proved to be in error and no definite loading plans could be made until Transron 15 passed through the Marianas in February.

[21] Units involved were: MAG–31 at Roi; 1st SepEngBn and 16th AAA Bn at Tinian; Corps Evac-Hosp No 2 and 2d AAA Bn at Guam; and 7th FldDep, 1st Prov MP Bn, and LFASCU–1 at Saipan.

[22] While returning from the rehearsal on 16 March, USS *Samuel Chase*, carrying one BLT of the 77th InfDiv, ran aground. Between 18 and 21 March, troops and cargo from the *Chase* were transferred to the USS *Pitt* and LST 990 so that the mishap caused no delay in mounting out. *CTG 51.1 AR*, Chap III, 4–6.

[23] Unless otherwise noted the material in this section is derived from CinCPac War Diaries for January, February, and March 1945.

[24] CinCPac-CinCPOA Bull 147–45, Translations and Interrogations No 32, 16Jun45, Dairy of unidentified superior pvt, 273d IIB.

of the classic understatements of the Pacific War. The raid which aroused his apprehension was merely his first taste of the destructive efforts of the Fast Carrier Task Force. On 22 January, when the naval pilots returned, his prose became more vehement.

> While some fly around overhead and strafe, the big bastards fly over the airfield and drop bombs. The ferocity of the bombing is terrific. It really makes me furious. It is past 1500 and the raid is still on. At 1800 the last two planes brought the raid to a close. What the hell kind of bastards are they? Bomb from 0600 to 1800![25]

In some ways this infantryman's reaction was typical of those contained in surviving personal records. The first carrier raid on 10 October 1944 had indicated the shape of things to come and the promise was fulfilled with each successive visit. The gutted remains of Naha furnished eloquent testimony of the effectiveness of that first raid and the hapless guess of one Japanese witness that "the enemy is brazenly planning to completely destroy every last ship, cut our supply lines, and attack us,"[26] was a concise summation of the American objective.

During January, Task Force 38 under Vice Admiral John S. McCain struck Formosa and the Ryukyus twice and paid an unfriendly visit to the ports of the South China Coast, while covering General MacArthur's landings on Luzon. After its last attack, TF 38 retired to Ulithi where reinforcing carriers were waiting to join. On 27 January, concurrently with the arrival of Admiral Nimitz at his advance headquarters on Guam, Admirals Spruance and Mitscher took over command of the Pacific Fleet's striking force from Halsey and McCain. When the carriers sortied again on 10 February, it was in the guise of Task Force 58, destined as usual to cover Marines in the assault.

Within the next four months, the amphibious forces of the Fifth Fleet, guarded by the planes and ships of TF 58, would mount, land, and support the expeditionary troops at Iwo Jima and Okinawa. To cover the landing of VAC on Iwo Jima, Admiral Mitscher's pilots struck heavily at the Tokyo area on 16–17 February and again on 25 February. On 1 March, while on its retirement route to Ulithi, TF 58 sent its planes over Okinawa to photograph enemy positions and hit defenses anew. The thoroughness with which the strafing, rocketing, and bombing covered the island led one veteran Marine flight leader to note that he had "never seen so many [planes] over one target at the same time."[27]

During the period when the fast carriers were ranging the Western Pacific, the Navy's submarines and patrol bombers were taking a steady toll of Japanese shipping. Working in close conjunction, the underseas wolf packs and seaplanes littered the bottom of the China Sea with the hulls of cargo vessels and the bodies of reinforcements who never reached their destination. By mid-February 1945 the enemy garrison was effectively isolated in the Ryukyus since "communications between the mainland of Japan and Formosa had been practically severed.[28]

From bases in China, India, the Philippines, Marianas, and Palaus, strategic bombers were smashing the industrial potential of Japan in a continuous series of strikes on the factories of the main islands and their outlying sources of raw materials. Giant B-29's, rising from fields in the southern Marianas in steadily increasing numbers, were staging 300-plane raids on Tokyo, Nagoya, Osaka, and Kobe by mid-March, increasing the fire-swept area of devastation on each occasion. In the interludes between carrier plane attacks, the superfortresses hit important targets in the Ryukyus with such frequency that the beleaguered Japanese troops referred to their visits as the "regular run."[29]

---

[25] *Ibid.*

[26] CinCPac-CinCPOA Bull 161–45, Translations and Interrogations No 34, 27Jun45, Diary of unidentified signalman, 5th Sea Raiding Base Hq.

[27] Statement of Maj D. C. Andre contained in VMF-(CV)–112 War Diary, March 1945, Strike Rpt 19–45.

[28] OCMH, Japanese Monograph No 135, Okinawa Operations Record, Revised Edition, November 1949, 45, hereinafter cited as *Okinawa Operations Record*. This study, prepared by surviving officers of the Thirty-second Army under the auspices of the Japanese First Demobilization Bureau, is a detailed account of the day-to-day operations of the army with supplemental sections covering the 24th InfDiv and 8th Air Div activities.

[29] CinCPac-CinCPOA Bull 147–45, Translations and Interrogations No 32, 16Jun45, Diary of unidentified superior pvt, 273d IIB.

NAHA, capital city of Okinawa, under aerial attack during the 10 October 1944 carrier strike. (Navy Photograph)

As L-Day approached, the tempo of covering operations increased throughout the Pacific. On 14 March, TF 58 sortied again from Ulithi for its final strike on Japan before the Okinawa operation began. Planes were launched on 18 March to interdict the airfields on Kyushu, and on the following day fighters and bombers swept over enemy installations on Shikoku and Honshu Islands. This time, however, the Japanese were ready and retaliated with powerful strikes on the task force. The retaliatory attack was sparked by suicide-bent *Kamikaze* (Divine Wind) pilots who were determined to crash on board an American ship. Five carriers, the *Franklin, Yorktown, Intrepid, Wasp,* and *Enterprise,* were hit, the *Franklin* so badly that it had to limp back to Pearl Harbor. The *Wasp* and *Enterprise,* temporarily out of action, were made part of a provisional task group for escort to Ulithi for repairs. The remaining carriers, the battleship force, and the protective screen were reorganized on 22 March into three relatively equal task groups. Admiral Mitscher's force then began its run to Okinawa for the opening of the pre-invasion bombardment.

SEIZURE OF KERAMA RETTO [30]

An essential feature of the ICEBERG operation plan was the seizure prior to L-Day of Kerama Retto and Keise Shima. Possession of a logistical support base close to the target would be an incalculable asset to the success of the operation. Emergency repair of battle damage, refueling and rearming operations, and the provision of "front line" supply and service support for the fleet meant maximum saving of lives and material. Once the proposed seaplane base was established in the anchorage, Navy patrol bombers could range from Korea to Indo-China in search, rescue, and antisubmarine operations. When the long-range guns of XXIV Corps artillery set up on Keise Shima, the complete cycle of preparations for the main assault would be completed. (See Map 7)

In the process of concentrating their defenses in southern Okinawa, the Japanese had gradually denuded the islands of Kerama Retto of defenders. Originally the garrison stood at 2,335 men, mostly personnel of the 1st, 2d, and 3d Sea Raiding Squadrons and Base Battalions. The conversion of the base battalions to infantry in February 1945 left about 1,000 men, who were augmented soon by 700 Korean laborers of the 103d Sea Duty Company. Before the 77th Division stormed ashore, however, many of these troops had returned to Okinawa during the general reinforcement of the Shuri-Shimajiri defenses in late March. Left as defenders were about 975 soldiers of varying combat value, distributed on four islands of the group— Zamami (400), Aka (300), Tokashiki (200), and Geruma Shima (75).

The real strength of Kerama Retto was centered around the more than 350 suicide boats of the sea raiding squadrons. Japanese records make it clear that the mission assigned them in the battle for Okinawa was destruction of the invasion transports lying off the Hagushi beaches. It is equally clear that, while it was

[30] Unless otherwise noted the material for this section is derived from *CTG 51.1 AR; 77th InfDiv OpRpt, Kerama Retto and Keise Shima;* AmphReconBn, FMFPac AR, Phase I and II, Nansei Shoto Operation, n. d., hereinafter cited as *AmphReconBn AR.*

SEIZURE of KERAMA RETTO
MARCH 1945
Scale 1:100,000

MAP 7

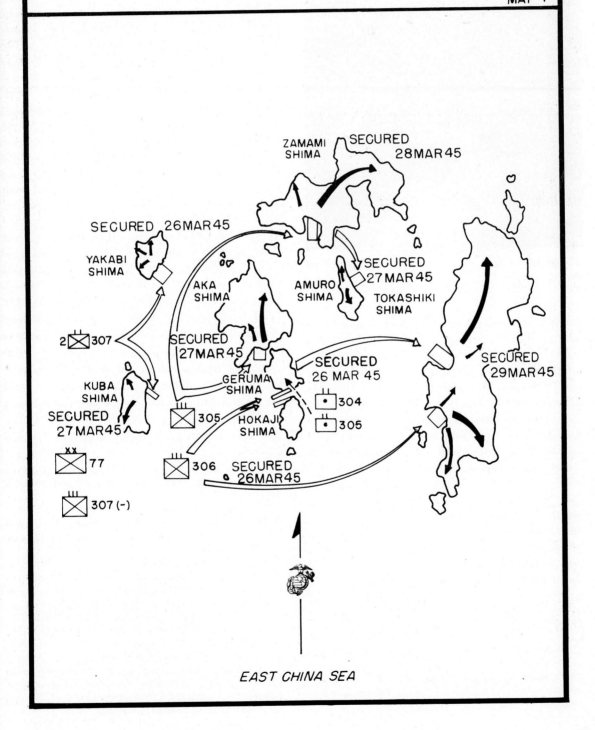

ZAMAMI SHIMA

SECURED 28MAR45

SECURED 26MAR45

YAKABI SHIMA

AKA SHIMA

AMURO SHIMA

SECURED 27MAR45

TOKASHIKI SHIMA

2 ⊠ 307

SECURED 27MAR45

GERUMA SHIMA

SECURED 26 MAR 45

SECURED 29MAR45

KUBA SHIMA

SECURED 27MAR45

⊠ 305

HOKAJI SHIMA

• 304

• 305

XX
⊠ 77

⊠ 306

SECURED 26MAR45

⊠ 307 (-)

EAST CHINA SEA

77TH DIVISION troops land on Hokaji Shima, Kerama Retto, on 26 March 1945 in the first amphibious attack of the Okinawa operation. (Army Photograph)

not dismissed, the concept of American seizure of the Kerama group prior to L-Day was lightly regarded. Perhaps too much depended on the success of these boats for the staff of the Thirty-second Army to entertain thoughts of complete destruction. If the Americans should attempt seizure of Kerama, orders were issued to shift the squadrons to the Naha area,[31] and to "employ the minimum strength necessary for self-defense" in holding the islands.[32]

Were it not for the protected anchorage in the lee of its islands, Kerama Retto would hardly have been classed as a priority target. There was nothing there to attract attention. So little flat land existed that the group could only support a population of 6,073 in 1940, and the main occupation of many of these people was fishing, not farming. Most of the area of the eight main islands, mountainous and blanketed with brush and trees, was inhospitable to the extreme. Except for small beaches at

the mouths of crooked, narrow valleys, steep slopes and cliffs extended to the water's edge.[33] In order to secure Kerama Retto it would be necessary to mount a series of semi-independent landing operations.

The mine sweepers of Admiral Blandy's Amphibious Support Force had cleared the way for the approach of the Western Islands Attack Group by nightfall of 25 March.[34] During the day members of UDT's (Underwater Demolition Teams) had reconnoitered the beaches of target islands in the Kerama group. The "frogmen" reported that no beaches were suitable for landing boats; all assaults would have to be made by amphibian tractors.[35]

The 77th Division's operation plans were flexible enough to allow for just such a contingency. Originally, two battalions had been slated to land on 26 March in LCVP's, 2/307 on Yakabi Shima and 3/306 on Kuba Shima.[36] When the UDT reports negated employment of landing boats, General Bruce notified unit commanders by dispatch that the preferred plan would be used with certain modifications. The four battalions originally scheduled for LVT-borne assaults would carry through their attacks on Zamami, Aka, Hokaji, and Geruma Shima. Those tractors which carried 3/305 into Aka Shima would immediately return to parent LST's and embark 2/307, which would meanwhile have transferred from its transport to the landing ships. A fifth landing of the day would then be made by 2/307 on Yakabi

---

[31] *Okinawa Operations Record*, 49.

[32] *CICAS Trans* No 231, 32d Army OpOrd A #115, 23Mar45.

[33] *CinCPOA Bull 161–44*, 56–58; CinCPac–CinCPOA Bull No 53–45, Okinawa Gunto, 2d Supplement, 28Feb45, 35–46.

[34] In order to avoid needless duplication, activities of TF 52 and TF 58 have been treated in this section only when they are intimately connected with Kerama Retto operations.

[35] Adm Kiland commended the "superb" performance of duty by these men from Underwater Demolition Group Able (Capt B. H. Hanlon, USN) whose accurate and timely reports "permitted changes to be made in the preferred landing plan which undoubtably saved many LCVP's and the lives of [many of] the 77th Division troops." RAdm I. N. Kiland Ltr to CMC, 28Oct54, hereinafter cited as *Kiland*.

[36] Because of the damage to the *Samuel Chase* in Leyte Gulf and the resultant commercial loading of 2/305 in the *Pitt*, 2/307 was assigned to assault Yakabi, originally part of 2/305's mission.

Shima. The remaining assault battalion, 3/306, would remain on board ship ready to land the following day as reserve in the 306th Infantry's operations against Tokashiki Shima, largest island of the group.

After TG 51.1 stood into the transport area in the early morning hours of 26 March, Admiral Kiland confirmed 0800 (M-Hour) as the time for the initial assaults on Kerama Retto.[37] LST's discharged their cargo of armored amphibians and troop-laden assault tractors for the run to the beaches. Carrier planes covered the transports and landing vehicles from Japanese suiciders who were beginning to filter through the outer fighter screen. Bombers plastered the landing beaches as mixed teams of LCI support craft formed to lead in the assault waves.[38]

A battleship and two large cruisers, supported by four destroyers, had been designated the NGF support unit for Kerama. The five-inch guns of the destroyers saw extensive service, but the larger ships, which remained on standby, were not called upon to fire. As each assault group approached its target, its support craft team commenced fire, with mortars opening up at 3,200 yards, rocket barrages beginning 1,100 yards, and automatic weapons within effective range. Fire was lifted at minimum range, and where possible these craft maintained steerageway to let assault waves pass through before retiring seaward. Destroyer support shifted to the flanks and inland to cover the landing when troops were 800 yards offshore.

Between 0801 and 0921 the four assault battalions landed on their objectives, which enclosed the Kerama anchorage from the west and north, although records disagree as to the

155MM GUNS of the 420th Field Artillery Group are set up on Keise Shima to shell the enemy's main defenses prior to the Tenth Army assault landing. (Army Photograph)

exact time each BLT came ashore.[39] By 1130, 2/306 had secured Hokaji Shima after finding no enemy and 1/306 had silenced the scattered opposition it had met on Geruma Shima. Both battalions reembarked on their LST's that afternoon to prepare for the 27 March assault on Tokashiki Shima which dominated the anchorage's eastern reaches. Two battalions of 105mm howitzers which landed in DUKW's on Geruma Shima to support further operations were emplaced and ready to fire at 1600.

The 3d Battalion, 305th Infantry landing on Aka Shima and that of 1/305 on Zamami Shima were met with light mortar and sniper fire at the beaches. Steady advances on both islands drove back the enemy defenders and secured beachheads by 1130. When night fell both units held secure positions from which they could launch the next day's attack.

While the units of the 305th and 306th Infantry were securing their objectives, the 2d

[37] Originally, Adm Kiland had delayed M-Hour, prompted by the necessity that he "be assured that a modification of the preferred plan had been received by all Attack Units concerned. . . . When assured that the changes in the landing plan were received and understood, it was possible to reestablish the original [M-Hour]." *Kiland.*

[38] The Support Craft Flotilla was composed of two mortar, three rocket, and four gunboat divisions. The 54 LCI's were organized into teams of various types and assigned to a specific beach and landing.

[39] *CTG 51.1 AR*, Chap III, 23–24 lists the landing times for Aka, Geruma, Hokaji, and Zamami Shima as 0804, 0801, 0921, and 0855, respectively. *77th InfDiv OpRpt, Kerama Retto and Keise Shima*, 29–31 gives the same landings as occurring at 0904, 0825, 0921, and 0900.

Battalion of the 307th was transferring to LST's. When the LVT's returned from Aka Shima, the troops embarked and made their unrehearsed assault. There was virtually no opposition, and Yakabi Shima was declared secure at 1600.

On 26 March the 77th Infantry Division had seized three islands of Kerama Retto and had a firm foothold on two others. Garrison elements on Aka and Zamami Shima had put up steady but light opposition, and the men of the 1st and 2d Sea Raiding Squadrons with their supporting base companies and Korean laborers had been driven back into the rugged island hills. Large numbers of suicide boats, which had not had time to get sea-borne because tactical surprise was achieved, had already been discovered hidden in caves and inlets along the rugged coast lines.[40]

While troops of the 77th Division awaited the next day's attacks, Marines of Major James L. Jones' FMF Reconnaissance Battalion (less Company B) made a night landing on the four reef islets of Keise Shima, discovered no enemy, and reembarked on board their destroyer transports.[41] During the night of 27–28 March Company A made a rubber boat landing on Aware Shima with the same result. No enemy were met by the scouts until 29 March when, in its last night landing before L-Day, the battalion reconnoitered two small islands, Mae and Kuro Shima, lying midway between Kerama Retto and Keise Shima. Although no garrison was present, the Marines' automatic weapons did destroy an enemy suicide boat which attempted to land on Mae Shima.

The story of enemy resistance was different on Zamami Shima, where the defending forces were bulwarked by the 1st Sea Raiding Squadron. During the night of 26–27 March, 1/305 repulsed ten separate counterattacks. One hundred and thirteen enemy dead lay in front of the battalion positions in the morning. During the day the 1st Battalion flushed out Japanese stragglers in the brush-covered hills to the north, while covering the administrative landing of 2/305, garrison for Kerama Retto. At 1300, Company B of 1/305 made a shore-to-shore assault on neighboring Amuro Shima; there was no opposition and the unit returned to Zamami at 1500. Both battalions made preparations that evening for a final clean-up drive on 28 March.

The remaining battalion of the 305th Infantry, the 3d, had spent a quiet night on Aka Shima. Extensive patrol action on 27 March developed an enemy position held by 75 men, reinforced by machine guns and mortars. An air strike, followed by a mortar barrage, enabled one company to scatter this pocket, and the battalion held up its attack at dusk.

The last remaining major target in the island group was assaulted by the 306th Infantry on 27 March. Preceded by rocket and destroyer fire, the 1st and 2d Battalions landed on separated beaches on Tokashiki Shima, with all elements coming ashore between 0908 and 0943. Resistance was light, but the broken terrain held up the attack. At 1300, 3/306 began landing in reserve with the mission of cleaning out the southern part of the five-mile long island. By nightfall the two assault battalions had joined and were ready for a drive to the north. On 28 March the scattered remnants of the 3d Sea Raiding Squadron were hunted down with relentless vigor.

One more island was added to the 77th's bag for 27 March when Company G, 2/307 moved via LVT from Hokaji to Kuba Shima and effected a bloodless occupation. After its second day of operations, General Bruce's division were ready to mop up Kerama Retto. On 28 and 29 March, units of the 305th and 306th Infantry did just that. Aka, Zamami, and Tokashiki Shima, where resistance had been centered, were secured and the few enemy remaining were incapable of organized resistance. After detaching 2/305 for garrison

[40] More than 350 suicide boats were captured or destroyed at Kerama Retto. The G–3 of the 77th InfDiv noted in a definite understatement "that the capture of these boats was of major assistance to the success of the main landings, for had they not been eliminated some damage would undoubtedly have been done to the landing force ships, particularly at night." Col. F. D. Miller Ltr to CMC, 22Oct 54.

[41] For operations in the Kerama area the ReconBn was split into two tactical groups, one under the battalion CO, the other under the battalion ExO. Co B, which was assigned to VAC for Iwo Jima, was not available until after L-Day.

duty, with the mission of patrolling the group from its base on Zamami, the 77th Division reembarked its troops. The last unit to board, 1/306, left Tokashiki Shima on 31 March.

While the division was securing the Retto, UDT's from TF 52 were blasting a path through the reefs of Keise Shima for the 420th Field Artillery Group's 155mm guns. Early on 31 March, 2/306 was landed on Keise in a last minute check for enemy opposition. Results were the same as those in previous searches—negative. Soon thereafter men and equipment of the 420th Group, whose tractor group had come up during the night, began landing. At 1935 the big guns began registration fire on selected targets in southern Okinawa where, as the Japanese reported, they "incessantly obstructed our movements by laying a great quantity of fire inside our positions." [42]

Within a few days the fire had become so galling that a special Japanese attack unit was formed to raid Keise. The 5th Artillery Command's 150mm guns were also ordered to concentrate on silencing the American "long toms." Neither measure proved to be successful, nor was the Thirty-second Army ever able to enforce its order to "stop the use of enemy artillery on Keise Shima." [43]

Between 26 and 31 March, at a cost of 31 killed and 81 wounded, the 77th Infantry Division, vanguard of Expeditionary Troops, had completely fulfilled its combat mission. Five hundred and thirty Japanese had been killed in the process, 121 had been taken prisoner, and 1,195 civilians had been rounded up. Although scattered enemy remained hidden in the hills of Kerama Retto and even communicated with Okinawa on occasion,[44] the Japanese garrison had ceased to exist as a threat to operation of the anchorage.

Before L-Day the floating naval base was performing all its planned functions. Sea-planes were already coursing the China Sea seeking out enemy submarines and ships. Repair vessels were busy patching up the damage caused by Japanese suicide planes, saving many of the ships concerned for further duty in Okinawan waters and a host of others from a permanent berth at the bottom of the ocean. Tankers and ammunition ships were engaged in a steady round of refueling and rearming operations. Without this logistic anchorage base "many more ships and personnel of the service force than were available in the Okinawa operation would have been required at sea to make replenishment an accomplished fact for all fleet forces." [45]

PRELANDING OPERATIONS[46]

Two days before the 77th Division's assault on Kerama Retto, the first elements of TF 52 were operating at the target. At daybreak on 24 March, sweepers of Mine Group One began clearing a channel outside the 100-fathom curve off the southeast coast of Okinawa. Then, while planes of TF 58 covered these operations and struck enemy installations ashore, the battleships of Admiral Mitscher's force, temporarily organized as TF 59, steamed through the swept area and opened fire on Okinawa. The impact of the 16-inch shells gave the garrison its first taste of "the ferocity of naval gunfire." [47] By late afternoon, as TF 59 was retiring to rejoin the carrier force, the mine vessels had finished their planned preliminary sweeps near Okinawa and Kerama Retto.

During this day's operations Task Force 54 with elements of TF 52, Admiral Deyo serving as Officer in Tactical Command, had completed their run from Ulithi and formed approach dispositions. Two fire support units separated themselves from the task force, one to cover

---

[42] *Okinawa Operations Record*, 49.

[43] *CICAS Trans* No. 266, 32d Army OpOrd A #127, 6Apr45. Although this order specifically directed the CO of the shipping engineers to organize a raiding unit and attack Keise on the night of 6 April, no contemporary records show that this operation was carried through.

[44] *Okinawa Operations Record*, 49.

[45] RAdm W. R. Carter, *Beans, Bullets, and Black Oil*, (Washington, 1953), 353.

[46] Unless otherwise noted the material in this section is derived from CinCPOA OpPlan 14–44, 31Dec44; CTF 51 OpPlan A1–45, 16Feb45; *CTF 51 AR; CTF 52 AR*.

[47] CinCPac-CinCPOA Bull 147–45, Translations and Interrogations No 32, 16Jun45, Diary of unidentified superior pvt, 273d IIB.

TORPEDO BOMBERS OF TF 58, each loaded with 18 100-pound bombs, fly over the *Bunker Hill* on a pre-L-Day strike mission against Okinawa. (Navy Photograph)

mine sweeping between Tonachi Shima and Kerama Retto and the other to cover mine sweepers off Okinawa and begin bombardment of the demonstration beaches. Underwater Demolition Group Able, mounted in high speed transports and covered by destroyers, formed for the next day's UDT and NGF operations at Kerama. The remainder of Admiral Deyo's force remained concentrated, ready to repulse any Japanese surface and aerial attacks.[48]

This concentration of strength was a carefully planned feature of the ICEBERG operation. To the east of the island group lay TF 58 with sea room and fighting power sufficient to overwhelm any or all of the remnants of the enemy navy. Closer in, on the west, the majority of the combat ships of the Amphibious Support Force were to concentrate, ready to stop any attempt to reinforce or evacuate the garrison. Those ships assigned to bombardment of the southeast coast of Okinawa were to retire together at night so that there would be no delay when they resumed their mission each morning. Each of the task groupings was able to sustain itself in any contemplated surface action.

As the mine sweepers cleared progressively larger areas around Okinawa, destroyers and gunboats moved in to patrol the intra-island waters and completely isolate the beleaguered garrisons. The ever present threat of enemy air was answered by the establishment of radar picket stations which eventually ringed the entire island group. Fighter director teams on board destroyers in each picket group controlled the combat air patrol which orbited over the station during daylight hours. These picket ships, which bore the brunt of the Navy's costly battle for Okinawa, were of incalculable value in protecting the vulnerable transport and service areas.

The devastating raids of TF 58 on the airfields of Kyushu had temporarily disorganized the attack plans of the enemy in the home islands. Once it was clear that an amphibious assault was in the offing, however, the Japanese began to mount an increasing number of strikes from the Formosa area on the inviting targets in the waters of Okinawa Gunto. Forward elements of the 8th Air Division, rising from fields in Sakishima Gunto, made their first *Kamikaze* attack on ships standing off Kerama Retto at dawn on 26 March.[49]

At 0624, the first of many ships to be crashed during the campaign, the destroyer *Kimberly*, was hit by a suicider which knocked out four five-inch guns, a 20mm cannon, and two depth charge throwers. Four men were killed, 33 wounded, and 17 were missing. During the hour-long attack four other ships were damaged by suicide planes crashing close aboard,

---

[48] Command relationships between CTF 52 (RAdm Blandy) and CTF 54 (RAdm Deyo) were somewhat complicated. CTF 52 as SOPA was in overall command of all operations at the target, while CTF 54 was responsible for the movement and approach to the objective of TF 54 and ships of TF 52 moving with TF 54, for fighting surface actions should there be any, and for night retirements.

[49] *Okinawa Operations Record*, Record of the 8th Air Div, Chart 1.

and the casualty list was swelled by three more killed and eight wounded.

The toll in ship damage and seamen's lives mounted each day as bombers and suiciders attacked the amphibious force in the half-light of dawn and dusk. On 26 and 27 March, Vice Admiral Sir Bernard Rawling's British Carrier Force (TF 57) struck the Sakishima Gunto as part of its planned schedule of preliminary operations supporting the assault. On 27 March, therefore, the Japanese carried the fight to the American task force with planes based on Okinawa. All available aircraft, including trainers, liaison planes, and a special attack unit which managed to fly in from Kyushu, were put into the air. By 29 March, after three suicide attacks, the air strength of the Okinawa garrison was expended.[50]

Before L-Day, the 8th Air Division sent 64 aircraft, 45 of them potential suiciders, against TF 52. Only 29 planes returned, but those that did brought back glowing reports of having sunk a battleship, a cruiser, and 11 other warships, while damaging 15 more.[51]

While the claims were as usual grossly exaggerated, the actual damage done was extensive. Starting on 27 March with work on the *Kimberly*, the repair ships at Kerama Retto handled a constant stream of cripples. Between 26 and 31 March six ships, including Admiral Spruance's flagship *Indianapolis*, were crashed by suiciders. Ten vessels were damaged by bombs and suicide misses. In addition, a destroyer and a mine sweeper that hit floating mines were sunk and an LCI(G) was damaged in an encounter with a Japanese torpedo boat. As a grim portent of things to come, TF 52's casualty list for the six days (26–31 March) showed 74 killed, 216 wounded, and 48 missing in action.

Steadily throughout this period of enemy air attacks, the support force proceeded with its main task of preparing the target for assault. Underwater Demolition Group Able, comprising four of the ten UDT's assigned to TF 52, cleared the beach approaches in Kerama Retto on 26 March and began working on the reefs of Keise Shima the next day. Although reconnaissance and demolition work off Okinawa's beaches had been scheduled to begin on 28 March, the need for additional offshore mine sweeping forced a delay. On 29 March, Underwater Demolition Group Baker made a reconnaissance of the Hagushi beaches while elements of Group Able scouted the demonstration beaches.

The pattern of support for the UDT's paralleled that used in previous operations. Successive lines of gunboats, destroyers, cruisers, and battleships smothered a 1,000-yard zone inland of the water line with suppressive fire. The cruisers and battleships, firing from stations 3,700 yards out, used their secondary batteries for UDT support while continuing main battery destructive fire on specific targets inland.[52]

During their reconnaissance on 29 March, the swimmers of Group Baker discovered approximately 2,900 wooden posts, six to eight inches in diameter, loosely set in rows into the reefs off the Hagushi beaches. Demolition operations were begun to remove these obstacles on 30 March, while UDT men operating off the demonstration beaches detonated charges of tetratol to persuade the Japanese that there would be a landing made on the southeast coast. Most of the posts were blown during the first day's operations, but two charges failed to explode and the teams returned on 31 March to remove the remainder. Only 200 scattered posts remained on L-Day and UDT guides with landing waves could lead the LVT's safely past

---

[50] The only air reinforcements to reach Okinawa, the 32d Makoto Special Attack Unit (nine planes), landed at Kadena during the night of 26 March. At dawn on the 27th it made an all-out suicide attack and some of its planes crashed the *Biloxi* and *Nevada*. On 28 and 29 March the seven aircraft remaining on the island were lost in similar attacks. *Ibid.*, 48–49.

[51] *Ibid.*, Record of the 8th Air Div, Table No 9, Part 2.

[52] The main departure from previous tactics of NGF support of UDT's was the circuitous approach used by the LCI(G)'s to avoid the appearance of an assault landing. At Iwo Jima, Japanese coast-defense guns had opened up on gunboats supporting UDT reconnaissance because the enemy thought a landing attempt was being made. See LtCol W. S. Bartley, *Iwo Jima: Amphibious Epic*, MC Historical Monograph, (Washington, 1954), 44–47, hereinafter cited as *Iwo Jima*.

these points.[53] After the reconnaissance and initial demolition operations had been completed on 29 and 30 March, troop observers with the UDT's were dispatched by ship to join the approaching attack groups with the latest intelligence information on the landing beaches.[54] The reports were generally favorable to a successful landing across the entire Tenth Army front.[55]

The principal deterrent to meeting the planned schedule of NGF preparation for ICEBERG was the presence of mines in the waters around Okinawa. Task Force 52 estimated its mine vessels swept and reswept over 3,000 square miles in the period 25–31 March, destroying 257 mines in the process. It was not until 29 March (L–minus 3) that the inshore approaches were declared safe enough for fire support ships to close to ranges of maximum effectiveness. Prior to that date, beginning with the first TF 54 bombardment of southeastern Okinawa on 25 March, the cruisers and battleships fired limited schedules which increased in scope as familiarity with the target and progressively closer ranges were obtained.

Although the full power of NGF bombardment was not realized until late in the preparation period, carrier air was able to strike the target repeatedly, hampered only by the AA fire of the defenders. The close air support unit (CASU) of TF 52 directed 3,095 sorties against Okinawa Gunto prior to L-Day. Special emphasis was laid on smashing submarine pens, airfields, suicide boat installations, bridges leading into the landing area, and gun positions. Each day's strike results were evaluated by CASU officers on board Admiral Blandy's command ship *Estes*, coordinated with NGF plans, and a revised schedule of missions issued for the next day's sorties.

Aerial observation and photo reconnaissance supplemented by reports of results obtained by fire support ships, enabled task force gunnery officers to maintain target information on a current basis. Ships were encouraged to conduct exploratory fire and seek profitable secondary targets in addition to completing priority fire missions. Because provision had been made in naval operation plans for ammunition replenishment at Kerama Retto, the expenditure of shells was high.

Despite the fact that 27,226 rounds of five-inch or larger caliber were fired in seven days of preliminary bombardment, losses to the deeply dug-in Japanese were slight. Damage to surface installations was extensive, however, especially in the vicinity of the airfields. By midafternoon of 31 March, Admiral Blandy had evaluated the effect of the air and NGF bombardment and could report that "the preparation was sufficient for a successful landing." [56]

During the period of prelanding preparation, the Thirty-second Army had been able to keep its tactical dispositions relatively concealed. Although the Americans knew generally where the enemy was disposed, actual revelation of many Japanese positions waited the probing attacks of ground elements. Overbalancing this enemy achievement was the American success in maintaining the illusion of a landing in southeast Okinawa. Naval bombardment and UDT operations convinced the enemy staff that "the possibility could not be ruled out that powerful elements might attempt a landing." [57] Accordingly, a substantial portion of the ene-

---

[53] Gen Shepherd noted "that many of these stakes were not in any sense a hazard to our ship-to-shore movement, they being primarily emplaced for either fishing purposes or deception. In any case, a UDT officer stated that he could remove most of them with his hands, without any demolitions required." *CMC Memo.*

[54] One officer for each battalion in assault, one for each RCT, division, and corps, and one for the army were assigned to go with the UDT's as reconnaissance and liaison personnel. Liaison officers briefed the UDT's on the scheme of maneuver to enable the teams to make certain that specific landing areas were cleared; they also observed the terrain in the vicinity of their assigned beaches. Tenth Army Tentative OpPln 1–45, 6Jan45, Appendix A, 1–z.

[55] In the 6th MarDiv zone of action "considerable question was raised as to the extent to which the defenses on the beaches were manned. The UDT personnel stated that they had been unable to detect any evidence of enemy in the beach emplacements while [the division] troop representative was of the opinion that those positions were in fact manned." *CMC Memo.*

[56] *CTF 52 AR*, Chap V, Sect C, 5.
[57] *Okinawa Operations Record*, 50.

ny's artillery and infantry strength was kept out of the first days' action by a threat that never materialized.

The Hagushi beaches, however, were still considered to be the most probable target. The scratch force formed from airfield personnel in this area to oppose the landing had been heartened by the reports of successes of *Kamikaze* attacks against the invasion fleet, but its commander cautioned his men not "to draw the hasty conclusion that we had been able to destroy the enemy's plan of landing on Okinawa Jima." [58] The regimental commander, Lieutenant Colonel Tokio Aoyanagi, was something of a prophet, since less than 24 hours after his message was distributed, the Northern and Southern Attack Forces were moving into their respective transport areas ready to launch the assault.

[58] CinCPac-CinCPOA Bull 107–45, Translations and Interrogations No 28, 14May45, 1st Specially Established Regt OpOrd No 1, 30Mar45.

Japanese Defensive Preparations[1]

CHAPTER **IV**

In early summer of 1944, as the tide of battle turned inexorably against the Japanese defenders of the southern Marianas, staff planners in Tokyo faced a thorny problem. Japan was losing the war it had started so confidently in December 1941. To the south and to the east, amphibious forces were steadily driving toward the core of the home island defenses. The steady attrition of air and undersea raiders had already cut off large numbers of garrison troops from effectual contact with Japan. A reasonable projection of Allied capabilities indicated that time for reinforcing the inner defenses was growing woefully short. For the next major Allied operation, aside from the inevitable return to the Philippines, Tokyo weighed probable targets of the South China Coast, Formosa, and the Ryukyus.

At Naha, headquarters of the newly formed Thirty-second Army, the choice of many potential objectives was narrowed to just one—Okinawa. Convinced that the main island of the Nansei Shoto would be invaded in the near future, staff officers hoped for enough time and men to make Okinawa a veritable fortress. Defensive planning was governed by bitter experience which had shown that "an army trained to attack on any and every occasion, irrespective of conditions, and with no calculation as to the real chances of success, could be beaten soundly."[2]

A new defensive concept had been forced on the Japanese by the failure of this accepted doctrine in the Solomons and on New Guinea. In turn, the theory of "impregnable defenses" designed to stop landing forces at the beaches of the Gilberts, Marshalls, and Marianas collapsed before the power of the American air-sea-land assault team. The Japanese finally adopted a defensive system aimed at prolonging each individual action to the utmost and inflicting maximum casualties.[3] In effect, the orders to the remaining island garrisons were to dig in, go underground, prepare for a protracted defense, and together with Japanese naval and air forces bleed Allied striking power to an

---

[1] Unless otherwise noted the material in this chapter is derived from *Okinawa Operations Record; IntelMono*; Tenth Army G–2 POW Interrogation Summaries Nos 1–19, July-August 1945, hereinafter cited as *POW InterSum*; Tenth Army G–2 Interrogation Rpt No 27, Akira Shimada (Secretary to LtGen Cho), 24Jul45, hereinafter cited as *Shimada Interrogation*; Tenth Army G-2 Interrogation Report No 28, Col Hiromichi Yahara (Senior Staff Officer, Thirty-second Army), 6Aug45, hereinafter cited as *Yahara Interrogation*.

[2] *IntelMono*, Part I, Sect A, 3.

[3] USSBS(Pac), NavAnalysis Div, *Interrogations of Japanese Officials*, 2 vols (Washington, 1946), Interrogation No 447, LtGen Torashira Kawabe, II, 426–427. This publication hereinafter referred to as *USSBS Interrogation* with interrogation number and name.

anemic standstill. For the Thirty-second Army the new concept was reflected in its battle slogans:

One Plane for One Warship
One Boat for One Ship
One Man for Ten of the Enemy
or One Tank [4]

THE THIRTY-SECOND ARMY

Lieutenant General Mitsuru Ushijima succeeded to the command of the Thirty-second Army in August 1944.[5] Exercising his recognized talent for choosing capable subordinates, he selected one of the ablest officers of the Japanese Army, Major General Isamu Cho, as his chief of staff. Cho, in turn, hand-picked from the "bright young men" of Imperial Headquarters a smoothly functioning staff exceptional for its alert and progressive attitude.

This command team, Ushijima and Cho, formed an effective combination in the tradition of Germany's Hindenburg and Ludendorf in World War I.[6] Ushijima, a senior officer slated for promotion to general in August 1945, was reputedly a quiet, competent man capable of inspiring great confidence and respect in his subordinates. Both he and Cho were veterans of the Burma campaigns early in the war, Ushijima as an infantry group commander and Cho as assistant chief of staff of the Southern Army. Prior to assuming command of the Thirty-second Army, General Ushijima served as Commandant of the Japanese Military Academy. During the same period, Cho was assigned to the General Military Affairs Bureau

of the War Department. General Cho, an extremely aggressive man with an Army-wide reputation as a strict disciplinarian, was the firebrand of the Okinawan defense. According to Japanese sources, he was relatively young for his rank and destined for high position in the service.[7] With his fiery faculties counterbalanced by Ushijima's soft-spoken demeanor, Cho effectively managed the strengthening of the Ryukyuan defenses.

Although units of division and brigade strength were added to garrisons on the other islands of the Nansei Shoto, notably Miyako Jima, the major reinforcement was made on Okinawa. Here the Americans were expected to land. To a large extent, in keeping with their flexible combat organization, the Japanese attempted to tailor the Thirty-second Army for the coming showdown battle. Many independent artillery, mortar, antiaircraft artillery (AAA), antitank (AT), and machine-gun units were assigned to the army to augment the firepower of its basic infantry strength.

Between June and August 1944, the major reinforcing units arrived from their former posts in China, Manchuria, and Japan. The 9th Infantry Division, first to arrive, was a veteran organization with battle honors dating from the Russo-Japanese War (1904–5). Considered by the Japanese to be the crack unit of the defensive force, it came directly from Manchuria. Fortunately for the Americans, however, the 9th Division was not destined to participate in the coming battle. The division left Okinawa for the Philippines in December by way of Formosa. MacArthur's landing on Luzon in January caught the 9th still on Formosa, where it stayed, shepherded by Allied submarines and planes, until the end of the war.[8]

In late June, about 600 men, survivors of the 44th Independent Mixed Brigade (IMB) landed on Okinawa. The brigade, later to become the headache of Tenth Army order of battle interpreters, had been raised at Kuma-

---

[4] CinCPac-CINCPOA Bull 122–45, Translations and Interrogations No 30, 1Jun45, 32d Army Battle Instructions, 15Feb45.

[5] The original commander of the Thirty-second Army, LtGen Hasao Watanabe, had been forced to retire due to chronic illness. His chief of staff, MajGen Kiyom Kitagawa, was replaced shortly thereafter by the new army commander.

[6] This famous relationship has been described by MajGen Hunter Liggett, commander of the First U. S. Army, A. E. F. "[Hindenburg] was the army's chief, [Ludendorf], his executive officer, but Ludendorf was the younger man, the greater organizer, more brilliant strategist, more resourceful mind; he was the greater in every respect but one—character." MajGen H. Liggett, *A.E.F.: Ten Years Ago in France*, (New York, 1928), 33.

[7] On 1Mar45, at the age of 51, Cho was promoted to lieutenant general.

[8] MIS, WD, Order of Battle for the Japanese Armed Forces, 1Mar45, 32.

moto, Kyushu in early June. Originally composed of the 1st and 2d Infantry Units (both approximately regimental size) with a combined complement of around 6,000, its organization and strength varied considerably over the course of the following months. While en route to Okinawa on 23 June 1944, its convoy was attacked by American submarines, and the *Toyama Maru* was sent to the bottom with more than 5,000 men. Replacements for one of the infantry units, the 2d, were raised in late summer on Kyushu and Okinawa.[9] The 1st Infantry Unit, however, existed merely as a headquarters and was never rebuilt. Instead, another newly-raised unit, the 15th Independent Mixed Regiment (IMR), was flown directly from Tokyo to Okinawa, and added to the 44th IMB in July, bringing its strength up to about 5,000 men. (See Chart 3)

The 24th Infantry Division, organized in December 1939 in Toan, Manchuria as part of the Kwantung Army, was the next major unit to arrive on Okinawa (July). Although this division, commanded by Lieutenant General Tatsumi Amamiya, was not battle-tested, it was well-trained and considered combat ready. The 24th, a triangular division, had been stripped of its infantry group headquarters, one battalion from each of its regiments, an artillery battalion, and an engineer company to help form various reinforcing expeditionary units sent from Manchuria to the Central Pacific in early 1944. For several months after their arrival, the 24th's infantry regiments, the 22d, 32d, and 89th Infantry, operated as two battalion units. In October over 1,200 Okinawan conscripts were added to the division for training and eventual absorption, and in January 1945 a general reorganization brought the unit very near its original strength. As the largest tactical unit in the Thirty-second Army on Okinawa, the 24th Division had over 14,000 Japanese troops and Okinawan conscripts assigned to its infantry, artillery, reconnaissance,

engineer, and transport regiments, and to divisional troops. (See Chart 4)

The last major unit assigned to the Thirty-second Army, the 62d Infantry Division, commanded by Lieutenant General Takeo Fujioka, arrived on Okinawa in August. The division had been activated in June 1943 in Shansi Province, China. Its internal organization, which varied considerably from that of the 24th Division, was typical of similar units in the Chinese Expeditionary Army. A square division whose brigades both had served in China as independent commands since 1938, the 62d fought as a unit in the April–June 1944 campaigns in northern Honan Province. Organic to each brigade were four independent infantry battalions (IIB); the 63d Brigade had the 11th, 12th, 13th, and 14th IIB's, and the 64th Brigade had the 15th, 21st, 22d, and 23d IIB's. In January 1945 two additional independent infantry battalions sent as reinforcements to Okinawa were attached to the division, which assigned the 272d IIB to the 64th Brigade and the 273d IIB to the 63d Brigade. The division had no organic artillery and few other supporting units, and its strength, even with the addition of the 272d and 273d IIB's, amounted to less than 12,000 men, almost all infantry. (See Chart 5)

Within the infantry components of the three major fighting organizations on Okinawa, there was some variance in strength. The 44th IMB's 2d Infantry Unit and 15th IMR each had three rifle battalions, an antitank company (4 37mm or 47mm AT guns), and a regimental gun company (4 75mm guns). Each battalion had three rifle companies, a machine-gun company, and an infantry gun unit (2 70mm howitzers) with a total strength of roughly 700 men. In the regiments of the 24th Division, the organization was similar except that one battalion in each regiment had a mortar platoon (4 81mm mortars) instead of the usual 70mm howitzers.

The 62d Division's organic battalions were the strongest infantry units on the island, each mustering 1,200 men in five rifle companies, a machine-gun company, and an infantry gun company with two 75mm guns and two 70mm howitzers. Available evidence indicates the

---

[9] The 2d InfUnit, although it was rebuilt and re-organized, never regained much of the organic equipment lost on the *Toyama Maru*. As a result it gained the nickname of *Bimbo Tai* (Have-Nothing Unit) among the Japanese troops.

THIRTY-SECOND ARMY OFFICERS sit for a formal portrait in February 1945. Numbers identify: (1) Rear Admiral Minoru Ota, Commander, Naval Base Force; (2) Lieutenant General Mitsuru Ushijima, Commanding General, Thirty-second Army; (3) Lieutenant General Isamu Cho, Army C/S; (4) Colonel Hitoshi Kanayama, Commanding 89th Regiment; (5) Colonel Kiuji Hongo, Commanding 32d Regiment; (6) Colonel Hiromichi Yahara, Army Senior Staff Officer. (Photograph courtesy of OCMH, DA)

attached 272d and 273d IIB's, with a reported strength of 700 men each, had one or two less rifle companies.

Because it was expected that the battle for Okinawa would develop into a relatively static position defense, Thirty-second Army was not assigned any strong armored force. The sole tank unit on the island, the 27th Tank Regiment, was organized in Manchuria in April 1944 from elements of the 2d Armored Division and reached Okinawa in July. The regiment was in effect an armored task force with a strength of 750 men organized into one light and one medium tank company, a tractor-drawn artillery battery, an infantry company, a main-

tenance company, and an engineer platoon.[10] Major armament of the regiment included 14 medium and 13 light tanks, four 75mm guns, two 47mm AT guns, and ten machine guns.

All artillery on Okinawa, with the exception of the 24th Division's organic 42d Field Artillery Regiment, was under control of Major General Kosuke Wada's 5th Artillery Command. In addition to the relatively weak 7th Heavy Artillery Regiment (the former Nakagusuku Wan Fortress Artillery Unit), General Wada's command included two medium regi-

---

[10] Originally the 27th TkRegt had two medium tank companies, but one was sent to the garrison of Miyako Jima.

ments, a heavy battalion, and the artillery units of the 44th IMB and 27th Tank Regiment. The combat-tested 1st Medium Artillery, which came from Manchuria in July, was a two-battalion regiment whose 1st Battalion was sent on to Miyako Jima.[11] The 23d Medium Artillery Regiment, which arrived in October, had been activated in 1941 and stationed since then in Japan. Together the two medium regiments mustered 2,000 troops to man 36 150mm howitzers. The 100th Independent Heavy Artillery Battalion had been formed in the fall of 1943 and brought its 500 men and eight 150mm guns directly from Japan to Okinawa in July 1944.

An unusual unit, of a type first encountered by Marines on Iowa Jima,[12] also operated under the 5th Artillery Command. This 1st Independent Artillery Mortar Regiment (or rather three of its batteries, since the other three had been sent from Manchuria to Burma in mid-1942) added 24 320mm spigot mortars to the Thirty-second Army's supporting fires.[13] In addition to these awesome weapons, whose 675-pound shells were dubbed "flying ashcans" by Americans, 96 81mm mortars in two light mortar battalions were available to Thirty-second Army. Although the 81mm mortar units were nominally under 5th Artillery Command, in actual practice they were assigned close support missions with the various infantry units and usually operated under sector defense commanders.

Besides the mortars and artillery gathered loosely under the 5th Artillery Command's aegis, many antiaircraft, antitank, and automatic weapons units were directly attached to the infantry during most of the campaign. Three independent AAA, three field AAA, and three machine cannon battalions performed a double role of air and ground defense with 72 75mm guns and 54 20mm machine cannon. Three independent AT battalions and one inde-

pendent company, all newly equipped with the effective 47mm gun, added 48 more high-velocity, flat trajectory weapons to the defense. Finally, rounding out the roster of nominal ground combat units, four independent machine-gun battalions with 96 heavy machine guns were closely integrated into infantry defensive positions.

In addition to the aforementioned line troops, the Thirty-second Army had many diversified supporting elements. Included in this number were thousands of potential infantry replacements of varying caliber, ranging from good in the two shipping engineer regiments to poor, at best, in the various small service units. One of the largest groupings of these units, numbering some 7,000 men, was under the 19th Air Sector Command Headquarters and consisted for the most part of airfield maintenance and construction troops stationed at the airstrips at Yontan and Kadena and on Ie Shima.

One category of Thirty-second Army troops, first encountered in the Philippines, deserves special mention: the sea raiding units.[14] Disguised in Japanese records by a variety of cover names, these super-secret organizations were designed to destroy amphibious invasion fleets with explosive-laden suicide boats. In the Okinawa Gunto, there was a total of seven sea raiding squadrons, three stationed in Kerama Retto, each with a strength of about 100 hand-picked men and 100 boats.[15] Supporting each squadron was a base battalion with a strength of 900 men whose duties included the construction and protection of the raiding base and the maintenance of the boats.

General Ushijima not only controlled all the Army air and ground units on the island, but was to assume command of the naval units on the island once ground combat was joined. Most of the 3,500 Japanese navy men and 6,000–7,000 civilian employees belonged to sub-units

---

[11] The 1st MedArtyRegt (also called the 1st FldHvyArtyRegt) was one of the original units to land at Lingayen Gulf in December 1941 and it participated in the struggle for Bataan. See L. Morton, *The Fall of the Philippines*, U. S. Army in World War II, (Washington, 1953), *passim*.

[12] *Iwo Jima*, 13–14.

[13] Each battery had in addition two 90mm mortars and two light machine guns.

[14] See M. L. Cannon and R. R. Smith, *Triumph in the Philippines*, U. S. Army in World War II, to be published in 1955.

[15] These men, mostly middle school graduates, were of a uniformly high caliber and considered officer candidate material. When one failed to return from a suicide mission, therefore being presumably successful, he was reportedly given a posthumous promotion to second lieutenant.

of the Okinawa Base Force under Rear Admiral Minoru Ota, an officer who had had considerable experience with Special Naval Landing Force units.[16] With the exception of a naval 81mm mortar battery (18 mortars), none of Admiral Ota's units were trained for ground combat prior to arrival on Okinawa. A small number of naval officers and enlisted men and most of the civilians were formed into maintenance, supply, and construction units for the large airfield on Oroku Peninsula and the harbor installations at Naha. At Unten-Ko on Motobu Peninsula, a torpedo boat squadron and a midget submarine unit were stationed. The major portion of the regular naval troops were formed into antiaircraft and coast defense batteries. Organized into four battery groups—emplaced mainly in the Naha-Oroku-Tomigusuku area—the AAA units manned 20 120mm guns, 77 25mm machine cannon, and 60 13mm machine guns. The 15 coast defense batteries were placed at strategic locations on the island's coast line, where their 16cm and 12cm rifles were under local Army sector commanders.

An important manpower augmentation of the Japanese Army was encountered for the first time on Okinawa. In June of 1944, faced with a steadily worsening military situation, Imperial Headquarters authorized the War Ministry to organize a Home Guard. The *Boeitai*, as the guard was called, consisted initially of all reservists in the 20–40 age group, including those who under the Japanese conscription system normally were not liable for regular service.[17] Local Army commanders, such as General Ushijima, assumed control of the *Boeitai* conscription set-up in their areas. These generals had wide latitude in details of conscription, organization, and utilization of the home guards. On Okinawa, almost as soon as the authorization was received, the Thirty-second Army began drafting men to help build up the island's defenses. These home guardsmen augmented the regular active service conscriptees, who may have numbered as many as 7,000. Exactly how many Okinawans eventually served in defense of their island is not known, but conservative estimates place the figure close to 20,000.

The *Boeitai* were a valuable addition to Thirty-second Army forces, although their capabilities as combat troops were slight. The majority bolstered regular units as labor details and rear echelon increments for service troops. Their drills, picks, and shovels steadily digging into the Okinawan hillsides over a period of almost nine months contributed substantially toward prolonging the battle for the island. Defenses that they helped dig were manned by combat troops they relieved from rear area duties. This additional manpower enabled the Thirty-second Army to stand off the American assault forces for three bitter and bloody months.

STRENGTHENING THE DEFENSES

"It became axiomatic in the Pacific War that the Japanese would dig and construct in a way and to an extent that an American soldier has never been known to do."[18] The pattern of organization of the ground on Okinawa paralleled that which assault forces found on Biak and Peleliu in late 1944 and on Iwo Jima in February 1945.[19] The most favorable defensive terrain was occupied and honeycombed with mutually supporting gun positions and protected connecting tunnels. Natural and man-made barriers were effectively incorporated into the defensive system in order to channelize an

[16] The Okinawa Base Force was activated 15Apr44 with RAdm Teizo Nippa in command. In January 1945, Adm Ota, who had commanded a SNLF battalion in the Shanghai Incident, the Munda SNLF, and the Sasebo Naval Barracks, relieved him.

[17] Nominally, Japanese conscription classes included seven categories of men in the 20–40 age group with the distinctions based on physical characteristics. Except for men considered unfit for even limited service (Class D) and those suffering temporary ailments (Class F), all eligible males were assigned either to active service or to units with varying liabilities for reserve training. Those men in the 2d National Army were generally considered, because of their poor physical condition or lack of height (between 4′ 9′′ and 4′ 11′′), to be available only for emergency call. WD, Handbook on Japanese Military Forces, 1Oct44, 2–4.

[18] *IntelMono*, Part I, Sect A, 5.

[19] For a discussion of Japanese defenses on these islands see R. R. Smith, *The Approach to the Philippines*, U. S. Army in World War II, (Washington, 1953); *Peleliu; Iwo Jima*.

344538—55——6

NORTH BANK of the Bishi Gawa shows the typical integrated tomb-cave-dugout defenses which characterized Japanese organization of Okinawan terrain.   (Army Photograph)

attack into prepared fire lanes and pre-registered impact areas.

Soon after General Ushijima took over the Thirty-second Army, its headquarters was split into two groups. The operations staff moved to Shuri, while a "rear headquarters" composed of the ordnance, veterinary, judicial, intendence,[20] and the greater part of the medical staff set up near Tsukasan. The separation of functions enabled the operations staff, under Colonel Hiromichi Yahara, to concentrate on developing a tactical scheme for effective utilization of Thirty-second Army manpower and firepower.

As each combat element arrived on Okinawa it was assigned a sector to develop and defend. By August 1944, the 44th IMB had occupied its area, Kunigami Gun, and was responsible for all of the island north of Ishikawa Isthmus, including Ie Shima and its airfields.   The

24th Division had begun to construct field fortifications around Yontan and Kadena airfields in an area bounded by Ishikawa Isthmus in the north and a line from Sunabe to Ozato in the south. Below the 24th's defensive zone the 62d Division was assiduously digging into the ridges, hillsides, and ravines north of Shuri. The 9th Division assumed responsibility for the entire southern portion of Okinawa below Shuri.

In late November, when orders were received to ship the 9th Division to the Philippines, the 24th Division began moving south to partially replace it. The 44th IMB, leaving two reinforced battalions of the 2d Infantry Unit behind on Ie Shima and Motobu Peninsula, took over an area stretching from Kadena airfield to Chatan. The sudden withdrawal of 14,000 combat troops also necessitated a readjustment in 62d Division lines. The northern divisional boundary dropped to Chatan-Futema and in the south the zone of responsibility was vastly increased to include Naha, Shuri, Yonabaru, and the entire Chinen Peninsula.

Throughout this period of troop movement, extensive fortification activities continued.   As

---

[20] The Intendence Service, which had no exact U. S. military equivalent, controlled clothing, rations, forage, contracts, pay, and the upkeep of Army buildings. In effect, it combined the functions of the U. S. Army Quartermaster Corps and Finance Department. WD, Handbook on Japanese Military Forces, 1Oct44, 50.

each unit occupied its new area, it added to existing installations. The Japanese planners meanwhile considered four possible defensive schemes, all aimed at denying the invasion force "the use of the island for as long a period as possible and [causing it] the greatest casualties."[21] Japanese sources list the following alternatives:

I. To defend, from extensive underground positions, the Shimajiri sector, the main zone of defenses being north of Naha, Shuri, and Yonabaru. Landings north of these defenses were not to be opposed; landings south of the line would be met at the beaches. Since it was impossible to defend Kadena Airfield [with available troops], 15cm guns were to be emplaced so as to bring fire on the airfield and deny the invaders its use.

II. To defend from prepared positions the central portion of the island, including the Kadena and Yontan airfields.

III. To dispose one division around the Kadena area, one division in the southern end of the island, and one brigade between the two divisions. To meet the enemy wherever he lands and attempt to annihilate him on the beaches.

IV. To defend the northern part of the island, with Army Headquarters at Nago, and the main line of defense based on Hill 220, northeast of Yontan Airfield.[22]

Eventually, after due consideration of the forces available, Plan I was selected as having the best chance of accomplishing the army's mission. Plan IV was rejected mainly because it conceded immediately the loss of the militarily important south. Similarly, Plan III, which attempted to defend these important objectives, was abandoned because it overextended Thirty-second Army troops. Plan II, appearing potentially the most dangerous to American staff officers, was given up reluctantly by the Japanese. Had it been followed by a Japanese army relatively untrained in fighting delaying actions[23] and subject to fragmentation by separate American landings, Ushijima considered that he might not be able to prolong the battle and inflict satisfactory casualties.

Under Plan I the rugged terrain surrounding Shuri was selected and developed as the main Japanese battle position with the strongest defenses oriented north toward the Hagushi beaches. To planning teams on both sides the Hagushi area seemed the obvious primary target. In addition, Japanese officers, "handicapped by their lack of ability to make an American logistics estimate for a landing operation,"[24] believed there would be another assault across the Minatoga beaches of southern Okinawa. The terrain inland from these beaches along the southeast coast of the Chinen Peninsula was so favorable to the defenders that they expected to exact a bloody price for a beachhead. Thanks to this flattering appraisal of American capabilities, a substantial portion of the Thirty-second Army's infantry and artillery strength which could have reinforced the Shuri bastion was to be held out of action during the first weeks of Tenth Army operations ashore.[25]

In January 1945, General Cho flew to Tokyo for a final round of conferences regarding the defense of Okinawa. Here he was told that sea and air suicide attacks would carry the entire burden of destroying American invasion shipping; Thirty-second Army artillery and coast-defense guns were to hold their fire. While great confidence was placed in the effectiveness of the suicide units, there was another telling reason for the "deathly stillness." As an army battle instruction explained, "The most effective and certain way of ascertaining the existence and organization of our firepower system is to have us open fire prematurely on

[21] *Shimada Interrogation.*

[22] *IntelMono*, Part I, Sect A, 1–2.

[23] In a delaying action a small, highly mobile covering force with relatively few troops employs elusive, fast-moving tactics to force the enemy into premature deployments. It avoids becoming heavily engaged before withdrawing to previously selected positions to the flank or rear since to do so would mean its destruction while unsupported by rearward defensive positions.

[24] *IntelMono*, Part I, Sect A, 3.

[25] In the Thirty-second Army staff there was sharp disagreement as to the probability of this additional landing. Col Yahara, senior staff officer, insisted that a diversionary landing, possibly the principal one, would be made in the Minatoga region. Maj Yakamaru, the intelligence officer, held that the only American landing would be in the Hagushi area. Prestige and seniority won the argument. "Yakamaru, bitterly disappointed at the final decision, went off the next few days to inundate his sorrows in prolonged draughts of expensive *sake*." *Shimada Interrogation.*

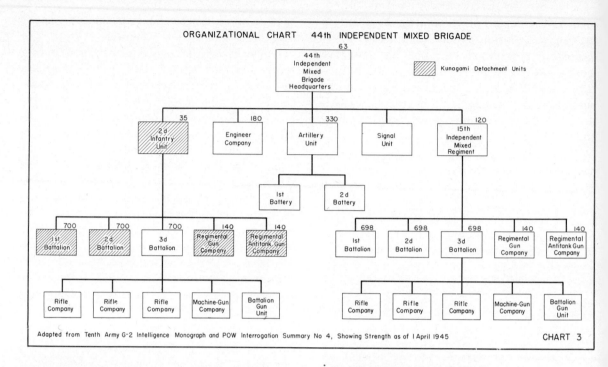

ORGANIZATIONAL CHART   44th INDEPENDENT MIXED BRIGADE

Adapted from Tenth Army G-2 Intelligence Monograph and POW Interrogation Summary No 4, Showing Strength as of 1 April 1945

CHART 3

a powerful force in a situation where it can maneuver."[26]

A healthy respect for the American air-NGF team resulted in the adoption of "the basic principle" of allowing "the enemy to land in full."[27] The Japanese command thought that the landing force would be effectively deprived of a large part of its supporting firepower once it became embroiled in the tangled skein of the island's defenses.

Either at Cho's January Tokyo conference or immediately thereafter, it became painfully apparent that the expected replacements for the 9th Division would not be forthcoming in time.[28] It now was necessary to find additional combat troops within the ranks of the Thirty-second Army. A drastic reorganization of army service troops took place in February and March 1945.

REINFORCING THE ARMY

On 1 January 1945, Thirty-second Army distributed to all units an order for total garrison mobilization. Under its terms all male islanders between 17 and 45, in good health, and possessed of "high morale" were adjudged "fit for direct battle." By the end of April mobilization was expected to be complete. Those "incapable of participation in battle"—most of the women, the aged, and children—were directed to move to northern Okinawa, thus clearing the projected battle zone.[29] Many of the rural people, however, managed to escape evacuation and stuck stubbornly to the area of their farmsteads.

The rate of induction of the Okinawans accelerated in the early months of 1945, adding to

[26] CinCPac-CinCPOA Bull 122–45, Translations and Interrogations No 30, 1Jun45, 32d Army Battle Instructions No 8, 8Mar45, 7.

[27] *Ibid.*

[28] On 23Jan45, Thirty-second Army received an Imperial Headquarters order to the effect that the 85th Division from Honshu would be sent to Okinawa. By nightfall the order was cancelled and the last hope of substantial reinforcement lost.

[29] *CICAS Trans* No. 83, Standards for the Establishment of Nansei Shoto Garrison Plans, 1Jan45. "In June of 1944 the governor of Okinawa Ken [Prefecture] 'suggested' that all women and children go to Kyushu or to northern Okinawa since they would be in the way if Okinawa became a battleground. Accordingly, from June to November about 50,000 . . . went to Kumamoto Ken in Kyushu. Passage was free, but they were expected to work in factories after their arrival." 1st MarDiv G–2 PrdRpt No 79, 19Jun45, Preliminary Interrogation Rpt No 110.

the pool of labor available for defensive construction. In February over 39,000 natives were temporarily assigned to Thirty-second Army units, divided into categories of Main Labor (22,383), Auxiliary Labor (14,415), and Student Labor (2,944).[30] In all probability, only a portion of this number actually entered military service, but the figure serves to confirm American estimates of 20,000 *Boeitai* who actually served in the Thirty-second Army. While comparatively few Home Guardsmen were integrated into front line units, their contribution to defensive preparations was substantial.

In addition to the *Boeitai*, the Japanese made a special effort to use the indoctrinated, politically reliable students of high school level in the Naha-Shuri area. In January, 750 of these young men were organized into Blood-and-Iron-for-the-Emperor-Duty-Units. A specialist from Japan trained them in the techniques of infiltration and guerrilla warfare. An additional 600 students were assigned to various headquarters as messengers, orderlies, and communications assistants. Before the campaign on Okinawa ended, many students, with a fanaticism comparable to that of the Hitler Youth Organizations, perished in attempts to destroy American tanks and rear area installations.

Although successive drafts of Okinawans were added to the Thirty-second Army, they did not compensate for the loss of the infantry strength of the 9th Division. It became imperative that additional riflemen be found within the army to reinforce combat units of the divisions and 44th IMB. In February the process of converting service troops to infantry began.

The seven sea raiding base battalions were the first elements affected by the reorganization. Between 13 and 20 February, these units, renamed the 1st, 2d, 3d, 26th, 27th, 28th, and 29th Independent Battalions, were removed from control of the sea raiding base headquarters and assigned to the major combatant units. Each battalion consisted of three companies, some reinforced by *Boeitai*, which varied in strength from 150–300 men.[31] A maintenance

[30] CinCPac-CinCPOA Bull 161–45, Translations and Interrogations No 34, 27Jun45, 32d Army-Assignment of Conscript Labor, February 1945.

[31] Although total strength varied, the organization of the 1st IndBn might be considered typical: a headquarters of 50 men and three companies of 150–180 men, each man armed with a rifle and five to ten grenades, with the companies having four light machine guns and two grenade dischargers apiece. Only one unit, the 1,100-man 29th IndBn, formed a machine-gun company, but its weapons (three heavy and six light machine guns) were redistributed to the rifle companies prior to entering combat.

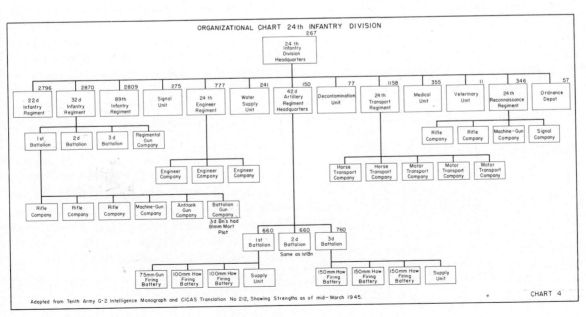

Adapted from Tenth Army G-2 Intelligence Monograph and CICAS Translation No 212, Showing Strengths as of mid–March 1945.

CHART 4

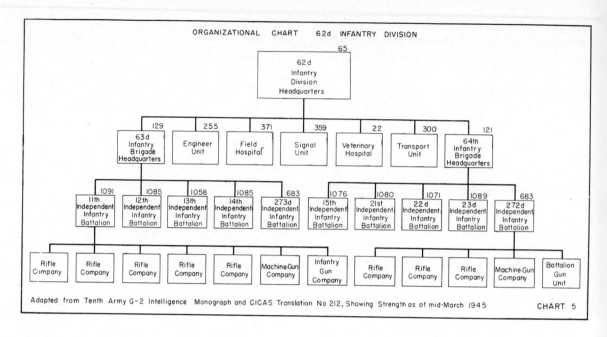

ORGANIZATIONAL CHART   62d INFANTRY DIVISION

65
62d Infantry Division Headquarters

129 — 63d Infantry Brigade Headquarters
255 — Engineer Unit
371 — Field Hospital
359 — Signal Unit
22 — Veterinary Hospital
300 — Transport Unit
121 — 64th Infantry Brigade Headquarters

1091 — 11th Independent Infantry Battalion
1085 — 12th Independent Infantry Battalion
1058 — 13th Independent Infantry Battalion
1085 — 14th Independent Infantry Battalion
683 — 273d Independent Infantry Battalion
1076 — 15th Independent Infantry Battalion
1080 — 21st Independent Infantry Battalion
1071 — 22d Independent Infantry Battalion
1089 — 23d Independent Infantry Battalion
683 — 272d Independent Infantry Battalion

Rifle Company / Rifle Company / Rifle Company / Rifle Company / Rifle Company / Machine-Gun Company / Infantry Gun Company / Rifle Company / Rifle Company / Rifle Company / Machine-Gun Company / Battalion Gun Unit

Adapted from Tenth Army G-2 Intelligence Monograph and CICAS Translation No 212, Showing Strength as of mid-March 1945   CHART 5

company remained under command of each sea raiding squadron to assist it in carrying out its suicide boat mission. The new independent battalions were poorly trained and equipped by comparison with regular infantry units, but their 4,500–5,000 men fed into existing combat formations provided an important source of Japanese strength during battle.

In March 1945 the Army forces defending Okinawa underwent their final reorganization to meet the imminent American assault. The Thirty-second Army published an order on 21 March directing "the various shipping, air, and rear echelon forces [to] set up organizations and dispositions for land combat." [32] In addition to their normally assigned functions, units named in the order were to give priority to construction of positions and training for infantry action. By 10 April the changeover was to be completed.

On paper the new organizations, two brigades and a regiment, looked impressive; in actuality, the lightly equipped, untrained service troops were of tactical value only as combat replacements. The 1st Specially Established Regiment, formed from units under 19th Air Sector Command Headquarters, was to defend, under 62d Division control, the area of Kadena and Yontan airfields. The 1st Specially Estab-

lished Brigade, three regiments of Thirty-second Army transport, ordnance, construction, and supply troops under the 49th Line of Communication Sector Headquarters, assumed support positions in the Naha-Yonabaru valley. The 2d Specially Established Brigade, three regiments composed mostly of shipping, sea transport, and engineer personnel under the 11th Shipping Group Headquarters, deployed in the 24th Division area to back up that unit in its defense of southernmost Okinawa. Thus, the 21 March order effected general mobilization for combat since Thirty-second Army further directed that all "Army rear echelon agencies not included in this order and their personnel will be under command of the front line unit in the vicinity where their duties are carried on, and will reinforce it in combat." [33]

By the time of the American landings in Kerama Retto (26 March), most of the Japanese Army ground and air troops on Okinawa had been integrated into the defensive organization. About the same time, the naval troops and civilian auxiliaries under Okinawa Base Force were ordered to organize for land combat. These units varied greatly in size, the only standard seeming to be that naval lieutenants should command those organizations

---

[32] *IntelMono*, Part I, Sect B, 14.

[33] *Ibid.*, 15.

named battalions and lieutenants (junior grade) should lead those named companies. Like the specially established units of the Army, the land combat organization of the Navy suffered from a lack of individual weapons. The only units adequately equipped were the 81mm mortar battery and two independent machine-gun battalions formed from the 13mm and 25mm AAA batteries. The addition of almost 10,000 naval troops to approximately 40,000 service troops and *Boeitai* doubled the potential combat strength of the Thirty-second Army.[34]

PRELANDING DISPOSITIONS

While the Okinawan populace and the ranks of the Thirty-second Army were being combed for combat replacements, the main defensive sector was readied for battle. The twisted, confused character of the terrain surrounding Shuri featured escarpments, steep slopes, and narrow ravines that showed no discernible pattern, making it "ideal for an enemy whose chief reliance was on large numbers of short range weapons, and whose propensities for digging enabled him to make each irregularity of the terrain into a fortress."[35] Routes of approach into the battle area were mined and swept by the fire of AT guns. Automatic weapons, mortars, and artillery were zeroed in on all possible attack objectives, especially hill crests and reverse slopes, so that even if the Americans did capture a commanding height they would be subjected to intense pre-registered destructive fires. Covered passageways connected many of the enemy positions, and natural and man-made caves afforded protection to troops, weapons, and supplies. The Japanese were determined to defend Shuri to the last man, capitalizing on every advantage given them by the wildly irregular terrain.

[34] For a complete Japanese Order of Battle see Appendix V.

[35] *IntelMono*, Part I, Sect A, 4.

TYPICAL BROKEN TERRAIN of the Shuri bastion viewed from the vicinity of Ishin looking west toward the heart of the enemy defenses. (Army Photograph)

During February the final enemy deployment for battle took place. Following the accepted plan, Kadena airfield and the rest of the area between the Hagushi beaches and Chimu Wan were left to the doubtful protection of 19th Air Sector Command units. The main battle force withdrew below an outpost zone north of Futema. (See Map 8)

Because of their belief that American troops would land on the Minatoga beaches, the Japanese positioned much of their reserve strength to oppose that landing. The 44th IMB took over the defense of the rugged hills of the Chinen Peninsula which commanded both the supposed landing area and the reaches of Nakagusuku Wan. The 24th Division continued to occupy the high ground inland from the southern coast, strengthening the positions begun by the 9th Division. On Oroku Peninsula, the Naval Base Force prepared to fight "the Navy Way," meeting the enemy at the beaches in a manner similar to that used at Tarawa.[36] The most significant realignment of forces, though, was the assignment of a major portion of the units under the 5th Artillery Command to the southern sector to back up the Minatoga beach defenses.

The battle-tested 62d Division, considered the most valuable combat unit on the island, was confirmed in its role as guardian of the heart of Okinawa's defenses. The Shuri bastion assumed the form of a series of concentric rings, each bristling with dug-in, mutually supporting weapons. If the Americans landed at Hagushi and Minatoga, plans called for making a fighting withdrawal to these prepared positions, extracting a terrific toll in lives for every yard of advance.

Isolated in the north, the Kunigami Detachment, under Colonel Takehiko Udo (Commanding Officer, 2d Infantry Unit), was charged with the defense of Motobu Peninsula and Ie Shima. Colonel Udo expected that Ie Shima would be attacked from the sea and that

Motobu, in turn, would receive an amphibious assault from the direction of that island. In so far as possible then, he emplaced his few artillery pieces to make the two positions mutually supporting. On 11 March, when Thirty-second Army ordered the destruction of the airfields of Ie Shima, the forlorn hope under Udo's command was ready for its part in the war of attrition.

Shortly before 1 April 1945, belated orders called for the destruction of airfields at Yontan, Kadena, and Oroku. By that time, carrier raids, Japanese suicide sorties, and finally the fires of Task Force 54 had combined to destroy most of the 30–31 planes that remained on Okinawa at the beginning of March.[37] Because the island was used mainly as a servicing and maintenance stop on the air route to Formosa and the Philippines, organic air power was never a significant factor in Thirty-second Army defensive plans.

The army did count, however, on the combat power of its own sea forces. It was expected that the sea raiding squadrons at Kerama Retto and those positioned along the coast of Okinawa would "blast to pieces the enemy transport groups with a whirlwind attack in the vicinity of their anchorages."[38] The Navy's midget submarines and motor torpedo boats stationed at Unten-Ko were unable to assist this grand scheme. By L-Day carrier airstrikes had knocked out all the submarines, and the torpedo boats had been destroyed or scattered in an abortive attack on the destroyer *Tolman* of TF 52.[39]

As both sides in the impending struggle made their final preparations, the Thirty-second

[36] Although the Base Force was under command of the Thirty-second Army and Adm Ota adopted a policy of full cooperation, certain of his staff were dissatisfied with local Army procedure and nurtured the spirit of fierce inter-service rivalry that hampered many Japanese Pacific operations. *POW InterSum* No 16, Naval Units on Okinawa, 28Jul45.

[37] The plane strength was compiled after an examination of unit reports contained in *POW InterSum* No 16, Naval Units on Okinawa, 28Jul45; *POW InterSum* No 19, Air-Ground Units, 25Jul45.

[38] *CICAS Trans* No 231, 32d Army OpOrd A #115, 23Mar45.

[39] Some POW's claimed that these boats were enroute to Sakishima Gunto and a fight "was not especially sought after." *POW InterSum* No 16, Naval Units on Okinawa, 28Jul45. TF 52's operation chronology for 28Mar45 notes, "From 0100 (I) to 0220 (I) *Tolman* on patrol south of Zampa-Misaki was under attack by 8 MTB. Two MTB destroyed, 2 probably destroyed, remainder driven off, *Tolman* undamaged." *CTF 52 AR*, Chap III, 9.

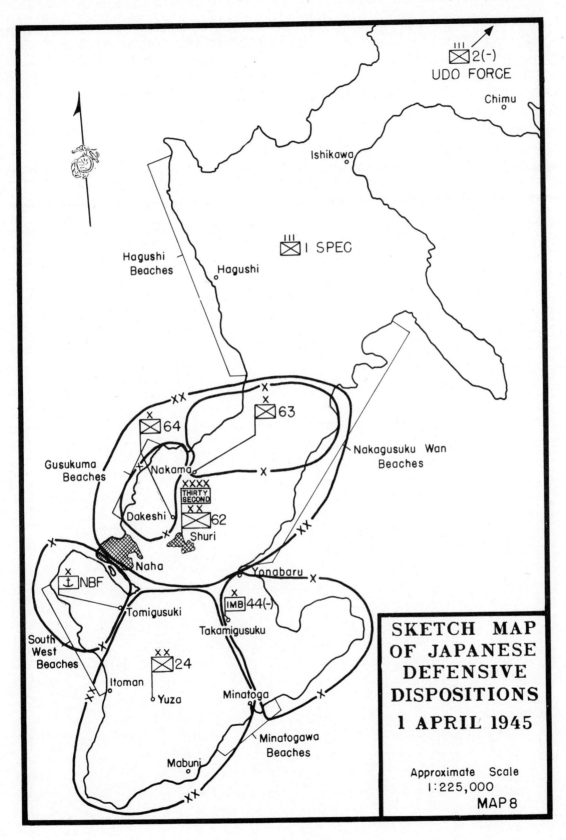

UDO FORCE

Chimu

Ishikawa

I SPEC

Hagushi
Beaches

Hagushi

Nakagusuku Wan
Beaches

64

63

Gusukuma
Beaches

Nakama

THIRTY
SECOND

Dakeshi

62

Shuri

Naha

NBF

Yonabaru

IMB 44(-)

Tomigusuki

Takamigusuku

South
West
Beaches

24

Itoman

Yuza

Minatoga

Minatogawa
Beaches

Mabuni

SKETCH MAP OF JAPANESE DEFENSIVE DISPOSITIONS 1 APRIL 1945

Approximate Scale
1:225,000

MAP 8

Army issued a battle warning to its troops. The news that Admirals King and Nimitz had met in Washington in early March was translated by the Japanese into a general alert "for the end of March and early April" based on a statistical estimate "that new operations occur from 20 days to one month after conferences on strategy are held." [40] The validity of this estimate was confirmed three days after the warning was issued, when repeated sightings of Allied ships and submarines enabled Japanese intelligence officers to predict that the target was "Formosa or the Nansei Shoto, especially Okinawa." [41]

[40] CinCPac–CinCPOA Bull 140–45, Translations and Interrogations No 31, 7Jun45, 32d Army Estimate of the Situation, 20Mar45.

[41] *Ibid.*, 62d Div IntelRpt on Findings Since the 20 March Rpt, 23Mar45.

CHAPTER V

Seizure of the Beachhead

By the early morning hours of 1 April 1945 more than 1,300 ships of the Central Pacific Task Forces had gathered in the darkness surrounding Okinawa. Transports and LST's bearing the III Amphibious Corps and XXIV Corps moved to their assigned areas off the Hagushi beaches. There the transports laid to, the LST's dropped anchor, and preparations were made to debark troops. On the other side of the island shipping carrying the 2d Marine Division stood off the Minatoga Beaches.

At 0406 Admiral Turner made the traditional signal "Land the Landing Force,"[1] and shortly before daylight the assault on Okinawa opened with a crash of naval gunfire.

L-DAY[2]

The dawn of L-Day brought enemy reaction in the form of scattered air attacks on the convoys. While carrier air and ship's antiaircraft guns accounted for most of the raiders, the transport *Hinsdale* and LST 884, standing off the southeastern beaches with elements of the 2d Marine Division, were crashed by enemy aircraft. The *Kamikazes* struck as the troops, mostly from the 3d Battalion, 2d Marines and its reinforcing units, were preparing to disembark for the feint on Minatoga. Eight Marines were reported killed, 37 were wounded, and eight listed as missing in action.[3] Thus, ironically, the first troop casualties were sustained by units not even scheduled to land.

At 0650 air support arrived over the target in force,[4] and ten minutes later the assault troops commenced debarkation. Troops embarked in APA's transferred to landing craft. Landing ships disgorged armored amphibians and amphibian tractors preloaded with troops and equipment. Simultaneously, landing craft, mechanized (LCM), carrying tanks, floated from the flooded well-decks of landing ships,

---

[1] CTF 53 Rpt of Participation in the Capture of Okinawa Gunto—Phases I and II, 20Jul45, Part III, 12, hereinafter cited as *CTF 53 AR.*

[2] Unless otherwise noted the material in this section is derived from R. E. Appleman, *et al Okinawa; The Last Battle, U. S. Army in World War II,* (Washington, 1948), hereinafter cited as *Okinawa: The Last Battle; CTF 51 AR; Tenth Army AR; XXIV Corps AR; IIIAC AR; 1st MarDiv SAR;* 1st MarDiv G–3 Jnl, 28Feb–13Jul45 hereinafter cited as *1st MarDiv G–3 Jul;* 1st Mar SAR, Nan Shoto, 25Jul45, hereinafter

cited as *1st Mar SAR;* 5th Mar S–3 Jnl, 15Jan–26Jul45, hereinafter cited as *5th Mar S–3 Jnl;* 7th Mar SAR, Phase I and II, 1May45, and Phase III, 11Jul45, hereinafter cited as *7th Mar SAR; 6th MarDiv SAR, Ph I&II;* 6th MarDiv Unit Jnl, Phase I and II, 1–22Apr45, hereinafter cited as *6th MarDiv Jnl, Ph I&II.* The action reports of the major component units of the 6th MarDiv are included as annexes to the division SAR and will be cited separately as *4th Mar SAR, Ph I&II; 1/4 SAR, Ph I&II; 6th TkBn SAR, Ph I&II;* etc.

[3] *2d MarDiv AR,* Annexes A–N. Ships crews suffered casualties of 1 KIA, 34 WIA, and 10 MIA.

[4] Between 0700 and 1000 more than 500 planes of the Fifth Fleet were engaged in troop support missions.

LVT(A)'s of the 1st Armored Amphibian Battalion form the first wave of the 6th Marine Division assault. In the background, the USS *Idaho* shells the landing area. (Navy Photograph)

dock (LSD's), and tanks rigged with T–6 flotation equipment debarked from LST's.[5]

The vicious pounding of the beaches by ten battleships, nine cruisers, 23 destroyers, and 177 gunboats elicited no reply from the shore other than desultory light artillery and mortar fire. Although the assembly areas in which the assault waves formed up were within range, this fire did no damage. The two battalions of the 420th Field Artillery Group on Keise Shima, however, received heavy fire during the early morning hours, which did no damage but caused a suspension of unloading operations.

Landing vehicles formed into waves behind the line of departure, marked by control vessels lying off each landing beach. At 0800 the pennants fluttering from the masts of the control craft were hauled down, signaling the first wave of LVT(A)'s forward behind a line of support craft. In its wake, hundreds of troop-carrying LVT's disposed in five to seven waves,

crossed the line of departure at regular intervals and swept toward the shore.

Throughout the 4,000-yard run to the beach scattered hostile artillery and mortar fire continued to fall ineffectively. As the landing force approached the beach, naval gunfire lifted and the LVT(A)'s took suspected targets under fire, while 138 planes that had been orbiting lazily over both flanks of the beaches, swooped down and saturated the landing area with bullets, explosives, and incendiaries.

With but little deviation from its schedule, the landing force went ashore according to plan. As the assault waves touched down, smoke laid on the high hills east of Yontan neutralized enemy observation of the landing beaches. Concurrently, the landing craft carrying elements of the 2d Marine Division, racing toward the Minatoga beaches, reversed their course as the fourth wave crossed the line of departure, and retired to the transport area behind a screen of smoke.

South of the Bishi Gawa (River) XXIV Corps met with no unexpected difficulties in negotiating the fringing reef. Mortar fire on the beaches did not interfere with the landing, and by H-plus 24 minutes six waves of LVT's had landed the eight assault battalions, which soon cleared the beaches and moved forward without opposition. (See Map 9)

Hard on the heels of the infantry, LVT(A)'s (which had moved to protect the flanks on landing), tanks, and amphibious trucks (DUKW's) pre-loaded with 4.2-inch mortars, poured through breaches battered in the sea wall by naval guns and rolled inland. In anticipation of an early build-up, additional beach exits were blasted in the sea wall by engineers who had landed with the first waves.

In the III Amphibious Corps zone north of the Bishi Gawa, the edge of the reef was ragged with fissures and boulders, becoming smoother toward the beach. Fortunately, the rising tide carried the landing vehicles water-borne over a large portion of the reef. However, on the northern flank of the 1st Marine Division, the tractors experienced particular difficulty in crossing the large offshore circular reef covering the approaches to the Blue Beaches and were delayed in reaching the shore.

---

[5] The T–6 flotation devices were utilized by medium tanks to proceed to the beach under their own power, using their tracks for propulsion. They consisted of flotation tanks welded to the outside of the medium, an improvised steering device, electrical bilge pumps, and electrically detonated charges to jettison the flotation tanks once the beach was reached. *6th TkBn SAR, Ph I&II*, 39–41.

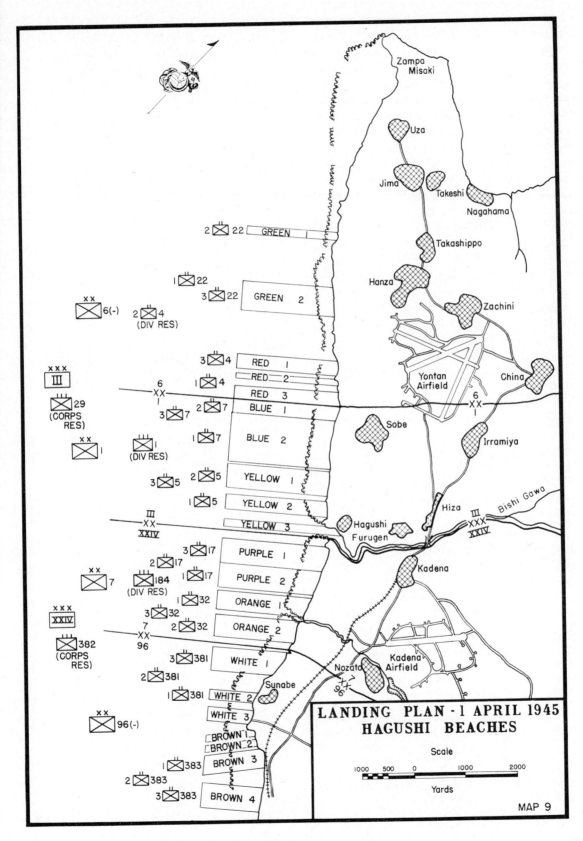

LANDING PLAN - 1 APRIL 1945
HAGUSHI BEACHES

Scale

1000 500   0   1000   2000

Yards

MAP 9

Several instances occurred where inexperienced wave guide officers followed incorrect compass courses with complete disregard for clearly recognizable terrain features ashore and landed troops out of position. The 3d Battalion, 4th Marines, assigned to Red Beach 1, landed on the right half of Green 2 (in the 22d Marines' zone) and on the rocky coast line between that beach and Red 1. Elements of the 7th Marines [6] were also landed in the 4th Marines' area but in insignificant numbers. On the extreme right of the 1st Division the fourth wave was diverted across the corps boundary and landed on the right flank of the 7th Infantry Division.[7] On the troop leaders' initiative, the fifth and sixth waves were forced to change course in order to make the proper beaches. Yet, despite these departures from the landing plan, by 0840 all the LVT(A)'s spearheading the IIIAC attack had reached the beach, and the eight assault BLT's were all ashore within a half hour.

The beaches were not mined and the scattered upright poles left on the offshore reef were easily pushed over by the LVT's. Enemy resistance to the landing consisted of sporadic mortar and small-arms fire, which inflicted a handful of casualties and caused no damage to the LVT's. "With utter consternation and bewilderment and with a great deal of relief the assault wave landed against practically no opposition." [8]

As the assault battalions surged up the terraced slopes behind the beaches and drove inland, the center of activity shifted from the line of departure to the transfer line. There, small boat, LVT, and DUKW control was established to unload support troops and artillery units on call.

Throughout the morning, as the attack progressed against negligible resistance, supporting units continued to pour ashore. At the transfer line at the edge of the reef, reserve infantry elements transferred from ship's boats to LVT's which had been employed earlier to land the assault battalions. Tanks equipped with flotation devices came in under their own power, others were landed on the beaches at high tide from LCM's, and the remainder were discharged directly onto the reef from medium landing ships (LSM's) and LCT's. Light field artillery battalions (75mm and 105mm howitzers) came ashore in DUKW's.

The assault waves of tanks of the 1st Division, which landed from LCM's and LCT's, were all on the beach by noon with the exception of one that drowned out in a reef pothole. The commander of the LST transporting the six T–6 flotation equipped tanks of the 1st Tank Battalion, disregarding the operation plan, refused to let them be launched until H-plus 60 minutes and then set them in the water ten miles off the landing beaches. It was not until 1445, after more than five hours in the water, that these tanks got ashore and then two were lost crossing the reef because of the falling tide. The LSM's carrying the reserve tanks of the battalion had extreme difficulty grounding on the reef on L-Day, losing the first tank off the ramp in an unseen pothole. Of the four LSM's employed, two finally landed their cargo late on L-Day, another at noon on L-plus 1, and the last on 3 April.

In the 6th Division zone tanks were landed early and with little difficulty, a different landing procedure being employed by each of the three companies of the 6th Tank Battalion. Tanks equipped with flotation gear swam easily to the edge of the reef, moved over the rough coral, dropped their pontoons on the beach, and were operational by H-plus 29 minutes. The company in LCM's came in at high tide (0930) and landed without incident. The third company landed directly from LSM's successfully, but experienced difficulty in fording the

---

[6] Throughout this monograph the designation "7th Marines," "22d Marines," etc., has been used interchangeably with Regimental Combat Team 7 (RCT 7), RCT 22, etc. Thus, reinforcing troops which make a regiment an RCT are considered included in the 7th Marines (22d Marines) designation. In like manner, the 1st Battalion, 5th Marines or 1/5 has been used synonymously with Battalion Landing Team 1/5 (BLT 1/5).

[7] This wave consisted principally of Co B, 5th Marines, the reserve company of the 1st Bn, and part of the command post group. By 0930 sufficient LVT's were sent to pick up all but one lieutenant and two squads who did not rejoin until L-plus 3. 1st Bn, 5th Mar SAR, Phase I and II, 29Apr45, 5, and Phase III, 9Jul45, hereinafter cited as 1/5 SAR.

[8] 4th Mar SAR, Ph I&II, 6–7.

7TH MARINES assault troops cross the sea wall on Blue Beach 2, seconds after landing on Okinawa.

deep water between the grounding point and the shore.[9]

On the open flank to the north, the accelerated pace of the assault caused the 22d Marines (Colonel Merlin F. Schneider) to become overextended soon after landing. Numerous detachments of troops made from the 2d Battalion (Lieutenant Colonel Horatio F. Woodhouse, Jr.) on the left of the regiment in order to guard the exposed flank, weakened the attacking echelon and reduced the frontage which the battalion could cover effectively. In consequence, a considerable gap developed between the 2d Battalion and the 3d Battalion (Lieutenant Colonel Malcolm "O" Donohoo) advancing on the right. Within a half hour after the landing Colonel Schneider ordered in his reserve battalion, less Company C which remained afloat. The remainder of the 1st Battalion (Major Thomas J. Myers) was committed in the center of the 22d Marines' zone of action.

[9] *6th TkBn SAR, Ph I&II*, 15–16, 39–41.

Still meeting no opposition and moving rapidly inland, by 1000 the left flank of the 22d Marines had stretched dangerously thin. Anxious to press the attack and exploit his initial success, General Shepherd (anticipating Schneider's request for reinforcements to cover his exposed flank) requested IIIAC to release one BLT of the 29th Marines to the 6th Marine Division.

While the 22d Marines continued to advance on Hanza unopposed, the 4th Marines (Colonel Alan Shapley) on the right moved on Yontan airfield against scattered resistance. Impeded only by isolated enemy pockets built around light machine guns, the regiment had swiftly penetrated several hundred yards inland and gained contact with the 7th Marines of the 1st Division on the right. Continuing the advance, the 4th reached Yontan airfield by midmorning.

The field was found to be essentially intact, but all buildings had been stripped and the antiaircraft emplacements contained only dummy guns. Unopposed, except for occasional sniper fire, the 4th Marines swept across the airfield and secured their objective to the east of it by 1300. This forward rush carried the regiment ahead of adjacent units, leaving an appreciable gap in depth between the left flank of the 4th Marines and the 22d Marines, then in the vicinity of Hanza.

At 1330 the 4th Marines again jumped off, meeting light resistance on its left. Tanks were called to reduce several cave positions, and the advance continued slowly through rugged, wooded terrain. In attempting to maintain contact with the 7th Marines on the right, the 4th Marines also became overextended. At 1500 the 2d Battalion (Lieutenant Colonel Reynolds H. Hayden) was released to the regiment from division reserve and immediately committed on the left of the line to establish contact with the 22d Marines.

Similarly, the 1st Battalion, 29th Marines (Lieutenant Colonel Jean W. Moreau) reverted to the 6th Division from corps reserve and was assigned the mission of protecting the critical left flank of the division. Released by IIIAC at 1300, Moreau's unit landed at 1500, and with its left flank anchored on Green Beach 1 completed tying in with the 22d Marines by 1700.[10]

Meanwhile, to the south of the 6th Division, the 1st Marine Division had encountered the same surprising lack of resistance. By 0945 the 7th Marines (Colonel Edward W. Snedeker) on the left had advanced through the village of Sobe, a first priority objective, and the 5th Marines (Colonel John Griebel) was 1,000 yards inland standing up. At this time, with the beaches clear and in order to avoid a loss of troops from anticipated enemy air attacks against the congested shipping, the division reserve was ordered ashore. Colonel Kenneth B. Chappell, commanding the 1st Marines, was directed to embark two BLT's immediately, and the third as soon as landing craft were available.

Before noon the LVT's had returned to the transfer line and shuttled the reserve battalions of both assault regiments to the beach. The 3d Battalion, 7th Marines (Lieutenant Colonel

Edward H. Hurst), landing in the center of the regimental zone of action, moved to the rear of the left flank unit, Lieutenant Colonel Spencer S. Berger's 2d Battalion. In the zone of the 5th Marines, the 3d Battalion (Major John A. Gustafson),[11] positioned on the right boundary of the division, followed the 1st Battalion at 400 yards.

Thus disposed in depth with reserve elements echeloned to the right and left, the division continued to advance steadily over the rolling checker-board terrain. In addition to the many caves that honeycombed the entire zone, the Japanese had begun to organize the ground, and numerous field fortifications in varying stages of development were encountered throughout the area. The conduct of the defense, however, was left to small, scattered groups of service troops and home guards.[12]

Below Hiza the principal bridge over the Bishi Gawa was still intact, and the local defense forces had exerted little effort to destroy the narrow bridges spanning the lesser streams. More of a hindrance than the enemy's abortive attempts to slow the advance by small-scale harassing action, was what one observer has described as "an excellent network of very poor roads." [13]

The bulk of the supporting troops and the artillery were ashore by 1530. All divisional artillery landed successfully, with the exception of one howitzer of the 15th Marines and three of the 11th Marines, which were lost when the DUKW's carrying them foundered on the reef.

---

[10] 1/29 SAR, Ph I&II, 8.

[11] At 1400 the 3d Battalion moved up behind the assault battalions, at which time Maj Gustafson went forward to reconnoiter. At 1500 Gustafson's group was fired on by a small bypassed enemy group, and Maj Gustafson was wounded and evacuated. The executive officer, Maj Martin C. Roth, took over temporarily until LtCol John C. Miller, Jr., assumed command on 5 April. 3d Bn, 5th Mar SAR, 1–21Apr45, 30Apr45, and 22Apr–22Jun45, 10Jul45, hereinafter cited as 3/5 SAR.

[12] A Japanese source describes these troops as ". . . a hastily organized motley unit, . . . facing extreme hardship in trying to achieve an orderly formation." Okinawa Operations Record, 52.

[13] 1st MarDiv SAR, Part VII. 1–2. "5th Marines was heckled by division because regimental supply couldn't keep up with the advance." Col. J. D. Muncie Ltr to CMC, 27Mar47, hereinafter cited as Muncie.

Although the artillery landed early, the rapid advance of the infantry and the resultant strain on communications made it difficult for forward observers to register their battalions. Corps artillery reconnaissance parties began landing at 1300, and found that all previously selected positions were suitable.[14]

Between 1600 and 1700 the advance was halted. The attacking infantry dug in, established contact all along the IIIAC line, and carried out extensive patrolling to the front.

Although General Shepherd's entire reserve had been committed early to maintain the impetus of the attack, the 6th Marine Division was well disposed to resume the advance the next day. The 4th and 22d Marines each still held a company in reserve, and the corps reserve (29th Marines, less 1/29) had landed at 1535 and was located northwest of Yontan airfield in the vicinity of Hanza.

The 1st Marine Division was unable to close the gap on the corps boundary before dark and halted 600 yards in rear of the 7th Infantry Division on the right.[15] Company L was taken from the 5th Marines' reserve and put in on the right of the 1st Battalion to refuse the open flank. The 1st (Lieutenant Colonel James C. Murray, Jr.) and the 2d (Lieutenant Colonel James C. Magee, Jr.) Battalions of the 1st Marines landed at 1757.[16] The 1st Battalion, attached to the 5th Marines for administrative control, moved inland to Furugen. The 2d Battalion, similarly attached to the 7th Marines, set up east of Sobe by 1845.[17]

The 15th Marines had established its fire direction center (FDC) by 1700, and all battalions were registered by 1830. Because of the late arrival of spotter planes, two battalions of the 11th Marines did not complete registration, but all battalions were prepared to fire night defensive missions. But aside from in-termittent mortar and machine-gun fire in the 4th Marines' sector, enemy action was confined to unsuccessful attempts at night infiltration, a tactic with which Marine units had long been familiar.

Except for the slow movement of supplies ashore after the tide had receded and exposed undesirable reef conditions, L-Day had been successful beyond all expectations. Besides the ground gained by III Amphibious Corps, XXIV Corps had captured Kadena airfield by 1000, driven inland to an average depth of 3,500 yards, and advanced south along the coast to the vicinity of Chatan. Over-all, Tenth Army had landed an estimated 50,000 troops between 0830 and 1600 and established a beachhead 15,000 yards long and 4,000–5,000 yards in depth. The cost in casualties for the entire day's advance by four assault divisions was reported to Admiral Turner as 28 KIA, 104 WIA, and 27 MIA. (See Map 10)

SEVERING THE ISLAND[18]

In the face of an optimistic announcement by Radio Tokyo on the morning of 2 April that the beachhead on Okinawa would be wiped out in "due time,"[19] the attack jumped off on schedule and without benefit or need of air strikes or artillery preparation. As the assault divisions progressed rapidly through spotty resistance, the 2d Marine Division effectively immobilized the Japanese main body by another feint against the Minatoga beaches.[20]

On the northern flank the early capture of the unoccupied Zampa Misaki (Point) region was directed by Admiral Turner so that a radar site could be established without delay. Con-

---

[14] *IIIAC Arty AR*, 19.

[15] "Coordinating the advance of the 1st Marine Division with the Army's XXIV Corps was tough on the 1st Marine Division which didn't have comparable transportation or road net." *Muncie.*

[16] The 3d Battalion, 1st Marines were on the transfer line at 1800 trying to transfer to LVT's. But unable to get LVT's they remained in the boats all night.

[17] Col R. E. Honsowetz Ltr to CMC, 9Oct54, hereinafter cited as *Honsowetz.*

[18] Unless otherwise noted the material in this section is derived from *IIIAC AR; 1st MarDiv SAR; 6th MarDiv SAR, Ph I&II; 1st Mar SAR; 4th Mar SAR, Ph I&II; 5th Mar S-3 Jnl; 7th Mar SAR; 22d Mar SAR, PhI&II; 29th Mar SAR, Ph I&II.*

[19] IIIAC G-2 PrdRpt No 2, 3Apr45.

[20] The operation order issued by Gen Ushijima at 1630, 2 April states in part: ". . . On the Minatoga front the enemy's plans cannot be disregarded. The Army will use the 62d Division to hold the main line of positions over a long period; it will use its main strength [24th Div and 44th IMB] to annihilate the enemy who plans new landings." *CICAS Trans* No 252, 32d Army OpOrd A–140, 2Apr45.

BEWILDERED CIVILIANS wait to be taken to military government camps in the wake of the swift American advance across the island.

the day against light opposition, reached an objective line well beyond the planned L-plus 5 line by 1600 and organized their defensive position for the night. On the other hand, the 4th Marines met with steadily mounting resistance.

Colonel Shapley's regiment had resumed the attack at 0730 in the same formation in which it had been disposed the previous evening. At 1100 a platoon of 3/4, entering the mouth of a steep ravine was met by a sharp fusillade of small-arms fire, which revealed a series of mutually supporting caves on both sides of the draw. In the fire fight that ensued, 12 wounded men were isolated and not recovered for four hours. "Every means of painlessly destroying the strongpoint was unsuccessfully tried and it was finally taken by a typical 'Banzai' charge, with one platoon entering the mouth of the draw and one platoon coming down one side of the two noses that formed the pocket." [23]

Meanwhile, because the 7th Marines was believed to be some 1,000 yards south of the division boundary,[24] an adustment was requested by the 6th Marine Division, and the regiment was ordered over to its left boundary. This movement placed 1/4 behind the 7th Marines, and in side-slipping back to its own zone 1/4 met with stiff opposition in strong enemy positions similar to those holding up 3/4. With the aid of a platoon of tanks,[25] this strong point was likewise reduced. Some 250 Japanese were

sequently, as the 4th and 22d Marines resumed the attack eastward, the 1st Battalion, 29th Marines moved northward to seize and secure that area. The advance of 1/29 progressed rapidly, encountering but few enemy soldiers who were speedily disposed of, and the Zampa Misaki peninsula was secured at 1125. At 1430 the battalion was ordered into division reserve, and at 1600 it occupied positions near Beach Green 2 with the mission of repulsing any counter-landings against the left flank.[21]

Clearing Zampa Misaki also uncovered the beaches on the peninsula, which were badly needed for unloading operations; however, they proved unsuitable for use by IIIAC. The 6th Reconnaissance Company (Major Anthony Walker) was ordered to scout the vicinity of Nagahama to determine the enemy situation and the character of the beaches there. Walker and his men passed between the 29th and 22d Marines, dispatched a few snipers in the village, made a complete reconnaissance of the beaches, finding them suitable for the use of small landing craft,[22] and returned by nightfall.

Meanwhile, the advance elements of the 22d Marines, which progressed rapidly throughout

---

[21] *1/29 SAR, Ph I&II,* 8; *CMC Memo.*
[22] *CMC Memo.*

---

[23] *4th Mar SAR, Ph I&II,* 8.
[24] "Lack of readily identifiable terrain features made it impossible to quickly identify the boundaries of zones of action in the rapid advance. Maps at this time were also poor and difficult to follow. Hill 165 [3,600 yards west of Yontan airfield] and certain towns were, however, unmistakable. [The] 7th Marines ZA was approximately 2,000 yards wide. While there was some slippage to the right all along the front, I know that 2/7 on the left and 1/7 on the right substantially covered their ZA's. My opinion is that the left flank of the 7th was not over 400 yards from the division boundary at any time. The slant distance from the actual right flank of the 4th Marines and the left flank of the 7th Marines may have been greater as the attacks of the two regiments were not at an even rate." *Snedeker.* "The maps were not accurate. The 7th felt that they were on the boundary and so did the 4th. Who was right was never determined." *Honsowetz.*
[25] *6th TkBn SAR, Ph I&II,* 16–17.

killed by the two battalions during the day's operations. The attack of the 4th Marines ceased at 1830, about 1,000 yards forward of the L-plus 3 line.

Screened by extensive advance patrols, the 1st Marine Division continued to advance with but little interference from the local defense units, a force officially designated the 1st Specially Established Regiment. Plans for this unit had been initiated in January, but it was not activated until L-minus 4. It was composed of 3,473 airfield service troops and *Boeitai*, less than half of whom had rifles. Additionally, the regiment was equipped with 55 light machine guns and 18 grenade dischargers. Its heaviest weapons were 10 heavy machine guns and five 20mm AA machine cannon. The unit was almost completely untrained, for even among the regular army service troops such elementary instruction as the operation of a light machine gun was incomplete on L-day.

When the combat troops moved south, this scratch outfit was assigned the mission of servicing any final traffic on Yontan and Kadena. With the commencement of an American landing, they were to destroy those airfields on order, and retire to positions from which they could deny their use to the invaders. One battalion, the 1st, was located in the 6th Marine Division zone of action; the 2d battalion and part of the 3d in the 1st Marine Division area; the remainder of the 3d Battalion faced the 7th Infantry Division; and the regimental reserve, the 5th Company of the 12th Independent Infantry Battalion was assembled at Hanza.[26]

That this motley crew made some attempt to slow the advance of the landing force is indicated in an order issued by the commanding officer, Lieutenant Colonel Aoyanagi, at 1400 on L-day. This operations order directed all battalions to hold all strong points, to carry out night raids, and to destroy all important bridges, and to construct tank obstacles; it exhorted "each and every one [to] carry out his duty with the conviction of certain victory."[27] But with their routes of escape to organized forces in the south cut off, poorly armed, without communications, and largely leaderless, this haphazard organization collapsed completely. The bulk of these troops probably fled to the northern hills, a few undoubtedly escaped to the south; 26 were captured and 663 killed by the 1st Marine Division alone. Most of those remaining in the combat area threw off all vestige of the military; however, some operated as snipers dressed in civilian clothes.

Because of the lack of firm contact with the enemy, intelligence was meager. But as tactical operations progressed rapidly against light resistance, hundreds of dazed civilians were encountered, interrogated, and sent back to the divisions' stockades. Attempts to obtain practical knowledge of the enemy situation from the local inhabitants encountered great difficulties imposed by the Okinawan dialect. But the younger natives, those of high school age, were used successfully as sources of information. While the civilians were cooperative, the information drawn from them which could be converted to immediate tactical use was disappointingly limited. It did, however, clarify the picture of the general withdrawal to the south, confirmed the presence of units suspected of being in the area, aided in establishing an order of battle, and revealed specific and general areas to which the civilian population had fled.

For the most part, the local inhabitants had moved with all their belongings to well dug caves near their homes to escape aerial and naval bombardment. Many were reassured by interpreters roving the area in trucks equipped with loud speakers and induced to leave their refuges voluntarily. But usually it was necessary, particularly in isolated regions, for language personnel "to enter the caves and verbally pry the dwellers loose."[28]

Patrols, specifically organized to corral civilians into areas designated by military government, were accompanied by language officers searching for documents. Most of the large

---

[26] None of the captured personnel knew that they were in this paper organization; only one had ever heard of it. Without exception they gave as their unit the service or home guard element with which they served at the airfields.

[27] CinCPac-CinCPOA Bull 107–45, Translation and Interrogations No 28, 14May45, 12–13, 1st Specially Established Regt OpOrd A2, 1Apr45.

[28] *1st MarDiv SAR*, Part VIII, 2.

amount of printed and written material found was civilian literature and of no military value. But documents containing pertinent information were translated verbally to the regimental S–2's, who took down details of local significance, and then forwarded to the division G–2 translators section for immediate attention.

Documents recovered in the 1st Division zone, supplemented by interrogations, revealed that the Japanese military authorities had engaged in active conscription of civilians of suitable age since the bombings of 10 October 1944. These men, between the ages of 17 and 45, had then been organized into three types of units: regular army units, specially organized engineer units, and coolie labor. In order to avoid the dangers arising from the presence of such a large element, from which varying degrees of hostility could be expected, all able-bodied males from 15 to 45 were retained with bona fide prisoners of war for further screening.[29]

In clarifying the status of these people, the Marines were aided by Army Counterintelligence Corps (CIC) detachments. CIC special agents interrogated and investigated each Okinawan male in the 15–45 age group. Eventually, after being cleared by the CIC, intelligent Okinawans were enlisted to assist in interrogations, and specially qualified natives were distributed throughout the villages and districts to act as informants.

Besides the difficulty in producing usable tactical intelligence resulting from the absence of significant enemy forces, the lack of resistance and the consequent rapid advance of the infantry imposed complicated problems upon supporting units and led to serious dislocation of the logistical plan. This plan had been predicated on the premise that the landing would be stubbornly contested, and unloading priorities had been assigned accordingly. But the landing being effected without opposition permitted the debarkation of large numbers of troops which were not expected ashore until L-plus 1 or L-plus 2. This necessitated the use

of landing craft originally scheduled to move cargo and caused a delay in unloading critical supplies which were to have been sent ashore on L-Day.

Because of the narrowness of the roads and trails, and in order to avoid traffic congestion, it was not practicable to employ LVT's very far inland, and transport for front line supply was restricted to jeeps, jeep trailers, weasels, and carrying parties. But as forward elements moved farther inland, the need for motor transport became urgent, which in turn necessitated a change in unloading priorities. Consequently, the highest priority was assigned to unloading cargo trucks from APA's and AKA's.

By the night of L-plus 1 displacement was necessary for all battalions of the 11th Marines and overdue for 1/11, the assault troops having moved beyond the range of that unit. Displacement was prevented though by the lack of transportation. However, two battalions were moved forward on L-plus 2 by shuttling and adding transport as it came ashore. The remainder of the regiment moved up the following day.[30] Corps artillery accomplished very little unloading on L-plus 1 because of the changes in priorities. But unloading continued and improved on L-plus 2.[31]

Although the organic divisional engineer battalions were relieved of mine removal tasks, the rapid advances of III Amphibious Corps imposed a severe strain on these units in road maintenance and repair.[32] Because of the celerity of the movement forward, the "narrow and impassable stretches of roads [and] lack of roads leading into areas in which operations against the enemy were being conducted, the engineers were called upon more than any other supporting unit." [33] The 6th Engineer Battalion had the additional task of reconditioning Yontan airfield in the first few days it was ashore. The first American plane to land on Okinawa, an observation type from VMO–2, was able to come down at Yontan late on 2 April, and by 4 April all three strips of the field

[29] The wisdom of these precautions was illustrated by several incidents which confirmed our suspicions. Many a Kimono hid a uniform, and a number of civilians were found to be armed." *Ibid.*, 7.

[30] 11th Mar SAR, n. d., 3, hereinafter cited as *11th Mar SAR.*

[31] *IIIAC Arty AR*, 19–20.

[32] *Tenth Army AR*, Chap II, Sect XI, 8–9.

[33] *4th Mar SAR, Ph I&II*, 29.

PATROLS of the 4th Marines work their way through the hilly terrain southwest of Ishikawa.

were ready for emergency fighter plane landings.[34] The first four-engine transports arrived from Guam and initiated air evacuation of wounded on 8 April.[35]

While the ever-present infiltration and occasional ambushing of patrols by small hostile groups did little to influence the tactical situation of the 1st Marine Division, "the weakness

of the resistance . . . was a source of astonishment" to General del Valle which led him to order a reconnaissance in force[36] late in the afternoon of 2 April. The 1st and 2d Battalions of the 1st Marines passed through 3/5 and drove toward the base of the Katchin Peninsula. This attack, which was unopposed, ceased at 2100 when 1/1 on the right reached Chibana and dug in for the night. After being relieved, 3/5 reverted to regimental reserve. Having landed during the morning, 3/1 constituted the division reserve.

On the right of the 1st Division, elements of the 7th Infantry Division, operating over less

---

[34] *6th EngBn SAR, Ph I&II*, Part VII, 2. The first plane was piloted by 1stLt Frank A Milliken. *2d MarDiv AR*, Annex L.

[35] *Blakelock*. This source continues: "These planes were required to make the return flight to Guam without refueling at Okinawa due to the shortage of AvGas ashore to refuel the planes. Okinawa had five flights daily from Guam on a non-fueling basis until 12 April when 500 gal/plane was furnished for the return flight."

[36] LtGen P. A. del Valle Ltr to CMC, 29Sept54, hereinafter cited as *del Valle*.

difficult terrain,[37] reached the east coast at 1600 on 2 April. Consequently, when the attack was resumed the following morning, General del Valle ordered his motorized 1st Reconnaissance Company (First Lieutenant Robert J. Powell) to reconnoiter the area along the corps boundary in order to gain contact with the Army units which were well in advance. Employment of this mobile covering force enabled units on the right to advance rapidly in column, and by noon the leading units of the 1st Marines were on the sea wall overlooking the northern extremity of Nakagusuku Wan. The reconnaissance company, having worked itself out of a job, was ordered to sweep the Katchin Peninsula and then patrol back up the east coast to the village of Hizaonna. During the execution of this mission a lightly held tank trap was the only military installation observed, and Powell returned to division headquarters before dark having covered virtually the entire division zone of action.

At 1700 all units of the 1st Division were ordered to halt on the most favorable terrain. The 1st Battalion, 1st Marines, with its right flank anchored on Nakagusuku Wan, occupied a line sealing off two-thirds of the Katchin Peninsula. The 2d Battalion, 1st Marines, meeting negligible resistance from armed civilians, had seized the high ground immediately west of Gushikawa from which the eastern shore could be covered by fire. During the day's advance "supply had been almost nonexistent and the troops were without water and still depending on the food they landed with."[38]

Meeting only a four-man patrol, the advance of the 5th Marines gained momentum throughout the day, the 1st Battalion reaching Agina where 3/5 was committed on the right to contact 2/1. On the left, separated by 1,000 yards, 2/5 had occupied the village of Tengan[39] and advanced within its zone of action to the east coast of Okinawa.[40]

While opposition on the right had been virtually nonexistent, the 7th Marines on the left had pushed forward over the increasingly difficult terrain[41] against light to moderate resistance. Nevertheless the assault battalions gained 2,700 yards of enemy territory and dug in for the night after neutralizing a strong point from which heavy mortar, 20mm, and small-arms fire had been received. Taking a calculated risk in order to exploit the enemy weakness, Colonel Snedeker asked and received permission from division to continue the attack. Late in the afternoon the reserve battalion (3/7) executed a passage of lines and moved out in column of companies toward the village of Hizaonna on the high ground overlooking the east coast.[42]

In the course of this advance, the 81mm mortar platoon, unable to keep up, broke contact with the main body of 3/7. Company K, fol-

[39] *1/5 SAR*, 6. "Our ever widening zone of action prohibited the 'hand-in-hand' advance of some small island operations and our units were able to maintain contact and clear their areas only by patrolling to the flanks and front." *1st Mar Div SAR*, Part VIII, 5.

[40] "This was accomplished by 1700 on 3 April. 2/5, commanded by LtCol W. E. Benedict, had marched approximately eight miles over hilly country since 0800 when they left their 2 April position near Ishimine." Col J. H. Griebel Ltr to CMC, 18Oct54.

[41] "The movement from the west coast landing beaches of Okinawa across the island to the east coast was most difficult because of the rugged terrain crossed. It was physically exhausting for personnel who had been on transports for a long time. It also presented initially an almost impossible supply problem in the Seventh's zone of action because of the lack of roads." Col E. W. Snedeker Ltr to CMC, 27Mar47, hereinafter cited as *Snedeker 1947*.

[42] *1st MarDiv G-3 Jul*, 3Apr45; Col E. H. Hurst Interview, 3Mar55. "The forced march of over three miles of the Third Battalion, Seventh Marines to Hizaonna, late on 3 April is noteworthy. Orders for the march were not issued until about 1430 on that date. Information received from the Division Reconnaissance Company indicated no substantial enemy strength on the east coast in the Seventh's zone. What might be encountered from the front line to the east coast was unknown. The march was made over rugged unfamiliar terrain, with the probable expectancy of meeting enemy forces at any time, and it resulted in advance elements, including the battalion CO reaching Hizaonna at 1830, 3 April. Hizaonna was at that time well beyond our front lines . . ." *Snedeker 1947*.

[37] "In the sweep across the island the most serious obstacle was the terrain, especially as no road existed in my zone of action, so that, as happened again later, I was obliged to employ the road on which the Seventh Infantry Division advanced, which was in their zone of action." *Ibid.*

[38] *1st Mar SAR*, 6.

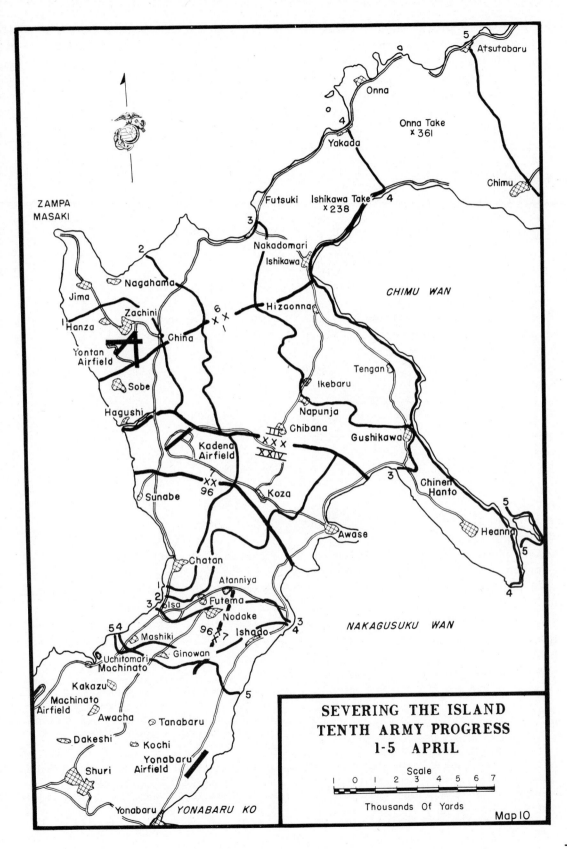

ZAMPA
MASAKI

Atsutabaru

5

Onna

Onna Take
× 361

4

Yakada

Chimu

Futsuki

Ishikawa Take
× 238   4

3

Nakadomari

Ishikawa

CHIMU WAN

Nagahama

Jima

Zachini

6
X X

China

Hizaonna

Tengan

Yontan
Airfield

Ikebaru

Hanza

Sobe

Hagushi

Napunja

Kadena
Airfield

III
Chibana

Gushikawa

Sunabe

XX
96

XXX
XXIV

Koza

3

Chinen
Hanto

5

Awase

Heanna

5

Chatan

Atanniya

Futema

NAKAGUSUKU WAN

4

1
2
Isa

Nodake

3

3
4

Ishado

5 4

Mashiki

96
X 7

Ginowan

Uchitomari
Machinato

Kakazu

Machinato
Airfield

Awacha

Tanabaru

Dakeshi

Kochi

Shuri

Yonabaru
Airfield

Yonabaru   YONABARU KO

5

SEVERING THE ISLAND
TENTH ARMY PROGRESS
1-5 APRIL

Scale
1 0 1 2 3 4 5 6 7

Thousands Of Yards

Map 10

lowing the mortars, became separated from the remainder of the battalion upon reaching a road fork after night had fallen. Lieutenant Colonel Hurst radioed the company to dig in for night defense after its repeated efforts to reach Hizaonna were defeated by the darkness and unfamiliar terrain. At daybreak Japanese troops in the hills surrounding the isolated company's perimeter began firing, and approximately 75 of the enemy attempted to assault the Marines' lines. The attack was repulsed and the remaining Japanese withdrew to the high ground to continue sporadic small arms and mortar fire. The fire fight gradually died out as the morning wore on and Company K moved out to rejoin the battalion. Tank patrols on the following day counted 126 dead Japanese in the area of the encounter.[43]

While the 1st Division drove to the coast and advanced its lines 3–5,000 yards,[44] the 6th Division, moving through difficult and heavily broken terrain honeycombed with innumerable caves, gained 3,500–7,000 yards of enemy ground. In the process the 4th Marines liquidated the resistance which had opposed it during the preceding two days, and minor pockets encountered by the 22d Marines were mopped up.

In order to develop the situation to the division's front, the 6th Reconnaissance Company, supported and transported by two reinforced platoons of the 6th Tank Battalion (Lieutenant Colonel Robert L. Denig, Jr.), was ordered forward on the north coast road and across the Ishikawa Isthmus from Nakadomari to the village of Ishikawa. This armored column was taken under mortar fire near Ishikawa and returned the fire at long-range. Before nightfall the reconnaissance was completed, revealing only small enemy groups in the isthmus area.

The 22d Marines, its deployment unchanged, moved out on L-plus 2 with 2/22 advancing up the west coast road to the isthmus and maintaining contact with 1/22 which was moving more slowly through extremely rough terrain. On the right 3/22 maintained contact with the 4th Marines. By 1700 2/22 had Nakadomari and the remainder of the 22d Marines occupied a position 400 yards south of this line.

Although the remnants of Japanese forces offered light and sporadic resistance to the 4th Marines, the greatest hindrance to that regiment's advance lay in the terrain and the difficulties of supply and evacuation engendered by the lack of roads. Yet the regiment had secured the formidable hill mass behind Yontan airfield when it ceased the attack at 1630, 3,000 yards short of the east coast.

In conjunction with the 58th Naval Construction Battalion (NCB), the 6th Engineer Battalion had continued improving the Yontan airfield. Light observation planes of VMO–6 operated from the field throughout 3 April, and a fighter plane negotiated a successful forced landing before dark. In anticipation of a possible airborne attack the division reserve (1/29) was ordered to Yontan field at 2000 to organize the airdrome for defense.[45]

After three days of vigorous activity, the 6th Division's left flank was at the base of the Ishikawa Isthmus and the 1st Division's right flank on Nakagusuku Wan, and operations in the IIIAC area were approximately 11 to 12 days ahead of schedule. (See Map 10) Earlier in the day, General Buckner signalled General Geiger:

I congratulate you and your command on a splendidly executed landing and substantial gains in enemy territory. I have full confidence that your fighting Marines will meet every requirement of this campaign with characteristic courage, spirit, and efficiency.[46]

[43] Hurst, *op. cit.,;* 1st MarDiv Interviews, Co K, 7th Mar, hereinafter cited as *1st MarDiv Interviews.* This last source consists of a series of interviews conducted by Sgt Kenneth A. Shutts and Sgt Paul Trilling, historians assigned to the 1st MarDiv for the Okinawa operation, which form a valuable record of the important actions of the campaign at the small-unit level.

[44] *Tenth Army AR*, Chap 7, Sect III, 3.

[45] *1/29 SAR, Ph I&II*, 8. During the morning 1/29 had again patrolled Zampa-Misaki with negative results, and had then assembled in reserve east of Yontan airfield. *Ibid.*

[46] *6th MarDiv Jnl, Ph I&II*, 3Apr45.

MEETING THE ENEMY[47]

On 4 April the attack was resumed at 0730. On the left of the 6th Marine Division 2/22, employing a mobile tank-infantry column, pushed vigorously up the west coast road, sending patrols inland to contact the flank patrols of 1/22 in the interior. The right element of the 22d Marines (3/22) drove across the base of the peninsula on Ishikawa, rapidly outstripping the 4th Marines which was laboring over steep ridges against moderate resistance.[48] With the 22d Marines swiftly racing northward, General Shepherd moved the division reserve within supporting distance. At 0835 he ordered 1/29 to entruck immediately and assemble in the vicinity of Nakadomari to await orders.

By midday the 4th Marines had reached the east coast and was pinched out of the line by the advance of Colonel Schneider's regiment to Ishikawa. The direction of the attack then shifted 90 degrees to the north. The 22d Marines, responsible for covering the entire division front from the east to the west coast, was reinforced by 1/29; and the 4th Marines, after clearing its zone, assembled in division reserve late in the afternoon.

The attack continued throughout the day against scattered resistance. The right battalion (3/22), also driving northward behind an armored spearhead, maintained contact with 1/22 by extensive flank patrolling.

At the time the 4th Marines was ordered into reserve at 1600, Colonel Schneider committed 1/29 in the center of the regimental zone,[49] and 1/22 (less Company C detached to 3/22 for night defense) passed into reserve. After an advance of 7,500 yards through rough, mountainous terrain the 22d Marines' attack was halted at 1700. A defensive position was set along a line through Yakada with both flanks anchored on the sea.

Because of the great distances that now separated infantry units of the 6th Division from Yontan airfield, General Shepherd requested relief from the responsibility for the defense of the airdrome. General Geiger assigned this task to the 29th Marines in corps reserve. Upon relief from this assignment the 29th Marines would revert to the operational control of the 6th Marine Division.[50]

The 4 April advance through the rugged, spinous mountain range had strained supply lines almost to the breaking point. In consequence, H-Hour on 5 April was delayed until 0900 in order that supplies could be moved forward to support the attack. During this temporary period of inaction, the assault battalions patrolled vigorously 500 yards to their front, and deep reconnaissances by armored columns were launched up both coastal roads. On the left (west) flank, the 6th Reconnaissance Company, reinforced with a tank platoon and tank dozer, was ordered out from Nakadomori to Chuda. Company F, 4th Marines, similarly reinforced, was assigned a like mission on the east coast.[51]

Company F advanced 14 miles before turning back in late afternoon. During the day the patrol was delayed three times by undefended road blocks but met no opposition until the tanks encountered the enemy at Chimu, where two Japanese were killed and a fuel truck was destroyed.[52] The reconnaissance company met no opposition, but was held up at Onna by a destroyed bridge which could not be bypassed. With these mobile covering forces searching out routes of advance, the assault battalions moved forward rapidly detaching companies as necessary to reduce enemy pockets of resistance inland. By the end of the day, although the terrain had become no less difficult and the enemy had become more active, the 6th Marine Division had gained another 7,000 yards. The 22d Marines held the general line Atsutabaru-Chimu, with the 4th Marines (less 1/4 bivouacked at Ishikawa)[53] located in assembly areas just behind its lines prepared to pass

[47] Unless otherwise noted the material in this section is derived from *1st MarDiv SAR*; *6th MarDiv SAR, Ph I&II*; *7th InfDiv AR*; *96th InfDiv AR*; *1st Mar SAR*; *4th Mar SAR, Ph I&II*; *5th Mar S–3 Jnl*; *7th Mar SAR*; *22d Mar SAR, Ph I&II*; *29th Mar SAR, Ph I&II*.

[48] *6th MarDiv Jnl, Ph I&II*, 4Apr45.

[49] *1/29 SAR, Ph I&II*, 8–9.

[50] *6th MarDiv Jnl, Ph I&II*, 4Apr45.

[51] *6th TkBn SAR, Ph I&II*, 19.

[52] *Ibid*.

[53] *1/4 SAR, Ph I&II*, 7.

HEAVY MACHINE GUNNERS of the 96th Division fire on enemy outpost resistance on 4 April. (Army Photograph)

through the following morning. The 29th Marines had been released to parent control by IIIAC at 1000 and had moved to the vicinity of Onna.[54]

During the afternoon of 4 April the 1st Marine Division also closed on the eastern shore of Okinawa. Meeting no enemy but encountering large numbers of civilians, the 1st Marines occupied the Katchin Peninsula by noon. In like manner the 5th Marines secured the shore line in its zone in the same period of time. Both regiments organized defensive positions and immediately initiated intensive patrolling to the rear to eliminate any bypassed positions, a task in which the reconnaissance company and the division reserve (3/1) also participated. The advance of the 7th Marines, however, was considerably more complicated.

At Hizaonna, Lieutenant Colonel Hurst had been joined by Company I and most of Company L the night before. The remainder of Company L, like Company K, took the wrong road at a junction and reached the beach south of Ishikawa late at night. There the company remained unmolested until daybreak enabled it

to move to Hizaonna. While Company K was breaking contact to rejoin the battalion, a supply party coming forward from the rear was ambushed, and Company L was dispatched to extricate it. Upon the completion of this mission, Company L returned and reported that the enemy had withdrawn to the north.

In the meantime, 1/7 and 2/7, attacking abreast, were advancing to the coast. Mopping up small pockets of resistance, 2/7 reached the sea at midday after an advance of 3,900 yards over difficult terrain. On the right 1/7 was delayed while it engaged and destroyed a force of some 50 Japanese and did not reach the eastern beaches until 1700.

In the early evening of 4 April 3/1 received orders to relieve the 29th Marines of the mission of defending Yontan airfield the following morning. Tentative plans were also formulated to release the 7th Marines to IIIAC in order to assist the 6th Marine Division in its northern drive. The next day, the 7th Marines (less 3/7 which was attached to 5th Marines) went into IIIAC reserve with orders to occupy and defend the village of Ishikawa pending further tactical developments.[55]

On 5 April, while the 6th Marine Division conducted vigorous reconnaissance north toward Motobu Peninsula, the 1st Marine Division entered a period primarily devoted to defensive activity. Besides bringing up supplies, camouflaging, and improving positions, heavy patrol activity was continued to the rear. A patrol from the 1st Marines on the Katchin Peninsula waded across the reef to Yabuchi Shima, captured five *Boeitai*, and reported the presence of some 350 civilians.

The near perfect weather which had prevailed since L-Day deteriorated in scattered rains in the early evening of 5 April. Although there was no organized resistance, enemy activity actually increased, but it was only from small scattered groups behind the lines. Of this period a regimental commander has noted:

There was almost daily patrol contacts with well-armed enemy groups . . . Some of these groups were wandering aimlessly about while others occupied well

---

[54] *IIIAC AR*, 35.

[55] *Snedeker 1947*, Enclosure A, A History of the 7th Marines on Okinawa Shima, 7, hereinafter cited as *7th Mar History*.

defended, organized, and concealed positions. These patrol operations were extremely valuable in giving to the officers and men of the regiment added confidence in each other and helped all to reach a peak of physical perfection. Conducting independent patrols, which were often under fire, added greatly to the ability of the leaders of small units.[56]

To the south of the 1st Division the tactical situation in the zone of XXIV Corps was also undergoing a radical change. Less hampered by supply difficulties than the units to the north, the assault divisions of the corps had aggressively exploited the initial lack of resistance. While 7th Division advance elements were cutting the island in half on 2 April, the 96th Division, moving south along the western shore, advanced its lines to the vicinity of Futema.

After clearing its zone of action on the trans-island axis of advance, the 7th Division reorganized and continued the attack to the south on 3 April, covering 3,000 yards to reach Kuba by nightfall. In the center of the 96th Division's zone, the 382d Infantry with two battalions abreast moved south to a line 200 yards north of Nodake, where contact was established with a small enemy force and the regiment dug in for the night. During the afternoon a platoon of the 96th Reconnaissance Troop passed through the 383d Infantry on the west coast and investigated as far south as Mashiki with negative results. Forward elements of the 383d occupied Isa and Chiyuna by nightfall. The 381st Infantry, coordinating its movements with the 32d Infantry of the 7th Division, completed wheeling to the south and at the end of the day was in position near Attaniya awaiting the passage of its lines the following morning by the 7th Division's 184th Infantry.

In a drive similar to the action involved in the compression of a strong steel spring, the 7th Division pushed south on 4 April to meet stiffening resistance from hostile infantry supported by field artillery at Hill 165.[57] During the day the Japanese were driven from this dominant terrain and the division gained approximately 1,000 yards.

Meanwhile, on the left of the 96th Division, the 382d Infantry was held up by the fire of an estimated enemy company. After driving this unit to the south, the regiment again ran into a reinforced company strong point north of Ginowan late in the afternoon. The 383d Infantry came under heavy machine-gun, mortar, and artillery fire during its advance, and 3/383, moving down the west coast road, was forced to hold up about 400 yards north of Uchitomari. The 2d Battalion, 383d Infantry also encountered mounting enemy resistance as it advanced on the positions holding up 3/383. The 381st Infantry reverted to divisional reserve during the day after the 184th Infantry moved through its lines, and the 7th Division took over the left of the 96th's zone of action.

By the night of 4 April the L-plus 10 line, originally planned as the southern limit of the Tenth Army beachhead, had been seized by the XXIV Corps. Both Army divisions moved out for their fifth day of ground action against an increasing volume of enemy defensive fires. On the corps left flank General Arnold's division continued its steady progress with the 184th and 32d Infantry advancing an average of 2,600 yards. Resistance was met mainly from small, scattered enemy groups in the hills and ridges bordering the east coast. Because of the 7th Division's wide turning movement to come into line with the 96th, its night positions forward of Ishado were still almost 1,000 yards to the rear of those of the 382d Infantry.

Both assault regiments of the 96th Division became heavily engaged with enemy outpost strong points during 5 April. On the division's left, the 382d Infantry's 2d Battalion took Ginowan during a 900-yard advance, but it was stopped on the outskirts of the village by intensive fire from ridge positions to the southwest. On the division boundary 1/382 made 400 yards through rugged high ground and with the aid of tanks and artillery broke up an enemy counterattack which was spotted forming in front of its lines about noon. For night defense, the regimental reserve (3/382) was moved to blocking positions from which it could cover by fire the gap between divisions.

---

[56] *Snedeker 1947.*

[57] It should be borne in mind that elevations on maps used at Okinawa were in meters. Thus Hill 165 if envisioned as feet by the reader seems a relatively insignificant terrain feature, whereas a height of 544 feet (165 meters) is an appreciable hill.

On the west coast, 3/383 consolidated its positions south of Mashiki won on 4 April and probed hard into the enemy defenses near Uchitomari, while 2/383 on the regimental left flank drove unsuccessfully against the first of a series of prepared ridge positions guarding the approaches to Kakazu. Four tanks were lost during the day's action, one to a mine and the others to enemy AT fire. In contrast to long advances during preceding days' actions, the 96th Division was able to take only about 400 yards on L-plus 4.

Over 2,200 Japanese, the majority in the XXIV Corps zone, had been killed or captured in five days of increasingly harder action at a cost of 300 battle casualties to American troops.[58] However, only the barest surface of Japanese resistance had been exposed. The men of the veteran 7th and 96th Divisions, as spearheads of the Tenth Army's main drive, stood on the threshold of the bitterest and most protracted battle of their experience. (See Map 10)

LOGISTICAL PROGRESS[59]

The absence of enemy opposition on the beaches had greatly simplified the problems of shore party control and facilitated the progress of unloading of assault shipping. By noon on L-Day division shore party commanders had begun to assume control of their sectors; by nightfall all shore parties were under division control. A steady procession of DUKW's and LVT's shuttled across the reefs bringing in supplies to build up inland dumps. For a period of four to five hours at each high tide ship's landing craft could make their runs directly to the beaches.

Before nightfall on L-Day, shore party officers had become painfully aware of what was to be their most pressing problem during the first days ashore. As the volume of cargo reaching the beaches increased, the number of

trucks available to haul it to dumps decreased. Plans had been made to use the organic motor transport of the assault divisions to assist the shore party. These plans had to be drastically modified. The unexpectedly rapid advance of forward elements required the divisions to commit their trucks to an effort to supply assault troops over the tortuous road system of central Okinawa. Even with the immediate and continuing aid of engineers and Seabees in improving beach exits and roads, the shore parties were hard put to keep up with their work load. By dint of improvisation and continuous improvement of materiel handling facilities, however, the flow of supplies continued unabated, although at times the situation was, to say the least, frustrating.

The favorable tactical picture influenced Admiral Turner to authorize night unloading under floodlights on 2 April and to direct that ship's holds be cleared of all assault cargo. Earlier on L-plus 1 the Joint Expeditionary Force Commander had directed that men and equipment of aviation engineer battalions and Marine air groups (MAG's) be unloaded as soon as possible. On 3 April General Geiger reinforced Turner's order with a request that all previous priorities of LST unloadings in IIIAC's zone be suspended until all the airfield headquarters, service, construction, and maintenance personnel were ashore.

This emphasis on getting Yontan and Kadena airfields operational, coupled with General Buckner's authorization on 3 April for the corps commanders to unload army troops at their discretion, brought about a steady increase in the volume of ship-to-shore traffic. Control vessels and beach parties soon noticed many instances of low priority units and equipment mingling with the shoreward flow of essential assault gear. In part this interruption of supposedly firm unloading schedules was due to ships' captains' natural desire to unload and get clear of the vulnerable Hagushi anchorage. The inability of the shore party with its inadequate transport to handle the vast quantities of supplies, forced many ships to stand off shore with half-empty holds awaiting the return of boats stacked up at control vessels.

The problem of control of ship-to-shore

---

[58] Tenth Army G-2 Rpt No 12, 7Apr45; *CTF 51 AR*, Part V, Sect H, 6.

[59] Unless otherwise noted the material in this section is derived from OpNav 34-P-0700, Amphibious Operations—Capture of Okinawa, 27Mar-27Jun45, 22Jan46, hereinafter cited as *CNO Record; CTF 51 AR; Tenth Army AR*.

SUPPLIES pour ashore on L-plus 2 from landing craft beached at the mouth of the Bishi Gawa.   (Navy Photograph)

traffic, while it was immense, was probably better handled at Okinawa than in any previous Pacific operation. Experience gained in the Marianas campaign had led Admiral Turner to recommend that only "the most experienced personnel available should be used in the Control Parties for assault landings." [60] Consequently, key members of the control group used at Iwo Jima served on board control vessels off Okinawa contributing their fresh experiences toward more efficient operations.

Individual coxswains of the landing boats further complicated the critical control problem by their efforts to "get to the beach at all costs." The commander of the 1st Marine Division's transport group commented on this unforeseen factor:

> There seemed to exist on the part of most coxswains an almost fierce determination to be first ashore with their individual boats, regardless of the orderly assignment to unloading points, which it is the function of the control vessel to carry out. Coxswains simply would not follow orders to form and remain in cargo circles, but jockeyed for positions of advantage from which to come along side the control vessel. Many even attempted to ignore the control vessel and bypass it, proceeding directly to whatever beach they had a preference for.[61]

By 4 April a good start had been made toward bridging the reef barrier off the Hagushi beaches with the aid of pontoon barges and causeways sidelifted to the target by LST's and

---

[60] CTF 51 OpRpt, FORAGER, 25Aug44, Recommendations, 2.

[61] Quoted in *CNO Record*, Chap 7, 55.

AKS's (General Stores Issue Ship).[62] The larger landing ships could now discharge their cargo directly onto causeways on Red Beach 1 opposite Yontan airfield and on Purple 1 and the Orange Beaches near Kadena. In addition, 80 self-propelled barges had been put into operation to shuttle supplies over the reef to the beach. To expedite the handling of the swarming small boat traffic off the IIIAC beaches, eight barge transfer points had been set up to provide temporary floating supply dumps.

Although heavy weather during the night of 4 April and most of the following day interfered with the orderly process of unloading,[63] the shore party continued to operate in an attempt to clear its jammed beach dumps. On 5 April, 32 empty transports and cargo vessels departed the target area. With the abatement of high winds on 6 April, unloading stepped up pace so that 13 additional APA's and AKA's were emptied and 60 LST's were reported cleared of cargo.

The planned process of transition of shore party control to progressively higher troop echelons continued throughout this early period. On 3 April the commander of the XXIV Corps shore party took over the southern beaches, and three days later the commander of the III Corps Service Group assumed control of the Marine divisions' unloading. As a result of a conference of responsible fleet and troop logistics officers on board Admiral Turner's flagship on 8 April, arrangements were made for Tenth Army to take over all shore party activities on the Hagushi beaches the following morning. The Island Commander, Major General Fred C. Wallace, was placed in charge and the 53d Engineer Special Brigade directed to operate all beaches except the newly opened one at Nago. IIIAC Service Group retained direct control of this landing point in order to operate a much-needed forward supply dump for the far ranging battalions of the 6th Marine Division.[64]

Between L-Day and 11 April when the first substantial increment of garrison shipping began to arrive, unloading over the Hagushi beaches was confined to assault shipping. By noon on 11 April, 532,291 measurement tons [65] of cargo had been unloaded, more than had been put ashore from assault shipping during the entire Marianas campaign.[66]

In large part the success of Tenth Army in early April was due to the untiring efforts of shore party personnel and ships' crews. The assault troops had seized a substantial beachhead and the support troops had made it secure by building up adequate reserves of supplies and equipment to meet the increasing demands of combat.

KAMIKAZE [67]

While assault battalions of the Tenth Army were probing the enemy outpost line on Okinawa, the fleet in the surrounding waters was engaged in a desperate battle to maintain its position. Crewmen of the destroyers and support craft on the picket line were on a continual alert. Radar screens searched the sky to detect the signs of enemy aircraft approaching the Hagushi anchorage. Many Japanese pilots

---

[62] *Blakelock.*

[63] Beaching difficulties and heavy weather seriously affected the resupply of ammunition to the 155mm guns on Keise Shima throughout the operation. On 8 April, when an LST due to discharge its cargo of vitally needed ammunition was unable to unload at Keise, orders were issued that an LCT be dispatched daily from the Hagushi beaches with resupply ammunition. *Ibid.*

[64] In the IIIAC zone of action many of the shore party troops were men from replacement drafts who trained with the divisions as infantrymen, accompanied the assault echelon to the target, and served in the vital role of beach and ship labor until the need for casualty replacements required their assignment to division combat units.

[65] The measurement ton is a unit of volume, not weight, used in describing ships' cargo. It is usually figured at 40 cu. ft.

[66] "The first garrison shipping to arrive carried assault cargo that could not be lifted in the assault shipping," and by 15 April 577,040 measurement tons of cargo, mostly assault supplies, had been unloaded against an estimated beach capacity of 529,790. *Blakelock.*

[67] Unless otherwise noted the material in this section is derived from CinCPac War Diary, April 1945; Fifth Flt AR, 1Apr–27May45, 10Jul45; *CTF 51 AR; Campaigns.* Casualty statistics for ship's crews are taken from *CTF 51 AR,* Part III, Sect H, 7–10, while figures on ship damage and losses are a result of a careful analysis of all the above sources for what is considered to be the most accurate information.

died, however, before they came within range of the pickets, shot down in furious battles with watchdog patrols of TF's 57 and 58 and the omnipresent fighters of TF 51's escort carriers.

Enemy planes that evaded the combat air patrols ran a gantlet of antiaircraft fire all the way from the outermost pickets to the AAA battalions on the beaches. Comparatively few pilots who took off from the airfields of Kyushu, Formosa, and the Sakishimas managed to reach their objective. Many of those who won through the curtain of fire were on conventional bombing and reconnaissance missions that held out some hope of survival. Others, far too many from the American viewpoint, were members of special suicide air attack units, the *Kamikazes*.

The first scattered *Kamikaze* attacks had been made in the Philippines in concert with the Japanese fleet's desperate bid for victory at Leyte Gulf. The development of the suicide philosophy, according to enemy sources, "originated in the feelings of all combatants in the Philippine area. All were beginning to think that there was no way but suicide to save the situation; there were many volunteers."[68] The motives of these *Kamikaze* pilots were explained to American interrogators after the war by a staff officer of the unit which made the initial attacks:

> We felt as follows: we must give our lives to the Emperor and Country, this is our inborn feeling. I am afraid you cannot understand it well, or you may call it foolish. We Japanese base our lives on obedience to Emperor and Country. On the other hand, we wish for the best place in death, according to *Bushido*. *Kamikaze* . . . was the incarnation of these feelings.[69]

The initial success of the special attack units at Leyte, Lingayen Gulf, and later at Iwo Jima heartened the Japanese leaders and public and encouraged them to a desperate gamble which had its culmination at Okinawa. The *Kamikaze* concept, "macabre, effective, supremely practical under the circumstances, supported and stimulated by a powerful propaganda campaign, . . . became virtually the sole method

used in opposing the United States striking and amphibious forces, and these ships the sole target."[70]

In contrast to the sporadic nature of the first suicide attempts, *Kamikaze* operations at Okinawa were well planned and organized. Army units of the 6th Air Force and naval squadrons of the 5th Air Fleet, with a combined initial plane strength of about 1,815,[71] were placed under a single commander, Admiral Soemu Toyoda, Commander in Chief, Combined Fleet.

The new headquarters was established at Kanoya, Kyushu on 13 February 1945 and the first all-out attack unleashed against TF 58's carriers during raids against Japan of 18–19 March. The results of the assault were considered satisfactory despite the loss of 161 attacking aircraft. The Japanese believed the damage to five American carriers reported by their scouting planes would effectively delay TF 58's regrouping for further operations. They were surprised, therefore, at the rapidity of the Fast Carrier Forces' reentry into action to cover the landings at Kerama Retto. Admiral Toyoda's units were not ready to attack again when Tenth Army began landing on Okinawa.[72]

Scattered flights of planes from Japan and the Formosa area carried the brunt of the attack on TF 51 during the first few days of April. The toll of ships damaged and sunk rose steadily. To the men of the transport fleet and picket line, especially those whose ships drew the attention of suicide pilots, the period from 1–5 April was nerve-racking. A battleship, an escort carrier, two destroyers, eight transport and cargo vessels, a mine sweeper, and two landing ships were damaged in aerial attacks; the APD *Dickerson* was hurt so badly by a suicide crash she had to be scuttled. Naval casualties continued to mount with 81 KIA, 294 WIA, and 60 MIA reported from the crews of the damaged ships.

By 6 April the Japanese were ready to mount a carefully planned *Kamikaze* attack from

---

[68] *USSBS Interrogation* No 62, Capt Rikibei Inoguchi, IJN, I, 60.

[69] *Ibid.*, 60–61.

[70] *Campaigns*, 286.

[71] RAdm T. Yokoi, "*Kamikazes* and the Okinawa Campaign," *USNI Proceedings*, May 1954, 508, hereinafter cited as *Kamikazes*.

[72] *Ibid.*, 507–508.

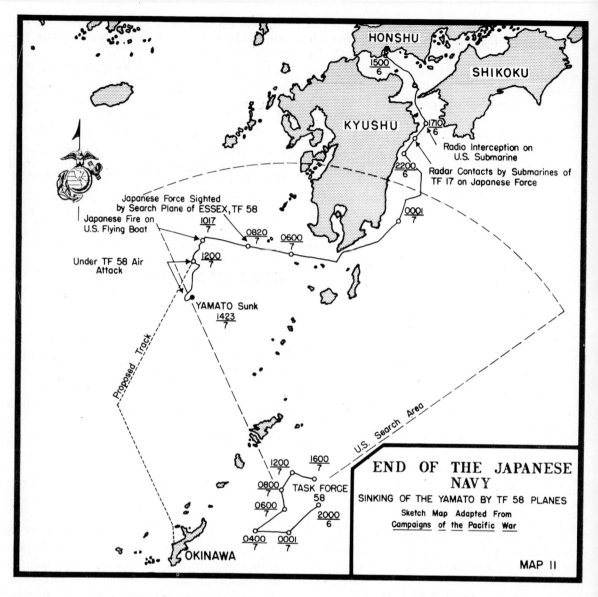

Japanese Force Sighted
by Search Plane of ESSEX, TF 58

Japanese Fire on
U.S. Flying Boat

Under TF 58 Air
Attack

1017
7

0820
7

0600
7

1200
7

YAMATO Sunk
1423
7

HONSHU

SHIKOKU

1500
6

KYUSHU

1710
6

Radio Interception on
U.S. Submarine

2200
6

Radar Contacts by Submarines of
TF 17 on Japanese Force

0001
7

Proposed Track

U.S. Search Area

1200
7

1600
7

0800
7

TASK FORCE
58

0600
7

2000
6

0400
7

0001
7

OKINAWA

**END OF THE JAPANESE
NAVY**

SINKING OF THE YAMATO BY TF 58 PLANES

Sketch Map Adapted From
Campaigns of the Pacific War

MAP II

Kyushu. In the early morning scout planes located TF 58 off Amami-O-Shima, and over 100 fighters and bombers were sent to engage the carrier force. Defending combat air patrols over Okinawa were drawn into battles with enemy fighters dispatched ahead of the main attack force. Covered by these advance fighter groups, approximately 200 *Kamikazes* began to drive in toward the Hagushi anchorage.

The main attack began about 1500 and lasted five hours. Although the weather was fair, visibility was severely limited as the smoke of burning planes and ships soon mingled with that of the protective screen over the transport

area. Entirely aside from the danger of suicide crashes, torpedoes, and bombs, crewmen in exposed positions and troops on the beaches were subjected to a deadly hail of shell fragments.[73] The hundreds of guns firing from beach and sea accounted for three friendly fighters which followed Japanese planes too closely into the lethal barrage.

The *Kamikaze* pilots started scoring at 1530 when the first plane crashed into the picket

[73] CTF 51 reported personnel injured by AA fragments on five APA's and one patrol craft during the attack. In addition CG, XXIV Corps reported 4 killed and 34 wounded by the falling shell fragments.

destroyer *Bush*. In short order two more suiciders piled into the hapless ship, despite valiant efforts by support craft and the destroyer *Calhoun* to drive off the attackers. The *Calhoun* itself was hit by three planes. Both ships eventually sank, the *Bush* at 1950 and the *Calhoun* under American gunfire at 0130 on 7 April when she began to break up under tow.

Meanwhile, the battle was raging all over the area with the barrier ring of pickets and patrol craft, lacking the protective cover of a smoke screen, getting the worst of it. Ships of all types were being damaged by plane crashes and near misses. The mine sweeper *Emmons* had 30 feet of her stern blown off at 1630; she was later sunk to prevent her drifting ashore in enemy territory. Shortly after the *Emmons* took its crippling suicide hit, *Kamikazes* dove into three ships in the Kerama area. All three, the LST 447 and the ammunition ships *Logan Victory* and *Hobbs Victory*, were total losses and eventually went to the bottom.[74]

After the fury of the main attack died down, the task force continued to get heckling raids throughout the night. The last ships were hit early on 7 April. The all-out attack had caused an impressive total of damage. In addition to the six ships sunk, the Japanese had damaged nine destroyers, four destroyer escorts, and five mine vessels. Over 500 more men had been added to TF 51's casualty list during 19 hours of savage action; the ships hit by *Kamikazes* reported losses of 94 killed, 264 wounded, and 178 missing.

Although the Japanese lost at least 135 planes during the attack to Admiral Turner's forces, they were elated by imaginative reports from their reconnaissance planes which backed up the claims of Thirty-second Army that more than

JAPANESE BATTLESHIP *Yamato* sunk by planes of TF 58 on 7 April during the abortive naval attack on Okinawa. (Navy Photograph)

30 ships were observed sinking and over 20 ships burning.[75]

During 6–7 April TF 58 reported splashing about 245 planes to bring the total Japanese loss to nearly 400. The damage to the heavily gunned and armored carrier force was much less than that to TF 51; only one carrier, the *Hancock*, and two destroyers were hit seriously enough to require retirement from the combat area.

In addition to driving off air raiders, Admiral Mitscher's flyers were busy on 7 April administering the death stroke to the largest battleship ever built, the 69,100-ton *Yamato*.[76] (See Map 11)

The sortie of the *Yamato* and its covering squadron, one light cruiser and eight destroyers, was planned as an aid to the *Kamikaze* attacks. Provided with only enough fuel for a one-way voyage,[77] the giant battleship's assignment was

---

[74] The loss of these two ammunition ships was a serious blow to Tenth Army resupply plans. A majority of the 81mm mortar ammunition in the U. S. was loaded on these ships and subsequent resupply shipments were in short supply of this type of ammunition. Air lift was resorted to in order to make up partially for this deficiency, and before the end of the campaign 117 tons of 81mm ammunition was flown to Okinawa by Army and Navy transport planes. *Blakelock*; *Tenth Army AR*, Chap 11, Part IV, 12.

[75] *Kamikazes*, 508.

[76] Capt K. Matsumoto and Cdr M. Chihaya, "Design and Construction of the *Yamato* and *Musashi*," *USNI Proceedings*, October 1953, 1105. The principal armament of the *Yamato* was nine 18-inch rifles. It had a radius of action of 7,200 sea miles cruising at 16 knots, an overall length of 863 feet, and a beam of 128 feet. It carried a crew of 2,500 men.

[77] *Kamikazes*, 509. Admiral Toyoda indicated there was extreme difficulty getting even the 2,500 tons of fuel oil necessary for the operation. Additional warships were available, but fuel for them was not. *Campaigns*, 327.

to shell the landing area and anchorage at Okinawa, drawing off the American air cover so that *Kamikazes* might have a clear shot at the amphibious force. It was definitely a suicide mission and Admiral Toyada felt the *Yamato* group had less than a 50–50 chance of even reaching its target. TF 58 reduced the mission from a gambler's risk to a forlorn hope.

Less than two hours after the Japanese force left Tokuyama naval base on Honshu (1520, 6 April) the submarines *Hackleback* and *Threadfin*, lying off the east coast of Kyushu, discovered the enemy ships and alerted Fifth Fleet. The submarines lost their contact later that night, but a search plane from the *Essex* picked up the *Yamato* group again at 0822, 7 April. At 1030 Kerama-based seaplane bombers began tracking the enemy ships. At the same time, the last of three strike groups, totalling 380 planes, was launched by TF 58.

A Japanese destroyer lagging at the rear of the enemy formation was attacked at 1210 and eventually sank. At 1240 the full fury of the first two American strike groups hit the main enemy force. The *Yamato* took two bombs and one torpedo, another destroyer was sunk, and the cruiser was stopped dead in the water. At 1333 the third group struck and finished the job in less than an hour. The *Yamato* took three additional bombs and nine torpedoes, capsized, blew up, and sank a full day's steaming from its Okinawan target. The cruiser and one other destroyer were sent to the bottom. Later that night a fourth heavily damaged destroyer was scuttled as the remaining ships withdrew to Japan—mission not accomplished. Despite the heavy curtain of antiaircraft fire put up by the beleaguered Japanese ships, TF 58's losses were phenomenally small—10 planes and 16 men.

Although this venture in aid of *Kamikaze* operations ended in abject failure, the Japanese High Command was convinced of the utility of suicide missions. Orders were issued to Fifth Air Fleet "to continue general attacks at all costs." [78] The pattern of air assault on 6–7 April was merely a grim portent of the future.

---

[78] *Kamikazes*, 509.

CHAPTER VI — Action in the North

SECURING THE EASTERN ISLANDS[1]

The rapid initial progress of Tenth Army had cleared the shore line of Chimu Wan and that of a large portion of the upper bay in Nakagusuku Wan by 5 April. Mine sweepers, operating under Admiral Blandy as Commander, Eastern Fire Support Group (CTG 51.1), were completing the dangerous job of sweeping the extensive reaches of both anchorages. Admiral Turner was anxious to make use of the eastern berths and beaches at the earliest possible moment. First, however, it was necessary to ascertain the Japanese strength on the six small islands that guarded the entrances to the anchorages. Major Jones' FMF Reconnaissance Battalion was again tapped for the scouting mission. (See Map 12)

Since preliminary intelligence had indicated that Tsugen Shima was the only island defended in any strength, it was selected as the first target. The island's size was not very significant, only 2,500 yards long by 1,200 yards wide, but its position southeast of Katchin Peninsula gave it effective control of the entrances to Nakagusuku Wan. The terrain of the island was generally flat, except in the south where a high ridge overlooked the village of Tsugen. Aerial reconnaissance had indicated that this ridge and the village below it were extensively developed strong points.

By midnight of 5 April the high-speed transports (APD's) lifting Major Jones' battalion were moving in toward the objective. The scouts embarked in rubber boats and made a landing on the northern coast of the island at 0200. Four civilians were encountered just inland from the landing point; two were captured, but the other two escaped, evidently alerting the garrison.[2]

Within minutes both assault companies[3] began receiving machine-gun fire, Company A from the vicinity of Tsugen and Company B from a trench system in the northwest part of the island. Japanese mortars soon found the range of the landing party, and the battalion withdrew to the beach under a steady rain of shells. Since Major Jones' assignment was to discover enemy opposition, not to engage it, he reembarked his unit at 0300. Despite Japanese claims of an easy victory over an "inferior" force,[4] the battalion had accomplished its mission although it cost two men killed and eight wounded, all from Company A.

That evening the amphibious scouts began to investigate the remaining islands of the off-shore group. At 0015, 7 April the entire battalion landed on Ike Shima, the northernmost

---

[1] Unless otherwise noted the material in this section is derived from *CTF 52 AR; 27th InfDiv OpRpt; AmphReconBn AR.*

[2] It is possible that these men were actually members of the garrison, perhaps *Boeitai*, since the unit that eventually captured the island, 3/105 of the 27th InfDiv, found no civilians there.

[3] Co B had rejoined the battalion on 3Apr45 after its release by VAC at Iwo Jima.

[4] *Okinawa Operations Record,* 55–56.

island. There was no sign of enemy troops or installations and only one aged civilian was discovered. Company B went on to Takabanare Shima, landing at 0530; 200 thoroughly cowed natives were the only inhabitants. At about the same time, two platoons of Company A made the trip to Heanza Shima and later, at 0800, used their rubber boats to cross over to nearby Hamahika Shima. Daylight reconnaissance confirmed the absence of Japanese soldiers, but added more than 1,500 civilians to the existing tally. These islands were later occupied by 3/5 in mid-April.[5]

After darkness had fallen on 7 April, Company B reembarked on its APD, circled Tsugen Shima, and made a landing on Kutaka Shima, opposite enemy-held Chinen Peninsula. A heavy surf capsized three of the boats as the company paddled in to shore and one man drowned. No enemy troops, installations, or civilians were found on the island and the Marines withdrew about 0100, 8 April.

While the reconnaissance battalion was searching the rest of the Eastern Islands on 7 April, swimmers of UDT 7 made a check of the proposed landing beach on the east coast of Tsugen Shima. They reported the water free of obstacles and the way clear for tracked vehicles to land. The UDT men spent the next two days looking over possible unloading beaches on Katchin Peninsula and the American-held portion of the Nakagusuku Wan shore line. While their tranport, the APD *Hopping*, was patrolling the entrance to the bay in the afternoon of 9 April, the hitherto silent garrison of Tsugen Shima opened up for a short period on the lightly-armed ship. Six hits were scored with 6-inch, 75mm, and 47mm shells, causing considerable structural damage, killing one and wounding 11 of the crew. In addition UDT 7 had one man killed and eight wounded by the enemy fire.

The guns that engaged the *Hopping* constituted the major armament of the Tsugen Shima defenders. A specially organized guard force with a strength of approximately 250 men, the garrison was built around the 1st Battery of the 7th Heavy Artillery Regiment. In addition to rifles, machine guns, knee mortars, and 81mm's the unit was equipped with three 6-inch naval guns, two 75mm and two 47mm guns. All but one of these weapons were located in the major defensive position in the ridge southwest of Tsugen; one 6-inch gun was covered by the trench system in the north of the island.[6]

The capture of the Eastern Islands had been assigned to the 27th Infantry Division as its part of Phase I of the Tenth Army preferred plan.[7] The information gained by the reconnaissance battalion on 6–7 April indicated that seizure of the islands did not warrant commitment of the entire division. Accordingly, General Buckner ordered General Griner to detach one regiment for the operation. At the same time, 8 April, in accordance with a request from General Hodge, the Tenth Army Commander directed the 27th Division to land on Okinawa and reinforce the XXIV Corps attack.

On 9 April as the main body of the 27th was coming ashore over the Orange beaches near Kadena, the ships of the 105th RCT (Colonel Walter S. Winn) were rendezvousing at Kerama Retto with Admiral Blandy's command ship, the *Estes*. The admiral had been designated Commander, Eastern Islands Attack and Fire Support Group (TG 51.19).

In addition to the *Estes*, Blandy's attack group consisted of the cruiser *Pensacola*, destroyers *Laws* and *Paul Hamilton*, three mortar gunboats, six control vessels, and four LST's, one lifting LVT(A)'s of the 780th Amphibious Tank Battalion and three carrying LVT's of the 534th Amphibious Tractor Battalion. The assault unit selected for the Tsugen Shima operation was the same one designated in the original comprehensive plan of the 27th Division to take the Eastern Islands—the 3d Battalion, 105th Infantry commanded by Major Charles DeGroff. The other two battalions of the 105th RCT were designated floating reserve for the operation, to be called up from Kerama if needed. The regimental commander in his headquarters ship, *Rutland*, would accompany the attack group to the target.

After the men of 3/105 had transferred to LST's at Kerama, TG 51.19 left the anchorage, swung wide around Okinawa during the night,

[5] *1st MarDiv G–3 Jnl*, 17–23Apr45.

[6] 27th InfDiv G–2 PrdRpt No 5, 14Apr45.
[7] Tenth Army Tentative OpPlan 1–45, 6Jan45, 13.

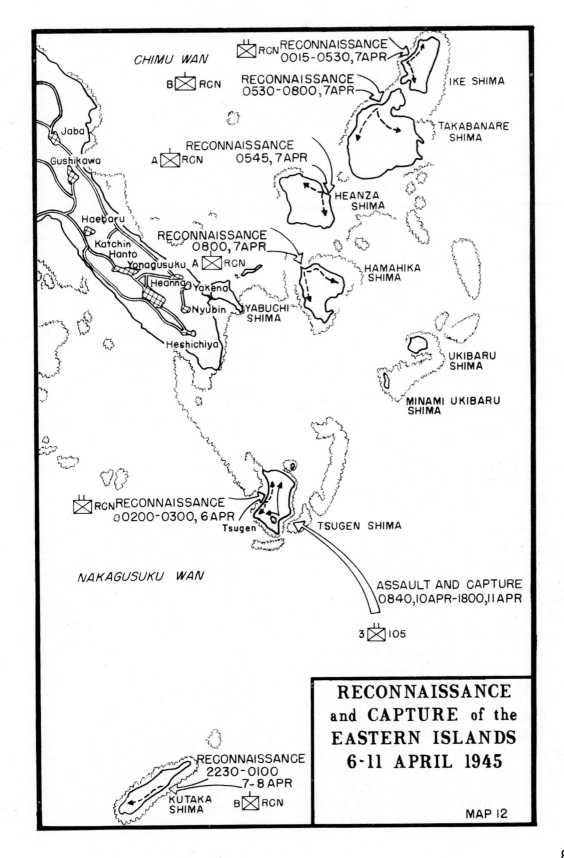

CHIMU WAN

Jaba

Gushikawa

Haebaru

Katchin Hanto

Yonagusuku

Heanna

Yakena

Nyubin

IYABUCHI SHIMA

Heshichiya

RECONNAISSANCE
0015-0530, 7APR

RCN

B RCN

IKE SHIMA

RECONNAISSANCE
0530-0800, 7APR

TAKABANARE SHIMA

A RCN

RECONNAISSANCE
0545, 7APR

HEANZA SHIMA

RECONNAISSANCE
0800, 7APR

A RCN

HAMAHIKA SHIMA

UKIBARU SHIMA

MINAMI UKIBARU SHIMA

RCN RECONNAISSANCE
0200-0300, 6 APR

Tsugen

TSUGEN SHIMA

NAKAGUSUKU WAN

ASSAULT AND CAPTURE
0840, 10APR-1800, 11APR

3 105

RECONNAISSANCE
2230-0100
7-8 APR

KUTAKA SHIMA

B RCN

**RECONNAISSANCE
and CAPTURE of the
EASTERN ISLANDS
6-11 APRIL 1945**

MAP 12

89

and came in on the target during the early morning hours of 10 April. Air and NGF had pounded Tsugen Shima intermittently since L-Day, especially after reconnaissance had developed the enemy defensive positions. On 10 April the support ships began firing at 0700, covering the area inland from the beach, the village of Tsugen, and its commanding ridge. At 0720, enemy mortars began returning the American NGF, reaching out for the LST's which had incautiously approached beyond prescribed distance. LST 557 was hit, two crewmen were killed and one wounded before the landing ships withdrew to a safer area. Just before the scheduled landing at 0830, a strafing run by 12 carrier planes was made on the beach zone. Only one pass was completed, however, as closing weather made it necessary for the planes to return to base.

When naval gunfire support shifted inland, the armored amphibians crossed the line of departure, hitting the beach at 0839. Two minutes later the first assault LVT's lumbered up out of the water and the men of 3/105 began advancing. Initial resistance was light, but the left flank company (Company I) soon became entangled in a day-long fire fight with enemy soldiers strongly entrenched in the stone and concrete rubble of Tsugen. Company L on the right, soon reinforced by the reserve company (K), swept through scattered opposition to secure the northern part of the island.

Hindered by a driving rain which served to conceal enemy strong points and curtail fire support capabilities, Company I made only limited advances during the day. As night fell, isolated enemy groups still held out in Tsugen and mortar fire from the heights above the village was causing a steady drain of casualties. Companies K and L, after securing the rest of the island, moved down into line with Company I to isolate the enemy holdouts.

With daylight on 11 April, Major DeGroff's rifle companies attacked in a concerted effort to wipe out the garrison. Opposition was stubborn at first, but gradually died out. By 1530 organized resistance had been eliminated, and shortly thereafter the battalion was ordered to reembark.[8] Very few Japanese survived the violent battle and these only by virtue of 3/105's early withdrawal. Enemy sources indicate that these survivors were able to rejoin the main body on Okinawa.[9]

In a day and a half's fighting Major DeGroff's battalion had lost 11 men, had 80 wounded in action, and three missing in action.[10] An estimated 234 Japanese had been killed and all enemy installations destroyed; no prisoners were taken.

Having struck the 27th Division's first blow in the battle for Okinawa, 3/105 rejoined its regiment at Kerama Retto during the night of 11–12 April. The battalion's action had opened the approaches to Nakagusuku Wan, insuring adequate supply from the sea to both flanks of the XXIV Corps drive toward Shuri.

6TH MARINE DIVISION ADVANCES[11]

While the FMF Amphibious Reconnaissance Battalion prepared the way for the seizure of the Eastern Islands, the 6th Marine Division moved into northern Okinawa with giant strides. Covering the rear of the division as it commenced its dash northward, the 7th Ma-

---

[8] *CTF 52 AR*, Part II, Sect C, 23; *27th InfDiv OpRpt*, 30 both say that the island was completely secured; RAdm Blandy's report states that Maj DeGroff reported all enemy soldiers killed. The *27th InfDiv History*, 530 claims, however, that the battalion reembarked under protest since a small enemy strong point still held out.

[9] *Okinawa Operations Record*, 61 has an entry under date of 10 April as follows: "An enemy force of about one battalion landed on Tsugen Island at 0830 hours. The Army issued an order to the garrison which was offering resistance from the base of Hill 36 [outside Tsugen] to rejoin the main force of the Army by way of Katchin Peninsula and by penetrating enemy lines from the rear. Several days later, the garrison unit commander, together with some 30 of his men, returned as ordered." A more contemporary enemy source, *CICAS Trans* No 136, 44th IMB Battle Lesson Urgent Rpt No. 8, Battle Lesson of the Tsugen Shima Garrison Unit, 16Apr54, supports the idea that at least a few of the garrison escaped.

[10] In this instance the casualty report of the *27th InfDiv OpRpt* has been taken. *CTF 52 AR*, Part II, Sect D, 4–5 lists 13 KIA and 84 WIA, while *27th InfDiv History*, 530 lists 13 KIA and 79 WIA.

[11] Unless otherwise noted the material in this section is derived from *6th MarDiv SAR, Ph I&II*; *4th Mar SAR, Ph I&II*; *22d Mar SAR, Ph I&II*; *29th Mar SAR, Ph I&II*.

rines in corps reserve patrolled the 6th Division zone south of the Nakadomari-Ishikawa line; [12] the 6th Reconnaissance Company mopped up Japanese remnants from this boundary up the Ishikawa Isthmus to the line Yakada-Yaka; and, after being passed through by the 4th and 29th Marines on the morning of 6 April, the 22d Marines reverted to division reserve and commenced active patrolling back to the area of responsibility of the reconnaissance company.

Preceded by an armored spearhead and with patrols probing inland, the 29th Marines drove up the west coast in column of battalions and reached its objective at Chuda by noon. The 4th Marines, similarly deployed, moved up the east coastal road in a contact imminent formation, with 2/4 reinforced by a platoon of tanks as the advance guard.

Because of the few roads inland, Colonel Shapley's plan was to move rapidly up the main road along the shore, detaching patrols from the advance guard to investigate to their source all roads and trails leading into the mountainous and generally uninhabited interior. In order to maintain control during the anticipated rapid advance, the regimental march CP moved out in a jeep convoy at the head of the main body.

By 1300, 2/4 had been used up by the detachment of small patrols and was relieved by 3/4 passing through. The 2d Battalion then reassembled at the rear of the column behind the 1st Battalion. The regiment halted in this formation at 1600 having advanced seven miles, despite the fact that three bridges destroyed by friendly air had restricted supply operations. (See Map 13, Map Section)

The 4th resumed its advance the following morning with battalions disposed in the same manner as they had halted the previous evening. The day's operations were virtually a repetition of those of 6 April. By noon the 3d Battalion had been dissipated by the commitment of security detachments to the flanks and the 1st Battalion passed through. Again opposition was limited to scattered stragglers,

BAILEY BRIDGE erected by 6th Division engineers over the ruins of a bridge blown by the enemy in an attempt to block the drive into northern Okinawa.

and the advance was retarded only by the condition of the road and enemy passive defense measures.

Japanese attempts to impede progress or destroy highway facilities during their retreat north were for the most part inept, and in very few instances was the forward movement of the 6th Division slowed to any great extent. Abatis, with neither mines nor booby traps attached or wired in place, were easily pushed aside by tank dozers and bulldozers. Mines in roads and defiles were not placed in depth and were not covered by infantry fire or protected by wire. In the main, mines constituted no more than a nuisance and caused very few casualties.[13] Japanese demolitionists often failed to destroy bridges completely, and much time was saved in hasty construction by using the remaining structural members as foundations for new spans.

When the 6th Marine Division wheeled northward up the Ishikawa Isthmus, one company of the 6th Engineer Battalion was placed in direct support of each assault regiment. One platoon of the engineer company was attached to the advance guard. This platoon cleared road blocks, removed mines, and built hasty bypasses for combat vehicles around de-

[12] *IIIAC AR*, 36. Effective 0600, 7 April, 6th MarDiv rear boundary was readjusted to exclude the area south of the Nakadomori-Ishikawa line. *Ibid.*

[13] *6th EngBn SAR, Ph I&II*, Chap VIII, 3.

GRINNING TROOPS of the 29th Marines hitch a ride on a tank in their swift advance toward Motobu Peninsula.

molished bridges. The remainder of the company followed up repairing and replacing bridges and widening the narrow thoroughfares to accommodate two-way traffic wherever possible. In the wake of the assault regiments, the third engineer company of the division followed closely, further improving the roads and bridges.

The coastal roads narrowed as the mountains came down to the sea, requiring increased exertion on the part of the engineers to widen these trails.[14] But despite these logistical difficulties and the fact that extensive patrolling through the rugged terrain was physically exhausting to the footsore infantry, another seven miles of enemy territory was penetrated by late afternoon when 1/4 reached the assigned objective just north of Ora. There, the 1st Battalion established a perimeter defense with the flanks secured on the coast. The regimental CP and Weapons Company set up in the village of Ora, while 3/4 and 2/4 established defensive perimeters at 1,000 yard intervals down the road.

On the western flank the 29th Marines had again seized its objective with little difficulty on 7 April. Advance armored reconnaissance elements reached Nago at noon, and by late afternoon the regiment had cleared the town and organized positions on its outskirts.

Behind the assault regiments, the 22d Marines

in division reserve had been actively employed during the day seeking out and destroying bypassed pockets of enemy resistance. Ahead of the division the 6th Reconnaissance Company, its mop-up activities ended, sought to determine the nature of enemy resistance on Motobu Peninsula.

After scouting the bomb- and shell-flattened town of Nago, at noon on 7 April one platoon of the reconnaissance company, supported by tanks, swung up the west coast road to the village of Awa.[15] At the same time, Major Walker led the remainder of his company and the tanks across the base of the peninsula to Nakaoshi. The patrol uncovered more enemy activity than had hitherto been revealed in the 6th Marine Division zone of action. The company met several enemy groups which were either destroyed or scattered.

Throughout the drive to the base of the Motobu Peninsula the 15th Marines was disposed with one battalion in direct support of each assault regiment and one in general support. Because of the rapidity of the advance, frequent displacements were necessary, averaging one a day for each battalion and regimental headquarters. The artillerymen were hard pressed to keep up with the fast moving infantry. But by stripping combat equipment to the bare minimum, substituting radio communications in place of wire, and leapfrogging units, at least one battalion of artillery was in direct support of each assault infantry regiment throughout the advance.[16]

To reinforce the fires of the divisional artillery, the 2d Provisional Field Artillery Group had been displaced to positions north of Nakadomari on the eve of the 6th Marine Division's drive up the Ishikawa Isthmus.[17] When resistance began to stiffen on the Motobu Peninsula, the 15th Marines was further augmented by the attachment of the 1st Armored

---

[14] *Ibid.*, 3-4.

[15] Intelligence sources later revealed that as the 6th RenCo moved westward toward Awa, the Japanese were close on the north flank of the company, observing its movement and holding fire. CMC Memo to Head, Historical Branch, G–3, 2Mar55, hereinafter cited as *CMC Memo 1955*; Ltr LtCol A. Walker to CMC, 3Jun55.

[16] *15th Mar SAR, Ph I&II*, Chap VII, n. p.

[17] *IIIAC Arty AR*, 19.

NAGO, objective of the 29th Marines' advance in early April, as it looked after the end of the battle for Motobu Peninsula. (Army Photograph)

Amphibian Battalion on 8 April,[18] and the following day the supporting corps artillery was moved forward to Besena Misaki at the southern extremity of Nago Wan, where it remained throughout Marine operations in the north.[19]

Because of the doubtful location of the enemy and a Tenth Army order to avoid destruction of civilian installations, unless there were clear indications or confirmation of the enemy's presence, naval gunfire support was not extensively used during the drive to Motobu. However, after 5 April, all naval units supporting IIIAC were diverted to the 6th Division zone of action. These ships paced the advance up the coast firing up the numerous ravines leading down to the beach. One call fire ship was furnished each assault battalion during the day, and each regiment was furnished an illuminating ship at night.[20]

As the zone of reconnaissance was extended to the west on 8 April, there were clear indications, confirmed by aerial observation and photos, that the enemy had selected the rugged mountains of Motobu in which to make a stand. It was therefore necessary to reorient operations in order to reduce the Japanese garrison on the peninsula. Consequently, the 22d Marines was deployed across the island from Nakaoshi to Ora to cover the right and rear of the 29th Marines attacking to the west. The 4th Ma-

[18] *15th Mar SAR*, Chap VII, n. p.

[19] *IIIAC Arty AR*, 20–21. At this time the 2d Prov FA Grp consisted of only the HqBtry and the 7th 155mm Gun Bn, the remainder of the IIIAC gun and howitzer battalions having passed to XXIV Corps on order of Tenth Army. *Ibid.*

[20] *Ibid.*, 39.

rines assembled near Ora in position to support the 29th on Motobu or the 22d in the north.

For the next five days, while the 4th and 22d Marines combed the wild interior and patrolled to the north, the 29th Marines probed westward to develop the enemy defense.[21] On 8 April, 2/29 moved across the base of the Motobu peninsula from Nago and occupied the village of Gagusuku.[22] Initially in reserve, 1/29 was ordered to send one company to secure the village of Yamadadobaru. This mission was accomplished by Company C at 0900. An hour later the 1st Battalion was directed to Narashido to assist Company H of the 3d Battalion [23] which had encountered stiff resistance.

Companies A and B moved out from Yofuke, just south of Nago, and at 1100 Company C set out from Yamadadobaru. At 1500 all companies converged on Narashido where heavy enemy machine-gun and rifle fire was encountered. Two hostile strong points were reduced, and the battalion dug in for the night.[24]

The following day saw the 29th Marines moving out in three columns to locate the enemy's main force: the 3d Battalion along the south coast; the 2d Battalion along the north coast; and the 1st Battalion up the center of the peninsula. All columns encountered opposition which indicated that a considerable

force confronted the division in the area from Itomi west to Toguchi.

On the left 3/29 found the roads rendered impassable by road blocks, mines, and demolitions.[25] In the center 1/29, ordered to occupy and defend Itomi, met stubborn resistance and was forced to dig in for the night 600 yards short of its objective. On the right 2/29 patrolled the north coast to the village of Nakasoni, destroying supply dumps and vehicles and dispersing small enemy groups.[26] This battalion also scouted Yagachi Shima with negative results.

On 10 April, 2/29 seized Unten Ko where the Japanese had established a submarine and torpedo boat base. Large amounts of abandoned equipment and supplies were found, and civilians reported that some 150 naval personnel had fled inland to the mountains. On the other side of the peninsula 3/29 captured Toguchi and sent patrols into the interior, while 1/29 pushed forward through Itomi and uncovered well-prepared positions on the high ground north of the village.

During this period numerous contacts were made in the difficult terrain to the northwest and southwest of Itomi. Ambushes were frequent and enemy artillery fire increased in intensity. Night counterattacks were also stepped up. A particularly vicious attack, supported by artillery, mortars, machine guns, and 20mm dual-purpose cannon, struck the defensive perimeter of 1/29 on the night of 10–11 April.

On 11 April, patrols sent out by 2/29 to contact 1/29 near Itomi met with little opposition. This tended to confirm the estimate that the Japanese battle position was located in the

---

[21] During this period "the 29th had a platoon of war dogs attached. These dogs gave an excellent account of themselves. Twenty-nine alerts were noted by the regimental S-3 section. All enabled the Marine patrol involved to avoid a Japanese ambush. In one instance a patrol leader chose to ignore the dogs and was badly wounded." LtCol A. M. Fraser Ltr to CMC, 24Mar55, hereinafter cited as *Fraser*.

[22] 2/29 *SAR, Ph I&II*, 4.

[23] Prior to a reorganization of Marine divisions in the spring of 1944, each infantry battalion had five companies: headquarters, weapons, and three rifle companies. When the weapons companies (D, H, and M) were absorbed, the rifle companies retained their original alphabetical designations, so that the three battalions of a regiment had companies lettered: 1st Bn, A, B, and C; 2d Bn, E, F, and G; 3d Bn, I, K, and L. The 2d and 3d Bns of the 29th Mar, formed after this reorganization took place, were lettered straight through in sequence after 1/29. Therefore, the rifle companies of the 29th Mar were A, B, and C in the 1st Bn, D, E, and F in the 2d Bn, and G, H, and I in the 3d Bn.

[24] 1/29 *SAR, Ph I&II*, 9–10.

[25] "From Nago westward on the Motobu Peninsula the enemy had done a more thorough job of demolition. Every bridge had been demolished and there were numerous tank traps blasted in the roads. The enemy was careful to place these obstacles at points where no bypass could be constructed for tanks. Those that were on the narrow coast roads were in spots at the foot of cliffs where no back fill was available, while those in the valleys were always located where the road passed through rice paddies. When the crater was in a cliff road, it was necessary to send the trucks long distances to find material to fill the crater." *6th EngBn SAR, Ph I&II*, Part VII, 4.

[26] 2/29 *SAR, Ph I&II*, 4.

area between Itomi and Toguchi. Consequently, the 2d Battalion (less Company F) was ordered to discontinue operations on the north coast of the peninsula, move to the vicinity of Itomi, and establish defensive positions tied in with those of 1/29. Company F continued on patrol.[27] Reconnaissance detachments from 1/29 encountered only light resistance during the day,[28] but 3/29, moving inland to gain contact with 1/29, ran into heavy resistance at Manna and was compelled to withdraw to Toguchi.[29]

In response to Admiral Turner's expressed desire for the early capture of Bise Saki, in order to establish radar facilities there, General Shepherd ordered the 6th Reconnaissance Company to investigate the region on 12 April. If opposition was light, the area was to be seized and held pending reinforcement. This mission was successfully accomplished against scattered resistance.

Meanwhile, the 29th Marines continued probing in an effort to fix the hostile battle position. Patrols from 1/29 moving west encountered strong resistance from well-organized positions on the high ground south of the Itomi-Toguchi road.[30] In the hills to the north of this road 2/29 also uncovered prepared positions.[31] From the vicinity of Toguchi, 3/29 sent Company G north to contact the reconnaissance company and to meet Company F at Imadomari; Company H was ordered to effect a juncture with 1/29 at Manna; and Company I was to patrol the high ground to the southeast.

On the march toward Manna Company H, pinned down by intense mortar, light machine-gun, and sniper fire, was unable to continue without incurring unacceptable casualties. Company I moving to the southeast came under a galling fire from all directions early in the afternoon. Although materially aided by prompt call fires from the destroyer *Preston*, and covered by LVT(A) fire and an 81mm mortar barrage, Company I was extricated only with difficulty, suffering losses of eight killed

and 33 wounded.[32] By midafternoon Companies H and I had withdrawn into a perimeter defense at Toguchi, and the command post of 3/29 was receiving artillery and mortar fire.[33]

With this significant resistance developing in the zone of 3/29, Company G, upon its arrival at Imadomari at 1415, was immediately ordered back to Toguchi.[34] At the same time, 3/22, which had been alerted during the morning after Company H had been hit,[35] was ordered to assemble in division reserve at Awa. Battalion headquarters and two companies completed the movement by 1700 and the remaining company arrived at 0900 the following morning.[36]

The night of 12 April found the 6th Marine Division confronted with a fourfold task: to continue to occupy and defend the Bise area; to secure the line Kawada Wan-Shana Wan and prevent enemy movement through that area; to seize, occupy, and defend Hedo Misaki, the northernmost tip of Okinawa; and to destroy the enemy forces on the Motobu Peninsula.[37]

Company F of the 29th Marines was ordered to reinforce the 6th Reconnaissance Company at Bise.[38] The 1st Battalion, 22d Marines had established a defensive perimeter at Shana Wan on 10 April. From this position 1/22 conducted vigorous patrolling to the north and eastward to the coast. By 12 April, patrols from 1/22 had contacted the 4th Marines on the east coast.[39] The 3d Battalion, 4th Marines was ordered to move to Kawada on 13 April.[40] The capture and defense of Hedo Misaki was assigned to 2/22, reinforced by Company A of the 6th Tank Battalion. The 2d Battalion, riding tanks and trucks, moved rapidly up the west coast on 13 April "beating down scattered and

[27] *Ibid.*, 5.
[28] *1/29 SAR, Ph I&II*, 10.
[29] *3/29 SAR, Ph I&II*, 3.
[30] *Ibid.*
[31] *2/29 SAR, Ph I&II*, 5.

[32] *3/29 SAR, Ph I&II*, 4–5.
[33] *6th MarDiv Jnl, Ph I&II*, 12Apr45.
[34] *3/29 SAR, Ph I&II*, 4–5.
[35] *6th MarDiv Jnl, Ph I&II*, 12Apr45.
[36] *3/22 SAR, Ph I&II*, 11–12.
[37] *IIIAC OpOrd 4–45*, 12Apr45.
[38] *6th MarDiv Jnl, Ph I&II*, 12Apr45.
[39] *1/22 SAR, Ph I&II*, 5.
[40] From 8 to 12 April the 4th Marines assembled in a condition of readiness near Ora and patrolled all areas within 3,000 yards of the regimental bivouac area. On 10 April, Company K was sent north on an extended patrol along the east coast. Company K was to rejoin the battalion at Kawada.

ineffective resistance," seized Hedo Misaki, and organized the defense of the area.[41]

THE BATTLE FOR MOTOBU PENINSULA[42]

While the first three missions facing the 6th Marine Division were being fulfilled by extensive patrolling which met with little or no enemy interference, the fourth task, destruction of the Japanese garrison on Motobu, posed a more complicated problem.

The ill-fated Company I of the 29th had evidently discovered the bulk of the enemy force on the peninsula. This was further confirmed during the night of 12–13 April when some civilians, who had lived in Hawaii and spoke English, fell into the hands of the 29th Marines. These people reported a concentration of about 1,000 Japanese on the high ground south of the Manna-Toguchi road. They further stated that this force was commanded by a Colonel Udo, and contained an artillery unit of some 150 men under a Captain Hiruyama.[43] Previous reports as to enemy strength and dispositions had been confirmed by the operations of strong combat patrols, and the hostile defenses were now firmly fixed in an area of some six by eight miles surrounding precipitous Mount Yae Take.

Around this towering 1,200 foot peak the Japanese had shrewdly selected and thoroughly organized the ground. The key terrain feature of the peninsula, the dominant heights of Yae Take commanded the outlying islands and all of Nago Wan. The steep and broken terrain precluded the use of armor and was of such an impassable nature that it also offered serious difficulties to the infantry. Moreover, the Japanese had obviously been organzing the ground over a considerable period of time. All likely avenues of approach into the position were heavily mined and covered by fire.

Intelligence indications placed enemy strength at 1,500 troops. This garrison, designated the Udo Force after its commander, was built around elements of the 44th IMB and included infantry, machine-gun units, light and medium artillery, Okinawan conscripts, and naval personnel from Unten Ko. In addition to 75mm and 150mm artillery, there were two 6-inch naval guns within the Japanese battle position which were capable of bearing on the coastal road for 10 miles south of Motobu, on Ie Shima, and all of Nago Wan.

The character of enemy resistance on Motobu made it apparent that the reduction of Yae Take was beyond the capabilities of a single reinforced regiment. Such being the case, the 4th Marines (less 3/4) was ordered to move from the east coast to Yofuke, just south of the juncture of the Motobu Peninsula and the main portion of the island. The 29th Marines was directed to continue developing the enemy positions on 13 April by vigorous patrolling and deploy for an early morning attack the following day.[44]

In compliance with General Shepherd's orders, on 13 April, Colonel Victor F. Bleasdale again attempted to clear the Itomi-Toguchi road[45] and link up his 1st and 3d Battalions. But Company A of 1/29, moving toward Manna, was ambushed and hit hard by fire from 20mm machine cannon. Patrols from 3/22, probing north from Awa, also came under fire and engaged in an hour-long fire fight before withdrawing under cover of 81mm mortars. During the afternoon the enemy placed artillery fire on this battalion's positions.[46]

At the same time Japanese counterbattery fire was placed on the artillery positions of 2/15. This heavy bombardment inflicted 32 casualties, including two battery commanders and the executive officer of the third battery, and destroyed the ammunition dump and two

---

[41] B. Cass (ed.), *History of the Sixth Marine Division*, (Washington, 1948), 57, hereinafter cited as *6th MarDiv History*. The early capture of this area was desired by Gen Buckner in order to secure a radar and fighter-director site. *CTF 51 AR*, Part III, 37.

[42] Unless otherwise noted the material in this section is derived from *6th MarDiv SAR, Ph I&II; 4th Mar SAR, Ph I&II; 22d Mar SAR, Ph I&II; 29th Mar SAR, Ph I&II;* MajGen L. C. Shepherd, Jr., "Battle for Motobu Peninsula," *MC Gazette*, August 1945; and Maj O. V. Bergren, "School Solutions on Motobu," *MC Gazette*, December 1945, hereinafter cited as *School Solutions*.

[43] *6th MarDiv Jnl, Ph I&II*, 13Apr45.

[44] *Ibid.*

[45] MajGen L. C. Shepherd, Jr., Memo for the OIC, Historical Div, 3Oct47.

[46] *3/22 SAR, Ph I&II*, 12.

105mm howitzers.[47]   Air strikes were called in on the suspected hostile positions and patrols from 3/22 also tried to locate the enemy batteries;[48] but as fires and exploding ammunition made the position untenable, 2/15 was forced to displace to alternate positions.[49]

Meanwhile, the 4th Marines (less 3/4) had moved on foot across the island to Yofuke. There, the leading battalion (2/4) was directed to continue on to a point on the southwest corner of the peninsula just below Toguchi. The 2d Battalion reached this area at 1700, after a difficult march of over 18 miles.   At 1630, while digging in at Yofuke, the 1st Battalion was similarly ordered to a position just west of Awa.   This move was accomplished before dark by shuttling a company at a time by truck.   Thus, nightfall found the 4th Marines disposed with the 1st and 2d Battalions in separate perimeter defenses three miles apart on the southwest coast of Motobu, the 3d Battalion 20 miles away on the east coast of Okinawa, and the regimental headquarters set up with the Weapons Company at Yofuke.[50]

A coordinated attack was planned for 14 April, which contemplated reduction of the enemy center of resistance by action from two opposing directions.   The 4th Marines, with 3/29 attached, were to attack inland in an easterly direction while the 29th Marines drove west and southwest from the center of the peninsula. Although the high Yae Take hill mass intervening between the two assault regiments left little chance of overlapping supporting fires, implementation of this rare scheme of maneuver nevertheless required careful coordination of artillery, air, and naval gunfire.   (See Map 14, Map Section)

In Colonel Shapley's zone of action, the 4th Marines was ordered to seize initially a 700-foot ridge some 1,200 yards inland from the coast. This high ground dominated the western coastal road, and it was immediately behind it that Company I of 3/29 had been ambushed, cut off, and badly mauled on 12 April.   Subsequently,

MAJOR GENERAL LEMUEL C. SHEPHERD, JR., Commanding General, 6th Marine Division at Okinawa.

sporadic machine-gun fire had also been received from that area.

Early on the morning of 14 April, a security patrol from 1/4, in regimental reserve, was fired on, and eight casualties were inflicted on the Marines before the Japanese were driven back.[51] But the attack jumped off according to plan at 0800.   From the vicinity of Toguchi, 3/29 attacked with two companies, G and H, in assault.   On the right of 3/29, 2/4 moved out in a similar formation with Companies G and E in assault.   Preceded by an intense artillery, aerial, and naval bombardment, the Marines advanced against surprisingly light resistance. Challenged only by scattered mortar and light artillery fire, both battalions were on the objective before noon,[52] with the left flank of 3/29 anchored on a very steep slope.

In order to protect the open right flank, the regimental reserve (1/4) moved up the coast during the morning to an assembly area to the right rear of 2/4.   At 1100, Company C of the 1st Battalion was ordered to seize a command-

---

[47] *15th Mar SAR, Ph I&II*, Chap X, n. p.; LtCol N. M. Pace Ltr to CMC, 22Mar55, hereinafter cited as *Pace*.

[48] *6th MarDiv Jnl, Ph I&II*, 13Apr45.

[49] *Pace.*

[50] Maj O. V. Bergren Ltr to CMC, 6Feb48, hereinafter cited as *Bergren*.

[51] *1/4 SAR, Ph I&II*, 8.

[52] *3/29 SAR, Ph I&II*, 4; *2/4 SAR, Ph I&II*, 7.

ing ridge to the right front of the 2d Battalion. Company C made contact with small groups of the enemy by noon, and soon thereafter began receiving mortar and machine-gun fire. Company A was committed on the left of Company C and the advance continued.[53]

Concurrently, the attack was resumed by 2/4 and 3/29 to seize the next high ground: another ridge 1,000 yards to the front. To cover the advance, heavy naval gunfire and artillery barrages were again laid down and two air strikes were called in.[54] But as the assault echelons moved into the low ground on the way to the next objective, enemy resistance began to stiffen appreciably. The broken terrain, covered with scrub conifers and tangled underbrush, was ideally suited to defense, and the Japanese exploited this advantage to the utmost.

Initial opposition consisted of small enemy groups. These hostile covering forces employed every available means to delay and disorganize the advance, and to mislead the attackers as to the location of the battle position. The Japanese would lie in concealment, with weapons zeroed in on a portion of a trail, allowing a considerable number of Marines to pass before opening up on a choice target. An entire platoon was permitted to pass a point on a trail without interference, but when the company commander reached that point with his headquarters section, a burst of machine-gun fire killed him and several others. Officer casualties were excessively high. In an area in which there had been no firing for over half an hour, Major Bernard W. Green, commanding 1/4, was killed instantly by machine-gun fire. No one else was hurt, although Major Green was standing with his operations and intelligence officers on either side of him. Lieutenant Colonel Fred D. Beans, Regimental Executive Officer, assumed command of the battalion.

"It was like fighting a phantom enemy."[55] For while the hills and ravines were apparently swarming with Japanese, it was difficult to close with them. The small enemy groups, usually built around a heavy Hotchkiss machine gun augmented by Nambus, would frequently change positions in the dense vegetation. Hostile volleys elicited furious Marine fusillades into the area from whence the firing had come. But after laboriously working their way to the spot, the Marines came upon only an occasional bloodstain on the ground. Neither live nor dead Japanese were to be found. One Marine registered his impression of these tactics by blurting out, "Jeez, they've all got Nambus, but where are they?"[56]

The first strong enemy contact was made at 1350, when Company G of 2/4 came under rifle, machine-gun, mortar, and artillery fire. Within five minutes Company E met similar resistance. The artillery piece was spotted and silenced by naval gunfire and artillery which were brought to bear on it.[57]

A considerable number of casualties having been inflicted on Company G, Company F (less one platoon in battalion reserve) was committed to its support; and despite their stubborn delaying action, the enemy covering forces were steadily driven in, and 2/4 took the ridge to its front by a combined frontal attack and envelopment from the right.[58]

By 1630, 3/29 and 2/4 were digging in on the regimental objective, with 2/4 in contact with 1/4 which held the high ground on the right. During the day's advance Company B had been committed on the right of Company C. The Regimental Weapons Company, denied effective use of its heavy weapons by the terrain, was organized as a rifle company to patrol the open right flank of Company B.

During the day 3/4 moved across the island by motor march and relieved 3/22 in division reserve, 3/22 returning to its patrol base at Majiya. Upon arrival at Awa, Company K of 3/4 was sent on a patrol mission along the south and west coasts of the peninsula to Bise. There Company K relieved Company F of 2/29 which returned to parent control on 15 April.[59]

[53] 1/4 SAR, Ph I&II, 8.
[54] 3/29 SAR, Ph I&II, 4.
[55] School Solutions, 3.

[56] Ibid.
[57] But not destroyed, inasmuch as the Japanese employed their familiar tactic of bringing the gun out of a cave, firing three or four rounds, and then withdrawing into the cave where counterbattery could not reach it. 2/4 SAR, Ph I&II, 6–7.
[58] Ibid.
[59] 3/4 SAR, Ph I&II, 6; 3/22 SAR, Ph I&II, 12; 2/29 SAR, Ph I&II, 5.

While the 4th Marines attacked to the east, the 29th Marines moved out from Itomi to the west in a column of battalions to eliminate the strong positions which had been located by patrols during the previous four days[60] and clear the Itomi-Toguchi Road. But as the attack developed, it became clear that an advance in a westerly direction would be difficult and costly. Consequently, the attack was reoriented to proceed initially in a southwesterly direction in order to take advantage of the high ground.

With 1/29 leading, the advance progressed 800 yards up steep slopes against determined resistance.[61] Late in the afternoon the 1st Battalion was pinned down by heavy enemy fire from the high ground to its front. The 2d Battalion was committed on the left flank and the troops were ordered to dig in for the night.

On 15 April, Colonel William J. Whaling assumed command of the 29th Marines from Colonel Bleasdale, and the regimental CP moved to Itomi.[62] During the day the regiment consolidated its positions on commanding ground and maintained constant pressure on the rear of the Yae Take position by vigorous patrolling to the west and northwest.

On the other side of the Yae Take massif, the attack of the 4th Marines jumped off at 0700[63] in the same formation in which it had halted for the night. Initially, small, scattered groups opposed the advance in a manner similar to that which had prevailed the previous day; but by noon, halfway to the objective, resistance sharply increased. From caves and pillboxes sited in dominating terrain, the enemy laid down heavy and effective fires on the assault units as they climbed the steep mountainside. (See Map 15, Map Section)

Engaging in numerous fire fights, 3/29 pushed forward to the east and south some 900 yards through intense machine-gun, mortar, and artillery fire.[64] But the advance was held up by an enemy strong point on Hill 210, 500 yards to the right front. Besides well-dug-in machine guns and mortars, this position also contained the cave-dwelling mountain gun located the day before. Despite the continued attempts of naval gunfire and artillery, and supporting air using 500-pound bombs and napalm to destroy it, this piece continued to function and do considerable damage with direct observed fire.

Fighting was extremely bitter all along the line, 2/4 again having tough going, as did 1/4 in its efforts to capture the high ground which dominated the right flank. Advancing with three companies abreast (less one platoon of Company E in battalion reserve), 2/4 came under fire at the outset of the attack. But after a day's hard fighting, Companies E and F seized Hill 200.

Company G, however, experienced the greatest difficulty. Five minutes after jumping off, this company came under heavy enemy fire which continued throughout the day. The battalion reserve was committed to support the attack, and Company G despite severe casualties (65 including three company commanders) eventually advanced three-fourths of the way up the hill just to the right of Hill 200, from whence it withdrew to a more suitable defensive position and tied in with Company F. On the right a 200-yard gap remained between 2/4 and 1/4 which was covered by fire. During the late afternoon 1/4 finally secured a key hill mass immediately southwest of Yae Take, from which it had been driven back earlier in the day.

The attack ceased at 1630 with the two battalions of the 4th Marines on the objective and 3/29 digging in on favorable ground slightly short of it. During the day the supply situation had become more acute, casualties had mounted, and the troops were very tired. But numerous caves had been sealed and 1,120 enemy dead counted. The handwriting was on the wall for Colonel Udo. That night he decided to shift to guerrilla operations, moving his command to the mountain fastnesses of northern Okinawa by way of Itomi.[65]

---

[60] *1/29 SAR, Ph I&II*, 10.

[61] *Ibid.*

[62] Col W. J. Whaling Ltr to CMC, 16Dec47, hereinafter cited as *Whaling*.

[63] *2/4 SAR, Ph I&II*, 7.

[64] *3/29 SAR, Ph I&II*, 4.

[65] *Okinawa Operations Record*, 114. "During the period 16–19 April while pressure was being applied to the Udo force on Mt. Yae Take a considerable number of the enemy either were directed to disband and directed to infiltrate or were cut off by our columns. They followed the natural lines of drift, were engaged by our CP at Itomi, particularly at night. Many were killed at our perimeter defenses. *Whaling.*

TOGUCHI and the first line of hills guarding the approaches to Mount Yae Take under naval bombardment on L–Day. In the right background is Sesoko Shima. (Navy Photograph)

By this time it was obvious that the 4th Marines was confronted by a force of at least two companies that had organized the difficult terrain to the best possible advantage. Moreover, it was apparent that the direction of attack was that which the Japanese had anticipated and for which they had prepared their defenses. Coupled with the fact that the advance was still toward friendly troops and artillery, these factors led to the decision to contain and envelop the strong point by flanking action from the right, shifting the direction of the main effort from east to north.

In view of these developments, 3/4 reverted to regimental control for the operations of 16 April, and 1/22 was ordered into division reserve at Awa.[66]

On 16 April the 6th Marine Division was oriented to launch a full scale attack on the enemy from three sides. The 29th Marines would continue to drive in from the east. The 4th Marines with 3/29 attached were to attack from the west and southwest. Strong combat patrols from 1/22 were to strike north into the gap between the 4th and 29th and effect a juncture between the two regiments.

Each of these three principal infantry elements was assigned a battalion of artillery in direct support. The artillery was so employed that the fires of two battalions of the 15th Marines, one company of the 1st Armored Amphibian Battalion, and a battery of the 7th 155mm Gun Battalion could be placed in any of the three zones of action.[67]

In the zone of the 4th Marines, the scheme of maneuver called for 3/29 to seize the high ground 500 yards to its front, which included the formidable Hill 210. On the right of this

[66] 6th MarDiv Jnl, Ph I&II, 15Apr45.

[67] 15th Mar SAR, Ph I&II, Chap VII, n. p.

battalion, 2/4 was to maintain its position and support by fire both the attack of 3/29 and that of 1/4 which was to swing its right flank to the north. Moving from its assembly area at 0700, 3/4 was to take the most direct route to its place on the division objective and tie in with 1/4. Inasmuch as 1/22 would not start from Majiya until first light,[68] the Weapons Company of the 4th Marines, was ordered to patrol thoroughly the area to the right rear of 1/4 and 3/4.

When the attack resumed at 0900, having been delayed by supply difficulties,[69] Company H on the right flank of 3/29 faced Hill 210 frontally. Consequently Company G in the center was ordered to break contact with Company I on its left and assault the flank of the stubborn strong point from the south. Company H was to move its support platoon into the gap left by Company G, and support that company by fire, as was 2/4 from the lofty heights of its position on the right.

The success of an envelopment is largely dependent on the ability of the secondary attack to contain the bulk of the enemy forces, and in this case the supporting fires effectively kept the defenders down until Company G had seized the top of the hill and swarmed over the forward slope. Blasted from their caves with grenades and demolitions, the demoralized Japanese hastily retreated, effectively pursued by fire from both assaulting and supporting units.

By 1200, 3/29 had captured its objective. The ubiquitous mountain gun had been silenced and 147 enemy dead counted. The positions of Companies H and G were inverted, with Company H in the center of the line and Company G on the right flank firmly holding Hill 210.

At the same time that 3/29 had secured its objective, 1/4 had completed its pivoting movement to the north, and had established contact with 3/4. This change in direction was accomplished by Company A, supported by fire from Company C, seizing a ridge directly below Mt. Yae Take, while Company B was sent to take the high ground on the right and remain in position until relieved by 3/4.[70] Well to the rear, 1/22 had begun its advance to cover the open flank of the 4th Marines.

Thus, at noon, 3/29 and 2/4 were solidly entrenched on high ground looking to the east, while the front of 1/4 and 3/4 formed a right angle to their positions, facing north. When the attack again jumped off, 3/29 and 2/4 remained in position to support by fire the advance of 1/4 and 3/4.

At 1230 the attack was resumed with the redoubtable Mt. Yae Take lying in the zone of 1/4. The 1st Battalion moved out with Company A on the left attacking frontally up the nose of the hill mass and Company C working up a draw to its right seeking an opportunity to envelop.

While progress up the steep slope was naturally slow, only light and scattered small-arms fire was encountered initially. But as Company A reached the summit, it was met with a withering fire at very close range. In the face of intense small-arms, grenade, and knee mortar fire the Marines withdrew below the crest and answered in kind with grenades and 60mm mortars. The fighting was close and fierce; the hilltop was untenable to either side until murderous fire laid down by 2/4 against the reverse (north) slope and effective artillery support enabled Companies A and C to push the assault home—this time to stay.

Although Companies A and C were in possession of Yae Take, the situation was nevertheless critical. The two companies had sustained over 50 casualties, and their ammunition was nearly exhausted. Moreover, the remaining enemy in the area were apparently gathering their strength for a counterattack. But

[68] *6th MarDiv Jnl, Ph I&II*, 15Apr45.

[69] "Supply and evacuation soon became a difficult problem. The road net was far from adequate, and engineers were working feverishly to improve it and to build new roads where necessary. However, the rugged terrain prevented them from catching up with the infantry, and usually the last 500 to 1,500 yards of the trip of the chow, ammunition, and water from the forward dumps to the front lines could be negotiated by no other means than manpower. For the next three days this was the case. Division sent up as many replacements from the division pool as could be spared. Battalion headquarters companies were used. Support platoons were used. Evacuation of wounded men was equally difficult if not more so." *4th Mar SAR, Ph I&II*, 13.

[70] *1/4 SAR, Ph I&II*, 8.

the effective artillery fire of the 15th Marines and the excellent supporting mortar and machine-gun fire of the 2d Battalion from its position in rear of the hostile strong point, held the Japanese in check until ammunition could be brought up.

Of this phase of the capture of Yae Take, the operations officer of the 4th Marines observed that:

If the supply problem was difficult before, it was a killer now. That 1,200-foot hill looked like Pike's Peak to the tired, sweaty men who started packing up ammunition and water on their backs. Practically everyone in the 1st Bn headquarters company grabbed as much ammunition as he could carry. A man would walk by carrying a five-gallon water can on his shoulder and the battalion commander would throw a couple of bandoleers of ammunition over the other! . . . The battalion commander, on his way up to the front lines to get a closer look at the situation, packed a water can on his way up. Stretchers also had to be carried up, and all hands coming down the hill were employed as stretcher bearers.[71]

The 1st Battalion received additional assistance in resupply and evacuation in the late afternoon, when men of Company K coming up from the rear to return to control of 3/4 aided in taking out the wounded of 1/4, and on their return trip carried in water and ammunition.[72]

Although 1/4 was resupplied with ammunition as quickly as possible, it was none too soon. At 1830, an hour after the capture of Yae Take, the enemy reacted with a fanatical *Banzai* charge against the 1st Battalion's front. An estimated 75 Japanese launched a strong attack, but with the help of the supporting fires of the artillery and 2/4, this force was virtually annihilated. By dark, Mt. Yae Take, dominating the entire area, was held securely.

During the afternoon 3/4 secured its objective against scattered small-arms and mortar fire, but met no organized resistance in any great strength. On the left, it was tied in with 1/4, Lieutenant Colonel Beans having committed Company B to establish contact. On the right, 1/22, retarded more by the terrain than the small enemy pockets of resistance which it had encountered and reduced, was unable to gain contact with the 4th or 29th and dug in an all-around defense for the night.[73]

While the 4th Marines was storming the fortified position on Mt. Yae Take, the 29th maintained relentless pressure against its rear. The opposition which faced the 29th was similar to that on the front of the 4th. From log-reveted bunkers and occasional concrete emplacements the enemy resisted the advance with increasing stubbornness, supported by machine guns, mortars, and artillery concealed in ravines and in caves on the high ground.[74] Rugged terrain and an acute supply situation also contributed to the difficulties confronting the 29th Marines in accomplishing its task of clearing the high ground flanking the Itomi-Toguchi Road.

The enemy displayed his usual ability to exploit the terrain and derived the maximum benefit from his weapons emplaced in caves and pits and concealed by natural cover. Particularly noteworthy was his use of 20mm dual-purpose cannon against personnel. Fire from these weapons on battalion CP's was a daily occurrence. All roads and natural avenues of approach were covered. Any attempt to move over the easier routes was met with bitter and effective resistance.

Consequently, "the method of reducing the enemy positions followed a pattern of 'ridge-hopping',"[75] covered by the fires of all supporting weapons. This tactic enabled the attacker to envelop the hostile defenses and reduce them in detail. Numerous abandoned positions and weapons encountered by the 29th indicated that the determination of the Japanese to resist diminished considerably when they were taken from the flank. In contrast to a coordinated advance with all units in contact across a broad front, the action in the zone of the 29th Marines was characterized by attacks that, even when delivered simultaneously, constituted a series of local patrol actions to seize critical positions, followed by mopping up activity within the area.

Throughout the advance westward from Itomi artillery and naval gunfire support had been habitually employed, but a particularly

[71] *School Solutions*, 6.
[72] *3/4 SAR, Ph I&II*, 7.

[73] *1/22 SAR, Ph I&II*, 6.
[74] *IIIAC AR*, 40.
[75] *29th Mar SAR, Ph I&II*, Part VII, 5.

heavy preparation was laid down on the morning of 17 April prior to resumption of the attack. At 0800 the 29th Marines advanced to effect a juncture with the 4th Marines along the Itomi-Toguchi Road. On the right, 1/29 moved out against light resistance, but over difficult terrain that made progress slow.[76] However, by 1300 the battalion had secured its objective, the highest hill in its area.[77] (See Map 16, Map Section)

The hostile positions confronting 1/29 were on the crest and face of the hill and presented a most difficult target for the USS *Tennessee*, in support, whose line of fire was almost parallel to the slope. Yet the intense bombardment delivered by the main and secondary batteries of this ship, together with the rapidity of the troops' advance,[78] was largely responsible for the capture of the hill without casualties. The Marines killed eight Japanese on the way up and 32 on the top; but the huge craters created by the *Tennessee* contained the bodies of more than 100 enemy dead.[79]

An hour after resuming the attack, 2/29 on the left flushed some 50 of the enemy, who fled to the northwest.[80] Thereafter, the 2d Battalion advanced steadily against sporadic resistance and destroyed a considerable amount of enemy equipment, ammunition, and supplies.[81] Before noon physical contact had been made with 1/22[82] which had reduced the positions met in its zone and captured large quantities of clothing and ammunition. After contacting the 4th Marines on the left, 1/22 was pinched out of the line and withdrawn to the vicinity of Awa.[83]

Because of the critical supply situation, the 4th Marines did not launch its attack until

ASSAULT TROOPS of the 4th Marines probe the hills of the peninsula after the capture of Mount Yae Take.

1200 on 17 April. At that time the 1st and 3d Battalions on the right of the regiment resumed the advance toward the regimental objective on the Itomi-Toguchi Road. The front of the two battalions on the left, 2/4 and 3/29, faced east at right angles to that of the assault units. They were therefore ordered to remain in place and support the assault battalions from present position until their fires were masked by the advance of 1/4 and 3/4.

The progress of the attacking echelon was rapid, being down hill all the way and impeded only by scattered stragglers. Elaborate fortifications, intricate communications systems, and several bivouac areas were overrun. The area was strewn with enemy dead and military impedimenta. Large quantities of equipment, weapons, food, and clothing were uncovered and either captured or destroyed. Sweeping across the front of 3/29, 1/4 found two 8-inch naval guns, five artillery pieces, eight caves full of ammunition, and over 300 dead Japanese in front of the position of Company G on Hill 210.[84] The 1st Battalion met only

---

[76] *6th MarDiv Jnl, Ph I&II*, 17Apr45.

[77] *1/29 SAR, Ph I&II*, 10.

[78] *Fraser*.

[79] In connection with this NGF performance the Commander, Northern Attack Force was "most gratified" to receive the following despatch from Gen. Shepherd: ". . . the effectiveness of your gunfire support was measured by the large number of Japanese encountered. Dead ones." VAdm L. F. Reifsnider Ltr to CMC, 21Mar55.

[80] *6th MarDiv Jnl, Ph I&II*, 17Apr45.

[81] *2/29 SAR, Ph I&II*, 5.

[82] *6th MarDiv Jnl, Ph I&II*, 17Apr.45.

[83] *1/22 SAR, Ph I&II*, 6.

[84] *3/29 SAR, Ph I&II*, 4.

one or two of the enemy, while the 3d Battalion killed 56 during the day without losing a man.[85]

As the axis of the attack of the 4th and 29th Marines gradually shifted to the northward, the desired juncture was effected between the two units, and 2/29 was withdrawn from the line to clear out any bypassed pockets of resistance remaining in the regimental zone.[86] The day's operations had revealed strong indications that the enemy was no longer able to maintain his position, that he was endeavoring to escape by retreat, and that the 6th Marine Division had broken the back of the Japanese defenses in the area. This estimate was confirmed when the 4th Marines captured an enemy map which showed the Yae Take position as the only organized resistance on Motobu.

Late afternoon saw the 4th and 29th Marines along the high ground overlooking the Itomi-Toguchi Road. Companies H and I of 3/29 were moved abreast of 1/4 and extended to the left around Toguchi, and Company G remained in a perimeter defense on Hill 210.[87] On the opposite flank 2/29, after mopping up, set up a battalion strong point on the high ground north of Itomi.[88]

After four days of vigorous combat, activity in the Motobu area on 18 April was confined to reorganization, consolidating the previous day's gains, patrolling the Itomi-Toguchi Road, and resupply. The now bypassed 3d Battalion of the 29th was detached from the 4th and moved around the base of the peninsula by truck to rejoin its parent unit at Itomi. Similarly, 1/22 returned to Majiya by motor march.[89] In the 4th Marines' area 1/4 went into reserve, bivouacking near Manna.[90]

Upon the return of 3/29 to regimental control, that unit was committed to a position on the right flank, north of Itomi, to block enemy escape routes to the east. The left of the 29th pushed northward to straighten out the lines with the 4th.[91] While 3/4 conducted local patrols, 2/4 thoroughly patrolled the area over which 1/4 and 3/4 had passed the previous day. Besides the presence of mines in the roads throughout the area, the enemy had lacerated the Itomi-Toguchi Road with six tank traps which greatly hindered supply.

The final drive to the north coast began on 19 April, with the 4th and 29th Marines abreast. Colonel Shapley passed 2/4 through 3/4 [92] and the regiment moved north with the former on the right. Colonel Whaling committed 2/29 on the right of 3/29 [93] and the regiment pushed forward on a three battalion front with 1/29 in contact with the 4th Marines. Elaborate systems of caves and trenches were encountered, the trenches littered with many enemy dead, presumably the victims of artillery, naval gunfire, and air. Resistance from stragglers was negligible, and the 4th and 29th Marines reached the north coast on 20 April, having eliminated all organized resistance on the Motobu Peninsula.[94]

At the conclusion of the battle for Motobu, the 6th Marine Division had lost 207 killed, 757 wounded, and six missing in action. Over 2,000 Japanese troops were counted who had given their lives defending their positions with characteristic tenacity. Garrison and patrol sectors were assigned the units on Motobu,[95] and mopping up operations continued throughout the zone of the III Amphibious Corps.[96]

THE MARINES' "GUERRILLA WAR"[97]

Colonel Udo's formidable Yae Take redoubt constituted the only significant organized resistance encountered by III Amphibious Corps during the month of April. But countering the activities of the ubiquitous guerrilla remained a continuing task in General Geiger's area of responsibility throughout the period. Independent or semi-independent groups of irregulars, employing tactics based on a small force

[85] 1/4 SAR, Ph I&II, 6; 3/4 SAR, Ph I&II, 7.
[86] 2/29 SAR, Ph I&II, 5.
[87] 3/29 SAR, Ph I&II, 4.
[88] 2/29 SAR, Ph I&II, 5.
[89] 3/29 SAR, Ph I&II, 5; 1/22 SAR, Ph I&II, 6
[90] 1/4 SAR, Ph I&II, 9.
[91] IIIAC AR, 42.

[92] 2/4 SAR, Ph I&II, 9.
[93] 2/29 SAR, Ph I&II, 10.
[94] IIIAC AR, 42.
[95] 6th MarDiv OpOrd 41–45, 20Apr45.
[96] Tenth Army AR, Chap 7, Part III, 11.
[97] Unless otherwise noted the material in this section is derived from IIIAC AR; IIIAC G–2 PrdRpts Nos 1–30, 1Apr–1May45; 1st MarDiv SAR; 1st MarDiv G–3 Jnl; 6th MarDiv SAR, Ph I&II; 6th MarDiv Jnl, Ph I&II.

striking a sudden blow against isolated detachments or convoys, attempted to harass, delay, and wear down the invaders.

In general, the scope and intensity of partisan operations increased progressively as the advance moved northward. The primitive wilderness of the north offered irregular troops the opportunity to exploit to the maximum the sources of information within the civil population, their thorough knowledge of the difficult terrain, and the lack of roads. At the same time, under these conditions, regular forces of superior strength and armament operating against guerrillas are often hindered by a lack of reliable information, dependence on an organized supply system, and difficulty in bringing the partisans to a decisive engagement.

In the southernmost portion of the IIIAC area, aside from picking off occasional stragglers, the principal activities of the 5th Marines were confined to improvement of the road net, sealing burial vaults, and demolishing the myriad caves. But to the north, as elements of the fast moving 6th Division neared the Motobu Peninsula and its lines of communication extended, positive guerrilla action emerged. During the night of 8–9 April a marauding party of undetermined strength, broke into the IIIAC Artillery area near Onna and destroyed a trailer and a small power plant. This was followed at dawn by an attempt to disrupt traffic through Onna, when other enemy groups rolled crudely made demolition charges from the bluffs along the road north and south of the village as vehicles passed.[98]

At 1000, on 9 April the 6th Marine Division rear boundary was established along the Chuda-Madaira road, and the northern boundary of the 1st Marine Division along the Nakadomori-Ishikawa line. The task of patrolling the region between division boundaries fell to the 7th Marines (less 3/7) in corps reserve at Ishikawa.[99] Consequently, 1/7 was moved to Chimu to cover the northern half of the regimental zone of responsibility while 2/7 and certain regimental troops remained in a perimeter defense around the rubble of battered Ishikawa with the collateral mission of patrolling the rugged terrain north and inland from the village.[100]

In the main, the defense of Ishikawa consisted of frustrating the night infiltration efforts of Japanese and Okinawan irregulars in search of food. These enemy groups, which rarely exceeded a half dozen men, occasionally probed the lines for safe routes of entrance. More often they moved through the gaps in the perimeter individually or in pairs; but most of them were killed or wounded either entering the village or leaving it. Initially, patrols combed the spinous heights of the narrow waist of the island without incident. But as pressure on the main Japanese forces in northern Okinawa increased, the "eerie feeling that Okinawa was a theater in which the enemy was not present, or in which he was a mysterious wraith"[101] was suddenly dispelled for the 7th Marines, when a combat patrol of 2/7 encountered a well laid ambush on Ishikawa Take—the highest elevation on the isthmus.

On 12 April, Company E moved into this difficult terrain, which had previously been patrolled by Companies G and F with negative results. Upon entering a saddle near the Ishikawa summit the leading platoon was ambushed, and the entire company soon was pinned down on the narrow trail[102] by heavy mortar, machine-gun, and rifle fire from an enemy force entrenched on the high ground, and estimated to be 100 to 150 troops.[103]

Inasmuch as at least a day would be required to attempt an envelopment through the rugged terrain, the Marines had no alternative but to withdraw. By the time Company E had fought its way out of the trap, under cover of indirect supporting fire from self-propelled 105mm howitzers of the Regimental Weapons Company, five Marines had been killed and 30 wounded.

The following day Lieutenant Colonel Berger closed in on the area with two companies. Company E was ordered to occupy the high ground

---

[98] Tenth Army G–2 Rpt No. 15, 10Apr45.

[99] IIIAC OpOrd 2–45, 8Apr45; BrigGen E. W. Snedeker Ltr to CMC, 10Mar55, hereinafter cited as *Snedeker 1955*.

[100] *7th Mar SAR*, 2–3.

[101] Capt V. E. Ludwig Memo for the Historical Branch, G–3, 28Oct54, hereinafter cited as *Ludwig Memo*.

[102] *Ibid.*

[103] *7th Mar SAR*, 3.

south of the saddle, and Company F was directed to move to a similar elevation on the other side. Advancing against token resistance, which nevertheless inflicted some casualties, both companies seized and occupied their objectives. The elusive enemy, however, had vanished into the tangled maze of ridge spines, deep gorges, and thickets of scrub pine and bamboo.

After an uneventful night on the twin peaks, the two companies were once more withdrawn in order to approach the infested area from a new direction. Upon their retirement, however, the enemy reappeared on the high ground to pursue by fire and inflicted a number of casualties on the Marines.[104] The two companies circled to the far side of the island, consolidated their lines, and moved in from the west on the enemy pocket which was well concealed on commanding ground. On 14 April 2/7 pinned down the Japanese, who did "not appear to be well organized,"[105] and ferreted them out by patrol action.

But at best, it was painstaking and time consuming business. The western slopes of Ishikawa Take were the least precipitous, but the lush vegetation there seriously hampered effective patrol action. Since the dense growth of bamboo and scrub conifers frequently limited visibility to three to five feet off the trails and precluded the use of flank patrols, war dogs proved a valuable asset.[106] To alleviate supply difficulties engendered by the configuration of the terrain and the lack of roads, the ban on the use of captured native horses (even for military purposes) which had hitherto prevailed was lifted and pack trains were organized to supply 2/7 while it operated in this isolated region. Resistance in the area continued until 23 April, and 2/7 accounted for about 110 enemy dead during the period.[107]

On the fringe of the pitched battle on Motobu, the tempo of partisan warfare increased as the fight for Yae Take threatened the destruction of the main Japanese forces in the Marines' area. Every afternoon at dusk, as the infantry was digging in, the enemy regularly harassed artillery positions, and in consequence delayed registration of night defensive fires.[108] When the 1st Battalion, 15th Marines, in direct support of the 22d, displaced to the vicinity of Taira on 12 April to cover the advance to the northern tip of Okinawa, forays against its perimeter occurred almost nightly. In addition to sporadic sniping and knee mortar fire, the ill-armed *Boeitai* threw grenades, demolition charges, and even antipersonnel land mines into installations on the rim of the battalion area. The hostile forces enjoyed excellent observation from the hills in rear of the area, and attacks against 1/15 were apparently coordinated. Charges were thrown near the fire direction center; a tractor was hit by rifle fire; and an enemy infiltrator, armed with demolition charges, was killed near an ammunition dump.[109]

From 14 through 16 April, at the climax of the battle on Yae Take, fires broke out in various villages along the west coast from the southern extremity of Nago Wan to the northernmost point of the island. At daybreak on 17 April, hostile raiders swept down on Nakaoshi, and simultaneously struck the water point and supply installations at the 6th Engineer Battalion CP nearby. In connection with these events, there were strong indications of civilian collaboration with the Japanese military forces. Investigation of the series of fires on the west coast revealed evidence of sabotage on the part of the natives. In the case of the dawn attack on Nakaoshi, the villagers left the settlement just before the onslaught, and fires in the buildings started shortly thereafter.

The security threat existing within the local populace, also appeared in the zone of the 1st Marine Division. On 9 April, 3/5 reported that many civilians seemed to be destroying their passes and staying out during the hours of darkness; and that there was "no reason to believe they [did] not contact the Nips at night."[110]

The 1st Division commenced herding all civilians into the Katchin Peninsula on 11

[104] *Ludwig Memo.*

[105] IIIAC G–2 PrdRpt No 15, 16Apr45.

[106] *Ludwig Memo.*

[107] *7th Mar SAR*, 3.

[108] *4/15 SAR, Ph I&II*, Chap VII, n. p.

[109] *1/15 SAR, Ph I&II*, Chap III, n. p.

[110] *5th Mar S–3 Jnl*, 9Apr45.

COMPANY B of 1/7 patrols the high ground in the Chimu area on 11 April.

April. The following day, the division began to take into custody all able-bodied men to determine their possible military status. Security and operational efficiency, however, are compatible only up to a certain point, where their interests will inevitably clash. The tactical situation governs which shall take precedence. Consequently, the establishment of control over the civilians in northern Okinawa was held in abeyance until organized resistance was broken and combat troops could be diverted to that task.

From the outset of the drive up the Ishikawa Isthmus an increasing number of Okinawans appeared on the roads. But inasmuch as the primary matter in hand was to find and fix the principal enemy forces as soon as possible, only the few men of military age encountered were detained. The remainder "were allowed to go about their business." [111] When the enemy situation was fully developed, the expeditious destruction of organized resistance was, of course, the paramount consideration. While questionable civilians were detained in the 6th Division area during the period of 12 to 16 April, tactical operations in progress at that time precluded a methodical collection of all able-bodied males, such as that being conducted in central Okinawa. But as soon as the hostile center of resistance on Motobu was reduced,

large numbers of Okinawans were brought in to Taira, the center of activities connected with control of the natives within the zone of the 6th Division. There, beginning 16 April, from 500 to 1,500 civilians were interned daily until the end of the northern operation.

General Geiger returned 3/7 to parent control on 15 April. This battalion moved to Chuda on the west coast and commenced active patrolling. The following day, as the 6th Division met with increasing resistance, the 7th Marines reverted to General del Valle's command and the boundary between divisions was readjusted along the Chuda-Madaira Road. At the same time the 3d Battalion, 1st Marines passed to General Shepherd's control. Upon moving north, 3/1 was attached to the 22d Marines and ordered to Kawada to assist that regiment in patrolling its extensive zone of responsibility, which covered an area of 140 square miles and included 95 miles of coast line. [112]

During the final drive of the 29th Marines to clear the Itomi-Toguchi Road on 17 April, an enemy group of 20 men attacked the quartermaster dump of the 22d Marines at Majiya. No stores were damaged and the intruders were driven off, but an hour later the Japanese man-

---

[111] *4th Mar SAR, Ph I&II*, 10.

[112] *22d Mar SAR, Ph I&II*, 14. On 15 April, 1/22 was alerted for employment as the division reserve on the Motobu Peninsula, and it moved to the vicinity of Awa on the following morning. *Ibid.*, 12.

aged the partial destruction of a bridge on the coastal road a mile west of Majiya.[113] As the enemy's Motobu defense crumbled, increasing evidence appeared that the Japanese were attempting to evade pursuit by shifting to partisan operations. During the afternoon of 17 April the 4th Marines reported that eight kimono-clad enemy had been seen firing light machine guns. A wounded woman was picked up who claimed she had been in company with 50 Japanese soldiers with plans to go to the Ishikawa Isthmus from Motobu.

Company G of 2/22, moving down from Hedo Misaki, joined with Company K of 3/22, which had crossed the island and was advancing from the south, at Aha on the east coast on 19 April. For the next few days units of the 6th Marine Division reorganized and commenced movement to assigned garrison areas to conduct vigorous patrols to locate any remaining enemy resistance. Additionally, the FMF Amphibious Reconnaissance Battalion was attached to the 6th Division, and preparations were set afoot to seize and occupy the small islands lying off the Motobu Peninsula.

Following a night reconnaissance in rubber boats, the battalion, transported by armored amphibians, seized Yagachi Shima on 21 April. A leper colony of some 800 adults and 50 children was located on this island, but no resistance was encountered.

Because aerial reconnaissance had reported Sesoko Shima to be occupied and defended, it was decided to launch an attack on that island with one reinforced regiment. But preliminary to the attack, a native was captured during an amphibious reconnaissance of the objective who revealed that the island was probably not occupied. A successive physical reconnaissance confirmed his statements.[114] Consequently, Major Jones' command was also assigned this mission, and the battalion occupied Sesoko Shima on 22 April. Although no opposition was met, the operation was interfered with by more than 100 civilians, moving by canoe from islands to the west where food was running low, and "considerable difficulty was involved in coralling and controlling" them.[115] On 23 April the 6th

Reconnaissance Company, also mounted on and supported by LVT(A)'s, executed a daylight landing on Kouri Shima, likewise finding no resistance.

Meanwhile, 1/22, patrolling the 6th Division rear area, killed 35 of the enemy in a fire fight near Nakaoshi on 22 April. The next day this battalion contacted a strong enemy force in the mountainous area to the east of Nago. These troops, numbering some 200 men who had escaped from the Motobu Peninsula, were firmly entrenched in previously prepared positions which included caves and pillboxes.

Companies A and B engaged this force and killed 52 of the enemy before a dwindling supply of ammunition made it necessary to break off the action. On 24 April, 1/22 returned to the scene of the previous day's engagement and with 4/15 in direct support reduced the strong point.[116] Toward evening a Japanese officer and two NCO's manning a mortar were killed and at their deaths the remainder fled. Patrol action continued in this trackless region on the 25th, and 1/22 completed the mission of eliminating the enemy pocket.[117]

On 23 April, a small group of IIIAC military police was extricated from an ambush by a detachment from the 7th Marines, and patrolling of the Ishikawa Isthmus was immediately intensified. The 7th was reinforced with 2/1, and all available war dogs were attached to that regiment. At the same time more stringent regulation of travel was imposed within the IIIAC area, and the movement of single vehicles within the corps zone in hours of darkness was prohibited.[118]

In the meantime, while the 29th Marines remained on the Motobu Peninsula, the 4th Marines moved to its assigned area in northern Okinawa. At Kawada 3/4 relieved 3/1, which returned to parent control on 23 April. In the succeeding two days the remainder of the regiment was disposed with 2/4 at Ora, and 1/4 with the regimental troops and headquarters in

[113] Ibid.

[114] CMC Memo 1955.

[115] AmphReconBn AR, 12.

[116] 22d Mar SAR, Ph I&II, 14.

[117] Ibid.

[118] "Ambushes could not be prevented by patrolling in the large rugged area, and the small enemy ambush groups would fade into the hills before patrols could destroy them." Snedeker 1955.

the vicinity of Genka, a small village five miles up the west coast from the juncture of the north coast of Motobu with the main portion of the island.[119] With Colonel Shapley's assumption of responsibility to seek out and destroy stragglers in what had been the southern half of the 22d Marines' area, 1/22 prepared to move to Hentona on the west coast midway between Motobu and Hedo Misaki, and just south of Ichi from whence 3/22 had been operating since 16 April.[120]

All units continued combing the mountainous interior for remnants of the Udo Force and semi-independent guerrilla bands.[121] With the exception of an occasional flushing of individuals or small groups, results of patrols were usually negative. But during the afternoon of 27 April a reconnaissance patrol of 3/4 sighted a hostile column of about 200 men moving through the northeast corner of the regimental area toward the east coast.[122] These enemy troops were believed to be survivors of the Battle for Motobu, who had infiltrated in groups of 20 to 40 from the peninsula by way of Taira, and would probably attempt to escape to the south. Immediate steps were taken to run the fugitives to earth. Two battalions of the 22d were ordered to proceed southward to intercept the column, while 3/4 moved inland from Kawada.

Soon after its arrival at Hentona in the late afternoon of 27 April, 1/22 commenced a forced night march which continued until 2300, at which time the battalion bivouacked until daylight. At dawn 3/22 (less Company I)[123] pro-

MORTARMEN of the 22d Marines proceed in route column toward the northern tip of Okinawa.

ceeded inland on a cross-island trail 1,000 yards to the north of, and parallel to, the advance of 1/22. Inasmuch as the quarry was expected to be in the zone of the 22d Marines when contact was made, 3/4 was attached to the 22d. Two battalions of artillery backed up the three infantry units, with 1/15 in direct support of 1/22 and 3/22, and 4/15 in direct support of 3/4.[124]

The 3d Battalion, 4th Marines moved out in the early morning of 28 April, and shortly before noon Company K established firm contact. Company L was immediately committeed to a flanking action, while Company I was employed for evacuation and trail security. During the three-hour fire fight that ensued Company K killed 81 and Company L 28 of the enemy with a loss of one killed and eight wounded.[125]

Meanwhile, 1/22 had resumed the advance at 0715 and had encountered small scattered groups of the enemy. But because of the difficult terrain this unit was unable to reach the scene of action and halted to go into bivouac at 1800. The 3d Battalion of the 22d was also still on the march at 1500 when 3/4 radioed that the enemy had been destroyed, whereupon

[119] 4th Mar SAR, Ph I&II, 17.

[120] 22d Mar SAR, Ph I&II, 14; 3/22 SAR Ph I&II, 13.

[121] "The 6th MarDiv reported it learned from civilians that small groups of Okinawa Home Guardsmen are in the hills in the northern part of the island, and that for a year they had been preparing for guerrilla warfare. They have established stockpiles in the interior. Some of these men, however, have returned to their homes and now are following civilian pursuits. Village home defense units were trained, the civilians said, by Okinawan veterans of China Service." IIIAC G–2 PrdRpt No 28, 29Apr45.

[122] 4th Mar SAR, Ph I&II, 18.

[123] 3/22 SAR, Ph I&II, 13. Between 21–28 April, Co I was on an extended patrol in the interior of the island with the mission of contacting Co F of 2/22 on a similar patrol moving down from the north.

[124] Ibid.; 22 Mar SAR, Ph I&II, 15.

[125] 3/4 SAR, Ph I&II, 8.

Colonel Schneider ordered 3/22 to continue on to the east coast. The 3d Battalion, 4th Marines returned to Kawada and reverted to the control of its regiment. The next day 1/22 returned to the vicinity of Momobaru on the west coast, but 3/22 remained on the eastern side of the island and patrolled the area in which 3/4 had fought the action of 28 April.[126]

The partisan warfare in the IIIAC area did little to delay the reduction of organized resistance in northern Okinawa, and the casualties the enemy inflicted did not impair combat efficiency. But the guerrillas attained their primary objective by forcing attrition in the sense that their activities necessitated the employment of a relatively inordinate number of combat troops on missions secondary to the main effort.

Inasmuch as the essence of guerrilla tactics is the avoidance of a decisive engagement, it follows that a multiple envelopment normally constitutes the quickest and most effective countermeasure of organized units for bringing the irregular to battle. In turn, this maneuver form requires that the counterguerrilla forces possess overwhelming numerical superiority over their adversaries.

The poorly trained and equipped *Boeitai* whose armament was often limited to grenades or sharp pointed bamboo spears,[127] made a substantial contribution to the over-all partisan mission. The native Okinawan, with his thorough knowledge of the terrain, for the most part avoided manning fixed fortifications and conducted a fluid defense in the broken terrain of the Okinawan hills. His offensive efforts consisted of individuals and groups of two or three of the *Boeitai* making night forays against supply installations; striking at corps switching centrals; cutting telephone wires and ambushing the line repair parties; and attacking water points and hospitals. While these assaults in themselves were essentially abortive, they nevertheless necessitated the provision of adequate security detachments, which were sometimes of platoon or company strength.

After Motobu Peninsula had been cleared

on 20 April, Tenth Army tightened the restrictions on the native populace. On this date all combat units were directed to intern all civilians in their areas regardless of age or sex, and prohibit their movement unless accompanied by an armed guard.[128] To carry out this directive, eight internment centers were designated by General Geiger for IIIAC units. Shortly thereafter the number of collection points in the Marines' area was reduced to three: Katchin Peninsula, Chimu, and Taira.

Despite these precautions harassment still continued during the last week of April. In the 7th Marines' area, a truck sent to pick up a patrol was fired on by an old man and a young boy. The driver was wounded, a lieutenant riding with him was killed, and the pair made off with the Marines' carbines when they left the scene. The same day the 7th killed a Japanese corporal with a kimono on over his uniform, and a patrol of the 1st Pioneer Battalion killed two of the enemy in a cave with their uniforms lying nearby.[129] On the last day of April a jeep was ambushed by what was believed to be a mixed group of soldiers and civilians.[130]

As the last significant combat by Marines was being fought in northern Okinawa on 28 April, Colonel Walter A. Wachtler, IIIAC operations officer, attended a conference at Tenth Army headquarters concerning the fu-

---

[126] *22d Mar SAR, Ph I&II*, 15; *3/22 SAR, Ph I&II*, 14.

[127] "Idiot-sticks" in American parlance.

[128] This order could not be complied with immediately by the 6th MarDiv because of the large numbers of civilians in its zone, and emphasis continued to be directed towards the detention of able-bodied men. Adding to the difficulties in this area was the fact that many of the civilians "were already in the category of displaced individuals, having fled to the north from Naha and other southern areas well in advance of the assault." *IsCom AR*, Chap 8, Sect XXV, 2–3.

[129] Evidence of a planned program of espionage and sabotage, carried out by higher Japanese headquarters, was revealed when the following document was recovered in the XXIV Corps area:

Permit

Army line probational officer Inoye Kuchi and two others: The above mentioned are permitted to wear plain clothes for the purpose of penetrating and raiding enemy territory from April 25, 1945, until the accomplishment of their mission.

IIIAC G–2 PrdRpt No 28, 29Apr45.

[130] Tenth Army G–2 Rpt No 36, 1May45.

ture employment of the corps in southern Okinawa. The 1st Marine Division had been placed in Tenth Army reserve on 24 April and plans were made to commit it in the south as a much needed reinforcement for the XXIV Corps attack. (See Map 13, Map Section)

CAPTURE OF IE SHIMA[131]

The rapid advance of the 6th Marine Division into northern Okinawa after L-Day, led to a reappraisal of plans as originally projected for Phases I and II. As it became evident that Okinawa north of the Ishikawa Isthmus could be taken by an overland advance, naval requirements were reduced to resupply and gunfire support operations. Ships which might have been needed for an amphibious assault on Motobu Peninsula, a possibility considered in all advance planning, were now available for the capture of Ie Shima. Admiral Turner lost no time in issuing an attack order directing the seizure of the island and its vital airfield. On 10 April, he designated Admiral Reifsnider, who commanded the Northern Attack Force, as Commander, Ie Shima Attack Group (TG 51.21). (See Map 17)

The landing force selected for the operation was the 77th Infantry Division. Its commander, General Bruce, who had remained on board his command ship at Kerama Retto since 26 March, was readily available for planning purposes. His staff and that of Admiral Reifsnider by working closely together were able to complete both the attack and field orders within two days. By 12 April, the 77th Division was committed to its second assault landing in less than a month. The day picked (W-Day) was 16 April and the moment of initial assault (S-Hour) tentatively set for 0800.

The men of the 77th had spent two weeks on board ship monotonously circling in an area about 300 miles southeast of Okinawa where they were relatively safe from air attack. The division's transron had not escaped unscathed, however. On 2 April, as the ships were sailing

for their open sea refuge, they were attacked by a flight of eight *Kamikazes*. All the Japanese planes were accounted for, but the count included three successful suicide crashes. Two transports and the APD *Dickerson* were hit.

The enemy pilot who dove his bomb-laden plane into the APA *Henrico* scored heavily. The commodore of Transport Division 50, the captain of the *Henrico*, and 48 of the ship's complement were killed, 120 others wounded. The 305th Infantry suffered almost as heavily, losing its commanding officer, Colonel Vincent J. Tanzola, who had led the regiment in combat on Guam and Leyte, plus the regimental executive, operations, and personnel officers and a number of key enlisted men of the headquarters detachment. Most of the surviving officers of the regimental staff were wounded. The 77th Division's total casualties during this attack were 22 killed, 76 wounded, and 10 missing. The *Henrico*, heavily damaged by fire, was towed back to Kerama for repairs where the headquarters of the 305th transferred to the transport *Sarasota*. A new regimental commander, Lieutenant Colonel Joseph B. Coolidge, was appointed by General Bruce, and officers were transferred from other units of the 77th to help rebuild the shattered staff.

Despite its tragic loss the 305th Infantry was ready for its next combat assignment, as were the other units of General Bruce's division. Their prospective target, Ie Shima, was an island plateau almost rectangular in shape, measuring five by two and a half miles, which jutted out of the sea three and a half miles northwest of Motobu Peninsula. Most of the island was flat land, broken only by low hills and scattered clumps of trees, a factor which influenced both Japanese and Americans to select it for extensive airfield development. Three mile-long runways had been laid out on the central plateau by the enemy, and CinCPOA planners intended to expand these existing strips and add others which would eventually accommodate an entire wing of VLR fighters.

In addition to the airfield, the only other prominent terrain features were a rugged, steep-sided 600-foot limestone mountain, Iegusugu Yama, located in the center of the eastern

---

[131] Unless otherwise noted the material in this section is derived from *CTF 53 AR; 77th InfDiv OpRpt, Ie Shima;* LtCol M. Myers (ed.), *Ours To Hold It High: The History of the 77th Infantry Division in World War II,* (Washington, 1947), hereinafter cited as *77th InfDiv History; AmphReconBn AR.*

part of the island, and the small village of Ie that lay at the foot of the mountain's southern slope. A fringing reef circled the island whose shore line on the south and east was broken by several beaches with gently sloping exits; a sheer bluff formed a barrier to landings on the north and west coasts.[132]

Reconnaissance flights over Ie Shima in January 1945 had indicated that an enemy force estimated at two infantry battalions plus airfield service troops was preparing to defend the island. Centers of resistance were sighted between the southern beaches and the west coast and the airfield and Ie village. Close photographic coverage of Iegusugu Yama failed to disclose any defenses, although the Americans were sure the mountain bristled with Japanese positions. As L-Day approached, the results of photographic sorties showed that guns that had originally been sited in the open had now disappeared and no sign of life could be seen anywhere on the island. As far as the observers were concerned, Ie Shima was a ghost island.

Although just prior to L-Day trenches, holes, and mines began appearing in the airfield runways, still no enemy soldiers could be seen. Low flying observation planes which skimmed over the island's tree tops daily from 27 March through 15 April sighted only five people. Some officers at Tenth Army were almost convinced the island had been abandoned. General Bruce and his staff were more skeptical; in fact, "the General successfully objected to an Army proposal that the 77th land two companies in daylight to reconnoiter the island."[133] The division's intelligence officers did not believe the evidence that photo coverage showed them; they suspected the enemy of perpetrating a gigantic hoax. And they were right.

The garrison of Ie Shima had performed a masterful camouflage job. Almost 7,000 people were concealed on the island. Iegusugu Yama boasted a maze of hidden firing positions, the village of Ie was a veritable fortress, and the intervening ground was honeycombed with caves, tunnels, bunkers, and spider holes. The skill and industry of the Japanese in preparing this hidden defense system presaged a bitter fight for the 77th.

Nominally, the Ie Shima garrison was part of the Kunigami Detachment, defenders of Motobu, and was under the command of Colonel Udo.[134] In actuality, the senior officer on the island, Major Masashi Igawa, directed the defense. Major Igawa, commanding officer of the 1st Battalion, 2d Infantry Unit, must have been an exceptional leader. Nowhere else in the ICEBERG campaign did native Okinawan's fight as hard or as successfully as they did on Ie Shima. "In the great majority of cases," the 77th Division was to find that "the difference in the fighting of civilians and soldiers could not be told."[135]

More than 1,500 men and women joined the regular garrison in a fanatic defense of their home island. The core of strength of Major Igawa's command was his own 930-man battalion which was reinforced by the 350 men of the 50th Specially Established Infantry Battalion, formerly the 50th Airfield Battalion. Rounding out the garrison strength of 2,000 was an aircraft maintenance unit, a construction detachment, and a special engineer unit made up of Okinawan conscripts. Every available weapon from crude spears to 75mm field guns was manned and ready to oppose an American landing.

The first assault mission of the Ie Shima operation was executed by the FMF Amphibious Reconnaissance Battalion. Major Jones' unit was directed to seize and occupy Minna Shima, a tiny island lying 6,500 yards southeast of the main target. Two 105mm and one 155mm howitzer battalions of the 77th Division's artillery were to be emplaced there to provide supporting fires during the battle for Ie Shima.

At 0445 on 13 April the Marine scouts landed on their objective and in less than two hours had scoured the island. No enemy soldiers and only 30 frightened civilians were found. On 13 and 14 April the battalion occupied positions on the island to cover naval UDT's preparing the reef and beach for the landing of artillery. Major Jones reembarked his men

---

[132] *CinCPOA Bull 161–44*, 31 *passim*.

[133] *77th InfDiv History*, 255.

[134] *Intel Mono*, Part I, Sect A, 10, 32d Army OpOrd AH–111, 11Mar45.

[135] *77th InfDiv History*, 280.

ASSAULT AND CAPTURE OF IE SHIMA
16-21 APR 45

Scale 1:100,000

MAP 17

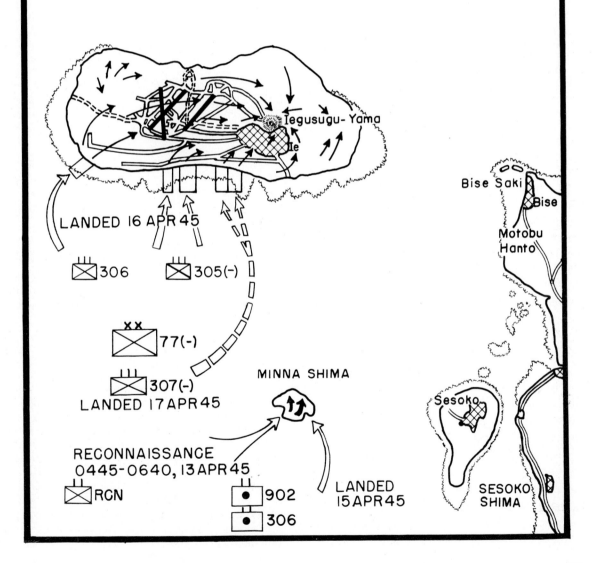

SECURED 21 APR 45

Iegusugu-Yama

Ie

LANDED 16 APR 45

Bise Saki

Bise

Motobu Hanto

306

305(-)

77(-)

307(-)
LANDED 17 APR 45

MINNA SHIMA

Sesoko

RECONNAISSANCE
0445-0640, 13 APR 45

RCN

902

306

LANDED
15 APR 45

SESOKO
SHIMA

before noon on 14 April, and the following morning (W-minus 1) the 305th, 306th, and 902d Field Artillery Battalions, using freshly blown UDT channels, landed and set up for firing.

The beaches and reefs of Ie Shima were also reconnoitered by UDT's on 13 and 14 April. No mines or obstacles were found, but the swimmers drew scattered rifle fire when they investigated the beaches on the southwestern shore of the island. Only silence greeted them when they checked the beaches near Ie village. Evidently, Major Igawa intended that the Americans would think that the beaches in the shadow of Iegusugu Yama were undefended. If that was the Japanese commander's purpose, then he failed.

Although the southwestern beaches, labeled Green T–1, Red T–1, and Red T–2, were much poorer than those farther to the east, General Bruce decided to make his initial assault landings there. Division planners were convinced that the western part of Ie Shima was lightly defended. They counted on rapid advances through this area to uncover the southeastern unloading points which were needed for the landing of tanks and heavy airfield construction equipment.

The plans for W–day envisioned landing the 306th Infantry with two battalions abreast over Green T–1 at S–Hour. The regiment's mission was to seize the airfield and reduce Iegusugu Yama in concert with the 305th Infantry. Coming ashore over Red T–1 and Red T–2 at S–Hour, the 305th's battalions (less 2/305 garrisoning Kerema Retto) would swing to the east, drive down the coast to secure the division's unloading beaches, take Ie village, and assist the 306th in the capture of Iegusugu Yama. Only the minimum of heavy equipment was to be landed on W–Day, although the division's remaining artillery battalion, the 304th Field Artillery, was slated to go ashore in direct support of the infantry's advance.

RCT 307, in floating reserve on W–Day, was directed to land on order over any of the preferred eastern beaches. The regiment was to advance north and assist the rest of the division in the reduction of Iegusugu Yama. There was a strong possibility that some part or all of the 307th would be withdrawn from the Ie Shima operation to take part in a demonstration landing off Minatoga during a XXIV Corps attack on 19 April. Division planners, therefore, intended to commit two battalions of the regiment on Ie Shima at the earliest possible moment in order to use their strength while it was available.

Slipping through a dense blanket of protective smoke laid over the Hagushi anchorage, the transports and landing ships of TG 51.21 sortied for the Ie Shima operation early on 16 April. Although the third major *Kamikaze* attack against Okinawa Gunto in less than ten days was underway, the Ie Shima Attack Group rendezvoused successfully with its covering force and was in position to launch its LVT's at dawn. Throughout the course of W–Day operations enemy planes attempted to get through the ring of radar pickets and CAP planes to Ie Shima. Very few succeeded and the seven that did were shot down by the gunners of Admiral Reifsnider's group. As usual the picket screen paid a heavy price in *Kamikaze*-caused damage for their successful defense.[136]

Despite the enemy air attack, the gunfire support vessels of TG 51.21 began their preliminary bombardment of Ie Shima as scheduled at dawn on 16 April. At 0725 the volume of fire was stepped up as missions in direct support of the landing attempt were fired. The entire island was covered by the NGF force of two battleships, seven destroyers, 17 mortar boats, and ten gunboats. Sectors of fire were assigned to each ship and special attention

---

[136] During the 16 April attack the destroyer *Pringle* was hit amidship on its torpedo tubes by a suicider; it broke in two and sank in six minutes. Prompt rescue action by sister picket ships saved 261 of a crew of more than 300. In addition to the *Pringle*, four destroyers, one destroyer escort, one mine sweeper, one fleet oiler, two LCS's, and one LCI of TF 51 were damaged by suiciders. *CTF 51 AR*, Part III, 43–44. Reported casualties were 102 KIA, 141 WIA, and 52 MIA. *Ibid.*, Part V, Sect H, 8–9. The carrier *Intrepid* of TF 58 was seriously damaged by a *Kamikaze* crash and had to return to Pearl Harbor for repairs. The price the Japanese paid for their success was 298 planes, 131 credited to the planes and ships of TF 51, 161 to elements of TF 58. CinCPac War Diary, April 1945, 52–57.

IE SHIMA'S AIRFIELD shows the scars of Japanese attempts to demolish the runways. Smoke from naval bombardment obscures Ie village. (Navy Photograph)

was paid to the Iegusugu Yama area. Five minutes before S-Hour, as the tractor waves were churning in toward the target, 16 fighter planes made a strafing and napalm attack on the beaches. Other fighters and bombers were orbiting over the island ready to protect the attack group and support the ground assault.

Within a minute of S-Hour (0800) the first waves of armored amphibians were ashore on all beaches. Assault troops soon followed, and there was little initial opposition in either regimental zone as the men advanced rapidly inland. The entire western part of the island was heavily mined, in most cases with buried, hastily laid, and camouflaged aerial bombs, and vehicles were severely limited in their attempts to support and supply the infantry.

By 1040, Colonel Aubrey D. Smith's 306th Infantry had reached its first phase line, a road approximately 2,000 yards inland from Green T–1. The reserve battalion, 3/306, was ashore and had begun to mop up behind the advancing front. Despite long-range machine-gun, AT, and mortar fire from Iegusugu Yama, the assault battalions pushed across the coverless airstrips during the afternoon. By nightfall, Colonel Smith's men had advanced almost 5,500 yards from Green T–1 and occupied a line with battalions abreast from 3/306's position on the north coast to 1/306's perimeter about 600 yards from the mountain and just north of Ie village.

At dusk a considerable gap, which was covered by a company-sized strong point of the

306th, existed between the front lines of the two assault regiments. The 305th Infantry had run into stiffened opposition as soon as the regiment had turned to drive down the south coast. Enemy delaying groups concealed in caves and fortified tombs contested every yard of advance. Late in the afternoon after 1/305 and 3/305 had reached their initial phase line about 500 yards east of Red T–2, Lieutenant Colonel Coolidge ordered his men to dig in and consolidate their positions. Throughout the night the regiment was subjected to repeated attacks and infiltration attempts which were all successfully beaten off. In the morning 199 dead were counted in and around the 305th's lines.

After its vigorous advance on W-Day the 306th Infantry remained in its night positions and patrolled forward into the northeast part of the island on 17 April. The men of the 305th, after an artillery preparation by the 105mm battalions on Minna and Ie Shima, jumped off to take the rising ground behind the preferred division beaches, labeled Red T–3 and T–4. By 1245, 3/305 on the left flank had driven through heavy enemy machine-gun and mortar fire to the outskirts of Ie village. The 1st Battalion, next to the coast, was able partially to clear the rear of Red T–3 by noon and continued on to Red T–4 where it held up at 1415 while the 307th Infantry passed through in attack.

Two battalions of the 307th, the 2d and 3d, had trans-shipped to LST's in Hagushi anchorage early on 17 April. The remaining battalion (1/307) of Colonel Stephen S. Hamilton's regiment remained on board its transport ready to participate in the 19 April demonstration landing. At 1030 these battalions arrived off Ie Shima ready to make an LVT-borne landing on Red T–3 and T–4. Because neither beach was completely secured and the Japanese were pouring machine-gun and mortar fire down on the area from Iegusugu Yama, the 307th made an assault landing.

By 1210 the regiment was ashore and at 1300 it attacked to the northeast through 1/305 behind Red T–4. The 3d Battalion of the 305th from its positions on the edge of Ie supported the drive of the 307th by fire. The route of advance was open and uphill, flanked by the Japanese defenses in the village and dominated by positions centered on a reinforced concrete building on a steep rise to the regiment's front. The troops soon named this terrain feature Government House and the hill on which it stood Bloody Ridge in dubious tribute to the cost of the battle to take it.

Mines and buried bombs were thickly strewn throughout the 307th zone, and tanks and self-propelled guns had considerable difficulty in closing to effective supporting range of the infantry. By the end of W–plus 1, 3/305 had been pinched out by the 307th's advance across its front and had reverted to division reserve. The 1st Battalion of the 305th had occupied a defensive line stretching from the 307th's left flank to the beach. Colonel Hamilton's regiment, retarded by heavy enemy fire from Bloody Ridge, had made only limited advances during the day, and the 307th set up for the night on a line about 400 yards from its beaches.

The 77th Division had adopted an efficient method of coordinating the combined arms effort to secure the limited land mass of Ie Shima. Although General Bruce and members of his staff went ashore each day, division headquarters remained on board ship where superior communications facilitated control of land, sea, and air activities. Direction of the ground fighting was given to Brigadier General Edwin H. Randle, Assistant Division Commander (ADC) of the 77th, who had landed on W-Day and set up a small advance headquarters with the 305th Infantry's command post.

On 18 April, General Randle ordered the 306th Infantry to secure all the ground north of Iegusugu Yama by a wide flanking movement, while the 307th continued its attack toward Government House, Bloody Ridge, and the mountain from the south. By the end of a day of bitter fighting every infantry battalion on the island was committed to the struggle to take the enemy strong points.

The wide sweep of the 306th was successful despite determined resistance from enemy holdouts in cave positions in the northeastern coastal bluff and a constant rain of mortar shells from the dominant mountain. Colonel Smith's men held positions at dusk that stretched from the northeast coast directly southwest to a point 300 yards from Iegusugu Yama.

The 307th Regiment, making the division's main effort, was able to seize most of the open ground below Bloody Ridge on 18 April. Fierce opposing fire from the ridge and Government House made the day's short advances costly, however. It was necessary to commit both battalions of the 305th to the fight.

To relieve pressure on the 307th's left flank, 3/305 attacked directly east into Ie. The battalion was soon engaged in a slow and deadly house by house advance through the stone rubble. Extensive mine fields again prevented supporting armor from being fully effective, and artillery was virtually useless against the dug-in fortifications hidden in the ruins. It was an infantryman's fight, and 3/305 was able to gain only about 400 yards against the fanatical Japanese defenders before it had to occupy night defensive positions.[137]

The 1st Battalion of the 305th was committed at 1500 on 18 April to protect the exposed right flank of the 307th. Encountering little opposition, the battalion advanced as much as a 1,000 yards during the afternoon covering much of the ground to the southeast of Iegusugu Yama. Because of this lack of resistance, 1/305 was far in advance of the heavily engaged 307th Infantry and was pulled back 600 yards to secure that regiment's flank for the night.

The weight of the American assault on 19 April was still centered in the south of the island. The 307th Infantry, supported by the 305th, spent the day attempting to secure Ie village and the approaches to Government House and Bloody Ridge. Gains were slight and the fighting in many instances was hand-to-hand as the defenders contested every inch of advance. At 1100, 1/305 was attached to the 30th, pulled out of its station on the regiment's right flank, and directed to seize the high ground east of

Government House by attacking through a gap that had developed between 2/307 and 3/307. Even the power of four battalions, all in direct assault, was not sufficient to breach the enemy defenses on 19 April.

For the following day's attack, the division decided to shift the direction of its main effort. The 306th Infantry, which had spent 19 April holding its positions in order not to mask NGF pounding Iegusugu Yama, was directed to seize the northern slopes of the mountain, while the 307th and 305th continued their efforts to reduce the defenses guarding its southern approaches.[138] The events of 20 April proved that the chink in the enemy armor had been found.

Attacking at 0915, after an intense artillery preparation, Colonel Smith's regiment, spearheaded by 1/306, broke through the mine field ringing the mountain and gained its lower slopes. The infantrymen then began a cave by cove, pillbox by pillbox, uphill advance aided by the flat trajectory fire of supporting weapons. Flame throwers and grenades were the principal weapons used to silence the heavy enemy fire. By noon the regiment was within 200 yards of the peak where it halted to reorganize. After another preparation by artillery and supporting weapons, the 306th attacked again in a spirited drive up the progressively steeper mountainside. Calling up mountain-trained infantrymen to lead the way and disregarding a rain of grenades and satchel charges hurled down on them from above, the men of 1/306 reached and held a point just short of the sheer peak to climax the day's advance. At the close of day the 306th held all of Iegusugu

---

[137] During the 18 April attack the famous war correspondent, Ernie Pyle, was killed by a Japanese machine gunner hidden behind 3/305's lines. Pyle was buried on Ie Shima in the 77th Division cemetery and the division erected a marker in his honor inscribed simply, "On this spot the 77th Infantry Division lost a buddy, Ernie Pyle, 18 April 1945." *77th InfDiv History*, 265.

[138] The original plan to seize Iegusugu Yama had contemplated its capture from the south and west. When unexpectedly heavy enemy opposition blocked that route it became necessary to determine if an attack from the north was possible. Ground reconnaissance was not feasible because of accurate observed fire from the mountain; aerial photos failed to supply the necessary terrain information. Therefore, General Bruce embarked on a Navy control boat on 19 April and made a personal reconnaissance of the unknown terrain from the sea. From the information gained at this observation post, in effect behind enemy lines, the decision was made to shift the division's main thrust to the 306th's zone of action.

Yama north of an east-west line through the center of the mountain.

The rest of the division was nearly as successful on 20 April, for the 307th after a grim grenade and bayonet battle finally gained the top of Bloody Ridge and took Government House. In spite of determined enemy counterattacks, 2/307 and 1/305 held on to the high ground. Both 3/305 and 3/307 were also able to advance through the maze of enemy pillboxes and mine fields during the day and set up perimeter defenses to guard the flanks of the newly-won ridge position.

On 21 April, six days after the 77th Division had landed on Ie Shima, the island was declared secure. General Randle directed the last coordinated assault which put the remaining enemy ground on the mountain into American hands. Because of the rapidly narrowing zones of action and the danger of hitting friendly troops, the ADC developed a scheme of allowing only one battalion in the closing ring to advance while the others took cover. Gradually, as the day progressed more and more units were pinched out of line until the last forward platoons completely circled the mountain's pinnacle. A small mountain-trained patrol of the 306th scaled this last obstacle at 1025 to plant the American flag on the summit, but sniper fire drove it off, and it was not until 1720 that the last vestiges of organized resistance on Iegusugu Yama were eliminated.

During the next four days the 77th Division hunted down surviving Japanese and Okinawans still disposed to resist. Mopping up activities added 88 killed and 30 prisoners to the enemy casualty list which totaled 4,706 killed and 149 prisoners on 21 April. Major Igawa's garrison had extracted a heavy price from the 77th for the division's victory: 239 KIA, 879 WIA, and 19 MIA. [139]

By 25 April it was apparent that further cleanup on Ie Shima could be safely left to the garrison—the 305th's Regimental Headquarters and 1/305. For the rest of the division there was to be no let-up after Ie Shima. From 25–28 April, LST's shuttled the 77th's units to Okinawa where their strength was needed to maintain the XXIV Corps drive on the Shuri bastion.

---

[139] *Tenth Army AR*, Corrections by CG, 77th InfDiv, 11Oct45.

Developing the Shuri Defenses

CHAPTER VII

By the morning of 6 April the Japanese noted that the "lines were drawn for a full scale battle."[1] Leading elements of the 7th and 96th Divisions, driving forward on the heels of the retreating 12th Independent Infantry Battalion, had run full tilt into the outpost zone of a series of concentric defense rings radiating from Shuri. The momentum of advance slowed appreciably as the bitter resistance of the veteran troops of the enemy 62d Division mounted. Defending from well-prepared positions on high ground liberally studded with machine guns and mortars and girded by barbed wire, AT ditches, and mine fields, the Japanese were prepared to fight a "prolonged holding action."[2]

PENETRATING THE OUTPOST LINE[3]

The 96th Division opened its attack at 0800 on 6 April after a preparation by carrier air. The 2d Battalions of the 382d and 383d Infantry drove against Japanese positions southwest of Ginowan, while flanking assault battalions supported the attack by fire. Japanese artillery and mortars hit the advancing troops

immediately and made the day's progress costly. Heavy machine-gun fire from hill positions to the front was silenced only when assault companies occupied the strong points and blasted and burned out the enemy gunners. At nightfall, after an advance of about 500 yards, the division consolidated defensive positions all along its front. The reserve battalion of the 383d Infantry was moved into the center of that regiment's line on the division right flank, while the three battalions of the 382d formed a chain that reached back to the forward positions of the 7th Division.

The 184th Infantry, attacking along the division boundary on 6 April, ran into the first strong enemy resistance encountered by General Arnold's troops. The concentrated fire of a company-sized enemy strong point surrounding a small hill peak about 1,000 yards southwest of Arakachi was sweeping the division front. Not until 1/184 reduced the outpost in a morning of fierce struggle was the 7th Division able to advance. The 184th Regiment took 1,000 yards of enemy territory while the 32d Regiment moved some 2,000 yards down the eastern coastal plain against scattered opposition. (See Map 18, Map Section)

On 7 April the XXIV Corps continued its drive to destroy the enemy outposts and contact the main line of resistance. In the 7th Division zone 3/184 led the attack on a hill

---

[1] *Okinawa Operations Record*, 55.

[2] *Ibid.*

[3] Unless otherwise noted the material in this section is derived from *Okinawa: The Last Battle; Tenth Army AR; XXIV Corps AR; XXIV Corps Arty AR; 7th InfDiv AR; 27th InfDiv OpRpt; 96th InfDiv AR.*

position 1,000 yards west of Minami-Uebaru that dominated the area of advance. Two frontal assaults, one supported by tanks, failed in the face of heavy fire; six tanks were lost to bomb-mines, AT and artillery fire, and the satchel charges of individual Japanese tank hunters. The hill which had been fanatically defended was finally taken when the battalion made a wide flanking movement to the right and drove up its slopes behind a heavy artillery and supporting weapons preparation. Again, as on 6 April, the reduction of an enemy strong point in the 184th Infantry zone enabled the entire division to advance, and probing patrols of the 32d Infantry reached the northern edge of Yonabaru airfield.

The interior assault battalions of the 7th and 96th Divisions, 3/184 and 1/382, tied in during the advance on L-plus 6. The 382d Infantry, moving through the broken ground fronting Kaniku, was able to secure about 300 more yards of hotly contested terrain, but halted its advance early in the afternoon generally 400–500 yards from the village in order to mop up bypassed positions and support the attack of flanking units. On the right of the corps advance, four battalions of artillery, three air strikes, and the 14-inch rifles of the *New York* were called upon to clear the path for the attack of 1/383 on the wooded ridges guarding the approaches to Kakazu. The battalion was able to advance 1,000 yards under cover of this supporting fire and reach positions approximately 500 yards north of Kakazu by 1600.

By 7 April it became apparent that the XXIV Corps was entering the Thirty-second Army's main defensive zone. General Hodge requested the attachment of additional artillery battalions to his corps to assist in the reduction of prepared positions. General Buckner, realizing that III Corps Artillery could not be used to maximum effectiveness in the north, ordered the assignment of most of the Marine 155mm units to the southern front. On 7 and 8 April, the 8th and 9th Gun Battalions and the 1st, 3d and 6th Howitzer Battalions were detached from IIIAC and moved south to support the XXIV Corps attack. The howitzer battalions were assigned to the 419th Field Artillery Group and paired off with similar Army

units in three firing groupments controlled by the respective Army battalion commanders. The gun battalions and a headquarters detachment joined the 749th Field Artillery (8-inch howitzers) in a provisional group named after and commanded by Lieutenant Colonel Frederick P. Henderson, G–3 of IIIAC Artillery.[4] General Sheetz, commanding XXIV Corps Artillery, now had four 155mm gun battalions plus an 8-inch and six 155mm howitzer battalions available to support the drive on the enemy's defenses.

The 8th of April was to have been the date of the first major Japanese counterattack on Tenth Army troops. Originally scheduled for 6 April during the all-out *Kamikaze* assault, the counterattack had been cancelled when aerial scouts reported a large enemy convoy in the waters off southern Okinawa. When the date of the attack was moved forward to the night of 8 April, the plans again had to be suspended because another large American convoy was sighted, this time off the western coast. Although the cooler heads among the Thirty-second Army staff officers were able to stave off an Army counterattack on each of these inauspicious occasions, it was only a question of time before the advocates of an offensive would win their way.[5]

Enemy resistance stiffened on 8 and 9 April as the Americans ran into increasingly stronger defensive positions. In the 7th Division zone, the 184th Infantry made the main effort in the face of heavy artillery and mortar fire. The regiment gained 1,600 yards in two days' action, taking and holding a tomb-studded hill that dominated both the coastal area and the high ground stretching to the boundary of the 96th Division. With the threat of flanking fire eliminated, the 32d Infantry was able to move its main strength forward on 9 April to the hills north of the village of Ouki. The 7th Division was now well within range of the enemy's first line of defenses after knocking out the major outposts in its zone of action, and its progress from now on would be measured in hundreds of feet rather than yards.

[4] *IIIAC Arty AR*, 20–21.
[5] *Okinawa Operations Record*, 53–59.

TANK–INFANTRY TEAM of the 382d Infantry advancing on 6 April. (Army Photograph)

In the center of the XXIV Corps front the 382d Infantry, using all three of its battalions in assault, drove on Kaniku and Nishibaru, its objective the ridges which dominated both villages. Enemy flat trajectory weapons in mutually supporting pillboxes and cave positions combed the high ground while artillery and mortars filled the defiles and terrain corridors with accurate fire. Assault units reaching intermediate objectives were subjected to severe flanking and frontal fire which pinned down the infantrymen. At the close of day on 9 April, the 382d was still short of its objectives and badly depleted by the punishment it had taken. The effective strength of its rifle and heavy weapons companies was 61 per cent.

The 383d Infantry was in even worse physical shape by dusk of 9 April with division accounting its assault units only 45 per cent effective. For two days the regiment had attempted to gain a toehold on Kakazu Ridge, the strongest enemy position yet encountered by the 96th Division. Moving forward through dense undergrowth and across low ground that was covered by pre-registered artillery, mortar, and machine-gun barrages, assault companies of

1/383 and 3/383 finally reached the ridge crest on 9 April. They immediately came under fire from hidden weapons emplaced in the ruins of Kakazu and were subjected to continual counterattacks by defending troops of the 13th Independent Infantry Battalion. All day long the beleaguered units on the ridge held out, taking a steady drain of casualties, while reinforcements were cut off from them by the enemy barrage. Finally ammunition was exhausted and the survivors withdrew to the previous night's positions; 23 men had been killed, 183 wounded, and 47 were missing in action as a result of the day's fighting on Kakazu Ridge.

On 8 April the 381st Infantry had been committed to the battle in the 96th Division's zone, 3/381 relieving 3/383 for the attack on Kakazu and then driving to the coast against stubborn resistance to capture Uchitomari and secure the division's right flank. On 9 April the battalion supported the attack of the 383d Infantry by fire. On the same date, following a request by General Hodge, three battalions of the 11th Marines displaced southward to reinforce the direct support battalions of the 7th and 96th Divisions. The 2d and 3d Battalions were

121

attached to the 96th and the 4th was assigned to the 7th Division. On 12 April the remaining battalion of the 1st Division's artillery regiment was also attached to the 96th Division.[6]

An even more significant event had taken place on 9 April. At noon, the 27th Infantry Division (less RCT 105) was assigned to XXIV Corps from Tenth Army reserve. General Griner and members of his staff reported to General Hodge for orders at 1300 and the division convoy which had come up during the night began unloading that afternoon. Personnel of the 106th and 165th Infantry, division artillery, and some special troops were landed before dark.

Torrential rains limited visibility and curtailed the effectiveness of supporting weapons on 10 April when XXIV Corps renewed its attack. The 7th Division was able to gain an average of 400 yards with the 184th Infantry using armored bulldozers to close enemy firing ports in the hill positions in its zone. On the division left, the 32d Infantry advance over the coastal flats was halted by a defended mine field and AT ditch outside Ouki and the regiment was forced into a slow advance along a series of finger-like ridges that jutted out from the higher hill mass to the west.

All three regiments of the 96th Division participated in the attack on the Kakazu Ridge area on 10 April. The rain, however, precluded aid from the three squadrons of carrier fighters that were to fly support, and the weight of bombardment was left to artillery and NGF. The long-range guns of corps artillery and supporting warships interdicted the enemy rear areas from 0530 to 1130 and division artillery, now six battalions strong, fired an intensive preparation for the attack from 0630 to 0700.

The 382d Infantry attacking with the 3d, 1st, and 2d Battalions from left to right met the strongest resistance it had yet encountered from Japanese positioned on high ground around Kaniku. Mud-bogged tanks were ineffective,

<hr>

[6] *11th Mar SAR*, n. p. Col W. S. Brown, CO of the 11th Mar, joined the staff of BrigGen Sheetz as liaison officer and remained there until 29 April when his battalions reverted to his command. MajGen W. S. Brown Ltr to CMC, 26Feb55, hereinafter cited as *Brown 1955*.

and their support was lost to troops advancing across fire-swept low ground. The 3d Battalion moving along the division boundary made only 200 yards before frontal and enfilade fire forced the unit to dig in. A strong Japanese counterattack, supported by machine guns and 320mm mortars, inflicted heavy casualties on 1/382 when it tried to move along a ridge line east of Kaniku and forced it to withdraw to defiladed positions north of the village to escape the crippling fire. Another counterattack struck 2/382 as it tried to outflank Kaniku on the west and drive a wedge between it and Kakazu. The Japanese overran some of the battalion's forward elements and wounded its commanding officer, but the unit clung to hill positions midway between the two enemy strong points. The men of 2/382 were already under fire from an even more formidable objective just a few hundred yards to the south, the precipitous ridge that guarded Nishibaru and paralleled the enemy position at Kakazu.

In the 383d Infantry zone, 2/383 passed through 1/383 in its position in front of Kakazu and attacked toward the ridge at 0700. Slowed immediately by enemy fire, the battalion was able to inch forward 300 yards by noon before the hail of artillery and mortar shells stopped its advance. On the regiment's right, 3/383 coordinated its attack with 2/381 which had driven forward from its reserve positions during the night. Wheeling wide around the end of the ridge under cover of 3/381's fire from Uchitomari, 2/381 was able to drive directly east and secure positions on the west end of the ridge line, a small hill called Kakazu West separated from the main ridge by a dip in the crest. The battalion was unable to advance farther on Kakazu Ridge because of the terrific wall of fire put up by the defenders. The 381st Regiment's reserve, 1/381, was called forward during the day to cover a gap between 2/381 on Kakazu West and 3/383 in position 300 yards north of the main ridge.

On the night of 10 April, as the fighting subsided all across the XXIV Corps lines, the Thirty-second Army, encouraged by overly optimistic reports of *Kamikaze* success on 6–7 April, issued orders for a counterattack on 12 April to coincide with a second round of major aerial suicide attacks. The assault units were to infiltrate American forward positions and inflict as much damage as possible in rear areas where their close intermingling with friendly troops would protect them from the fire of naval guns and artillery. The counterattack objective was an area 1,500 yards north of Futema stretching roughly from Chatan on the west coast to Shimabuku in the center of the island.

Fresh troops were to be used in the assault. The 22d Regiment of the 24th Division was to move from its positions on Oroku Peninsula on the night of 11 April and launch an attack the following evening against the left of the XXIV Corps line. The 62d Division was to commit three fresh battalions, the 23d and 272d IIB's to attack up the road between Kakazu and Nishibaru and the 273d IIB to attack up the west coast. The 5th Artillery Command was directed to support the counterattack by laying harassing fires on the areas immediately in the rear of the front lines.[7]

Colonel Yahara, Thirty-second Army operations chief, strongly opposed the counterattack plan, feeling that it was not in keeping with the army's defensive mission and that it would waste men. He succeeded in getting the 1st Battalion of the 22d Regiment and elements of the 23d IIB cut from the counterattack force. He made a dire prediction that the infiltrating units, unfamiliar with the terrain in their attack sectors, would get lost, confused, and cut to pieces during a night assault.[8]

While the Japanese readied fresh infantry units for a counterattack, the 7th and 96th Divisions spent 11 and 12 April consolidating their gains of the previous week. The 1st Battalion of the 381st Infantry pushed forward 300 yards on 11 April by dint of desperate hand-to-hand fighting to improve the regiment's hold on Kakazu West and its northeastern slopes. On 12 April the battalion was repulsed in three separate attacks on Kakazu Ridge by intense enemy mortar, machine-gun, rifle, and grenade fire. Even an air strike and the combined fire support of 2/381 and 3/381 were unable to beat down the enemy resistance.

Although heavy surf conditions during this period hampered unloading of the 27th Division's heavy equipment, its infantry was committed to strengthen the XXIV Corps position. On 11 April the 106th Regiment was attached to the 96th Division and closed on that division's reserve area at 1500, while the 165th Regiment, with elements of the 27th Reconnaissance Troop attached, relieved the 17th Infantry of the 7th Division of the mission of defending the corps service area. On 12 April 2/106 relieved 3/381 on its positions west of Uchitomari in the first movement of 27th Division troops into the XXIV Corps front line.

The opening move of the combined enemy attack was made by *Kamikazes* which began to pour into the Okinawa area at 1300 on 12 April. During the next seven hours 147 enemy planes were accounted for by TF 51, but again some of the suicide pilots were successful. The destroyer *M. L. Abele* was sunk after hits by a suicide plane and bomb, and LCS 33 exploded and sank quickly after a *Kamikaze* plunged into her magazines. Two battleships, three destroyers, three destroyer escorts, three mine vessels, an LSM, and an LCS were damaged in the air attacks. The casualty list of ships' crewmen was increased by 124 killed, 364 wounded, and 130 missing in action.[9]

Shortly after midnight on 12–13 April enemy mortars laid down a barrage on the 381st and 383d Infantry's positions, and three company-sized counterattacks were launched against the American front lines. All were driven back as artillery and small-arms fire caught the attackers in the light of NGF star shells. At 0300 a 1,000-round artillery concentration began falling on the 96th Division's forward area and enemy attacked again, this time in battalion strength. At dawn the Japanese survivors withdrew, followed all the way by a hail of American artillery, mortars, and naval gunfire.

In the 7th Infantry Division sector, the Japanese 22d Regiment attacked simultaneously with the battalions of the 62d Division, trying to penetrate the lines with small infiltrating groups.[10] Illuminating flares caught the enemy in the open, and the men of the 32d and 184th

---

[7] *Okinawa Operations Record*, 63–64.
[8] *Yahara Interrogation.*

[9] *CTF 51 AR*, Part III, 33–35; Part V, Sect H, 8–9.
[10] *CICAS Trans* No 198, 22d Regt OpOrd No 63, 1600, 12Apr45.

Infantry drove off the attackers with mortars, grenades, and small-arms fire.

The XXIV Corps spent 13 April strengthening its infantry positions in anticipation of renewed counterattacks, while artillery, air, and NGF hammered enemy troop concentrations. The last two small Japanese attacks were made at 2000 and 0315 on the night of 13–14 April against 96th Division positions; both were driven off by small-arms and supporting weapons fires. In the two days' action, XXIV Corps reported it had killed 1,594 of the enemy and taken four prisoners.[11]

A partial explanation of the lack of success of the enemy counterattack is offered by Japanese sources which state that:

> When the Army chief of staff, after the opening of the offensive, visited the headquarters of the 62d Division he learned that the senior staff officer, Colonel Yahara, after the issuance of the Army order for the attack, personally communicated to the responsible operational officers of both the 24th and 62d Division that committment of a few shock troops would suffice for the attack instead of employing a major force, since the attack was bound to fail.[12]

Despite Colonel Yahara's efforts to conserve the lives of trained infantrymen for later defensive action, the attack was very costly to the Japanese. They reported that the fate of the 3d Battalion, 22d Regiment was "unknown," but that it failed to rejoin its parent unit after the night of 12–13 April and presumably disintegrated under American shell fire. The 2d Battalion of the regiment was reported to have "suffered heavy casualties, losing the bulk of its strength" to defending forces.[13] On the right of the enemy line one half of the personnel of 272d IIB was lost, while the 273d IIB was deemed to have suffered a "lethal blow," because "almost all personnel, from the battalion commander down, were killed or injured in action." The Japanese considered "the night assault resulted in a complete failure.[14]

BUILD-UP IN THE SOUTH[15]

Despite the fact that XXIV Corps estimated that it had accounted for 6,883 enemy

dead by 14 April,[16] its identifications of front line units opposing its advance still consisted mainly of the 12th, 13th and 14th IIB's of the enemy's 63d Brigade. Even the addition of elements of four new battalions to the line after the 12–13 April counterattack did not account for the continued presence of infantry units that should by all rights have been virtually destroyed. The resultant difficulty in maintaining an up-to-date enemy order of battle at Tenth Army headquarters was a direct result of the operation of the Thirty-second Army's replacement system. Individuals and small groups from service and support troops were being gradually fed into forward units while whole companies and battalions not yet committed as integral units were absorbed temporarily, permanently in some cases, into the existing defensive setup.

The 12th Independent Infantry Battalion's first reorganization serves as an excellent example of this practice. On 23 March the strength of the unit's organic elements was 1,043 and attached special guard, labor, and naval elements raised the total to 1,333. The battalion's armament included 49 light and nine heavy machine guns, 42 grenade dischargers, two 70mm howitzers, and two 75mm guns. On 12 April, after more than a week of continuous fighting with XXIV Corps, the Japanese listed the 12th IIB's total strength as 1,257. Only 414 men were left of the original battalion and 61 from the original attached units, but the 2d Battalion, 22d Regiment (less one rifle company) and the entire 1st Light Mortar Battalion had been added to its strength.[17] If anything, the battalion armament was more powerful than it had been before L-Day: 45 light and 13 heavy machine guns, 45 grenade dischargers, 19 90mm mortars, and three 75mm guns.[18]

The capture of classified enemy maps and documents during the first two weeks of battle

[11] Tenth Army G–2 Rpts Nos 18–20, 13–15Apr45.

[12] *Okinawa Operations Record*, 65.

[13] *Ibid.*, Record of the 24th Div, 10.

[14] *Ibid.*, 65.

[15] Unless otherwise noted the material in this section is derived from *Okinawa: The Last Battle; Tenth Army AR; 7th InfDiv AR; 27th InfDiv OpRpt; 96th InfDiv AR.*

[16] Tenth Army G–2 Rpt No 19, 14Apr45.

[17] IIIAC G–2 Rpt No 38, JOB Supplement, 9May45.

[18] 1st MarDiv G–2 PrdRpt No 37, 8May45, Translation No 46, Organization of the 12th IIIB, 12Apr45.

had given Tenth Army intelligence officers a fairly accurate picture of Japanese defensive plans. They also had been forced to revise their L-Day estimate of enemy troop strength upward from 65,000 to 72,000 which was "deemed a conservative minimum." [19] It was clear that the reduction of the Shuri fortress would be a tedious process involving tremendous expenditures of men and materiel.

Command restrictions on the expenditure of ammunition had been applied as early as 9 April when it became evident that the rate of arrival and discharge from ships could not keep up with the tremendous volume of fire poured out by battalions supporting the XXIV Corps. [20] The nature of the enemy defenses surrounding Shuri dictated the maximum use of artillery to reduce these prepared positions, strip off the camouflage that concealed them, and if possible close the firing ports and collapse the warren of interconnecting tunnels that housed and protected the defending troops. Corps and division artillery formed the backbone of the assault support since, unlike air and NGF, their firing was little restricted by weather or enemy air attacks.

General Hodge, convinced that an all-out effort was necessary to penetrate the Thirty-second Army's lines, scheduled a corps attack with three divisions abreast for 19 April. The period from 15–18 April was spent in preparing for the assault. Reserves of artillery ammunition were stockpiled at battery positions and distribution points while the guns and howitzers kept up a steady hammering at enemy forward positions and troop concentration areas. During the four-day preparation planes from TAF and TF 51 flew 905 sorties in support missions for XXIV Corps, dropping 482 tons of bombs and expending 3,400 rockets and over 700,000 rounds of .50-caliber and 20mm ammunition on Japanese installations. [21] In addition, TF 51 maintained a strong force of battleships, cruisers, and destroyers offshore

both day and night during the preparatory period in direct support of XXIV Corps. [22]

Combat troops were as vitally needed as supporting fires for the coming attack. Part of the requirement was met by narrowing the division zones of action and committing the 27th Division on the right of the corps line. Some attempt was made to alleviate the battle losses of the 7th and 96th Divisions by dividing between them 1,117 replacements that arrived from Saipan on 13 April. All Army divisions remained short of infantrymen even after the replacements joined, however, since losses sustained in their previous campaigns sent them to the target understrength. The 27th Infantry Division, originally assigned only reserve roles, was nearly 2,000 men short of table of organization (T/O) strength, while the 96th Division was short 1,000, and the 7th almost 400. In contrast, the Marine divisions' attached replacement drafts enabled them to embark with a five per cent T/O overage.

Front line units were in a constant state of flux before the 19 April assault. Small local attacks were made to improve forward positions, and strong patrols were sent into the maze of enemy defenses to pinpoint locations of defending weapons and troops. With the entrance of the 27th Division into the line, a reshuffling of assault battalions took place. (See Map 18, Map Section)

On 15 April General Griner assumed responsibility for the corps right flank, and 3/106 relieved 2/381 on Kakazu West. The 381st Infantry, in turn, took over the positions of the 383d which then moved to the corps service area to relieve the 165th and enable its release to 27th Division reserve. The following day elements of the 105th Infantry, which had been released from army reserve after the capture of Tsugen Shima, began moving into the left of the 96th Division's positions enabling the 381st Infantry to shift correspondingly and narrow the 382d's zone of action. Thus, two days before jump off, the initial assault dispositions had been made.

The 106th Infantry at Uchitomari faced the precipitous Urasoe-Mura Escarpment across

[19] Tenth Army G-2 Rpt No 22, 17Apr45, JOB Summary, 8–14Apr45.

[20] For an examination of this artillery ammunition problem see Chap VIII, "Logistical Progress."

[21] *XXIV Corps Arty AR*, Annex C, Enclosure 2.

[22] *CTF 51 AR*, Part V, Sect C, 39–42.

the estuary separating XXIV Corps front lines from Machinato. The 105th Infantry occupied positions on Kakazu West and to the north of Kakazu. The 381st Infantry, holding a salient in the enemy lines, occupied the ground in front of Nishibaru Ridge and the lines of the 382d stretched back to the hills before Kaniku. On the left of the corps line, the 184th Infantry was positioned in the rugged hills 1,500 yards north of Tanabaru and the 32d faced a prominent ridge rising abruptly south of its lines at Ishin and Ouki.

The Japanese, aware that a major attack was pending, used the preparatory period to reinforce their lines with supporting weapons, especially AT guns. Defending the west coast area south of the Machinato Estuary were the relatively intact 15th and 21st IIB's of the 64th Brigade. At Kakazu the 23d IIB, reinforced by the remnants of the 273d IIB, held the high ground. The 12th, 13th, and 14th IIB's and the 22d Regiment occupied Nishibaru, Kaniku, and the hills and ridges forward of Tanabaru. The 11th IIB had been committed on the east coast and the 3d Battalion, 89th Regiment of the 24th Division had been moved up to Conical Hill northwest of Yonabaru to back up its line.[23]

The success of the XXIV Corps attack on the right depended in large part upon the ability of the 27th Infantry Division to seize and hold an adequate bridgehead across the Machinato Estuary. General Griner made his plans with this in mind and intended that the estuary would be completely secured by H-Hour on 19 April. (See Map 19, Map Section)

At 1630 on 18 April, Company G of the 106th Infantry made a daring daylight crossing of the water barrier in engineer assault boats under cover of a heavy smoke barrage. Taking the enemy by surpise, the company secured Machinato at dusk. While artillery and mortars fended off enemy counterattacks, the 102d Engineer Combat Battalion began construction

of a foot, a pontoon, and two Bailey bridges.[24] By midnight the footbridge was completed and the rest of 2/106, with the 27th Reconnaissance Troop attached, crossed the estuary to Machinato. At 0400 the assault companies, undetected by the Japanese, moved 1,000 yards through the darkness to a position at the western end of the Urasoe-Mura Escarpment and made ready to assault the heights at dawn.

ATTACK OF 19 APRIL[25]

At 0512 on 19 April Admiral Blandy, commanding a demonstration attack group, ordered his ships to open fire on the Japanese positions along the southern coast of Okinawa. In conjunction with the main attack of XXIV Corps on the Shuri defenses, a diversionary landing feint was again to be made on the Minatoga beaches. Admiral Mitscher sent three of his battleships from TF 58 to provide support for this operation and Admiral Turner added two battleships, two cruisers, and four destroyers to Blandy's bombardment force. A 48-plane strike group spent 25 minutes plastering the target beaches, and at 0742 the first waves of troops crossed the line of departure. These men, from the 1st Battalion, 307th Infantry, had been held out of the Ie Shima assault force to fake the landing attempt. At 0817 the last waves of LCVP's turned back toward their transports and the feint was over.[26]

It is doubtful that the demonstration landing on 19 April succeeded as had those on L-Day and L-plus 1 in persuading the Thirty-second Army that its southern flank must be defended

[23] *Okinawa Operations Record*, 67–69; Record of the 24th Div, 11.

[24] See *27th InfDiv History*, 543–547 for the interesting story of how this engineer unit masked its materiel build-up for the bridging operation from the Japanese. During the five days prior to the attack, the battalion literally learned from the bottom up how to erect the Bailey bridge, a piece of equipment they had had no occasion to use in previous operations.
[25] Unless otherwise noted the material in this section is derived from *Okinawa: The Last Battle; XXIV Corps AR; 7th InfDiv AR; 27th InfDiv OpRpt; 96th InfDiv AR.*
[26] *CTF 51 AR*, Part V, Sect C, 4Z; *CTF 52 AR*, Part III, 34–35; Part V, Sect E, 8; *Tenth Army AR*, Corrections by CG, 77th InfDiv, 11Oct45.

at all cost. Although enemy staff officers were still convinced that the Minatoga landing was a logical move for Tenth Army to make, the threatened collapse of 62d Division's defenses before the XXIV Corps attack outweighed this consideration. Consequently, on 20 April, headquarters of the 24th Division was ordered north in preparation for the commitment of its units to the battle line.[27]

The preparatory and supporting fires delivered on Japanese positions for the main attack on 19 April were awesome in their magnitude. Admiral Turner allotted six battleships, six cruisers, and nine destroyers to direct support of XXIV Corps, and his air support control officer, Captain Richard F. Whitehead, USN, arranged for 650 Navy and Marine planes, over 300 of them from TF 58, to hit enemy defenses, assembly areas, and supply points.[28] Beginning at 0600, 27 battalions of artillery, firing everything from 75mm to 8-inch howitzers, covered the 5-mile front with a density greater than one weapon to every 30 yards. Nineteen thousand rounds fell on the enemy before the jump-off at 0640. It seemed as if no one could survive the massive preparation, but unfortunately almost all the Japanese did.[29]

Hidden in their caves deep within the hill-ridge complex, protected by walls of solid limestone, the enemy troops waited for the fire to lift. At 0620 the American artillery shifted its impact area 500 yards to the rear and the infantry feinted an attack to draw the Japanese out into the open. The ruse failed and the artillery came down again on the forward areas.

The attack plans called for the units on the left of the XXIV Corps line to advance first so that advantage could be taken of successive massed fires across the front. Initially, the assault troops of the 7th and 96th Divisions made rapid progress, but as the defenders

[27] *Okinawa Operations Record*, 69–70; Record of the 24th Div, 8.
[28] *CTF 51 AR*, Part III, 50; Part V, Sect C, 42; *XXIV Corps Arty AR*, Annex C, Enclosure 2.
[29] BrigGen Sheetz, CG, XXIV Corps Arty, later said he doubted that as many as 190 Japanese were killed by the morning's artillery preparation. Quoted in *Okinawa: The Last Battle*, 194.

4.2-INCH MORTAR fires in support of the 7th Division attack on 19 April. (Army Photograph)

manned more and more of their positions the advance slowed and finally ground to a stop.

On the extreme left of the corps front, Skyline Ridge, the knife-like height forward of 32d Infantry's lines, was the initial objective. Tanks and armored flame throwers moving through Ouki burned and blasted a toehold for 3/32 on the base of the ridge. The counterattacks of Japanese defenders holding the reverse slopes, although they were repulsed, prevented the battalion from gaining the crest or flanking the ridge. Finally, the unit was forced to relinquish its precarious hold when 2/32 on its right was unable to penetrate a pre-registered mortar and machine-gun impact area that guarded the approaches to the western end of Skyline Ridge. In the 184th Infantry zone of advance along the division boundary, the attacking companies were also caught in an impact zone and raked by fire from two rocky knolls (Rocky Crags) that guarded the approaches to Tanabaru. The net result of the day's action in terms of ground gained and held was nil.

The 382d Infantry, attacking to the east of Kaniku with two battalions abreast, was able to move forward about 500 yards before a hail of machine-gun and rifle fire coming from a low tomb-studded ridge on its right swept its front. The enemy position, dubbed Tombstone Ridge by the men of the 382d, bristled with well dug-in, interlacing automatic weapons. Using all the fire available from its supporting tanks and assault guns, 1/382 gained and held the northern tip of the ridge and 2/382, with the lessening of fire on its right flank, moved up parallel to the 1st Battalion's positions. A gap which had developed between the two battalions during the day's advance was covered by 3/382 which moved into the center of the regimental zone.

The 1st Battalion, 381st Infantry, in position north and northwest of Kaniku at the start of the attack, moved rapidly through the western part of the village and came abreast of 3/381 at 0715. Both battalions then jumped off with their objective the Nishibaru-Tanabaru ridge line. After garnering 300 yards of enemy territory in an almost unopposed advance, the 381st came under extremely heavy machine-gun fire that pinned down the assult troops. Enemy positions on the ridges to the front, at Kakazu to the right of 3/381 and Tombstone Ridge to the left of 1/381, dominated the area. The volume and accuracy of the Japanese fire made further advances impossible during the day, and forward units pulled back to protected defensive positions late in the afternoon.

The impetus given the 27th Division's attack by 2/106's night advance was responsible for substantial gains along the west coast on 19 April. The estuary was crossed by 1/106 at 0515 and a half hour later the 2d Battalion, backed by the 1st, mounted the Urasoe-Mura Escarpment and attacked to the southeast. During the day the 3d Battalion was committed in the center of the regimental zone, and by nightfall the regiment held a 2,000-yard line, forward of the escarpment along the low coastal plain and on the crest of adjoining high ground for the rest of the distance. Resistance, which had been negligible at the start of the day's action, increased sharply as the Japanese in reverse slope positions fought doggedly to halt the 106th's progress.

Kakazu Ridge, whose formidable defensive network had blocked the 96th Division's advance for over a week, proved just as tough for the 27th Division to take. The 105th Infantry,

with 1/105 in assault, attacked the ridge at 0730, preceded by the full power of the corps artillery preparation. The defenders were not intimidated, and their damaging fire drove the 1st Battalion to cover soon after the jumpoff. The 3d Battalion was committed on the right of 1/105 and bypassed the ridge and village to the west, moving into the low, uneven ground dominated by the Urasoe-Mura Escarpment.

The 2d Battalion of the 105th, preceded by a reinforced company of tanks, also attempted to bypass the ridge by moving along the division boundary through the cut between Kakazu and Nishibaru. The Japanese were waiting for this move and had emplaced mortars, machine guns, AT guns, and AA cannon to cover the Ginowan-Shuri road that crossed through the cut. The tank company was cut off from accompanying infantry by planned barrages of mortars and grenade dischargers and the fire of machine guns manned by infiltration groups sent forward on the night of the 18th.[30] The tanks swung in behind the ridge and shot up Kakazu, demolishing what little was left of the village, but without infantry support they were forced to withdraw. Only eight from the original 30-tank force made it back through the cut. The fire of AT and AA guns, mines in Kakazu, and the suicidal attacks of Japanese with satchel charges accounted for 22 tanks.[31]

After this repulse, 2/105 moved back around Kakazu and came up on the left of 3/105 which by now had occupied positions tying in with 1/106 on the escarpment. A gap of more than a thousand yards existed between the left of the 105th Infantry and the right of the 381st. The flank battalions of each division were unable to advance because of the withering enfilade fire that criss-crossed their front lines from Kakazu and Nishibaru. (See Map 20, Map Section)

The XXIV Corps resumed its slow, grinding advance on 20 April at 0730, after a half hour artillery preparation. On the 7th Division front heavy fire from Skyline Ridge and Rocky

[30] CinCPac-CinCPOA Bull 212–45, Translations and Interrogations No 39, 30Aug45, 62d Div Battle Lessons Priority Dispatch No 19, 20Apr45, 47–49.

[31] Of these 22 tanks all but five were eventually salvaged by maintenance men of the 193d TkBn and the 27th InfDiv. *27th InfDiv History*, 619.

Crags continued during the day. Company B of the 17th Infantry was committed on the extreme right of the division zone to reinforce 3/184's attack and the fresh troops gained a purchase on the northernmost height of the Rocky Crags position. Action in the 32d Infantry zone centered on the hill at the western extremity of Skyline Ridge. Late in the afternoon, under cover of a 4.2-inch mortar smoke and shell barrage, leading elements of 2/32 wrested the summit of the hill from the Japanese. Despite counterattacks and constant shelling, the small advance party, supported by fire from 2/184 and 3/32 on its flanks, held its lines throughout the night.

In the center of the corps line the second day of all-out assault yielded Tombstone Ridge to the attackers and placed elements of two battalions on the crest of the Nishibaru-Tanabaru ridge line. The 3d Battalion of the 382d Infantry, covered by 1/382 in the positions it had seized on 19 April, pushed south down Tombstone Ridge and succeeded in wiping out enemy resistance by the end of day. When 3/382 came abreast of 1/381, that battalion was able to launch its attack on Nishibaru Ridge and by noon two companies were dug in on its top. At 1320, 2/381 was committed on the right of 1/381 and despite punishing flanking fire from Kakazu managed to get two companies up on the ridge. Neither of the 96th Division's flank battalions, 3/381 and 2/382, was able to advance during the day because of accurate fire laid down by the Japanese on Kakazu Ridge and Rocky Crags.

The 27th Division continued its advance along the west coast on 20 April, with the 1st and 2d Battalions of the 165th Infantry passing through the positions of 2/106. The regiment attempted to take Gusukuma during the day, but was held up north of the village by intensive fire from a complex of ridge and ravine positions that completely dominated its zone of advance. This Japanese position, called Item Pocket,[32] was to prove fully as trouble-

ITEM POCKET, scene of a bloody, protracted battle in the 27th Division zone of action. (Army Photograph)

some as Kakazu Ridge. (See Map 19, Map Section)

The 106th Infantry, delayed two hours in its jump-off by a heavy enemy artillery shelling, moved down off the Urasoe-Mura Escarpment on 20 April, mopping up reverse slope positions as it progressed. Gains of 500–800 yards were registered by 3/106 and 1/106 as well as 3/105 which moved up on the left of the regiment. The 2d Battalion of the 105th, attempting to advance over the escarpment near Nakama (also called Awacha) was driven back to its original positions by a strong enemy counterattack which came late in the afternoon. The 105th's 1st Battalion, which had been mopping up Kakazu, had to be committed on 2/105's left to prevent a breakthrough. By sundown the 27th Division had made substantial progress on its right although at a cost of over 500 casualties, but its left flank was still dominated by the bypassed Kakazu ridge position.

Casualties had been heavy in all the attacking divisions, but the Japanese were taking a beating. Front line units were being whittled down to skeleton size and only the natural strength of the enemy positions held the XXIV Corps in check. On 21 April, the 32d Infantry seized the entire military crest of Skyline Ridge from the depleted defending companies of the 11th IIB. On the 7th Division's right flank, the 184th Infantry secured its hold on the north peak of Rocky Crags and gained an average of 300 yards throughout the regimental zone.

---

[32] The position was named for its location on the 1:25,000 tactical map used by Tenth Army. Its major strong points were located within the 200-yard grid square 7777-I (or Item in the military phonetic alphabet).

Both 1/381 and 2/381 were unsuccessful in their attempts to improve their hold on Nishibaru Ridge during the day. Deadly machinegun fire from Nishibaru village pinned the advancing battalions down, and a heavy mortar barrage forced the leading troops to withdraw. Although the 381st's forward progress was halted, 3/382 moved through the 381st's zone of action and captured positions on the crest of the ridge. At 1300, 3/383, previously in division reserve, was committed in the center of the 382d's zone and attacked toward the ridge line. By nightfall the battalion had reached a point 200 yards north of the ridge to the left rear of 3/382.

As had been the case in the preceding two days of action, 3/381 was unable to advance on 21 April because of flanking fire from Kakazu Ridge. The 105th Infantry, attempting to move east along the Urasoe-Mura Escarpment was unable to hold any appreciable gains because of heavy enemy fire from Nishibaru and Kakazu which covered its rear. On the right of the 27th Division, the 165th Infantry hammered fruitlessly against Item Pocket. Small gains were made on either flank of the position, but the core of enemy resistance remained intact. The 106th Infantry, in the center of the division zone of action, consolidated its hold in the area southeast of Gusukuma during the day.

In an effort to relieve the pressure on the Thirty-second Army's front line, Admiral Toyoda sent his *Kamikazes* against TF 51 on 22 April. According to the Japanese, they expected "to destroy the remaining enemy shipping in the waters around Okinawa."[33] Attacking at dusk, the suicide pilots were unable to make good on the boast although LCS 15 and the mine sweeper *Swallow* were sunk. Four destroyer types were damaged by suicide hits, near misses, and bomb fragments. In return for 54 enemy planes shot down TF 51 had to add 24 KIA, 44 WIA, and 36 MIA to the spiralling naval casualty list.[34]

Although little terrain was secured during ground action on 22 April, the continual attacks of XXIV Corps were beginning to tell on the enemy. On that date the Thirty-second

Army issued orders to the 24th Division to begin moving its "main force" to the north, preparatory to taking over the right half of the depleted 62d Division's line.[35]

While the 32d Infantry consolidated its gains on Skyline Ridge, the 184th repeatedly attacked the southernmost of the Rocky Crags. Even the direct fire of a 155mm howitzer, added to that of tanks and self-propelled guns, was not enough to blast a way for the assault troops on 22 April.

In the center of the corps line, the 381st Infantry held its position of 21 April and covered with fire the relief of the 382d by the 383d. By 1000, 2/383 had relieved 3/382 on the crest of the ridge east of Nishibaru, and an hour later the regiment attacked to the southeast toward Tanabaru. After an afternoon of bitter fighting, the 383d had secured about 200 yards on its right and 150 yards on its left. The 96th Division ended the day with three battalions firmly ensconced atop the ridge (2/381, 1/381, and 2/383) and with two battalions (3/383 and 2/382) ready to push to the top on 23 April.

On the west coast the 27th Division conducted mopping up operations on the fourth day of the corps attack. Unit positions were consolidated and contact was established all across the line. General Hodge, concerned about the gap between the 27th and 96th Divisions, directed Brigadier General William B. Bradford, ADC of the 27th Division, to coordinate efforts to reduce the Kakazu position. The 3d Battalion of the 106th Infantry, with the 27th Reconnaissance Troop attached, cleaned out the village of Kakazu by nightfall but held up in the face of mounting opposition from enemy units that still held out on the reverse slopes of the ridge.

Action on 23 April was confined to mop up and consolidation in the 27th Infantry Division's zone while General Bradford organized a variegated task force to reduce the Kakazu position. The infantry elements were 3/106 (27th Reconnaissance Troop attached) in Kazazu village, 2/165 which held the ground between the 105th's lines on the escarpment and Kakazu, 3/17 which had been assigned as 27th Division reserve on 22 April, and 3/381 in position just north of the gap between

[33] *CICAS Trans* No 246, 32d Army OpOrd No 170, 0830, 22Apr45.

[34] *CFT 51 AR*, Part III, 54–57; Part V, Sect H, 9.

[35] *CICAS Trans* No 246, 32d Army OpOrd No 170, 0830, 22Apr45.

Kakazu and Nishibaru. In addition, elements of the 27th and 96th Divisions' attached tank battalions, the Cannon Company of the 105th Infantry, and signal and engineer detachments from the 27th Division were included in the Bradford Task Force. An operation order directed that the force seize Kakazu Ridge and establish firm contact between the two divisions.

The 96th Division made its main effort on 23 April in the 383d Infantry's zone and by nightfall had managed to get one more battalion, 3/383, into position on top of the Nishibaru-Tanabaru ridge line; 2/382, on the division left, held up just short of the crest after a 200-yard advance during the day. Rocky Crags, on the left of 2/382, had been taken by 1/17 earlier in the day after a relatively brief struggle which showed that the previous days of fighting had wiped out the garrison.

The XXIV Corps was ready to throw its full power against the remnants of 62d Division holding the outer defense ring when the attack was renewed on 24 April. But the day was marked by sweeping advances all along the line. During the night, under cover of "the most intensive artillery fire yet experienced on the XXIV Corps front," [36] the enemy had withdrawn his defending forces from the line that had held up the 7th and 96th Divisions for two weeks. Only on the west of the 27th Division's zone, where American advances could outflank the second line of defenses stretching from Gusukuma through Maeda to Kochi, Onaga, and Kuhazu did the stubbornness of the defense remain unabated. The Bradford Task Force had little difficulty in mopping up Kakazu Ridge, the enemy fortress whose defenders had completely stopped attacks of the 96th and 27th Divisions for so long.

ASSAULTING THE SECOND DEFENSE RING [37]

With the withdrawal of defending forces from the Kakazu, Nishibaru, Tanabaru, and Skyline Ridges, the left and center of the XXIV Corps line advanced 600–1,000 yards on 24 April. The 17th Infantry, passing through the 184th on the right of the 7th Division zone, thrust its assault companies forward to the eastern outskirts of Tanabaru and took the high ground on the right of the 32d Infantry positions on Skyline Ridge. The 383d Infantry, encountering the same lack of resistance, advanced rapidly on the left of the 96th Division, securing Tanabaru Ridge and taking Tanabaru itself. The 381st Infantry, led by 3/381 which finally gained the top of Nishibaru Ridge, came within 400 yards of the Urasoe-Mura Escarpment forward of Maeda. All units put patrols out to locate the next enemy defense line.

While the Bradford Task Force mopped up Kakazu, the 105th Infantry strengthened its positions on the escarpment and conformed to the advance of 2/165. By 1600, firm contact had been established on the division boundary between 2/165 and 3/381; 1/105 was tied in to the right of 2/165. The 106th Infantry, in an afternoon attack advanced its lines 400 yards to a point where they paralleled Gusukuma, but the 165th Infantry was unable to make any progress against Item Pocket and its lines remained substantially the same.

The following day, in preparation for a planned corps attack on 26 April, the 105th and 106th Infantry remained in position, sending strong patrols to the front. The 165th Infantry, with the 1st and 3d Battalions in assault, continued its attempt to reduce Item Pocket. Due to the broken nature of the ground, individual platoons and companies with scattered tank support battled throughout the day and into darkness. Gains were made all around the periphery of the pocket and elements of 1/165 occupied Gusukuma, but the defending 21st Independent Infantry Battalion still held the pocket itself.

The 96th Division attempted no advances on 25 April, but prepared for the next day's attack. Aggressive patrols of the 383d Infantry probed the hills 400–500 yards in front of its lines without encountering strong resistance. The 17th and 32d Infantry moved forward about the same distance to establish a strong position on

[36] Tenth Army G–2 Rpt No 30, 25Apr45.
[37] Unless otherwise noted the material in this section is derived from *Okinawa: The Last Battle; XXIV Corps AR; 7th InfDiv AR; 27th InfDiv OpRpt; 96th InfDiv AR.*

FLAME TANK clears a path for 7th Division assault troops attacking Skyline Ridge.   (Army Photograph)

high ground which the 7th Division could use as a base for further advances.

The disposition of enemy forces facing XXIV Corps changed considerably after the advance of 24 April. The 1st and 2d Battalions of the 22d Regiment occupied the Onaga-Kochi area, and the depleted independent infantry battalions of the 63d Brigade gradually withdrew from the east coast and moved cross-island to positions near Nakama and Maeda. The 1st Battalion of the 32d Regiment was committed at Kuhazu on 25 April and on the 28th moved to positions north of Shuri. The rest of the 32d Regiment reached the Maeda area between 27 and 29 April and immediately initiated a vigorous defense of the dominating escarpment. The 89th Regiment, also committed by battalion as the need arose, was concentrated in the

Gaja-Kuhazu region by the end of the month. The strength of enemy forces opposing the XXIV Corps rose steadily as General Hodge's forces threatened the second ring of Shuri defenses.[38]

The corps attack on 26 April in the 27th Division area opened at 0700 after a 30-minute artillery preparation. The 105th Infantry advanced against moderate resistance through the village of Nakama and set up a defense position on its outskirts. At the end of day all three of its battalions were on line. The 106th Infantry made rapid progress to the east of Yafusu, but had to stop short of that village when the line stretching back to the 105th's positions

[38] *Okinawa Operations Record*, 69–76; Record of the 24th Div, 10–14.

became overextended. On the west coast, although Item Pocket still held out, the 165th Infantry was able to make further encroachments on all sides of the enemy position and advance patrols to the northern edge of Machinato airfield.

Assault battalions of the 96th Division reached the northern slopes of the Maeda Escarpment on 26 April. Progress in the morning was rapid against light resistance, but the fury of enemy fire mounted as men of the 381st and 383d Infantry attempted to cross the escarpment and reach its southern slopes. The escarpment itself, an extension of the Urasoe-Mura heights, was a sheer cliff throughout most of the 96th Division zone and tanks and assault guns could not accompany the attacking infantry. In the face of determined enemy resistance the division dug in late in the morning to hold its gains and spent the rest of the day locating and destroying enemy weapons' positions in its zone of action.

The 17th Infantry bore the brunt of the attack in the 7th Division zone on 26 April. Attempting to envelop Kochi Ridge (between Kochi and Onaga) on either flank, 1/17 and 2/17 were driven back by heavy enemy fire. The nature of the compartmented terrain prevented effective cooperation between the assault units. The 32d Infantry, because its right flank was vulnerable to enemy fire from Kochi and Onaga, did not advance but sent strong combat patrols into Unaha and Kashukai to the west and south of Yonabaru airfield.

Scattered rains of 25 and 26 April increased to such an extent on 27 April that supply operations and tank support were considerably curtailed. Most action on L-plus 26 was confined to bitter and bloody close quarter infantry combat. The 17th Infantry again failed to take Kochi Ridge and 32d Infantry patrols ran into sharp opposition as they probed the Unaha area.

In the 96th Division zone enemy fire made the top of the escarpment untenable and prevented the 381st Infantry from advancing. Average gains of 200 yards were made on the division left by the 383d and elements of 1/381 against extremely intense machine-gun and small-arms fire. During the day the eastern part of Maeda was seized by 2/283, and 3/383 moved to a position generally parallel with Kochi.

Item Pocket was bypassed by the 165th Infantry on 27 April and left to be mopped up by two rifle companies. The northern third of Machinato airfield was secured by 3/165 against heavy machine-gun and mortar fire, and 2/165, after an initial repulse, drove through an enemy artillery barrage to occupy most of Yafusu. The 106th Infantry confined its action during the day to extensive patrolling and adjusting front line positions to conform to the advance of 2/165. The 105th Infantry, with its lines already stretched thin, made no attempt to advance during the day. (See Map 20, Map Section)

Most of the assault troops of the 77th Infantry Division, fresh from their capture of Ie Shima, were ashore on Okinawa by 27 April. Aware that his division would probably be committed on Okinawa, General Bruce had had his staff keep current on the progress of the fighting on the main island. Despite the fact that it had fought two major amphibious operations in the short space of a month, the 77th Division was ready to enter the XXIV Corps front line. Plans had been made for it to begin relieving the badly-battered 96th Division on 29 April.

As early as 24 April, the need for substantial increments of fresh troops in the main battle line had been officially recognized when General Buckner directed General Geiger to designate one division of IIIAC as Tenth Army reserve, with one regiment of that division ready to assemble and move south on 12 hour's notice. General Geiger selected the 1st Marine Division, and General del Valle placed the 1st Marines on alert status.[39] On 27 April, Tenth Army declared its intent to attach the 1st Division to XXIV Corps at an early date in order to relieve the 27th Division for garrison duty under Island Command.[40]

On 28 April, as the first infantry elements of the 77th Division moved into position to relieve the 96th, a conference at General Buckner's headquarters considered the future employment

[39] *Tenth Army AR*, Chap 7, Sect III, 13.

[40] *1st MarDiv G-3 Jnl*, 27Apr45.

of IIIAC. The plan presented proposed attachment of the 1st Marine Division to XXIV Corps on 30 April. It then would begin moving south to relieve the 27th Infantry Division. Upon relief, the 27th Division would shift to northern Okinawa as garrison troops of Island Command and relieve the 6th Marine Division. The 6th Division would then assemble near Chibana and on or about 7 May the IIIAC would take over the zone held at that time by the 1st Division. Simultaneously, Tenth Army would assume tactical control of the two-corps front and a coordinated army attack would be made soon thereafter.[41]

1ST MARINE DIVISION JOINS XXIV CORPS[42]

As preparations were being made to effect the relief of two divisions on the XXIV Corps front, the attack to the south continued. On 28 April, 3/165, using tanks and assault guns to neutralize fire from enemy pillboxes on its flanks, completed the capture of Machinato airfield. The remainder of the 27th Division made slight advances during the day, securing Yafusu and destroying enemy emplacements in the respective battalion zones of action. On the 105th Infantry's left the stubborn defense of reverse slope positions on the escarpment by the Japanese prevented the 381st Infantry from gaining the fire-swept top. An air strike and the fire of tanks brought up by means of a road bulldozed through the broken ground east of Maeda enabled the 383d Infantry to advance its lines 300 yards during the day.

The enemy's savage reaction to the 96th Division's progress featured counterattacks, infiltration attempts, and repeated barrages of artillery and mortar fire. Possession of the Maeda Escarpment was vital to the Thirty-second Army's plans because the terrain offered a commanding view of the whole of the Japa-

nese positions as far as the foothills of Shuri and blocked similar enemy observations within American lines.[43] The region surrounding Maeda became the focus of continuous enemy attempts to regain the dominating ground of the second ring of Shuri defenses.

The 7th Division's moderate advances on 28 April secured Kochi and Onaga, but the 17th Infantry was still unable to maintain a purchase on Kochi Ridge. The 32d Infantry managed to advance armored flame throwers into the village of Kuhazu, but accompanying riflemen were stopped by heavy mortar concentrations. The story on the following day was much the same. The 17th Infantry advanced slightly on both flanks of Kochi Ridge while the 32d pushed reconnaissance patrols as far forward as Gaja. Any attempt to put more than a few men into the broken, abrupt terrain in the Kochi-Onaga-Kuhazu area was instantly met by deadly concentrations of small-arms, mortar, and artillery fire.

The 307th Infantry of the 77th Division, which had moved into reserve positions in the 96th Division zone on 28 April, began relieving the 381st Infantry the following morning. As soon as the assault battalions, 1/307 and 3/307, attempted to attack they ran into the same furious wall of devastating fire that had met the 381st. Constant pressure was maintained during the day but gains were slight against the highly developed defense system.

The 3d Battalion of the 383d Infantry on 29 April again pushed its lines forward despite the heavy fire from enemy positions on its exposed right flank. A platoon from the 763d Tank Battalion, covering the advance of 3/383 on the left of the regimental zone, managed to reach positions from which it delivered direct fire on the town of Shuri, 1,000 to 1,500 yards to its front. The 3d Battalion held up for the night in firm possession of Hill 138, 500 yards forward of American lines on either flank.

The last 34 defenders of Item Pocket charged 165th Infantry lines early in the morning of 29 April and were cut down by troops of Company K, 3/165, ending nine days of fanatical resistance from this enemy strong point. The lines of the 27th Division were advanced

---

[41] *IIIAC AR*, 44.

[42] Unless otherwise noted the material in this section is derived from *Okinawa: The Last Battle; XXIV Corps AR; 1st MarDiv SAR; 7th InfDiv AR; 27th InfDiv OpRpt; 77th InfDiv OpRpt, Okinawa; 96th InfDiv AR; 1st Mar SAR;* 5th Mar SAR, 22Apr–23Jun45, hereinafter cited as *5th Mar SAR; 7th Mar SAR.*

[43] *Okinawa Operations Record,* 74.

through Kuwan and Miyagusuku during a day-long drive which revealed deeply dug-in enemy positions, protected by mine fields, throughout the rugged hills and ridges to the east and southeast of Machinato airfield.

Major air attacks by Japanese *Kamikaze* units were made on 27, 28, and 29 April in another ineffectual effort to isolate the Tenth Army from its supporting fleet. During the three days of intermittent attack defending forces accounted for over 150 enemy planes but again the Japanese exacted a heavy price for their losses. The ammunition ship *Canada Victory* was sunk and seven destroyer types and two LCI's were damaged. The APH *Pinckney* was gutted amidships by fire after a *Kamikaze* hit, and another suicide pilot dove his plane into the casualty-loaded *Comfort* which was sailing to Guam under full hospital ship procedure. Twenty-two patients were rewounded and five killed in this tragic attack, and six nurses were killed and four wounded.[44]

The American build-up in southern Okinawa continued despite the harassment of enemy air raids which hampered orderly unloading and severely curtailed the night movements of vehicles. At 0600 on 30 April the 1st Marine Division was attached to XXIV Corps and march serials of the 1st Marines and 1st Tank Battalion began moving south to the 27th Division area. The Army division, meanwhile, had continued its attack in the area south of Machinato airfield. At 1000 as the first Marine units began moving into the front lines, the 27th Division halted its forward progress and disengaged its advance patrols which had been caught in a heavy fire fight.

On the extreme right of the corps line, Company B of 1/1 with a platoon of Company C attached took over the whole of the sector of 1/165 which stretched in a half-circle around the end of the airfield from Nakanishi to the northern outskirts of Kuwan. The rest of Lieutenant Colonel Murray's battalion took up reserve positions in the low coastal area north of Kuwan. Since no orders were issued for the

MAJOR GENERAL PEDRO A. DEL VALLE, Commanding General, 1st Marine Division at Okinawa.

resumption of 1/165's attack, the Marines spent the rest of 30 April digging in, improving defenses, and registering normal barrages.[45]

On the left of 1/1, Lieutenant Colonel Sabol moved his 3d Battalion into the positions of 2/165 which had met the heaviest resistance during the 27th Division's morning attack. Notified by the Army battalion commander that there were still Japanese holdouts in Miyagusuku, Sabol directed Companies K and L to mop up the village as they moved toward 2/165's forward positions. Scattered mortar and rifle fire peppered the Marines, and late in the afternoon enemy artillery started falling in the forward area. The Japanese began infiltrating back to Miyagusuku in some strength, and at 1715 Company L reported it was pinned down in the ruins of the village by concentrated enemy fire. The company was forced to withdraw at 1830 and set up for the night north of the village. Company I, the battalion reserve, was committed on the left of Company

[44] *CTF 51 AR*, Part III, 64–70. Ships' crews suffered 38 KIA, 80 WIA, and 24 MIA as a result of the three-day attack. *Ibid.*, Part V, Sect H, 9.

[45] 1st Bn, 1st Mar SAR, 23Feb–21Jun45, n. d., 3, hereinafter cited as *1/1 SAR*.

L at dusk in order to tie in with the lines of the 106th Infantry.[46]

While the 1st Marines took over the right of the 27th Division's lines, the 77th Division completed the relief of the 96th. The Hill 138 position of 3/383 occupied on 29 April was taken over by 3/306, and 1/306 relieved 2/383 on its lines southwest of Maeda. At noon General Bruce assumed command of the area from General Bradley. Throughout the day the 307th Infantry attempted to improve its positions on the escarpment. Infantry-engineer teams with scaling ladders and cargo nets negotiated the vertical cliffs at the escarpment's top under cover of every available supporting weapon the regiment could muster. Once on the naked top, however, attackers met a storm of enemy fire they described as "all hell rolled into one." [47] Eventually the sheer weight of punishing metal thrown forced them back to defensive positions of the previous night.

The character of Japanese resistance met on 30 April by the 307th Infantry was typical of the type the 96th Division had faced since L-Day. When General Bradley withdrew his troops for a short rest and rehabilitation period, the ranks of the "Deadeye Division" [48] were sadly depleted. The infantry regiments had suffered 2,504 battle casualties with 353 men killed in action. The division left an estimated 7,170 enemy dead in the wake of its advance,

The major gains on the XXIV Corps front on 30 April were made by the 32d Infantry. With the 17th Infantry stalled in its attacks on Kochi Ridge, General Arnold shifted the 7th Division's main effort to the left flank. Behind a wall of artillery, air, and NGF support 1/32 gained the ridges southwest of Kuhazu after a 1,200 yard advance. That night the battalion was subjected to a ceaseless round of counterattacks and infiltration attempts that delayed

its relief by 1/184 the following morning. As the 184th Infantry took over the 32d's lines on 1 May, both units had to fight their way into position and little progress was made during the day's action.

The savage resistance that thwarted the 307th Infantry's attack on 30 April continued on 1 May. With the 306th supporting its advance with fire into the flank and rear of Japanese positions on the escarpment, the 307th jumped off with all three battalions in assault. When the troops dug in early in the afternoon to meet the inevitable nightly counterattacks, they had pushed at heavy cost through some 300 yards of hotly-contested ground on the right and gained 100 yards on the left.

The 1st of May marked the official entrance of the 1st Marine Division as a unit into the southern front although the 11th Marines had supported the 96th and 27th Divisions throughout most of the April fighting.[49] The artillery battalions of those units remained in position to continue support of the 1st and 77th Divisions in their drive southward.[50] General del Valle assumed command of the 27th Division's former zone of action at 1400, and the Army troops assembled for movement north the following day. General Griner's men killed or captured an estimated 5,019 enemy in their battles for Kakazu Ridge, the Urasoe-Mura Escarpment, Machinato airfield, and Item Pocket. However, during the 12 days since it had jumped off in attack on 19 April, the 27th Infantry Division had paid a price of 2,661 battle casualties, 316 of them listed as killed in action. Had the division's casualty rate of 19–30 April been continued, the end of the Okinawa campaign would have found every man in the original T/O buried or hospitalized.

Indicative of the battle-riddled condition of 27th Division front line units was the fact that

[46] 3d Bn, 1st Mar SAR, Phase I and II of the Nansei Shoto Operation, 10Jul45, 9, hereinafter cited as *3/1 SAR*.

[47] *77th InfDiv OpRpt, Okinawa*, 37.

[48] According to the division history, the 96th received its nickname from the constant insistence of BrigGen C. M. Easley, ADC, on crack marksmanship from all ranks during its training period. O. R. Davidson, *et al*, *The Deadeyes: The Story of the 96th Infantry Division*, (Washington, 1947), 5, hereinafter cited as *96th InfDiv History*.

[49] "On 29 April, Headquarters, 11th Marines assumed command of its scattered battalions in the zone of and reinforcing the 27th Division, the two battalions with the 7th and 96th Divisions displacing into that area. All four battalions of the 11th Marines were commended by the Army divisions with which they had served." *Brown 1955*.

[50] Only one battalion, the 249th Field Artillery, went north with the 27th Div to furnish support during mop-up activities. This unit returned to the southern front on 29 May to reinforce the fires of IIIAC Arty.

ENEMY FIRE sweeps the gorge south of Machinato airfield as Marines of 1/1 dash across the open ground on 2 May

rifle companies of 2/5 each relieved a battalion of the 105th Infantry when the 5th Marines took over the remaining positions of 27th Division during the afternoon of 1 May. Lieutenant Colonel William E. Benedict's men did not attempt to do much more than consolidate the positions they had occupied on the south edge of Awacha (Nakama). The Marines got a taste of what was in store for them during the next 50 days, however, when four of five Army tanks, attempting to pass through Awacha to support the 307th Infantry's attack, were hit by 47mm AT fire as soon as they cleared the village.[51]

The 3d Battalion, 5th Marines relieved the 106th Infantry in the center of the division line at about 1400, suffering a few casualties in the process. All reliefs by Colonel Griebel's regiment were completed by 1700, and patrols reconnoitered the zone of advance in preparation for a division attack on 2 May. General Hodge had instructed General del Valle earlier in the day that he was to do all he could by fire and movement to assist the advance of the 77th Division,[52] an assignment that would fall to the lot of the 5th Marines.

The Japanese had been forced to re-form their battle line on the west coast to block the threat of penetration after the 27th Division took Gusukuma. Most of the 62d Division was now positioned along a general line from Awacha through the ridges north of Dakeshi

---

[51] 2d Bn, 5th Mar SAR, Okinawa, 1Apr–22Jun45, n.d., 2–3, hereinafter cited as *2/5 SAR*.

[52] *1st MarDiv G–3 Jnl*, 1May45.

to Uchima and Jichaku. The Thirty-second Army was well aware, however, that "powerful elements of the Division scattered and remaining in the cave positions within the [American] lines [were] still offering resistance."[53] It was these enemy holdouts that faced the 1st Marines.

Lieutenant Colonel Murray had no attack order for 1 May, but kept reconnaissance patrols forward of 1/1's lines to check the terrain over which the battalion would have to advance for routes of tank approach. A deep L-shaped ravine cut across his entire front, and the retreating enemy had blown out the fill where the main north-south highway had crossed it. Artillery and AT guns were registered on the area and it was obvious that a warm reception awaited any armor attempting a penetration. A patrol from Company A sent to investigate approach routes near the mouth of the ravine on the west coast was driven back by fire from the steep cliffs on the far side. The enemy had perfect observation of the 1st Battalion's zone of advance from positions on high ground south and southeast of the Asa Kawa, and the resistance encountered by patrols portended a stiff fight to reach the river.[54]

The 1st Tank Battalion sent three gun and four flame tanks to 3/1 on 1 May to provide direct support for the infantry's second attempt to secure Miyagusuku. Tank guns blasted the remaining houses and walls, and 300 gallons of napalm were expended to gut the ruins.[55] As soon as the village had cooled sufficiently, a small patrol from Company L passed through it without incident. At 1315, the battalion advanced with Company L moving into the smoking ruins on the left and Company K covering the right flank. The intermittent artillery and mortar fire that had been falling all night and morning increased as the battalion cleared Miyagusuku and enemy riflemen and machine

gunners opened up on the advancing troops. At 1530, Company K reported it had already taken 30 to 40 casualties and was attempting to evacuate them under cover of a smoke and mortar barrage. The company commander requested permission to withdraw which Lieutenant Colonel Sabol granted, and by 1900 the battalion was back in the positions it had occupied on 30 April.[56] (See Map 21, Map Section)

A driving rain fell throughout 2 May and limited visibility and the effectiveness of air support. During the night one company of 3/184 advanced as far as Gaja Ridge, the last high ground before Conical Hill, the key Japanese position on the east coast. This advantage was lost at the end of day when company officers withdrew their men because of excessive casualties suffered. Positions held by 1/184 near Kuhazu were extended despite extremely strong resistance. The Japanese positions on Kochi Ridge and the hills to the south again proved too much for the 17th Infantry, and the men of 3/17 and 2/17, pinned down by fires from front and flanks, were unable to gain the ridge.

The pattern of assault for the 77th Division on 2 May followed that used the day before. The 307th attacked along the top of the escarpment and the 306th supported the movement by fire. Again the ferocious defense put up by the enemy 32d Regiment and elements of the 63d Brigade limited advances to a few yards, each one taken only after close quarter grenade and satchel charge exchanges. Machine-gun and cannon fire swept all exposed areas, and pillboxes continued to resist even after explosive charges had been dropped into the vents and gun ports. The 307th was forced to use all its organic weapons in order to retain the ground won.

Fire from reverse slope positions facing the 307th Infantry pinned down the left flank company (E) of 2/5 when the battalion attempted to advance at 0900 on the morning of 2 May. After Companies F and G had moved about 200 yards against moderate opposition, they too came under the withering fire and were showered with grenades and knee mortar shells

---

[53] *Okinawa Operations Record*, 80.

[54] *1/1 SAR*, 3–4.

[55] 1st TkBn Summaries of Tank Action, 15Apr–23-Jun45, hereinafter cited as *1st TkBn Summary*. According to the *3/1 SAR*, 10, the tanks supporting them were Army mediums, but 1st TkBn lists them as belonging to its own Co A. The flame tanks were from Co B, 713th TkBn (USA) which was attached to the 1st MarDiv and later IIIAC.

[56] *3/1 SAR*, 10–12.

from high ground to their immediate front. By 1100 casualties in assault platoons were so heavy that the battalion had to withdraw under cover of a smoke screen to reorganize. Enemy artillery followed the men back over the broken ground causing further losses.[57] The remainder of the day was spent concentrating supporting weapons fire on the high ground in the 307th's zone.

The frontal and flanking fire that had driven back 2/5 stopped the 3d Battalion shortly after it had crossed the line of departure on 2 May. "The advance was untenable and had to be withdrawn to initial positions."[58] The battalion spent the day in limited patrolling and extensive mopping-up action. Because the 5th Marines had failed to advance, Company L on the left of 3/1 was stopped when Lieutenant Colonel Sabol's battalion made its attack. Company K, however, was able to move out through Miyagusuku and progress beyond the edge of the town.

At 1446, Colonel Chappell received orders from division to change the direction of his regiment's attack from due south to southeast. This change would bring pressure to bear on the flank of many of the positions holding up the 5th Marines and enable Company L to advance.

Jumping off at 1630 after a ten-minute artillery preparation, 3/1, with Company K leading, fought its way to a series of small hills about 300 yards south of Miyagusuku. Machine-gun fire and knee mortar shells fell continually on the forward elements, and when the companies were ordered to dig in at 2000 and hold the ground they had taken, a series of heavy infiltration attempts began. The night was marked by violent hand-to-hand clashes on the hill held by Company K as the Japanese and Marines struggled to gain possession of the high ground. Company K won, but only after enduring the grimmest night it was to spend on Okinawa.[59]

The 1st Battalion ran into equally heavy opposition during its attack on 2 May. Lieutenant Colonel Murray's plan called for Com-

FIRING LINE of 1st Division Marines engages the enemy defenses in the broken ground southeast of Machinato airfield.

pany C to move through Nakanishi and cross the ravine where it angled north toward Miyagusuku. At the same time Company B was to force the mouth of the ravine and take the high ground to the south. The battalion reserve, Company A, was to be committed on either flank of Company B as the situation dictated.

Company C attacked through Nakanishi at 0920 and was ready to plunge into the ravine by 1000. The slowness of the attack on his left led Colonel Chappell to warn Murray to proceed with caution in order not to expose his troops to enfilade fire.

Self-propelled assault guns had been used against the enemy positions on the south side of the ravine since the attack opened in the morning. Company B was able to move into the mouth as these positions were partially silenced. However, when the men reached the floor of the defile they were caught in the rear by fire from Japanese in caves on the northern side. Heavy flanking fire from a nose of ground at the bend in the ravine poured down on them. Company C was also punished by fire from this position, and although the men managed to brave the fusillade and reach a defiladed position, the unit was cut off front and rear by the enemy fire. A general withdrawal was ordered at 1300 and the companies pulled back to high ground using smoke cover to evacuate their casualties.

[57] *2/5 SAR*, 3–4.
[58] LtCol M. C. Roth Ltr to CMC, 18Mar55.
[59] *3/1 SAR*, 13.

When the division order shifting the direction of attack was relayed to Murray, he secured permission to take the plateau across the ravine in order to protect his flank before making the change. Because both Companies B and C were badly shot up, he requested a company from 2/1 to support the attack, and Company F started moving up.

At 1630, Company A moved through B's lines and attacked straight across the ravine west of the mouth. Maintaining the impetus of its drive, the company approached Jichaku and dug in at dusk. Company F, ordered to move up to support Company A, did not cross the ravine until after dark and consequently elements of the unit became separated. Fortunately, the night passed comparatively quietly for the assaut companies, and a firm line was established by morning.[60]

The last major element of the 1st Division moved south on 2 May when the 7th Marines shuttled its battalions to the vicinity of Uchitomari. The following day, Colonel Snedeker moved his command post to a point 200 yards north of Gusukuma, and the 1st and 2d Battalions displaced to beach defense positions northwest of Machinato airfield.

For the attack on 3 May, the 1st Division designated two objective lines for the 1st Marines, the first stretching along the railroad track from the bridge across the Asa Kawa to a point opposite Miyagusuku and the second from the same bridge to Uchima and including Dakeshi. The boundary between regiments was switched to intercept the corps boundary just north of Dakeshi. The 5th Marines was given the job of cleaning out the tangled gorges and precipitous hills that became known as the Awacha Pocket.

The day's attack netted about 300–600 yards in the 5th Marines' zone, but the 1st made only limited gains. Company F ran into a stubborn defense in Jichaku, and Company A was badly cut up while attempting to reduce the elbow position in the ravine that had checked Company C on 2 May. Both assault units were subjected to murderous fire throughout the morning and it seemed impossible for them to advance without the protection of tanks. Colonel Chappell granted Lieutenant Colonel Murray's request to withdraw his forward units under cover of smoke late in the morning. Plans were made for engineers to remove mines that blocked a tank approach along the west coast as soon as darkness hid the men from enemy observation posts in the Shuri heights.[61]

Company L on the left of 3/1's line was not to move out on 3 May until attacking units of 3/5 seized a hill to the company's left front. At 1555, 3/5, which had taken the objective, was driven off by heavy artillery fire. Company L was then ordered to attack the same hill and gained its top within a half-hour behind an 81mm mortar barrage. It was unable to move forward, however, because the Japanese on high ground to the front and flanks pinned down the assault platoons. Company K, which had attempted to come up on the right of L, was unable to maintain its position and had to fall back. Company I was committed on the right of K to close a gap that developed along the battalion boundary; therefore, regiment assigned Company G of 2/1 to back-up the 1,200-yard 3d Battalion front.[62]

Company K of 3/5, driven off the hill on 3/1's left during the afternoon's attack, fell back 100 yards to escape heavy machine-gun and mortar fire. Advances for the battalion on 3 May were limited to 200–300 yards because of the strong opposition. The 1st Battalion (Lieutenant Colonel Charles W. Shelburne) passed through 2/5 with Companies C and A in assault in the morning and gained 400–600 yards, but had to bend back its lines to tie in with Company I at 1620.[63] Upon its relief 2/5 had swung to the left and taken over part of the lines of the 307th

---

[60] 1/1 SAR, 4–7. The CO of Co F, Capt Edward R. Tiscornia, was killed by a sniper as his unit moved up and as a result of the necessary reorganization the advance across the ravine was delayed until after dark.

[61] Ibid., 7–8. The infantry-engineer patrol which moved out that night was almost cut off by a large enemy unit that attempted to work its way around to the patrol's rear. The patrol discovered that the coastal road was blocked by a huge crater flanked by rice paddies and consequently was unsuitable as a tank route.

[62] 3/1 SAR, 14.

[63] 1/5 SAR, 1–2.

Infantry on the outskirts of Awacha. The volume and intensity of enemy fire received during the day indicated that the 1st Division's turning movement to cut off the Awacha Pocket was to be bitterly contested and costly to the attackers.

When 2/307 was relieved by 2/5 at Awacha, the Army battalion shifted to the left and took over part of 1/307's zone. The regiment, using all three of its battalions, mopped up the top of the escarpment and the upper part of its reverse slopes during the day. Supported by fire from the 306th Infantry, the assault companies worked over enemy emplacements and sealed caves and pillboxes to consolidate their hold on the high ground. After the day's action the 307th held lines that commanded the Japanese positions all the way to the Shuri foothills. The enemy, although pushed back, was still making a determined resistance from caves on the reverse slope and counterattacking with company- and platoon-sized units to regain key ground.

The 306th Infantry from its positions forward of Maeda and on Hill 138 also supported the attack of the 17th Infantry at Kochi during the day. Both 1/17 and 3/17 tried again to take Kochi Ridge but the enemy laid down a massive artillery and mortar concentration, backed up by small-arms and machine-gun fire, to drive the assault troops back. The 184th Infantry maintained a constant pressure against the outlying positions blocking the approach to Conical Hill but advances for the day were negligible.

All along the XXIV Corps front the ferocity of enemy resistance was undiminished. As veteran Japanese units were decimated, they were rebuilt with rear area replacements and new infantry elements were introduced to the line. The prediction of General Hodge at the start of the 19 April attack that "it is going to be really tough . . . and that I see no way to get [the Japanese] out except blast them out yard by yard," [64] was being grimly fulfilled.

---

[64] CG, XXIV Corps Ltr to CGAFPOA, 17Apr45, quoted in *Okinawa: The Last Battle*, 185.

CHAPTER VIII

IIIAC Enters the Lists

The steady attrition of the XXIV Corps drive to the south was reflected in mounting Japanese casualty figures. By the end of April the 62d Division, which bore the brunt of the early fighting, had been reduced to less than half its original combat strength. Many officers of the Thirty-second Army, although pessimistic regarding the chances of eventual Japanese victory on Okinawa, were encouraged by a significant fact. They considered it to be "an unprecedented occurrence since the start of the Pacific War that after thirty consecutive days of systematic fighting the main body of one of [their] fighting forces should remain intact."[1] Most of the units of the 24th Division, 44th IMB, and 5th Artillery Command were as yet untouched by the fury of the battle for the Shuri defenses. The sentiment at enemy headquarters was overwhelmingly in favor of committing these fresh troops *en masse* in a concerted effort to stop the American advance.

JAPANESE COUNTERATTACK[2]

The fear of an American landing at Minatoga dominated Thirty-second Army planning during early April; in fact, the army staff decided that "such a landing could be executed relatively safely and easily, and, moreover, it would bring a prompt ending to the fighting."[3] The Japanese officers felt that successful exploitation of a beachhead south of Shuri would enable General Buckner's men to cut the Thirty-second Army in two and defeat it in detail.

By 20 April it was apparent to both sides that the overextended 62d Division could not hold its lines much longer without substantial reinforcement. If the Thirty-second Army persisted in keeping the majority of its troops positioned below the Naha-Yonabaru valley to meet a threatened American landing, that could only lead to the swift collapse of the Shuri defenses. So the Japanese made a reappraisal of their objectives. Since General Ushijima's mission was to prolong the battle and inflict the heaviest casualties possible, he decided to concentrate the Thirty-second Army in defense of the strongest position on Okinawa—the Shuri bastion.

Consequently, orders were issued to the 24th Division and the 44th IMB to begin moving north on 22 April. The 24th Division was to recover control of its 22d Regiment from the 62d Division and take over the right sector of the defensive position, occupying a line from Gaja on the east coast to Maeda at the eastern end of the Urasoe-Mura Escarpment. The 62d Division's shattered battalions were to concen-

---

[1] *Okinawa Operations Record,* 75–76.

[2] Unless otherwise noted the material in this section is derived from *Okinawa Operations Record; Intel-Mono; Shimada Interrogation; Yahara Interrogation; Tenth Army AR; XXIV Corps AR; 1st MarDiv SAR; 7th InfDiv AR; 77th InfDiv OpRpt, Okinawa; 1st Mar SAR; 5th Mar SAR; 7th Mar SAR.*

[3] *Okinawa Operations Record,* 69.

trate in the area from Maeda to the west coast near Gusukuma. Backing up the 62d from positions on the high ground to the south and east of the Asa Kawa, the 44th IMB would cover Naha and the ridges and draws on Shuri's western flank.

The area below the Naha-Yonabaru valley was not to be completely denuded of Japanese troops. Admiral Ota's naval force was still charged with the defense of Oroku Peninsula, and a makeshift guard organization formed from miscellaneous artillery, engineer, service, and supply elements was assigned to protect the Chinen Peninsula area. Should the Americans attempt a landing, the orders to Army troops were to make a fighting withdrawal to Shuri where the battle would be continued to the death of the last defender.

By 27 April the 24th Division had completed movement to its sector north and east of Shuri, and the 44th IMB was in position below the Asa Kawa. The steady advance of XXIV Corps assault battalions was continuing despite the infusion of new strength into the Japanese front line. On the west coast near Machinato airfield and in the center at Maeda and Kochi, the defending troops were gradually pushed back as small, local counterattacks failed to regain lost ground. At Thirty-second Army headquarters below Shuri Castle the proponents of aggressive action, led by General Cho, were able to convince General Ushijima that the time was ripe to use the relatively intact 24th Division as the spearhead of an all-out Army counterattack. There was one lone dissenter to this plan, Colonel Hiromichi Yahara, senior staff officer and operations chief.

The colonel pointed out that "to take the offensive with inferior forces against absolutely superior enemy forces is reckless and would only lead to certain defeat." He noted further that the Japanese would have to attack the Americans in positions on commanding ground, making it "more and more definite that the offensive would end in failure." Yahara maintained that the only sensible course in keeping with the army's mission was the continuation of:

. . . its current operation, calmly recognizing its final destiny—for annihilation is inevitable no matter

what is done—and maintain to the bitter end the principle of a strategic holding action. If we should fail, the period of maintaining a strategic holding action as well as the holding action for the decisive battle for the homeland would be shortened. Moreover, our forces would inflict but small losses on the enemy, while on the other hand, scores of thousands of our troops would be sacrificed in vain as victims of the offensive.[4]

Although Colonel Yahara strove desperately to make his views prevail, General Cho, backed by the division and brigade commanders, won the decision. The plan of attack that evolved was exceedingly ambitious. Its aim was the destruction of the XXIV Corps and its ultimate objective the area around Futema which the Japanese believed to be the location of Tenth Army headquarters.[5]

The day of attack (X-Day) was tentatively set as 4 May and the hour (Y-Hour) as 0500. The 24th Division was to make the initial assault with three regiments abreast. On the east, the 89th Regiment attacking at Y-Hour was to penetrate the front of the U. S. 7th Division and advance to the hills near Minami-Uebaru by sunset. In the center, the 22d Regiment was to hold its positions near Onaga and Kochi and support the attack of flanking units by fire. When the Japanese attack reached an east-west line through Tanabaru, the 22d was to move out, destroy the American units to its front, and follow up the assault in the center rear of the advancing units. On the west of the 24th Division zone, the 32d Regiment, making the division's main effort, would drive forward at Y-Hour, seize the U. S. 77th Division's positions southeast of Maeda, and take the heights west of Tanabaru by sundown on X-Day. (See Map 22, Map Section)

The 27th Tank Regiment, moving from positions near Ishimmi, was to penetrate the 77th Division's lines to the west of Kochi and support in turn the attacks of the 32d and 22d Regiments. The 44th IMB was to shift to the area northeast of Shuri on 3 May ready to follow the attack of the 32d Regiment by an advance to the west coast at Oyama. The brigade was then to turn south isolating the 1st Marine

---

[4] *Ibid.,* 76–77.

[5] Actually the Futema area was the location of the CP of the 96th InfDiv.

Division and annihilating it with the help of the 62d Division, the only major Japanese unit not committed to the attack.

The full power of General Wada's 5th Artillery Command was assigned to support the assault. During the night of 3–4 May the guns, mortars, and howitzers were to move out of their hidden firing positions into the open where they would be free to use maximum elevation and traverse. Even the naval base force was to play its part. Admiral Ota was directed to form four "crack" infantry battalions as an exploitation reserve to be committed on Thirty-second Army order.

The open flanks of the XXIV Corps position were not forgotten in the Japanese attack plan. The main strength of the 26th Shipping Engineer Regiment, using a miscellany of landing barges, small boats, and native canoes, was to embark at Naha on the night of 3–4 May and land behind the 1st Marine Division front at Oyama. At the same time elements of the 26th, 28th, and 29th Sea Raiding Squadrons were to bypass the Marine lines by wading the reef and move inland in support of the counterlanding. In all about 700 men were committed to the west coast attack. On the east coast, the same plan was to be followed with approximately 500 men from 23d Shipping Engineer Regiment and 27th Sea Raiding Squadron attempting to come ashore at Tsuwa behind the 7th Division's front lines.

Both regiments were to infiltrate American rear areas in small groups using grenades and demolition charges to destroy equipment and harass command posts. The raiders were not to make a concerted attack unless they had at least 100 men together. If all went well the two units were to join up near the center of the island and assist the 24th Division's advance.[6]

The Thirty-second Army was able to get air support from Japan and Formosa for its proposed attack. Starting at dusk on 3 May, flights of enemy bombers from Kyushu were slated to hit Yontan and Kadena airfields in an attempt at catching TAF planes on the ground. After this preliminary air raid, the fifth major *Kami-*

kaze attack in less than a month was to be made on the support vessels of TF 51.

Although both Tenth Army and XXIV Corps considered a full scale counterattack to be a definite enemy capability, the weight of evidence on the evening of 3 May favored a delaying action from successive positions with the Japanese "defending each position until the troops on the position are nearly annihilated." [7] Elements of the infantry regiments of the 24th Division had been identified as part of the enemy force opposing the 7th and 77th Divisions, but there were no indications that a major attack was imminent. No particular significance was attached to the determined attempts of the 32d Regiment and the 62d Division to regain the commanding heights at the eastern end of the Urasoe-Mura Escarpment. Local counterattacks to retake lost ground had been part of the enemy defensive pattern since L-Day, and the stiffened nature of Japanese resistance was easily attributed to the presence of fresh troops in the front lines. The Japanese were successful in masking their counterattack preparations, but the XXIV Corps was alert and ready to handle the assault when it came.

At 1800 on 3 May enemy planes approaching Okinawa from the direction of Formosa made the first attack of a two-day struggle which Colonel Yahara called "the decisive action of the campaign." [8] For more than two hours Marine and Navy pilots and antiaircraft gunners, afloat and ashore, fought off a determined assault, downing 36 planes.[9] The enemy bombers, harassed by AA fire, unloaded at high altitudes over Yontan airfield and the Hagushi anchorage causing only superficial damage. It was a different story with the *Kamikaze* pilots whose will to die drove them through a wall of shell fragments and explosions toward their favorite targets, the picket ships. The destroyer *Little* and LSM 195 were sunk; two mine layers and an LCS were damaged.[10]

Shortly after midnight the first of an esti-

[6] 1st MarDiv G–2 PrdRpt No 39, 10May45, POW Interrogation No 38, Superior Pvt, Hq, 2d Co, 26th Shpg-EngRegt (CO's orderly).

[7] Tenth Army G–2 Rpt No 33, 28Apr45; Tenth Army G–2 Rpt No 39, 4May45.

[8] *Yahara Interrogation.*

[9] *CTF 51 AR*, Part III, 75–76.

[10] *Ibid.* Naval casualty figures were increased by 28 KIA, 128 WIA, and 77 MIA in this attack. *Ibid.*, Part V, Sect H, 9–10.

mated 60 enemy bombers began attacking Tenth Army rear areas. Again AA fire kept the planes high and the bombing erratic. The only serious damage was suffered by IIIAC Evacuation Hospital No. 3 near Sobe where a string of bombs demolished two dug-in surgery wards, killing 13 and wounding 36.[11] The use of "window" by the attacking enemy planes prevented radar-directed TAF night fighters from closing with the bombers.[12]

With daylight the *Kamikazes* resumed the attack, timing their approach to coincide with Thirty-second Army assaults ashore. From 0600 to 1000 the suicide pilots attempted to reach the Hagushi anchorage; only one succeeded and he crashed into a turret on the cruiser *Birmingham*, leaving 25 dead, 60 wounded, and 17 missing in his wake. On the picket line losses and damage again were heavy. Two destroyers, *Luce* and *Morrison*, and two LSM's went to the bottom; two more destroyers, a mine sweeper, and an LCS were damaged. In addition the light mine layer *Shea* was hit by a *baka* bomb [13] and suffered severe fire damage and flooding, with 25 men reported killed.

Early in the evening of 4 May, suicide planes made another attack, this time striking the escort carrier group of TF 51. A *Kamikaze* plunged right through the flight deck of the *Sangamon*, and the resultant explosion damaged both elevators and destroyed 21 planes. The toll of Japanese planes downed on 4 May reached 95 as this last attack subsided. But the cost in naval casualties was also impressive: 91 KIA, 280 WIA, and 283 MIA.[14]

The Navy's contribution to the repulse of the coordinated Japanese attack was not confined to beating off aerial assaults. Cruisers, destroyers, and gunboats on "flycatcher" [15] duty off both coasts discovered the attempts of the shipping engineer regiments to slip behind American lines and aided ground forces with illumination and gunfire in meeting the counterlandings. When the full strength of the Japanese attack revealed itself at dawn on 4 May, the NGF force assigned to XXIV Corps for daylight support, two battleships, five cruisers, and eight destroyers, joined with artillery and air to smash the advancing infantry and silence enemy supporting weapons.

Japanese artillery had begun firing with darkness on 3 May and as the night wore on the volume of fire steadily increased with shells falling mainly on the forward positions of the 7th and 77th Divisions. A regular gun duel ensued as American artillery battalions replied.

On the quiet sector of the front shortly after 0100, LVT(A) crews guarding the shore near Machinato airfield opened up on unidentified persons they heard on the beach. Naval support craft were soon observed directing low angle fire at targets in the water just offshore.[16] Less than an hour after this initial outbreak of firing the 1st Marines reported enemy barges heading in for shore at Kuwan.

The landing craft, which carried the bulk of the attacking forces, had had trouble with the reefs and lost their way.[17] Instead of reaching their objective, Oyama, well in the rear of Marine lines, the Japanese turned shoreward at the exact point where Company B of 1/1 had anchored its night defense position. The stealthy approach was undetected by beach sentries until the enemy set up a terrific din of screeching battle cries that revealed their pres-

---

[11] Tenth Army G-2 Rpt No 40, 5May45.

[12] Window is a term used to denote the fragments of metal foil scattered by planes to confuse radar operators and cloud their screens with multiple sightings of nonexistent aircraft. Its use by the Japanese enabled many of their night attacks to reach Okinawa relatively unscathed.

[13] The *baka* ("foolish") bomb was a piloted, rocket-driven suicide missile carried to the target by a twin-engined bomber. Although it was potentially very dangerous, the *baka* achieved limited success because of low fuel capacity, poor maneuverability, and the lack of training of its doomed pilots.

[14] *CTF 51 AR*, Part III, 77–79; Part V, Sect H, 9–10.

[15] During the operation support craft were assigned nightly to an anti-small boat screen. Heavier fire support ships were designated to control the screen, to illuminate points of activity on request, and to harass suspected boat locations. These ships were dubbed "flycatchers" as the result of their success on a night following a warning by Adm Turner to "be particularly alert as this looks like a fine night for flycatching." *Ibid.*, Part V, Sect C, 6.

[16] 3d ArmdAmphBn SAR, Nansei Shoto Operation, 1Jul45, 12–13.

[17] 1st MarDiv G-2 PrdRpt No 39, 10May45, POW Interrogation No 38, Superior Pvt, Hq, 2dCo, 26th ShpgEngRegt (CO's orderly).

WOUNDED MARINES are placed in the shelter of an LVT while mopping-up operations proceed against survivors of the Japanese counterlanding. (Navy photograph)

ence. It was all the warning the Marines needed.

Mortars and heavy machine guns sited to cover the reef began firing at the crowded barges, some of which carried as many as a hundred men. Rifle grenadiers from the defending platoon of Company C (attached to Company B) which held the extreme right flank of the 1st Battalion's line found targets in the open boats. Soon a weird half-light from flares, tracers, and burning barges suffused the area. Riflemen and machine gunners fired at bobbing heads in the water and raked the reef to stop the determined attackers.[18]

Reinforcements had been dispatched by Colonel Chappell as soon as word of the attack was received. The 2d Battalion, in regimental reserve, sent Company E to close on the right flank of the Company C platoon. LVT(A)'s from the 3d Provisional Armored Amphibian Battalion helped to seal off the landing area by taking up positions on the reef above Kuwan. By 0245 the ring of fire was complete and the Japanese survivors on the beach were being steadily pounded by all available weapons.

Some of the first enemy troops to get ashore had been able to infiltrate into the rear of 1/1's lines before the trap was sprung. Company F, holding the right flank forward of Company B's position, engaged these raiders in an intense

fire fight that ended with 75 enemy dead lying scattered in and around the Marines' positions.[19]

After the dispatch of Company E to Kuwan to contain the enemy attack, Colonel Chappell was left with one rifle company (G) as regimental reserve. The uncertainty of the situation prompted him to request the attachment of a battalion of the 7th Marines to his regiment. Division approved his request, and at 0300 2/7 began moving south through moderate enemy shelling to report to 1/1 for orders. Lieutenant Colonel Berger and his S–3 preceded the unit and at 0500 arrived at the 1st Battalion command post. The situation was well in hand. Except for scattered enemy groups hiding out in Kuwan, the bulk of the 300–400 who had attempted the main landing were dead, sprawled on the beach along the seawall or aimlessly floating amid the gutted hulks of their landing craft. At 0645, 2/7 was given the mission of mopping up the counterlanding area and began relieving the right flank elements of 1/1 so that the 1st Battalion's attack to the south could continue.[20]

The landing at Kuwan was not the only one attempted behind the 1st Division front that night. Scattered small enemy groups, most using native canoes, were able to get ashore farther up the coast, an estimated 65 landing near

---

[18] *1/1 SAR*, 8.

[19] 2d Bn, 1st Mar Narrative Rpt-ICEBERG, 23Feb–22Jun45, n. d., 4, hereinafter cited as *2/1 SAR*. "Some of the enemy troops who got ashore were able to work their way well inland. One enemy soldier was located the following evening within 50 yards of 3/5's CP where he attempted to run from a small cave, at dusk, carrying an explosive charge." Col J. C. Miller, Jr. Ltr to CMC, 22Mar55.

[20] 2d Bn, 7th Mar SAR, 2 May–22Jun45, 2Jul45, 4, hereinafter cited as *2/7 SAR*. "The final pocket of Japanese was wiped out early in the afternoon when a Company E patrol from 2/7 encountered about 30 enemy in the pandanus growth along the seawall. Company mortars, walking fire in from the water to bring their 60mm rounds within 15 yards of friendly troops, finally destroyed the enemy. From the time of their night landing until engaged by the patrol, the Japanese, digging through the twisting roots of the thick pandanus, had completed three trenches, one behind the other, at right angles from the seawall. The waist-deep trenches were approximately 30 feet long and were joined by connecting trenches parallel to the seawall." Capt V. E. Ludwig Interview, 13Dec54.

Isa in the vicinity of the division command post. The more usual fate of the attackers was to die in the water as the combined fire of naval vessels, LVT(A)'s, infantry, and service troops caught their boats before they could make the beach. Those few score Japanese able to reach shore were doomed with the coming of daylight to be hunted down and killed. A carrier pigeon found in the possession of one of the raiding groups was released to carry back a message to enemy headquarters that said: "We are returning your pigeon. Sorry we can not return your demolition engineers." [21]

At approximately the same time the 26th Shipping Engineers were attempting to wreak havoc behind the Marine front, the 23d Regiment attempted to put its boats ashore in the 7th Infantry Division zone. Naval patrol vessels spotted the attempt, illuminated the area with star shells, and opened fire. On shore the 7th Division Reconnaissance Troop, guarding the Yonabaru airfield area, cut loose with all its firepower and joined the naval craft in completely destroying the attack. Only an estimated 20 men were able to get to the beach and these were soon eliminated. Those lucky few engineers whose boats escaped the holocaust turned back to their starting points, leaving behind some 400 dead. [22] With the defeat of counterlanding attempts on both coasts, the flanks of XXIV Corps were secure, and the opening move of the Thirty-second Army ground attack had ended in abject failure.

The steady fury of enemy artillery fire reached a screaming crescendo at 0430 when the Japanese began a half-hour preparation for the 24th Division's attack. More than 7,600 rounds were fired in the preparatory phase, and 5th Artillery Command's guns hurled 8,600 more during the course of the day's action. [23] In addition, many thousands of mortar rounds fell on the front lines as attacking troops sought to penetrate XXIV Corps defenses. In the gray light of dawn the 24th Division's assault units moved forward through their own supporting fire, taking heavy casualties in order to reach the American lines. Most of the company- and battalion-sized attacks died aborning in the smother of destruction laid down by NGF, air, and 16 battalions of division artillery, backed up by corps artillery's 12 battalions of 155mm guns and 155mm and 8-inch howitzers. With daylight the first of 134 planes to fly supporting missions for XXIV Corps on 4 May made its initial bombing run. By 1900, 77 tons of bombs, 450 rockets, and 22,900 rounds of machine-gun and cannon fire had been expended on Japaneses troop concentrations and artillery positions. [24] Despite the fact that the area was under heavy enemy air attack, NGF support vessels, whose power ranged from the 14-inch rifles of the *New York* and *Colorado* [25] to the mortars and 20mms of the ubiquitous support craft, ranged the coastal waters delivering observed and called fires on enemy targets.

Because Thirty-second Army had directed that a heavy screen of smoke be laid on American lines to cover the Japanese advance, staff observers on the heights of Shuri could not see the progress of their battle. However, "good news" had poured into the army command post at the start of the attack telling of "the success of the offensive carried out by the 24th Division." [26] Unfortunately for the Japanese, the overly imaginative reports of assault commanders did not reflect the true situation.

On the east coast, the initial attack of the 89th Regiment was repulsed by 7th Division defenders, and all subsequent attempts by the enemy unit to reorganize and renew its advance were prevented by the storm of supporting fire that covered assembly areas and routes of approach. By noon the threat of attack was gone, and front line regiments were mopping up the scattered and demoralized elements of the 89th that had penetrated to the American positions.

In the center of the line the Japanese 22d Regiment was never able to fulfill its role of following up the "successful" advance of flank

[21] 1st MarDiv War Diary, May 1945, 5.

[22] Tenth Army POW Interrogation Rpt No 10, Sgt Hiroshi Tamae, Hq, 23d ShpgEngRegt.

[23] *XXIV Corps AR*, 29. Estimated figures for this preparation and support vary in most sources, but in this instance the report of the unit commanding the area attacked has been accepted.

[24] *XXIV Corps Arty AR*, 8; Annex C, Enclosure No 2, 8.

[25] *CTF 51 AR*, Part V, Sect C, 53.

[26] *Okinawa Operations Record*, 81.

units, and the regiment spent the day locked in a violent fire fight with men of 3/306, 3/17, and 1/17 holding the Kochi-Onaga area. The Japanese reported the 22d "was not able attain results worth mentioning."[27]

The highest hopes and greatest strength of the 24th Division were centered in the 32d Regiment's attempt to gain control of the escarpment near Maeda, thus breaching the 77th Division's lines and opening a hole through which the waiting 44th IMB could pour into the 1st Marine Division's rear area. The 1st and 3d Battalions of the 306th Infantry, holding the left of the 77th lines, turned back the first tank-led assaults launched by the 32d Regiment. Rebuffed in this attempt to gain the high ground flanking the central island corridor leading to Futema, the Japanese concentrated their efforts on driving the 307th Infantry off the top of the Urasoe-Mura Escarpment.

A day-long succession of strong enemy counterattacks hit all along the front of 307th as the regiment attempted to gain the south slopes of the hill mass. Attackers and defenders, often locked in hand-to-hand combat, seesawed back and forth over the ridge crest, but the constant pounding of supporting weapons whittled the strength of the 32d Regiment down, and nightfall found all three battalions of the 307th firmly dug-in on the south slope of the escarpment. The major effort of the Japanese counterattack had failed and XXIV Corps could report that its troops had either securely held their original positions or taken more enemy ground on 4 May.

The farthest advance of XXIV Corps during the day's action was made in the 1st Division zone. The time of the Marines' morning attack had been successively delayed from 0800 to 0900 to 1000 while unit reorganization and ammunition replenishment necessitated by the counterlanding attempt took place. When the assault battalions of the 1st and 5th Marines moved out, they were hit immediately by heavy fire from well-integrated defensive positions of the Japanese 62d Division.

Company F attacking on the right of 1/1 was soon pinned down in the ruins of Jichaku, and Company A, which attempted to bypass the village, was stopped by murderous fire coming from a defile in a ridge to its front. Japanese heavy machine guns emplaced in the ruins of a sugar mill on the south bank of the Asa Kawa had a clear field of fire through the gap, which was itself strongly defended by dug-in enemy positions. Lieutenant Colonel Murray, noting the moderate opposition on his left where 3/1 was advancing, decided to exploit the weak flank of the gap position.

At 1600 Company C in assault with B following immediately to the rear crossed the low ground to the right of 3/1 and drove to the heights overlooking the left of the defile and the river to the front. Casualties were surprisingly light and the two companies dug in for the night in firm possession of their attack objective. Except for a short stretch of enemy ground from the gap to the eastern edge of Jichaku, the 1st Battalion was only a few hundred yards from its final objective, the north bank of the Asa Kawa.[28]

Lieutenant Colonel Sabol's 3d Battalion had not had an easy time of it on 4 May, but the commander was able to keep the positions won by his forward elements. Company I on the right flank moved out at 1000 and gained a hold on a ridge 300–400 yards to its front where it was exposed to damaging enemy fire from three sides. The steady drain of casualties was slowed by noon as Companies K and C came up on either flank and took the defending positions under fire. With Company L keeping pace with the 5th Marines' flank in that regiment's eastward drive, a gap quickly opened between it and Companies K and I. Late in the afternoon, the 2d Battalion (less Company F) was moved to a blocking position south of Yafusu to cover this space and stop any enemy breakthrough attempt.[29] Although all three of its battalions were now committed to hold the ever-widening regimental front, the 1st Marines had a sure grasp on the ground taken during the day's advance.

In the 5th Marines' zone, 2/5, holding the high ground on the 77th Division boundary, remained in position during the day's action and

[27] *Ibid.*

[28] *1/1 SAR*, 8–10.
[29] *3/1 SAR*, 15–16.

supported the advance of 3/307 and 1/5 on its flanks. Lieutenant Colonel Shelburne's 1st Battalion pivoted on 2/5 and its own left company and swung its right through 400 yards of hotly-contested broken ground during the day. On the right of the regimental zone 3/5 continued the plan of cutting off the strong enemy pocket in the gorge forward of Awacha and pushed Company L on its left up to tie in with the right of 1/5. Company I, moving forward about 250 yards along the battalion boundary, kept pace with the advance of 3/1. By early afternoon the 3d Battalion's front, moving both south and southeast, had stretched very thin, and a sizeable hole had developed between Companies L and I. At 1500, division attached 3/7 to the 5th Marines and Colonel Griebel moved the battalion to a blocking position behind 3/5. In order to strengthen the lines for night defense, Company K of 3/7 was committed to cover the gap.

An aura of gloom pervaded the Japanese Thirty-second Army command post on the evening of 4 May. It was obvious to even the most rabid fire-breathers that the ground offensive had failed. But hope dies hard, and General Amamiya, commanding the 24th Division, ordered the 32d Regiment to try again under cover of darkness what it had failed to do during the day. At 0200 on 5 May, following a heavy mortar and artillery barrage, the regiment smashed into the front lines of the 77th Division, attempting to penetrate the positions of the 306th Infantry. American artillery broke up this effort, but the enemy returned to the attack at dawn, this time led by tanks. Again the assault was stopped, six tanks were knocked out, and the remnants of the 32d forced to withdraw. The 3d Battalion had been badly mauled, the 2d wiped out,[30] and the 1st, although it scored an initial success, was doomed to the same fate.

In the confusion of the counterattacks a substantial portion of 1/32 was able to infiltrate the 77th Division's lines on the east side of the Ginowan road. Moving cross-country in column, the enemy battalion retook Tanabaru and established a defensive position on the escarpment to the northeast of the village where it was joined by other scattered infiltrating groups that had been able to slip through the lines on 4 May.

The task of reducing this strong point, which was just within the 7th Division's zone, fell to the 17th Infantry's reserve battalion, 2/17. A dogged battle was fought behind the lines for three days before the last of more than 400 enemy troops was eliminated. Some elements of 1/32, led by the battalion commander, managed to escape the Tanabaru death trap and return to the Shuri lines. General Ushijima commended the skeletal battalion for its "success" behind the American lines, but the gesture was a hollow one.

The Thirty-second Army needed such a morale boost, however empty or futile it may have been. One Japanese platoon leader, probably a member of the 15th IMR, noted in his diary on 6 May that "there's an unsavory rumor current that the situation at the front is critical." [31] The actions of 5 May may well have prompted his concern. Taking advantage of the dazed condition of enemy 24th Division units, the 7th and 77th Infantry Divisions had sent strong patrols into the counterattack area to mop up enemy remnants and count the numerous bodies left in the wake of American air, NGF, and artillery defending fires. Survivors of the various counterattacks were relentlessly hunted down while the Army divisions consolidated their positions and prepared for further advances. Only in the 1st Marine Division area was the pattern of resistance the same as it had been before the counterattack started.

Made even more desperate by the failure of the 24th Division's grand attack, the rag-tag battalions of the 62d Division made every yard of advance count in Marine lives. Concentrating their strength on the left of the 1st Division zone, the defenders fought to the death to guard the vital western approaches to Shuri. Each pillbox, cave, and tomb was the center of a storm of fire that hit attacking platoons from

---

[30] *Okinawa Operations Record*, Record of the 24th Div, 17–18 states: "The 2d Battalion was completely enveloped by the enemy and its escape became impossible."

[31] CinCPac-CinPOA Bull 212–45, Translations and Interrogations No 39, 30Aug45, Diary of unidentified platoon leader, 32d Army.

all sides. Despite this desperate resistance, the Marines were able to make substantial progress during the day.

The 5th Marines advanced its lines an average of 300 yards in the center and on the left, with 1/5 making the main effort. The battalion, attacking at 0730 with the support of 15 gun and two flame tanks,[32] managed to gain the nose of the high ground stretching west from Awacha before it was stopped by enfilade fire from both flanks. On the left, 2/5 moving through a deluge of enemy artillery fire, had made 250 yards, guiding its advance on 3/307 which was mopping up the reverse slopes of the escarpment. On the right, 3/5 had made no appreciable forward progress but had spent the day cleaning up the complex of enemy defenses in the vicinity of its night defense position. At dusk the regiment tied in solidly across its front, faced with the prospect of another day's painful advance into the fire lanes and impact areas of the enemy's Awacha defenses.

In the 1st Marines' zone the attack got off at 0800 with 2/1 moving through the 3d Battalion and advancing with 1/1 toward the Asa Kawa. By 1123 the 1st Battalion, with five rifle companies under its command (A, B, C, F, and I), had seized the high ground along the river to its center front against light resistance. Pockets of enemy on both flanks were destroyed during the afternoon, and by evening the battalion was dug in on commanding ground along the river line. The 2d Battalion, which had met much heavier enemy fire coming from its front and the village of Asa to the southwest, progressed slowly during the day. At 1600, Lieutenant Colonel Magee ordered his men to begin preparing strong night defenses to hold the ground between 3/5 and 1/1. Company L of 3/1 was positioned on high ground to the 2d Battalion's rear to cover any gaps in the line, and at 1735 Company F was released from attachment to 1/1 and moved to defensive positions in the vicinity of 2/1's command post. Although the 1st Division was ready for a renewal of the enemy counterattack in its zone, the night passed quietly.

A recapitulation of the cost of the two days' action in XXIV Corps zone showed that the 7th and 77th Divisions, which had blunted the full force of enemy counterattack, had lost 714 soldiers killed, wounded, and missing in action, while the 1st Division which had continued its drive to the south had taken corresponding losses of 649 Marines.[33]

It was the Japanese, however, who had taken the significant losses during the counterattack period. XXIV Corps counted 6,227 enemy dead, almost all of whom were irreplaceable veteran infantrymen. In addition to loss of men and equipment in the front lines, the enemy had 59 artillery pieces destroyed during the short time they were set up in open positions by the American air-NGF-artillery team. Tenth Army troops were never again to encounter artillery fire as heavy or as destructive as that which had covered the Japanese assault.

Colonel Yahara, who had vehemently opposed wasting men and materiel in an operation that had no chance of success, was vindicated in his prediction of the utter failure of the enemy counterattack. He won a tearful promise from General Ushijima that the army would follow Yahara's counsel in the future. The pattern of defense in the 62d Division zone was to be reinstituted across the entire enemy front. The 24th Division and 5th Artillery Command were directed to reorganize and shift to a holding action designed to bleed American strength by forcing the Tenth Army to continue its slow, deadly, yard-by-yard advance into the fire of prepared positions.

The definitive estimate of the value of the Japanese counterattack in the defense of Okinawa was furnished by its prime motivator, General Cho. "After this ill-starred action," the fiery Thirty-second Army chief of staff was reliably reported to have "abandoned all hope of a successful outcome of the operation and declared that only time intervened between defeat and the 32d Army."[34]

---

[32] *1st TkBn Summary*, 5May45.

[33] *Okinawa: The Last Battle*, 302; 1st MarDiv War Diary, May 1945, 5–6.

[34] *Shimada Interrogation*.

THE BATTLE LINES ARE DRAWN[35]

On 6 May Tenth Army subordinate units received Operation Order 7–45 which marked the beginning of a full strength drive to destroy the enemy's Shuri bastion. At 0600 on 7 May General Geiger was directed to take command of the 1st Marine Division's portion of the XXIV Corps front. At the same time General Buckner would assume direct tactical control of the two-corps attack. Geiger was further ordered to move the 6th Marine Division south from its concentration points near Chibana to take over the right of the 1st Division's zone of action. In preparation for a co-ordinated army assault, IIIAC and XXIV Corps were directed to advance and seize a jump-off line running generally east from Asa through Dakeshi to a road junction 1,000 yards northeast of Shuri and then southeast to the outskirts of Gaja. (See Map 23, Map Section)

On 6 May action in the 7th Division's zone was limited to aggressive patrolling in strength to develop the approaches to Conical Hill and wipe out the scattered remnants of the abortive Japanese counterattack. In the center of the XXIV Corps front the 77th Division during the night of 5–6 May smashed the last enemy effort to maintain a hold on the Urasoe-Mura Escarpment. Both the 306th and 307th Infantry beat back infiltration attempts, and 3/307 counted 250 enemy dead in front of its lines after repulsing a savage counterattack. Capitalizing on the severe losses it had inflicted on the Japanese defenders, the 307th, with 3/305 and 3/307 in assault, drove 800 yards down the division boundary during the day to lock its hold on the south slope of the escarpment. Cost of the bitter seven-day contest for the dominant high ground north of Shuri had been high to both sides, and "in the most severe

fighting any of the troops had ever experienced,"[36] the 77th Division had lost 197 men killed in action, while the enemy left behind more than 17 times as many—an estimated 3,417 dead.

Along the west coast, while preliminary plans were drafted for the movement of the 6th Marine Division into the front lines, the attack of the 1st Division on the Dakeshi-Awacha hill complex continued. The 7th Marines took over the right coastal flank of the division's line at 0730 when 2/7 relieved 1/1. At 0900 the 2d Battalion's left flank assault units attacked behind an artillery and NGF preparation to complete the seizure of the north bank of the Asa Kawa. Within 45 minutes Lieutenant Colonel Berger's men had advanced 400 yards to their objective and begun to dig in. Regimental and battalion supporting weapons were moved up to silence the enemy artillery, mortars, and machine guns firing from the hills across the estuary.

The new regimental boundaries narrowed the attack zone of the 1st Marines considerably and enabled the assault battalion commanders to concentrate their forces against the western approaches to the Dakeshi hill defenses. Concentration of power was urgently needed since the front line in the 1st Marines' area cut back sharply from the Asa Kawa to the positions of the 5th Marines north of the Awacha Pocket. Attacking units were subject to brutal frontal and flanking fire from a 1,000-yard-long maze of heavily organized hills and ridges that guarded Dakeshi's western flank.

When Lieutenant Colonel Sabol's 3d Battalion, with Companies I and L in assault, attacked to the south, the Japanese defenders from the 62d Division smashed the attempt handily. The enemy permitted Company I to reach its objective and then pinpointed the exposed assault platoons with a hail of machine-gun, mortar, and artillery fire. Although the men attempted to dig in, the effort was unsuccessful and the company withdrew under a continuous barrage of mortar fire.[37]

In 2/1's zone the story was much the same. Company F moved through the lines of Com-

[35] Unless otherwise noted the material in this section is derived from *Okinawa: The Last Battle; Tenth Army AR; XXIV Corps AR; 1st MarDiv SAR;* 6th MarDiv SAR, Okinawa Operation, Phase III, 30Jun45, hereinafter referred to as *6th MarDiv SAR, Ph III* (Rpts of subordinate units included as annexes to this SAR will be cited separately as *4th Mar SAR, Ph III; 1/4 SAR, Ph III;* etc.) ; *7th InfDiv AR; 77th InfDiv OpRpt, Okinawa; 96th InfDiv AR; 1st Mar SAR; 5th Mar SAR; 7th Mar SAR; 22d Mar SAR, Ph III.*

[36] *77th InfDiv OpRpt, Okinawa,* 43.
[37] *3/1 SAR,* 16–17.

pany L at 0945 and attacked west toward Hill 60 which commanded the battalion front. Tanks and assault guns accompanied the infantry, blasting caves and pillboxes to clear the path. A well-concealed enemy 47mm AT gun knocked out three tanks,[38] and continuous heavy AT fire neutralized the efforts of the rest of the armored support. Company F, like Company I, was able to reach its objective but equally unable to maintain its hold in the face of fierce enemy fire. Heavy casualties, coupled with the loss of tank support, made it doubtful that the assault platoons could hold against an enemy counterattack, and Lieutenant Colonel Magee ordered his men to withdraw. Company G furnished fire and smoke cover to the embattled unit, and by 1630 Company F had evacuated its casualties and drawn back to its jump-off positions where it was relieved by Company E.[39]

The enemy forces defending the gorge and ridges of the Awacha Pocket, the 23d Independent Infantry and 14th Independent Machine Gun Battalions,[40] held the 5th Marines to small gains during 6 May despite an intensive four-battalion artillery attack preparation[41] and the call missions fired by NGF and air. The 1st and 3d Battalions blasted and burned out caves and bunkers that had held up their advance the previous day with the help of relays of gun and flame tanks.[42] On the regimental left flank 2/5, which beat off a heavy counterattack at dawn, fought its way down the division boundary to link its lines with the 307th Infantry. By noon the battalion held an L-shaped front with all three companies on line, Companies G and F holding 450 yards along the division boundary and Company E joining its front with that of 1/5. The Army's advance on the left flank made it possible for 2/5 to concentrate its fire on the enemy reverse

slope positions that were holding up the rest of the regiment.

The lead message entered in the 1st Division G–3 Journal for 7 May was a commendation from General Hodge for the Marines' work while under his command.[43] During six days of desperate action the division had suffered 1,409 battle casualties, including 199 men killed in action and died of wounds, while securing the north bank of the Asa Kawa and the outer defenses of Dakeshi. At 0600 General Geiger officially assumed control of the 1st Marine Division zone of action and of the IIIAC artillery battalions that had been attached to XXIV Corps.[44] The 27th Infantry Division's artillery remained in position to reinforce the fires of Marine artillery in support of the III Corps attack.

Heavy rains on the morning of 7 May delayed the projected IIIAC advance until tanks were able to negotiate the muddy terrain. In the 1st Marines' zone, the new regimental commander, Colonel Arthur T. Mason,[45] ordered 3/1 to support the attack of the 2d Battalion on Hill 60 with all available weapons by firing into the enemy reverse slope defenses. All morning long the regiment's mortars concentrated on the enemy position, and at 1400 when tanks finally reached the front lines the battalion attacked with Company E in assault.

Artillery fire covered the foot of the objective while mortars and assault guns blanketed the crest and reverse slopes. The company swept to the top of Hill 60 by 1422 in a vivid demonstration of "the effect of properly massed, sup-

---

[38] *1st TkBn Summary*, 6May45.

[39] *2/1 SAR*, 4–5.

[40] *Okinawa Operations Record*, 86.

[41] This artillery preparation was typical of the interunit, inter-service efforts of the southern Okinawa campaign. The firing battalions were 2/11 (1st MarDiv), 104th FA Bn (27th InfDiv), 3d 155mm HowBn (IIIAC Arty), and 145th FA Bn (XXIV Corps Arty), *11th Mar SAR*, S–3 Rpt, 7May45.

[42] *1st TkBn Summary*, 6May45.

[43] *1st MarDiv G–3 Jnl*, 7May45.

[44] To support the IIIAC attack BrigGen Nimmer organized his artillery battalions into three groups: 2d Prov FA Grp (3d 155mm HowBn, 6th 155mm HowBn, 145th FA Bn) and the 27th InfDivArty (less 249th FA Bn) to provide reinforcing fires to the 11th and 15th Mar and a group of 155mm gun battalions (7th, 8th, and 9th) under LtCol E. P. Foley to deliver long-range reinforcing, counterbattery, interdiction, and harassing fires. The 1st 155mm HowBn remained under XXIV Corps Arty until 23 May when it reverted to parent control; on the same date the 145th FA Bn was returned to XXIV Corps. During the time IIIAC Arty battalions supported XXIV Corps (7Apr–6May) they fired 53,988 rounds of ammunition in a total of 2,344 missions. *IIIAC Arty AR*, 22–26.

[45] Col Mason relieved Col Chappell on 6May45.

CONICAL HILL, eastern anchor of the Shuri defenses, looms in the background of this shot of the 96th Division's zone of advance.   (Army Photograph)

porting fires in front of assault troops."[46] Once the company entered the impact zone, however, and supporting fires were shifted to other targets the enemy defenders emerged from their caves and engaged the Marines in hand grenade duels. Gradually the volume of Japanese fire of all types "grew noticeably stronger and progressively more intense so that it was evident that the enemy was receiving large reinforcements."[47] The threat of a strong counterattack measured against the dwindling strength of Company E forced Lieutenant Colonel Magee to adjudge the company's advanced position untenable and to order a withdrawal to the previous night's lines.[48]

The deep draw that cut across the front of 1/5 and the right of 2/5's positions was the heart of the enemy's Awacha defenses. At 0900 on 7 May, General del Valle and Colonel Griebel met with Lieutenant Colonels Shelburne and Benedict and their staffs to discuss methods of reducing the deeply dug-in Japanese positions that rimmed the draw and studded its steep slopes.[49] An extensive preparation by artillery, rockets, and air was planned, and a reinforced company of tanks was moved up in time to support the infantry when it jumped off at 1200.[50] In the center of the regiment's line, 1/5 methodically worked its way forward 300–400 yards to the edge of the draw while 3/5 and 2/5, aided by Company L of 3/7 which moved into the line on the 1st Bat-

---

[46] *2/1 SAR,* 5.

[47] *Ibid.* During this period the Thirty-second Army attached the 3d Bn, 2d InfUnit to the 62d Div "in order to relieve the crisis of the troops fighting in the vicinity of Dakeshi." *Okinawa Operations Record,* 85.

[48] *2/1 SAR,* 5–6.

[49] *2/5 SAR,* 8.

[50] *1st TkBn Summary,* 7May45.

talion's right,[51] maintained flanking pressure with small local advances. The day's progress was marked by intense close-quarter fighting with flame-thrower and demolition teams burning out and sealing enemy cave defenses. Although the gains made by 1/5 indicated the 62d Division's hold on the Awacha Pocket was slipping, the fury of opposition met gave no grounds for undue optimism.

The 77th Infantry Division, advancing through the same type of terrain that confronted the 1st Marine Division, garnered 400–500 yards of enemy territory on 7 May against increasingly stiffer resistance. The Japanese had completed the reorganization of their defenses after the disastrous 4–5 May counterattack and were well dug in to block the most direct route to Shuri. The 305th Infantry (less 2/305 at Kerama Retto), relieved of its garrison duties on Ie Shima by 27th Division units, moved into the 77th Division's line to replace the 307th Infantry and gave General Bruce a fresh regiment for use in the proposed Tenth Army attack.

Fresh troops were being readied behind the rest of the XXIV Corps front as the 96th Infantry Division, which had absorbed 4,000 replacements, terminated its rehabilitation and training activities and prepared to replace the 7th Division along the east coast. The 7th's assault regiments, the 17th and 184th Infantry, did not passively await relief, however, but drove ahead on 7 May to take Gaja Ridge and inch their way into the tangled network of defenses that guarded the western approaches to Conical Hill.

A cold, driving rain began to fall late in the afternoon of 7 May and continued through the night and the next day, immobilizing tank support along the entire Tenth Army front. The 17th Infantry, still hammering at the enemy ridge positions south of Kochi, fought an infantryman's battle where gains were measured in Japanese dead rather than yards of ground seized. The lack of effective cover and the loss of tank support on 8 May prevented the 184th Infantry from gaining ground in the flatlands along the coast and held its advances to

limited objectives in the foothills of the broken inland plateau near Kibara. During the day the 96th Infantry Division moved into assembly areas in the rear of the 7th's lines in preparation for relief operations.

Along the rest of the Tenth Army front on 8 May the rain effectively cancelled out planned offensive operations. Assault units mopped up in the vicinity of their night positions and sent patrols forward to spot enemy dispositions. In the 1st Division zone 75mm pack howitzers from 1/11 were manhandled into the front line in an unsuccessful effort to place direct fire on enemy emplacements.[52] During the morning the news of the victory in Europe was spread through the infantry units, drawing a universally apathetic reaction[53] from rain-soaked men whose immediate future was tied irrevocably to the battle plans of a deadly enemy in positions scant yards from their own. Exactly at 1200 every available artillery piece and naval gun fired three volleys at vital enemy targets to apprise the Japanese of the defeat of their Axis partner.

The 22d Marines, which General Shepherd had selected to lead the 6th Division's attack in southern Okinawa, moved out from Chibana on 8 May, and by 1530 2/22 and 3/22 had relieved 2/7 on its lines along the Asa Kawa. At 1600 the 6th Division commander assumed responsibility for his zone of the corps front.

The 22d Marines began their offensive action

---

[52] "One battery was sent to the 1st Marines, another to the 5th Marines (over artillery protest). Since neither the organic M–7's of the infantry nor the tanks would function satisfactorily, it was obvious that the truck-drawn pack howitzers could not. Neither battery accomplished anything. The battery with the 5th Marines was never used. Both batteries were returned on 11 May, but their parent battalion was emasculated throughout the period of their absence. 1/11 was then built up to a strength of 24 guns by adding LVT(A)'s. 75mm ammunition was plentiful, as contrasted with heavier calibers, so 1/11 (reinforced) was used to fire interdiction, harassing, and 'appeasement' missions across the front. Later two more batteries of LVT(A)'s were formed as artillery to thicken the fires of 2/11 and 3/11." *Brown 1955.*

[53] When the word of the defeat of Germany reached 3/1 the rifle companies were immediately notified and the most favored comment, typical perhaps of the reaction along the entire front, was "So What?" *3/1 SAR,* 18.

---

[51] 3d Bn, 7th Mar SAR, Phase III, 1Jul45, 1, hereinafter cited as *3/7 SAR.*

against the Japanese at daybreak on 9 May when patrols from Companies I and K of 3/22 were dispatched to reconnoiter the Asa Kawa and the ruined bridge that spanned it. The patrols reported that the bridge was impassable to foot and motorized traffic, that the depth of water in the estuary at high tide in its shallowest point was four feet, and that the river bed was mud. At noon the same companies sent out other patrols to find suitable crossing sites and to determine the strength and dispositions of the enemy.[54]

The Company I patrol crossed upstream and drew fire from positions along the river bank, but it noted that other caves and pillboxes farther south seemed unoccupied. Company K's patrol, which waded across the river at its mouth, met sufficient opposition to force it to withdraw, and its report included the finding that the soft river bed would not support a tank ford.

The 2d Battalion, in position near Uchima, also patrolled to its front during the day. Although no enemy activity was noted by Company E, which sent men out to the left flank and front, a Company G patrol that crossed the Asa Kawa promptly drew heavy fire. The patrol was able to rescue the pilot and observer of an artillery spotting plane which was shot down over enemy territory before it disengaged itself and withdrew. From the information gathered by all the patrols the division and regiment were able to formulate a workable plan for crossing the river and seizing a bridgehead which could be effectively exploited.

The 6th Engineer Battalion was ordered to move light bridging material up to the 22d Marines' area prepared to lay a footbridge across the estuary near the ruined bridge site after darkness. The 3d Battalion with 1/22 in support was to cross the river at 0300 on 10 May, secure the bank, and be ready to attack south at dawn. The 2d Battalion was to establish a strong point on high ground southwest of Uchima from which it could support the attack of 3/22 and 1/22.[55]

The plans of the 6th Marine Division to breach the Asa Kawa line were part of the over-all preparations for the Tenth Army attack. On 9 May Tenth Army Operation Order 8–45, which set the date of the attack for 11 May, was put into effect by dispatch. The immediate army objective was the envelopment and destruction of the enemy forces occupying the Shuri defenses and the ultimate mission was the total defeat of the Japanese Thirty-second Army.

The 1st Marine Division made substantial advances on 9 May which materially aided in straightening the division line. The division attack was first called off because of the muddy condition of the ground but then rescheduled for 1200 as it became evident that tanks would be able to furnish support to assault troops.

Colonel Mason decided to commit his 1st Battalion to crack the Hill 60 defenses. During the two days 1/1 had been in regimental reserve it had reorganized and absorbed 116 replacements to fill partially the gaps left by the 259 casualties it had suffered between 30 April and 6 May. The battalion moved into positions behind 2/1 and at 1205, following an artillery preparation, jumped off with Company C in assault to seize the finger ridge that commanded the eastern slopes of Hill 60. By 1240 Company C was partially on its objective, and as resistance stiffened Company B was sent in on its right. The success of 1/1 in penetrating the high ground east of Hill 60 enabled Colonel Mason to put into effect the next stage of his attack plan, and he ordered 2/1 under cover of fire from 3/1 to advance and seize Hill 60.[56]

Company E with tanks and assault guns in direct support moved rapidly to the crest of its objective. By 1400 it had full control of the hill and its reverse slope, and engineers were busy blowing the numerous cave entrances.[57] Resistance to 1/1's advance continued to mount and assault companies suffered heavy casualties, especially from fire coming from their left front. As a result there was a general shift to the left as Company C moved into the 5th Marines' zone to wipe out the opposition, and Lieutenant Colonel Murray committed Company A on the right of Company B to close the gap to

[54] 3/22 SAR, Ph III, 2.
[55] 2/22 SAR, Ph III, 2.
[56] 1/1 SAR, 13.
[57] 2/1 SAR, 6

AWACHA POCKET, showing the gorge which was the scene of much bitter fighting by the 5th Marines.

2/1's lines on Hill 60. Exhaustion, crippling casualties, and lack of contact almost stopped the attack, but it was renewed at 1600, and the battalion battled its way through 150 more yards of broken terrain and stubborn resistance to reach its initial objective and tie in with Company I of 3/5 on the left and E of 2/1 on the right.

Late in the afternoon Lieutenant Colonel Murray, who had come up to the front to supervise the disposition and defense preparations of his companies, was wounded by a sniper. Before he was evacuated Murray designated Captain Francis D. Rineer, commanding Company B, as temporary battalion commander, and Rineer conducted 1/1's night defense until he was relieved the following morning by Lieutenant Colonel Richard P. Ross, Jr., regimental executive officer.[58]

Company K of 3/7 which had been acting as reserve for 3/5 reverted to parent control on 9 May and moved into the front line on the right of Company L so that 3/7 had two companies in assault for the 5th Marines' attack. The battalions facing the Awacha Draw, 1/5 and 2/5, were directed to furnish supporting fire for the attack of 3/7 and 3/5 on the rugged ground at the mouth of the draw. At 1200, after an air, NGF, artillery, and mortar preparation, the assault battalions jumped off.

Initial progress was rapid, and the advance reached its first objective, the same ridge line faced by 1/1, before the volume of enemy fire from 3/7's exposed left flank forced a halt. At 1515 it was necessary to commit 1/7 (Lieutenant Colonel John J. Gormley), which had moved up from the Gusukuma during the morning, to close the gap that had opened between 3/7 and 1/5.[59]

[58] *1/1 SAR*, 13–14. LtCol Austin C. Shofner, Division Provost Marshal, relieved LtCol Ross as CO of 1/1 on 13 May. LtCol Ross resumed his duties as 1st Mar ExO.

[59] 1st Bn, 7th Mar SAR, 22Apr–22Jun45, 29Jun45, 5, hereinafter cited as *1/7 SAR*. Both 1/7 and 3/7 were attached to the 5th Mar on 9 May; 7th Mar (–) was the division reserve.

New division orders were issued during the afternoon of 9 May to meet the problem raised by the bitter defense of the Awacha Pocket and the absolute necessity of continuing the division attack to the south in order to reach Tenth Army objectives. The 5th Marines (less 3/5) was assigned a limited zone of action on the left of the division front and given the mission of reducing the Awacha defenses. The 7th Marines (with 3/5 attached) and the 1st Marines were given new boundaries that placed them across the division front in position to jump-off for the 11 May attack.[60] At 1855 Colonel Snedeker relieved Colonel Griebel of responsibility for the new 7th Marines' zone and took control of the front lines of 3/5, 3/7, and 1/7 in preparation for a division attack the following morning.

The decision to concentrate the 5th Marines' efforts on the Awacha Pocket was welcomed by the 77th Division since its right flank had suffered galling fire from the enemy defenses there. On 9 May this division, using tactics it was to employ throughout its drive toward Shuri, concentrated its offensive effort on one small sector of its front. All available supporting fire was delivered against the limited ridge line objective of 3/305 in the center of the division zone. After the assault battalion had gained a hold on the ridge, it was in a position to deliver flanking fire on similar objectives in front of other elements of the division. This system of advancing by seizing salients in the enemy line was the most effective that could have been employed by the 77th, which faced an interminable series of hills and ridges whose main axis was generally perpendicular to its direction of advance.

The 17th Infantry, which had fought doggedly to secure Kochi Ridge and the high ground to the west of Conical Hill was relieved by the 382d Infantry of the 96th Division on 9 May. At the same time the 383d Infantry moved to forward assembly areas behind the 184th, and on 10 May it relieved the 184th on its lines directly north of Conical Hill. Both fresh regiments were able to destroy enemy strong points that had held up the battle-weary 7th Division's advance and improve the posi-

tions of their division for the 11 May offensive by seizing key hills that guarded the approaches to Conical. General Bradley assumed command of the east coast sector from General Arnold at 1420 after the last front line unit of the 184th Infantry was relieved.

The 77th Division continued to improve its jump-off position on 10 May and concentrated its offensive effort in the zone of 3/305 which seized additional high ground that led toward the key road junction north of Shuri. The 306th Infantry again supported the 305th's attack and in addition fired across the division boundary into the reverse slopes of the hill positions in front of the 382d. Progress for the 77th Division in the area southwest of Maeda had been steady since 5 May, but the enemy was now ready with a reorganized and reinforced 32d Regiment and the dug-in tanks and 90mm field guns of the 27th Tank Regiment to dispute any further movement down the main highway that led to Shuri.[61]

The readjustment and reinforcement of enemy lines necessary after the 4–5 May counterattack had been completed by 10 May. Remnants of the 62d Division that had fought the 77th Infantry and 1st Marine Divisions in the tangled ridge network between Maeda and the Asa Kawa were being gradually withdrawn toward Shuri to be rebuilt to some slight semblance of their former strength with drafts from the *Boeitai*, Naval Base Force, and service and supply troops. The 24th Division, whose main reinforcements at this stage of the battle were taken from former sea raiding base battalions and division troops, held the front from Dakeshi to Gaja with the 22d and 89th Regiments facing the U. S. 96th Division.

The 44th IMB with the full strength 15th IMR as a nucleus and strong reinforcements from the 3d Battalion, 2d Infantry Unit, 7th Independent Antitank Battalion, 1st and 2d Independent Battalions, and the 26th Shipping Engineer Regiment faced IIIAC. Although the 3d Battalion, 2d Infantry Unit had been committed at Dakeshi, the main strength of the brigade was screened from the Marines by outposts and scattered strong defensive posi-

[60] 1st MarDiv War Diary, May 1945, 8.

[61] *Okinawa Operations Record*, Record of the 24th Div, 21–22.

MARINES of Company B, 1/7 cautiously advance toward the smoking slopes of Dakeshi Ridge on 10 May.

tions still held by units of the 62d Division. Once the 6th Marine Division crossed the Asa Kawa, however, and the 1st Division reached Dakeshi Ridge, IIIAC would be deeply immeshed in the Japanese brigade's highly organized defensive position.

During the night of 9–10 May 1/5 repulsed two counterattacks and turned back numerous enemy infiltrators in fighting that sometimes closed to bayonet range. In the morning more than 60 enemy bodies were counted in front of the battalion's lines. Lieutenant Colonel Shelburne issued his attack order at 0600 after the excitement died down, and at 0800 the battalion moved out in a column of companies with Company A in the lead. A swift advance of 400 yards reached the corps boundary, and Company C was committed on the left of A to deepen the battalion front.

Tanks, which had been scheduled to move up in support, were blocked from joining the assault companies by lack of a suitable approach route. About 0845 heavy machine-gun and mortar fire coming from the front, both flanks, and the rear pinned down the battalion in its advanced position and casualties skyrocketed. It was impossible to evacuate the wounded by carrying parties, and amphibious tanks, which were called up to do the job, were unable to negotiate the rugged terrain. Finally at 1700 Shelburne requested a heavy smoke barrage and ordered his men to withdraw under its cover and bring back their casualties. By 1945, 1/5 was back in the lines it had held the evening before.[62]

---

[62] *1/5 SAR*, 4–5.

Despite the fact that 1/5 was repulsed in its attempt to isolate the Awacha Pocket, the 5th Marines made significant gains against the enemy position on 10 May. Lieutenant Colonel Benedict, using 12 gun and three flame tanks with his infantry fire teams, was able to overcome all effective enemy resistance in that part of the Awacha Draw which lay in 2/5's zone of action. Streams of flame were played over the northern slope of the draw while tanks working in relays blasted enemy positions in front of 2/5 and 1/5. Company G, accompanying the tank firing line, moved into the draw and cut down the enemy troops flushed out of caves by the armored flame throwers. Companies E and F then advanced in their sectors to and through the draw, mopping up the enemy as they went. By nightfall 2/5 had broken into the heart of the Awacha defenses, but there were still many pockets of desperate resistance to be accounted for.

In the 7th Marines' zone of action, the 3d Battalion on the right was pinned down on its line of departure by accurate shelling from artillery and mortars. Heavy small-arms fire from caves and pillboxes to its front prevented any appreciable advance during the day. As a result 1/7, which paralleled the advance of 1/5, attacked at 0800 with an open flank. Initial progress was rapid against scattered opposition, and at 0842 Lieutenant Colonel Gormley committed Company A on the left of the assault company (B) to strengthen his front. Mortar and machine-gun fire from Dakeshi Ridge increased steadily during the morning despite artillery and 81mm mortar concentrations laid on the ridge and village.

At 1145 enemy machine guns firing from a draw in the 5th Marines' zone on the rear of Company B effectively slowed the advance. A smoke barrage by 81mm mortars and the mop-up efforts of Company G of 2/7 failed to eliminate fire from the draw, and Gormley was forced to order a halt. When 1/5 began its withdrawal at 1700, 1/7 came under direct fire from three sides and its left rear and gradually was driven from its forward positions. At 1754 Gormley gave permission for all his assault units to pull back to their original lines.[63]

The road leading out of the west end of Dakeshi was the objective of the 1st Marines' attack on 10 May. The 3d Battalion jumped off at 0800, advanced swiftly to the railroad cut which bisected the regimental sector, and held up awaiting the attack of 1/1. The tanks which were to support the 1st Battalion had been delayed by a 6th Division tank which struck a mine and blocked the only tank road into 1/1's area. At 1020, the tanks having arrived, both battalions resumed the attack, advanced steadily, and reached the low ridge that overlooked the Dakeshi road. All attempts by the assault companies, K and L of 3/1 and A and B of 1/1, to move beyond the road were ineffective. Vicious enfilade fire from Dakeshi Ridge drove back all combat patrols and made it evident that the ridge would have to be taken before any further advance to the south could be made. During the day, Company I of 3/5 kept pace with the attack of 1/1 and at nightfall linked the lines of the 1st and 7th Marines.[64]

Shortly after dark on 9 May engineers began construction of a footbridge across the Asa Kawa in front of 3/22, using the approaches of the old bridge. At 0300 Company K, followed closely by Company I, began crossing the footbridge, and shortly thereafter Company A of 1/22 started wading the shallow eastern portion of the stream. At about 0530 two Japanese "human demolition charges" rushed out of hiding and threw themselves on the south end of the footbridge, destroying it.[65] The possible loss of the bridge had been provided for in attack plans, and engineer demolition parties with the assault troops breached the sea wall to provide direct access to the front lines by LVT's loaded with supplies and reinforcements.

At daybreak the assault companies of 3/22 attacked to the south. Company K, moving along the coast in broken terrain, was pinned down immediately by enemy fire from all sides. In the center, Company I was able to advance slowly with the aid of covering fire from Company A. At 0900 Lieutenant Colonel Donohoo

[63] 1/7 SAR, 6.

[64] 1/1 SAR, 14; 3/1 SAR, 20–21.

[65] 6th EngBn SAR, Ph III, Part III, 2. Some reports credit heavy enemy mortar fire with knocking out the bridge, but in this instance the SAR of the engineers who built the bridge has been accepted.

ordered Company L to cross the river and support the attack. Artillery and supporting ships fired continuously to clear the path for the infantry but could not bring their fire in close enough to the front lines to destroy the enemy emplacements. The situation called for the direct fire of tanks, but the tanks were unable to ford the Asa Kawa despite repeated attempts.[66]

The stubbornness of the enemy resistance led Colonel Schneider to order 1/22 to attack and relieve the pressure on the 3d Battalion. Companies B and C moved up on either flank of Company A and assaulted the first of a series of ridge positions southeast of Asa at 1345.[67] Supporting fire from the left flank was delivered from the 2/22 strong point established by Company G at 0730.[68] The regimental advance continued along the entire front during the afternoon despite heavy rifle and machine-gun fire, with the longest advances being made in the center of the line by 1/22. At dusk the attack was halted and the assault companies dug in with firm control of a bridgehead 1,400 yards long and 350 yards deep. At 2200 the 6th Engineer Battalion began erecting a Bailey bridge to enable tanks to cross the Asa Kawa and support the 22d Marines in the Tenth Army attack of 11 May.

TENTH ARMY ATTACKS[69]

The Japanese furnished the prelude to the Tenth Army attack of 11 May. At 0630 combat air patrols intercepted the first of series of enemy raiders that attempted to reach the Ie Shima and Hagushi anchorages during the morning. *Kamikazes* crashed and seriously damaged a Dutch merchantman, the *Tjisdane*, and the destroyers *Evans* and *Hadley*, while a bomb crippled LCS 88. The *Hadley* was credited with shooting down 19 planes and the

Evans with 15 out of a total of 93 credited to ship's AA and defending air patrols.[70]

Naval gunfire assignments of five battleships, six cruisers, and 13 destroyers [71] to support the army's attack were not affected by the enemy air raid. Planes from TF 58, TF 51, and TAF were constantly on station to fly strike missions and augment the fire support of artillery and NGF. The attack got off on time at 0700 all along the front, and assault troops advanced slowly against bitter resistance.

Tanks and self-propelled guns were not available to the 22d Marines at the start of its attack. Intermittent shelling by enemy artillery during the night had slowed engineer progress in the construction of a Bailey bridge across the Asa Kawa. With daylight enemy observers on the Shuri heights were able to see the engineer working parties, and the tempo and accuracy of the shellfire increased. The time set for the completion of the bridging operation was successively delayed from 0400 to 0600 to 1000, and the first tanks actually crossed the river at 1103.[72]

During the morning close-in support for the infantry was limited to the 75mm howitzers of the 1st Armored Amphibian Battalion firing into the seaward face of the cliffs on the right flank of 3/22. Lieutenant Colonel Donohoo sent Company K into this area to clean out its caves and pillboxes while Companies I and L moved up the coastal road to outflank the 147-foot hill northeast of Amike that dominated his zone of action. Intense enemy fire from the steep and rocky hillside raked the open ground along the road and pinned down the assault troops. At 1150 Company B of the 6th

---

[66] *3/22 SAR, Ph III,* 2–3; *6th TkBn SAR, Ph III,* 5

[67] *1/22 SAR, Ph III,* 2.

[68] *2/22 SAR, Ph III,* 2.

[69] Unless otherwise noted the material in this section is derived from *Tenth Army AR; IIIAC AR; 1st MarDiv SAR; 6th MarDiv SAR, Ph III; 77th InfDiv OpRpt, Okinawa; 96th InfDiv AR; 1st Mar SAR; 5th Mar SAR; 7th Mar SAR; 22d Mar SAR, Ph III; 29th Mar SAR, Ph III.*

[70] *CTF 51 AR,* Part III, 89–90. Naval casualties in this attack were 46 KIA, 105 WIA, and 19 MIA. *Ibid.,* Part V, Sect H, 10.

[71] *Ibid.,* Part V, Sect C, 58.

[72] 6th MarDiv Unit Jnl, Okinawa Operation, Phase III, 23Apr–30Jun45, 11May45, hereinafter cited as *6th MarDiv Jnl, Ph III; 3/22 SAR, Ph III,* 3. The CG, 6th MarDiv observed that "the task of constructing the Bailey bridge across the Asa Kawa Estuary was a splendid feat of combat engineering. It was not only built under observed fire, both artillery and small arms, but it was built in a difficult locality where the actual engineering constituted a considerable problem. Even the dump site where the bridging material was stacked was occasionally under fire." *CMC Memo 1955.*

Tank Battalion moved into position to support the infantry, and the attack was renewed. Enemy AT guns registered hits on three tanks, destroying one, before the tanks were able to silence the fire.[73] By midafternoon 3/22 was fighting its way up the hill in a close quarter battle with the enemy defenders, and at 1600 after an 800-yard advance the battalion reported that it had established control of the high ground which overlooked Naha.[74] General Shepherd, who had observed 3/22's attack from the 22d Marines' observation post, sent Lieutenant Colonel Donohoo a message commending "every officer and man who participated in this assault for his personal bravery and the fine team work exercised by all units in capturing this precipitous and strongly defended terrain feature."[75]

The fire from the tanks of Company B that supported 3/22 also aided the advance of the 1st Battalion in the center of the regimental zone of action. Extremely heavy small-arms fire coming from a coral ridge that overlooked the left flank of the bridgehead had driven back 1/22's assault company (C) during the morning's attack. The direct fire of the NGF support ships assigned to IIIAC was laid on the objective, and the 6th Division sent several urgent messages to corps requesting assignment of flame-throwing tanks to sear the caves and covered positions that infested the upper reaches of the ridge.[76]

Four of the armored flame throwers were detached from the 1st Division, but they did not arrive in time to support the attack which was renewed when the Shermans of Company C, 6th Tank Battalion reported to 1/22. Heavy fire from the ridge halted the first tank-infantry assault. However, when the tanks with 3/22 were directed to cover the reverse slopes with fire while those of Company C hit the forward face, the infantry was able to advance swiftly and seize the objective.[77] Portable flame throwers and satchel charges were used to silence the defenders in rugged close-in fighting

ATTACKING under enemy fire, men of 1/22 race through the ruins of the sugar mill south of the Asa Kawa.

for what proved to be an extensive headquarters and supply installation.

The main effort of the 22d Marines' attack had been made by 1/22 and 3/22. The 2d Battalion's mission was to advance and seize a hill that paralleled the general line of objectives facing the other battalions and to maintain contact with 1/22 and the 1st Division. The battalions on both flanks were pinned down almost immediately after the morning's attack began, but Company G in assault for 2/22 was able to maintain its initial steady momentum against moderate opposition. Rather than hold up his men to keep contact, Lieutenant Colonel Woodhouse committed Companies E and F on the left and right flanks respectively to link up the front lines. Advances on both flanks later in the day served to straighten the line, and the battalion dug in on its objective at 1700.[78]

The banks of the railroad cut that ran down the division boundary furnished 2/1 with a covered route of advance on 11 May. The battalion's objective was the high ground west of Wana, but attempts to attack through 1/1's lines on the approaches to Dakeshi Ridge were stopped by accurate machine-gun fire from its

[73] *6th TkBn SAR, Ph III,* 5–6.
[74] *3/22 SAR, Ph III,* 3.
[75] *6th MarDiv Jnl, Ph III,* 11May45.
[76] *Ibid.*
[77] *6th TkBn SAR, Ph III,* 6–7.

[78] *2/22 SAR, Ph III,* 3.

6TH DIVISION ZONE OF ACTION on 11 May showing tanks moving across the Asa Kawa in the foreground.

reverse slopes and the forward slopes of Wana Ridge. Company E on the left was pinned down, but Company F, moving down the railroad cut, made steady progress toward the objective. By 1300 Lieutenant Colonel Magee found it necessary to commit Company G in column behind F to back the attack and keep contact. Tanks, which deployed to silence opposition from Dakeshi Ridge, drew heavy artillery and mortar fire on Company E's area.[79] At 1600, when Company F was partially on its objective and holding up so that 2/22 could tie in, Company G was caught in a terrific artillery bombardment which caused casualties to mount alarmingly. All available artillery and air was concentrated on suspected enemy gun

positions to free Companies G and E, but finally it was necessary to order the companies to dig in where they stood.[80] A gap which had opened between 2/1 and the 7th Marines during the day was closed by the 3d Battalion which took cover from the persistent artillery fire[81] by occupying the east bank of the railroad cut.

In addition to providing close-in fire support, the tanks working with the 7th Marines on 11 May also evacuated the wounded; some were

---

[79] *1st TkBn Summary,* 11May45.

[80] *2/1 SAR,* 6–7.

[81] The ammunition dump of the 3d Bn's 81mm MortPlat was hit by enemy artillery fire at 1115 and totally destroyed: two mortars were knocked out; three men were killed and 17 wounded. LtCol Sabol ordered the shattered platoon to the rear to reorganize, and Col Mason arranged for a platoon of Army 4.2-inch mortars to support 3/1 in place of its knocked-out 81mm's. *3/1 SAR,* 21–22.

WHITE PHOSPHORUS SHELLS screen the advance of the 5th Marines on 11 May.

taken up through the escape hatches and others rode out on the back of the tanks which provided an armored shield between stretcher cases and enemy fire.[82] The need for tank protection to evacuate the wounded was indicative of the fury of opposition met by 1/7 and 2/7 which carried the brunt of the regiment's attack. Both battalions advanced about 800 yards during the day, converging in front of 3/7 in a double envelopment of the enemy position and gaining a firm hold on Dakeshi Ridge.

Company F, in assault for 2/7 on the right, worked some elements over the crest of the ridge and into the outskirts of Dakeshi village by 0948, but the intensity of enemy fire from coral caves and pillboxes on the reverse slopes mounted as the men penetrated into the core

of defenses. Further progress was impossible, and the rest of the day was spent in mopping-up action along the ridge to consolidate the battalion's hold.[83] The same heavy fire from reverse slope defenses met Company C of 1/7 when it reached the top of the ridge at 1116, and Lieutenant Colonel Gormley sent Company A forward early in the afternoon to strengthen the line and fill in on the left toward the division boundary. Both companies used tank fire, flame throwers, grenades, and demolitions to seal the caves and emplacements that infested the newly-won ground and finally gained a secure hold on the objective.[84]

The last organized resistance in the Awacha Pocket was eliminated on 11 May by 2/5, while

---

[82] *1st TkBn Summary*, 11May45.

[83] *2/7 SAR*, 4.

[84] *1/7 SAR*, 7–8.

1/5 moved up behind 1/7 and wiped out by-passed enemy strong points. At nightfall the 1st Battalion linked the positions of the 7th Marines and 305th Infantry to provide a solid front line along the division boundary. The 2d Battalion made contact with 2/307 which had moved up to support positions behind the 305th Infantry during the day.

Assault battalions in the 77th Division's zone of action gained 400–500 yards during the 11 May attack. The broken nature of the terrain that guarded the approaches to Shuri gave the enemy ample opportunity to take the flanks and at times the rear of advancing troops under telling fire. The progress of 1/305 on the division right "was won inch by inch against fanatical resistance from enemy strongpoints," [85] and flame-throwing tanks were used extensively to burn out the defenders. The 3d Battalion of the 306th Infantry, advancing along the division's left boundary, made slow progress, and attempts by 2/306 to turn the enemy flanks were halted by withering fire. The division consolidated its gains at sundown and dug in under sporadic mortar and artillery bombardment.

A company-sized counterattack hit 1/382 on the right of the 96th Division during the night of 10–11 May, and the battalion was still engaged in a heavy fire fight at the 0700 jump-off hour. It was not until 0930 that tank-infantry teams were able to advance around the flank of the last stubbornly resisting enemy pockets. Because of mounting casualties and critical ammunition shortages, the battalion, after gaining over 400 yards during the day, was forced to withdraw from its advanced positions on the forward slopes of the next objective, 400-foot-high Dick Hill. The same murderous machine-gun cross-fire and mortar bombardment that thinned the ranks of the 1st Battalion kept 3/382 from making any appreciable gains during its attack on the ridges northwest of Kuhazu. The 383d Infantry on the left of the division front made substantial progress on 11 May with the 1st and 2d Battalions battling their way forward 600 yards to a firm hold on the northwest slope of Conical Hill.

The following day's attack netted few yards for the 383d but enabled the assault battalions to consolidate their positions on Conical Hill's forward slopes and wipe out enemy resistance in the vicinity of the front lines. Advance elements of 1/382 again reached Dick Hill and again were driven back by a veritable wall of enemy fire despite flank support from 2/306 and 3/382. The division's lines were straightened during the day when 3/382 advanced 400 yards to seize high ground that brought it abreast of 1/382 and 1/383.

The 306th Infantry's mission in the 77th Division's 12 May attack was to furnish fire support to flanking units. While elements of the 2d Battalion worked with 1/382, the 1st Battalion concentrated its mortars and machine guns on the reverse slopes of hills and ridges facing the 305th Infantry. Attacking into a maze of heavily defended hills, ravines, and gullies, the regiment advanced 400–500 yards to gain the crest of one ridge only to be confronted with killing fire from the next. Mopping up in the rear of the assault battalions, 2/307 shifted its positions 300 yards to the south in order to maintain contact with the 305th and protect the division right flank.

The 400-yard gap along Dakeshi Ridge between the night positions of the 1st and 2d Battalions, 7th Marines was closed on 12 May. The 2d Battalion with Companies E and F in assault, E on the left, cleaned out the reverse slopes of the ridge with the aid of gun and flame tanks. Carrier strikes were called down on targets directly in front of Company E as it moved into the ruins of Dakeshi. The hail of mortar and artillery fire which had been falling intermittently since the start of the Tenth Army attack, increased sharply in intensity as the enemy attempted to stop the battalion's forward progress. Company F, moving along a spur of Dakeshi Ridge toward the regimental boundary, was hit especially hard by mortar concentrations and was found to have a total strength of 93 at the end of the day's action.[86] At 1522 Company E made contact with Company C of 1/7 on the ridge above Dakeshi, and both battalions consolidated their hold for the night along the northern outskirts of the village and on the high ground on its flanks. (See Map 27, Map Section)

[85] *77th InfDiv OpRpt, Okinawa*, 49.

[86] *2/7 SAR*, 5.

Company C of 1/7 repulsed a determined counterattack at 0235, driving off the enemy who left 65 known dead in front of the battalion's lines, 30 of whom were credited to artillery defensive fires. At 0737 orders were received from Colonel Snedeker to mop up Dakeshi Ridge, advance to an objective line just beyond the village, and support the advance of 2/7 by fire. Company A moved out in assault at 0821 and meeting no opposition, walked into Dakeshi at 0912, while Company C cleaned out cave positions on the ridge. By 1330 the battalion had reached its objective line, and Company B had been committed to the left rear of A to back up the forward positions. Resistance to the day's advance on the left of the regimental front was erratic, but it stiffened as night fell and reconnaissance indicated that the ground directly north of Wana Ridge was strongly organized in depth.[87]

The attack of the 1st Marines to improve its positions west of Wana was held up for three hours until 2/1 could be resupplied by air with rations, ammunition, water, and medical supplies. Heavy and accurate shelling and small-arms fire covered the whole battalion area, causing mounting casualties and forcing Lieutenant Colonel Magee to consolidate the remnants of Companies E and G under the Company G commander in order to obtain an effective striking force.

At 1030 these companies attacked in an attempt to come abreast of Company F's forward positions. Every step of the way was contested by swarming enemy snipers and heavy machine-gun fire from the vicinity of Wana. Japanese artillery and mortar observers on the heights to the left front had perfect observation of the battalion's routes of supply and evacuation. Under these circumstances, gains by the depleted companies were negligible, and most assault elements were pinned down almost as soon as they moved out. As dusk approached the companies were forced to dig in where they stood, at best only a few score yards forward of their 11 May positions.[88]

The 3d Battalion, attacking on the left of 2/1 with Companies K and L in assault, was forced to pull up short of the eastern extension of the ridge line along which the 2d Battalion was strung out. Partially protected by the cover along the banks of the southern tributary of the Asa Kawa, 3/1 was able to advance 300 yards to the southeast toward Wana Draw before the volume of enemy fire forced a halt. At 2230, after the troops had dug in, Company L reported that it was undergoing a counterattack by an unestimated number of enemy troops. Division alerted the 5th Marines at 2300 to be prepared to support the 1st against the counterattack, but 3/1 was able to drive off the Japanese without the aid of reinforcements.[89]

The 6th Division front on 12 May began to assume the shape it was to hold throughout most of the month's fighting. The formidable enemy position at Wana, 1,000 yards to the northeast of the 6th Division's lines, effectively blocked the advance of the 1st Division. Consequently, the left flank units of the 6th Division were open to observation and direct fire from the western slopes of the Shuri massif and were unable to match the advances made by troops moving down the west coast toward Naha.

On the second day of the Tenth Army attack, the 22d Marines concentrated its efforts in the center of the line where opposition from enemy hidden in caves and tombs was steady and heavy. The 1st Battalion, with a company of tanks in support and Companies A and B in assault, advanced steadily and seized its objective line, the high ground north of the Asato Gawa, by 1400. On the right of the division front, 3/22, from its advanced positions secured the previous day, reached the commanding ground at 0920 and sent patrols through the suburbs of Naha to the river where they found the bridge demolished and the river bottom muddy and unfordable. Both battalions dug in for the night with their lines on the northern outskirts of the Naha suburbs.[90]

The 2d Battalion, moving down the division left flank, hit the roughest opposition encountered during the day. A bulldozer tank con-

[87] 1/7 SAR, 9–10; 1st MarDiv G–2 PrdRpt No 42, 13May45.
[88] 2/1 SAR, 7.
[89] 3/1 SAR, 22–23.
[90] 1/22 SAR, Ph III, 2; 3/22 SAR, Ph III, 3–4.

structed a crossing on the upper branch of the Asa Kawa and enabled tanks, which had not been available on 11 May, to move up to support the infantry.[91] At 0807 when the tanks arrived in position, Companies E and G jumped off in attack.

Extremely heavy enemy fire coming from the 1st Division zone effectively slowed Company E's advance, but Company G kept pace with the progress of the rest of the regiment. By 1400 Company G had reached high ground that overlooked Naha near the positions of 1/22, and regiment had informed Lieutenant Colonel Woodhouse that 3/29 would take over Company E's front on the overextended left flank. At about the time the relief was being completed, Company G's leading platoon was caught in a terrific mortar barrage. After concentrated artillery fire failed to knock out the enemy mortars, the whole of Company G and a platoon of tanks attacked to extricate the trapped platoon. A rain of small-arms and automatic weapons fire from the enemy-held ground to the front and flanks punished the rescue party severely, and two tanks were lost to mines[92] before the 75 men remaining in the company withdrew under a withering cross-fire. For night defense Company F was moved into the line on the left to contact 3/29 and Company E was recommitted in the center to bolster the badly battered remnants of Company G which tied in with 1/22.[93]

During the night of 12–13 May the Japanese attempted a counterlanding behind the 6th Division's lines, but the landing craft were detected by the naval antiboat screen lying offshore and sunk. The 40 survivors who managed to swim to the reef's edge were cut down by the men of 3/22.

The battalion's assignment for the day was reconnaissance of the northern suburbs of Naha. The first patrol was turned back, however, by heavy fire from a village that had been empty and silent on 12 May. Battalion 81mm mortars were laid on its houses, and Company L was ordered to send a platoon with tanks into the village to destroy resistance. One tank was knocked out by a suicide-bent Japanese with a satchel charge, and the infantry was stopped by strong machine-gun and rifle fire. Another tank-infantry force from Company L attacked from a different direction to rout out the defenders. At 1830 the troops and tanks withdrew after a four-hour battle in the narrow streets with a well covered and concealed enemy.[94] The 1st Battalion's patrols encountered similar opposition from defenders outposting the houses on the north bank of the river.[95]

The division attack on 13 May was scheduled for 0730 with 2/22 making the main effort and 3/29 attempting to clear the high ground along the division boundary which offered commanding fields of fire into the 2d Battalion's left flank. The jump-off was delayed until 1115 because of the difficulty in getting vitally needed supplies and the rocket trucks scheduled for preparation fires up to the front lines over the broken, trackless terrain.

The heavy rocket and artillery bombardment preceding the attack seemed to have no effect on the enemy defenders, and the tank-infantry assault teams were subjected to murderous fire from the hill complex to the front and flanks as they slowly advanced. By late afternoon Company E on the right reached the high-water mark of the 12 May attack, an insignificant-looking, low, rounded hill backed up on three sides by rugged ridge lines, before it was forced to give ground in the face of enemy fire. Company F, which waited through the morning for 3/29 to come abreast before it attacked, was also slowed, halted, and finally driven back by the accurate defending fire.[96] On the left flank, 3/29, with Company H in assault, was able to move forward about 300 yards just before darkness and seize the forward slopes of a hill whose defenders had fired on the left rear of 2/22

[91] 6th TkBn SAR, Ph III, 7–8.

[92] Ibid., 8. The losses suffered by the three dismounted tank crews in this action (one other tank was stuck in a shell hole and abandoned) were indicative of the density and accuracy of enemy fire received—13 of the 15 crew members were KIA or WIA.

[93] 2/22 SAR, Ph III, 3–4.

[94] 3/22 SAR, Ph III, 4.

[95] 1/22 SAR, Ph III, 2. In an apparently successful effort to confuse the Japanese, Company A used captured grenade dischargers to support its combat patrols on 13 May.

[96] 2/22 SAR, Ph III, 4–5.

throughout the day's action. (See Map 24, Map Section)

The 22d Marines had suffered about 800 casualties in its advance from the Asa Kawa, and the regiment's combat efficiency was clearly impaired when General Shepherd redisposed his troops during 13 May to maintain the impetus of the division attack. The remainder of the 29th Marines moved to positions behind 3/29 and stood ready to strengthen the division effort the following day. The IIIAC reserve, the 4th Marines, moved south to take over the old positions of the 29th, defend the 6th Division's rear areas, and back up the LVT(A)'s which were set up to guard the open seaward flank.

In the 1st Marine Division zone the hills, ridges, and ravines that guarded the western approaches to Shuri spawned two heavy pre-dawn counterattacks against the positions of 3/1, but they were broken up by point-blank machine-gun, bazooka, and small-arms fire. At 1200 Company L, supported by the fire of Company K, attacked southeast to gain the high ground at the mouth of Wana Draw. As the tank-infantry teams reached their objective, they began receiving heavy machine-gun fire from three sides and were caught in a maelstrom of mortar, grenade, and rifle fire. A withdrawal was necessary, and tanks furnished fire and smoke cover for casualty evacuation as the troops moved back to their original lines. The same devastating flanking fire that forced Company L to withdraw prevented 2/1 from moving up its left flank to extend Company F's hold on the high ground west of Wana.

Dakeshi was secured by the 7th Marines on 13 May. The 2d Battalion cleaned out the village, while 1/7 hunted down snipers and closed caves on the ridge above, and 3/7 mopped up in the regiment's rear areas. Tanks, assault guns, and 37mm AT guns supported Company G's attack, but the last organized resistance was not silenced until late in the afternoon. A cave-pocked center of enemy resistance in the reverse slope of Dakeshi Ridge, later found to be a brigade CP, was discovered during the afternoon and taken under close assault,[97] so close

that the Japanese noted that the brigade commander and his men had exchanged grenades with the attackers. Retreat orders for the few score men remaining in the enemy 64th Brigade were executed that night, and survivors attempted to infiltrate American lines to reach Shuri and re-form.[98]

The 305th Infantry made contact with the left flank of the 7th Marines at noon on 13 May as the Army regiment continued its dogged advance into the extremely rugged terrain north and northeast of Shuri. To insure that the 305th retained firm possession of newly-won ground, tank-infantry-engineer teams followed directly behind assault elements to clean out and seal cave and tomb positions that might harbor snipers and infiltrators.

On the left flank of 77th Division the 306th Infantry attacked in conjunction with the 382d of the 96th Division to capture the hills along the road from Kochi to Shuri. The assault battalion, 2/306, drove through heavy mortar barrages to reach the northern slopes of its initial hill objective, but repeated attempts to advance farther to the south were blocked by strong enemy fire which seriously depleted the ranks of assault infantry.

The coordinated attack was more successful in the 382d Infantry's area where that regiment seized enemy positions that had been softened up by two day's of constant bombardment and bitter close-in fighting. The 1st Battalion advanced 400–500 yards and dug in for the night at the base of Dick Hill, while the 3d Battalion gained 600 yards in an advance to the southwest onto the forward slopes of a prominent height, dubbed Oboe Hill, 1,000 yards due east of the outskirts of Shuri.

The most significant gain on the Tenth Army front on 13 May was made by the 383d Infantry. Attacking astride Razorback Ridge which extended north and south from the peak of Conical Hill to its base, the left company of 2/383 reached a position within 50 yards of the highest point of the hill. A threatened counterattack against the advance positions of the 2d Battalion was broken up by artillery and 4.2-inch mortars zeroed in by an artillery observer

[97] 2/7 SAR, 5.

[98] Okinawa Operations Record, 86.

flying overhead. The fact that the battle for Conical Hill was far from ended with 2/383's success was demonstrated by the bitter opposition met by 1/383 as it attempted to advance over the ridges west of the peak; only 100 yards of ground were occupied during a day-long attack. To protect the division's left flank, 2/381 was attached to the 383d at 1100 and moved into position on Gaja Ridge.

The following day 2/381 moved one company up on the eastern slopes of Conical Hill abreast of the left flank of 2/383. The 383d, with elements of all three battalions in line, advanced its forward positions approximately 200 yards on either flank and in the right center to establish a hold on high ground on both sides of Conical's peak. Assault companies encountered numerous pillboxes and mutually supporting strong points on the slopes of the hill that were only reduced after extensive tank-infantry action.

The attack of the 382d Infantry to secure Dick Hill and the other highly organized hill strong points guarding Shuri's eastern flank ran into increased enemy opposition on 14 May. Tanks were needed to carry resupply ammunition across the fire-swept ground leading to the positions of the assault companies. An all-out effort by 1/382 and 3/382 to seize Dick Hill was driven back, and the lines held for the night were substantially those occupied on 13 May.

The 77th Division's 306th Infantry, whose three battalions had been cut by combat attrition to the T/O strength of one, attempted a consolidated attack on the northern and western approaches of the hill defenses that blocked the 382d's advance. Seeking the weakest points in the enemy positions and exploiting them, the regiment advanced several hundred yards into the valleys and ravines that ringed the hills, but forward progress was stalled by accurate barrages of artillery and mortar fire and intense opposition from machine gunners and riflemen. The 307th Infantry moved during the day to support positions behind the 306th, prepared to attack through the front lines on 15 May.

In the attack zone of the 305th Infantry the Japanese had noted on 12 May "that little shift in friendly or enemy lines" was evident "due to

intermingling of both forces in depth together with the complicated terrain of that combat area."[99] By nightfall on 14 May the 305th had made important progress, but its gains were measured in tens rather than hundreds of yards over terrain which entirely favored the defense. Armored bulldozers had to prepare approach roads before tanks could reach the front lines, resupply operations were complicated by the broken ground, and in most cases infantrymen had to fight their way forward at grenade range to achieve even minimal gains. Cross fire from mutually supporting pillboxes and cave emplacements met every attempt to advance, and artillery and mortars were zeroed in on all possible approach routes.

The fighting in the IIIAC zone on 14 May was especially bitter in the center where attempts to breach the enemy line west of Wana and northwest of Naha were unsuccessful. Attacking infantry suffered heavy casualties, and the two division tank battalions had 18 tanks destroyed or damaged by antitank, artillery, and mortar fire, mines, and suicide attacks.[100] The Marines were now squarely up against the Japanese main line of resistance.[101]

The 2d Battalion, 7th Marines jumped off for Wana Ridge at 0730 with 1/7 prepared to pass through and continue the attack if 2/7 was stopped by enemy resistance. Once the left assault Company (E) was clear of Dakeshi village it was pinned down in the open by enemy fire. Company G on the right, followed by Company F, swung through the zone of 1/1 and by late afternoon had driven to a point within 100 yards of the ridge crest north of Wana. Machine-gun and mortar fire from the front and left flank forced the assault troops to take cover, and Companies F and G were ordered to hold their positions until 1/7 could relieve them.[102]

The 1st Battalion received its orders to take over 2/7's lines at 1107 and was in position to pass through at 1252. The renewed attack was delayed, however, in order that all supporting

[99] *Okinawa Operations Record*, 87.
[100] *1st TkBn Summary*, 14May45; *6th TkBn SAR, Ph III*, 9.
[101] *Okinawa Operations Record*, 88.
[102] *2/7 SAR*, 5.

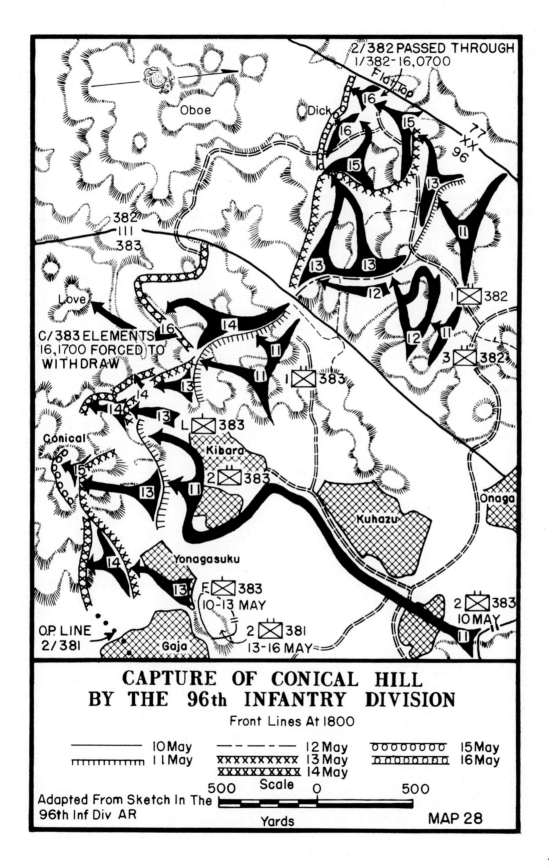

CAPTURE OF CONICAL HILL
BY THE 96th INFANTRY DIVISION
Front Lines At 1800

———————— 10 May	— — — — 12 May	ooooooooo 15 May
┬┬┬┬┬┬┬┬ 11 May	xxxxxxxxx 13 May	∩∩∩∩∩∩∩∩ 16 May
	xxxxxxxxx 14 May	

Scale

500   0   500

Adapted From Sketch In The
96th Inf Div AR

Yards

MAP 28

weapons assigned to 2/7 could be brought under control of 1/7. An intensive NGF, artillery, and rocket preparation was fired on the ground over which the battalion was to advance and the assault troops moved forward at 1615. Company B made the main effort, moving through Dakeshi and attempting to cross the open ground where Company E had been pinned down. The torrent of fire received from the direction of Wana and Shuri again proved to be too strong for the attackers, and the company was ordered to pull back to Dakeshi for night defense. Company C's mortars and machine guns laid down a heavy barrage to cover the withdrawal.

Company A had been ordered to take over the positions of Company G of 2/7, and while moving south through unfamiliar terrain had to fight numerous small infiltrating groups that were attempting to penetrate American lines. Both the commander and the executive officer of Company A became casualties before the relief was effected at about 1900. Company C was instructed at 1853 to tie in between Companies A and B, but enemy machine-gun fire coming from the right stopped it from making contact with A before darkness set in.[103]

The attack of the 7th Marines to reach Wana Ridge was paralleled by the advance of the 1st Marines. The 1st Battalion was to make the regimental assault with its initial objective the western tip of Wana Ridge, while the 2d and 3d Battalions supported its advance by fire. Company C jumped off at 0730 without tank

support and moved swiftly up the approaches to the ridge. When the tanks joined about 0830, the company forged ahead onto its objective under a protective cover of 75mm, machine-gun, and mortar fire. By noon Company C reported that the western tip of the ridge was entirely secured and that its men were digging in to hold the newly captured ground despite heavy enemy fire. Company A had moved up to the right rear of Company C, and the gap between units was covered by the fire; there was no contact with the 7th Marines on the left.

By late afternoon there was still no contact on the left and enemy troops swarming on the unoccupied portion of the ridge started to counterattack the exposed company in force. Despite concentrated mortar and artillery barrages the Japanese attack continued and broke into the lines of Company C. There was no time to send reinforcements, and the company commander requested and received permission to withdraw. The men drew back in good order, a few at a time, to the lines of Company A while machine guns and mortars covered their rear.[104] The company built up a strong line for night defense on the left of Company A in contact with the positions of the 7th Marines.[105] At 2200 units of the 5th Marines began relieving the assault companies of the 1st so that a relatively fresh regiment could renew the attack on Wana the following morning.

In the 6th Division zone of action the objective of the 14 May attack was the north bank of the Asato River. On the right 3/22 moved out at 0900 with Companies I and L in assault. Company L cleaned out the village which had held up its advance the day before and occupied its objective by 1230. Company I, on the left of the battalion zone, was slowed by artillery and mortar fire and did not secure the river heights until 1730. Because of the heavy machine-gun and mortar fire received from across the Asato, the company was unable to occupy its defensive position until after dark.[106]

The 1st Battalion started its advance at 1200, and Companies A and B reached the objective line five hours later after undergoing terrific

[103] *1/7 SAR*, 11–12. The S–3 of 1/7 commented that this action "involved a standard Japanese tactic that gave our forces trouble throughout the war. There was always a reluctance on our part to withhold an attack that was continuing to gain ground. Also, there was a general tendency to tie in the defenses and establish ourselves in a defensive posture prior to dark. These two factors often over-lapped and we found ourselves in the position of frantically establishing a night defense in the few remaining minutes of twilight. The Japanese, of course, had long since reacted to this procedure and were wont to send infiltration groups and LMG teams against us in the awkward period between BENT [Beginning of Evening Nautical Twilight] and EENT [End of Evening Nautical Twilight]. It was in this period that the relief of G/2/7 by A/1/7 took place." Maj D. P. Wycoff Ltr to CMC, 25Mar55, hereinafter cited as *Wycoff*.

[104] *1st MarDiv Interviews*, Co C, 1st Mar, 14.
[105] *1/1 SAR*, 15–16.
[106] *3/22 SAR, Ph III*, 4.

shelling from Japanese defenses south of the Asato and in the zone of 2/22. By darkness the 22d Marines had moved up to the river along a front of 1,100 yards, but defense lines were manned by skeletal companies as a result of the heavy casualties suffered since crossing the Asa Kawa.

The fury of enemy opposition increased in direct ratio to the nearness of the assault troops to the Shuri bastion. In 2/22's zone the focus of Japanese resistance was the central hill (named Sugar Loaf by Lieutenant Colonel Woodhouse) that had turned back the battalion's assault troops on two previous days. The triangular pattern of strategically-located high ground with Sugar Loaf at its apex enabled the defenders to cover the front, rear, and flanks of any portion of the position with interlocking bands of automatic-weapons fire and murderous barrages from mortars, grenade dischargers, and artillery. The Sugar Loaf position constituted the western anchor of the Japanese Shuri defenses. (See Map 24, Map Section)

Company G consolidated its remaining men into one rifle platoon to assist Company F in the attack, and Companies E and F moved forward very slowly at 0730 toward the Japanese position. Enemy fire from the left rear, in the 29th Marines' area, punished Company F severely. Company E, aided by flanking fire from 1/22, was able to seize the forward slopes of a small hill to the right front of Sugar Loaf but was not able to advance any farther in the face of the withering enemy fire. Company F managed to gain a foothold on the high ground directly north of Sugar Loaf and advance one platoon across the intervening open ground to the hill itself.

The forward platoon, despite the support of every available weapon within range, was unable to maintain its position against the enemy fire barrier. Survivors pulled back to Company F's lines across the open ground which was signposted by the burning hulks of three tanks hit by 47mm AT fire.[107] At 1500 Lieutenant Colonel Woodhouse, "considering his losses and the obvious strength of the enemy to the front requested more troops to aid his battalion to hold what had been taken."[108] Woodhouse received direct orders from division to continue the assault on the battalion objective, and Company K of 3/22 was attached at 1545[109] to back up his attack.

At 1722 Company F, moving behind a line of tanks and an artillery smoke screen, attacked Sugar Loaf a second time. At 1930 approximately 40 survivors of Companies F and G were in position at the foot of the hill under command of Major Henry A. Courtney, Jr., battalion executive officer. Snipers were everywhere and mortar fire was being received from both flanks as well as the reverse slopes of Sugar Loaf. The exposed group was low on all kinds of ammunition, and Woodhouse sent a carrying party of 26 replacements up to Courtney to replenish supplies and thicken the lines. The Japanese were rolling grenades downhill into Courtney's position and he decided that the situation called for an immediate attack to throw the enemy off balance and seize the hill crest. At 2300 Courtney and the 40-odd men still with him stormed up the hill throwing grenades ahead of them and dug in at the top to face a night of continued heavy mortar fire and constant counterattacks.[110]

Perhaps the primary reason for 2/22's heavy going on 14 May was the enfilade fire received on its left from flanking hills in the 29th Marines' zone of action. The assault battalion of the 29th, 3/29, had attempted to bypass enemy strong points on its left and drive abreast of 2/22 after its jump-off at 0730. Fire from enemy positions on the rear of the 3d Battalion proved so troublesome that the advance was halted and fighting was deadlocked around this center of resistance throughout all of the morning and most of the afternoon. At about 1630 the 29th Marines attacking forces were regrouped and 1/29 was moved into the line on the left of 3/29. The attack was renewed with Companies H and A working on both flanks of the enemy position, which was slowly com-

---

[107] 6th TkBn SAR, Ph III, 9.

[108] 2/22 SAR, Ph III, 5.

[109] 3/22 SAR, Ph III, 4. At 1635 the 22d Mar reported 2/22 was 60% effective and that it was short 472 men from its T/O strength. 6th MarDiv Jnl, Ph III, 14May45.

[110] 2/22 SAR, Ph III, 5–6.

pressed and partially neutralized. Company G of 3/29 continued the attack to the south and after a running assault across 200 yards of open ground gained the forward slopes of the hill northwest of Sugar Loaf and tied in with 2/22.[111]

By nightfall on 14 May the assault troops of IIIAC and XXIV Corps were deeply enmeshed in the enemy main line of resistance. Despite the fact that Tenth Army estimated that almost half of the enemy garrison had been killed—with the heaviest toll among first-line infantrymen—there was no sign of weakening on the part of the Japanese. There was little prospect of cracking the enemy defenses without bitter, prolonged, and close-quarter tank-infantry combat. (See Map 23, Map Section)

LOGISTICAL PROGRESS[112]

By the end of April all assault and first echelon transports and landing ships had been completely discharged. Some idea of the magnitude of this task at Okinawa can be gained through comparison with comparable unloading figures for previous Central Pacific operations, as follows:

Operation	Number of ships	Personnel	Measurement tons
Gilberts	63	35, 214	148, 782
Marshalls	122	85, 201	293, 792
Marianas	210	141, 519	437, 753
Leyte [113]	110	57, 411	214, 552
Palau	109	55, 887	199, 963
Iwo Jima	174	86, 516	280, 447
Okinawa	458	193, 852	824, 567

Some elements of the garrison forces and their equipment as well as regular resupply shipments were also being unloaded during this same period, thus adding greatly to the complexity of the logistics schedules for Okinawa.

The most pressing supply problem facing Tenth Army, however, was not caused by the jammed condition of its beach dumps or vehicle and personnel shortages in its shore party or the rapidly increasing length of supply routes from beach to front line, although all these factors served to some extent to decrease unloading efficiency. The dogged nature of the Japanese defense of Shuri was the determinant of the primary problem, which was the maintenance of an adequate reserve of artillery ammunition at the target. The tremendous expenditure of shells from all types of supporting weapons needed to blast a path through Japanese positions seriously depleted initial supplies and ate up replenishment shipments as fast as they came in.

Because "ammunition resupply had been based on an estimated 40 days of combat" [114] it became necessary early in April to revise the shipping schedules drastically upward. On 17 April, General Buckner requested CinCPOA to load five LST's with 155mm gun and howitzer ammunition from Saipan dumps to arrive at Okinawa by 27 April. This was the first of many special requests made to keep abreast of the ever-expanding rate of fire.

The sinking of the *Canada Victory* during the *Kamikaze* attack of 27–28 April brought to three the number of ammunition ships lost since L-Day. Loss of their cargo of over 22,000 tons of vitally needed munitions was an added burden at a time when combat requirements dictated an expansion of original expenditure estimates. Reserve stocks in the Marianas and at Oahu where drawn on repeatedly to maintain the massive weight of fire support for assault troops. Cancellation late in April of contingent operations originally slated for Phase III of ICEBERG released substantial quantities of ammunition for employment at Okinawa. For the duration of the campaign,

---

[111] *3/29 SAR, Ph III*, 2.

[112] Unless otherwise noted the material in this section is derived from *CTF 51 AR; Tenth Army AR*.

[113] "The number of ships and cargo tonnage listed under 'Leyte' represents that loaded for the Palau-Anguar-Yap Operation which was diverted to the Leyte Operation but which was unloaded under direction of Com3dPhibFor." *CTF 51 AR*, Part V, Sect I, 33.

[114] *Tenth Army AR*, Chap 11, Sect IV, 21. "In the preliminary planning the Tenth Army Ordnance Officer envisaged heavy ammunition expenditures. Original requests far exceeded the supplies made available initially and had to be drastically modified downward to fit availability of ammunition stocks and shipping to transport same." BrigGen D. H. Blakelock Ltr to CMC, 22Mar55, hereinafter cited as *Blakelock 1955*.

DUMP AREA behind Yellow Beach 2 appears in an aerial photograph taken on 1 May.

however, the problem remained critical, and Tenth Army was never able to maintain more than a barely satisfactory level of reserve supplies in its artillery ammunition points.

Aggravating the situation in the early stages of the operation was the fact that supply ships carried "balanced" loads, so that excessive amounts of small-arms ammunition had to be unloaded to get at vital artillery cargo. As the nature of enemy resistance revealed itself and expenditure rates of ammunition types could be more properly projected, logistics officers were able to schedule resupply shipments that better met the needs of ground combat on Okinawa.

The bitter and protracted Japanese defense of their Shuri bastion taxed to their limit the unloading facilities of the Hagushi beaches. As some of the beaches used for the assault landing were unsuitable for sustained and heavy operation and others selected for eventual use were not uncovered on schedule by Tenth Army's steady but slow advance, estimated beach unloading capacity gradually became an unrealistic figure. By 5 May the optimum point was reached and thereafter cargo unloading never equalled planned goals.[115]

Between 17 April and 17 May four new beaches were opened on the eastern coast of Okinawa in Chimu and Nakagusuku Wan to support base development activities and the XXIV Corps southern drive. Even the addition of these discharge points to the available beach capacity could not bridge the gap between planned and actual unloading totals.

---

[115] "One of the most important factors in preventing the unloading from reaching planned goals after 5 May was the weather. Frequent interruptions were also caused by Red alerts and enemy air raids. During May there were 17 days of heavy seas and torrential rains (14.68 inches fell in May with over 11 inches falling between 21 and 30 May) which materially interfered with unloading operations. During June there were 15 days when typhoon warnings and heavy weather materially interfered with unloading." *Blakelock 1955.*

344538—55——13

Although the threat of enemy air attacks made it desirable that cargo ships at Okinawa be limited to those that could be expeditiously unloaded, more ships than could be efficiently handled had to be called up. The change in the mission of IIIAC and the resultant opening of a four-division attack on Shuri defenses vastly increased consumption of all classes of supplies. Since a six-day lapse occurred between call-up and arrival of replenishment echelons, a calculated risk of *Kamikaze* attack had to be taken in order to maintain an immediate reserve of essential supplies in the target area.

Extensive efforts were made by naval and army authorities to expedite unloading and processing of supplies as the demands of ground combat increased in late April and early May. On 25 April Admiral Hall (SOPA Hagushi), acting in concert with General Wallace, Island Commander, recommended to General Buckner that more cranes, transportation, and labor be used to empty beached landing ships and craft; that more LVT's and crane barges be employed at the reef transfer line; that intermediate transfer dumps be established to prevent excessive hauls from the beach by shore party vehicles; and that ammunition and fuel dump dispersion requirements be modified to conserve personnel and transport.[116] The Tenth Army commander approved these recommendations immediately, but the increasing magnitude of the supply task swallowed up the gains made by the resulting improvements.[117]

While there was no real danger that the Americans would lose their hold on Okinawa at any time after attack forces landed the assault troops, the problem of sustaining the impetus of ground attack was acute during April and early May. During this critical phase Admiral Turner as Commander, Joint Expeditionary Force was solely responsible for coordinating the air, ground, and naval effort to maintain adequate supply levels of ammunition, fuel, and rations and replenishment stocks of troop material vital to the success of Tenth Army operations.

On 17 May Admiral Spruance, acting in accordance with the planned ICEBERG command pattern, announced that the amphibious phase of the Okinawa operation was ended. At 0900 on that date Vice Admiral Harry W. Hill, Commander, Fifth Amphibious Force, relieved Admiral Turner of his control of naval activities and air defense as CTF 51. Admiral Hill was directed to report to General Buckner who took command of all forces ashore and assumed Turner's responsibility to Admiral Spruance for the defense and development of captured objectives. At the same time a representative of Commander, Service Squadron Ten, logistical support force in forward areas, took over all of Turner's logistics duties.

During his period of command responsibility at Okinawa, Admiral Turner had successfully directed the largest amphibious operation of the Pacific War. His forces had killed 55,551 and captured 853 enemy troops in ground action and accounted for 1,184 enemy planes. From L-Day through L-plus 45 (16 May), 1,256,286 measurement tons of assault, garrison, maintenance, and ground ammunition cargo had been unloaded over Okinawa's beaches. Covering force guns from 5- to 16-inch had expended 25,000 tons of ammunition in support of Tenth Army and to protect the ships of TF 51.[118]

---

[116] RAdm Hall also recommended that the beach at Nago Wan be transferred to IsCom control from IIIAC. The size of the IIIAC shore party detachment necessary to handle a maximum capacity of five LST's or LSM's is indicative of the magnitude of the supply task involved on even this relatively small beach. On 26 April the detachment numbered over 600 men with 491 Marines and 123 members of the 11th Spec NCB.

[117] "Another factor contributing to the lower rate of unloading was the increased need of service troops, particularly engineers, to improve roads and to endeavor to make existing roads passable as a result of the extremely heavy rains. These additional troops came from airfield construction projects and the beach areas, the latter causing corresponding slow down of unloading. The arrival of engineer and service troops

---

on the island never kept pace with the requirements for unloading, base development, and the support of combat troops." *Blakelock 1955.*

[118] Comparative figures of tons of naval ammunition expended in other Central Pacific operations follow: Tarawa (1,833); Makin (1,800); Kwajalein (3,937); Roi-Namur (2,251); Eniwetok (2,020); Saipan (10,-

Although only a small portion of Okinawa's total area remained in Japanese hands on 17 May, the enemy had exacted a terrible price for what they had lost. Tenth Army had sustained 3,964 men killed in action, 18,258 wounded, and 302 missing, plus 9,295 non-battle casualties.[119] Admiral Turner's naval forces had lost 1,002 killed, 2,727 wounded, and 1,054 missing in action. Defending air forces had lost 82 planes to all causes, while TF 51 had had 156 ships sunk or damaged by enemy action: 25 sunk, 86 severely damaged, and 45 damaged but still operational.[120]

---

965) ; Tinian (3,627) ; Guam (8,000) ; Peleliu (5,579) ; and Iwo Jima (14,190). ComPhibsPac Amphibious Gunnery Bull No 2, Assault on Okinawa, 24May45.

[119] Of this number hospital ships evacuated 10,188 casualties, APA's 4,887, and air transports 5,093.

---

[120] The breakdown of loss or damage by ship type was:

Sunk: 8 DD; 1 DMS; 1 APD; 2 AM; 3 XAK; 1 LST; 3 LSM; 2 LCS; 1 LCI; 1 YMS; 1 PGM; 1 LCT.

Damaged: 7 OBB; 2 CA; 2 CL; 2 CVE; 38 DD; 6 DM; 9 DMS; 5 DE; 4 APD; 5 AM; 20 AP types; 1 AGS; 1 AO; 4 LST; 2 LSM; 9 LCS; 2 LCI; 2 YMS.

Reduction of the Shuri Bastion

CHAPTER IX

The 11 May attack of Tenth Army was a massive, coordinated effort to destroy the defenses of Shuri. It inaugurated two weeks of bloody, close-in combat that took the lives of thousands of men. For each attacking division the battle for Shuri took the name and shape of a different terrain feature. Conical Hill dominated the front of the 96th Division. The 77th Division fought for Shuri. The objective of the Marines of the 1st Division was Wana Draw. And for the 6th Division the goal was the capture of Sugar Loaf.

SUGAR LOAF HILL[1]

The three mutually supporting hills of the Sugar Loaf position rose abruptly from surrounding bare terrain. The flanks and rear of Sugar Loaf Hill were blanketed by fire from extensive cave and tunnel positions in Half Moon Hill to the southeast and the Horseshoe to the south. The 6th Division's analysis of the terrain pointed out that:

. . . the sharp depression included within the Horseshoe afforded mortar positions that were almost inaccessible to any arm short of direct, aimed rifle fire and hand grenades. Any attempt to capture Sugar Loaf by flanking action from east or west is immediately exposed to flat trajectory fire from both of the supporting terrain features. Likewise, an attempt to reduce either the Horseshoe or the Half Moon would be exposed to destructive, well-aimed fire from Sugar Loaf itself. In addition, the three localities are connected by a network of tunnels and galleries, facilitating the covered movement of reserves. As a final factor in the strength of the position it will be seen that all sides of Sugar Loaf Hill are precipitous, and there are no evident avenues of approach into the hill mass. For strategic location and tactical strength it is hard to conceive of a more powerful position than the Sugar Loaf terrain afforded. Added to all the foregoing was the bitter fact that troops assaulting this position presented a clear target to enemy machine guns, mortars, and artillery emplaced on the Shuri heights to their left and left rear.[2]

The strength of Major Courtney's embattled group of Marines atop Sugar Loaf on the night of 14–15 May fell away to a mere handful under the ceaseless bombardment and counterattacks of the Japanese. Shortly after midnight Courtney was killed leading a grenade attack against the reverse slope defenders, and the situation of the few remaining men steadily worsened.[3] At 0230 Lieutenant Colonel Woodhouse ordered his reserve, Company K, to reinforce Sugar Loaf, and the woefully understrength unit moved to the top of the hill and dug in. Counterattacks and infiltration attempts hit all along 2/22's thin lines during the

---

[1] Unless otherwise noted the material in this section is derived from *6th MarDiv SAR, Ph III; 6th MarDiv Jnl, Ph III; 4th Mar SAR, Ph III; 22d Mar SAR, Ph III; 29th Mar SAR, Ph III.*

[2] *6th MarDiv SAR, Ph III*, Part III, 5.

[3] *6th MarDiv History*, 112.

night, and at 0630 Company D of 2/29 was attached to the 22d Marines to help mop up the enemy that were fighting throughout the 2d Battalion's area.

At dawn less than 25 men, many of them badly wounded, remained within 2/22's perimeter on Sugar Loaf. At 0800 the seven survivors of the Courtney group were ordered off the hill by Lieutenant Colonel Woodhouse and shortly thereafter the Japanese again attacked the American outpost. As soon as Company D of 2/29 moved into position on the hill just north of Sugar Loaf, Woodhouse sent a reinforced platoon forward to relieve the remnants (1 officer and 8 men) of Company K. The enemy pressure on Sugar Loaf continued to mount and eventually drove the Marines off the hill. At 1136 the 11 remaining men of the original 60-man platoon drew back to hastily-constructed defenses manned by the rest of Company D.[4]

The series of enemy counterattacks begun at Sugar Loaf reached at least battalion strength and spread out along a 900-yard front into the zones of 1/22 and 3/29. An intensive preparation fired by NGF, air, and artillery to support the 6th Division attack set for 0800 temporarily stopped the Japanese assault but it soon regained momentum. Until 1315 when the last counterattack effort finally subsided, the troops manning the center of the division line beat off repeated attempts to penetrate their positions. A heavy loss was suffered by 1/22 as a result of the incessant artillery and mortar bombardment that supported the enemy attack. The battalion commander, Major Thomas J. Myers, was killed, and the commanders of all three rifle companies and the supporting tank company were wounded when the battalion observation post was hit by artillery fire.[5] Major Earl J. Cook, the executive officer, took over the battalion and began its reorganization. Companies A and B moved forward on the left of the battalion front during the morning to

seize the hill northwest of Sugar Loaf and blunt the force of enemy counterattacks.

The fear of a breakthrough in 2/22's area caused Colonel Schneider to order Company I of his 3d Battalion to move into blocking positions behind the 2d's thin lines. At 1220 he notified Lieutenant Colonel Woodhouse that his badly depleted battalion would be relieved by 3/22 as soon as possible and that it would then take over the 3d Battalion's old positions on the right of the division line.[6] By 1615 the relief was completed with Companies I and L occupying 2/22's old front lines.[7] Company D of 2/29 reverted to parent control. The 2d Battalion received a draft of 50 men from regiment to bolster its strength as it moved into new positions along the Asato Gawa.

An abortive counterlanding attempt on the night of 14–15 May had been smashed by naval support craft, but the prospects of further raids prompted division to reinforce its beach defenses. The 6th Reconnaissance Company was attached to 2/22 for night defense, and 2/4, which had been moved across the Asa Kawa at the height of the counterattack threat, went into position west of Asa. Lieutenant Colonel Woodhouse was given control of 2/4, which was still in corps reserve, for defense coordination purposes.

During the day the 29th Marines, besides contributing substantially to the repulse of the enemy counterattack, improved its hold on the high ground north of Half Moon Hill. The 1st Battalion, with Company C in assault and A following closely to the right rear, wiped out the pocket of resistance on the regiment's left flank which had held up the advance on 14 May. By late afternoon Company C had reached the valley north of Half Moon where its supporting tanks came under direct 150mm howitzer fire. Assault troops engaged the enemy reverse slope defenders in a grenade duel and dug in along the ridge north of the valley. Elements of Company A moved up on the right of C to contact 3/29, and Company B linked the 1st Battalion's lines with the 5th Marines along the division boundary. Freed from enfilade fire

---

[4] 2/22 SAR, Ph III, 6–7.

[5] 6th TkBn SAR, Ph III, 9. On hearing of the death of Maj Myers, Gen Shepherd remarked, "It's the greatest single loss the Division has sustained. Myers was an outstanding leader. Whenever I called on him for a job he never failed me." 6th MarDiv History, 117.

[6] 2/22 SAR, Ph III, 6–7.

[7] 3/22 SAR, Ph III, 4.

by the reduction of the pocket on its left flank, Company I of 3/29 moved abreast of 1/29 at dusk and tied in with Company G which had borne the brunt of the Japanese counterattack during the day's action.

The Japanese 15th Independent Mixed Regiment, which faced the 6th Marine Division, suffered heavy casualties on 15 May as a result of its unsuccessful counterattack and the advance of 1/22 and the 29th Marines. The division counted over 585 enemy dead within its zone and estimated that 446 more had been killed by supporting fires or sealed in caves and tombs during mopping-up activities.[8] Anticipating General Shepherd's all-out effort to destroy the Sugar Loaf position, the Thirty-second Army reinforced the 15th IMR on the night of 15–16 May with a "crack" battalion picked from the service and support units of the 1st Specially Established Brigade.[9]

The seizure of Half Moon Hill was the key to the success of the 6th Division attack plan for 16 May. Once the 29th Marines had cleared the high ground on its left flank, 3/22 was to advance and capture Sugar Loaf. Heavy enemy fire swept the entire front as the assault companies attempted to jump off at 0830. A platoon from Company B of 1/29, accompanied by tanks, passed through the right flank of the battalion line to clear the reverse slope of the ridge occupied by Company C. Devastating small-arms, artillery, AT, and mortar fire hit the tank-infantry teams as soon as they moved out of defilade and drove them back to cover. The fury of opposing fire from the reverse slopes also prevented Company C from moving over the crest of the ridge. The only gain of note in the battalion sector was made by the remainder of Company B which advanced 300 yards down the division boundary to positions abreast of Company C before it too was stopped by vicious frontal and flanking fire.[10] At 1400 Lieutenant Colonel Moreau was seriously wounded by an artillery shell which exploded in his observation post, and Major Robert P. Neuffer took command of the battalion.[11]

The 3d Battalion of the 29th (Lieutenant Colonel Erma A. Wright) spent most of the morning moving into favorable attack positions while the enemy bombarded its front lines with heavy mortars and artillery. At about 1400 tanks moved through the railroad cut northeast of Sugar Loaf and swung into the open valley that constituted the approach to Half Moon. While the tanks fired into the reverse slope of the ridge in front of 1/29 and delivered close-in supporting fire,[12] Companies G and I made a swift advance across the bare ground and reached the northern slope of Half Moon. Initial resistance was light, but by 1500 the battalion was in serious trouble. Showers of grenades from caves and emplacements on the south slope of the hill hit the men as they attempted to dig in. Machine-gun, rifle, and mortar fire coming from both flanks and the rear crisscrossed the exposed positions. An attempt to give the battalion protection with smoke cover failed to lessen the enemy fire, and slightly before dark Lieutenant Colonel Wright authorized a withdrawal. The assault companies pulled back to their jump-off positions for night defense.[13]

On the right of the division attack zone 1/22 met intense automatic weapons fire from the outskirts of Takamotoji as it attempted to move into position to support the attack of the 3d Battalion. The Takamotoji area had previously been quiet, and the presence of determined enemy defenders revealed that the Japanese had moved reinforcements into position to block any attempt to flank Sugar Loaf from the direction of Naha. The battalion was unable to occupy the high ground assigned it because of this fire and that coming from the direction of Sugar Loaf and the Horseshoe.

Lieutenant Colonel Donohoo planned to have Company I make 3/22's main effort as soon as 3/29's advanced covered his flank. The company was to circle and assault Sugar Loaf from the left while Company L advanced its lines to the next high ground to its front and covered the assault with fire on the west and south

---

[8] 6th MarDiv G–2 PrdRpt No 45, 16May45.

[9] Okinawa Operations Record, 88.

[10] 1/29 SAR, Ph III, 2.

[11] Maj P. D. Carleton, The Conquest of Okinawa: An Account of the Sixth Marine Division, (Washington, 1947), 69.

[12] 6th TkBn SAR, Ph III, 9–10.

[13] 3/29 SAR, Ph III, 2.

SUGAR LOAF HILL, western anchor of the Shuri defenses, seen from a point directly north.

slopes of the hill. Company I moved out with its supporting tanks at 1500 and reached the hill without meeting any serious opposition. Once the assault platoons attempted to drive to the crest, however, they began receiving machine-gun and mortar fire from the enemy defenders. The supporting tank company attempted to flank the hill and fire on the reverse slope but it was stopped by a mine field which claimed one tank.[14] Despite the heavy enemy fire the company had fought its way to the top of the hill by 1710 and begun to dig in.

Company L, which had moved out to support the attack shortly after 1500, was pinned down almost immediately by fire from three sides. With 1/22 and Company L unable to get into position to furnish supporting fire on the right and 3/29 forced to withdraw from Half Moon on the left, Company I's precarious hold on the top of Sugar Loaf was impossible to maintain. Excessive casualties inflicted by enemy gunners on both flanks and the determined defenders of Sugar Loaf itself forced the company back down the hill. Division and corps artillery fired harassing and interdictory fires to prevent

the Japanese from attacking Company I as it slowly withdrew to its former positions. During the necessary reorganization of 3/22's night defenses, enemy artillery shelled the front lines and Lieutenant Colonel Donohoo was wounded. The battalion executive officer, Major George B. Kantner, assumed command.[15]

At the close of a day of action that the division called the "bitterest" of the Okinawa campaign, in which its "regiments had attacked with all the effort at their command and had been unsuccessful,"[16] the offensive capabilities of the 22d Marines had been reduced to a point where further effort was inadvisable. After assessing his losses in the 16 May attack, Colonel Schneider reported that his regiment's combat efficiency was down to 40 per cent. Clearly, the 29th Marines would have to carry the burden of the fighting on 17 May. The regimental boundary was shifted to the west to include Sugar Loaf within the 29th Marines' zone because of the difficulty of coordinating an attack on both Sugar Loaf and Half Moon. (See Map 25, Map Section)

---

[11] *6th TkBn SAR, Ph III,* 9–10.

[15] *3/22 SAR, Ph III,* 5.

[16] *6th MarDiv SAR, Ph III,* Part III, 7.

The 29th Marines attacked with three battalions abreast at 0855 on 17 May. The 2d Battalion on the right, with Company E in assault, was assigned the mission of seizing Sugar Loaf while the 1st and 3d Battalions attacked the Half Moon. In an effort to neutralize the powerful enemy defensive system, an intensive preparation including the fires of 16-inch naval rifles, 8-inch howitzers, and 1,000-pound bombs was laid down on the regiment's objectives. The assault companies advanced behind a heavy and continual artillery barrage, and each infantry battalion had the support of a company of tanks.

Company A, attacking on the right of 1/29, drove west against the Japanese who occupied the reverse slopes of the battalion's ridge position. Tank fire, flame, and demolitions finally weakened the enemy fire enough for Company C to cross the crest of the ridge and attack down the hotly-contested southern slope. While Company C mopped up the remaining enemy defenders, Company A renewed its attack and made a swift advance across the valley floor to the forward slopes of Half Moon Hill. Fire from caves and trenches on the hill, from Sugar Loaf, and from the direction of Shuri stopped Company B when it attempted to cross the open ground and extend the battalion's lines on the left. The positions of the exposed assault platoons of Company A proved untenable without the planned reinforcement, and Major Neuffer authorized a withdrawal to a defiladed area approximately 150 yards forward of the morning's jump-off line.[17]

Freed from some of the heavy enfilade fire that raked its front by the advance of Company A on its left, 3/29, with Company H in the lead, fought its way across the valley floor to Half Moon. By midafternoon the battalion was digging in on the forward slopes of the hill but there was no contact between its positions and those of 1/29. At 1635 Colonel Whaling ordered two platoons of Company F to move up and close the gap. The hastily established defensive positions on Half Moon were subjected to terrific bombardment, and the failure of repeated attacks by 2/29 to secure Sugar Loaf exposed the right flank of 3/29 to

heavy and accurate fire from the enemy strong point.[18] In order to set up a secure night defense that would meet the threat of Japanese counterattacks, 3/29 pulled back when Company A was forced to withdraw on its left. The battalion took up strong positions only 150 yards short of Half Moon and tied in by fire with 1/29 and 2/29 on its flanks.

The first attempt by Company E of 2/29 to reach Sugar Loaf, a wide turning movement using the railroad cut for cover, was checked by enemy artillery fire as soon as the Marines debouched into open ground. A second assault, a close flanking attack around the left of the hill, was stopped by the precipitous nature of its southeastern face. The company reoriented its lead platoons to move up the northeast slope, and at 1700 the climbing assault started. Three times the troops, attacking through extremely heavy mortar fire coming from covered positions in the Horseshoe, reached the crest. Each time a frenzied counterattack drove them off.

At 1830 the fatigued and seriously depleted company made its final assault, once more gaining the fire-swept hill top. A determined counterattack was beaten back, but the company's ammunition supply was completely exhausted and casualties were so heavy that no men could be spared to evacuate wounded. At 1840 the battalion commander, Lieutenant Colonel William G. Robb ordered the company to withdraw from Sugar Loaf for the night. During one day's action 160 men had been killed or wounded in Company E, and Sugar Loaf was still in Japanese hands. At dusk some small measure of repayment for the day's terrible losses was gained when the enemy was caught attempting to reinforce Sugar Loaf by moving troops across the open ground at its base. Artillery observers concentrated the fire of 12 battalions on the hapless Japanese and completely smashed the attempt.

On 18 May tanks provided the key to a successful assault of Sugar Loaf. Despite mine fields and accurate AT fire which claimed six tanks, a company of mediums reached positions on each flank of the hill from which they could cover the reverse slopes. Company D of

[17] 1/29 SAR, Ph III, 2.

[18] 3/29 SAR, Ph III 3.

HALF MOON HILL and the corridor leading to the Kokuba Gawa as seen from Sugar Loaf.

2/29 advanced with the tanks and made a double envelopment of the objective. At 0946 the assault platoons reached the top of Sugar Loaf and held their ground despite a fierce grenade and mortar duel with the enemy defenders. The attackers soon moved over the crest to mop up and destroy the caves and emplacements on the south slopes. Deadly mortar fire from covered positions in the Horseshoe blanketed Sugar Loaf, and Company D dug in at about 1300 to hold its gains.

Lieutenant Colonel Robb committed Company F on the right of the battalion zone to reduce the Horseshoe defenses. Supported by fire from the troops on Sugar Loaf and 1/22 on its right, Company F reached the ridge that marked the lip of the Horseshoe depression before it was halted by an intense mortar and grenade barrage. The company withdrew slightly to the forward slopes of the ridge and dug in a strong defensive position for the night.

Impassable terrain prevented the tanks with

1/29 and 3/29 from enveloping Half Moon Hill.[19] Their fire support was invaluable, however, to the assault troops of the two battalions who had spent most of 17 May improving and consolidating their positions along the base of Half Moon. The continued strong resistance of enemy defenders in the Horseshoe and on Half Moon after the fall of Sugar Loaf Hill pointed up the importance of the Sugar Loaf position to the Thirty-second Army's defensive scheme.

During the 6th Division's advance to the Asato Gawa, the Japanese had countered the threat of a breakthrough at Naha by moving four battalions of naval troops to the area south of the 44th IMB's front lines. The motley naval units had a thin backbone of men trained for land combat, but most of their strength was derived from inexperienced service troops, civilian workers, and Okinawans attached to Admiral Ota's Naval Base Force. The lack of training was in part compensated for by a generous allotment of automatic weapons taken from supply depots on Oroku and the wrecked planes that littered the peninsula's airfield.[20] The naval force was to back up the Sugar Loaf position, hold the hills northwest of the Kokuba Gawa, and guard Shuri's flank should be the 44th IMB's defenses collapse. The Japanese considered that the fate of the left flank of the Shuri position hinged directly on their success in holding the defense area which stretched from the Naha estuary near Kobakura to the outskirts of Shuri.[21]

By nightfall on 18 May the combat efficiency of the 29th Marines had been seriously impaired by its fight for the Sugar Loaf position. The 6th Division had suffered 2,662 battle and 1,289 non-battle casualties since the start of the Tenth Army attack, almost all of them in the ranks of the 22d and the 29th Marines. A fresh unit was needed to continue the attack with undiminished fervor and General Geiger released the 4th Marines to General Shepherd at 1830. The 29th Marines was to become division reserve subject to IIIAC's control. The attack plan for 19 May called for the 2d and 3d Battalions of the 4th Marines to relieve the 29th and consolidate the gains of the previous day's fighting. (See Map 26, Map Section)

At 0300 the Japanese counterattacked the open right flank of Company F of 2/29 on the edge of the Horseshoe depression. The enemy assault, supported by a heavy bombardment of white phosphorus shells, was strong enough to force the leading elements of the company to withdraw to the southern slope of Sugar Loaf.[22] At daybreak Companies K and L of 3/4 began relieving the units of 2/29 on Sugar Loaf, while Companies F and E of 2/4 took over the rest of the 29th Marines' front. The reliefs were effected smoothly despite the difficult terrain, steady bombardment, and opposition from small enemy groups which had infiltrated the lines during the night. Some advances were made along the regimental front as assault companies seized the most favorable positions from which to attack on 20 May.

The area that had spawned the counterattack on Company F was partially neutralized during the day's action. The 22d Marines under its new commander, Colonel Harold C. Roberts,[23] advanced its left 100–150 yards to the high ground on the flank of the Horseshoe. Companies A and B of 1/22 dug in under enemy artillery and mortar fire to hold the new positions which materially aided in strengthening the division's line.

Company E of 2/4, which had taken over 3/29's advanced positions on Half Moon Hill,

[19] *6th TkBn SAR, Ph III*, 11.

[20] *IntelMono*, Part I, Sect B, 15–16; *CICAS Trans No. 202, Naval Attack Force T/O&E*, 4May45. While there was no organization or equipment standard for these units, the make-up of one of the battalions is indicative of that of the rest. On 4May45 the 3d Bn of the Iwao Force, a three battalion group organized to reinforce the Thirty-second Army, had 415 men disposed in two companies that were armed with 28 machine guns, 258 rifles, 27 grenade dischargers, 191 mines, and 1,744 grenades.

[21] *Okinawa Operations Record*, 89–90.

[22] The position of Co F on 18 May constituted a deep salient into the Japanese front. "Close examination of the aerial photo available was the cause of some concern since it appeared that the long ridge occupied by Co F was honeycombed with caves at, and slightly above, the level of the valley floor. . . . The counterattack which dislodged Co F apparently was initiated by Japanese from those caves." *Fraser*.

[23] At 1430 on 17 May, Col Roberts and LtCol August Larson relieved Col Schneider and Col Karl K. Louther as CO and ExO of the 22d Mar, respectively.

sustained a strong counterattack in the late afternoon which began shortly after the relief was completed. By 1700, after a two-hour fire fight, the company had turned back the attackers. However, since its exposed position was still vulnerable to attack from three sides, Lieutenant Colonel Hayden ordered the company to draw back its left flank elements approximately 150 yards to a point where they could tie in physically with Company F.[24] For night defense the 4th Marines established firm contact across its front linking up with positions of the 22d on the right and the 5th on the left.

Promising gains were made by both assault battalions of the 4th Marines on 20 May. Jumping off at 0800 behind heavy artillery barrages and tanks, the attacking troops moved rapidly ahead for 200 yards before encountering fierce opposition from the Horseshoe and Half Moon. The 22d Marines on the right furnished fire support to 3/4 in its attack on the high ground which formed the western end of the Horseshoe.

Infantrymen with demolitions and flame throwers followed closely behind the tanks which blasted the cave positions honeycombing the forward slopes of the Horseshoe. By 1600 when the regiment called a halt to the attack to prepare strong night defenses, Companies K and L held dominating ground that overlooked the Japanese mortar emplacements in the Horseshoe depression. Shortly after noon Lieutenant Colonel Bruno A. Hochmuth had committed elements of the 3d Battalion's reserve, Company I, which had mopped up Sugar Loaf Hill during the morning, to maintain contact with 2/4 on the left and strengthen the front line. Colonel Shapley, anticipating a counterattack in 3/4's area, alerted 1/4 to back up the Horseshoe defenses. Company B was designated for the job and briefed on 3/4's situation, routes of approach, possible support, and methods of support.[25]

The attack of 2/4 on Half Moon developed into a replica of the Sugar Loaf Hill battle during 20 May. Heavy and accurate flat trajectory fire coming from the direction of Shuri heights raked the battalion's flank, and mortars firing from defiladed positions on the reverse slopes of

TANKS evacuate wounded as men of the 29th Marines continue the attack on the Sugar Loaf position.

Half Moon covered the entire zone of advance. Resistance increased sharply throughout the morning as the enemy strove desperately to hold the commanding ground.

At about 1000 Company E, which had been replaced by Company G for the attack, was committed again on the left of the battalion line to maintain contact with the 5th Marines. With all three of his rifle companies in assault and the casualty toll mounting, Lieutenant Colonel Hayden decided to reorient his attack objectives from the front to the flanks of Half Moon. While Company F held its lines in the center and supported the advance by fire, Company E was to attack south down the division boundary and Company G was to drive past Sugar Loaf and then turn to attack the reverse slopes of Half Moon from the southwest. One company of tanks would furnish overhead fire support while a second company split to attempt a double envelopment with Companies G and E.

By 1245 the details of coordination were completed and the attack was renewed. The tanks with Company G negotiated the mine field that guarded the right flank of Half Moon and provided neutralization fire that enabled the infantry to seize and hold the western end of the hill. The tanks with Company E were unable to reach positions where they could fire on the

[24] 2/4 SAR, Ph III, 3.
[25] 3/4 SAR, Ph III, 2–3.

reverse slopes of Half Moon because of the operational failure of a tank bulldozer which attempted to make an approach route to the east of the hill.[26] Consequently, Company E was subjected to heavy grenade and mortar barrages as it advanced, and it eventually had to dig in on Half Moon's forward slopes.[27] The night positions of 2/4 and the Japanese were close but separated by a killing zone along the hill crest swept by continual enemy and friendly mortar and artillery fire.

The anticipated counterattack against the 4th Marines materialized at about 2200 when a Japanese group of battalion-size struck the positions of Companies K and L of 3/4. Prepared concentrations by six artillery battalions were fired as soon as the attackers revealed themselves, and constant illumination was maintained over the area by naval support ships.[28] In a two-hour-long wild melee fought by the weird light of flare shells, the battalion beat back the attack. Lieutenant Colonel Hochmuth committed Company B, which moved "with perfect timing"[29] to join the close-quarter combat and help blunt the attack spearheads. By midnight the few Japanese who had penetrated the lines were either dead or attempting to withdraw. Investigation in the morning light revealed 494 enemy dead and indicated that the attack had been made by fresh units, including some naval troops.[30] The frenzied

counterattack showed how determined the enemy was to safeguard Shuri's western flank.

The division attacked on 21 May with its objective the upper reaches of the Asato Gawa. The 4th Marines made the main effort with the 22d conforming to its advance and delivering supporting fire. Under its new commander, Lieutenant Colonel George B. Bell,[31] the 1st Battalion, less Company C in regimental reserve, attacked in the center of the line down the south slopes of Sugar Loaf toward the eastern extremity of the Horseshoe. Progress was slow and the fighting bitter as Companies A and B struggled to reach the river. A steady, soaking rain fell throughout the morning and most of the afternoon, making the loose, shell-torn ground muddy and treacherous. Adequate supply and evacuation through the thick, clinging cover of mud were almost impossible. The day's advance of approximately 200 yards was won only by dint of prodigious efforts by men who had to fight the weather as well as the numerous enemy pockets that held out all along the river approaches.[32]

The 3d Battalion drove down into the extensively tunneled interior of the Horseshoe, using demolitions and flame throwers to wipe out resistance in the nest of enemy mortar positions. Companies K and I halted their advance in midafternoon and set up a solid defense line approximately halfway between the Horseshoe and the river.

Advances in 2/4's zone of action were negligible because of the rugged terrain which prevented effective tank support and the intense mortar and artillery fire brought to bear on all ground exposed to the Shuri heights. After the fifth day of limited advances in the Half Moon area General Shepherd was convinced that the enemy power that prevented the capture of Half Moon was centered in the Shuri area, outside of the division zone of action. As a consequence, after a thorough estimate of the situation was prepared, he determined to establish a strong reverse slope defense on his left, "making no further attempt to drive to the

[26] *6th TkBn SAR, Ph III*, 12.

[27] *2/4 SAR, Ph III*, 3–4.

[28] An interesting sidelight on this action was related by the CO of 4/15, whose unit, assigned to direct support of the 4th Mar, controlled artillery fires directed at the counterattack. He stated that "I was able to talk directly to the front line commander of 3/4, LtCol Bruno Hochmuth, during the entire action . . . . This proved to be very handy indeed, because as usually happens when a large number [15 battalions were firing by 2315] of artillery units are firing in close proximity to our own front, 3/4 started receiving an uncomfortably large number of our own rounds. Because of the fact that I was talking directly to LtCol Hochmuth, who was observing the action from his OP, we were able to pick a lull in the fight, straighten out our 'shorts,' and still continue the very heavy artillery support he had requested early in the attack." Col B. T. Hemphill Ltr to CMC, 28Feb55.

[29] *3/4 SAR, Ph III*, 3.

[30] 6th MarDiv G–2 PrdRpt No 51, 22May45.

[31] LtCol Bell assumed command of 1/4 on 1 May replacing LtCol Beans who resumed his duties as 4th Mar ExO.

[32] *1/4 SAR, Ph III*, 2.

southeast in the face of Shuri fire, and to concentrate the division's effort on a penetration to the south and southwest."[33] He felt that such a maneuver would partially relieve the division of the menace to its left flank, and at the same time give added power to the drive to envelop Shuri from the west.

At midnight on 21 May heavy rains again began to fall, seriously impeding efforts to resupply assault troops and replenish forward dumps. The major obstacle to the success of the 6th Division's new plan of attack was not the fiercely resisting enemy defenders, but the unrelenting torrents of water that poured out of the heavens and rapidly turned southern Okinawa into a sea of mud.

WANA DRAW[34]

On 14 May a mop-up patrol from the 1st Engineer Battalion discovered a leaflet on the body of an enemy infiltrator in the 1st Division's rear area. Purportedly written by a wounded prisoner from the 96th Division it warned in atypical English that:

> . . . the battles here will be 90 times as severe as that of Yusima Island [Iwo Jima]. I am sure that all of you that have landed will lose your lives which will be realized if you come here. The affairs of Okinawa is quite different from the islands that were taken by the Americans.[35]

If the crude Japanese propaganda was intended to halt the Marine attack, it was patently unsuccessful. The promise of bitter resistance, however, was amply fulfilled by the defenders of Wana Draw.

In constructing the Wana position the Japanese had "taken advantage of every feature of a terrain so difficult it could not have been better designed if the enemy himself had the power to do so."[36] With this natural advantage, the enemy had so organized the area that in order to crack the main line of resistance it was necessary for the 1st Marine Division to wheel towards Shuri and attack directly into the heart of the city's powerful defenses. Any

attempt to drive past Shuri and continue the attack to the south would mean unacceptable losses inflicted by artillery, mortar, automatic-weapons, and rifle fire coming from the heights that commanded the division's flank and rear areas. (See Map 27, Map Section)

The southernmost branch of the Asa Kawa wandered across the gently rising floor of Wana Draw and through the northern part of Shuri. The low rolling ground bordering the insignificant stream was completely exposed to enemy fire from positions along the reverse slope of Wana Ridge and the military crest of the ridge to the south. At its mouth Wana Draw was approximately 400 yards wide, but it narrowed drastically as it approached the city and the ridge walls closed on the stream bed. Guarding the western end of the draw was Hill 55,[37] rugged terminus of the southern ridge line. The hill bristled with enemy guns whose fields of fire included the whole of the open ground leading to the draw. Defending the Wana position was the 64th Brigade of the 62d Division with remnants of the 15th, 23d, and 273d Independent Infantry Battalions, the 14th Independent Machine Gun Battalion, and the 81st Field Antiaircraft Artillery Battalion under its command.[38]

At 0630 on 15 May the 5th Marines completed the relief of the 1st, and Colonel Griebel assumed command of the zone of action west of Wana. The 2d Battalion was in assault with the 3d in close support and the 1st in reserve. On the recommendation of the regimental and battalion commanders of both the 1st and 5th Marines, the division decided to subject the high ground on both sides of Wana Draw to a thorough processing by tanks and self-propelled 105mm howitzers before 2/5 attempted to advance across the open ground at the mouth of the draw.[39]

With Company F of 2/5 providing fire teams for protection against suicide attackers, nine tanks from Company B, 1st Tank Battalion

---

[33] *6th MarDiv SAR, Ph III*, Part III, 11.

[34] Unless otherwise noted the material in this section is derived from *1st MarDiv SAR; 1st MarDiv G–3 Jnl; 1st Mar SAR; 5th Mar SAR; 7th Mar SAR.*

[35] 1st MarDiv G–2 PrdRpt No 44, 15May45.

[36] 1st MarDiv G–2 PrdRpt No 47, 18May45.

[37] This hill was also known as Hill 57 and Hill 59 because of the topographical inaccuracies of the first two versions of the official battle map. The designation shown on the third and most accurate revision, issued late in May, has been used in the text.

[38] 1st MarDiv G–2 PrdRpts Nos 44–50, 15–21May45.

[39] *2/5 SAR*, 11.

spent the morning working on the positions at the mouth of the draw. The tanks drew heavy small-arms, mortar, artillery, and AT fire, and accompanying infantry was dispersed to reduce casualties. Because of the open area of operation, the fire teams were still able to cover the tanks at relatively long-ranges. Both sides of the draw were honeycombed with caves and the tanks received intense and accurate fire from every sector at their front. During the morning one 47mm AT gun scored five hits on the attacking armor before NGF silenced it.

About noon the tanks withdrew to allow an air strike to be placed in the draw and then return to the attack in reinforced strength. Naval gunfire again silenced a 47mm gun that took the tanks under fire, this time before any damage was done.[40] With the approach of darkness the tanks pulled out of the draw pursued by a fury of enemy fire. The 5th Marines, convinced "that the position would have to be thoroughly pounded before it could be taken,"[41] scheduled another day of tank-infantry processing for Wana Draw before making its assault.

The 7th Marines spent 15 May reorganizing its companies, improving its positions, and mopping up the area around Dakeshi. Forward observers, liaison parties, and spotting teams concentrated on reducing known enemy strong points on Wana Ridge with extensive artillery, air, and NGF bombardment. At 2100 the 1st Battalion received orders from regiment to execute a fake attack on 16 May, with troops to concentrate for the jump-off while all supporting weapons fired a preparation.[42]

At daylight the troops moved into position, and at 0755 the preparatory barrage for the feint began. The area to the front was smoked by 81mm and 4.2-inch mortars. After 15 minutes the barrage was lifted to induce the Japanese to leave their covered cave positions and man open emplacements and entrenchments to repulse the expected attack. At 0825 supporting weapons opened fire again with undetermined results.

At 0950 the 7th Marines notified Lieutenant Colonel Gormley that an air strike on Wana Ridge was scheduled for 1000 and that he was to send patrols forward immediately following the strike to feel out enemy resistance. When the planes were delayed, Gormley requested cancellation of the mission and dispatched patrols from Company C to the ridge under cover of a mortar barrage. The patrols advanced without meeting any resistance until they approached the western end of Wana Ridge, where they came under vicious grenade and machine-gun fire. Counterfire was immediately laid down by the battalion's 81mm mortars and the patrols were able to occupy the western end of the ridge.

Orders were issued to the outpost to hold its ground, and reinforcements from Company C were dispatched to the ridge. At 1240 one platoon of Company A was sent forward to assist Company C, and at 1536 the rest of Company A was committed. Assault teams attempting to expand 1/7's hold on the ridge were met by showers of grenades from enemy troops hidden among the burial vaults and jagged coral outcroppings. A counterattack attempt was broken up by supporting weapons, but stiff resistance continued. With darkness the battalion's forward elements were forced to withdraw to secure night defense positions on the plateau just north of the ridge where contact was established with 2/5 to right rear and 3/7 to the left rear. During the day the 3d Battalion had occupied 1/7's former positions on Dakeshi Ridge.[43]

Tanks assigned to the 7th Marines had furnished direct overhead fire support to 1/7 from positions on Dakeshi Ridge, while the tanks with 2/5 had spent another busy day burning and blasting positions in Wana Draw. Working in relays, the tanks, supported by fire teams of Company F, ranged as far into the draw as Wana where three mediums and a flame tank completed the job of destruction of the village started by artillery, air, and NGF. Antitank fire disabled two tanks during the morning's action, but observers spotted the gun flashes of two 47mm's, and the main battery of the *Colorado* was brought to bear on the positions, destroying both guns.[44] Another tank was lost to

[40] *1st TkBn Summary*, 15Mar45.
[41] *5th Mar SAR*, 4.
[42] *1/7 SAR*, 12.
[43] *Ibid.*, 13–14.
[44] *2/5 SAR*, 12.

OBJECTIVES of the 1st Division's advance during May.

a mine and had to be abandoned and written off. Although strenuous attempts were made to retrieve tanks that were temporarily disabled, enemy fire usually blocked rescue attempts. If the tanks were left in the field overnight they were invariably destroyed by Japanese demolition parties and quite often used as pillboxes by the enemy defenders. At nightfall when the tanks retired, they had expended almost 5,000 rounds of 75mm and 175,-000 rounds of .30 caliber ammunition plus 600 gallons of napalm on targets on the ridge and in the draw.[45] After two days of intensive preparatory fire the 5th Marines was ready to attempt the attack on Wana Draw.

Throughout the morning of 17 May tank-infantry teams of 2/5 again worked on enemy positions in the mouth of the draw. Company F kept contact with the 7th Marines in its

attack on Wana Ridge, but was unable to hold advanced positions near the western tip of the ridge when a heavy enemy mortar and artillery barrage forced the advanced elements of the 7th to withdraw. On the right of 2/5's zone of action, Company E was more successful in penetrating the Wana Draw defenses.

The company's objective was Hill 55 at the mouth of the draw. Using the railroad embankment along the division boundary for cover and advancing across the open ground behind tanks, the company reached the base of the hill before it was pinned down by heavy small-arms and mortar fire coming from the left and left front. Two supporting tanks were disabled by mines,[46] and it was decided to withdraw the company under cover of fire from the two remaining tanks. A reorganization was effected behind the protection of the railroad

[45] *1st TkBn Summary*, 16May45.

[46] *Ibid.*, 17May45.

embankment, and at 1700 a platoon of Company E with six tanks attacked toward the hill again. This time a strong point was established on the western nose of the hill and held. Supplies and ammunition were brought up to the platoon outpost by tanks since the low ground leading to the hill was swept by machine-gun and rifle fire coming from Wana Draw.[47]

The 3d Battalion, 7th Marines relieved 1/7 at daybreak on 17 May and attacked with two companies toward Wana Ridge. Company I on the right seized and held the plateau that led to the western nose of the ridge line, while Company K, with the support of 12 gun and two flame tanks, attempted to secure the ridge crest northeast of Wana village. As soon as the company reached the ridge the enemy concentrated his fire against the assault platoons. Smoke grenades were used in an attempt to blind the tanks and limit the effectiveness of their supporting fire.[48] As the day wore on the position of Company K, beset from the front and both flanks, became untenable, and at 1700 the Marines pulled back to Dakeshi to set up night defense.[49] Late in the afternoon Lieutenant Colonel Hurst sent his reserve, Company L, up to reinforce Company I, prepared to assist the attack on the ridge the following morning.[50]

After a night of sporadic bombardment from enemy artillery and mortars, 3/7 again attempted to gain a foothold on Wana Ridge. During the morning supporting weapons concentrated their fire on the forward slopes and crest of the objective and at noon Company I, followed by a platoon of Company L, jumped off and fought its way to the ridge. The assault troops' gains "were measured in yards won, lost, and then won again." [51] Finally, mounting casualties inflicted by enemy grenade and mortar fire forced Lieutenant Colonel Hurst to pull back his forward elements and consolidate his lines on positions held the previous night.[52]

On the right flank of the division front the isolated platoon from Company E of 2/5 was unsuccessful in exploiting its hold on the western slopes of Hill 55. The men were driven to cover by intense enemy fire, and tanks again had to be called upon to supply ammunition and rations to the outpost.

During the morning operations the 5th Marines laid protective fire with tanks and assault guns along Wana Ridge to support 3/7's advance. At noon, under cover of this fire, Company F sent one rifle platoon and an attached platoon of engineers into Wana village to use flame throwers and demolitions against the enemy firing positions in the ruins. Numbers of grenade dischargers, machine guns, and rifles were found in Wana and the tombs behind it and destroyed. Further advance into the draw was not feasible until the 7th Marines could occupy the high ground on the eastern end of the ridge and furnish direct supporting fire to troops advancing in the draw below. At 1700 the troops were ordered to return to their lines for the night.[53]

In many ways the action of 19 May was a repetition of that on the previous four days. The 7th Marines again made the division's main effort, and the 5th Marines operated against the Japanese positions at the mouth of Wana Draw. All morning the ridge underwent a thunderous preparation from artillery, tanks, mortars, and weapons company howitzers in an effort to neutralize enemy fire. However, when Company I of 3/7 jumped off shortly after 1200 it ran into immediate enemy opposition. The company succeeded in reaching the western nose of Wana Ridge by 1555 by dint of fighting its way through a heavy mortar barrage. The weary troops then withdrew a short distance under enemy fire in order to be relieved by elements of 3/1.[54] The 1st and 2d Battalions of the 7th Marines had been relieved by their opposite numbers of the 1st Marines in their positions near Dakeshi earlier in the day. With the relief of 3/7 by 3/1 Colonel Mason assumed responsibility from Colonel Snedeker for the

---

[47] *2/5 SAR*, 12–13.
[48] *1st TkBn Summary*, 17May45.
[49] *1st MarDiv Interviews*, Co K, 7th Mar, 7.
[50] *3/7 SAR*, 2–3.
[51] *1st MarDiv SAR*, Part VII, OpAnnex, 6.
[52] *3/7 SAR*, 3.

[53] *2/5 SAR*, 13.
[54] *3/7 SAR*, 3. In its three-day battle for Wana Ridge 3/7 lost 20 KIA and 140 WIA.

WANA RIDGE, rugged barrier in the path of the 1st Division, is shown looking southeast toward Shuri.

capture of Wana Ridge, and the 7th Marines became division reserve.

Despite the fact that tanks with the 5th Marines had worked on the defenses at the mouth of Wana Draw for almost a week, new positions were noted daily and old positions, exposed by tank fire, were rebuilt and recamouflaged each night.[55] The defenses that blocked the mouth of the draw were duplicated and multiplied as the ridges on either side narrowed and grew steadily higher and more rugged. The eastern terminus of Wana Ridge, 110 Meter Hill [56] on the northwestern outskirts of Shuri, overlooked the zones of action of both the 1st and 77th Divisions, and its defending fire was a potent barrier to the capture of Shuri and the reduction of Wana Draw. On 20 May 110 Meter Hill was made the objective of a coordinated attack by the 1st Marines and the 305th Infantry with 2/1 moving into the 77th Infantry Division's sector to gain the most favorable route of approach.

Sparked by the presence of the rested and rebuilt [57] 1st Marines, the 1st Division made substantial progress on 20 May. Using the road running east from Dakeshi as a line of departure, Company G of 2/1 jumped off at 0815 sup-

---

[55] *1st TkBn Summary,* 19May45.

[56] This terrain feature was also known as 100 Meter Hill, Knob Hill, and Conical Hill by assault troops, but the designation of 2/1's SAR has been accepted here.

[57] On 16–17May45 the 1st MarDiv received 25 officer and 652 enlisted replacements from IIIAC, former members of the 46th Replacement Draft, and most of these men were allocated to the 1st Marines in division reserve.

ported by tanks, self-propelled guns, 37mm's, and overhead machine-gun fire. The assault troops surged ahead rapidly covering 600 yards to the base of the battalion objective, 110 Meter Hill. Enemy reaction was violent, and Company G suffered heavy casualties, including the company commander, from mortar and machine-gun fire. At about 1230 Lieutenant Colonel Magee ordered Company F to be prepared to pass through Company G and continue the assault.

At 1525 Company F attacked toward the high ground, passing through Company G which delivered suppressive fire on the ruins of Wana. Company F was unable to occupy the crest of the objective in the face of bitter resistance from reverse slope defenders. The assault troops dug in on the hill, and Lieutenant Colonel Magee sent Company E forward to extend the battalion's line on the left. A considerable gap that existed between the Marine and Army forward positions was thoroughly covered by interlocking bands of machine-gun fire and mortar concentrations.[58]

The 3d Battalion of the 1st Marines tied in with 2/1's lines for night defense after seizing a firm hold on the rest of the northern slope of Wana Ridge during the day's attack. Companies I and K moved out at 0845 and shortly thereafter closed to grenade range with the defenders of the ridge. The assault platoons, closely supported by tanks and armored flame throwers, spread out along the ridge, burning and blasting the innumerable caves, pillboxes, and weapons emplacements that defended the forward slopes. At 1140 two platoons of Company L, in compliance with Colonel Mason's orders, started carrying 55-gallon drums of Napalm up to the positions of Company I with the intention of splitting them open, rolling them down the steep slopes of the ridge into the Japanese positions at the head of Wana Draw, and setting the flame mixture afire with white phosphorous grenades.

The working parties were only able to manhandle three of the heavy and awkward drums up to Company I's positions by 1500. When these were split open at 1630, rolled into the draw, and set afire, their forward progress was

stopped about 50 yards down the reverse slope by an enemy entrenchment. The flame seared a small part of the Japanese defenses, but its effect was not potent enough to give Company I an entering wedge into the reverse slope positions. While it was still light, the 3d Battalion set up night defenses along the ridge crest with Company K tied in with 2/5 and Company I with 2/1. Because the troops could not dig in very deep in the hard coral that formed the ridge, casualties from enemy mortar and artillery shelling were high. The night positions of the defenders of Wana Draw and the Marines were separated by a few scant yards of shell-blasted ground.[59]

The objective of the 5th Marines' attack on 20 May was the low ridge running roughly southwest from Hill 55 along the Naha-Shuri Road. While Company G maintained contact with the 4th Marines at Half Moon Hill along the division boundary, Company E made the main assault. The time of attack, originally scheduled for 0730, was delayed an hour to increase the effect of the tank, assault gun, and artillery preparation. The assault progressed exceedingly well behind a continuous artillery barrage, and at 0930 Company E was involved in close fighting against Japanese in positions along the ground that bordered the road. Engineer mine-removal teams cleared a path for tanks to circle the battle from the direction of Wana Draw and take the defenders from the rear. By noon tank-infantry action had enabled Company E to secure its objective.

The next high ground to the south, Shuri Ridge, was the western extension of the height on which Shuri Castle was situated. Heavy small-arms and mortar fire from this ridge raked Company E's position throughout the afternoon, but continual artillery fire, point-blank tank fire, and two heavy rocket barrages finally silenced the enemy guns. Night activity, except for the usual sporadic mortar and artillery fire, was negligible, and shortly before dawn the troops were relieved on the front line by Company C of 1/5.[60]

The mission of 1/5 on 21 May was to maintain sufficient troops in the vicinity of Wana Draw

---

[58] 2/1 SAR, 9.

[59] 3/1 SAR, 26–27.
[60] 2/5 SAR, 13–14.

at Hill 55 to assist the attack of the 1st Marines and to patrol aggressively forward toward Shuri Ridge and the high ground to the east of Half Moon Hill. Tank-infantry patrols from Companies B and C scouted the ground to the south against intense machine-gun and mortar fire. Tank commanders, using their vehicles as armored observation posts, successfully called down artillery fire on point targets at close ranges.[61] Front line positions on Hill 55 and along the division boundary were advanced slightly to put the troops into more favorable positions for an all-out attack.

On 21 May Lieutenant Colonel Ross assumed command of 3/1 to replace Lieutenant Colonel Sabol who was transferred to the 7th Marines as regimental operations officer.[62] Ross' attack plan called for fire teams of Company L to work with relays of tanks in Wana Draw during the morning in an attempt to clean out the reverse slope positions on Wana Ridge. Companies K and I would support Company L's advance from the ridge crest and be prepared to attack across the draw on order with Hill 55 and the ridge line to the east as their objective.

During the early part of the afternoon the tank-infantry teams of Company L continued to work on positions in the draw against increasingly stiffer enemy opposition. At about 1500 Company K started across the mouth of the draw, and Ross asked Colonel Mason for a company from 1/1 to set up a secondary line on Wana Ridge to back up 3/1's attack. Company I, attempting to follow Company K's assault, was pinned down in the draw by heavy machine-gun and mortar fire. By 1800 Company K had fought its way up Hill 55 and tied in with 1/5, but it was unable to advance any farther to the east toward Shuri. Since Companies I and L were unable to reach the southern ridge line and advance up Wana Draw in the

face of withering enemy fire, Ross ordered them to withdraw to Wana Ridge for the night defense.[63]

In response to Lieutenant Colonel Ross' request, Colonel Mason attached Company C of 1/1 to the 3d Battalion. For night defense Company C occupied Company I's 20 May position tied in with Company L on the right and Company F of 2/1 on the left.

The 2d Battalion made repeated attacks on 110 Meter Hill and the rest of Wana Ridge in its zone on 21 May. The terrain was so steep and irregular that tanks were limited to overhead supporting fire. The deep cleft at the head of Wana Draw prevented the armor from reaching the reverse slopes of 110 Meter Hill, and the enemy defenders continued to hold out. On the left of the battalion, Company G mopped up enemy opposition in the northern outskirts of Shuri, but it was unable to exploit its success by turning the flank of the commanding hill. Resisting the advance of Company G were elements of the 22d Independent Infantry Battalion, the Thirty-second Army's last remaining first-line infantry reserve, which had been thrown into the battle to hold the area round 110 Meter Hill.[64]

Lieutenant Colonel Magee concentrated the fire of all his battalion's supporting weapons on positions in Wana Draw, but Companies E and F were unable to move down the reverse slopes of Wana Ridge in the face of bitter opposing fire from extremely close range. The accuracy of enemy mortar and artillery fire made it clear that the battalion was holding a preregistered impact area, since lowering skies and occasional rain squalls obscured the view of both enemy and friendly observers. Despite a steady drain of casualties the battalion maintained its forward positions. Company G linked 2/1's lines by fire with the 77th Division on the left, and Company F tied in for night defense with Company C of 1/1.

At midnight the day's intermittent rain increased to a steady downpour, and at 0200 the Japanese, capitalizing on the poor visibility, swarmed up Wana Ridge to attack Company C.

---

[61] *1st TkBn Summary*, 21May45.

[62] On 18May45 1stLt Peter I. McDonnell, CO of Co I, 3/7, was KIA. The ExO of 3/7, Maj John F. Corbett, assumed temporary command of Co I and was himself WIA in the attack of 19 May. The 7th Mar S–3, Maj Walter Holomon, was reassigned to 3/7 as ExO on 22 May. LtCol Sabol replaced Maj Holomon as 7th Mar S–3 and LtCol James S. Monahan, CO of HqBn, 1st Mar Div, replaced LtCol Ross as ExO of the 1st Mar.

[63] *3/1 SAR*, 27–29.

[64] 1st MarDiv G–2 PrdRpt No 50, 21May45.

For four hours a grim hand grenade battle see-sawed back and forth across the crest of the ridge before the Marines were able to restore their lines at daylight.[65] The enemy lost 180 men in their unsuccessful attempt to break the line held by Company C.[66]

So much of the success of the 1st Division's attack depended upon the tank-infantry team that the beginning of heavy rains was a major disaster. The ferocity of enemy resistance at Wana Ridge, where tank support was severely limited by terrain barriers, seemed undiminished. With the only tank country, that in the zone of the 5th Marines, rapidly turning into a veritable swamp, the 1st Division faced the prospect of a bloody stalemate with the odds distinctly in favor of the Japanese. (See Map 23, Map Section)

SHURI HEIGHTS AND CONICAL HILL [67]

For the XXIV Corps the period from 15–21 May was marked by a series of costly battles for the possession of hill strong points that guarded the approaches to Shuri and Yonabaru. Determined and agonizingly slow advances brought brief and bloody fame to rugged hills and ridges called Chocolate Drop, Flat Top, Ishimmi, Hog Back, Dick, Love, Oboe, and Sugar. And finally, when success was in sight and Shuri's flank was turned, driving rain and seas of mud bogged the attack to a virtual standstill.

The 77th Infantry Division was faced, as was the 1st Marine Division, with the unenviable task of maintaining steady, grinding pressure on the defenses of the core of enemy resistance at Shuri. On 15 May the 305th Infantry continued its dogged advance through the irregular terrain west of the main Ginowan-Shuri highway and east of Dakeshi. No prominent terrain features stood out in the regiment's zone of advance to keynote its action. Its objective was the northern outskirts of Shuri, and its path on this day and succeeding days was blocked by

countless small hills, ridges, and ravines fiercely defended by elements of the Japanese 64th Brigade and 32d Regiment.

On the left of the 77th Division sector several prominent hills and ridges completely dominated the rolling ground east and northeast of Shuri. The 306th Infantry had exhausted its strength in ten days of constant battling to reach these objectives and it was relieved on the morning of 15 May by the 307th Infantry. From right to left across the front of the fresh assault regiment the key ground was Ishimmi Ridge, 500 yards long and 110 meters high, which overlooked the Ginowan-Shuri highway; Chocolate Drop Hill, a rounded peak 130 meters high that rose abruptly from the rough plateau between the highway and the division boundary; and 140-meter Flat Top Hill, a companion peak to Dick Hill in the 96th Division zone, which effectively blocked the road from Kochi to Shuri that generally paralleled the division boundary.

On 15 May 3/307 fought its way up the forward slopes of Chocolate Drop and reached the base of Flat Top Hill against determined resistance. On the right of the regiment's zone the 2d Battalion, driving toward Ishimmi Ridge through the open highway valley, managed to gain a tenuous hold on a low finger ridge that extended southwest from Chocolate Drop. For night defense the regiment withdrew its assault troops from their forward slope positions to guard against the inevitable grenade duels and infiltration attempts.

The 382d Infantry of the 96th Division supported the attack of 3/307 on Flat Top Hill on 15 May in conjunction with its own assault against Dick Hill, which extended south from Flat Top along the division boundary. Behind a covering barrage of artillery fire placed on known enemy gun positions and observation points, 3/382 worked its companies up the steep slopes of the hill by infiltration. By 1700 three companies of the 3d Battalion and one of the 1st had reached the hill crest, but all attempts to cross the skyline were driven back by raking machine-gun fire. Night positions were taken up just short of the crest, only 50 yards from the Japanese defenders.

The 383d Infantry, with 2/381 attached, made

[65] *1/1 SAR*, 17.

[66] 1st MarDiv G–2 PrdRpt No 52, 23May45.

[67] Unless otherwise noted the material in this section is derived from *Okinawa: The Last Battle; Tenth Army AR; 77th InfDiv OpRpt, Okinawa; 96th InfDiv AR*.

little forward progress during the day against the extremely heavy enemy fire coming from the hill complex southwest of Conical's peak. Supporting weapons were used effectively to knock out enemy emplacements in the vicinity of the front lines and to cover strong probing patrols that felt out the reverse slope defenses of Conical Hill. The defenses were formidable, well-organized, and manned by the enemy's 89th Regiment which was determined to hold the vital eastern flank of the Shuri bastion.[68] (See Map 28)

The following day 2/383, attempting to capitalize on the information its patrols had gained on 15 May, attacked down the southeast slopes of Conical Hill. The battalion made only slight gains but one of the supporting tank platoons on its left flank broke through the cordon of enemy fire that swept the coastal flats and advanced 1,000 yards to the northern outskirts of Yonabaru. The tanks immediately started bombarding the town, but the intense enemy fire prevented the infantry from exploiting the armor's success and the tanks withdrew after exhausting their ammunition supply.

The 1st Battalion of the 383d again attempted to penetrate the hill fastness southwest of Conical and again was pinned down almost immediately. One platoon that did slip through the enemy fire barrier was practically annihilated on the forward slopes of the battalion's objective, Love Hill, by the crossfire of an estimated 50 machine guns that opened up from front, rear, and both flanks.

The hold that the 382d Infantry had seized on Dick Hill was exploited on 16 May. Early in the morning 2/382 passed through the lines of 1/382 and attacked across the crest of the hill. By 1400 the battalion had successfully wrested 100 yards of the southwest slope from the enemy in a violent bayonet and grenade battle. The 3d Battalion, attacking with 2/382, managed to get a few men onto the reverse slopes of the hill, but murderous heavy machine-gun fire from Oboe Hill (also called 150 Meter Hill), 500 yards due south, completely covered the exposed terrain of Dick Hill in 3/382's sector and effectively blocked the advance.

Fire from many of the same positions that had contained the advance of the 382d Infantry beat back the assault companies of the 307th on 16 May when the 77th Division renewed its attack on Flat Top and Chocolate Drop Hills. The 3d Battalion, led by tanks, made three attacks on Flat Top, reaching the crest each time only to be driven back by barrages of machine-gun and mortar fire. Attempts to flank Chocolate Drop were similarly stopped by bitter close-quarter combat and accurate long-range supporting fires. The reverse slope defenders of Chocolate Drop succeeded in pinning down the left flank of 2/307 driving toward Ishimmi Ridge, and the fire from the ridge held the right flank to moderate gains.

The 305th Infantry on 16 May concentrated its firepower in the attack zone of 3/305. Supported by armored flame-throwers and medium tanks mounting 105mm howitzers, the battalion advanced slowly along the finger ridges leading to the high ground of Shuri. The Japanese had turned the burial vaults that dotted the broken ground into mutually supporting strong points which could only be reduced by vicious close-in action. The day's advance netted about 200 yards and brought 3/305 to within 500 yards of the northern outskirts of Shuri.

On 17 May the 77th Division surprised the Japanese with a very successful pre-dawn attack. Both assault regiments made substantial gains, and Chocolate Drop Hill fell to 3/307. Only on the extreme right of the division where 1/305 came under fire from 110 Meter Hill and the sprawling fortress houses of Shuri's suburbs did the attack bog down. The 3d Battalion of the 305th and 2/307 dug in only a few hundred yards north of Shuri and Ishimmi in the highway valley. Flat Top was outflanked by 3/307, but heavy mortar and machine-gun fire drove back the assault companies when they tried to move into the exposed terrain south of the hill. The swift and silent advanced had bypassed many enemy strong points and the daylight hours of 17 May were spent mopping up and sealing caves to secure the ground taken. Constant pressure was maintained along the new front line to keep the enemy off balance and consolidate forward positions.

[68] *Okinawa Operations Record*, Record of the 24th Div, 18.

The day's attack had practically wiped out the Japanese 22d Regiment which had defended Chocolate Drop and still held the reverse slopes of Flat Top and Dick Hills with the help of the 1st Battalion, 32d Regiment. General Amamiya, 24th Division commander, issued orders on 17 May for the 32d Regiment to take over the defense of Shuri along a line from Ishimmi to Dick and Oboe Hills. The dwindling manpower available to both regiments was disposed in depth to contain any penetration and take advantage of the natural strength of Shuri's eastern defenses.[69]

The 96th Division's attack plan for 17 May called for the 382d Infantry to seize the hill mass south of Dick Hill that centered on Oboe Hill. The 2d Battalion cleaned up a host of fortified cave positions on Dick's western and southern slopes, making a hotly-contested advance of 200 yards. The 3d Battalion, encountering heavy fire from Oboe Hill to the south and Love Hill to the east, pushed mop-up patrols into the high ground that led to the regiment's objective. The intensity of enemy resistance met by the 382d indicated the need for further softening-up of the Oboe Hill area before a full-strength attack was renewed.

In the 383d Infantry's zone of action strong tank-infantry patrols of 1/383 operated to the left front of the 382d Infantry to clean out some of the multitude of machine-gun and mortar positions that barred any advance to Love Hill. The 2d Battalion atop Conical Hill maintained steady pressure on the reverse slope defenses and gave up part of its extended front to the 381st Infantry during the day when the 96th Division committed a third regiment to the attack. While 2/381 continued its mop-up activities and patrolling along the coast, 3/381 took over the left of 2/383's sector on the eastern slope of Conical Hill and brought forward its supporting weapons in preparation for an attack.

The following day 3/381 made the 96th Division's main effort while the remainder of the assault battalions concentrated on mopping up the vicinity of their front lines with tank-infantry, flame-thrower, and demolition teams. Medium tanks operating to the west of the

[69] *Ibid.*, 20–22, Map 5.

coastal road furnished excellent direct fire support against machine gun positions in the high ridge (Hogback Ridge) that extended south from Conical Hill. Despite this armored fire support, 3/381 was subjected to heavy and continual mortar and small-arms fire from Hogback, and its advance over the finger ridges that sloped down to the coast was limited to approximately 400 yards. Nevertheless, the battalion's progress was encouraging and indicated the possibility of opening the coastal corridor for a drive through Yonabaru to outflank Shuri.

The 77th Infantry Division on 18 May drove its attack wedges farther into the inner core of Shuri defenses with 3/305 gaining 150 yards along the Ginowan-Shuri highway and 2/307 advancing as much as 300 yards toward Ishimmi. Resistance was fierce and unrelenting and the ground taken was won at a high cost in casualties. Enemy gunners on 110 Meter Hill, Ishimmi Ridge, and the reverse slopes of Flat Top and Dick Hills had good observation and fields of fire across the whole front of the division's advance.

On 19 May the division undertook a systematic elimination of the enemy firing positions on the high ground to its front, using every available weapon for the task. The 306th Infantry, rested and partially rebuilt while it was in reserve, began moving up to replace the 305th, and 3/306 relieved 3/305 and portions of 2/307 along the low ground bordering the highway leading to Shuri. Small counterattacks, mounting in fury and strength as darkness approached, hit all along the 307th's lines and were finally turned back at dawn on 20 May after all available artillery was brought to bear.

The 3d Battalion of the 381st Infantry again made the 96th Division's main effort on 19 May while the 382d and 383d Infantry concentrated on destroying the cave positions and gun emplacements in the wildly irregular ground between Conical and Dick Hills. Prior to 3/381's attack two platoons of medium tanks and six platoons of LVT(A)'s, plus artillery and infantry supporting weapons, bombarded Hogback Ridge and Sugar Hill which rose sharply at the ridge's southern tip where it overlooked

Yonabaru. At 1100 the battalion attacked south and west toward Sugar Hill but gained very little ground in the face of the heavy defending fires. Numerous enemy positions spotted in the 18 May attack were destroyed, however, and the net result of the day's action was a steady whittling down of the Japanese 89th Regiment's defensive potential.

When 3/381 returned to the attack on 20 May, it made a slow, steady advance down the east slopes of Hogback, reaching the foot of Sugar Hill despite incessant grenade duels with the enemy fighting desperately to hold every inch of ground. The rest of the 96th Division also made significant gains as a result of three days of intensive preparatory firing and mopping-up activities. The 1st and 2d Battalions of the 383d Infantry fought their way to jump-off positions within 300 yards of Love Hill and in the process destroyed enemy strong points that had blocked their forward progress for a week. The 382d Infantry supported a successful attack of the 77th Division on Flat Top Hill and finally reduced all enemy resistance on the south and east slopes of Dick Hill. The 3d Battalion of the 382d making its first all-out attempt to take Oboe Hill was forced to withdraw by mortar concentrations and grazing machine-gun fire that made its forward positions untenable. The 383d concentrated its efforts through most of 20 May on destroying newly located defenses.

The fire support furnished the 77th Division by 2/382, coupled with the morning-long battle fought by 3/307 for Flat Top Hill, spelled the end of effective resistance from the enemy strong point. The 307th Infantry had now knocked out the second of the three hill fortresses that faced it on 15 May and was ready to attack south to Ishimmi Ridge and Shuri. The 305th Infantry, with 1/305 and 3/306 in assault, coordinated its attack with the 1st Marines on its right and made a slow, grinding advance of 100–150 yards that brought it to within 200 yards of the outskirts of Shuri in the highway valley. To exploit the gains of 20 May General Bruce, his commanders, and staff planned a pre-dawn coordinated attack across the entire 77th Division front.

At 0415 on 21 May in the 305th Infantry's

TANK DESTROYER of the 306th Infantry supports the attack of the 77th Division on Shuri. (Army Photograph)

sector 3/306 jumped off and advanced 200 yards without meeting any opposition. By 0520 the leading platoons had entered the northern suburbs of Shuri and were fighting on the eastern slopes of 110 Meter Hill. The relief of the 305th Infantry by the 306th was completed during the morning, and 2/306 moved into the division line on the right making visual contact with the 1st Marines. Much of the day was spent in mopping up bypassed enemy positions, and the regiment set up for night defense along a line from the forward slopes of Ishimmi Ridge through Shuri's outskirts to 110 Meter Hill.

The pre-dawn attack of the 307th Infantry got off at 0300 when 1/307 passed through the lines of 3/307 and attacked toward the regiment's next objective, three small hills which formed a triangle in the open ground 350 yards to the south of Flat Top. The leading company reached the objective at dawn but the enemy discovered the attackers and opened up with every type of weapon from the front and right flank pinning down the following units. No further progress was made, and at dusk the battalion dug in to hold its gains under continuous and accurate enemy fire.

The 96th Division made the most significant advances in the XXIV Corps zone on 21 May. The 1st Battalion of the 382d Infantry passed through the lines of 3/382 and advanced swiftly against moderate opposition to Oboe Hill. The 2d Battalion on the right paralleled the advance, moving southwest over the open ground to a hill 400 yards from Shuri. At 1130 both units noted enemy troops withdrawing from their fronts towards the high ground at Shuri and fired on the retreating Japanese. A series of counterattacks by isolated enemy troops hitting all along the regimental front prevented any further advances during the day.

The Japanese defenders of Love Hill, who had blocked a week of incessant attempts by the 383d Infantry to advance southwest from Conical Hill, again succeeded in turning back the attack of 1/383. Although tank-infantry spearheads of the 1st Battalion reached the base of the hill, heavy and accurate artillery concentrations forced a withdrawal. Units on the right of 2/383 were also driven back by this artillery barrage, but the rest of the battalion, cooperating with the 381st Infantry's attack, secured the western slopes of Hogback Ridge.

Fierce hand-to-hand combat cleared the eastern slopes of Hogback and brought 3/381 to the top of Sugar Hill by noon. Despite fanatical resistance which marked every foot of the day's progress, the battalion drove its advance elements to positions within 200 yards of the Naha-Yonabaru highway. The success of 3/381's attack on 21 May opened a 700-yard corridor down the east coast which promised to be the key to the reduction of the Shuri bastion. (See Map 23, Map Section)

General Hodge, confident that the steady progress of the 96th Division would give him the chance to outflank Shuri, had moved the 7th Infantry Division to assembly areas just north of Conical Hill on 20 May. Before dawn on 22 May the 7th attacked toward Yonabaru and the high ground south of the village. The rain that had fallen intermittently throughout 21 May had increased to a steady, torrential downpour by the time the assault troops of the 7th were in position to jump off. In short order "the road to Yonabaru from the north—the only supply road from established bases in the 7th Division zone . . . became impassable to wheeled vehicles and within two or three days disappeared entirely and had to be aban-

doned." [70] Rain and mud, normally impartial signs of nature's seasonal changes, became active and tremendously effective reinforcements for the Japanese Thirty-second Army.

STRUGGLE IN THE RAIN [71]

Paralleling the coast of Nakagusuku Wan between Yonabaru and the Chinen Peninsula was the forbidding Ozato hill mass,[72] a tangled area of rugged peaks and ridges whose heights rivalled and surpassed those at Shuri. On the north the hill mass commanded the eastern end of the Naha-Yonabaru valley. Before the XXIV Corps could cut off the Japanese in Shuri by attacking west through the valley, it was imperative that strong blocking positions be seized in the Ozato hill mass to guard the left flank and rear of the assault force. The mission of the 7th Division's 184th Infantry on 22 May was to capture Yonabaru and secure the heights that overlooked the valley and the village. (See Map 29, Map Section)

Led by 2/184, the regiment moved out at 0200 from its positions at Gaja Ridge, passed swiftly and silently through Yonabaru, and by daylight had gained the crest of its first hill objective south of the village. Surprise was complete; at dawn the defenders of the hill were shot down as they emerged from their cave shelters to man entrenchments and gun positions. The Thirty-second Army had not expected an attack, still less a night attack, believing that the Americans would not advance without tank support.[73]

Capitalizing on its initial advantage, the 184th Infantry committed 3/184 on the right of the 2d Battalion and drove forward to seize the key points of the terrain. Despite the rain

---

[70] *XXIV Corps AR*, 31.

[71] Unless otherwise noted the material in this section is derived from *Okinawa: The Last Battle; Tenth Army AR; IIIAC AR; XXIV Corps AR; 1st MarDiv SAR; 6th MarDiv SAR, Ph III; 7th InfDiv AR; 77th InfDiv OpRpt, Okinawa; 96th InfDiv AR; 1st Mar SAR; 4th Mar SAR, Ph III; 5th Mar SAR; 22d Mar SAR, Ph III; 29th Mar SAR, Ph III.*

[72] The hill mass derived its name from its location in the Ozato Mura (township) area in same manner that the Urasoe Mura Escarpment encountered by XXIV Corps in April was named. In both instances the terrain feature was located in close proximity to the township designation on the 1 : 25,000 battle map.

[73] *Yahara Interrogation.*

105MM HOWITZER of the 15th Marines is almost swamped, but still in firing order, after ten days of rain.

and mud which severely hampered supply operations and curtailed the effectiveness of supporting weapons, the regiment advanced 1,400 yards during the day and set up secure night positions holding most of the ground on its assigned objectives.

On the opposite flank of the Tenth Army front on 22 May the 4th Marines attacked to bring its lines up to the Asato Gawa. While 2/4 held its position on Half Moon Hill and maintained contact with the 1st Division, 1/4 and 3/4 slogged slowly through the "gooey slick mud" [74] to the bank of the rain-swollen river. Enemy opposition was sporadic and ineffective, and assault troops seized their objective by 1230. Patrols immediately crossed the Asato and advanced 200 yards into the outskirts of Naha before drawing scattered enemy fire. The troops dug in along the north bank of the river for night defense while tentative plans were

[74] *3/4 SAR, Ph III, 3.*

laid for a crossing in force on 23 May. (See Map 30, Map Section)

In sharp contrast to the sweeping advance of the 7th Infantry Division and the encouraging progress of the 6th Marine Division was the situation in the center of the Tenth Army front. For the 1st, 77th, and 96th Divisions 22 May marked the beginning of a week of bitter frustration and fruitless pounding against the Shuri defenses. Deprived of vital tank support by the mud which blanketed the zone of attack, the infantrymen of the three divisions could do little more than probe and patrol to the front. Small local gains were made each day and relentless pressure was maintained against the defenses of the enemy fortress city; but each time a full-scale coordinated attack was planned, a fresh onslaught of driving rain cancelled the operation.

The floor of every draw and gulley became a sticky morass of knee- and thigh-deep mud while the precipitous slopes of the hills and ridges, treacherous footing under the best conditions, were virtually unassailable. Every ration box, water can, and round of ammunition needed to maintain the assault troops had to be manhandled up to the front lines when lowering skies prevented air drops. Reserve units, depleted from days of heavy fighting for Shuri's heights, had to provide many of the necessary carrying parties. Every type of vehicle, including LVT's and wide-tracked bulldozers, eventually bogged down in the mud, and the gap between forward supply dumps and the battle line steadily widened despite day and night efforts by engineers to maintain the vanishing road net. Under these conditions it was impossible to build up adequate supply reserves which would be needed to sustain an all-out assault. Day after wearying day the sodden infantrymen left their flooded foxholes to attack the Japanese positions, sometimes gaining, sometimes losing a small patch of ground, but the net result was stalemate.

Aided by the fact that their open seaward flanks gave them a route of supply denied to units in the center of the Tenth Army's front, the 6th Marine and 7th Infantry Divisions drove back the Japanese who held the coastal flats. Once their direction of attack shifted toward Shuri's heights, however, they encountered the same fierce resistance met by the 1st, 77th, and 96th Divisions. This opposition, coupled with the continued bad weather, was enough to lose the "opportunity to isolate completely the main enemy force in Shuri." [75]

On 23 May the enemy Thirty-second Army served notice on the 7th Infantry Division that a drive west through the Naha-Yonabaru valley would be bitterly opposed. While the 184th Infantry with its 2d and 3d Battalions in assault drove further into the Ozato hill mass securing the mouth of the valley, the 32d Infantry moved through Yonabaru and struck west and southwest to cut off the defenders of Shuri. Enemy opposition increased steadily during the day with mortar and machine-gun fire coming from a series of low hills to the front near Yonawa. The tanks which had been counted upon to exploit the breakthrough were

immobilized by the mud of the flooded valley, and 2/32 and 3/32 were forced to dig in along a line a mile to the southwest of Yonabaru.

During the night of 22–23 May a patrol from the 6th Reconnaissance Company scouted the south bank of the upper reaches of the Asato Gawa. Returning through the lines of 1/22 the patrol reported:

> Reconnaissance conducted successfully. Stream fordable at low tide. Routes steep but will accommodate infantry. Covered half of bluff on south side of river. No occupied emplacements found. Met 2 Nip patrols 1–6 man, 1–3 man. Japs threw grenades. Killed 1. [76]

Since the night reconnaissance indicated to General Shepherd that "it might be feasible to attempt a crossing of the Asato without tank support," [77] he ordered the 4th Marines to intensify its patrol activities south of the river during the early morning of the 23d. If resistance proved light, the regiment was to be prepared to execute the Asato crossing. The patrols received long-range machine-gun fire from high ground around Machisi, but there was little evidence of determined resistance at the river's edge.

At 1000 General Shepherd made the decision to force the Asato line, and at 1030 Companies A and B of 1/4 and I and L of 3/4 began wading the stream. By 1100 a firm bridgehead had been secured on the south bank. [78] The day's objective was a low east-west ridge 500 yards south of the river, and resistance increased sharply as the assault troops approached it. Many Okinawan tombs on the forward face of the ridge had been fortified, and the reverse slopes were studded with mortar positions. The heavy fire slowed the advance to a crawl, and the troops dug in on the ridge approaches as darkness fell.

At the time of the assault crossing the Asato had been ankle deep, [79] but a steady driving rain turned the stream into a chest-high torrent. While engineers struggled to put in a bridge

---

[75] *XXIV Corps AR*, 31.

[76] *6th Mar Div Jnl, Ph III*, 23May45. Some abbreviations in the original recorded message have been spelled out.

[77] *6th MarDiv SAR, Ph III*, Part III, 12.

[78] Col G. B. Bell Ltr to CMC, 7Mar55, hereinafter cited as *Bell*.

[79] *6th MarDiv Jnl, Ph III*, 23May45.

under intense artillery and mortar fire, men stood for hours in the water forming a human chain to pass supplies and casualties between the muddy banks.[80] Two foot bridges had been constructed by midnight, but attempts to bring up materials for a Bailey bridge during the afternoon were beaten back by accurate enemy artillery fire.[81]

General Geiger shifted the boundary of the 1st Division to the right during the morning of 23 May so that 2/4 could close up its extended lines and better protect the left flank and rear of the 4th Marines' bridgehead. The 5th Marines on the right of the 1st Division committed 3/5 to take over the extended front. No forward progress was made by either assault regiment of the 1st Division although combat patrols rooted out the enemy defenders in the vicinity of the front lines. The 77th and 96th Divisions also limited their activities to patrolling and mopping up near the positions they had reached on 21 May.

By nightfall on 23 May the Japanese command had evaluated the threat to the flanks of the Shuri bastion by the American advances along both coasts. Even though the 4th Marines "had broken into the city of Naha," the enemy commanders believed their forces were "still able to halt the collapse of all positions by holding positions in depth to the line of Shichina and Kokuba." However, the Thirty-second Army believed that it had to eliminate the 7th Infantry Division spearhead that had reached the Naha-Yonabaru valley or it would "be unable to maintain the Shuri front."[82] Every man that could be spared from the positions checking the advance of XXIV Corps north and east of Shuri was thrown into a defense line that stretched from the southwest slopes of Conical Hill through Yonawa to the road junction village of Chan.

Proof of this heavy enemy reinforcement was met by the 32d and 184th Infantry as they attempted to expand their hold on the valley and the high ground to its south. Steadily increasing resistance which culminated in a series of heavy counterattacks during the night of 24–25

[80] 3/4 SAR, Ph III, 4.
[81] 6th EngBn SAR, Ph III, Part III, 3.
[82] Okinawa Operations Record, 90.

A BULLDOZER, an assault gun, and a jeep all fight the mud that blanketed Okinawa in late May.

May served to slow and finally halt the western progress of the 7th Infantry Division. Patrols of the 184th Infantry continued to thread their way through the Ozato hill mass toward the Chinen Peninsula, meeting sporadic opposition, but any attempt to drive towards the road net directly south of Shuri was blocked by fanatical defenders.

Again on 24 May the action in the center of the Tenth Army line was limited by the muddy terrain and lack of adequate supply reserves to local attacks. Fervid close-quarter grenade duels and point-blank exchanges of small-arms fire indicated that the enemy was still determined to hold Shuri. Although very little rain fell during the day, the condition of the ground was by now so bad that little advantage could be taken of the break in the weather. The enemy, however, perhaps in support of his counterattacks on the 7th Infantry Division, mounted a combined *Kamikaze*-airborne attack against Okinawa during the night of 24–25 May.

The *Kamikazes* concentrated on the radar picket stations, damaging the APD *Bates* and the LSM 135 so severely that the former eventually capsized and the latter had to be beached and abandoned. Eight other ships, mostly destroyer types, received varying degrees of dam-

TRACERS interlace the sky as AAA guns repulse a Japanese air raid on Yontan airfield.

arms fire that crisscrossed the open field and 18 were injured.[85] Judging from the damage done by eight to ten trained men, if even one or two more enemy transports had landed, the amount of destruction would have been staggering. Fortunately, the antiaircraft defense of Okinawa was superlative, and even the one plane that penetrated the fire barrier was riddled with shell fragments.

The clear weather on 24 May which had allowed the Japanese to make an intensive air attack had been preceded by a night of steady rain. Consequently, the 6th Marine Division with the supply line to its assault battalions bisected by a raging, rain-swollen stream had to concentrate its efforts on establishing vehicular crossings. Any attempt to continue the attack to the south without adequate reserves of ammunition and rations below the Asato could well have been disastrous. Patrols of the 4th Marines probed the enemy defenses near Machisi, and a heavy air strike plus a continuous artillery bombardment was laid on the regiment's objectives. By midafternoon a Bailey bridge had been constructed despite accurate artillery and mortar shelling that plagued the engineer working parties. An earlier attempt to install a makeshift bridge built on LVT's had failed because of the large number of enemy mines encountered along the river bank; two LVT's of the five used had been severely damaged before the effort was abandoned.[86]

During the morning of 24 May 3/22, commanded by Lieutenant Colonel Clair W. Shisler,[87] was detached from its parent unit, ordered to relieve 2/4, and given responsibility for the defense of the division's left flank. After its relief by 3/22, 2/4 crossed the Asato and relieved the badly battered 3d Battalion[88] on the right of the 4th Marines' line. To pro-

age, and the Japanese pilots exacted a toll of 38 killed, 183 wounded, and 60 missing in action from the crews of the stricken vessels. Over 150 enemy planes were shot down by combat air patrols and ship and ground AA.[83]

In a night characterized by the heaviest ground antiaircraft action of the campaign, Marine and Army AAA battalions guarding Yontan and Kadena airfields repulsed an enemy airborne attack by shooting down 11 twin-engined planes and driving off the remainder. Most of the planes fell before the guns of the Marines' 1st Provisional AAA Group emplaced around Yontan airfield. Only one of the aircraft, each of which carried about 14 men of the Japanese 1st Air Raiding Brigade, reached the ground safely and eight of the occupants were dead when the plane ground to a wheels-up stop on one of Yontan's runways.[84]

The few Japanese who survived the crash landing created extensive havoc with their demolition charges and grenades before they were killed by Marine air personnel defending the field. Eight aircraft were destroyed and 24 were damaged by flame and explosives. Two Marines lost their lives in the hail of small-

---

[83] ComFifthPhibFor AR, Capture of Okinawa Gunto, Phases I and II, 17May–21Jun45, Part III, 20–26, hereinafter cited as *CTF 31 AR*.

[84] 53d AAA Brig AAR, 21Jun45, 40–43; Tenth Army G–2 Rpt No 61, 25May45, Annex A, Organization of the 1st Raiding Brig.

---

[85] 2d MAW War Diary, May 1945, 11. One of the planes destroyed was the headquarters transport of MajGen James T. Moore, CG, AirFMFPac, who had landed on Yontan that morning to confer with MajGen Mulcahy on the relief of pilots and other problems.

[86] *6th EngBn SAR, Ph III*, Part III, 3.

[87] At 1815 on 20 May Maj Kantner was relieved of his temporary command of 3/22 by LtCol Shisler and once again became Bn ExO.

[88] None of the companies of 3/4 could muster more than 90 men when the battalion was relieved.

vide the assault regiment with a strong reserve, General Shepherd attached 1/29 and ordered Major Neuffer's battalion to take up positions south of the river.

Despite the heavy rains which closed in once more, the 6th Division was able to expand its bridgehead on 25 May. The immediate objective of the attack was the high ground in and around the village of Machisi. In 1/4's zone of action on the left of the regimental line, Company C led the assault and Company B was fed in gradually on the left to keep contact with Company A which remained tied in with 3/22.[89] Tanks which had crossed the river on the new engineer bridge furnished overhead fire suport but were unable to negotiate the muddy terrain between the river and the front line. The ridge in Machisi was taken by 1030 against stiff resistance from reverse slope defenders, and the assault troops forged ahead slowly, taking heavy fire from the front and left flank. At 1630 Colonel Shapley halted the regiment's attack and ordered the assault troops of the 1/4 and 2/4 to dig in and establish firm contact across the front.

The 2d Battalion with Companies F and G in assault made 400 yards during the day against extremely thick mortar and small-arms fire. By mid-afternoon it was necessary to commit Company E on the left of the battalion line to maintain the impetus of attack and bridge a gap that had developed between 2/4 and 1/4. Deprived of tank support by the mud, the attacking troops suffered heavy casualties from Japanese defending the walled houses and tomb-studded ridges along Naha's eastern outskirts.[90]

A canal 20 yards wide with a thick mud bottom and banks of stone three to five feet high, connecting the Asato Gawa and the Kokuba Gawa estuary, effectively divided urban Naha into two distinct zones of action. On 25 May as the 4th Marines fought the enemy defending the city east of the canal, Major Walker's 6th Reconnaissance Company crossed the Asato near its mouth and quickly cleared an area about 300 yards deep of snipers and scattered enemy defenders. The engineers put in a foot bridge

near the river's mouth behind the reconnaissance company's defensive perimeter, and 2/22, which now held the whole 22d Marine's front north of the river, readied Company G to support or relieve Walker's men as necessary.[91]

The Marines west of the canal spent a quiet night, but the Japanese staged heavy counterattacks against the positions of 1/4 and Company E of 2/4. A railroad cut ran along the 1st Battalion's left boundary about 150 yards from the positions of Company A. At 2000, under cover of darkness and smoke shells, a company-sized counterattack was mounted against 1/4's lines. Spotted immediately by observers with Company A, the attack died a-borning as a solid two hours of artillery and mortar shelling blanketed the Japanese assembly area.[92] A lighter counterattack hit Company E which was down to a strength of one officer and about 40 men after the day's fighting. A platoon from 1/29 helped drive off the Japanese amid a lethal shower of hand grenades.[93]

Across the remainder of the Tenth Army front on 25 May the reports of the assault units reflected the havoc wrought by the rain. With its lone supply road rapidly disappearing into the mud and the Japanese providing greatly stiffened resistance, the 7th Infantry Division was hard put to maintain the impetus of its attack. Despite the losses suffered by the enemy in night-long counterattacks and constant pressure by the 32d Infantry, the enemy defense line west of Yonabaru remained "materially unchanged."[94] The troops of the 96th Division holding the broken ground south and west of Conical Hill were almost isolated from division rear areas. Constant small counterattacks and infiltration attempts bled the strength of assault rifle companies to the point where every available man in service and support elements had to be committed to the front lines or assigned the tremendously debilitating task of packing supplies forward through the muddy terrain. A capsule description of progress in

[89] 1/4 SAR, Ph III, 2.
[90] 2/4 SAR, Ph III, 4.

[91] 6th MarDiv Jnl, Ph III, 25May45.
[92] 1/4 SAR, Ph III, 3.
[93] 2/4 SAR, Ph III, 5. On 26May45 Maj Edgar F. Carney assumed command of 2/4.
[94] Tenth Army G–2 Rpt No 61, 25May45.

the 96th's zone of action was provided by one of its officers who reported:

Those on the forward slopes slid down. Those on the reverse slopes slid back. Otherwise, no change.[95]

The monotonous sameness of reports of thread-thin supply lines and continual small unit pressure on enemy positions that resulted in little or no forward progress marked 25 May's action in the sectors of the 1st Marine and 77th Infantry Divisions. However, on the following day a definite break in the solid front of enemy opposition at Shuri occurred. Front line observers of the 1st and 5th Marines noted considerable enemy movement south of Shuri, and Lieutenant Colonel John W. Scott, Jr., the 1st Division G-2, requested air observation at 1200.[96]

Despite the rain and poor visibility a spotter plane from the battleship *New York* sighted large numbers of enemy troops and vehicles crowding the roads south of Shuri. Within 13 minutes the cruiser *New Orleans* fired the first salvo of a thunderous NGF barrage that pounded the enemy troop concentrations.[97] Every artillery piece and mortar within range chimed in. Less than a half-hour after the *New York's* spotter had confirmed the 1st Division's reports, and despite the hazardous flying conditions, more than 50 Marine fighters took off to strafe and bomb the lucrative targets. An estimated 3,000–4,000 Japanese with tanks, trucks, and artillery pieces had been caught in the open, and the pilots and gunners had a field day. Observation planes zoomed dangerously low through the overcast to tally more than

500 enemy dead as a result of the combined bombardment. General del Valle's message to TAF at the day's end applied equally to all the supporting units who received the front line infantrymen's "congratulations and thanks for prompt response this afternoon when Nips were caught on road with kimonos down." [98]

The obvious fact that large numbers of enemy troops were pulling out of Shuri seemed to make little difference in the stubbornness of the Japanese defense of the area. While the heavy rains prevented all but local attacks, patrols probing toward the city met mortar and machine-gun fire that indicated the inner perimeter defense was still strongly held. Only along the coasts where the 6th Reconnaissance Company checked the ruins of western Naha and the 184th Infantry patrolled toward the Chinen Peninsula was the resistance light.

During the night following the discovery of the Japanese troop movement, artillery and naval support ships fired continuous interdictory and harassing missions on all roads, crossroads, and road junctions leading south from Shuri. On 27 May General Buckner issued the following instructions by dispatch to both corps:

Indications point to possible enemy retirement to new defensive position with possible counteroffensive against our forces threatening his flank. Initiate without delay strong and unrelenting pressure to ascertain probable intentions and keep him off balance. Enemy must not repeat not be permitted to establish himself securely on new position with only nominal interference.[99]

Although continued heavy rains precluded the possibility of a successful army-wide attack, strong combat patrols were dispatched toward the Japanese positions all along the front. Stiff resistance was encountered immediately, indicating that the enemy still held his Shuri defenses in force. Typical patrol reports read, "No indication of Japanese withdrawal," or, "Does not appear that resistance has lessened." [100]

The 7th Infantry Division assault troops attempting to drive west from Yonabaru were met by elements of the Japanese 62d Division

---

[95] Quoted in *96th InfDiv History*, 159.

[96] IIIAC G-2 Prd Rpt No 56, 27May45.

[97] *CTF 31 AR*, Part III, 27. Regarding the circumstances of this NGF support, the IIIAC NGFO recalled that "the *New York* was some distance from the beach but the *New Orleans* was close in. The *New Orleans* heard the report of the *New York's* plane and asked the spotter for coordinates. She positioned herself and began adjustment by full salvos of main battery. . . . Other firing ships and support craft with H&I [Harassing and Interdiction] missions or otherwise in the area, noticed the increased activity, sent up planes, and got into the act. Ships without planes asked to be cut in with ships that did have them and often a plane spotter was firing two or more ships at the same time." LtCol W. M. Gilliam Ltr to CMC, 16Mar55.

[98] 2d MAW War Diary, May 1945, 12.

[99] *Tenth Army AR*, Chap 7, Sect III, 24–25.

[100] *1st MarDiv G-3 Jnl*, 27May45.

hastily committed to brace the enemy's right flank. Patrol spearheads of the 184th Infantry on the left flank of the army reached Inasomi two miles southwest of Yonabaru without encountering any organized resistance. The Japanese were well aware of the threat of this deep penetration, however, and additional troops of the 62d Division were moved down from Shuri to contain it.[101]

Evidence that the Japanese had virtually abandoned Naha was discovered by the 6th Marine Division on 27 May. Early morning patrols of Company G of 2/22 operating west of the canal and of 2/4 and 1/4 on the east met only scattered fire. At 0950 Lieutenant Colonel Woodhouse of 2/22 received orders to move the rest of his battalion across the Asato, and at 1115 came a directive to attack with two companies abreast at the earliest practicable time to seize an objective line about 1,100 yards from the Kokuba estuary.[102] At the same time division ordered the 4th Marines to attack to seize the same general objective line as it extended into eastern Naha. The 3d Battalion, 4th Marines was ordered to fill in on the left of 1/4 as the assault progressed to maintain contact with 3/22.

At noon after a nine-battalion artillery preparation the division attack jumped off. In effect it amounted to occupying the ground that the morning patrols had found to be lightly defended. By 1600 the objective had been taken and the troops were dug in amidst the rubble of the city. The 4th Marines after ten days in the line were sorely in need of rest and replacements. Consequently, General Shepherd ordered the 29th Marines to effect a relief beginning at 0630 the following morning.

At midnight on 27 May another important replacement occurred at sea off Okinawa. The Third Fleet relieved the Fifth Fleet and Admiral William F. Halsey assumed Admiral Spruance's responsibility to CinCPOA for supporting ICEBERG. For the troops ashore the change passed without notice since the same ships and task groups continued to support ground operations as before but under new numerical designations (i. e., TF 31 for TF 51). General Buckner now became directly responsible to Admiral Nimitz for the defense and development of captured positions in the Ryukyus.[103]

Admiral Halsey assumed command in the midst of the eighth major Japanese *Kamikaze* attack since L-Day. Starting early on the morning of 27 May and continuing after dark that evening, enemy suicide planes and bombers attempted to support the withdrawal of the Thirty-second Army from Shuri. The destroyer *Drexler*, crashed by two *Kamikazes*, exploded and sank within a minute, and 11 other ships suffered varying degrees of damage. The enemy lost over 100 planes in the attack to AA fire and CAP's, but again the personnel losses of the fleet were substantial: 52 men killed, 288 wounded, and 290 missing in action.[104]

"The morning of 28 May was clear with no rain,"[105] but large-scale movements remained impractical because of the condition of the ground. General Buckner's 27 May directive to maintain strong and unrelenting pressure against the Shuri defenses had passed through the chain of command and been reinforced by local attack orders suited to the situation and terrain. The 7th Infantry Division deepened its hold on the Ozato hill mass as 2/184 moved to a point within 1,000 yards of Shinazato at the neck of the Chinen Peninsula.

Fierce but spotty resistance was met from isolated platoon-sized enemy groups. The attempts of 1/184 and the 32d Infantry to drive west through the Japanese 62d Division's blocking positions made little headway. To the north the 96th Infantry Division had equally tough going against the strong points southwest of Conical Hill, and the 77th Division met bitter and determined resistance from the defenders of the Shuri heights.

The results of the fighting on 28 May in the XXIV Corps zone of action were inconclusive. Although sightings of enemy troop withdrawals continued to mount, the opposition met on the approaches to Shuri was "intense," and there

[101] *Okinawa Operations Record*, 95–98.
[102] 2/22 *SAR, Ph III*, 8.
[103] ComFifth Flt AR, 1Apr–27May45, Ryukyus Operation, 10Jul45, Part III, 7.
[104] *CTF 31 AR*, Part III, 30–34.
[105] 2/1 *SAR*, 11.

was little evidence that the inner defenses of the Japanese fortress were cracking.[106]

In the IIIAC sector the pattern of resistance met by the Army divisions was duplicated. Long advances were made on the corps' right flank and center, but the stubborn defenders of Shuri prevented any significant gains on the left. In the 1st Marine Division zone Companies E and G of 2/1 attacked 110 Meter Hill covered by fire of 3/1 and the 3d Battalion, 306th Infantry on its flanks. The forward elements of Company E gained the hill crest but were forced to withdraw by vicious enemy fire which raked their positions. Lieutenant Colonel Magee felt that his depleted battalion, down to a total strength of 277 men in the rifle companies, might recapture the hill, but "it could not possibly hold it against a strong enemy counterattack."[107] Although new replacements were available to regiments for training or other use, a division order prevented their being sent to front line units during a battle situation that called for the utmost in skill and knowledge of veterans.[108] Throughout most of the morning and all of the afternoon, 2/1 concentrated the fire of its supporting weapons on the reverse slopes of 110 Meter Hill and engaged the Japanese in a fierce and continuous fire fight. Nightfall brought no cessation of enemy resistance, and many infiltrators were killed in the battalion's lines.[109]

Patrols from Company I of 3/1 penetrated 300 yards into Wana Draw on 28 May against enemy rifle and machine-gun fire coming from the direction of Shuri. At 1600 Colonel Mason ordered 3/1 to clear all the Japanese from the draw, but Lieutenant Colonel Ross requested and received a delay in the attack hour until the following morning so that he could concentrate his forces for the operation.[110] During the day Company K of 3/1 had patrolled 600 yards due east from its position on Hill 55 and made no contact with the enemy. Patrols of 1/5 on Company K's right had also encountered no opposition in a 500-yard advance through the terrain south of Hill 55.[111] A key enemy hill position guarding the approaches to Shuri Ridge which had held out through days of artillery, NGF, and air bombardment was taken during the late afternoon.[112] The way seemed clear for a drive deep into the heart of Shuri.

On the right flank of the 1st Division 3/5 with Company F attached, under its new commander, Major Frank W. Poland, Jr., attacked at 1015 towards the Asato Gawa. Resistance was weak, mainly long-range mortar and machine-gun fire from the hills between the Asato and the Kokuba, and the battalion had seized its objective by noon.[113] (See Map 31, Map Section)

The 4th Marines, which had suffered over 1,100 casualties in nine days of fighting, was relieved by the 29th Marines on 28 May. The 3d Battalion took over the positions of 1/4 and 3/4 on the left of the regimental zone of action, while 1/29 moved into the lines of 2/4 east of the Naha canal. Most of the day was spent by 3/29 in familiarizing the troops with the area of combat and bringing up supplies and supporting weapons. The 1st Battalion, however, staged an attack in conjunction with the advance of the 22d Marines in western Naha. Pivoting on Company A on the battalion boundary, Company C gained 250 yards through the city's ruins against heavy small-arms fire and scattered shelling from mortars and artillery.

[106] Tenth Army G–2 Rpt No 64, 29May45.

[107] 2/1 SAR, 11.

[108] Col A. T. Mason Ltr to CMC, 10 May 47, hereinafter cited as Mason. According to the CO of the 1st Mar "the existence of a replacement pool which could not, at the moment, be used for combat proved to be extremely valuable. At the end of May, when the rainy period had rendered the roads and the countryside impassable to anything on wheels or tracks, the supply of forward troops became most critical. Something like 500 replacements, if my recollection is correct, were available to the 1st Marines; these men were formed into man-pack trains, under the direction of the executive officer. Their exhausting struggles, heavily laden, through mud which even an unburdened man found difficult to negotiate were the solution to the supply problem at this time, though with no margin to spare."

[109] 2/1 SAR, 12.

[110] 3/1 SAR, 34–35.

[111] 1st MarDiv G–2 PrdRpt No 58, 29May45.

[112] MajGen P. A. del Valle, "Old Glory on Shuri," MC Gazette, August 1945, 17.

[113] 3/5 SAR, n. p. LtCol Miller was taken sick and evacuated on 17 May and Maj Poland, ExO of 1/5, was assigned to command the 3d Bn.

For night defense a line 800 yards from the Kokuba was occupied in visual contact with the 22d Marines across the canal and 3/29 on the left flank.[114]

The 1st Battalion, 22d Marines passed through the lines of 2/22 under cover of darkness [115] on 28 May and attacked toward the shore of the Kokuba estuary west of the mid-city canal. The advance was rapid against negligible resistance, and with 2/22 protecting its flanks and rear the 1st Battalion was on its objective at 0845. In order to release the 22d Marines for further offensive action against the Kokuba hills, division assigned the 6th Reconnaissance Company the mission of defending western Naha. Major Walker, the company commander, heard of his new assignment at 1030 when he received the following message from Lieutenant Colonel Victor A. Krulak, the division G–3:

Reposing great confidence in your integrity and political ability you are hereby named acting mayor of Naha. The appointment effective [at 1600] carries all pay and emoluments accruing to office. To be collected from Imperial Treasury.[116]

At 1345 the 6th Engineer Battalion had been directed to erect at least three foot bridges across the Naha canal to permit the 22d Marines to attack east along the Kokuba on 29 May. The engineers, working at night in torrential rain and ahead of the Marine lines, manhandled the bridging material into position and completed their task by 0420.[117] Ten minutes later Companies A and B of 1/22 crossed the canal and reorganized on the eastern shore.

At 0500 the battalion jumped off in attack against scattered rifle and machine-gun fire. Resistance increased steadily as the day wore on, and it became evident that the Japanese were holding the hills north of the Kokuba in strength. Contact with 1/29 was made at 0845,

MARINES of Company A, 1/5 cautiously approach the ruins of a Japanese barracks in their drive toward Shuri Castle.

and the attack continued with both battalions driving on the newly developed enemy position. At 1500 the 2d Battalion, 22d Marines was alerted to relieve 1/22 as soon as the tactical situation permitted. Major Cook's assault companies were heavily engaged in a fire fight at this time and he advised against the relief. Instead, Companies E and G of 2/22 moved into the front line on the right to strengthen the regiment's night position.[118]

The strong enemy defensive installations developed during the day's 700-yard advance were located on small hills covered by the thick stone rubble of the houses on Naha's eastern outskirts. Routes of approach were across open ground with relatively little cover or concealment; Colonel Roberts reported that "tanks would be of great value." [119] Unfortunately, the mud and rain still prevented effective armored support, and the conquest of the Kokuba hills would rest with the infantryman.

The 29th Marines executed a wheeling assault on 29 May with 1/29 pivoting on 3/29 and attacking south and then east to bring the regiment on line with the 22d Marines. The ultimate objective of the 1st Battalion's attack was the high ground northwest of Shichina. The approach to the objective was over low and open terrain which drew the comment from regiment

<hr />

[114] 1/29 SAR, Ph III, 3. At 1600 on 29 May LtCol Samuel S. Yeaton relieved Maj Neuffer of his temporary command of 1/29. Maj Neuffer then became battalion ExO.

[115] LtCol E. G. Kurdzeil Ltr to CMC, 24Mar55.

[116] 6th MarDiv Jnl, Ph III, 28May45. The new "Mayor's" command was reinforced by an officer and 40 men from 6th MT Bn. Ibid.

[117] 6th EngBn SAR, Ph III, Part III, 4; 6th MarDiv Jnl, Ph III, 29May45.

[118] 2/22 SAR, Ph III, 8.

[119] 6th MarDiv Jnl, Ph III, 29May45.

that it was "about as suitable to fighting as a billiard table." [120] Fire from strong points in tombs and caves on the small hills and ridges to the front kept the advance to a slow pace, and the assault companies, A and C, dug in slightly to the left rear of the positions of the 22d Marines at nightfall.[121]

Ordered to keep contact on both flanks during the day's action, 3/29 had paced the advance of 1/29 by moving its front forward slightly on the right. On the left, however, the swift advance of 3/5 of the 1st Division made it necessary to bring the lines forward 600 yards. In the afternoon Company I in the center of the battalion zone made a limited objective attack that eliminated most of the re-entrant formed by the day's unequal progress on its flanks.[122]

Attacking at 0735, Company L of 3/5 had moved down the division boundary and reached a point 2,000 yards from the village of Kokuba before being held up by machine-gun, mortar, and small-arms fire. Later in the day Companies I and K, attempting to come up on the left of Company L, were caught in a mortar barrage fired from positions west of Shuri. Bazookas were brought into play against the mortars,[123] but the two assault companies were held to small advances. At dusk 3/5's front line cut back sharply from Company L's forward position to Shuri Ridge where contact was made with Company B of 1/5.

The 1st Battalion of the 5th Marines had started its attack on 29 May with Companies B and C in assault and Company A following in trace of Company C. The Marines quickly gained the crest of Shuri Ridge and Lieutenant Colonel Shelburne requested permission for one of his companies to storm Shuri Castle which commanded his position. Although the castle was in the zone of action of the 77th Infantry Division, General del Valle gave his assent to the request in view of the great danger of enemy action from the strong point. The 1st Marine Division commander felt that "at that time the position of the 77th Division was such that it would have taken several hard day's fighting

through enemy resistance" [124] before the castle could be taken.

Company A drove east along the muddy ridge line, overwhelming the few Japanese in its path, and by 1015 the castle, core of the Shuri bastion, had been secured. The 77th Division, which had scheduled air strikes and a heavy artillery bombardment on the castle heights for 29 May, received little prior warning of the Marines' assault and "was barely able to avert [its] called strikes in time." [125] Without taking any credit away from Company A of the 5th Marines for its feat of capturing Shuri Castle, its success was clearly the result of the combined effort of all the assault and support troops of Tenth Army which had maintained relentless pressure on the enemy defenses and paved the way for the breakthrough. (See Map 31, Map Section)

Taking advantage of 1/5's success, General del Valle quickly revised the division's plan of attack and ordered Colonel Mason to send 3/1 through the 5th Marines' zone of action to relieve 1/5 on Shuri Ridge. By midafternoon the relief was completed and 1/5 had renewed its attack to the south. Lieutenant Colonel Ross set up a perimeter defense around the crumbled walls of the castle with Companies K and L and was joined at dusk by Company I which had been engaged in a stiff fight for Wana Draw through most of the morning. Two companies of 1/1 which had been assigned to Ross' operational control fought their way into positions facing north that tied in with 3/1's lines on the castle heights.[126]

The 1st Battalion (less Company C) had originally been ordered to follow 3/1's advance around Hill 55 towards the castle and then to attack east into the northern sector of Shuri. As soon as the line of departure in front of Hill 55 was crossed, the assault units came under heavy machine-gun fire from a deep and rugged cut a few hundred yards south of Wana Draw. Unable to drive past this strong point, the battalion gradually moved to the right and eventually contacted 3/1 south of the city.[127] The 2d Bat-

---

[120] *Ibid.*

[121] *1/29 SAR, Ph III*, 3.

[122] *3/29 SAR, Ph III*, 3.

[123] *3/5 SAR*, n. p.

[124] del Valle, *op. cit.*

[125] *77th InfDiv History*, 357.

[126] *3/1 SAR*, 35–36.

[127] *1/1 SAR*, 18–19.

talion with Company C attached had been ordered to hold Wana Ridge while 3/1 and 1/1 attacked Shuri from the west. All battalion headquarters personnel, cooks, wiremen, and stretcher bearers were sent forward to help man the lines against undiminished enemy fire from 110 Meter Hill and northern Shuri.[128]

The enemy defenders of the hill complex in northern Shuri evinced no desire to break off the fight, despite the American lodgement in their rear at Shuri Castle. The 77th Division after "a day almost entirely spent in hand-to-hand combat"[129] was unable to break through the cordon of defending fires. To the south the picture was the same, fanatical resistance that seemed little weakened by the thrust to the castle heights. The 7th and 96th Divisions, attacking toward the road net south of Shuri, were met by fierce opposition that held the assault elements to insignificant gains. However, no organized resistance was met by the 7th Reconnaissance Troop which scouted a good part of the area of the Chinen Peninsula during the day.

The lack of serious opposition along the coasts proved by the advances of the 6th Marine and 7th Infantry Divisions offered sharp contrast to the bitter defense of the corridor leading south from Shuri. Although elements of both corps of Tenth Army were heavily engaged in trying to cut through these barrier defenses and spring a trap on the city's defenders, the overwhelming weight of evidence pointed to the fact that the quarry had escaped.

JAPANESE WITHDRAWAL[130]

The success of Tenth Army's steady advance into the maze of Shuri defenses had forced the Japanese to reevaluate their battle plans. Threatened on either flank with penetrations into the Naha-Yonabaru Valley and pressured all along its front by constant American attacks, the Thirty-second Army was gradually being encircled in its Shuri fortress. On the night of 22 May, principal enemy staff officers and commanders were called to a conference at army headquarters to consider the alternatives to a last-ditch defense of Shuri.

Although the holding of the heights surrounding the city had been the keystone of the Japanese pre-L-Day preferred plan, several factors now militated against its retention. There were an estimated 50,000 surviving officers and men to be crammed into a final defense zone less than a mile in diameter. Once these troops were surrounded, the Japanese believed that they would be rendered ineffectual and become "easy prey"[131] to overwhelming American fire superiority. In addition, Japanese long-range artillery pieces, many of which were still intact, could not be effectively utilized within the limited space that would be available.

Army planners had narrowed the choice of alternative defensive positions to two areas, the Chinen Peninsula and the southernmost part of the island, the Kiyamu Peninsula. The rugged Chinen cliffs and hills and the lack of roads made the peninsula ideal antitank country. However, there were not enough caves and prepared positions to accommodate all of the Thirty-second Army, and the munitions stockpile was inadequate. The poor road network would prevent a speedy reconcentration of forces from Shuri, and there was a strong possibility that the Japanese would have to fight their way into the peninsula. The weakened defending forces on the right flank of the Japanese line could not be trusted to hold out while the withdrawal took place. These disadvantages weighed heavily against the natural strength of the peninsula in the minds of the Thirty-second Army staff.

The best chance of prolonging the battle for Okinawa seemed to rest in defending the Kiyamu Peninsula region which was dominated by the Yaeju Dake-Yuza Dake Escarpment. Natural and artificial caves, sufficient to accommodate the whole of the surviving army, abounded in the area. The 24th Division, which had organized the terrain, had left a considerable amount of ammunition and weapons there when it moved north to the Shuri lines. The principal roads in southern Okinawa led directly to the proposed position, thus facilitating

[128] 2/1 SAR, 12.

[129] 77th InfDiv OpRpt, Okinawa, 61.

[130] Unless otherwise noted the material in this section is derived from Okinawa Operations Record; Yahara Interrogation; Shimada Interrogation.

[131] Okinawa Operations Record, 90.

RUINS OF SHURI after weeks of incessant bombardment as seen from the castle heights.

the movement of large bodies of men in the shortest possible time. These roads also gave American tanks an excellent route of advance, but only to the outposts of the defensive zone where cliffs, hills, and precipitous ridges barred the way.

The 62d Division commander, General Fujioka, opposed the move to the south. He felt that thousands of seriously wounded men would have to be abandoned in the withdrawal. Since the defense of Shuri had originally been charged to his division, and the majority of its officers and men had fallen protecting the city, the survivors were desirous of being allowed to fight to the end in their present positions.

Major General Shigeru Suzuki, commanding the 44th IMB, supported the move to abandon Shuri but wanted the final defensive position to be the Chinen Peninsula which his brigade had developed. Generals Amamiya and Wada of the 24th Division and 5th Artillery Command agreed with Thirty-second Army's staff estimate that retirement to the Kiyamu Peninsula would best fulfill the Japanese mission. To add weight to his argument, General Amamiya indicated that his 24th Transport Regiment had preserved enough trucks to move the Shuri munitions reserve to the new position within five nights if weather conditions permitted.

General Ushijima, after considering the respective positions of his staff and commanders, decided to order the move to Kiyamu. At midnight on 23 May transportation of wounded men

and munitions reserves to the south began. The main body of the Thirty-second Army was scheduled to begin withdrawal on 29 May.

The 44th IMB was to move from its positions on the west flank of the Shuri front to a defense line stretching between Hanagusuku on the east coast and Yaeju Dake. The 24th Division was to occupy the heights of Yaeju Dake and Yuza Dake, the ridges at Kunishi and Mezado, and Nagusuku on the west coast. Elements of these units would defend an outpost zone forward of this main battle line from Itoman through Yunagusuku to Gushichan. The badly shattered 62d Division would occupy the coast in the rear of the main battle line, reorganize its troops, and be prepared to reinforce any threatened portion of the front. General Wada's artillery would be emplaced in a triangle bounded by Komesu, Makabe, and Medeera ready to fire in support of the entire Japanese defense line. The Okinawa Naval Base Force was to move to the center of the Kiyamu area as a reserve. Each unit withdrawing from the Shuri front would leave behind sufficient troops to delay the advance of the Tenth Army. (See Map 33)

The gravest threat to the success of the Japanese withdrawal plan was the 7th Infantry Division spearhead that had penetrated through Yonabaru. On the night of 25 May, the remnants of the 62d Division were to pull out of the Shuri line and move through Tsukasan to counterattack the Americans. The relatively strong 22d Independent Infantry Battalion, which had been in reserve throughout most of the fighting in April and May, was directed to hold the Shuri front in place of the division. The orders to General Fujioka were "to annihilate the enemy rushing from the Yonabaru area." [132] Failing this, the division was at least to stop the American advance long enough to allow the main body of the Thirty-second Army to retire.

In order to gain time to organize the new positions, the holding force left on the Shuri front was to fight on until 31 May. Withdrawing units were to leave behind strong rearguards which would defend a line along the Kokuba Gawa to the hills north of Tsukasan and Chan and then south through Karadera to the east

[132] *Ibid.*, 95.

coast until the night of 2 June. Then a second line centered on Tomusu, approximately 2,000 yards farther south, would be held until the night of 4 June. By that time the Thirty-second Army would be firmly set up within its Itoman-Yunagusuku-Gushichan outpost zone. Admiral Ota's naval force was directed to hold the west flank of the withdrawal corridor and begin its own retreat when ordered by Thirty-second Army.

By 23 May, the steady pressure of the Tenth Army advance had forced the Japanese to throw all their available replacements into the crumbling Shuri line. Walking wounded started to pull out of their hospital caves on 24 May, while those who were too seriously hurt to move were either abandoned or, in some cases, given lethal shots of morphine.[133] On the night of 25 May, according to the withdrawal plan, the 62d Division began moving its remaining 3,000 men to meet the thrust of the 7th Infantry Division. The Japanese hoped to capitalize on the continued bad weather which limited visibility and severely curtailed American air, NGF, and tank support.

The rain proved to be a more potent barrier than the division which unsuccessfully tried to drive back the advancing Americans. The

defending forces on the Chinen Peninsula, organized around the 7th Heavy Artillery and 23d Shipping Enginner Regiments, which had evacuated their stronghold, came under the command of the 62d Division and took over the right of the Japanese holding positions.

The lack of success of the 62d Division in driving back the break-through forces confirmed General Ushijima's resolve to evacuate Shuri while this was still possible. Confirmatory orders were issued on 28 May to initiate the withdrawal the following evening. Admiral Ota's naval force, which had misinterpreted the original Thirty-second Army order and was already retiring toward Kiyamu Peninsula, was intercepted and sent back to Oroku Peninsula where its strength was needed to bulwark the western side of the escape corridor.

Leaving one-third of the 32d Regiment and the 22d IIB as a covering force, the 24th Division moved out according to orders on the night of 29 May. The 44th IMB held its lines outside Naha and the 62d Division its positions near Chan and Karadera while the 24th Division slipped through to the south.

By dawn of 30 May, the major portion of Thirty-second Army had evacuated the Shuri lines and successfully escaped the flanking drives of IIIAC and XXIV Corps. Japanese headquarters was now established in a cave deep within Hill 89 outside Mabuni, 11 miles to the south of Shuri Castle. General Ushijima, with the aid of a continual curtain of rain, had been able to execute his planned "properly deft withdrawal,"[134] and his covering forces were in position to give him time to organize the defense of Kiyamu Peninsula.

---

[133] 1st MarDiv G–2 PrdRpt No 63, 3Jun45, POW Interrogation Rpt No 54, Superior Pvt, 5th Co, 22d IIB. This POW gave the following depressing description of conditions in his hospital cave, which was not unusual judging from the reports of other wounded Japanese captured: "At one time there were almost 90 men in the cave, lying on the ground in the mud in pitch darkness, except when a doctor or corpsman would come around with a light and ask them how they felt. Medical supplies were very low, so very little could be done to care for the wounded. Men died on all sides. Filth accumulated. In the heavy rains, water poured into the cave and the wounded almost drowned. The smell was so bad that they could hardly breathe."

---

[134] 1st MarDiv G–2 PrdRpt No 64, 4Jun45, Translation No 85, Matters for the Attention of Unit Commanders During the Change in the Direction of Advance, n. d.

CHAPTER **X**

Ushijima's Last Stand

BREAKOUT TO THE SOUTH[1]

Rain squalls on 30 May continued to hamper Tenth Army operations, as forward elements maintained a steady pressure on the collapsing enemy front. The problem of keeping an adequate supply of rations and ammunition up with assault troops were almost impossible to solve although both corps attempted to maintain minimum levels by use of amphibious craft and vehicles along the costs. Seas of mud effectively blocked inland approach routes for trucks, and TAF planes were called upon to make 11 supply drops to front line battalions despite the terrible flying weather. But the weather on 30 May was responsible for one unique event in the bloody two-month history of the Okinawa operation—"For the first time no enemy planes were detected in the area for the 24-hour period."[2]

General Hodge's troops secured all the broken ground east and northeast of Shuri during the day's advance. At noon a change in the boundaries between the Army divisions became effective; the direction of advance of the 77th and 96th was oriented toward the corps bound-

ary below Shuri, while the 7th was assigned the zone below the Naha-Yonabaru valley. Strong patrols of the 184th Infantry penetrated the Chinen Peninsula fastness, encountering only light enemy resistance. To the north and west the 32d Infantry advanced 400–1,200 yards through the hills and hamlets flanking the rail line to Kokuba. Opposition was sporadic but bitter as Japanese 62d Division units guarded the withdrawal corridor.

General Bradley employed elements of all his regiments to push the 96th Division's attack. Approximately 1,200 y a r d s were gained throughout the zone of advance against relatively light resistance. Small enemy strong points held out on each successive hill until they were wiped out or withdrew to the next high ground. By nightfall the division had taken most of the ground north of the Naha-Yonabaru road in its assigned area and pushed a company of 1/381 forward to the new boundary where it tied in with 2/32 of the 7th Division and 2/382 of its own.

The 382d Infantry had coordinated its drive toward Shuri with that of the 307th attacking on the left of the 77th Division. The holding forces of the enemy 32d Regiment resisted fiercely as they attempted to gain time for the last elements of Thirty-second Army to evacuate the abandoned fortress. During the day the 306th Infantry captured Ishimmi and mopped up the gutted ruins of the village. The enemy defenses north and east of Shuri were penetrated all along the division front, but gains

---

[1] Unless otherwise noted the material in this section is derived from *Okinawa: The Last Battle; Tenth Army AR; IIIAC AR; XXIV Corps AR; 1st MarDiv SAR; 6th MarDiv SAR, Ph III; 7th InfDiv AR; 77th InfDiv OpRpt, Okinawa; 96th InfDiv AR; 1st Mar SAR; 4th Mar SAR, Ph III; 5th Mar SAR; 7th Mar SAR; 22d Mar SAR, Ph III; 29th Mar SAR, Ph III.*

[2] *CTF 31 AR*, Part III, 41.

were limited to 600 yards in the face of the fanatical rear guard action.

Although the 3d Battalion, 1st Marines was in complete possession of Shuri Castle, the enemy forces north of the castle heights in the city and on the ridges at its outskirts still held out. The supply situation was so bad that Lieutenant Colonel Ross sent a message to Colonel Mason requesting that an adequate supply and evacuation route be established before any major attack was carried out. He indicated that his men had been without food for two days and that the ammunition on hand was grossly inadequate to support an all-out drive. Attempts to succor the battalion by air were only partially successful as the low ceiling and stormy weather obscured the drop zones. Each man, however, did receive one-third of a K ration and a canteen of water from supplies that were recovered.

During the morning of 30 May, General del Valle sent G-2 representatives up to Shuri Castle to look for the Thirty-second Army headquarter's caves. He also sent along the division colors with a request that they be raised over the castle. Lieutenant Colonel Ross located the remnants of a Japanese flagpole and scaled the southern wall of the ruins to plant the American flag on the ancient citadel of the Okinawan kings. Ross and all nearby observers rapidly cleared the vicinity of the flag raising since this event was expected to draw Japanese artillery fire.[3]

Colonel Mason confined the activities of his regiment to vigorous patrolling on 30 May while the supply deficit was somewhat alleviated by carrying parties and air drops. The 2d Battalion was relieved on the left by elements of the 306th Infantry and in turn took over part of 1/1's zone. Patrols of the 1st Battalion scouting to the north through the city ruins were driven back by 47mm and machine-gun fire from strong enemy positions in a ravine southwest of Wana Draw.

The 5th Marines on the right of the division zone of action also confined its day's activities to patrolling. The 2d Battalion, in reserve, furnished carrying parties to build up supply dumps for assault units and to evacuate casualties. Although enemy resistance was negligible, the barrier of mud prevented any effective advance that would strain the already overextended supply route.

Taking full advantage of the water route on its flank, the 6th Division advanced 600–800 yards during 30 May, seizing the key high ground overlooking the Kokuba Gawa from the north. The day's attack, originally scheduled for 0900, was delayed an hour while division language personnel and prisoners of war attempted to persuade enemy holdouts in front of the 22d Marines to surrender. The only response to the loudspeakers was a rain of enemy mortar and small-arms fire from the 44th IMB defenders. An intense artillery preparation was fired on the uncooperative enemy, and the assault battalions of the 22d and 29th Marines jumped off at 1000.

A network of Japanese machine gun positions hidden in the clusters of tombs on the low hills to the Marines' front made progress slow and costly. Heavy sniper fire whipped the lines and killed Lieutenant Colonel Woodhouse of 2/22 who was forward controlling his battalion's attack. Major John G. Johnson, the executive officer, took command immediately and continued a steady pressure. The advance consisted of a series of local assaults and mop-up actions that brought the battalion to secure hill positions overlooking the Kokuba Estuary and the rail line leading to the north by nightfall.[4]

Lieutenant Colonel Shisler's 3d Battalion passed through 1/22 during the morning's attack and behind a screen of artillery, mortars, naval gunfire, and rockets drove onto the high ground at the eastern outskirts of Naha. By means of a series of holding attacks and flank assaults, Shisler was able to move his companies into the maze of enemy defenses where close quarter grenade and small-arms exchanges decided the issue. Once the dominating ground was won, the battalion was subjected to intense artillery and mortar fire.[5]

The 1st Battalion, 29th Marines moving forward on the flank of 3/22 made the main effort

---

[3] 3/1 SAR, 36–38.

[4] 2/22 SAR, Ph III, 9.
[5] 3/22 SAR, Ph III, 6–7.

in Colonel Whaling's zone of action on 30 May. Initially, Companies A and C were in assault, but the blowing up of a tomb full of enemy explosives caused 25 casualties in Company C, and Company B was passed through to maintain the impetus of advance.[6] Machine-gun emplacements and snipers hidden in tombs stubbornly resisted 1/29's advance, but the battalion was able to fight its way through 600 yards of enemy territory before it held up for night defense. The 3d Battalion, which had supported the attack of 1/29 by fire during the day, linked with 3/5 on the division boundary in the early afternoon to present a solid line tied in all across the 6th Division front.

The volume of enemy harassing artillery and mortar fire falling on Tenth Army front lines decreased noticeably during the night of 30–31 May. However, when assault troops jumped off against the Shuri positions in the morning, they were not prepared for the eerie silence, broken only by scattered sniper and machine-gun fire, that greeted them. Following their withdrawal plan, the Japanese holding forces from the 44th IMB, 32d Regiment, and 22d IIB had evacuated their positions during the hours of darkness and pulled back behind the second line of blocking positions north of Tsukasan.[7]

The immensely strong Shuri bastion, labeled "a perfect final defensive position"[8] was an empty shell. By 1000 on 31 May, the 77th Infantry Division had driven to all its objectives, and the 305th Infantry had taken over the entire zone with orders to mop up and cover the right rear of the XXIV Corps advance. The rest of the division, less its artillery battalions which continued to fire supporting missions for the corps, moved to the rear areas for sorely needed rest, rehabilitation, and absorption of replacements.

In the 96th Division zone, attacking battalions also moved quickly to their assigned objectives and spent most of the day mopping up isolated enemy holdouts. Only on the extreme left flank where elements of 1/381 encountered enemy forces defending the Tsukasan line did the division fail to reach the corps boundary. At 1255 the encirclement of Shuri was completed when patrols of 3/383 contacted Marines from Company C of 1/5 south of the city.[9]

Attacking in concert with the 77th Division on its left, the 1st Marine Division completed the occupation of Shuri on the last day of May. Like a bright omen, the sun broke through the solid overcast and rain that had shrouded the battle front for over ten days. It considerably cheered the sodden infantrymen as they went about their mop-up tasks. The troublesome positions on the northern outskirts of Shuri and the formidable Wana Draw were cleared by noon. The 1st Marines was ordered into division reserve and given the task of thoroughly patrolling Shuri.

The 1st Division advance on 31 May was continued by the 5th Marines with 3/5 making the main effort. At 1445, fifteen minutes after it had received an air drop of badly needed water and ammunition, Major Poland's battalion moved out against scattered resistance. When it reached the hills just north of Shichina machine-gun and rifle fire from the Thirty-second Army's second holding line forced the Marines to dig in for the night. Company F of 2/5 was attached to the battalion to bridge the gap between it and 1/5 on the corps boundary.[10]

Resistance was much stronger on both flanks of the Tenth Army attack on 31 May than it was in the center where the 1st, 77th, and 96th Divisions profited from the Japanese withdrawal from Shuri. The 6th Division moved forward rapidly during the morning, but the assault companies of the 22d and 29th Marines soon contacted the hill complex to the west of Shichina and Kokuba where naval troops and units of the 32d Regiment were dug in to delay the advance. At 1300 a heavy artillery preparation and the long-range supporting fire of a company of tanks, which had moved up as close to the front lines as mud and mine fields permitted,[11] enabled the division to gain another 400 yards before nightfall.

Although leading platoons of both 2/22 and 1/29 were able to reach the dominating high ground in their respective regimental zones, the

---

[6] 6th MarDiv Jnl, Ph III, 30May45.

[7] Okinawa Operations Record, 99.

[8] 3/1 SAR, 38.

[9] 1/5 SAR, 9.

[10] 3/5 SAR, n. p.

[11] 6th TkBn SAR, Ph III, 14.

intensity of enemy fire from reverse slope and flank defenses drove them off. After this repulse, the five assault battalions (1/22 had been committed during the morning's attack) consolidated their lines on a series of low hills just west of the core of enemy resistance. Preparations were made for a coordinated attack on 1 June, and an all-night artillery preparation was called down to silence the Japanese guns.

On the eastern shore of the island the 7th Infantry Division continued its drive down the Nahá-Yonabaru valley on 31 May. A chain of hill strong points, stubbornly defended by 62d Division troops, were taken by the 32d Infantry which advanced an average of 800 yards and reached the corps boundary at Chan and along the main valley road. During the day, the 184th Infantry sent strong combat and reconnaissance patrols into the Chinen Peninsula and the mass of hills and ridges that guarded its neck.

The last day of May had seen the end of organized resistance at Shuri and the development of a new defensive position along the Kokuba Gawa and around Tsukasan. In two months of constant, steady fighting the Tenth Army had killed an estimated 62,548 Japanese defenders and taken 465 military prisoners; it had occupied all but eight miles of the island; and it was rapidly driving the remnants of the Thirty-second Army into a pocket where its only possible end would be surrender or annihilation. The cost of this success was considerable: 5,309 had been killed or died of wounds, 23,909 had been wounded, and 346 were missing in action in Tenth Army units.[12]

On 1 June the XXIV Corps changed the direction of its main attack. The 381st and 383d Infantry relieved the 7th Division's 32d Infantry along lines that paralleled the corps boundary north of Chan and turned to the east at that village to reach a point 1,000 yards due north of Karadera. The 96th Division regiments reorganized on their new lines and prepared to attack south the following day with their objective the hill mass in the Tomui-Aragusuku-Meka area. The 77th Division assumed responsibility for the former 96th Division zone, and 2/305 moved out along the corps boundary

to guard the right rear of the XXIV Corps advance.

With a much narrower zone of action and orders to advance directly south, the 7th Division attacked early on 1 June with the 17th and 184th Infantry in assault. The reconnaissance patrols of the previous two days had done their work well and the division's front lines were advanced 1,100 yards despite steadily mounting resistance. The defending elements of the 7th Heavy Artillery and 23d Shipping Engineer Regiments gave way slowly during the day, retiring in the direction of Itokazu.

In the IIIAC zone a coordinated attack by both divisions secured all the high ground overlooking the main east-west road in the Kokuba Gawa valley. Two battalions of the 5th Marines were the attacking force of the 1st Division. Enemy resistance was light, and the regiment advanced 1,500–1,800 yards before setting up on the hills east of Shichina.

The story of rapid advances against light opposition was the same in the 6th Division zone where the enemy defenses that had held up the 22d and 29th Marines collapsed during a combined tank-infantry attack. By nightfall the assault battalions held the high ground north of the Kokuba Gawa, and 6th Division patrols were scouting the river banks looking for suitable crossing points. Having fulfilled their mission of delaying the American advance, the Japanese second holding force had withdrawn during the night, and the way was open for a crossing of the Kokuba Gawa. (See Map 32, Map Section)

General Geiger had instructed General Shepherd early in the morning of 31 May to study the practicality of a shore-to-shore landing on Oroku Peninsula. Plans were immediately laid to use Major Walker's 6th Reconnaissance Company to make an amphibious reconnaissance of the peninsula that evening. At 1110, III Corps issued a warning order that stated the 6th Division would probably reorient its attack and go into Oroku to secure Naha harbor and seize the big naval airfield. A directive was issued to all units to restrict the use of flares and illuminating shells between 2030 and 0300 while the reconnaissance was being made.[13]

---

[12] Tenth Army G–3 Rpt No 67, 1Jun45.

[13] *6th MarDiv Jnl, Ph III*, 31May45.

RAIN-SWOLLEN STREAMS, mud, and water-filled shell holes typified the terrain south of Shuri in the early days of June.

At 2100 four teams, each with four men, used plastic boats to move silently across the mouth of the Naha estuary and land on the northern part of the peninsula. After six hours deep in enemy territory, during which they drew some fire and observed and heard considerable activity, the scouts returned to Naha. Major Walker estimated on the basis of the team reports that the high ground to the north and east of Oroku airfield was occupied but not in great strength.

Before the reconnaissance was completed General Shepherd issued a warning order to all his units to alert them for a possible amphibious assault on Oroku Peninsula.[14] General Geiger, acting on orders from General Buckner, confirmed the 6th Division's alert for Oroku operations late on 1 June and directed that the 1st Marine Division take over the zone of the 6th the following day.

The 7th Marines, which had been in 1st Division reserve, moved up to relieve the 22d and 29th Marines on 2 June. The 2d Battalion took over the 22d Marines' zone along the north bank of the Kokuba Gawa and 3/7 replaced the 29th Marines on the hills west of Kokuba village. At 1215 General del Valle assumed command of the former 6th Division zone, and Colonel Snedeker ordered Lieutenant Colonel Berger to move 2/7 across the river to the hills on the south bank. Picking a path over the wreckage of a bridge in the battalion zone,[15] Company E made the first crossing and quickly moved onto the northern nose of the high ground that overlooked the river. While Company G was filing over the bridge ruins, Company E engaged and repulsed a group of 50–100 Japanese that attempted to turn its right flank. By 1930 Company F had joined the rest of the battalion in a solid defensive line to the south of the river, and the crossing site was safe.

The 5th Marines established a bridgehead across the north branch of the Kokuba on 2 June. Using a railroad bridge that the withdrawing Japanese had left intact, 1/5 and 3/5 crossed early in the morning and moved to the ridge line that guarded the approaches to Tsukasan. When the assault companies attempted to advance beyond this ridge, a storm of ma-

chine-gun and rifle fire from the front and flanks pinned them down. Although further gains south of the river were very limited, the day's advance by the 5th Marines had placed the entire Naha-Yonabaru road in American hands.

On the left of the 1st Division General Bradley's assault regiments drove back 62d Division defenders 800–1,200 yards all along the front. Moving down the corps boundary, 2/383 cleaned out Chan and then attacked in conjunction with 3/383 to seize high ground just north of Tera and Kamizato. The 381st Infantry made repeated attacks on hill positions that held up its advance and succeeded in penetrating to Kamizato and Karadera.

The 7th Division maintained relentless pressure against the retreating garrison of the Chinen Peninsula and advanced its lines 2,400 yards. Rain had begun to fall again on the night of 1–2 June, and as a result air drops and carrying parties shouldered most of the burden of supplying the infantry spearheads of General Arnold's division. Despite the debilitating effects of their rapid advance over steep ridges and through muddy draws, at the end of day the 17th and 184th Infantry were in position to make a drive to the southeast coast and close the mouth of the Chinen Peninsula.

As the east flank of Tenth Army continued to sweep in on Kiyamu Peninsula on 2 June, the 6th Division prepared for its assault landing. An analysis by the division staff of intelligence available indicated that the most successful scheme of maneuver would be an amphibious assault against the Nishikoku beaches which opened directly onto low, rolling ground that offered access to Oroku airfield and the shore of Naha harbor. Except at these beaches, which were northeast of the airfield, the shore of the peninsula was ringed by a sea wall and dominated by high ground immediately inland.

Only 72 LVT's were available to the division for the landing, and many of these were in poor shape from continual use during the extended rainy spell when the sea and reef offered the most practical supply route. Largely because of this shortage of amphibious craft, the decision was made to land only one regiment as division assault troops. Colonel Shapley's 4th Marines was designated for the task, and he in turn

[14] *Ibid.*
[15] *7th Mar History*, 21.

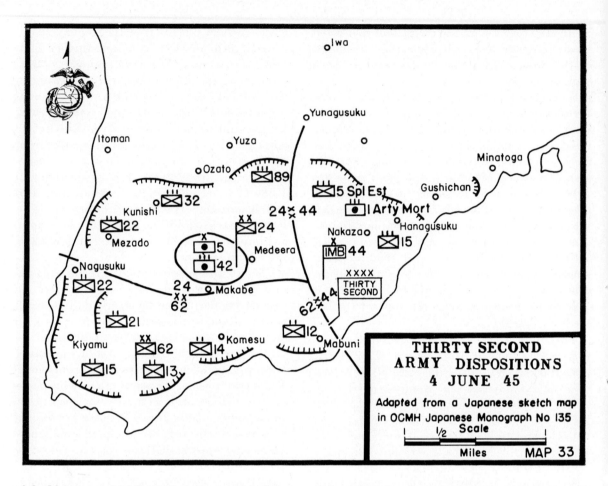

THIRTY SECOND
ARMY DISPOSITIONS
4 JUNE 45

Adapted from a Japanese sketch map
in OCMH Japanese Monograph No 135

Scale

Miles MAP 33

picked his 1st and 2d Battalions to spearhead the movement. The 29th Marines was alerted to move in behind the 4th as soon as the beachhead allowed and sufficient LVT's were available. Since it was not feasible to supply the assault troops entirely over water, the 6th Reconnaissance Company, reinforced by a company of LVT(A)'s, was to seize Ono Yama Island in the middle of the Naha estuary and provide protection for the 6th Engineer Battalion which would replace the demolished bridge that had crossed the island from the capital city to the peninsula. D-Day was set as 4 June and H-Hour as 0500 for Ono Yama and 0545 for the main landing.

Preparation for the assault continued through 3 June as the Tenth Army attack to the south picked up momentum. Jumping off from positions it had seized on 2 June, the 7th Division, spearheaded by 1/184, advanced to the coast of Okinawa southeast of Kakibana by late afternoon. The Chinen Peninsula was completely cut off, and General Arnold moved the 32d Infantry into its rugged hills to mop up any surviving members of the garrison. The front lines of the 17th and 184th Infantry were consolidated in the hills above Itokazu and Toyama in readiness for an attack to the southwest against the Kiyamu Penninsula.

General Bradley's 96th Division met with similar success on 3 June. By noon the 383d Infantry had secured Kamizato and Tera against relatively light resistance. The 381st Infantry after assisting in the capture of Kamizato moved on to take Inasomi. Both regiments, despite continued bad weather and extremely difficult supply conditions, were able to garner 1,400 yards of enemy territory before they held up for night defense. Stiff resistance from the Japanese defending forces marked the last few hours of daylight as the 96th Division fought its way to dominating positions in the hill mass north of the road and rail junction at Iwa. The pace of the XXIV Corps advance had widened the already existing gap between

Army and Marine units, and General Hodge kept the 305th Infantry advancing down the corps boundary during the day to guard his exposed flank.

When the 5th Marines sent probing patrols forward during the morning of 3 June, they were pinned down by heavy fire from Japanese positions south of Tsukasan and west of Gisushi. With 1/5 and 3/5 unable to advance without taking excessive casualties, Colonel Griebel received permission to move his reserve battalion through the XXIV Corps zone and outflank the enemy strong points. At 1330 Lieutenant Colonel Benedict and his men, stripped of all nonportable gear, started a wide swing through the rear areas of the 383d Infantry. After an exhausting struggle in the morass of mud that covered the broken countryside, 2/5 arrived at a position 400 yards east of Gisushi at 1800. Attacking immediately with Companies E and G in assault, the battalion quickly seized the ridge line west of Gisushi against negligible resistance.

Before digging in for the night the Marines attempted to blast shut the many cave openings in the ridge beneath them. A white phosphorus grenade thrown at two Japanese holdouts evidently ignited a hidden ammunition dump, and the ground in Company E's sector erupted with a terrific explosion that killed three and wounded 17 of the men. Isolated as it was ahead of the 1st Division's main battle line, 2/5 faced a tremendous task in evacuating these casualties, and only through the "invaluable assistance" of the 96th Division units on its left was it able to move the wounded Marines to the rear.[16]

At 1530 as 2/5 was moving on Gisushi, Colonel Griebel ordered a resumption of his regiment's attack. The volume of enemy fire had slackened considerably since morning, and the 1st and 3d Battalions were able to move through Tsukasan in a 1,500 yard advance that brought them to the hills south of the former Thirty-second Army rear command post. The success of the day's attack made it evident that Japanese holding forces were again withdrawing toward Kiyamu. (See Map 33)

On the right flank of the 1st Division, the 7th Marines, preceded by patrols of the 1st Reconnaissance Company, made a steady advance against small enemy delaying groups. Harassing fire from mortars, machine guns, and machine cannon emplaced in the hills guarding the entrance to Oroku Peninsula hit the right flank of the battalion and the attached reconnaissance company throughout the day. Supply and evacuation were conducted solely by carrying parties which had to plod through a gantlet of sniper fire to reach the only bridge leading over the Kokuba Gawa in the regimental zone. Air drops were again resorted to in order to keep a minimal level of rations and ammunition available on the front lines.[17] At dusk Colonel Snedeker had both his assault battalions across the Kokuba and firmly dug in on the southern edge of the hill mass below the river; the 3d Battalion had established contact with 1/5 and the regiment was tied in across its front.

Preparations for the 6th Division's shore-to-shore assault were completed on 3 June. At 1215 the beacon lights marking the line of departure 1,200 yards north of the Nishikoku beaches were set in place.[18] The various assault units prepared for the landing the next morning by moving to positions along the west coast where their LVT's could pick them up. General Geiger placed the 22d Marines in corps reserve in and around Naha and moved the regimental weapons company to the shore of the estuary where its 37mm's and self-propelled assault guns could support the 4 June attack. In addition to artillery, NGF, air, and their own organic weapons, the assault troops were to have the supporting fires of a company of LVT(A)'s, a company of tanks, a company of 4.2-inch mortars, and a detachment of mobile rocket launchers. At 2300 the 6th had completed all its preparations and was ready for the Oroku operation.

THE CAPTURE OF OROKU PENINSULA[19]

The units of the 4th Marines designated to make the assault on Oroku, the 1st and 2d Battalions, received the landing order during the

[16] 2/5 SAR, 16.

[17] 2/7 SAR, 7.

[18] CTF 31 AR, Part III, 49.

[19] Unless otherwise noted the material in this section is derived from 6th MarDiv SAR, Ph III; 6th MarDiv Jnl, Ph III; 4th Mar SAR, Ph III; 22d Mar SAR, Ph III; 29th Mar SAR, Ph III.

ASSAULT TROOPS of the 4th Marines pause to reorganize just after their landing on Oroku Peninsula.

late afternoon of 3 June and immediately began loading supplies and equipment. The next morning at 0300 the troops of 1/4, bivouacked farthest from the line of departure, commenced embarkation and an hour later were underway. Moving out to sea in column, the 1st Battalion turned south to pick up the 2d Battalion off its loading-out area.[20] At 0446, 3/15 opened fire on Ono Yama, and armored amphibians put the 6th Reconnaissance Company ashore there 15 minutes later. Simultaneously, the guns of one battleship, two heavy cruisers, and a destroyer started pounding the landing area on Oroku Peninsula. As the leading waves of the 4th Marines approached the line of departure, in the first "gray light of dawn," [21] the two by three mile peninsula rocked under the impact of the shells of 15 artillery battalions joining in the bombardment.[22]

In the meantime, the waterborne assault battalions rendezvoused according to plan. But almost immediately difficulties beset the 1st Battalion, when tractors started falling out because of mechanical failures. By the time the red beacon marking the line of departure was reached, nine LVT's had broken down and only six were present for the assault. Lieutenant Colonel Bell radioed the regimental commander

that only two platoons of the right assault company and one of the company on the left were on the line of departure. Colonel Shapley ordered the attack to proceed on schedule with the troops on hand,[23] and at 0530 the first wave of troop carrying vehicles started for shore in the wake of a line of LVT(A)'s.[24]

At 0600 the assault platoons landed under sporadic machine-gun fire and pushed on to the high ground 300 yards inland against minor resistance. In little more than half a hour all of the 2d Battalion was ashore. By 0700 Companies A and C of the 6th Tank Battalion were on the beach, together with four self-propelled guns of the Regimental Weapons Company. But the troops of the 1st Battalion, delayed by tractor breakdowns, continued to come ashore throughout the remainder of the morning.[25]

After the initial foothold had been secured the attack ground ahead slowly against mounting resistance on the left. Dense mine fields also impeded the advance and the heavy rains of the preceding 10 days had made a veritable morass of the ground. Movement of armor was restricted to the roads, which were blown in numerous places, thus denying the infantry tank support until repairs could be effected.[26]

Inasmuch as Company B, in reserve, was the only unit of 1/4 to land at anywhere near full strength, it was immediately committed to seize the high ground on the right flank of the beach. The company soon overran its objective and in doing so was instrumental in maintaining the impetus of the attack, for enemy resistance from that point had held up the entire battalion.[27]

The regimental reserve, 3/4, reached the peninsula at 0845 and within 20 minutes was committed on the right of 1/4 where it pushed forward to the edge of the airdrome.[28] By 1000 the beachhead had been expanded sufficiently to

[20] *1/4 SAR, Ph III*, 4.

[21] *Bergren.*

[22] Between 0445 and 0545 over 4,300 rounds of high explosive ammunition, varying from 75mm to 14-inch, were placed on the high ground immediately fronting the landing beaches.

[23] *Bell.*

[24] *1/4 SAR, Ph III*, 4; *2/4 SAR, Ph III*, 5.

[25] *Ibid.*

[26] *6th TkBn SAR, Ph III*, 15. During the battle on Oroku Peninsula the need for engineer support grew so critical that the armored dozers of the 6th EngBn and a liaison officer were attached to the 6th TkBn. In addition, the tank battalion was given first priority on engineer work and equipment. *Ibid.*, 26.

[27] Maj J. R. Kerman Ltr to CMC, 7Jan48, hereinafter cited as *Kerman.*

[28] *3/4 SAR, Ph III*, 5.

warrant landing a second regiment. Accordingly, Colonel Whaling was directed to start embarking the 29th Marines immediately.

Although rain was coming down in driving sheets and it appeared that it might be difficult and dangerous to cross the bay, Colonel Whaling's regiment completed loading and landing on schedule.[29] By 1300 the 2d Battalion was ashore and relieving the left flank elements of 2/4. The remainder of the zone of that battalion was taken over by 3/29 an hour and a half later, and 2/4 passed to regimental reserve.

While the 29th Marines was moving to Oroku, division wiremen ferried a four-trunk cable across the mouth of the Naha Harbor, overheaded it to the mast of a sunken ship, and established wire communication with the assault units by 1100. In the early afternoon bridging operations were set afoot between Naha and Ono Yama, which had been secured against negligible resistance concurrent with the main landing.

Despite the harassment of continuous fire from hostile automatic weapons emplaced on the high ground along the northern Oroku coast, the division engineers had a Bailey bridge installed by 1845. Although pontoons had been readied in the meantime to span the estuary between Ono Yama and the peninsula, the emplacement of this bridge was held in abeyance pending neutralization of the enemy machinegun fire which might well have punctured and sunk the pneumatic pontoons.

The afternoon storm prevented the movement of the remainder of the 6th Tank Battalion to the Oroku area; but the 1st Battalion, 29th Marines was landed and assembled in regimental reserve by nightfall. The end of the day found the assault battalions 1,500 yards inland with the left of the 29th secured on the bay of Naha, while on the right the open flank of the 4th was firmly anchored on the sea. There, the perimeter of 3/4 contained approximately one-third of Naha airfield which was swampy, overgrown with grass, and harbored only a few planes that had been "bombed and strafed to a mess of useless wreckage."[30]

During the day development of the enemy's defense had revealed an inordinate number of

OROKU AIRFIELD and the terrain inland towards Naha is shown during a carrier strike. (Navy Photograph)

automatic weapons, ranging in various calibers up to 40mm. Subsequently, it was disclosed that the Japanese had stripped the armament from the air defenses and damaged aircraft in the area and integrated these weapons into the ground fortifications to stiffen materially the resistance on Oroku. Besides meeting with the most extensive mine fields yet encountered during the campaign, on this day the 6th Division had its first contact with an awesome weapon: an 8-inch rocket that exploded with terrific concussion. However, there was little fragmentation and accuracy was poor. While the noise the huge projectiles made, tumbling through the air end over end, sounded "like a locomotive from hell"[31] to the troops, the rockets were mainly a source of annoyance and caused few casualties. Rockets continued to fall in the rear areas during the night, snipers and infiltrators were active, and the entire front came under intermittent heavy mortar fire. (See Map 34, Map Section)

[29] *Whaling.*

[30] *3/4 SAR, Ph III,* 5.

[31] Maj P. D. Carleton, *The Conquest of Okinawa: An Account of the Sixth Marine Division,* (Washington, 1947), 104.

The 1st Battalion, 22d Marines reverted to the 6th Division from corps reserve at 0700 on 5 June and moved to the division left flank to give protection to the right (west) flank of the 7th Marines pushing south from the Kokuba Gawa. Shortly thereafter, the attack on Oroku jumped off and progressed slowly but steadily against uniformly stubborn resistance until about noon, when the 4th Marines was halted by a heavily fortified locality north of Toma.

This strong point lay in the zone of 3/4 where Company I came under fire from its left front. While Company K patrolled the high ground on the right with negative results, Company I pushed forward and swung southeast to clean out the pocket. Artillery was not too effective against the deep caves of the hill fortress, and although 37mm guns were used to advantage, the infantry badly needed the support of direct fire weapons of heavier caliber.[32]

Tanks were ordered up but were immobilized by the soft mud and impassable roads. However, one platoon of Company C, 6th Tank Battalion worked its way along the reef on the seaward side of the airdrome to a rift in the sea wall. Passing through the breach, the platoon crossed the airfield and made contact with 3/4.[33] Aided by the tanks and the fires of self-propelled 105's located in the zone of the 1st Battalion, the infantry overran the noxious position late in the afternoon. As soon as Company I had cleared its area, Company L was committed to establish contact with 1/4 on the left.

The 1st Battalion had met stiff resistance along its entire front. Company C on the left slowly fought its way forward. But Company A was pinned down almost immediately by the heavy fire from its right front. After the Toma fortifications were cracked by 3/4, Company A advanced to the high ground overlooking that village. When the attack ceased at 1700, Company C, suffering heavy casualties, had inched its way to commanding terrain southeast of "Oroku-Mura."[34]

Despite bitter opposition and difficulties of

supply and evacuation engendered by the water-soaked ground, the lines were advanced about 1,000 yards, securing three-fourth of the airfield. The 4th had also encountered heavy concentrations of artillery fire. Counterbattery of the 15th Marines silenced four 120mm dual-purpose guns, one 6-inch rifle, and several smaller field pieces, but enemy shelling still made it necessary for Company K, returning from the ridge at 1600, to move behind the sea wall and back along the defended lines to the battalion reserve area. Hostile artillery also prevented LVT's from using the route the tanks had taken, and supplies had to be hand-carried to 3/4.[35]

Meanwhile, the 29th Marines had experienced enemy opposition similar in nature to that met by the 4th. Progress was slow against intense rifle, machine-gun, and mortar fire. As the advance continued, thickening mine fields provided an additional impediment. Roads and bridges, damaged beyond local repair facilities, together with the soggy terrain, served to immobilize the tanks. However, their direct fire destroyed several automatic weapons and a 3-inch dual-purpose gun.[36]

Resistance was overcome painfully and laboriously. By 1400 the 29th was heavily engaged with a strong center of resistance near Hill 57, which was also delaying the left of the 4th Marines. An enemy counterattack against 3/29 was successfully broken up, and the battalion pushed forward almost 1,000 yards before its attack was stalled by heavy fire from the areas of the adjacent battalions.[37]

The 2d Battalion, 29th Marines continued to push its left flank along the estuary and cleared the bridge site. Covered by security detachments from 2/29, a 300-foot pontoon bridge was floated into position, despite enemy machine-gun fire from the vicinity of Oroku village. Before dark the first tractor had rumbled over to the peninsula from Ono Yama, opening a ground supply line to the assault troops.

---

[32] 1/4 SAR, Ph III, 5; 3/4 SAR, Ph III, 6.

[33] 6th TkBn SAR, Ph III, 16.

[34] Ibid.; 1/4 SAR, Ph III, 5; 3/4 SAR, Ph III, 6. Actually this village was unnamed on the map, but because the name Oroku-Mura (denoting the township within which the peninsula lay) was superimposed over it, the settlement was designated by that name during the operation for clarity and simplicity. Kerman.

[35] 3/4 SAR, Ph III, 6; 6th TkBn SAR, Ph III, 16.

[36] 6th TkBn SAR, Ph III, 16.

[37] 3/29 SAR, Ph III, 4.

Supported by a platoon of tanks firing overhead from a high ridge, 2/29 moved forward slowly on 6 June. On the left of the 2d Battalion, another tank platoon was able to move along the shore line and assist the advance until halted by a destroyed bridge.[38] After a gain of several hundred yards, 2/29 was pinned down by heavy fire, and the advance came to an abrupt standstill.

On the right of the 29th Marines the attack was stymied from the outset. The terrain confronting the 3d Battalion there "consisted of a series of small temple-like hills, each of which had been converted into a fortress . . . from which mutually supporting automatic weapons could cover adjacent positions and deny the open ground between the hills."[39] These gun positions were well dug-in and impervious to artillery fire. Because the narrow roads in the area had been made impassable by mines and shell cratering, tank support was not forthcoming, and a day of bitter fighting netted 3/29 a gain of a scant 150 yards.[40]

The baneful strong point, dubbed Little Sugar Loaf, which had frustrated the efforts of 3/29 rendered the attack of the 1st Battalion, 4th Marines equally futile. Denied tank support for the same reasons as 3/29, the left flank of 1/4 (where Company B had passed through Company C) remained stationary in the outskirts of "Oroku-Mura." On the right Company A, in an attempt to turn the flank of the enemy position, became involved in a vicious fire fight. One platoon was pinned down for the better part of six hours, and was able to pull out only after the direct fire of self-propelled 105's was brought to bear on Little Sugar Loaf. By the time tank dozers and armored bulldozers had painstakingly repaired the mine-infested roads so that armor could be brought up, insufficient daylight remained to execute the attack. Consequently the 1st Battalion fell back to the lines it had occupied in the morning with little to show for a day of hard fighting.[41]

Although the coordinated attack of two regiments accomplished little in the center, the operations of 6 June revealed that the major enemy defenses were located in the area of the axial ridge, running northwest to southeast along the length of the peninsula. Progress was found to be less difficult on the right of the 4th Marines, and every effort was made to push 3/4 to the south in order to place the regiment on the flank of the principal resistance.

Preceded by air strikes on the ridges to its front, the 3d Battalion moved out on 6 June with Companies I and L in assault. Company I on the right began to receive fire from 20mm machine cannon and an artillery piece of heavy caliber located on Senaga Shima, a small island 500 yards west of the midpoint of Oroku's southern shore. Counter fire from tanks, artillery, and support craft was immediately laid down. An urgent call for an air strike on the island was answered in less than half an hour, and "as rack after rack of bombs fell on the Nip positions, the troops stood up and cheered."[42]

The artillery piece was soon silenced, but 20mm fire was received spasmodically. Nevertheless, 3/4 pressed forward with its open flank covered by continued air strikes on Senaga Shima and completed the capture of Naha airfield before noon. While maintaining contact with the stalemated units in the center as the attack swept down the coast 3/4 became overextended and Company K was committed on the right of Company I. In addition, Colonel Shapley ordered the 2d Battalion to relieve the left flank company of the 3d. Company E took over the zone of Company L about 1600, and the latter unit moved over to the coast to tie in with the right of Company K.[43]

The day had been warm and clear, and the ground was drying out. Engineers went to work on the main north-south road and disarmed 83 mines of various types. Company B, 6th Tank Battalion landed at noon with the remainder of the division tanks which were assembled in reserve.[44] By the next day wheeled transportation was available to lessen the supply difficulties of the assault troops.

The 4th Marines resumed the advance on 7 June and again made the most rapid progress

[38] *6th TkBn SAR, Ph III*, 16.

[39] *29th Mar SAR, Ph III*, 8.

[40] *3/29 SAR, Ph III*, 5.

[41] *1/4 SAR, Ph III*, 5; Kerman.

[42] *3/4 SAR, Ph III*, 6.

[43] *Ibid.*

[44] *6th TkBn SAR, Ph III*, 16.

along the seaward flank. But resistance increased in the late afternoon when Company L, on the right of 3/4, attempted to secure the last high ground on the west coast of the peninsula, near Gushi village. A report at 1615 that the hill had been taken proved to be premature. Soon thereafter, murderous machine-gun fire from the left and front, coupled with a heavy mortar barrage, forced the company to pull back to the next ridge for the night.[45] (See Map 35, Map Section)

Stiff resistance and bitter fighting characterized the action in the center and on the left of the 4th Marines' area. However, the attack forged ahead against machine-gun fire coming "from everywhere," while "countless caves were methodically cleaned out and sealed by the old process of direct fire, flame, and demolitions."[46]

On the left 1/4 reverted to regimental reserve during the morning of 7 June, when Major Carney's 2d Battalion passed through its lines with Companies F and G abreast. It was 1000 before the attack could be coordinated with 3/4 and all supporting units. But by that time tanks, M–7's, and 37mm guns were all brought to bear on Little Sugar Loaf. Company F commenced to advance slowly and steadily against the enemy entrenched in the most dominant piece of terrain of central Oroku.

Covered by the fire of Company E from the positions it had occupied the previous afternoon, Company G executed a wide envelopment from the right (south) and was on its objective by noon. Major Carney immediately ordered Company E to attack on the right of G. After Company E had also taken its objective from the right flank and Company F had wrested the position in its zone from the stubborn enemy,[47] the formidable bastion was overrun late in the afternoon.

On the left of the 4th Marines, 3/29 began three days of heavy combat, during which very little enemy territory was captured. But in this period Lieutenant Colonel Wright's command brought about the demise of some 500 Japanese, destroyed large quantities of all types of their weapons, and sealed numerous caves filled with troops, weapons, and equipment.[48]

Progress continued to be slow throughout the 29th Marines' area. The 37mm guns were manhandled to commanding positions, and did effective work with direct fire against hostile automatic weapons. The division engineers replaced the destroyed bridge that had impeded the advance of the tanks along Naha Bay, and armored support enabled 2/29 to enter the village of Oroku on 7 June. The following day 1/29 was committed partially, when Company C entered the lines on the left of the 2d Battalion, while A and B remained behind it in reserve. Company C continued to tie in the flank of 2/29 with the estuary on 9 June and sent patrols toward Hill 53, which were met by heavy artillery, mortar, and machine-gun fire.[49]

The original scheme for the capture of Oroku had envisioned a southeasterly drive toward the base of the peninsula by the 4th and 29th Marines abreast. By 8 June, however, as the attack developed, the changing tactical situation demanded a shift in the axis of the main effort. While the 29th Marines was stalled at the key ridge line on the left, the 4th had pushed far forward along the beach and lower ground on the right, pivoting to the east in a counterclockwise movement which faced its lines northeast, approximately at right angles with the 29th. Consequently, Colonel Shapley's direction of attack was reoriented northward toward the core of enemy resistance.[50]

At the same time the general attack of the Tenth Army pressed southward, and the 7th Marines swept past the base of Oroku and the unguarded flank of the 6th Marine Division along its boundary with the 1st Division. General Geiger released the 22d Marines to General Shepherd for the purpose of covering the left of the 6th Division zone and giving protection to General del Valle's exposed flank. As the 7th Marines advanced to the sea on 7 June, 3/22 captured Hill 103.[51] Thus, the 22d began to

[45] 3/4 SAR, Ph III, 6.
[46] 4th Mar SAR, Ph III, 11.
[47] 2/4 SAR, Ph III, 6.

[48] 3/29 SAR, Ph III, 5.
[49] 1/29 SAR, Ph III, 4.
[50] Bergren.
[51] Ibid.; 3/22 SAR, Ph III, 8–9. Hill 103 proved to be an important observation post. Although it was occupied in strength, the defense was weak inasmuch as the Japanese elected to stay in their caves. This definitely restricted the fields of fire which could be easily outflanked by way of covered routes of approach. Ibid.

SENAGA SHIMA and the tangled ridges on the west coast of Oroku photographed shortly after the peninsula was secured.

swing to the west across the peninsula to face the 4th and 29th.

Early in the morning of 8 June 1/4, covered by smoke from the artillery, skirted the eastern edge of Naha airfield and moved to positions on the right of 3/4. At 1030 the 1st Battalion attacked, with Company A in assault, to seize the high ground at the base of the peninsula just south of Gushi. Only one platoon was committed initially, and this was pinned down at once by a hail of rifle, machine-gun, and mortar fire.

Although tanks had been positioned on the north bank of a stream to support the attack, their fires were masked by the configuration of the terrain until the vehicles succeeded in crossing the creek and moving farther south. Under cover of smoke fired by the tanks, the harassed platoon was withdrawn to cover, and preparations were made to launch a coordinated assault. After a 20-minute preparation of direct overhead fire by two platoons of tanks, while two more pounded the reverse slope of Gushi Ridge from positions on the reef, Company A attacked to the south and within 15 minutes overran the strong point which had held up 1/4 for almost half a day.

As soon as the objective was reached, Company A changed its direction of advance to the northeast. At the same time Company C continued the attack to the south, on the right of A, and cleared the high ground down to the last hill overlooking the sea wall. Meanwhile, Company B swung in on the left of A and attacked north.

Thus, Lieutenant Colonel Bell was in the unusual position of having each of his three rifle companies attacking in a different direction. But the maneuver was successful, and the end of the day found the 1st Battalion in possession of the dominant terrain at the base of Oroku. Company B tied in for the night with 3/4, while Company C covered the exposed flank by moving into a position on the right rear of A, commanding the north-south road to Itoman.[52]

In changing its direction of advance to cross the peninsula, the 3d Battalion, 4th Marines attacked into rugged terrain consisting of a maze of interlaced ridges. Every hill was honeycombed with mutually supporting caves which were often dangerous to blow because of the enormous amounts of explosives and ammunition which some of them contained.[53] Progress was slow but steady, requiring much maneuver, close cooperation between units, and careful coordination of supporting fires. Mines continued to be detected and removed, and hundreds of pounds of demolitions were used to seal caves.

The advance on the left of the 4th Marines' zone of action was resumed by the 2d Battalion on 8 June at 1000. All three rifle companies were on the line; but in order to shift the axis of the attack toward Oroku village, only Company E on the right moved out initially while Companies F and G supported by fire. After Company E had gained about 300 yards, Company G attacked on its left and by 1130 both companies had completed the swing to the northeast. Only 200 yards from the day's objective, G and E reorganized to continue the attack and shortly after 1300 resumed the advance, with Company F supporting by fire. Although forward progress was contested with determination, the assault companies were on the objective by 1530 and digging in for the night.[54]

In reaching this goal, Major Carney's men employed a tactical maneuver which had been used successfully by the 96th Division in the fighting southwest of Conical Hill. The center

of bitterest resistance in the 2d Battalion's area was Hill 39 northeast of Tamikamiya. Rather than move down the forward face of the hill, which was swept by blistering automatic weapons fire, Company E passed through instead of over its objective. A fire team, quickly followed by a light machine gun section was sent through a Japanese tunnel. The line rapidly built up on either side of the exit, and the troops were soon on their way to the next hill. This technique proved highly successful on two other occasions during the day.

In the meantime the 22d Marines continued to pivot on its right, wheeling the left flank clockwise toward a juncture with the 4th. On the morning of 8 June, 1/22 was ordered to send strong patrols to seize Hills 55 and 55(1). The 3d Battalion, 22d Marines with Company B attached, moved out toward the sea to contact the 4th Marines. Late in the afternoon 2/22 moved down the Kokuba Gawa to positions in rear of the 1st Battalion. Hill 55 was in the hands of 1/22 at 1800. But heavy mortar fire, coupled with an ammunition shortage, forced the battalion to pull back 150 yards after dark.[55]

Meanwhile, Company B, meeting only an occasional sniper, patrolled to the coast but failed to contact the 4th Marines. At the same time the advance of 3/22 was gradually reoriented to the northwest as Company I probed toward Chiwa. During the day patrols worked north to a ridge line half a mile south of the village, meeting little local resistance but receiving heavy fire from Hills 55 and 55(1).

Company B reverted to 1/22 at 0500 on 9 June.[56] All units were scheduled to jump off at 0830: the 1st Battalion to regain Hill 55; the 2d to seize Hill 55 (1); and the 3d with its objective Hill 28 on the outskirts of Chiwa. At 0700, however, the time of attack was delayed until 0900, at which time 1/22 moved on Hill 55. As soon as the 1st Battalion had taken its objective the 2d was to pass through and capture Hill 55(1).[57]

After hard fighting and suffering heavy casualties, 1/22 secured Hill 55 late in the afternoon. Although 2/22 had been ready to attack

[52] 1/4 SAR, Ph III, 6; 6th TkBn SAR, Ph III, 17; Kerman.
[53] 3/4 SAR, Ph III, 7.
[54] 2/4 SAR, Ph III, 6–7.

[55] 1/22 SAR, Ph III, 4.
[56] 3/22 SAR, Ph III, 9–10.
[57] 2/22 SAR, Ph III, 12.

all day, 1/22 had not progressed as rapidly as had been expected, and it was decided to postpone the assault of the 2d Battalion until 10 June.

Similarly, hostile fires from Hill 55 (1) prevented 3/22 from occupying Hill 28, but Company I secured the high ground just south of it by 1000 and contacted the 4th Marines when patrols of that unit cleaned out Chiwa. Company K manned the positions vacated by I in the morning, while Company L returned from mopping up the coastal area to fill the gap between K and 2/22.[58]

The action in the zone of the 4th Marines on 9 June remained unchanged from that of preceding days:

> The advance was still slow and tedious against bitter resistance. Every Jap seemed to be armed with a machine gun, and there was still the same light and heavy mortar fire. Casualties continued to mount and the number of Japs killed soared over the maximum of 1500 which were supposed to be defending and there were still plenty left.[59]

On the right of the 4th the 1st Battalion moved out with Companies A and B in assault to seize the high ground near Hill 55 (2) and Uibaru. The attack was delayed until armor could be brought to bear from the road running along the right flank of the battalion. But when the tanks were in position, a rail-mounted 75mm gun, firing from two cave ports in the face of a small cliff south of Chiwa, forced them to scurry for cover.[60]

Nevertheless, the attack moved out through machine-gun and mortar fire at 1230. Each of the innumerable caves had to be demolished before it could be passed, and progress was slow. Late in the afternoon, after 1/4 had pushed through Gushi, a tank was moved through the village on to the Oroku-Itoman road. The tank came in on the flank of the cliff-dwelling 75mm gun, "knocking it out with only two shots fired—one from the gun which missed and one from the tank which did not."[61] By evening

SATCHEL CHARGES, such as this one being flung into an enemy dugout on Oroku, were often the only means of silencing Japanese opposition.

the right of 1/4 was anchored on a ridge northwest of Chiwa, while the left rested in the outskirts of Uibaru, which 3/4 had taken as its day's objective.[62]

As the infantry regiments converged from three directions to compress the Oroku garrison in the southeast corner of the peninsula, restrictions upon the employment of supporting arms (an inherent difficulty in the execution of a double envelopment) conspired with the ruggedness of the terrain and the tenacity of the defenders to retard the progress of 2/4 on the afternoon of 9 June. Since the 2d Battalion was attacking toward its own artillery and across the front of the 29th Marines, only tanks, M-7's, and 37's could be used. Consequently, when it was necessary to effect road repairs to move tracked vehicles forward, and neither tank dozers nor armored dozers were available, the advance of 2/4 bogged down after a scant gain of 150 yards.

But on 10 June the momentum of the attack accelerated. Early in the morning equipment was obtained to clear all tank approaches to the front lines of 2/4. By 0815 supporting arms were moving into position to cover the advance, and the 2d Battalion launched a three-company assault at 0945 which was coordinated with the 29th Marines. An hour later 2/4 had broken

---

[58] Ibid.; 3/22 SAR, Ph III, 10.

[59] 4th Mar SAR, Ph III, 12.

[60] 1/4 SAR, Ph III, 6. "The gun seemed as surprised by the arrival of the tanks as the tanks by fire from the gun, because it fired only HE [High Explosive] and no AP [Armor Piercing] and the tanks were able to get to cover without loss." Kerman.

[61] Kerman.

[62] 1/4 SAR, Ph III, 6; 3/4 SAR, Ph III, 7.

through, seized the last commanding ground in its zone, and commenced preparing defensive positions from which it supported the adjacent units by fire for the next two days.[63] (See Map 36, Map Section)

The battle for Oroku was entering its final stages. In the remainder of the 4th Marines' area the 1st and 3d Battalions also advanced against decreasing resistance. In the center 3/4 moved forward on a narrow, one-company front until 1400, when it was squeezed out of the line by 1/4 converging on 2/4 at Hill 58. On the right 1/4 occupied Hill 55(2).[64]

Meanwhile, the 22d Marines moved northeast toward Tomigusuki and abreast of the 4th. While 1/22 retained its positions and supported 2/22 by fire, the attack of the latter battalion jumped off in column at 0845 with Company F in assault, followed by Company E. Company G, reinforced by a 37mm platoon, assisted by pounding the reverse slope of Hill 55(1). At 1045 Company F was on the crest of the hill which was declared secure just before noon. By 1500 Company G rejoined on the high ground at 55(1).[65]

Concurrently, 3/22, which had also supported the attack of the 2d Battalion, was ordered to advance to the northeast in concert with 1/4. Company K remained in position, but Company I occupied Hill 28 and tied in with the 4th Marines. Company L was ordered to positions in the 1st Battalion sector.[66]

Although the 29th Marines made only limited gains on 10 June, it had clearly defined the last major pocket of resistance in the high ground west of Oroku village. Up to this point enemy resistance had continued without faltering, but the defense of Oroku was beginning to crumble. In one case during the day's advance, elements of 1/4 overran the retreating Japanese who were trying to pull out toward Tomigusuki.[67] Further evidence of the extreme pressure to which the enemy was subjected appeared during the night in a series of local counterattacks all along the front. The heaviest of these were against the perimeter of 1/4, where 200 enemy dead were counted after daylight.

To break through the remaining resistance, a concerted attack was launched on 11 June by the greater part of eight battalions. In the zone of the 22d Marines, the 2d Battalion was to seize Hill 62 north of Tomigusuki, while the 3d Battalion, less Company I which was to support the 4th Marines until the advance of that unit masked its fires, moved to an assembly area near Hill 55. After 2/22 secured its objective, 3/22 was to pass through to Hill 53 overlooking the Kokuba Estuary.

Preceded by a half hour of intense artillery preparation,[68] 2/22 jumped off at 0825 on 11 June with the assault companies, E and F, in column, Company G standing fast to support the attack by fire initially. By 0900 the attacking echelon held the high ground south of Tomigusuki. But at 0950 it was still there with an open left flank. Consequently, Lieutenant Colonel Johnson ordered Company E to remain in place until contact was established by the 4th Marines approaching from the left rear. Company G was directed to move forward with Company F to attack the strongly fortified Hill 63. After a five-minute M–7 bombardment, the advance was resumed at 1115, and less than an hour later a heavy fire fight was in progress on the slopes of the objective.[69]

In the meantime Lieutenant Colonel Shisler, who had been directed to render assistance, ordered Company L of 3/22 to seize the eastern shoulder of Hill 63 and support 2/22 by fire. At 1145 Company L was in position to execute this mission, and 2/22 moved onto the objective. By 1220 Tomigusuki was declared secure.[70]

Without artillery preparation,[71] but preceded by a half hour 81mm mortar barrage, 3/22 launched the assault against Hill 53 at 1435. Company K passed through the 2d Battalion to attack, while Company L moved to envelop the hill from the east. Company I rejoined in bat-

---

[68] Six battalions of 105mm and one of 155mm howitzers.

[69] 2/22 SAR, Ph III, 12.

[70] Ibid.; 3/22 SAR, Ph III, 10.

[71] "As the three regiments came closer together, it became dangerous and finally impossible to use even 60mm mortars, and some casualties were incurred from friendly fire on both flanks." Bergren.

---

[63] 2/4 SAR, Ph III, 7–8.

[64] 1/4 SAR, Ph III, 6–7; 3/4 SAR, III, 7.

[65] 2/22 SAR, Ph III, 12.

[66] 3/22 SAR, Ph III, 10.

[67] 1/4 SAR, Ph III, 7.

talion reserve. Company K on the left met stiff resistance, and although it was unable to participate in the assault with Company L, it contributed materially by reducing pressure on L which occupied Hill 53 at 1450.[72]

The 29th Marines made repeated attacks against the high ground west of Oroku village with only limited gains in the heavily fortified hills. In the 4th Marines' zone the 1st and 2d Battalions remained in position while 3/4 passed through 1/4. Company I seized the hill to its front after a day of hard fighting. But Company K on the right fell 300 yards short of contacting the left of 2/22.[73]

Nevertheless, the ramparts of the Oroku fortress were cracking, and Admiral Ota released his last dispatch to General Ushijima:

Enemy tank groups are now attacking our cave headquarters. The Naval Base Force is dying gloriously at this moment . . . We are grateful for your past kindnesses and pray for the success of the Army.[74]

During the night of 11–12 June artillerymen killed or dispersed a group of Japanese troops attempting to cross the Kokuba Gawa,[75] while 51 infiltrators were killed trying to pass through the lines of the 22d Marines. The following day saw the first real break in the enemy's stubborn, well-coordinated defense. Units of the 22d Marines consolidated their positions and mopped up the area which had been secured the day before. The 4th and 29th continued to compress the enemy pocket west of Tomigusuki.

The 3d Battalion, 4th Marines resumed the attack and proceeded slowly and methodically, eliminating all resistance and sealing caves as the troops advanced. By 1550, 3/4 tied in with the 22d Marines and as the day ended only one hill intervened between the battalion and Naha Harbor, 500 yards to the front. (See Map 37, Map Section)

During the day the 29th Marines broke through the hard core of the enemy defense that had been holding it up for a week. The 2d Battalion completed cleaning out Oroku village, and before dawn the 1st Battalion successfully launched the first of a series of coordinated attacks against the mutually supporting tactical localities west of Oroku.[76]

By 1540, 1/29 had overrun the center of resistance, permitting 2/29 to move up on the left. Company F moved out from Oroku to seize Easy Hill, immediately south of the village—the last strong point in the zone of the 29th Marines. The capture of this key terrain feature forced the enemy into the alluvial flats along the coast between Oroku and Hill 53. "In the late afternoon enemy troops began displaying flags of surrender. Language officers equipped with loud speaker systems were dispatched to the front line areas to assist in the surrender of those Japs who desired to. The attempt was partially successful, 86 enemy soldiers voluntarily laid down their arms." [77]

At daybreak on 13 June, 3/29 relieved 1/29 in the lines and jumped off with 2/29 to destroy the remaining enemy in the regiment's zone of action. Their advance to the southeast was rapid, sweeping past 2/4 and 1/4 to pinch them out of the line. Concurrently, 3/4 also drove swiftly toward the beach. Advancing in skirmish lines, the assault companies flushed the demoralized Japanese from the brush in the marshy ground along the waterfront. Reserve companies followed with flame throwers and demolitions sealing bypassed caves.

The battle turned to a rout. Some of the enemy threw down their arms and fled at the Marines' approach. Large numbers surrendered; but some fought back with hand grenades in desperate, individual last ditch stands, while many more used grenades to destroy themselves in despair.

The sea wall was reached at noon, and the remainder of the day was spent running to earth small groups hiding in the cane fields and rice

---

[72] *3/22 SAR, Ph III*, 10.

[73] *3/4 SAR, Ph III*, 7–8; *2/22 SAR, Ph III*, 13.

[74] *Okinawa Operations Record*, 105.

[75] *IIIAC Arty AR*, 30.

[76] By the afternoon of 9 June, the heavy fighting of the previous three days had seriously depleted the ranks of 3/29. Consequently, the 3d Bn was reinforced by the attachment of Co B from the regimental reserve. The following evening 1/29 relieved 3/29, Co A taking over from Cos G and H, while Co I remained in the line attached to the 1st Bn. On 11 June Co H was attached to 2/29, replacing Co C on the left flank of that battalion. After the initial attack of 12 June, Co I was squeezed out of the line passing to 1/29 reserve. The evening of 12 June both H and I reverted to the control of 3/29. *3/29 SAR, Ph III*, 5.

[77] *6th Mar Div SAR, Ph III*, Part III, 21.

FINAL SWEEP on Oroku brings a skirmish line of Marines into action against Japanese hiding out in the marshes north of Tomigusuki.

of the Battle for Oroku:

> The ten day battle was a bitter one from its inception to the destruction of the last organized resistance. The enemy had taken full advantage of the terrain which adapted itself extraordinarily well to a deliberate defense in depth. The rugged coral outcroppings and the many small precipitous hills had obviously been organized for defense over a long period of time. Cave and tunnel systems of a most elaborate nature had been cut into each terrain feature of importance, and heavy weapons were sited for defense against attack from any direction.
>
> Despite the powerful converging attacks of three regiments, the advance was slow, laborious, and bitterly opposed. The capture of each defensive locality was a problem in itself, involving carefully thought out planning and painstaking execution. During ten days fighting almost 5,000 Japs were killed and nearly 200 taken prisoner. Thirty of our tanks were disabled, many by mines. One tank was destroyed by two direct hits from an 8″ naval gun fired at point blank range. Finally, 1,608 Marines were killed or wounded.[78]

The most notable aspect of this operation, however, was that during a critical phase of the campaign Tenth Army was able to exploit fully an amphibious capability despite the fact that the extremely short notice precluded major preparations. Besides the complications arising from a lack of time for rehearsals, or even the detailed briefing of participating units, the approach and landing were executed for the most part in the darkest hours of the early morning with inadequate navigation aids. Moreover, it was done without wave guides, control boats, or any other control feature common to an amphibious assault. Yet, in a period of 36 hours the operation was effected on schedule and according to plan.[79] Thus, the significant point in an analysis of the seizure of Oroku Peninsula is that "with trained troops and competent staffs in all echelons, the amphibious landing of a division is not of excessive complexity."[80]

KUNISHI RIDGE[81]

As the 6th Marine Division initiated operations on Oroku Peninsula, the 1st Marine Division continued its resolute, albeit slogging pursuit of the Japanese forces withdrawing from the Shuri battle position. The atrocious weath-

paddies. In the late afternoon General Shepherd notified General Geiger that all organized resistance on Oroku had ceased.

At noon of 13 June orders were issued to the 6th Reconnaissance Company to secure Senaga Shima, which that unit had scouted on the night of 10 June. The island had been subjected to intense bombardment for four days and was kept under interdiction all night. Company C of 1/29 was attached to the reconnaissance company, and at 0500, 14 June, the attack was launched. No resistance was encountered, but as mopping up continued on the peninsula, Major Walker's men thoroughly combed the island, finding only the victims of artillery, air, and naval bombardment: enemy dead and the silenced guns which had been used against the troops on Oroku.

Operations of 14 June marked the completion

[78] *Ibid.*, 22.
[79] *CMC Memo 1955*.
[80] *6th MarDiv SAR, Ph III*, Part III, 60.

er had converted the already muddy roads to impassable morasses. Transport was hopelessly mired north of the Kokuba Gawa. South of the river the "trails were only negotiable by foot troops—vehicles could not have been used" even if it had been possible to bring them across the inlet.[52] The acute supply situation could be coped with only by carrying parties and air drop. Yet, despite the difficulties imposed by the weather and the terrain, the 1st Division chalked up gains of as much as 1,800 yards on 4 June as the drive southward from the Naha-Yonabaru valley began. (See Map 38, Map Section)

While the 4th Marines secured the initial foothold on the northwest tip of Oroku, the 7th Marines, on the right of the 1st Division, moved south from the bridgehead at the mouth of the Kokuba to isolate Admiral Ota's force on the peninsula. The hill mass at the base of Oroku was the dominating terrain in the division zone of action, culminating in Hill 108 overlooking the East China Sea and the objective town of Itoman. Thus as the 7th moved forward, its open right flank was exposed to constant harassment from the commanding ground along the boundary between the 1st and 6th Divisions. On the other hand, the left of the division where the corps boundary ran generally southward from Shuri to Iwa was secure. The adjacent 96th Infantry Division was well ahead at the outset of the advance from the line of the Kokuba Gawa.

Upon the collapse of the Shuri line, the 1st Marines had remained behind to patrol and mop up in the vicinity of the city while the 5th drove forward in pursuit of the retreating enemy. But at 0430 on 4 June the 1st joined the chase as the 3d Battalion left Shuri to make a wide envelopment through the 96th Division zone in order to seize the high ground north of Iwa and Shindawaku in concert with the 1st Battalion which

was to pass through the 5th Marines' lines near Tomusu.[83]

By 0930, 3/1 had reached the village of Tera immediately south of Chan.[84] At 1300 the point was pinned down by hostile fire, and Company L, which constituted the advance guard, attempted to clean out the enemy pocket. Because he lacked mortar ammunition and had no communications with artillery or NGF support ships, Lieutenant Colonel Ross ordered the company to disengage, and the battalion bivouacked in rear of the 383d Infantry. At 1500, 3/1 was brought under enemy artillery fire, but as the battalion was in defilade no casualties were sustained.

Torrential rains continued all day, making rivers of the roads and churning the fields into seas of calf-deep mud, of such viscosity that the soles were torn from the shoes of many of the men. Food was scarce, but through the whole-hearted cooperation of the 96th Division the Marines procured two meals of K rations per man.[85] It was the considered opinion of at least one member of 3/1 that "this day probably was the most miserable spent on Okinawa by men of this battalion."[86] To compound these problems and discomforts, the 3d Battalion also found itself without a supply route or communications with the regiment 11,000 yards to the rear.[87]

The day's events proved to be no more propitious for the 1st Battalion, 1st Marines than for the 3d. The occupation of the high ground across the front of the 5th Marines had been completed shortly after daylight, when Company F of 2/5 secured Hill 107 without opposition, and Lieutenant Colonel Benedict's battalion held the entire frontage of the regimental position.[88] After a long, wet, and tedious march 1/1 took over from 2/5 about noon. The latter

[51] Unless otherwise noted the material in this section is derived from *Tenth Army AR; 1st MarDiv SAR; 1st MarDiv G-3 Jnl; 1st Mar SAR; 5th Mar SAR; 7th Mar SAR; 22d Mar SAR, Ph III; 7th Mar History;* MajGen P. A. del Valle, "Southward from Shuri," *MC Gazette,* October 1945, hereinafter cited as *Southward from Shuri.*

[52] *2/7 SAR,* 7.

[83] *1/1 SAR,* 20; *3/1 SAR,* 41.

[84] This locality is not to be confused with the Tera near Itoman on the west coast.

[85] In the opinion of the CG, 96th InfDiv these Marines "were not equipped or organized for a protracted campaign. I was glad to assist in supply, air drops, and the care of their wounded. They were fine comrades and cooperated to the fullest extent." MajGen J. L. Bradley Ltr to CMC, 22Oct54.

[86] *3/1 SAR,* 41.

[87] *Ibid.*

[88] *2/5 SAR,* 16–17; LtCol W. E. Benedict Ltr to CMC, 28Mar47, hereinafter cited as *Benedict.*

unit maintained its positions as a secondary line while passing into corps reserve with the remainder of the 5th Marines.

Lieutenant Colonel Shofner immediately began preparations for an attack at 1400 against the Iwa-Shindawaku Ridge with Companies A and C in assault, the former on the right. But as the rain increased to cloudburst proportions to aggravate the supply problem, General del Valle ordered the attack cancelled.[89] The 7th Marines on the right, however, had already moved out, and counterorders for 1/1 to resume the advance were received an hour later. At 1630 the assault companies of 1/1 started for a ridge 1,500 yards ahead. Meeting no opposition, the advance progressed rapidly until the troops reached a stream some 300 yards short of the objective. The day's downpour had transformed the rivulet into a raging torrent. Shofner could see no way of getting his battalion across until a reconnaissance upstream to his left resulted in the discovery of a bridge.

An attempt was made to cross and redeploy on the other side, and two platoons of Company C negotiated the narrow span without molestation. But as they floundered forward through the mud, the enemy suddenly opened up with mortars and machine guns, pinning down those men who were south of the stream. Inasmuch as 3/7 on the right was held up[90] by the flooded water course, and the bridge area was covered by pre-arranged fires from the 200-foot ridge to the front, Shofner recognized the futility of further attempts to force a crossing and ordered a withdrawal to the 2/5 sector. The battalion had suffered a number of casualties, and a covering force was left behind which brought the wounded out after dark. The next day 1/1 was ordered to bypass the entire area by swinging east into the 96th Division zone and moving in the trace of 3/1 to Iwa.[91]

Because the advance of the 1st Marines southward, in common with those of other regiments, was so extended, the sole means of contact between Colonel Mason's headquarters and his two assault battalions was by radio at extreme range. But this was considered so precarious that the movement orders provided that in the event communications broke down completely, the senior battalion commander would assume tactical control of both battalions.[92] In consequence on 5 June, after a long, tiresome, and muddy trek to the south, during which the 1st Battalion lost 50 men from exhaustion and outran its communications, 1/1 came temporarily under the over-all command of Lieutenant Colonel Ross of the 3d Battalion.[93]

Meanwhile, 3/1 had received no word from the regiment since leaving Shuri. But the corps objective had not been taken, so the battalion commander departed on reconnaissance with his command group early in the morning of 5 June. While this preliminary reconnaissance was underway, the shivering troops built fires and tried to dry out as much as possible before moving. Intermittent showers continued, but between rain squalls 19 plane drops were made to 3/1. A battalion observation post was established by 0700, and information was received from 2/383 that Iwa had been patrolled with negative results. The 3d Battalion left its bivouac at 1030, and upon its arrival in the assembly area Lieutenant Colonel Ross issued his orders for the capture of the Iwa-Shindawaku Ridge.[94]

The attack jumped off at 1230. A delay occurred while a small pocket of the enemy was cleaned out, but the advance continued against moderate machine-gun and rifle fire and at dusk the battalion was on the objective west of Iwa, having advanced more than 3,000 yards to effect the envelopment. During the day 2/1, in regimental reserve, moved to a bivouac area within supporting distance between Tsukasan and Chan. The advance echelon of the 1st Marines had also moved forward, and the regimental commander was able to issue oral orders for 6 June. The 3d Battalion was directed to continue the attack and secure the village of

[89] *1/1 SAR*, 20; *2/5 SAR*, 16.

[90] "There was no bridge in the 3/7 ZofA. Several men were drowned attempting to carry lines across the stream in an attempt to get troops across." LtCol W. Holoman Ltr to CMC, 22Mar55, hereinafter cited as *Holoman*.

[91] *Ibid.*; Notes on Interview with LtCol Austin C. Shofner, USMC, by Capt James R. Stockman at HQMC, 19Mar47, hereinafter cited as *Shofner Interview*.

[92] *Mason*.

[93] *1/1 SAR*, 21.

[94] *3/1 SAR*, 42.

Shindawaku, while the 1st Battalion eliminated all enemy resistance in the regimental zone from the rear of 3/1 to the stream which had stalled the 4 June advance.

Striking out at dawn, 1/1 swung down to Iwa and wheeled to the north. With all three companies deployed in skirmish lines, the 1st Battalion swept northward over the bypassed area on an extremely broad front, passing 3/7 attacking south in its zone. The ridge from which the enemy had stymied the advance two days before was overrun from the rear, surprising the few enemy soldiers remaining there to the extent that some were caught in the act of shifting to civilian clothes, and all were wiped out before they could return a single shot. This curious maneuver was completed by 1400 and 1/1 went into reserve near Tomusu.[95]

Although the rain had finally stopped, supply was still practically nonexistent. But 3/1 obtained one and a half meals of field rations from the 383d Infantry and jumped off at 0900.[96] The battalion attacked to the west and reached the outskirts of Shindawaku at 1045. By 1800 3/1 had pushed on to the ridge running from the northwest to the village and 2/1 had moved to the vicinity of Iwa. The left flank of the 3d Battalion was tied in with the 383d Infantry, but its right was not in contact with the 7th Marines. Early the next morning 2/1 moved up on the right of 3/1 to close the gap.

Enemy resistance on the front of the 1st Marine Division consisted of relatively small groups, of approximately company strength and aggregating about two battalions, bent on restricting or diverting the advance. Orthodox tactics, however, provided the 1st Division with the means for driving in these covering forces. Patrols were used to find them and feel them out. A secondary attack fixed them by applying pressure frontally, while the main attack took them in flank or rear to finish them. And in spite of the prevailing terrain and weather conditions, the division commander felt that "it was refreshing to be able to maneuver again, even on a modest scale."[97]

On the critical right flank of the 1st Division, the 7th Marines drove steadily south against mounting resistance with the 2d and 3d Battalions in assault. The 1st Battalion followed in their tracks, patrolling and mopping up. On the open right flank, the attached 1st Reconnaissance Company screened the advance of 2/7, and the deep patrols of this unit initially furnished the regiment with valuable information. But the reconnaissance company's lack of effective communications and supply organization subsequently imposed severe restrictions upon its employment.[98]

In addition to the exposure of 2/7 to harassment from outside the division zone, a potential threat also existed on the interior flank. There, knowledge of the location of adjacent units was often nebulous because of communication difficulties and the leap-frogging tactics of the 1st Marines. But artillery fire served to neutralize the first threat effectively, and the reserve battalion was held in readiness to counter the second. For the 7th Marines as well as the 1st, river crossings, communications, weather, terrain, supply, and evacuation proved far more difficult to cope with than the enemy.

With adverse weather and difficult terrain conspiring to slow down time and space factors, each day's attack was inevitably delayed until air drops could be made. Supply by air delivery reached unprecedented proportions, marking the route of advance of the 7th with a trail of bright-colored cargo parachutes. As the lines of communication extended, eight to ten litter bearers were needed to move a single casualty through the rain and mud over distances of as much as five miles.[99]

The initial attack from the Kokuba Gawa bridgehead on 4 June carried 1,100 yards in the zone of 3/7, and 2/7 seized Takanyuta. On 5 June the waters of the swollen stream to the front of 3/7 subsided revealing a causeway over which part of the battalion passed, while the remainder crossed in the zone of 2/7.[100] The 7th Marines drove to positions just north of Hanja, scoring gains up to 1,000 yards. During the day the 1st Division received blanket clearance from IIIAC for artillery fires in the 6th Division's zone until cancelled by the latter. At the same time the 22d Marines began mov-

[95] 1/1 SAR, 21; Shofner Interview.
[96] 3/1 SAR, 43.
[97] Southward from Shuri, 39.
[98] 2/7 SAR, 7; Snedeker 1947.
[99] 7th Mar History, 22–23.
[100] Holoman.

WOUNDED MARINES are evacuated by liaison plane from a temporary airstrip north of Itoman.

ing to close the widening gap on the division boundary.

When the advance resumed on 6 June, the 22d Marines had not yet closed on the right of 2/7. Consequently, although Hill 103 was in the zone of the 6th Division, its hostile automatic weapons and mortars were a constant source of annoyance, and it was determined to clean up this threat before proceeding across the base of the peninsula. The 2d Battalion had almost reached the crest of the hill when the 22d Marines arrived and 2/7 continued the attack toward Hill 108, advancing 1,000 yards before meeting stiff resistance and digging in for the night near Dakiton. On the left 3/7, changing its direction of attack to the southwest, pushed through Dakiton to the high ground south of the village.

Under the clearing skies of 7 June, the 1st Division broke to the sea and slammed the door on the Naval Base Force on Oroku. Following an air, naval gunfire, artillery, and mortar preparation Company G of 2/7 seized Hill 108. The fleeing Japanese were pursued by the fires of machine guns and supporting weapons, and the 2d Battalion pushed on to the high ground overlooking the beach. The 3d Battalion overran Hanja, established contact with 2/1 on the left, and dug in just north of Zawa.[101] The attack veered south again on 8 June, and resistance stiffened as 3/7 passed through Zawa and advance elements of 2/7 probed positions in the Itoman area.

The break-through to the sea had cut the last escape route of the enemy facing the 6th Division and brought the troops of the 1st Division into position to swing south for the final drive against the Kiyamu defenses. In addition, the expansion of the foothold on the west coast opened a water supply route to the forward areas. The first LVT's, supported by LVT(A)'s, arrived at the newly-uncovered beaches at noon on 8 June, and shortly thereafter General Hodge sent General del Valle "congratulations for cutting the island in two." [102]

After more than a week on reduced rations, supply by LVT made it possible for the men of the 7th Marine to receive a full issue on 9 June. On the return trip the amphibious vehicles evacuated casualties to ships offshore. Evacuation soon was further improved by the use of a narrow concrete road north of Itoman as a landing strip from which cub planes carried out the wounded by air. Moreover, the rains were becoming light and infrequent, some bridges had been constructed over the streams to the north, and a few wheeled vehicles were beginning to make their appearance. Even the enemy contributed towards improving the supply situation. During the night of 8 June Japanese planes dropped several cases of demolitions into the 2/7 area, which were used to seal enemy caves the following morning.

When the axis of the 1st Division attack shifted to the southwest on 7 June, the 1st Marines paced the 7th Marines' drive to the sea with substantial advances. The 2d Battalion of the 1st, filling the gap between 3/1 and the 7th Marines with Company E, secured Hill 75 just north of Zawa. The 3d Battalion, moving on Yuza along the corps boundary, made gains up to 1,200 yards against moderate artillery fire on the right and occasional machine-gun fire on the left.

Logistical difficulties, however, still dogged the regiment. Air delivery continued to be the only means of supply, and by the time this could be accomplished the assault companies were far forward of the drop zone. Supplies were then manhandled by headquarters personnel to for-

[101] *3/7 SAR*, 4.

[102] *1st MarDiv G–3 Jnl*, 8Jun45.

ward dumps, from whence reserve company men carried them to the assault units. Water supply by air was not practicable and it was necessary for the troops to use stream water treated with halazone.[103]

The continuing good weather of 8 June eased the supply situation, but enemy resistance stiffened. Nevertheless the 3d Battalion maintained its advance toward Yuza, secured its objective at 1600, and after being relieved by 1/1, went into reserve north of Shindawaku. The 2d Battalion, 1st Marines moved rapidly against increasing resistance to its objective on the high ground overlooking the Mukue Gawa. During the night pressure on the enemy was maintained by patrols. The next day advance elements of the 1st Division probed the outposts of the last defense line on Okinawa in preparation for a major assault on 10 June.

Driving the enemy's outer shell of covering forces from the line of hills running generally northeast to southwest through Zawa had been accomplished without too much difficulty; but as the 1st Division closed on the outpost line of resistance in the Tera-Ozato area, the going got tougher. All units on the division front dispatched strong patrols south of the Mukue Gawa on 9 June. Both the 1st and 7th Marines were met by heavy rifle and machine-gun fire and found that the only means of forcing the stream was by infiltration of individuals and small groups. Because of the severity of hostile fire, 2/1 was obliged to await the fall of darkness before evacuating casualties sustained by its patrols.[104]

On the right of the division zone the 1st Battalion, 7th Marines relieved the 3d on the interior flank and made two attempts to seize a hill overlooking the northern edge of Tera. While trying to negotiate the deep gorge of the Mukue Gawa, Company B observed the Japanese reinforcing commanding ground to the southeast, and 1/7 withdrew under cover of smoke. A second attempt was driven back by heavy fire.[105]

On the seaward flank of the regiment the initial attempt of 2/7 to seize the ridge north of Itoman [106] was also frustrated by a fusillade from the 1st Battalion's zone of action. A platoon from Company E was allowed to cross the river, but was pinned down immediately at the base of the ridge by heavy and accurate fire from the front and left flank. Lieutenant Colonel Berger, operating from a mobile LVT(A) observation post some 100–200 yards offshore, had a clear view of the action and came ashore to order the rest of Company E to cross the Mukue at its mouth and reinforce the patrol. Enemy machine-gun fire turned back the first attempt to cross on foot and repulsed a later effort to move the Marines forward by LVT. At dusk, Berger ordered the exposed platoon to withdraw north of the river under cover of LVT(A) fire.[107]

The following morning Companies G and F passed through Company E's night defense positions, dropped over the ten-foot sea wall, and waded 400 yards to a point opposite the ridge. Following a terrific LVT(A) preparation, the assault platoons mounted the sea wall and attacked the ridge and town.[108] Five officers were lost to enemy fire in the first seven minutes of fighting, but the assault continued, clearing the ridge and sweeping through the rubble-strewn streets to positions on the high ground on the southern edge of the town.

While 2/7 was securing Itoman, the 1st Battalion with Company A in assault made a swift, unopposed advance to the crest of the hill north of Tera which had been the center of enemy opposition to the 7th Marines' advance on 9 June. Lieutenant Colonel Gormley sent Company C forward to reinforce Company A, and both units patrolled the ruins of Tera after a white phosphorus barrage by the battalion's 81mm mortars had fired most of the buildings

---

[103] 2/1 SAR, 13. Halazone is a chemical compound used to disinfect water; tablets were carried by every individual in the field to meet just such emergencies.

[104] Ibid.

[105] 1/7 SAR, 18.

[106] Although on the 1:25,000 battle map a large inhabited area north of the Mukue Gawa was labeled Itoman, the town was actually south of the river. Snedeker 1947, Enclosure D; 2/7 SAR, 8. The misnamed village was actually a suburb of Itoman, undefended and constituting no obstacle to the advance of 2/7. Interview with Capt V. E. Ludwig, 27Jan55, hereinafter cited as Ludwig Interview.

[107] Ludwig Interview.

[108] 2/7 SAR, 8.

VIEW FROM YUZA HILL looking toward Yuza Dake. In the background a flame tank sears enemy positions in Yuza village.

still standing. A number of dazed civilians were found in the village and directed to the rear, but there was no enemy opposition. As the battalion dug in for night defense, orders were received to seize Kunishi Ridge on 11 June.[109]

Although the rains had ceased, movement of transport was still difficult. But wheeled vehicles were beginning to appear in appreciable numbers to facilitate supply from the beaches, and a number of tanks had struggled through the mud to the forward areas.

With armored support at last available on 10 June, the 1st Marines with 2/1 on its right succeeded in cleaning out the southern slopes of the dominant ridge between Tera and Yuza,

which Company G occupied late in the afternoon. Fairly heavy mortar and artillery fire fell on the battalion during the night, but an anticipated counterattack failed to materialize. The following day the 2d Battalion was ordered to seize Hill 69 just west of Ozato.

The battalion jumped off at 1030 in column of companies, Company F in assault followed by Company E. Company G maintained its position and supported the attack with overhead fire. At the outset progress was rapid, but as the leading company moved into the low ground forward of the hill hostile mortars and artillery began to inflict losses. As the left flank of Company F neared Ozato, heavy machine-gun and rifle fire added to the toll. With mounting casualties slowing the advance, Company E was committed on the right of F. The massed fires

---

[109] *1/7 SAR*, 18–19.

of supporting weapons did little to diminish the enemy fire. But disregarding its waning strength and the loss of three supporting tanks, the attacking echelon pushed the assault home late in the afternoon. By dark the lines were consolidated on the objective and defensive fires established. During the night the battalion frustrated continual attempts on the part of the Japanese to infiltrate and repulsed one moderately heavy counterattack.[110]

In the meantime, the left battalion of the 1st Marines had likewise been heavily engaged. During the morning of 10 June, Army units succeeded in coming up on the flank of 1/1, and at 0915 the 1st Battalion moved against Yuza Hill, immediately west of the village. Although the attack was made in the face of withering machine-gun and artillery fire the advance was rapid. Leaning against a rolling barrage laid down by the 11th Marines, Company C in assault swarmed up the western nose of the hill and onto the crest. But the price was high. Some 70 men of the 175 composing the company were killed or wounded in the assault.

The seizure of Yuza Hill, however, carried 1/1 well ahead of the 96th Division which had been halted in its tracks before the heavily fortified Yuza Dake escarpment. In consequence the eastern flank of Company C was dangerously exposed to the dominant positions before the units on the left. Lieutenant Colonel Shofner ordered Company B to work through Yuza village and tie in with the left of C and the 96th Division. Intense mortar and artillery fire from the Yuza Dake area, however, prevented this movement, and late in the afternoon Company B was sent around to the right to join C on the hill. Company C had lost all its officers and during the night was commanded by a mess sergeant.[111] Company A, in reserve, occupied positions in rear of the open flank.

The excellent artillery support had pinned the Japanese garrison down until the Marines were right on top of them. However, there was considerable fighting on the hill after its capture. The two assault companies suffered 120 casualties during the day, but the issue was never in doubt. The battle continued well into the night with the enemy laying heavy mortar and artillery concentrations on the hill. Machine-gun fire from Yuza Dake grazed the position from time to time, adding to the toll of casualties, and at 0400 on 11 June, Company C lost another 20 men repulsing a counterattack. For the next three days the 1st Battalion remained in position on Yuza Hill awaiting the reduction of Yuza Dake. Although 1/1 had no real difficulty holding the hill, the battalion was under constant fire for two days until advances by adjacent units straightened out the salient.[112]

On June 11 the 7th Marines pushed forward against mounting resistance for gains of 400 to 1,000 yards during the morning. The 1st Battalion cleared Tera and attacked to reach the heights immediately south of the village, while the 2d Battalion mopped up in Itoman and advanced 500 yards beyond. Ahead of the 7th Marines, some 800 yards from the southern fringes of the two settlements, lay "the scene of the most frantic, bewildering, and costly close-in battle on the southern tip of Okinawa" [113]— Kunishi Ridge.

This precipitous coral escarpment constituted the western-most anchor of the last heavily defended line on Okinawa. The ridge contained innumerable caves, emplacements, and tombs on both the forward and reverse slopes. The intervening area between this formidable fortress and the lines of the 7th Marines was a broad valley of grassy fields and rice paddies which offered no protection to advancing infantry. The supporting tanks were restricted to two approaches into the position: a road across the valley which cut through the center of the ridge and another along the coast line. Both of these routes were covered by antitank guns. (See Map 39)

Shortly after noon patrols from the 1st and 2d Battalions moved out with armored support to probe the Japanese defenses. Intense frontal fire from Kunishi Ridge, enfilade fire from the enemy on Hill 69 opposing the attack of 2/1, and artillery concentrations directed at the tanks forced a withdrawal at 1447.

Because of the complete fire coverage of the

---

[110] 2/1 SAR, 14.

[111] Col A. C. Shofner Interview, 22Mar55.

[112] 1/1 SAR, 21–22; Shofner Interview.

[113] Okinawa: The Last Battle, 451.

open valley enjoyed by the Japanese, both from the heights and slopes of the ridge itself and from the Yuza Dake area, it was apparent that a daylight assault of the position would be a costly affair. Consequently, after Colonel Snedeker had made a personal reconnaissance of the objective from a light liaison plane,[114] it was determined to attack at night.

The commanding officers of the 1st and 2d Battalions were oriented on the general plan during the afternoon. The central road and a line of telephone poles was designated as the boundary between battalions upon which the assault units would guide. The scheme of maneuver contemplated a penetration of the ridge where the road passed through it, followed by an expansion of the initial foothold to the right and left flanks to secure the remainder of the objective in the regimental zone of action. Normal artillery would be placed alternately on Kunishi Ridge and Mezado Ridge (500–600 yards southwest of Kunishi) until H-Hour and thereafter on the latter.

For several days General Buckner had been sending messages to the Japanese commander by radio broadcast and air drops pointing out the hopelessness of the enemy situation in an attempt to persuade General Ushijima to surrender. During the afternoon of 11 June, Tenth Army representatives were conducted to the 2d Battalion OP overlooking Itoman to await any enemy party that might desire to negotiate. At 1700 all fire was suspended in the 7th Marines' area pending the doubtful appearance of a white flag. About 15 Japanese wearing white headgear appeared in the 1/7 zone in front of Company A at 1740, but dispersed when hailed. Six of the enemy surrendered to Company C at 1802, but the situation returned to normal two minutes later when hostile mortar fire fell on the captors' position.[115] Final orders for the resumption of the attack were issued by Colonel Snedeker about 2000 setting H-Hour at 0330, 12 June.

Both 1/7 and 2/7 were to make the assault with one company each, and at 0225 Company C moved out to establish contact with Company F on the line of departure. The attack was launched on schedule at 0330 and at 0500 Companies B and G moved out in support of the assault companies. Concurrently, Company F reached the objective at a point 500 yards north of Mezado village, as Company C came up on its left to extend the line eastward. The enemy was completely surprised and several small groups were wiped out by Company C while they were engaged in preparing breakfast. But the enemy quickly recovered, and the Japanese on Kunishi Ridge braced for the final stand in southern Okinawa.

At daylight the companies moving up to reinforce those on the ridge were pinned down by murderous machine-gun fire and forced to withdraw. Tanks were sent up to support a second attempt, but upon clearing Tera were driven back by enemy artillery. The troops moved out again at 0815 under cover of a smoke barrage and once again recoiled under withering fire from the Japanese battle position. The tanks were ordered to destroy tombs and suspected emplacements in the valley north of Kunishi, and a third and equally abortive effort to cross the fire-swept plain under smoke cover was beaten back at 1300.

At 1555, 1/7 began sending tanks forward with critical supplies for the beleaguered companies on Kunishi. When these had been delivered, the tanks undertook reinforcement of the ridge.[116] Troops were loaded in concealment at Tera and disembarked through the tank escape hatches upon arrival on the position. Before darkness suspended these operations, nine tanks had carried a reinforced platoon of 54 men of Company A forward to bolster Company C and brought out 22 wounded.[117]

After nightfall Company B moved forward again and reached the ridge without incident,

---

[114] Maj J. S. Hudson Ltr to CMC, 27Mar47.

[115] *1/7 SAR*, 20. The message from Gen. Buckner, offering Ushijima an opportunity to surrender did not arrive at Thirty-second Army Headquarters until 17 June, a week after it had been dropped behind the Japanese lines. Col Yahara stated that the delay was

normal for frontline headquarters communications at that stage of the operation. *Yahara Interrogation*. When the message was delivered, "Cho and Ushijima both laughed and declared that, as *Samurai*, it would not be consonant with their honor to entertain such a proposal." *Shimada Interrogation*.

[116] *1/7 SAR*, 21–22; *2/7 SAR*, 7–8.

[117] *1st TkBn Summary*, 12Jun45.

WESTERN END OF KUNISHI RIDGE as seen from the air, showing the exposed terrain over which the 7th Marines had to advance.

building up the line on the left of C which was tied in with 2/7. The front of the 2d Battalion was similarly extended to the west at 2030 when Companies G and E arrived on the escarpment.[118] By midnight the positions there could be considered reasonably secure.[119] But as General del Valle put it, "The situation was one of those tactical oddities of this peculiar warfare. We were *on* the ridge. The Japs were *in* it, both on the forward and reverse slopes."[120]

While the desperate, bloody battle of the 7th Marines was in progress during 12 June, patrols of the 1st Marines ranged southward along the corps boundary through Ozato. On Hill 69 outside of this village 2/1 continued to mop up and seal caves under sporadic fire from Kunishi Ridge, towards which the battalion sent patrols the next day preparatory to a pre-dawn attack on the 14th.[121]

Preparations to commit the 1st Marines to the struggle for Kunishi Ridge was the principal consideration throughout the 1st Division zone on 13 June. The entire southern portion of the

island still in the hands of the Thirty-second Army rocked under continual bombardment from the guns of the artillery and the ships offshore. Rocket craft stood in to the southern tip of the island to augment naval gunfire by raking reverse slope defenses. The villages of Makabe and Komesu alone were saturated with more than 800 5-inch rockets in a single hour.

The tanks available to the 1st Marines were not committed, but those with the 7th performed yeoman service. Some worked over the western nose of the ridge in the 2/7 sector, while others with 1/7 pounded enemy positions on Kunishi and covered that unit's supply route. This road, through the center of the ridge, had been blocked late in the preceding afternoon when a bridge caved in. But a tank dozer constructed a bypass and several tanks were able to provide fire support, continue to transport troops and supplies, and evacuate the wounded, some of them strapped to the sides and sandbagged in for protection against enemy fire. More than 50 more men of Company A dropped through the tank hatches onto the battle position, and 35 wounded were carried to the rear.[122] The excellent performance of the armored workhorses of the 1st Tank Battalion in building up supply reserves was matched by the equally outstand-

---

[118] *1/7 SAR*, 21–22; *2/7 SAR*, 7–8.

[119] ". . . the large amount of artillery support available could destroy any enemy counterattack which might be made against the initial ridgehead seized on Kunishi Ridge." *Snedeker 1955.*

[120] *Southward from Shuri*, 40.

[121] *2/1 SAR*, 15.

[122] *1st TkBn Summary*, 13Jun45.

ing aerial delivery service of the torpedo bombers of VMTB–131 and –232.[123]

Infantrymen of the 7th Marines concentrated on consolidating their positions on hard-won Kunishi and expanding to both flanks. The enemy, however, continued to lace the ridge with shells and bullets from both the front and flanks, and very little progress was made. Patrols of 1/7 probed eastward along the ridge line seeking the enemy. The Japanese were observed using screening smoke in the village of Kunishi, and a heavy 81mm mortar concentration was laid there. Mopping-up operations netted two 90mm mortars, a light machine gun, and a grenade discharger destroyed. Late in the afternoon the 1st Battalion placed heavy mortar and small-arms fire on a concentration of hostile troops observed on Mezado Ridge.[124]

The 2d Battalion patrolled along the west coast but was pinned down by heavy fire from the eastern reaches of Kunishi Ridge, necessitating a withdrawal under cover of smoke. Despite the excellent counterfire of a supporting battleship during which four direct hits on gun emplacements were observed and main battery fire was brought within 250 yards of the troops, enemy opposition continued to be intense and several tanks were put out of action by AT fire in the 2/7 area.[125]

After half an hour's artillery preparation, the 2d Battalion, 1st Marines moved out with Companies E and G in assault at 0330, 14 June to take up positions on Kunishi Ridge east of the 7th Marines. Although flares from adjacent units illuminated the 600 to 800 yards of open valley floor between the line of departure and the objective,[126] initial advances were made without resistance, and by 0500 two platoons of Company E were on the topographical crest of the objective. But the support platoon and the company headquarters were stopped cold, well below the summit, by intense machine-gun fire. Company G on the left met heavy mortar, machine-gun, and rifle fire 300 yards short of the objective, but one platoon succeeded in working up and tieing in with Company E. With the coming of dawn the severity of enemy fire increased, halting the support platoons in their tracks and isolating the assault platoons on the high ground. In like manner the battalion headquarters and reserve were effectively cut off from the assault companies.[127]

This situation continued throughout the day as the heavy fire continued unabated. Casualties rose to staggering proportions; one company lost six of its seven officers. Tanks were brought forward; but they were so sorely needed to evacuate the wounded and bring up critical supplies of ammunition, water, and blood plasma that their tactical employment was relegated to a minor role. The troops clung grimly to their precarious toehold, and after dark Company F, in reserve, moved up to tie in with both G and E and establish a perimeter defense on the ridge.

Enemy small-arms, grenade, mortar, and artillery fires continued throughout the night, and the following day brought no respite. There was no relaxation of pressure on the part of the Japanese, and casualties mounted. Supply and evacuation by tank continued, but the 1st Marines was less fortunate than the 7th with air delivery. A drop scheduled for 0900 was not made until midafternoon and then two-thirds of the ammunition and rations fell within the enemy lines and could not be recovered. Company G, however, with the aid of gun and flame tanks, clawed its way along the ridge and extended the line about 200 yards to the left. But despite the heroic efforts of the men, Kunishi Ridge was still far from being secured when 2/5 relieved 2/1 that night.[128]

The 5th Marines, which had been bivouacked in reserve near Gisushi,[129] began relieving the

[123] "The air drops were mostly well made and were largely successful. Some drops did fall where they could not be retrieved but they were in the minority." *Snedeker 1947.*

[124] *1/7 SAR,* 22.

[125] *2/7 SAR,* 9 with marginal note by LtCol S. S. Berger.

[126] Besides the constant fire of Japanese artillery, mortars, and small arms, continual enemy attempts to infiltrate during the night were equally characteristic of the fighting on Kunishi Ridge. Although it was standard procedure to forbid the use of flares during a night operation, the orders did not always reach all units.

[127] *2/1 SAR,* 15.

[128] *Ibid.*

[129] Less 1/5 which had been covering the western boundary of the division since 11 June. *1/5 SAR,* 11.

1st during the morning of 15 June. By noon 3/5 (Lieutenant Colonel Robert E. Hill)[130] had taken over 1/1's lines on Yuza Hill and relieved its reserve company which had moved forward to blocking positions on Hill 69 to the left rear of 2/1. During the afternoon 1/1 assembled at Dakiton and 3/1 at Shindawaku.

Because the area for 1,000 yards in rear of 2/1 was still being swept by small-arms fire, it was impossible for Lieutenant Colonel Benedict of 2/5 and his company commanders to make an adequate reconnaissance, adding greatly to the normal difficulties involved in the relief of a unit engaged in a fire fight. All company commanders of 2/5 were taken to the 2/1 area in tanks and returned at 1600 to report that the situation on the ridge had not improved. The 1st Marines' troops held only a 75-yard sector on the crest with no contact with adjacent units. The bulk of the battalion was pinned down in a small pocket on the forward slope by fire from the rear and both flanks. After a conference between Lieutenant Colonels Benedict and Magee it was decided to begin the relief immediately after dark.

The battalion commander of 2/5 also decided to commit only Company G initially to prevent congestion in the restricted area under control. At 2000, Company G moved out and arrived on the position half an hour later without suffering any casualties.[131] The relief was completed by 2300 and 2/1 moved to Dakiton. The 1st Marines reverted to division reserve after 12 days in the line, during which the regiment had sustained almost 500 casualties.

Meanwhile, on 14 June, the 7th Marines had continued "the slow, methodical destruction of enemy emplacements on the ridge, to which the descriptive word 'processing' had come to be applied."[132] In the zone of 1/7, Company A attacked east to seize the remainder of the reverse slope of Kunishi Ridge in the regimental zone of action, with Companies B and C mopping up the area held and supporting by fire. The attack encountered exceedingly difficult terrain, and the enemy resisted stubbornly. Short-

ly after noon Company B was ordered to move east through Kunishi village and attack north over the ridge to secure the forward slope of the 7th Marines' objective.

Company B gained control of the village, but in assaulting the high ground to the north was met with machine-gun fire. The company continued to press the attack until two rifle squads reached the ridge line. But a strong Japanese counterattack drove the troops from the high ground, and Company B was ordered to withdraw under cover of a heavy mortar barrage. The battalion established its lines as of the previous night.[133]

On the front of 2/7 enemy fire continued to mount in intensity, despite the use of suppressive barrages, and that unit made only negligible gains. Tanks supported the 7th Marines, logistically and tactically, until 1530 when all tanks were withdrawn for employment with the 1st Marines.[134] During the day 48 men were ferried forward to the 7th Marines on Kunishi by Company C, 1st Tank Battalion, and all three of the tank companies evacuated a total of 160 wounded.[135]

Although an overwhelming amount of naval gunfire, artillery, air, rockets, and 81mm mortars was brought to bear on the enemy on 15 June, the progress of 2/7 was again limited to no more than local gains. However, with armored support, patrols from the 2d Battalion were able to probe the northwest slope of Mezado Ridge and destroy numerous caves and emplacements.[136]

On the left of the regiment, the action of 1/7 was similar to that of the previous day. After preliminary patrolling and artillery preparation Company C attacked directly east along the ridge, while Company B again swung down through the village of Kunishi to assault the ridge line from the south. Company B encountered considerable resistance, and Company C was unable to advance far enough east to relieve the pressure on B. Consequently, at 1600 the companies were again withdrawn to the defensive positions of 13–14 June.

[130] LtCol Hill assumed command of 3/5 on 8 June while the battalion was in reserve.

[131] 2/5 SAR, 19–20.

[132] 7th Mar History, 31.

[133] 1/7 SAR, 23.

[134] Ibid.; 2/7 SAR, 9.

[135] 1st TkBn Summary, 14Jun45.

[136] 2/7 SAR, 9.

Before resuming the attack on 16 June, the left flank troops of 1/7 were withdrawn about 200 yards to the west in order to permit an extremely heavy concentration of artillery, mortars, and rockets to be placed on the ridge. These preparatory fires commenced at 0700 and continued unabated until the troops moved out at 0945. The attack began with Company A working along the northern slope of Kunishi Ridge and Company B patrolling Kunishi village. Both units were covered by Company C in reserve.

Company A advanced cautiously, demolishing caves and emplacements. As it continued forward slowly and methodically destroying all enemy resistance, Company C followed on its heels, building up the line from the west, consolidating the gains of Company A and mopping up. Although the progress of Company B was slowed by the large number of civilians encountered in the village,[137] the company destroyed numerous groups of the enemy who were found "wandering through the town of Kunishi in a confused, disorganized, and bewildered state."[138]

During the afternoon Company A cracked a particularly difficult strong point called "The Pinnacle," which had defied reduction for two days, breaking through to the eastern boundary of the regimental zone of action. But even after the fall of this bastion, a single sniper remaining killed or wounded 22 Marines before he could be located and eliminated. On the right, despite heavy casualties and a continuing loss of tanks to 47mm guns and land mines, 2/7 extended the lines some 400 yards to the west to complete the capture of the objective in its zone. By the end of the day 2/7 occupied the first high ground of the Mezado hill mass, and the 1st Battalion held its sector of Kunishi ridge with Company A on the left, C in the center and B on the right.[139]

The ground that had been so tenaciously defended and the approaches to Mezado had been virtually cleaned out. Kunishi Ridge was no longer a major obstacle in the 7th Marines' zone of action, and operations were set afoot for a passage of lines to continue the attack the following morning. The 22d Marines, in assault for the 6th Division, were to take over the front of 2/7 while 3/7 would attack through the lines of the 1st Battalion.

As 1/7 had advanced eastward on 16 June, visual contact had been established with 2/5 attacking toward the west. At daybreak Company G of 2/5 assaulted a coral peak on the ridge which commanded its position. Bitter close-quarter combat broke out almost immediately and continued until 0900 when two fire teams managed to reach the summit. The company commander then ordered an attack on his left flank to extend the front eastward along the crest of the ridge. Two gun tanks and an armored flame thrower went forward at 1130 to assist. Mortar and small-arms fire was extremely heavy all along the company front, and at 1330 a smoke screen was requested to enable a tank to evacuate casualties. Fighting continued throughout the day with Company G making slow but steady progress.

On 17 June, as on the previous day, 3/5 continued to mop up in its area and maintain contact with the 96th Infantry Division. The 2d Battalion resumed its attack to secure the 800 yards of Kunishi Ridge remaining in Japanese hands. The battalion moved out at 0800 with Company E working along the ridge to the left and Company G attacking to the front to destroy enemy reverse slope defenses. A rocket barrage was laid down at 0820 to assist the advance of Company E, and by 1030 an armored bulldozer had opened a road around the right flank enabling tanks to join the fighting on the southern face of the escarpment. This eased the pressure on Company G considerably, but armored support was hamstrung throughout the afternoon by the necessity of using tanks to evacuate casualties under heavy fire. Stretcher cases posed a particularly difficult problem, inasmuch as they could not be loaded through the escape hatches and many of them were wounded again while being carried to the aid station lashed across the rear of the tanks.

From the outset fighting was heavy all along the line, and at 1130 the entire front of Company E was enfiladed by murderous machine-gun fire from the XXIV Corps area. Although

[137] 1/7 SAR, 23–24.
[138] 7th Mar History, 32.
[139] 1/7 SAR, 24; 2/7 SAR, 9–10.

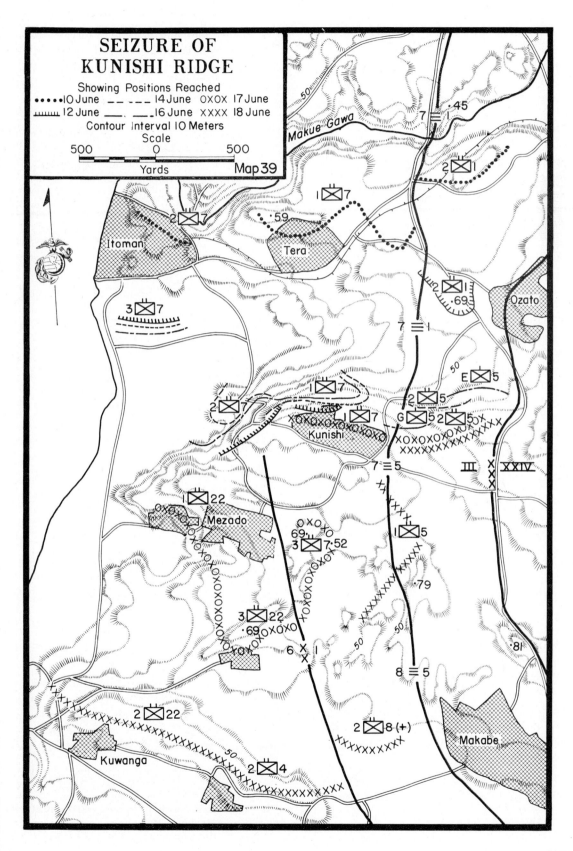

SEIZURE OF KUNISHI RIDGE

Showing Positions Reached

•••• 10 June   ⸺ ⸻ 14 June   OXOX 17 June

ﬧﬧﬧ 12 June   ⸺ ⸺ 16 June   XXXX 18 June

Contour Interval 10 Meters

Scale

500   0   500

Yards   Map 39

Makue Gawa

Itoman

Tera

Ozato

Kunishi

Mezado

Makabe

Kuwanga

it was impossible to advance against this devastating fire on the crest of the ridge, Company E continued a gradual extension to the left along the forward slope. During the afternoon tank-infantry teams working over the valley north of the ridge secured a route of approach to the battle position. It was therefore determined to commit Company F shortly before dark, and by 1745 the company had reached positions in rear of E. At 1800, Company F attacked eastward along the ridge, and by nightfall 2/5 held all but 400 yards of the 1,200 yards of Kunishi in the 5th Marines' zone.

Company K of 3/5 was attached to 2/5 and moved into position to protect the battalion rear at dusk. Towards midnight the enemy launched a frenzied counterattack which was broken up by Companies G and E. The few Japanese who managed to infiltrate were cut down by Company K.[140]

The 6th Marine Division having been assigned the coastal zone of action, effective 17 June, the 22d Marines began the passage of lines through 2/7 at 0300 that morning. The relief of 2/7 proceeded without incident, and dawn found the 22d in position on the north slope of Mezado Ridge prepared to attack with the 1st and 3d Battalions in assault, the former on the right.

The 3d Battalion, 7th Marines, which had relieved 1/7 during the night, jumped off with the 22d Marines at 0730 to seize the high ground just east of Mezado village. The battalion moved out in column with Company K in assault, followed by I and L. As Company K approached the objective, Company I maintained contact with the 22d Marines, and Company L occupied positions on the left of K to cover the increasing gap between 3/7 and the stalemated 5th Marines.[141] An advance of 1,400 yards was made before heavy enemy fire from the commanding heights protecting the Kuwanga-Makabe road forced the battalion to dig in. Because 2/5 had been unable to advance, 3/7 bent its left flank well to the rear for night defense.

In the rear of 3/7 and the 22d Marines, the 1st and 2d Battalions of the 7th Marines remained in position on Kunishi Ridge to complete mopping up. As these units continued "processing" the escarpment during the day, enemy fire in the valley north of Kunishi almost ceased and supply lines were opened to normal traffic.

Die-hards holding out in caves on the southern face of Kunishi halted the attack of 3/22 soon after the 22d moved out on 17 June. After the troops on the ridge had cleaned out the infested area, Lieutenant Colonel Shisler ordered Company L to positions on Kunishi from which it could support Company K in assault.

Preceded by a 20-minute mortar barrage, Company K resumed the advance at 1130. By noon the company had secured the hill just north of the village of Mezado, and Company L immediately moved up to reinforce K, mop up, and prepare to attack the final objective. After a 15-minute artillery preparation 3/22 jumped off at 1415, supported by tanks. Company I passed through the eastern edge of Mezado village and attacked on the left of K, which was trailed by Company L. Company I reached the high ground east of the village at 1620 and tied in with 3/7 on the left.

The right of the company was in contact with Company K on the southern slope of Mezado Ridge, and Company L filled the gap between K and 1/22. Company E of 2/22 was attached to the 3d Battalion to tie in with 3/7 and 1/22 for all-around night defense. Orders were issued shortly after dark providing for a passage of the lines of the 3d Battalion by the 2d on 18 June. While 3/22 mopped up Mezado and delivered overhead fire support, 2/22 was to assault the next objective to the south in the 6th Division sector: Kuwanga Ridge.[142]

On the right of the 22d Marines, 1/22 also secured a foothold on Mezado Ridge after a day of hard fighting, but it was prevented by heavy fire from penetrating the reverse slope defenses. Companies A and B, the former on the right, were pinned down early in the assault, and the battalion commander was wounded.[143] Company C which was committed on the right of A, also met heavy fire from caves in the steep, brush-covered hillside. Although Companies

[140] 2/5 SAR, 20–21.

[141] 3/7 SAR, 5.

[142] 3/22 SAR, 11; 6th MarDiv Jnl, Ph III, 17Jun45.

[143] The battalion commander, Maj Earl S. Cook, was wounded about 0800. The executive officer, Maj Norman R. Sherman, took over temporarily until 1300 when LtCol Gavin C. Humphrey assumed command. LtCol G. C. Humphrey Ltr to CMC, 27Jan48.

A and C were unable to advance, Company B on the left worked a platoon through the zone of 3/22 to the top of the hill mass. The remainder of the company built up on this precarious foothold and secured positions from which the crest of the ridge could be enfiladed.

About 1500, after repeated futile attempts to gain the ridge, Company C was withdrawn and positioned in reserve in rear of A and B. With Company B and the battalion mortars providing a base of fire, Company A pushed up the hill to the right, but in doing so opened a gap in the center of the battalion. Company C moved into the breach. With the assistance of the supporting fire of Company B, A and C continued the attack and secured positions on the military crest of Mezado about 1700.[144]

After nightfall about 50 Japanese launched a last gasp counterattack against 1/22; but it was a gesture of despair, for the remnants of the enemy 22d Regiment had been completely annihilated during the afternoon, thus collapsing the Japanese left flank and opening the way for an envelopment of the enemy 32d Regiment standing at bay near Makabe.[145] (See Map 39)

Fresh troops were available to exploit the success the following day. For at the height of the 7th Marines' battle on Kunishi Ridge, the 8th Marines (Reinforced) had been landed and attached to the 1st Marine Division. As the battered 7th prepared to pass into reserve, the 8th Marines of the 2d Division moved to assembly areas in readiness to pass through 3/7 before dawn and continue the attack.[146]

IHEYA-AGUNI OPERATION

Elements of the 2d Marine Division had reappeared on the Okinawa battle scene on 3 June as the landing force of an operation that had been planned early in May. Admiral Turner, deeply concerned at the heavy damage suffered by his light fleet units on picket duty, had requested General Buckner to initiate a study for the capture of outlying islands of Okinawa Gunto on which long-range radar and fighter director facilities could be established. The result had been a decision that Tori, Iheya, Aguni,

and Kume Shima would be taken in the order listed. On 12 May a reinforced company of the 165th Infantry had made an unopposed landing on the rocky little island of Tori Shima about 45 miles west of Okinawa. The next step in the plan was the occupation of Iheya and Aguni Shima.

General Buckner felt that the forces on Okinawa were nearing the crucial stage of their struggle with the Japanese and should not be diverted to secondary operations. Therefore the 8th Marines of the 2d Division, suitably reinforced, was selected to conduct both landings, and Brigadier General LeRoy P. Hunt, ADC of the Division, was designated the landing force commander. General Hunt and key members of his staff flew to Okinawa on 15–16 May and were briefed on the operation plan during the next few days.

The 8th RCT (Colonel Clarence R. Wallace) began loading on LST's at Saipan on 21 May and the troop convoy departed three days later, arriving off Okinawa on 30 May. A regular schedule of air and NGF support was set up for the Iheya landing, and detailed plans were made to meet any foreseeable opposition that might develop on the island. Early on 3 June the attack force, commanded by Admiral Reifsnider, sortied from the Hagushi anchorage for the target island 15 miles northwest of Hedo Misaki.

H-Hour was 1045 and the preliminary bombardment and assault landings by 2/8 and 3/8 went off on schedule. There was no opposition and no enemy troops, only 3,000 docile civilians to be cared for by military government teams of Island Command. General unloading commenced late in the afternoon and on 4 June the island was officially declared secure.

After several delays because of inclement weather, on 9 June BLT 1/8 under Lieutenant Colonel Richard W. Heyward executed a similar unopposed landing on Aguni Shima, 30 miles west of Okinawa. On both islands seized by the 8th Marines, immediate steps were taken to set up air warning and fighter director installations to strengthen the defensive perimeter surrounding Okinawa.

The instructions to General Hunt and Colonel Wallace in the Iheya-Aguni operation orders

[144] *Ibid.*
[145] *Okinawa Operations Record,* 29–30.
[146] *IIIAC AR,* 64.

were to be prepared for future operations against the enemy. Thus, when the need for additional troops arose in the last stages of the battle to reduce the Kiyamu Peninsula the regiment was ready.[147]

YAEJU DAKE-YUZA DAKE[148]

The outpost line of Kiyamu Peninsula was fully manned on 4 June. Japanese Army headquarters estimated that the strength of its now concentrated forces totaled 30,000, distributed as follows: 24th Division and attached units, 12,000; 62d Division and attached units, 7,000; 44th IMB and attached units, 3,000; 5th Artillery Command and attached units, 3,000; and units directly under Thirty-second Army command, 5,000. The difference in total strength between the 50,000-man estimate late in May and the 30,000 left in Kiyamu Peninsula was attributed to "attrition during retirement operations."[149] (See Map 33)

Only about 20 per cent of the remaining troops were survivors of the original crack infantry-artillery units; the rest were untrained rear echelon personnel or *Boeitai*. Most senior commanders at battalion level and above were still alive, however, and capable of bolstering the fighting spirit of their motley collection of men. But the Thirty-second Army had suffered grievous losses in weapons and equipment since L-Day. Hand grenades and explosives were almost entirely expended. Four out of every five machine guns had been destroyed, and the supply of heavy infantry cannon and mortars had been reduced to the vanishing point. Despite the fact that two 150mm guns, sixteen 150mm howitzers, and ten AAA guns had been successfully withdrawn to the Kiyamu battle position, artillery ammunition levels were insufficient for more than ten days of sustained firing.

General Ushijima's Thirty-second Army was in desperate straits, its destruction merely a question of time, but the tradition, discipline, and indoctrination of Japanese military forces promised only a violent, last-ditch, man-to-man struggle before the battle for Okinawa was ended.

Taking cognizance of the assault forces available and the relative strength and importance of enemy strong points in Kiyamu Peninsula, General Buckner shifted the corps boundary to the west on 4 June. The 1st Marine Division, attacking in the narrowed IIIAC zone, was made responsible for cutting off Oroku Peninsula, capturing Itoman, reducing the Kunishi and Mezado ridge positions, and driving to the southernmost point of the island, Ara Saki. The XXIV Corps was assigned the commanding Yaeju Dake-Yuza Dake Escarpment as its primary objective. Both of the towering crags that gave the escarpment its name fell within the 96th Division zone of advance. Capture of the remaining high ground of the escarpment, dominated by Hill 153 northeast of Medeera, was left to the 7th Division.

Substantial gains were made by all assault units of XXIV Corps on 4 June. Driving down the corps boundary, 2/383 and 3/383 hit isolated but strong enemy delaying groups. Heavy machine-gun fire from hill positions in the IIIAC zone pinned down the 2d Battalion on the right flank until neutralizing fire from the regimental reserve, 1/383, smothered the enemy opposition. The outskirts of Iwa were secured by dusk and the regiment held a line 1,400–2,000 yards forward of its night positions on 3 June.

Matching the progress of the 383d, the 381st Infantry with the 1st and 3d Battalions in assault drove in enemy outposts all the way to the hills north of Aragusuku. Fire from an isolated ridge, over 325 feet high, which guarded the approaches to the village stopped the regiment's attack. Resistance to the 96th Division's advance increased steadily as the day wore on, but it was obvious that the bulk of enemy defenders had not as yet been engaged.

While the 32d Infantry completed the mop up of Chinen Peninsula on 4 June, the 7th Division's assault regiments advanced rapidly to the southwest. Resistance was spotty and ineffective, and the 184th Infantry reached and crossed the shallow river north of Minatoga. On the

---

[147] CT 8, 2d MarDiv AR–Iheya and Aguni Operations. n. d. The only casualties in the Iheya operation were two Marines killed and 16 wounded by short NGF rounds and aerial rockets.

[148] Unless otherwise noted the material in this section is derived from *Okinawa: The Last Battle; CTF 31 AR; Tenth Army AR; XXIV Corps AR; 7th InfDiv AR; 96th InfDiv AR; Okinawa Operations Record*.

[149] *Okinawa Operations Record*, 101.

division right flank the 17th Infantry established positions controlling the Minatoga-Meka road. By nightfall General Arnold's men had secured the high ground backing the much feinted demonstration landing beaches. Investigation of the abandoned but highly developed defensive network covering the beaches indicated that their capture would have required a major and costly operation. (See Map 38, Map section)

The rainy weather which had been a decisive factor in delaying the reduction of Shuri, aiding the Japanese withdrawal, and slowing the Tenth Army pursuit, continued on 5 June. The vast sea of mud surrounding the hills and ridges and the absolute lack of usable roads in southern Okinawa prevented tanks and artillery from fulfilling their vital role of close support for the infantry. Until the sun dried the ground and cleared the air, Tenth Army assault troops would be denied their most effective weapons.

Infantry spearheads of XXIV Corps continued to penetrate the enemy outpost zone on 5 and 6 June, developing the fringes of the main Japanese battle position. After two days of progressively harder action the 7th Division stood at the outskirts of Gushichan, and the 96th Division, having captured Iwa and Aragusuku, held forward positions in Shindawaku and Tomui. A deadly barrier of enemy fire shielded the looming heights of the escarpment to the front of the Army infantrymen.

The Japanese position was extremely strong. Low, rolling ground marked by small hill fortresses led to the foot of the escarpment on the north and northeast. A precipitous bluff line rising 160 feet above this low ground extended throughout the zones of the 96th Division and 17th Infantry. On the west the escarpment barrier continued to the coast in the 1st Marine Division sector at Kunishi Ridge. The 184th Infantry, on the left of the XXIV Corps, faced the only natural avenue of approach into the enemy position: the narrow Gushichan-Nakaza Valley. The valley, however, was completely dominated by high ridges on either flank, notably Hill 95 along the coast, which paralleled the direction of advance and offered fields of fire along the eastern face of the escarpment. (See Map 40, Map Section)

The plateau which topped the bluffs was wildly broken by outcroppings of coral and limestone and riddled with cave positions. Two hill strong points on the northern edge of the plateau, Yuza Dake which rose 340 feet over the plain at its foot and Yaeju Dake which towered to 400 feet, possessed perfect observation of the American zone of advance. Hill 153, the apex of a triangle which had Yuza Dake and Yaeju Dake at its base, blocked the path of advance from the Gushichan-Nakaza Valley.

It was obvious to General Hodge from the volume of enemy fire received and the natural strength of the position his corps faced that reduction of the escarpment required an all-out effort. On 7–8 June the principal offensive efforts of the 7th and 96th Divisions were directed at probing enemy defenses and advancing assault battalions to more favorable positions for an attack. The small port of Minatoga which had been opened on 6 June handled a steady flow of ammunition and supplies to replenish dwindling stocks. Clear skies and drying roads allowed the tanks, assault guns, and artillery that had been bogged down far to the rear to move up to supporting positions. The ground was still muddy, however, and engineers had to work feverishly to maintain the access roads throughout the 8,000–10,000 yard zone that the XXIV Corps had penetrated in a week of rapid advances.

On 9 June when the corps attack opened, the 96th Division confined its activities to an intensive effort to soften the enemy positions on the escarpment to its front. A day-long barrage of artillery and NGF, coupled with air strikes and direct tank fire, hit all along the heights, concentrating on the northern faces of Yaeju Dake and Yuza Dake.

The key objectives in the 7th Division zone were Hill 95 on the coast and the southeastern extremity of Yaeju Dake at a point just north of Nakaza where the steep slopes offered a path to the top of the escarpment. The 32d Infantry had replaced the 184th in its lines before Gushichan during the afternoon of 8 June, and at 0730 the following morning the leading company of 1/32 attacked the eastern end of Hill 95. Machine-gun, knee mortar, and rifle fire pinned down the assault troops before they could move a hundred yards. A flanking attack from the north was driven back, but not before the most troublesome sources of enemy fire had been located and marked for destruction. The net gain of enemy territory in the 32d's zone was zero, but the groundwork had been laid for a successful attack on 10 June.

To the north 3/17, making its regiment's main effort, managed to gain a precarious toehold on its objective. Assault companies had to crawl across open ground swept by waves of machine-gun fire. Individuals and small groups broke through the fire barrier and climbed the escarpment, wiping out the Japanese as they struggled upward. By nightfall 20 men from Company I had wrested a small area on the lip of the escarpment from the enemy and Company K had secured positions on the southeastern slope of Yaeju Dake. Despite showers of grenades and three determined counterattacks, the enemy failed to dislodge Company I from its entering wedge in the Kiyamu battle position.

The entire 711th Tank Battalion moved into the 7th Division's front lines on 10 June as the 17th and 32d Infantry renewed their attack. Under cover of tank guns on the landward side and NGF from the sea, 1/32 made a slow but steady advance onto the eastern slopes of Hill 95, while 2/32 moved through Gushichan toward Hanagusuku as its left flank was gradually uncovered. Armored flame throwers were brought up to burn the enemy out of the jagged coral outcroppings that crowded the crest and sides of the ridge. The 17th Infantry's forward progress during the day's attack was limited as the 3d Battalion strengthened its tenuous hold on the escarpment and 1/17 blasted the southeastern face of Yaeju Dake from its positions near Tomui. The division for the first time since the rainy season began was able to employ the full power of its supporting weapons.

Tanks and artillery also played an important part in the 96th Division's 700-yard advance on 10 June. A constant drumfire of shells exploded on and against the escarpment, seeking out enemy guns and reserve assembly areas. Under cover of the supporting fire the four assault battalions attempted to cross the open areas at the foot of the slope. In the 383d Infantry zone the 1st and 3d Battalions were able to secure the railroad track that led from Itoman to Iwa be-

fore their advance was stopped. Enemy machine guns firing from Yuza Dake and a hill near Yuza just within the 1st Marine Division sector raked both battalions with murderous fire and forced them to dig in. The combined fire of tanks, assault guns, artillery, and experimental 57mm and 75mm recoilless rifles [150] was insufficient to silence the enemy opposition, and the 383d was forced to dig in just south of the rail line.

The sheer bluff at the foot of Yaeju Dake was interrupted by a secondary escarpment, relatively easy to ascend but completely dominated by guns on the higher ground. Moving behind a barrage of flat trajectory weapons and a heavy smoke screen, 1/381 fought its way to positions on the lower escarpment by midafternoon. The torrent of fire that poured down on the exposed men prevented any further advances. On the left of the 1st Battalion, 3/381 attempted to take Yaeju Dake from the northeast by moving through Tomui. Once the assault companies cleared the village ruins, they were stopped by the accurate fire of Japanese guns emplaced in the deep caves and fissures that scarred the slopes of the escarpment. Night positions that offered some protection from the galling fusillade were taken up on the northwestern and southern edges of Tomui.

The defense of the escarpment from Hill 95 to Yaeju Dake was the responsibility of the 44th Independent Mixed Brigade, while the 24th Division held the remainder of the high ground including Yuza Dake. The immense natural strength of the positions along the northern edge of the escarpment enabled the Japanese to hold back the assaults of the 96th Infantry Division with only one reinforced regiment, the veteran 89th.

The enemy troops that manned the front in

---

[150] The War Department sent teams of ordnance men to Okinawa to test the combat utility of recoilless rifles. Demonstration firing against enemy caves and pillboxes were conducted late in May, and after air shipments renewed the extremely limited ammunition supply the new weapons were used by both the 7th and 96th Divisions against the Yaeju Dake-Yuza Dake Escarpment. The destructive power, accuracy, and portability of the recoilless rifles impressed unit commanders who had the opportunity to use them in action and led to recommendations by both divisions that they be adopted as standard infantry weapons.

the 7th Infantry Division zone, however, were not of the same caliber as those holding Yuza Dake. Miscellaneous shipping engineer, sea raiding, mortar, and line of communication troops loosely organized as provisional infantry regiments held most of the 44th IMB line. The survivors of the 15th IMR were entrusted with the vital Hill 95-Nakaza Valley area. On 11 June the steady, punishing pressure of General Arnold's attack began to crack the front of the enemy brigade on both flanks, imperiling the whole of the Thirty-second Army position. Attempts to reinforce the crumbling battle line with makeshift infantry units composed of service and support troops proved to be "as ineffective as throwing water on parched soil."[151]

Seas of flame engulfed Hill 95 on 11 June as 1/32 slowly advanced toward the crest of the enemy position behind the jets of armored flame throwers. Flame fuel was pumped and sprayed from hoses over portions of the ridge inaccessible to tanks and then ignited. Infantrymen moved among the still hot and smoking rocks and drove back the surviving defenders. That night the battalion dug in just short of the Hill 95 peak.

Although little forward progress was made by 2/32 or the 17th Infantry on 11 June, the enemy position was considerably weakened. Intensive fire from supporting weapons was concentrated against the slopes of Yaeju Dake, and strong patrols cleaned out enemy groups that held positions near the 7th Division front lines.

Reinforcements had been able to cross the open ground to join forward elements of 1/381 on the lower escarpment during the night of 10–11 June. With daylight, however, the enemy fire from Yaeju Dake prevented the battalion from doing more than consolidating its newly-won positions. Advances throughout the 96th Division zone were negligible in the face of this killing fire. Although tank-infantry teams of 2/383 working with 1/1 along the corps boundary were able to penetrate Yuza, they were driven back by heavy machine-gun fire from the heights south of the village. Most of the day was spent ferreting out bypassed enemy holdouts and silencing some of the guns on the

<hr />

[151] *Okinawa Operations Record,* 106.

PATROL of the 381st Infantry advances toward Yaeju Dake on 10 June. (Army Photograph)

escarpment whose fire raked the division sector.

Pre-dawn attacks were planned for vital points all along the Tenth Army front on 12 June. The 29th Marines on Oroku Peninsula, the 7th Marines at Kunishi Ridge, and the 17th Infantry at Yaeju Dake were all successful in catching the enemy off guard and gaining vital territory.

A dense fog blanket hid the men of Companies A, B, and L of the 17th Infantry who moved out at 0400 to climb the escarpment. The surprise was complete. By 0530 the assault companies had reached their objectives and joined Company I which had held its advanced position against all comers since 9 June. The men of 1/17 and 3/17 had a field day when the startled Japanese emerged from their holes and caves at dawn. Many of the enemy were shot down before they were even aware that the Americans had established themselves in a position that threatened the collapse of the Thirty-second Army's entire eastern flank. During the day Company C of 1/17 mopped its way up the escarpment to join its parent unit, while 2/17 with Company L attached relieved 3/17 and enlarged the regiment's hold on the escarpment's edge.

The 381st Infantry was able to capitalize on the 17th Infantry's successful night attack on 12 June. Company L of 3/381 moved through the 7th Division's zone to the top of the escarpment and then advanced north to take up positions on the slopes of Yaeju Dake that guarded the rest of the battalion in the valley immediately below the peak. The 2d Battalion, 381st Infantry joined 1/381 on the secondary escarpment during the day's advances and delivered suppressive fire that enabled 3/383 to cross the open ground and extend the division front on the face of the main escarpment. Yuza was secured during the morning by 2/383 and hill positions were captured south of the village despite continuous machine-gun fire. The ferocity of enemy opposition seemed undiminished along the front of the 89th Regiment, but 12 June had been the beginning of the end for the 44th IMB. Urgent pleas for reinforcements secured the release of two battalions of the 62d Division to the brigade commander but the time for their effective use had passed.

Repeated counterattacks were launched against 7th Division positions during the night of 12–13 June, but the assault battalions held their ground. In the morning the attack was resumed against the rapidly disintegrating remnants of the 44th IMB. On the left the 32d Infantry completed the capture of Hill 95 and cleaned out the ruins of Hanagusuku. Nakaza was secured, and the 17th Infantry expanded its hold on the escarpment top. Three objectives now lay ahead of the division: Hill 153 which covered the rear of Yaeju Dake and Yuza Dake; Hill 115, a fingerlike ridge which extended northeast along the coastal side of the Nakaza Valley; and Hill 89, location of General Ushijima's headquarters, just south of the village of Mabuni. The approaches to these positions lay across a rolling tableland broken by jagged outcroppings of coral and garrisoned by desperate groups of last-ditch defenders.

The clear weather enabled General Hodge to bring all his supporting agencies into play. Air, artillery, and NGF pounded the reinforcing units of the 62d Division that were attempting to bolster the shattered 44th IMB. Enemy communication with Yaeju Dake was lost on 12 June, and the brigade commander was unable to regain it the following day after the remainder of 3/381 fought its way to the top of the escarpment.

The 89th Regiment, reinforced by the 24th Reconnaissance Regiment, still held Yuza Dake, but the danger to its rear and flank from the penetration south of Yaeju Dake was acute. Although 3/383 and 2/381 could not gain the top of the escarpment west of the peak despite repeated attacks, the strength of the defenders was seriously whittled down by the tremendous volume of covering fire.

On the right flank of the 96th Division, substantial progress was made on 13 June by 1/383 which passed through Yuza at 0730 and drove south to Ozato. The strongly defended village in the shadow of Yuza Dake was secured in a day of bitter fighting, but mine fields prevented further advances. On 14 June, the battalion mopped up Ozato and cleared the mines from the littered streets. Direct fire of tanks and AT weapons were directed against Yuza Dake before 1/383 withdrew from its exposed position to tie in for night defense with 1/1 and 2/383. Tank fire was invaluable in aiding 2/383 and 3/383 to beat down enemy fire from the escarpment and advance during the day. At nightfall the 3d Battalion held positions just under the lip of the escarpment west of Yaeju Dake.

The remaining defenders of the enemy stronghold had been annihilated during the day by 3/381 which secured the peak at 1125 and pushed forward down its south slopes. A coordinated regimental attack, making full use of tanks and armored flame throwers which had worked their way up tortuous paths to the plateau, had been responsible for the success. Advancing despite heavy mortar and machine-gun fire, 2/381 and 1/381 had kept constant pressure on the northern face of Yaeju Dake and finally gained the top of the escarpment.

Night lines of the 381st Infantry tied in with the 7th Division which had made no spectacular gains on 14 June. The 200–300 yard average advance by the 17th and 32d Infantry had, however, smashed the 13th Independent Infantry Battalion which had been committed in an unsuccessful effort to stop the division's drive.

After a night of disorganized counterattacks and infiltration attempts, the 7th Division attacked toward Hills 115 and 153. A sweeping 1,200-yard advance was made all along the front which brought the assault troops to the outlying slopes of the hill positions. As a result of the

7th Division's advance, General Ushijima was forced to commit his last reserves, the remaining battalions of the 62d Division, in an effort to delay the inevitable end.

The 89th Regiment continued to hold the north and west slopes of Yuza Dake on 15 June, and its fire prevented 1/383 from moving south of Ozato. Forward progress in the rest of the 383d's zone was significant, however. A fresh battalion, 2/382, relieved 2/383 on the outskirts of Yuza and fought its way well up on the north slopes of Yuza Dake before digging in for the night. The attack of the 381st Infantry and the left flank battalion of the 383d, 3/383, was very successful. The escarpment between Yuza and Yaeju Dake, considered by the Japanese to be "the strongest defensive zone," [152] was taken and the flank of the 89th Regiment exposed to crippling attacks.

On 16 June the enemy position continued to contract as steady advances by the Americans eliminated more and more of the remaining strong points. The 32d Infantry, driving down the coast, took Hill 115, while the 17th Infantry pushed its assault companies onto the forward slopes of Hill 153. The Japanese Thirty-second Army headquarters lost all contact with the last cohesive element of the 44th IMB during the day's fighting when the 15th IMR was wiped out by the three battalions of the 32d Infantry attacking abreast.

The 62d Division, attempting to move from its reserve positions southwest of Makabe to back up the crumbling Japanese lines, was savagely battered by artillery, ships' guns, and planeloads of rockets and napalm. The 96th Division took advantage of the confusion caused by continuous bombardment of the enemy rear areas and smashed its battalions through the Yuza Dake perimeter. The 382d Infantry moved into the lines of the 383d and drove forward over the crest of the enemy peak in a coordinated attack with 3/383 (attached to the 382d) making the final effort. By 1800 the battalion was in complete control of the highest ground, and the 382d had tied in all along its front with 3/382 in Ozato, 1/382 and 2/382 on the high ground southwest of Yuza, and 3/383 on Yuza Dake. The 381st Infantry gained some

600 yards along its front and reached the saddle between Yuza Dake and Hill 153. Heavy enemy fire from the south and west slopes of Hill 153 in the 7th Division zone appreciably slowed the 381st's attack during the day.

The 17th Infantry relieved this pressure on the 96th Division's flank with its successful attack on 17 June. The peak of Hill 153 fell after dogged resistance by the makeshift enemy forces that attempted to stem the tide of advance. On the left the 32d Infantry secured the reverse slopes of Hill 115 and readied an attack on Mabuni and Hill 89. At 1730 the 184th Infantry moved into the front lines of the 17th and took over Hill 153 and the intervening high ground to Hill 115. Its final objective was that portion of the Medeera-Makabe-Komesu triangle in the XXIV Corps zone lying 1,000–2,000 yards to the front.

All organized enemy resistance in the Yuza-Ozato-Yuza Dake area was eliminated by the 382d Infantry on 17 June. Using flame and demolitions, assault guns and tanks, and artillery and NGF, the infantry mopped up the peak and surrounding escarpment. The 96th Division's front lines were advanced 600 yards on the right and 200 on the left as the assault battalions converged on Aragachi and Medeera.

By nightfall on 17 June the XXIV Corps controlled all the commanding ground on the Yaeju Dake-Yuza Dake Escarpment. Between its front lines and the southern coast of the island were a heterogeneous mixture of units and individuals from the 62d Division, 44th IMB, and 89th Regiment, most of whom were determined and destined to die fighting in a hopeless attempt to protect the headquarters of the Thirty-second Army. (See Map 40, Map Section)

END OF ORGANIZED RESISTANCE [153]

The intensity of enemy resistance steadily lessened in the face of Tenth Army advances

---

[152] *Ibid.*, 108.

[153] Unless otherwise noted the material in this section is derived from *Okinawa: The Last Battle; Tenth Army AR; IIIAC AR; XXIV Corps AR; 1st MarDiv SAR; 6th MarDiv SAR, Ph III; 7th InfDiv AR; 77th InfDiv OpRpt, Okinawa; 96th InfDiv AR; 4th Mar SAR, Ph III; 5th Mar SAR;* 8th CT AR, Okinawa Operation, 11–22Jun45, hereinafter cited as *8th CT AR; 29th Mar SAR, Ph III; Okinawa Operations Record.*

THE 8TH MARINES cross Oroku airfield en route to assembly areas behind the 1st Division battle positions.

on 18 June. Isolated pockets of stubborn defenders clung to ridge and hill positions until they were driven off or killed by advancing tank-infantry teams. Two major areas of resistance developed during the day, one around Medeera and the other at Mabuni. The Medeera position was held by the remnants of the 24th Division, while elements of the headquarters and troops of the other major Thirty-second Army units centered their lines on Hill 89, south of Mabuni.

General Buckner's attack on 18 June was highlighted by the first introduction of a fresh unit to the Okinawa battle line in two months. The 8th Marines had been attached to the 1st Division upon landing on 15 June. By 0630 on the 18th, 2/8 had relieved 3/7 on Mezado Ridge and 3/8 had taken over the positions of 1/7 on Kunishi Ridge.[154] In order to split the Japanese defenses in two again, General del Valle decided to commit Colonel Wallace's regiment in column of battalions "for a quick decisive thrust" to the sea at the southern tip of the island.[155]

After a thorough preparation by artillery, the 8th Marines jumped off with 2/8 (Lieutenant Colonel Harry A. Waldorf) in assault to seize the Kuwanga-Makabe Road. Moderate machine-gun and rifle fire, interspersed with mortar and light artillery rounds, hit the Marines from the left front and flank as they made a spirited advance of over 1,400 yards. Tanks from Company A, 2d Tank Battalion delivered suppressive fire on the high ground around Makabe.[156] By late afternoon the battalion had reached its objective and begun to dig in. Company B of 1/8 was attached for night defense to refuse the open left flank.

Colonel Wallace's observation post on Mezado Ridge was visited by General Buckner at midday. After watching the steady progress of 2/8 in the valley for about an hour, the Tenth Army commander decided to move on to another front.[157] Almost simultaneously with this decision, the Japanese, perhaps attracted by the cluster of figures on the ridge heights, zeroed in five artillery shells on the observation post. Fragments of jagged coral filled the air and mortally wounded General Buckner. He died within minutes, just a few scant days short of his goal, the capture of Okinawa. General Geiger, as senior troop commander, assumed temporary command of Tenth Army and directed its final combat operations.

Hill 79 northwest of Makabe was the objective for the 5th Marines' attack on 18 June.[158] Lieutenant Colonel Shelburne's 1st Battalion moved around the east end of Kunishi Ridge through the zone of the 8th Marines and attacked at 0730 to take the troublesome hill position from the flank. Almost immediately after jump-off the assault companies were pinned down by heavy and accurate machine-gun fire. Tanks were called for, and after they came forward the attack was renewed at 1100. A suspected AT gun position on Hill 81 just north of Makabe was smoked so that the tanks could operate successfully. An experienced tank officer flying above

[154] 1st MarDiv G–3 Jnl, 18Jun45.

[155] LtGen P. A. del Valle Ltr to CMC, 9 Mar 55, hereinafter cited as del Valle 1955.

[156] 1st TkBn Summary, 18Jun45.

[157] R. W. Johnston, Follow Me: The Story of the Second Marine Division in World War II, (New York, 1948), 270.

[158] The rapid advance of the 8th Mar left Gen del Valle's eastern flank uncovered. Consequently, "the battle-weary and decimated infantry of the 1st MarDiv had to be employed in attacking the various hill positions along the [eastern] flank simply to cover it. . . . We knew that the XXIV Corps could not keep up with the penetration executed by fresh troops, so we planned our maneuver to provide for this expected contingency." del Valle 1955.

the battlefield during the day's action spotted enemy AT guns and directed their reduction.[159] With the help of armored firepower, 1/5 was able to gain the lower slopes of Hill 79 at dusk. During the day 3/5 moved up from reserve to a support position behind the 1st Battalion, and tank-infantry teams of 2/5 eliminated the last organized resistance on Kunishi Ridge.[160]

Another of the enemy-infested ridges in the IIIAC zone was secured on 18 June. Passing through 3/22 in a column of companies, 2/22 attacked under smoke cover across the valley between Mezado and Kuwanga. In less than an hour the leading Company (E) was astride Kuwanga Ridge, and the men, aided by direct fire of tanks, swung left to push their attack toward the division boundary. The rest of the battalion mounted the ridge and fanned out to flush the defenders from their caves and crevices. A hot, dusty day-long struggle secured the 1,800-yard ridge line, but the understrength 2d Battalion was spread too thin to cover the whole of the position. At 1406 General Shepherd ordered the 4th Marines to attach one battalion to the 22d for night defense,[161] and Colonel Shapley ordered 3/4 forward to occupy the eastern end of the ridge.

Small enemy groups still occupied considerable stretches of the reverse slopes of Mezado Ridge, and 1/22 and 3/22 spent a busy day hunting down the desperate holdouts and silencing their fire. Observation posts on the ridge and positions on its crest were all subjected to the sporadic fire which also struck down men from 2/22 on Kuwanga.[162] At 1430 Colonel Roberts, commanding the 22d Marines, was killed by a sniper near his observation post, and Lieutenant Colonel August Larson, the regimental executive officer, assumed command.

The 96th Infantry Division, attacking the Medeera position from the east in a coordinated effort with the 1st Marine Division attack on the west, tightened the deadly ring around the enemy-held area on 18 June. On the north 3/382 smashed through a rugged cave and pillbox complex in a 600-yard advance to the base of

the rock-studded ridges north of Aragachi. The 381st Infantry with the 1st and 2d Battalions in assault moved rapidly across the plateau against scattered resistance to seize high ground only 400 yards north of Medeera.

The 7th Division assault regiments made a two-pronged attack with elements of 1/184 and 3/184 driving down the reverse slopes of Hill 153 to close on Medeera and the division and corps boundary from the southeast. The 32d Infantry moved down the coast toward Mabuni with all three battalions in line against increasingly stiff resistance. The night was marked by infiltration attempts and scattered small attacks all along the Tenth Army front in which the Japanese lost at least 340 men.[163] (See Map 41, Map Section)

General Ushijima, realizing that his "Army's fate had been sealed" sent farewell dispatches to Japan and Formosa on 19 June and a last message to all Thirty-second Army units that still had contact with Mabuni, congratulating the survivors on performing their "assigned mission in a manner which leaves nothing to regret" and exhorting them "to fight to the last and die for the eternal cause of loyalty to the Emperor."[164] Most of the army staff officers were directed to leave the command post disguised as native Okinawans in order to infiltrate American lines and escape to northern Okinawa. Some men, like Colonel Yahara, were given the mission of reaching Japan to report to Imperial General Headquarters, while others were directed to organize guerilla operations and harass the rear areas of Tenth Army and Island Command.[165]

Not all of the Thirty-second Army survivors were imbued with a will "to die for the eternal cause of loyalty to the Emperor." Loudspeakers mounted on tanks in the 7th Division's front lines and on LCI's that cruised up and down the coast line were successful in convincing over 3,000 civilians to surrender. Far more significant, however, were the 106 Japanese soldiers and 238 *Boeitai* who voluntarily gave up during the division's advance on 19 June.[166] The relentless attack of American troops, coupled

---

[159] *Ibid.*

[160] *2/5 SAR*, 22.

[161] *6th MarDiv Jnl, Ph III*, 18Jun45.

[162] *2/22 SAR, Ph III*, 15.

[163] Tenth Army G-2 Rpt No 86, 20Jun45.

[164] *Okinawa Operations Record*, 110–111.

[165] *Shimada Interrogation; Yahara Interrogation.*

[166] Tenth Army G-2 Rpt No 86, 20Jun45.

with intensive efforts by psychological warfare teams, brought in increasing numbers of battle-weary Japanese and Okinawans who had decided that the war was lost and their cause was hopeless. It is not inconceivable that every enemy soldier who surrendered meant one less American casualty as the wind-up drive of Tenth Army continued.

Despite the influx of civilian and military prisoners that slowed the advance of assault units, the 32d Infantry reached positions only 200 yards from the outskirts of Mabuni. Tanks delivered direct fire on the cave openings in Hill 89, inadvertently timing their bombardment to coincide with General Ushijima's farewell supper for his departing staff officers.

On the right of the division zone the 184th Infantry operated in concert with the 381st to close on Medeera from the south and east. While the volume of enemy fire was not as heavy as had previously been encountered, the small enemy groups that defended the hills and ravines guarding the 24th Division headquarters had to be wiped out before the front lines could advance. The story was much the same north of Aragachi where the 382d Infantry overcame determined resistance in reaching the ridges that overlooked the village. While observing this fighting, Brigadier General Claudius M. Easley, ADC of the 96th Division, was killed by enemy machine-gun fire.[167]

Hills 79 and 81 which bulwarked that part of the Medeera defensive position in the 1st Division sector were repeatedly assaulted by the 5th Marines on 19 June. The 1st Battalion was directed to seize Hill 79 and continue its attack to Hill 81.[168] Despite covering fire from a company of medium tanks Lieutenant Colonel Shelburne's men were unable to seize the crest of Hill 79, and the tank company lost three tanks to enemy action.[169] Colonel Griebel then committed 2/5, which had been relieved of its mop-up responsibilities on Kunishi Ridge by 3/7

at 1500, to take Hill 81 from the south and relieve some of the pressure on the 1st Battalion.

Lieutenant Colonel Benedict moved his battalion out at 1515 in a wide, swinging movement through the 8th Marines' zone and arrived opposite Hill 79 at 1700. As soon as 2/5 attempted to attack Hill 81 through Makabe, which had been secured by 3/5 earlier in the day, it came under heavy sniper fire from Hill 79. Company G which led the battalion column was forced to run a 1,000-yard gantlet of fire to reach cover at Makabe, and as a result 20 men were reported to be exhaustion cases. Lieutenant Colonel Benedict, wishing to attack as soon as possible, passed Company F through Company G's lines and accompanied the assault platoon which was pinned down as soon as it tried to move up the slope of the objective. The volume of enemy fire, the lateness of the hour, and the condition of his men caused Benedict to call off the attack and order the battalion into a perimeter defense southwest of Makabe.[170]

The desperate defense that met the 5th Marines on 19 June was not matched in the rest of the 1st Division zone of advance. The 8th Marines passed 3/8 (Lieutenant Colonel Paul E. Wallace) through 2/8 at the opening of the morning's attack, and the fresh battalion, moving against light resistance, took Ibaru Ridge, the last high ground before the sea. Company K, the battalion reserve, was then passed through the assault companies "more for the experience rather than for any tactical necessity"[171] and led the advance to the coastal cliffs which it reached at 1623. By 1634 the entire battalion line was established on the sea and the Kiyamu Peninsula defensive position was severed. The 5th Marines' 3d Battalion, which had secured Makabe during the morning, kept pace with 3/8 during the day's 2,500-yard advance and reached the coast at almost the same instant as Company K.[172] The 8th Marines, with 3/5 attached, took charge of the coastal zone for night defense and tied in with the 5th and 4th Marines along a crescent-shaped line from Komesu to the boundary between Marine divisions.[173]

---

[167] *96th InfDiv History*, 182–183.

[168] *1/5 SAR*, 12.

[169] *1st TkBn Summary*, 19Jun45. One tank was hit by enemy AT fire, abandoned, and then destroyed by friendly tank fire. Two others, temporarily abandoned because of mine damage to tracks on 18 June, had to be destroyed because Japanese machine gunners had converted them into pillboxes.

[170] *2/5 SAR*, 22–23.

[171] 3d Bn, 8th Mar AR, 6, Enclosure to *8th CT AR*.

[172] *3/5 SAR*, n. p.

[173] *1st MarDiv G–3 Jnl*, 19Jun45.

On the right of the 1st Division, the 4th Marines, making the 6th Division's main effort on 19 June, paralleled the advance of the 8th Marines during most of the day but was unable to reach the coast. A strong enemy position developed along the Kiyamu-Gusuku hill mass that shielded the southern tip of the island, Ara Saki. The assault battalions, 3/4 and 1/4, were forced to dig in at the foot of the cliff-like hills under a heavy rain of machine-gun and mortar fire. The 2d Battalion, which had been committed to cover the regiment's open west flank [174] during the day's advance and which had taken part in the attack on Kiyamu-Gusuku, was relieved by the 29th Marines at 1900.

In accordance with orders to be ready to move his regiment into the front lines on the right of the 4th Marines on 20 June, Colonel Whaling had started his men marching south from Oroku Peninsula at 0800, 19 June. At 1415 he received orders to commit 1/29 and 2/29 immediately. The two battalions jumped off from Kuwanga Ridge at 1705 and, moving rapidly against light resistance, reached the base of the Kiyamu-Gusuku hill mass and linked up with the 4th Marines before darkness fell.

After a night of unorganized infiltration attempts all along its front, the 6th Division launched its attack on the hill mass with 3/4, 1/4, 1/29, and 2/29 in assault. The key points on Kiyamu-Gusuku, Hills 72 and 80, were in the 4th Marines' zone, and the regiment concentrated its efforts on reducing these enemy positions. Lieutenant Colonel Bell of 1/4, whose line of departure was directly beneath Hill 72, was unable to get enough of his men to the top of

the cliff to his front to maintain a foothold. Enemy defenders hidden among the boulders and brush that screened the narrow paths to the top drove back the points of Company C's assault platoons. Attempts to cut a tank road to the crest on the flank of the position were stopped when a satchel charge thrown from about 15 feet completely demolished an armored bulldozer. Blind fighting raged all day at grenade range, and the battalion dug in for the night in the same positions it had held on 19 June, barely 20 yards from the enemy on the hill above.[175]

The ridge to the front of 3/4 was steep, with irregular rock cliffs ranging from 50 to 200 feet in height covered by heavy undergrowth. Lieutenant Colonel Hochmuth's estimate of the situation indicated that a frontal assault against the enemy holding this tangled ground would be futile. Accordingly, he ordered Company I to pass around the east end of the ridge by moving through the zone of the 8th Marines and to mount its attack up the nose of the ridge from the flank. After the leading company had mopped up the eastern slope, Company L was committed on the left to link up with the 8th Marines and extend the battalion's hold on the ridge. By late afternoon 3/4 held strong positions on the left flank of Hill 72 and was ready to close on the enemy strong point.[176]

The regimental reserve, 2/4, had been alerted at the start of the day's attack to support either assault battalion. At 1040 Major Carney was ordered to move his unit into the front lines and take over the right 400 yards of 1/4's zone of action. The battalion objective was Hill 80, and Company G reached it at 1330 after overcoming moderate resistance. Company E was held up at the base of the hill by an enemy pocket, which Major Carney decided to contain with one platoon while he moved the rest of the company around through the right of Company G and assaulted the objective from the west. By 1645 Company E had overrun the hill crest and 2/4 had sealed the right flank of the Hill 72 position.[177]

Except for enfilade fire from the reverse

---

[174] An impromptu amphibious assault against a small islet 300 yards off Nagusuku was organized by WpnsCo, 4th Mar after a POW revealed the presence of enemy troops and the regimental CP reported it was receiving fire from there. A POW was sent over to induce the Japanese to give up. "The answer that came back was a definite no, and also included a remark that was not exactly complimentary to Marines. So a task force was immediately organized from [3] LVT(A)'s, two 37mm platoons organized as infantry, and the 1st War Dog Platoon. Under the Weapons Company CO, the island was stormed and cleared without a casualty." *4th Mar SAR, Ph III*, 15. Several machine guns and knee mortars were captured, 20 enemy killed, and 5 POWs were taken.

[175] *1/4 SAR, Ph III*, 8–9.
[176] *3/4 SAR, Ph III*, 9–10.
[177] *2/4 SAR, Ph III*, 9.

slopes of Hill 80, the attack of the 29th Marines on 20 June met only light resistance and swept forward to the south coast on a two-battalion front. When General Shepherd decided to envelop the Kiyamu-Gusuku position from the left, he shifted the boundary of the 29th Marines to the east to include all of Ara-Saki. The regiment's night lines tied in with the 4th Marines and barred escape from the tip of the island.

The attack of the 6th Division had been greatly hampered during the day as an ever-increasing horde of enemy civilians and soldiers attempted to surrender. Loudspeakers mounted on LCI's persuaded many to give up and leave the inaccessible caves on the coastal cliffs that had been their refuge. Over 4,000 natives and 800 military were herded through the front lines before dark.[178]

Action in the 1st Division sector on 20 June centered on Hills 79 and 81. The 7th Marines at Kunishi Ridge, the 8th Marines along the south coast, and 3/5 around Komesu conducted extensive mopping-up operations and added about 50 POW's and 2,000 natives to the IIIAC total.[179] Fire support to 7th Division operations was given by 3/5 from positions on Komesu Ridge, and patrols from the Marine battalion linked up with 1/184 at 1520. For night defense physical contact between the corps was broken, but the battalions occupied high ground near Komesu and Udo and covered the gap by fire.[180]

A pre-dawn soaking rain turned the roads around Makabe into quagmires and prevented effective support of 2/5 by tanks and assault guns until late in the morning. In 1/5's zone of action, however, the tanks were able to move up with the assault troops at 0730 and fire on enemy emplacements on Hill 79. Lieutenant Colonel Shelburne had reoriented his direction of attack from northwest to southeast and jumped off with three companies in line. By

[178] IIIAC G–2 PrdRpt No 81, 21Jun45. Most of the enemy surrendered in 3/4's zone of action where a few men were detailed to strip and search the military prisoners. Before the POW's were sent to the rear, they were used to distribute air-dropped supplies. *3/4 SAR, Ph III*, 10.

[179] IIIAC G–2 Rpt No 81, 21Jun45.

[180] *1st MarDiv G–3 Jnl*, 20Jun45.

1300 Company C had fought its way to within 75 yards of the hillcrest and Companies A and B with flame and gun tanks in support, were burning and blasting out the enemy machine gun nests and snipers that infested the hillside. At 1635 Company A reported it had seized the top of the hill, but two hours later it was forced to withdraw because its understrength platoons were unable to consolidate their positions in the face of heavy and accurate enemy small-arms fire.[181] The battalion dug in for the night in possession of most of Hill 79 and with good prospects of cleaning up the enemy position the following day.

After being freed from the mud which had bogged down their earlier efforts, the tanks supporting 2/5 were stopped by road blocks in Makabe when they tried to pass through the village towards Hill 81. An armored bulldozer cleared the streets by 1400, and the tanks moved to the road along the corps boundary to deliver direct fire on the hillside.

The battalion jumped off from the northern outskirts of Makabe at 1520 with Companies E and F in assault. Company F was pinned down in the low ground south of the hill almost immediately, but Company E, attacking from the southeast, was able to secure about 100 yards of the eastern slope before fire from the front and right rear stopped the advance. Company F and then Company G were ordered to pass through Company E and continue the attack, but enemy machine-gun and mortar fire prevented both moves. After the tanks ran out of ammunition at 1910 and withdrew, and the assault companies had tried for another hour to gain more ground, Lieutenant Colonel Benedict ordered his men to pull back to better night defensive positions.[182]

Two enemy strong points remained in the XXIV Corps zone at the close of the fighting on 20 June. One was centered on Hill 89 south of Mabuni, the location of the Thirty-second Army headquarters cave, and the other was in Medeera and on Hills 79 and 85 to the west of the village which together with Hill 81 in the 1st Division sector formed Makabe Ridge.

The 2d Battalion, 32d Infantry reached the

[181] *1/5 SAR*, 12–13.

[182] *2/5 SAR*, 24.

eastern slope of Hill 89 on 20 June despite desperate resistance from enemy hidden in coral outcroppings and caves along the coastal cliffs, and 1/32 halted its attack on the northern outskirts of Mabuni. The 3d Battalion, reinforced by a company of the 17th Infantry, held a long looping line northwest of the village that paralleled the axis of 32d Infantry's attack and joined the positions of 3/184 and 1/184 in the hills above Udo. Company-sized strong points of 2/184 south and southeast of Medeera blocked escape routes from the final defensive position of the enemy 24th Division.

The last courier contact between the two enemy pockets was made during the night of 20 June after Lieutenant General Amamiya, 24th Division commander, had directed all his units "to fight to the last man in their present positions." [183] The general had few of his infantrymen left to protect the Medeera position at the time he issued the order, since IIIAC had virtually destroyed the 22d and 32d Regiments during its advance to the coast, and the 96th Division had annihilated the 89th Regiment at Yuza Dake and Aragachi. The remaining defenders were a conglomeration of artillerymen, drivers, corpsmen, engineers, *Boeitai*, and headquarters personnel from virtually every unit of the L-Day island garrison. Those who did not surrender or take their own lives fought with the determination of fanatics.

The 382d Infantry cleaned out Aragachi on 20 June and the 381st seized the northern outskirts of Medeera. The 305th Infantry of the 77th Division, which had been fighting a vigorous mopping-up action behind the lines of the 96th Division since its attachment on 16 June, was designated by General Bradley to wipe out the Makabe Ridge position in the XXIV Corps zone. To allow for detailed reconnaissance and assembly of troops and supporting weapons, the time of attack was delayed until noon on 21 June; the direction of attack was to be northwest through the lines held by 2/184.

At 1027 on 21 June, General Shepherd informed General Geiger that organized resistance had ended in the zone of the 6th Marine Division. Colonel Shapley had directed 2/4 and 3/4 to make a double envelopment of Hill 72 on Kiyamu-Gusuku ridge. Both battalions began their turning movements at 0800 and by 0930 had linked up and were driving north over the reverse slopes of the hill. In less than an hour the objective was secured and the troops, aided by tanks and armored flame throwers, were cleaning out the last enemy defenders. The 29th Marines encountered very light resistance in its sweep of Ara Saki, and Company G of 2/22, attached to 1/29, planted the division colors on the southernmost point of the island during the day. [184]

The task of flushing out Japanese holdouts and handling the mounting stream of soldiers and civilians who wanted to surrender fell to to the 7th and 8th Marines on 21 June. The 5th Marines concentrated its efforts on reducing Hills 79 and 81. The 1st Battalion completed the capture of Hill 79 by late afternoon after a day of small unit mop-up actions by tank-infantry teams. Hill 81 was a tougher nut to crack.

Lieutenant Colonel Benedict delayed the attack of 2/5, originally scheduled for 0900, until 1104 in order that approach routes for tanks could be prepared, and the battalion could take advantage of an intense rocket barrage on the hill. [185] The scheme of maneuver called for the leading company (E) to seize the eastern slope of the hill and for Companies F and G to be committed successively from the left until the hill was taken. By 1214 Company E had occupied its objective after destroying two machine guns that had temporarily stopped its advance, and Company F had begun to fight its way up the hill, burning and blasting caves as it ascended. Company G attacked shortly

---

[183] *Okinawa Operations Record*, Record of the 24th Div, 30.

[184] Co G was also the first unit to raise the flag over the northernmost point of Okinawa, Hedo Misaki. *6th MarDiv History*, 174–175. The 22d Mar evidently had a proclivity for securing the extremities of island objectives since units of the regiment duplicated the Okinawan feat during the recapture of Guam. Maj O. R. Lodge, *The Recapture of Guam*, MC Historical Monograph, (Washington, 1954), 154.

[185] LtCol W. E. Benedict Ltr to CMC, 28Mar47. Because of the compression of the Japanese defenders into a restricted area at Hill 81, no artillery support was available on 21 June. *Brown 1955*.

MEN OF THE TENTH ARMY pay final tribute to their gallant commander, General Buckner.

thereafter and also began the tortuous climb in the face of heavy fire from the interconnected cave positions.

The slow advance by all companies continued throughout the afternoon. About 1300 word was received at the battalion command post, incorrect as it turned out, that Hill 81 was the last organized enemy position on Okinawa, and there was considerable pressure to effect its capture. Benedict's several requests for reinforcements were refused, and at 1430 he was ordered to report to the regimental commander. He turned over the battalion to his executive officer,

Major Richard T. Washburn. At 1500 Lieutenant Colonel Hill of 3/5 assumed joint command of both battalions, and Company L started moving to Makabe to support the Hill 81 attack. Enemy fire slackened off as 2/5 neared the crest, and at 1700 all assault companies reported the hill secured, marking the end of organized enemy resistance in the IIIAC zone.[186]

The 1st Battalion, 305th Infantry attacked Hill 79 at 1200 behind a concentrated 4.2-inch

---

[186] 2/5 SAR, 25.

mortar preparation. The battalion mortars and machine guns of both 1/305 and 3/305 furnished supporting fire, and gun and flame tanks led the assault. The intensity of enemy rifle and machine-gun fire from caves and pillboxes on Makabe Ridge increased sharply at 1315 when the explosion of an ammunition-filled cave disrupted the battalion advance and disorganized the leading company. Firm control was quickly recovered, however, and 1/305 continued its advance behind a heavy mortar barrage. The troops gained the forward slopes of the hill and at 1630 launched a successful attack on its crest. The battalion dug in in control of Hill 79 and in contact with 3/305 which had followed the attack during the day and was slated to pass through the front lines in the morning to seize Hill 85.

A series of small local attacks and mopping-up actions, frequently halted to allow large numbers of civilians and soldiers to surrender, occupied most XXIV Corps units on 21 June. Where resistance was met it was bitter and costly; enemy pockets were silenced only when the defenders were wiped out. The 32d Infantry secured Mabuni and drove to the table-land atop Hill 89. Flame tanks enabled the attacking infantry to scour and burn out the enemy defenders who tried to protect the entrances to the headquarters cave. By nightfall the hill was secured and the enemy within were reduced to desperation attempts to break out from their massive tomb.

The rapid progress of assault units during 21 June and the obvious collapse of major enemy opposition led General Geiger to declare that the island of Okinawa was secure and that organized enemy resistance had ended by 1305. A formal ceremony at 1000, 22 June, attended by representatives of all elements of Tenth Army, marked the official end of resistance by the Japanese Thirty-second Army.

CHAPTER XI

Campaign Summary

THE CLEAN-UP DRIVE[1]

Lieutenant General Mitsuru Ushijima and Lieutenant General Isamu Cho, respectively commander and chief of staff of the Japanese Thirty-second Army, fulfilled their last obligation to the Emperor on the night of 21–22 June. In the traditional manner of adherents to the warrior code of their homeland, they atoned for their failure to stem the tide of American advance by committing *hara-kiri*.

At 0300 on 22 June both generals, wearing their bemedaled full field uniforms, led a party of aides and staff officers out onto the narrow ledge of a cave entrance that overlooked the ocean. U. S. soldiers of the 32d Infantry who held the crest of Hill 89 less than 100 feet away were unaware of the silent preparations for the suicide ceremony. First Ushijima, then Cho, bared his abdomen to the ceremonial knife and thrust inward while a simultaneous slash of the headquarters adjutant's saber struck his bowed neck. The men were secretly buried and not uncovered until 25 June when patrols of the 32d Infantry found the bodies at the foot of the seaward cliff-face of Hill 89. General Cho had written his own simple epitaph:

22d day, 6th month, 20th year of the Showa Era. I depart without regret, fear, shame, or obligations.

---

[1] Unless otherwise noted the material in this section is derived from *Tenth Army AR; IIIAC AR; XXIV Corps AR; 1st MarDiv SAR; 6th MarDiv SAR, Ph III; 7th InfDiv AR; 77th InfDiv OpRpt, Okinawa; 96th InfDiv AR.*

Army Chief of Staff; Army Lieutenant General Cho, Isamu, age of departure 51 years. At this time and place I hereby certify the foregoing.[2]

While the enemy generals were preparing to take their own lives in a rite peculiar to Japanese philosophy, the theme of military suicide was carried out in the skies overhead by *Kamikaze* pilots making the last major organized air attack of the Okinawan campaign. About 1830 on 21 June, a small group of raiders showing friendly radar recognition signals[3] penetrated to Kerama Retto where one dived into the seaplane tender *Curtis*, starting night-long fires that severely damaged the ship. Other planes of this flight crashed LSM 59 and the decoy ship ex-*Barry*,[4] sinking both. Between 0001 and 1130, 22 June Okinawa underwent a total of 30 air raids. Admiral Hill reported that the "magnificent work of CAP and northern pickets prevented all but a few stragglers getting through. Those that did penetrate were knocked down by AA fire, and only insignificant damage was reported by one LST and one DE."[5] The

---

[2] Tenth Army G–2 Rpt No 92, 26Jun45, Annex A, Rpt by 7th InfDiv G–2.

[3] CinCPac War Diary, June 1945, 75.

[4] The APD *Barry* was hit and severely damaged by a suicider late in May. A Board of Inspection and Survey recommended that she be decommissioned and canabalized. The hulk was under tow to its final station as a *Kamikaze* decoy when it fulfilled its mission. *Ibid.*

[5] *Ibid.* The toll of naval casualties on 21–22 June was 30 KIA, 154 WIA, and 19 MIA. *CTF 31 AR*, Part III, 95–97.

strength if not the ferocity of Japanese air attacks diminished as the tide of battle turned against the Thirty-second Army on Okinawa. In preparation for the final defense of the home islands, the enemy high command adopted a policy of extreme conservatism, saving its remaining plane strength for the last battle when thousands of *Kamikazes* were scheduled to hit the American invasion fleet.[6] After the cessation of the last suicide air attack, TF 31 and TAF shot down or turned back all the enemy raiders that attempted to penetrate to Okinawa.[7]

Ground combat action on Okinawa did not stop with the official declaration of the end of organized resistance. Although unprecedentedly large numbers of Japanese soldiers, both officer and enlisted, surrendered, die-hard groups and individuals continued to fight until they were annihilated. An extensive, coordinated mop-up of southern Okinawa was necessary before the area could be considered safe for the planned build-up of supply depots, airfields, training areas, and port facilities.

A line of blocking positions manned by companies of the 1st Marines and 307th Infantry was set up in the hills above the Naha-Yonabaru valley to stop the attempts of the Japanese to infiltrate to the north. On 22 June the four assault divisions that had smashed the Kiyamu Peninsula defenses were ordered to conduct a sweep to the north, destroying any resistance encountered, blowing and sealing all caves, burying all dead, and salvaging friendly and enemy equipment left on the field of battle. Three phase lines were established across the island for coordination of the effort, and the pace of advance was to be set by the progress of the 96th Division, moving up the center of the island on the left of the XXIV Corps zone. Ten days were allotted for the completion of the mopping-up action which was to be controlled by the new Tenth Army commander, General Joseph W. Stilwell. General Stilwell, former Command-

ing General, Army Ground Forces, formally relieved General Geiger on 23 June.

The final reduction of the 24th Division defensive position also took place on 23 June as elements of the 381st Infantry mopped up the last holdouts in the ruins of Medeera. Hill 85, which had been seized by 3/305 on 22 June, was thoroughly probed, and the 96th Division concentrated its efforts in the Medeera-Aragachi area. Units of the 1st and 6th Marine Divisions worked over Komesu and Kiyamu-Gusuku Ridges, while the 7th Division probed Hill 89 and Mabuni. On 25 June after the area of most recent battle action south of the Yaeju Dake-Yuza Dake escarpment had been intensively combed, the Tenth Army began its clean-up drive to the north with both corps responsible primarily for the ground they had taken during the previous month.

Kume Shima, the last and largest of the islands of Okinawa Gunto chosen as radar and fighter director sites, was secured during the mop-up period. The FMF Amphibious Reconnaissance Battalion, attached to Island Command on 23 April for garrison duty in the Eastern Islands, was released to Tenth Army control on 21 June for use as the landing force on Kume Shima.[8] Patrols from Company B had scouted the beach areas of the 40-square-mile island on the night of 13–14 June and learned from captured civilians that there was only a 50-man enemy garrison present. Although this estimate later proved to be correct, the possibility of a stronger Japanese force being met was answered by attaching Company A and the 81mm Mortar Platoon of 1/7 to the 252-man reconnaissance battalion for the operation.[9]

After the landing had been delayed two days by adverse weather conditions,[10] the assault took

---

[6] *Campaigns*, 12, 339; *USSBS Interrogation* No 62, Capt Rikibei Inoguchi, IJN, I, 63. The enemy air forces in the Formosa area called off their part of the attack against Okinawa in early June because they were convinced that the Sakishima Gunto would be invaded in the near future. *Okinawa Operations Record*, Record of the 8th Air Div, 30.

[7] *CTF 31 AR*, Part III, 97–106.

[8] During the early planning for ICEBERG, Kume Shima was considered as a possible target for Phase III if further reconnaissance proved the island suitable for airfield development. The assault force tentatively allotted for the operation was 25,736 men, including one infantry division, and the estimated casualties were set at 4,000. *ICEBERG Study*, Appendix H.

[9] *1/7 SAR*, 25. It was necessary to transfer men from other companies of 1/7 into Co A in order to build that unit up to the three-quarter strength called for in the attachment order.

[10] *CTF 31 AR*, Part III, 99.

STOCKADE housing some of the thousands of Japanese troops who surrendered in the last stages of the campaign on Okinawa. (Army Photograph)

proximately 42,000 civilians had fallen victim to artillery, NGF, and air attacks because of their unfortunate proximity to Japanese combat troops and installations.[12]

American losses were heavy. Tenth Army reported 7,374 Americans killed or died of wounds, 31,807 wounded or injured in action, and 239 missing. In addition there were 26,221 non-battle casualties. The combat divisions reported their battle casualties as: [13]

	KIA-DOW	WIA-IIA	MIA	Total
1st Marine Division	1,115	6,745	41	6,901
6th Marine Division	1,622	6,689	15	7,326
7th Infantry Division	1,122	4,943	3	8,068
27th Infantry Division	711	2,520	24	3,255
77th Infantry Division	1,018	3,968	40	5,026
96th Infantry Division	1,506	5,912	12	7,430

place at 0644 on 26 June. There was no opposition. Company A of 1/7 took over the initial beachhead from the reconnaissance companies which then sent out patrols to contact the garrison. On 30 June, after five days of intensive patrolling had failed to uncover any enemy opposition, Major Jones, the battalion commander, declared the island secure.[11]

The end of June also brought the end of the mop-up campaign in southern Okinawa which had accounted for an estimated 8,975 Japanese killed and added 2,902 military and 906 unarmed labor troop prisoners of war to the Tenth Army total. A recapitulation of enemy losses for the entire Okinawan campaign showed 107,539 counted dead plus 23,764 estimated to be sealed in caves or buried by the Japanese themselves. A total of 10,755 prisoners of war had been captured. Since this casualty total of 142,058 was "far above a reasonable estimate of military strength on the island," Tenth Army intelligence officers concluded that ap-

Army units absorbed 12,277 replacements between 1 April and 30 June, while Marine units joined 11,147 Marines and naval corpsmen.

The United States Pacific Fleet and attached British carrier forces suffered a severe mauling in supporting and maintaining the operations of Tenth Army in Okinawa Gunto. During the three-month ICEBERG Campaign 36 ships were sunk and 368 were damaged, 763 aircraft were lost to all causes, and 4,907 seamen were killed or missing in action and 4,824 were wounded. In grim return for these losses, ships and ground AAA and planes operating under Navy coordination or control accounted for 7,830 Japanese aircraft and 16 combatant ships.[14]

On 1 July 1945, in accordance with the planned progression of operational control,[15] General Stilwell established Headquarters, Ryukyus Area. He assumed responsibility as a joint task force commander directly under

---

[11] *AmphReconBn AR*, Phase III, Encl A, The Assault and Capture of Kume Shima, 15 Aug 45. Two fire fights with the lightly-armed enemy garrison in early July resulted in the capture of three of the four machine guns that had been its principal armament and the death of six Japanese. Constant aggressive patrolling forced the survivors to scatter into the hills in the interior of the island where they offered no threat to the successful operation of air warning facilities.

[12] *IntelMono*, Part I, Sect B, Chap 2, 3. Japanese sources indicate that approximately 75,000 soldiers and 50,000 Okinawan noncombatants were killed during the campaign and that half of the survivors were wounded. *Okinawa Operations Record*, 125.

[13] See Appendix VI for the final compilation by unit of all Marine casualties.

[14] *Campaigns*, 331.

[15] Tenth Army Tentative OpPlan 1–45, 6Jan45, Annex 1, 4.

INFANTRYMEN of Company K, 3/305 advance against the last organized enemy positon on Okinawa on 22 June (Army Photograph)

Admiral Nimitz for the defense and development of all captured islands and the waters within 25 miles. CinCPac dissolved Task Force 31 and Admiral Hill and his staff departed for Pearl Harbor; Rear Admiral Calvin H. Cobb took over as Commander Naval Forces, Ryukyus under General Stilwell. In like manner, TAF, Tenth Army became TAF, Ryukyus. It would be General Stilwell's mission to coordinate and control the vast effort necessary to support the coming operations against the Japanese home islands.

TACTICAL AIR FORCE, TENTH ARMY[16]

More than a month before the destruction of the Thirty-second Army was completed, planes of General Mulcahy's Tactical Air Force had joined those from carriers and superfortress bases in bringing the war to the Japanese home islands. The primary mission of the fighter squadrons that comprised the bulk of TAF's complement was the defense of the Okinawa area from enemy air attack. Efficient execution of that mission demanded destruction and interdiction attacks against staging fields in the northern Ryukyus and air bases on Kyushu that harbored the swarms of *Kamikazes*.

By 30 June reconnaissance flights reported that two-thirds of the known aircraft strength available to the Japanese had been withdrawn from fields within range of TAF squadrons. With this withdrawal, forced by frequent fighter sweeps and nightly intruder missions flown against the enemy bases after 13 May,[17]

---

[16] Unless otherwise noted the material in this section is derived from R. Sherrod, *History of Marine Aviation in World War II*, (Washington, 1952), hereinafter cited as *Marine Aviation History; TAF AR;* 2d MAW War Diary, April–July 1945; MAG–43 War Diary, April 1945; TAF Air Defense Command War Diary, May–July 1945.

[17] The first strike mission and first night fighter mission were both flown off Okinawa on 13 May. Fighter-bombers of VMF–441 attacked the airfield at Kikai Jima and night fighters of VMF(N)–543 hit targets on Amami-O-Shima.

MAJOR GENERAL FRANCIS P. MULCAHY, Commanding General, Tactical Air Force, Tenth Army, throughout most of the Okinawa campaign.

the potential of the Japanese for seriously interfering with the development program on Okinawa ceased to exist.

The most important element of TAF was Brigadier General William J. Wallace's Air Defense Command which controlled the air warning squadrons of MAG–43 and the Marine and Army fighter groups assigned to Tenth Army. General Wallace considered the *Kamikaze* menace to be his primary problem, and from 7 April when Corsairs of VMF–311 splashed TAF's first suicide plane while flying in to Yontan, the emphasis of his command was placed on meeting and stopping the destructive attacks. Tactical flights were airborne from Yontan and Kadena on the first day that squadrons of MAG–31 and –33 reached their new bases from CVE transports. Despite frequent bombing and shelling that damaged both planes and runways, aviation engineers and ground crews kept the fields operative and the planes aloft. Before the end of April TAF had flown 3,521 combat air patrol sorties and downed or helped to down 143 3/4 potential suiciders.

The tempo of air defense stepped up during May as additional planes from MAG–22 and the Army's 318th Fighter Group increased TAF strength. Long-range Army P–47's, rising from airfields on Ie Shima, hit Kyushu in the first of many attacks on 17 May. A barrier combat air patrol was established north of Okinawa, and more than 6,700 sorties were flown to protect troops on the island and picket ships on its defensive perimeter. Despite foul weather which severely hampered air operations and worked to the benefit of enemy raiders during much of May, the total of planes shot out of the air by TAF rose to 369. During the same period (7 April–31 May) only three American planes were shot down by Japanese pilots out of 109 aircraft lost to all causes including operational accidents.

Throughout June and especially after the termination of organized resistance on Okinawa, increasingly stronger attacks against Japanese bases were mounted. MAG–14 and the remaining two groups of the Army's 301st Fighter Wing were added to the TAF strength during the month. Unfortunately, General Mulcahy, who had commanded the joint Marine-Army aerial task force since its inception, was in such poor health that he was unable to finish out the campaign with his pilots. On 11 June, Major General Louis E. Woods assumed command of both TAF and the 2d Marine Aircraft Wing.

On 30 June the score card for air defense showed 600 Japanese planes shot down by TAF with 484½ kills credited to Marine squadrons. Only 41 Marine aircraft were reported lost to enemy air or antiaircraft action during the course of the campaign.[18]

Although the majority of the more than 29,000 sorties flown by planes of General Wallace's Air Defense Command were combat air patrols and far-ranging fighter sweeps, direct support of ground operations was an important part of the TAF mission. Plans for ICEBERG had provided that TAF would assume full responsibility for air defense of Okinawa as soon as the amphibious phase of the operation was ended. However, because of "the all out efforts of Japanese aircraft and the success of their *Kamikaze* suicide attacks directed against

---

[18] *Campaigns,* 331.

TWO DIVISIONS OF VMTB-232 fly over the scarred terrain of southern Okinawa while returning from a strike against Kiyamu Peninsula defenses

naval units, operational control of aircraft in the Ryukyus remained with the Navy until the area was secured." [19] As much as 60 per cent of ground support missions were flown by Navy and Marine [20] carrier pilots, while the Tenth Army's air force made its main effort against the *Kamikazes*. The allocation of planes—both land- and carrier-based—for each day's missions were made on board Admiral Turner's and later Admiral Hill's flagship by the Commander Air Support Control Units (CASCU) on the basis of intelligence reports and availability data furnished by subordinate commands.

To at least one TAF air group commander

"it seemed strange for planes off the carriers to come in for close support missions, passing Marine planes flying out for CAP duty, when it was the Marines who were supposed to be close support experts." [21] Even the CVE's *Block Island* and *Gilbert Islands*, which arrived in the Ryukyus in May with an all-Marine flight complement and a primary mission as designated by Admiral King of close troop support,[22] spent

---

[19] *Tenth Army AR*, Chap 11, Sect VII, 5.

[20] For the story of the operations of carrier-based Marine squadrons that supported the Okinawa operation see *Marine Aviation History*, 357–368.

[21] *Ibid.*, 386.

[22] Adm King had followed the recommendations of senior Marine troop commanders in the Marianas campaign (LtGen H. M. Smith, MajGen H. Schmidt, and MajGen R. S. Geiger) in designating four CVE's for close troop support with an all-Marine flight complement embarked. See Maj O. R. Lodge, *The Recapture of Guam*, MC Historical Monograph, (Washington, 1954), 109, 168.

A FULL SALVO of eight 5-inch rockets is fired by a Marine Corsair against an enemy target in northern Okinawa.

more time blasting targets in Sakishima Gunto than they did bombing and strafing ahead of Tenth Army lines. Rear Admiral Calvin C. Durgin, who commanded the escort carriers at Okinawa, provided a partial explanation of this anomaly when he pointed out that Navy CVE squadrons were similarly specially trained in close air support techniques and that:

> The advent of Marine Air Groups in CVE's should not be permitted to complicate the support carrier picture any more than is necessary. . . . Marine Air Groups should be and probably are as flexible as Navy squadrons and groups, and should remain so, and should expect no preferential treatment. To assign all Marine squadrons to direct support work would probably work to the detriment of morale of the Navy groups and squadrons and this command sees at present writing no reason for such assignments and has no intention of allowing it to occur.[23]

The aerial support of ground operations at Okinawa was handled through a smoothly functioning system of coordinating agencies. Once the operation was underway Marine Landing Force Air Support Control Units (LAFASCU's), commanded by Colonel Vernon E. Magee, acted as the representatives ashore of the Navy CASCU and relayed all orders con-

cerning aircraft direct to TAF. At Tenth Army headquarters LAFASCU-3 coordinated the work of LAFASCU-1 and -2 which handled the air support requests of IIIAC and XXIV Corps respectively. Front line direction of close support missions by both TAF and carrier aircraft was provided by Air Liaison Parties (ALP's) from the Joint Assault Signal Companies (JASCO's) attached to each division. LAFASCU-3 "screened all requests for air support of the ground troops and ordered Tactical Air Force to fulfill such of those missions as was consistent with the required Combat Air Patrol." [24]

Navy ASCU's on board amphibious force flagships directed 6,908 ground support sorties during the first days of April before the Marine control units were set up ashore. After the LAFASCU's took over they controlled 10,506 close support sorties during which carrier and TAF planes expended 4,725 tons of bombs, 37,653 5-inch rockets, and 1,116 tanks of napalm on enemy targets.

The value of close air support was proven repeatedly on Okinawa where "ground troops attacking with close air support were materially aided in taking enemy strong points." [25] The actual instances of bombing and strafing friendly troops were surprisingly few considering the quantities of flame and explosives dropped on the Japanese from a sky that seemed at times to be actually crowded with planes attacking targets as close as 100 yards [26] to American lines. Foul weather and the requirements of aerial defense limited the number of air support requests that could be granted.[27] Army units getting their first real taste of close air support were "insatiable in their demands" [28] for aerial attacks, matching the Marines in their enthusiasm for this tactic.

The senior Marine commanders, who had worked steadfastly throughout the Pacific War

---

[24] *TAF AR*, Chap 6, Sect III, 1.

[25] *7th InfDiv AR*, 42.

[26] *96th InfDiv History*, 154.

[27] IIIAC requested 704 air support missions and had 562 filled. *IIIAC AR*, Appendix 3, Summary of Air Support. XXIV Corps requested 945 missions and received 630. *XXIV Corps AR*, 47.

[28] Col V. E. Magee quoted in *Marine Aviation History*, 411.

---

[23] Quoted in *Marine Aviation History*, 397, which adds that "the core of this argument resembles nothing so much as the Army's thesis that 'anybody can do amphibious operations.' "

to increase the quality and quantity of close air support, were convinced that more extensive use of the Air Liaison Party at division, regimental, and battalion levels would sharply increase its effectiveness. They believed that the ALP's, with proper communication equipment and training, were capable of taking over control of strike groups from LAFASCU's and "talking" the pilots directly onto their targets.[29] The reason this procedure of direct ground-air communication and control between ALP's and planes (developed by the Marine Corps and utilized by the 1st and 6th Division in their training cycle) was not used was explained by Colonel Magee who commented that:

> . . . to have permitted each battalion liaison party to control striking aircraft on a corps front of only ten miles, when many simultaneous air strikes were being run, would obviously have led only to pandemonium and grave hazard for all concerned. On the other hand, where conditions approximated those in the Philippines, i. e., battalion or regimental actions in an uncrowded area, actual control of aircraft was frequently delegated to the air liaison party.[30]

The air support missions flown for Tenth Army by TAF were not limited to strikes against ground targets. Numerous observation flights were made to provide intelligence officers with first-hand information of enemy dispositions. The Army's 28th Photo Reconnaissance Squadron rephotographed the entire Okinawa Gunto area to help correct errors found on L-Day maps and provided assault commanders with large-scale aerial photographs of masked terrain features in their zones of action. Hundreds of air supply drops enabled assault troops to maintain the impetus of attack when terrain and weather cut off the front lines from regular supply channels.

Between 3 and 18 April 70 planeloads of ammunition, rations, and water, packaged and loaded by teams of the Air Delivery Section of

AIR DROP was often the only means by which front line troops could be supplied.

IIIAC, were parachuted from CVE-based torpedo bombers to isolated units of the 1st and 6th Marine Divisions. In the battle for southern Okinawa, two Marine squadrons, VMTB–232 (from 20 April) and VMTB–131 (from 30 May),[31] provided the planes and pilots that pinpointed air drop zones with 760 loads of vitally needed supplies for both Marine and Army units. In all, 495,257 pounds of variegated supplies were dropped with a 98 per cent recovery rate by ground troops.[32]

The contribution of these highly-skilled pilots and equally proficient air delivery specialists is evidenced by the letter of appreciation sent to Major Allen L. Feldmeier and the members of VMTB–232 by General del Valle on behalf of the 1st Marine Division. In it he noted that during the period 30 May–9 June his assault

[29] *IIIAC AR*, 197–198; *1st MarDiv SAR*, Air Support Annex; *6th MarDiv SAR, Ph I&II*, Part X, 24–26.

[30] Quoted in J. A. Isely and P. A. Crowl, *The U. S. Marines and Amphibious War*, (Princeton, 1951), 567, hereinafter cited as *The U. S. Marines and Amphibious War*. For the story of Marine close air support in the recapture of the Philippines, see Maj C. W. Boggs, Jr., *Marine Aviation in the Philippines*, MC Historical Monograph, (Washington, 1951).

[31] The TBF's of these squadrons were included in TAF primarily for antisubmarine warfare, but VMTB–232 was not equipped with essential sound ranging gear and the job of day antisubmarine patrol was taken over by Kerama-based seaplanes until VMTB–131 arrived at the target.

[32] Air Delivery Sect, IIIAC H&S Bn AR, ICEBERG, 24 Jun 45, 1–3.

units were almost entirely supplied by air deliveries and that the "unerring accuracy of VMTB–232 in making drops during all types of weather and enemy fire contributed immeasurably to the continued advance of this division during a period when supply routes were impassable."[33]

On 24 June, General Geiger, a naval aviator himself, culminated the stream of commendatory messages that flooded TAF from ships and ground units when he wrote to General Woods that the air support provided by TAF was "outstanding, and contributed materially to a speedy and successful completion of the campaign."[34]

Between 7 April, when the first Corsair of MAG–31 touched down on Yontan airfield, and 30 June when it had over 750 planes under its control, TAF swelled enormously to meet the constantly changing pattern of air operations in the Ryukyus. At the end of the third month of the Okinawa operation, General Woods commanded a Marine Aircraft Wing with four fighter groups, an Army Fighter Wing with three groups, and a Bomber Command with one light, one medium,[35] and two heavy bomb groups assigned.

The character of the air war in the Ryukyus shifted swiftly from fighter defense to bomber offense after the completion of the ground campaign on Okinawa. On 14 July, its mission completed, TAF was dissolved, and the Far Eastern Air Force assumed control of the widening span of attacks against Japan.

ISLAND COMMAND ACTIVITIES [36]

Major General Fred C. Wallace's Island Command had perhaps the most complex task of any major element of Tenth Army participating in ICEBERG. It had the concurrent missions of providing administrative and logistical support of combat operations, executing the Cin-

CPOA base development plan, and assuming, as directed by the Commanding General, Tenth Army, the responsibility for garrison and defense of Okinawa and its outlying islands. In order to accomplish these diversified assignments, Island Command was set up as the controlling and coordinating agency of a vast multipurpose joint task force. In much the same manner that the Air Defense Command encompassed a large part of TAF's groups and squadrons, Island Command directed the efforts of a substantial portion of Tenth Army's service and support troops. "In effect, Island Command [operated] as a combined Army Service Area and advance section of a Communication Zone."[37]

As the area of active combat steadily decreased, the scope of command delegated by Tenth Army to General Wallace correspondingly increased. By the end of June he controlled 153,000 men and was responsible for the defense and development of every major island in the Okinawa Gunto.[38] Reporting to him were the commanding officers of the Naval Operating Base, Joint Communication Activities, Hydrographic Survey, Army and Navy Air Bases, Construction Troops, Military Government, and Ground Defense Forces. In addition to these type commands, General Wallace exercised control over a considerable body of service troops assigned directly to his headquarters.

The cancellation of Phase III operations against Miyako and Kikai Shima late in April transferred the bulk of base development operations and troops slated for other islands in the Ryukyus to Okinawa. Revised plans called for

---

[33] 2d MAW War Diary, June 1945, 3. Showing the versatility of the TBF pilots and the various types of jobs they performed, this same squadron received a letter of commendation from the CG, XXIV Corps for "the outstanding performance, excellent cooperation, and enthusiasm which VMTB–232 has shown in accomplishing close support, heckler, and observation missions." *Ibid.*

[34] *Ibid.,* 9.

[35] The B–25's of the 47th and 48th BombSqn(M) of the 41st BombGrp(M) arrived on Okinawa on 28 June and the first strike on Kyushu, escorted by P–47's of the 301st FtrWing, was made on 1 July.

[36] Unless otherwise noted the material in this section is derived from *IsCom AR;* MilGovtSect, IsCom, Histories of MilGovtOpns on Okinawa, April-August 1945; *27th InfDiv OpRpt.*

[37] *Tenth Army AR,* Chap 11, Sect XXVI, 1.

[38] Izena Shima to the north of Okinawa was scouted on 23 June by patrols of the 2d MarDiv RcnCo operating from its base on Iheya Shima. No enemy soldiers were found and the 4,000 civilians were reported to be friendly in attitude. The island passed to IsCom control on 24 June. On 29 June, Kume Shima, seized by the FMF AmphRcnBn (Reinf), came under IsCom.

TRAFFIC CIRCLE south of Kadena airfield handled as many as 20,000 vehicles a day by mid-August.

double the number of airfields originally scheduled and a corresponding increase in supply installations and troop staging, rehabilitation, and training areas. However, until the enemy Thirty-second Army was destroyed, first priority on the services of Island Command units was given to direct combat support of Tenth Army air and ground operations.

As an instance of this singleness of purpose, General Buckner directed all airfield construction units to concentrate on maintenance of supply roads during the period of heavy rains in late May and early June when mud threatened to halt the Tenth Army attack. Despite such delays incident to the weather, the first American-built airstrip on Okinawa, a 7,000-foot runway at Yontan, was completed by 17 June. Before the end of the month five airfields were

operational and eight of the 18 proposed and sited were in the process of rehabilitation or construction to meet the demands of a burgeoning bomber force.

The engineering task of the construction troops of Island Command during the campaign was not confined to air base development and road maintenance. Over 160 miles of existing native roads were widened to take two-lane traffic, and 37 miles of new two-, three-, and four-lane highway were built to accommodate the increasing load of supply and troop traffic. New beaches were opened, piers constructed, and dump areas cleared to handle the supply buildup. A water system adequate for the needs of hundreds of thousands of soldiers and civilians was developed. Pipelines and tank farms capable of handling vast quantities of aviation gas to meet current and projected needs were built. A good start was made on the job of constructing the hundreds of headquarters, hospital, and storage buildings necessary for operations against Japan.

Island Command's responsibilities became so complex as the campaign progressed that they defy complete description. For example, elements of General Wallace's organization handled such widely separated tasks for Tenth Army as the maintenance of communications with higher headquarters, the processing of casualties evacuated by air and sea, the handling of all classes of supply from ship to combat boundaries, and the administration of enemy civilians and control of prisoners of war. In short, Island Command eventually became responsible for every logistical task necessary for the successful continuation of Tenth Army combat operations.

After the end of organized resistance, the emphasis of the logistical effort shifted to preparation for future operations. Tremendous areas were pre-empted in southern Okinawa and on Motobu Peninsula for base development, which substantially altered the pre-invasion topography and way of life on the island. For the duration of the war, at least, much of the arable land and many of the most heavily populated areas were lost to the native inhabitants, who became, in effect, wards of Island Command.

Military government, as it operated on Okinawa, was, like so many Tenth Army activities, a joint service effort. The JCS had assigned the task of governing the Ryukyus to the Navy, but Admiral Nimitz requested and received permission for the Army to assume that responsibility since ICEBERG would be primarily an Army effort once the amphibious phase was over. Although the War Department was unable to provide sufficient trained personnel to take over the entire military government operation, it provided 183 officers including the Deputy Commander for Military Government, Brigadier General William E. Crist, and the Navy furnished the remainder of the officers and all of the enlisted men necessary to operate the various teams at division, corps, and army level.

27TH DIVISION PATROL scouts a stream bed during the three-month mop-up drive in northern Okinawa. (Army Photograph)

During the initial stages of ground combat, military government on Okinawa took on the aspect of a "disaster relief operation—food, water, clothing, shelter, medical care, and sanitation—and evacuation of civilians with speed from the fighting front to rear areas, so as not to hamper military operations" [39] was the primary consideration. In this situation, the talents of many specialists in civil government processes, assigned to teams at corps and division level, were not adequately realized. As the area of actual combat diminished and the civilian population was concentrated in northern Okinawa, strong efforts were made to develop a self-sustaining economy and to reinstitute most normal civil governmental functions with an increasing participation by the Okinawans themselves.

Largely because of the fairness and decency of military government personnel in dealing with the natives, the Okinawans overcame their Japanese-inspired fear of Americans and were surprisingly cooperative. "A deep impression was made by American failure to discriminate against the poor and ragged," [40] and the strict impartiality of treatment that characterized military government operations. The magnitude of the task performed by the few hundred men assigned to military government agencies

---

[39] *Tenth Army AR*, Chap 11, Sect XXVII, 3–4.

[40] History of MilGovtOpns on Okinawa, July 1945, 31Aug45, 8.

can be gauged by the fact that 261,115 civilians were in their charge on 30 June 1945 and an additional 100,000 before the end of the war.

General Wallace's mission of garrison and defense of occupied areas involved considerable mopping-up operations that assumed at times the magnitude of pitched battles. Most of the resistance was encountered on Okinawa proper where the 27th Infantry Division was the main garrison force, but enemy outbreaks occurred from time to time in Kerama Retto also.[41]

On 2 May when the 27th Division officially passed to Island Command control, the 165th Infantry was assigned responsibility for the former 1st Marine Division sector, and the 105th and 106th [42] Infantry were sent north to relieve the 6th Marine Division on Motobu Peninsula and in the areas farther north. The next two weeks were spent in intensive patrolling, assisting military government teams in the collection of civilians, and in blowing caves and prepared positions found within zones of responsibility. Gradually the toll of Japanese killed rose from an average of three or four to 15 a day, and increasing evidence of recently occupied assembly and bivouac areas was found. The decision was made to make a thorough sweep of northern Okinawa and clean out the remaining Japanese.

On 17 and 18 May the regiments, leaving small detachments behind to protect their bivouac areas, assembled at the base of the Ishikawa Isthmus and on 19 May began a sweep northward with three regiments abreast. Five days later the men had reached Onna Take, a heavily forested 1,000-foot hill mass in the center of the island just north of the isthmus. The Japanese had extensively fortified the area, and the 106th and 165th Infantry fought a ten-day battle in the rain without artillery or air support

to reduce the position. When 1/165 and 1/106 finally broke through the defenses they found 195 bodies and the evidence that the enemy had buried many more. Others of the strong point's garrison had escaped northward, and the 27th Division's drive continued.

When the fighting in the south of Okinawa ended, the 27th was still sweeping Motobu Peninsula, soon to be the rest camp and training area of the 1st Marine Division. It was 4 August before the mop-up campaign was completed at Hedo Misaki and the division was able to move down out of the hills to return to its bivouac area. Over 1,000 Japanese had been killed and 500 captured in the course of the operation.[43]

TACTICAL EVALUATION[44]

The Okinawa operation represents "the culmination of amphibious development in the Pacific War." [45] Before it was ended "more ships were used, more troops put ashore, more supplies transported, more bombs dropped, more naval guns fired against shore targets" [46] than in any previous campaign. But even the staggering wealth of data regarding ICEBERG can not obscure the trenchant demonstration of the validity of fundamental amphibious doctrine. As General Geiger pointed out, the battle for Okinawa "reemphasized most clearly that our basic principles of tactics and technique are sound, are 'in the book,' and need only to be followed in combat." [47]

Interservice cooperation was the keystone of success at Okinawa where "Army artillery supported Marine infantry and vice versa," where "Marine and Army planes were used interchangeably and operated under the same tactical command," where "each contiguous infantry unit was mutually supporting and interdependent," and where "the Navy's participation was

---

[41] On 23 May 2/305 was relieved as the garrison of Kerama Retto by a provisional infantry battalion formed from the 870th AAA(AW) Bn. The former AAA men were given some infantry training by experienced 27th InfDiv officers and NCO's and operated against the numerous survivors of the sea raiding battalions hidden out in the rugged hills of the island group until the end of the war.

[42] The 106th InfRegt operated throughout the mop-up of northern Okinawa without its 2d Bn, which relieved elements of the 305th Inf as the garrison force for Ie Shima on 6 May.

[43] *27th InfDiv History*, 649.

[44] Unless otherwise noted the material in this section is derived from *U. S. Marines and Amphibious War; Tenth Army AR; IIIAC AR; XXIV Corps AR; 1st MarDiv SAR; 6th MarDiv SAR, Ph I&II; 6th MarDiv SAR, Ph III.*

[45] *U. S. Marines and Amphibious War*, 551.

[46] *Ibid.*

[47] *IIIAC AR*, 194.

vital to both throughout." [48] Instrumental in ensuring the most efficient utilization of the power of the various supporting agencies was the Tenth Army's system of centralization of target information and assignment.

At each staff level down to the battalion, the artillery officer acted as the target coordinator for infantry support. Working in close conjunction with the NGF and air liaison officers, and using the facilities of a Target Information Center which collated intelligence regarding enemy defenses, he allocated fire missions to the support elements whose capabilities promised the most effective results. The system stood the test of combat without major difficulties and drew unanimous praise from the divisions using it and a recommendation from Tenth Army that it be adopted for all future amphibious operations.[49]

The majority of ground support missions assigned to TAF planes were pre-planned and did not come as a result of ALP requests. Strikes were usually asked for and assigned through the LAFASCU's well in advance to allow, where possible, thorough target briefing. As the strength of *Kamikaze* attacks gradually waned in May and June, more planes became available to ground units and the tempo of close air support stepped up considerably.

The main complaint of the assault battalions concerned the length of time which elapsed between request and execution of a mission. Because the ALP's could not enter the Support Air Direction (SAD) net linking LAFASCU's and strike groups, but had to relay their information for the pilots through the control units, many lucrative but fleeting targets escaped aerial destruction. Although Tenth Army did not go as far as the Marine units in recommending more extensive use of ALP's, it did call for authorization for the ALP's to enter the SAD

net "in an emergency or when necessary to give information to flight units." [50]

The role of aerial supply drops in sustaining isolated front line assault units impressed Tenth Army with the need for the formation of a unit similar to the III Corps Air Delivery Section to work with each field army or independent corps. At the same time Tenth Army recommended the disbandment of the JASCO's that were assigned to each assault division. The marked dissimilarity of training and duties between the various components of these signal companies pointed to more efficient operations if separate air liaison, naval gunfire, and shore party communication units were formed. The NGF spotting and liaison teams were singled out for special commendation because of their competence in handling the tremendous volume of naval shells fired at shore targets.

Approximately 579,000 rounds from 5-inch or greater caliber naval rifles were expended in shore bombardment on Okinawa. On L-Day alone, in "the heaviest concentration of naval gunfire ever delivered in support of the landing of troops," [51] 3,800 tons of shells from battleships, cruisers, and destroyers, and from the rocket racks and mortars of support craft, exploded ashore. Throughout the campaign naval support was readily available to assault units, with ships of TF 54 (later TF 34) alternating between ammunition resupply at Kerama Retto and shore bombardment at Okinawa. At least one call fire ship and one illumination ship were assigned to each front line regiment during most of the campaign, and on occasion, such as the 6th Marine Division's drive into northern Okinawa, each assault battalion had a destroyer on call.

Because fire support ships were not rotated to the screen but remained on station, their value increased as their gunnery officers and ground and aerial observers became increasingly familiar with the Okinawa terrain and the character of enemy defenses. In most cases, especially when ships were firing directly on observed targets, the high velocity, flat trajectory, and destructive power of the naval rifles enabled them to disrupt enemy activities and neutralize

[48] *U. S. Marines and Amphibious War*, 578.

[49] Regarding this fire support system, the CO of the 11th Mar commented that "for the first time in the Pacific, coordination of naval gunfire and air support with artillery was prescribed in army orders, a forerunner of the present FSCC [Fire Support Coordination Center]. Examination of the records will show that each division and corps, Army and Marine, used a different modification of it. It is worthy of note that the system used by the First Marine Division was most like what we have today." *Brown*.

[50] *Tenth Army AR*, Chap 10, Sect III, 5.

[51] *Ibid.*, Chap 11, Sect V, 6.

his installations. However, even the weight of broadsides from battleship main batteries was insufficient to penetrate many of the enemy cave positions. The task of reducing the intricate network of deeply dug-in defenses was impossible for any single supporting arm to accomplish. Even the artillery, which used every expedient including the use of antiaircraft guns and LVT(A) howitzers to supplement regular fires, were stymied continually by the impenetrability of the Shuri and Kiyamu fortifications.

During most of the battle for southern Okinawa, the artillery battalions of all six divisions were in line to support the attack. While infantry units were rotated on the front lines, artillery outfits stayed in position and maintained a constant drumfire of support. Marine and Army corps artillery provided 12 battalions for general support to reinforce the fires of the 24 divisional battalions. In addition, IIIAC organized, trained, and used its two LVT(A) battalions as field artillery, giving each the equivalent reinforcing power of a four-battalion regiment of 75mm howitzers.

During the campaign field artillery battalions alone fired 1,766,352 rounds [52] in support of the infantry. The governing factor in the assignment of artillery units to general and direct support roles was need. The centralized fire direction and target assignment system enabled artillery officers to mass the fires of all guns within range of any given target in minimum time. Coordination between Marine and Army units was exceptional, and a pervading spirit of cooperation placed the protection and support of the infantryman ahead of all other considerations.

The strength of the Japanese defenses on Okinawa and the expectation that future ground operations against the enemy home islands would call for vastly increased firepower led Tenth Army to recommend a heavy increase in Corps artillery. In addition to a field artillery observation battalion and four group headquarters and headquarters batteries, the proposed new strength included the following firing battalions: one 105mm howitzer (self-propelled); three 155mm howitzer; one 155mm howitzer (self-propelled); two 155mm gun; one 155mm gun (self-propelled); two 8-inch howitzer; one 8-inch howitzer (self-propelled); and one 240mm howitzer. Both the self-propelled units and the additional heavy artillery were added to meet the threat of naturally strong cave positions which were best reduced by direct fire of the heaviest calibers. General Geiger, impressed by the penetrating and destructive power of the 200-pound shells of the 8-inch howitzer as compared to the 95-pound rounds of 155mm weapons, asked for the inclusion of 8-inch battalions in Marine Corps artillery in future campaigns against the Japanese.

The attack on heavily fortified enemy positions is an example of teamwork, or rather the work of many interrelated teams, such as the air-NGF-artillery team, the infantry-tank-artillery team, the infantry-engineer team, and the tank-artillery team. But the partnership of actual assault operations is shared primarily by the tank and the infantryman. On Okinawa, in the judgment of General Shepherd, "if any one supporting arm can be singled out as having contributed more than any others during the progress of the campaign, the tank would certainly be selected." [53] The Marine general was supported in his opinion by the commander of the Japanese Thirty-second Army who issued a battle lesson which stated that "the enemy's power lies in his tanks. It has become obvious that our general battle against the American forces is a battle against their M–1 and M–4 tanks." [54]

Tenth Army units lost 153 tanks to all causes during the battle for Okinawa. The loss figure to Japanese action undoubtedly would have been much higher had accompanying infantrymen not been charged with the protection of the tanks from enemy attackers. An elaborate Japanese plan for destroying armored vehicles by close-in assault with hand-thrown mines and demolition charges failed miserably in the face of infantry covering fire. Only seven tanks from the five Army battalions in Okinawa were

---

[52] The breakdown by type shows: 75mm How—166,068; 105mm How—1,104,630; 155mm How—346,914; 155mm Gun—129,624; 8-inch How—19,116.

[53] *6th MarDiv SAR, Ph III*, Part III, 28.

[54] Quoted in the preface to *1st MarDiv SAR*, Tank Support Annex.

initially put out of action by individual attackers, while the 6th Marine Division had only three disabled, and the 1st Marine Division reported no tanks lost because "the alertness of the covering infantry and the tank crews prevented the successful completion of these attacks." [55]

Armor was used entirely as an infantry weapon on Okinawa, and the one time the tanks attempted to operate without infantry support, during the 27th Division's attack at Kakazu Ridge on 19 April, the results were disastrous. The success of the tank-infantry team was due to the stress laid in training and in combat on mutual cooperation: the tank supported and protected the infantryman and vice versa. When the heavy rainfall of late May prevented tank support of assault battalions, Tenth Army's attack on the Shuri defenses bogged down.

Companies of the Army's 713th Armored Flamethrower Battalion, the first of its type to be formed and see sustained action, supported both Marine and Army units in Okinawa, eliciting only the highest praise for a "consistently outstanding record of performance." [56] Covered by the fire of infantry and standard medium tanks, the flame tanks were particularly effective in burning out enemy positions in rocky crags, on reverse slopes, and in the fortified ruins of villages. Both IIIAC and XXIV Corps recommended increased use of the armored flame throwers, with General Hodge asking for the attachment of two battalions in future operations and General Geiger recommending that a company of these tanks be made organic to each Marine tank battalion.

Another Army supporting weapon which found favor with the Marine infantrymen was the 4.2-inch chemical mortar. Each division of IIIAC had a company of these heavy mortars attached to furnish high angle fire on targets which were not suitable for artillery howitzers or 81mm mortars. The accuracy, long-range, and terrific destructive power of the rifled mortars convinced General del Valle that each Marine division should add a 4.2-inch mortar company to its T/O.

The battle for Okinawa was not marked by startling innovations in infantry tactical methods. As General Geiger reported: "No new or unusual features of infantry combat were disclosed or developed during the campaign on Okinawa which would tend to modify or annul current standard principles or doctrines." [57] Aspects of the Okinawan fighting frequently cited as new developments in the Pacific War, like the extensive use of night attacks and the refinement of tank-infantry tactics, were merely logical applications of existing combat principles stemming from increased familiarity with the enemy and his methods of fighting. In the final analysis the success of battle rested on the quality of the individual infantryman and his training. American material and numerical superiority was insufficient to root the enemy out of his massively strong defenses without prohibitive losses unless the infantryman was thoroughly trained to operate with maximum effectiveness as a member of an assault team.

Trained infantrymen were at a premium on Okinawa once the fighting intensified before Shuri. Replacements that came in during the campaign were often insufficiently trained to take their places in the front lines, yet had to be used to fill the ranks of hard-hit assault units. Attempts were made to give the new men battle indoctrination and unit orientation before they met the enemy and to feed them into their new organizations in periods when these were in reserve. However, the exigencies of the combat situation often dictated that replacements enter combat before they were completely "shaken down" into their units.

In the case of IIIAC where General Geiger "had only two divisions to fight," it was impossible to effect the "relief of front line divisions for rest and assimilation of replacements." The use of the triangular organization of a corps for extended operations provided an "automatic reserve," and without it the Marine

---

[55] *Ibid.*, 23–24.

[56] *Ibid.*, 41. All standard tank battalions on Okinawa had some tanks equipped with small flame throwers of limited range capable of firing through either the bow gunner's or a periscope mount. Of the three types used, the gun tube flame thrower of the 713th TkBn was considered "an all around better weapon and the most practicable of the three." *Tenth Army AR*, Chap 11, Sect IX, 12.

[57] *IIIAC AR*, 103.

divisions had to remain on line in assault continually. A corps of at least three divisions was considered necessary for maximum effectiveness in any future operations that had the features of infantry combat on Okinawa.[58]

The practice of Marine divisions training replacement drafts with infantry units and then taking them to the target as shore party labor until casualties forced their use as infantry was duly noted by the understrength divisions of XXIV Corps. Although the 1st and 6th Marine Divisions were severely hampered by the limited training of replacements arriving during the later stages of the campaign, the replacement drafts which accompanied the divisions to the target were quickly integrated when the need for them arose. Tenth Army recommended that each Army division in future operations include a strong replacement company which had been trained with its parent unit. XXIV Corps went further and asked that infantry battalions be allowed to carry a 25 per cent overage of strength to the target and that balanced 1,000-men battalions of infantry replacements be attached to and loaded out with each division.

The concern with the infantry replacement system reflected the high degree of training necessary to make the assault operations of a complex military unit effective. The teamwork of infantry and supporting arms was vital to victory on Okinawa and in the words of Tenth Army's final action report:

The support rendered the infantry by naval gunfire, artillery, air and tanks was adequate in every respect. Without such magnificent support, little progress could have been made by the infantry in their advance against the heavily organized enemy positions in southern Okinawa. Supporting fires enabled the infantry to carry out the tremendous task of repeated assaults against strongly fortified positions.[59]

KEY TO CONQUEST [60]

Fleet Admiral King in his post-victory report to the Secretary of the Navy observed that "the outstanding development of this war, in the field of joint undertakings, was the perfection of amphibious operations, the most difficult of all operations in modern warfare." [61] ICEBERG was the culmination of that development in the Pacific, but it was merely a foretaste of the operations that were planned against Japan itself. Okinawa was destined to play a major part in these operations as a staging and supporting base, thereby more than justifying the heavy cost of its capture in human lives.

In the fall of 1945, a three-pronged assault on southern Kyushu, code-named OLYMPIC, was to be mounted by the Sixth Army with ten infantry divisions and three Marine divisions (2d, 3d, and 5th). Early in the spring of 1946, operation CORONET was planned to bring the Eighth and Tenth Armies ashore in assault on the Tokyo Plain, with the First Army transshipped from Europe to furnish a ten-division reserve. In CORONET, the 1st and 6th Marine Divisions together with the 4th Marine Division were to strike the Japanese again as part of IIIAC.

By the beginning of August 1945 Tenth Army had lost a large part of its striking force as infantry units were shifted to other islands in the Pacific for rest, rehabilitation, and training. The 77th Division and part of the 96th were in the Philippines, and headquarters of IIIAC and the whole of the 6th Division were located in the Marianas. The time of the combat troops remaining on Okinawa was divided between routine mopping-up activities and preparations for the coming assault on Japan.

The influx of garrison, service, and support troops kept pace with the departure of infantry units as southern Okinawa assumed the aspects of a vast supply and munitions dump. Fleet logistical operations at Kerama Retto were rapidly transferred to Chimu Wan and Buckner Bay [62] after 1 July as construction battalions

---

[60] Unless otherwise noted the material in this section is derived from *War Reports*; 1st Information and Historical Service, Documents Relating to the Surrender of Japanese Garrison in the Ryukyus and the Occupation of that Area by Elements of the Tenth Army, September and October 1945, 9Dec45, hereinafter cited as *Surrender Documents*.

[61] *War Reports*, 658.

[62] Early in July Nakagusuku Wan was renamed Buckner Bay in honor of the deceased Tenth Army commander. RAdm W. R. Carter, *Beans, Bullets, and Black Oil*, (Washington, 1953), 365.

---

[58] *Ibid.*, 195.

[59] *Tenth Army AR*, Chap 11, Sect IX, 1.

SURRENDER of all Japanese Forces in the Ryukyus takes place on 7 September at Tenth Army Headquarters. (Army Photograph)

worked feverishly to complete the development of naval operating base installations. It is doubtful if the assault troops that landed on 1 April would have recognized their battleground by August, for the topography of Okinawa underwent a drastic change as soon as engineers could turn their full attention from combat support to base development activities. Hills were leveled and ravines filled, and enormous storage areas came into being where Americans and Japanese had struggled short weeks before. New highways interlaced the island, connecting the camps, airfields, dumps, and headquarters that studded the altered landscape.

As the preparations to support projected amphibious operations against Japan kept pace with target schedules, the fury of aerial destruction mounted from Okinawa increased. By mid-August the Far Eastern Air Force had four heavy bomber, five light and medium bomber, and nine fighter groups striking the enemy homeland. Plans called for 47 groups, including 12 of B-29's, to be based on Okinawa in time to support OLYMPIC.

The news of the dropping of atomic bombs on Hiroshima and Nagasaki came with startling suddenness in the midst of all-out war preparations. On 10 August, "at 2113 hours a spontaneous celebration broke out all over Okinawa when the local radio station interrupted its evening musical broadcast program with a dramatic announcement that Japan desired to surrender under the terms of the Potsdam Declaration."[63] Offensive operations continued unchecked, however, until the last day of the war to emphasize to the Japanese that delay in meeting the ultimatum of unconditional surrender would be disastrous. The end of nearly four years of bitter fighting in the Pacific was signaled on Okinawa early on the morning of 15 August. Acting on directive from higher headquarters, the commander of the 7th Air Force messaged his subordinate tactical groups to "cancel all missions against Japan. Recall all airborne aircraft."[64] The war with Japan was over.

On all the conquered islands of the Pacific wide distribution was given to the Imperial Rescript ordering the Japanese to lay down their arms. Intensive efforts were made to persuade enemy holdouts to surrender and prevent needless bloodshed. On Okinawa, as the word of defeat was gradually spread and believed, hundreds of enemy soldiers and sailors turned themselves in to Tenth Army forces. Large organized groups[65] surrendered near Machinato, Kunishi, Nago, Oroku, and Mabuni during August and September. Stragglers continued to come in for months after the fighting ended. After the war, surviving officers of the Thirty-second Army, using Japanese demobilization records, estimated that approximately 10,000 Japanese Army and Navy personnel and 8,000 Okinawans (*Boeitai* and conscripts) had survived the battle for Okinawa.[66]

On 26 August 1945, General of the Army MacArthur, appointed Supreme Allied Commander in the Pacific to accept the Japanese surrender, authorized General Stilwell to negotiate the capitulation of enemy garrisons in the Ryukyus. In accordance with Stilwell's orders, the top enemy commanders appeared at Tenth Army headquarters on 7 September to sign "unconditional surrender documents representing the complete capitulation of the Ryukyus Islands and over 105,000 Army and Navy forces."[67] Appropriately enough, the ten-minute surrender ceremony took place in the presence of representative Army and Marine infantry and tank platoons while hundreds of planes flashed by overhead.

When surrender teams were organized to supervise the actual disarmament of enemy garrisons, their infantry components were made up of converted AAA battalions. The combat troops that had seized Okinawa Gunto had been chosen to take part in the occupation of Japan and Korea and the repatriation of Japanese troops from North China. The 4th Marines of the 6th Division, inheritors of the name and traditions of the regiment captured at Corregidor, went ashore at Yokosuka Naval Base on 30 August, three days before the formal surrender ceremony aboard the USS *Missouri*. The remainder of IIIAC was sent to China in late September and early October: corps headquarters and the 1st Division to Tientsin and Peiping and the 6th Division (less the 4th Marines) to Tsingtao. The 27th Division was airlifted to Honshu and the 7th Division, as the advance force of the XXIV Corps was shipped to Korea in September.

The transfer of control of the Nansei Shoto to the United States in the brief surrender ceremony at Tenth Army headquarters on 7 September 1945 marked the beginning of a new era of American influence in the Pacific. Okinawa and its satellites in the Ryukyus, wrested from the Japanese at heavy cost, were entrusted to American hands by the United Nations. The strategic position of the islands in relation to China, Japan, and the Philippines, their potential in terms of airfields, anchorages, and forward supply bases, made them too important to relinquish in the face of unsettled world conditions. Okinawa's post-war destiny was to serve as the western bastion of the defenses of the United States.

[63] HqSqn, Air Defense Command–2 War Diary, August 1945.

[64] 2d MAW War Diary, August 1945, 5.

[65] On 28Aug45 the commander of the enemy 32d Regt brought in 55 officers, 342 enlisted men, and 105 civilians who had been hiding out in caves in the Itoman-Kunishi area. Tenth Army G–2 Weekly Summary, 26Aug–1Sept45, in Tenth Army G–3 Jnl and File, 6Sept45.

[66] *Okinawa Operations Record*, 125. On 15Sept45 the official total of POW's was 10,988 combat and 3,842 labor troops. Tenth Army G–3 Weekly Summary, 9–15Sept45, in Tenth Army G–3 Jnl and File, 19Sept45.

[67] News Release contained in *Surrender Documents*.

APPENDIX I

Bibliography

OKINAWA: VICTORY IN THE PACIFIC

The main sources consulted in the preparation of the narrative of the Okinawa operation have been the reports, journals, war diaries, orders, and plans of the units involved. Descriptions of specific actions have been based mainly on the records of the units most directly concerned. In general, the lowest echelons have been considered the best source for details, while the reports of higher units familiar with overall concepts have been used in evaluating progress and results.

More than 200 key participants in the campaign, including representatives of all the services, have been asked to read the preliminary drafts of the narrative. The resulting comments, corrections, and additions have been included in the final manuscript after careful checking against contemporary records. The majority of the draft comment has been supplementary in nature and has not substantially altered the picture presented by official sources.

Much of the material consulted had only a very general or indirect bearing on the progress of the campaign and therefore, is not listed in the bibliography. Only the most useful sources, including all those cited in the text, have been included below. Material marked (OCMH) is held by the Office of the Chief of Military History, Department of the Army. Material marked (TAGO) can be obtained from The Adjutant General's Office, Department of the Army. Copies of all other material listed are available in the Records and Research Section, Historical Branch, G–3 Division, Headquarters, U. S. Marine Corps.

DOCUMENTS

Joint Chiefs of Staff Documents, Letters, and Notes Relating to the CAUSEWAY, DETACHMENT, and ICEBERG Campaigns, Compiled by LtCol Whitman S. Bartley.

Chief of Naval Operations 34–P–0700, Amphibious Operations—Capture of Okinawa, 27Mar–21Jun45, dtd 22Jan46.

Military Intelligence Service, War Department, Survey of the Nansei Shoto and the Nanpo Shoto, dtd 15Feb43.

CinCPac–CinCPOA Operations in the Pacific Ocean Areas During the month of October 1944, dtd 31May 45; November 1944, dtd 1Jun45; December 1944, dtd 25Jun45.

CinCPac–CinCPOA Bulletin 161–44, Okinawa Gunto, dtd 15Nov44.

CinCPac–CinCPOA Bulletin 53–45, Okinawa Gunto, 2d Supplement, dtd 28Feb45.

CinCPac–CinCPOA Bulletin 107–45, Translations and Interrogations No 28, dtd 14May45.

CinCPac–CinCPOA Bulletin 122–45, Translations and Interrogations No 30, dtd 1Jun45.

CinCPac–CinCPOA Bulletin 140–45, Translations and Interrogations No 31, dtd 7Jun45.

CinCPac–CinCPOA Bulletin 147–45, Translations and Interrogations No 32, dtd 16Jun45.

CinCPac–CinCPOA Bulletin 161–45, Translations and Interrogations No 34, dtd 27Jun45.

CinCPac–CinCPOA Bulletin 212–45, Translations and Interrogations No 39, dtd 30Aug45.

CinCPOA Joint Staff Study—ICEBERG, dtd 25Oct44, with Changes of 2Dec44, 21Dec44, 5Feb45, and 28Feb45.

CinCPOA Operation Plan No 14–44, dtd 21Nov44.

United States Army Forces, Pacific Ocean Areas, Participation in the Okinawa Operation, 2 vols, dtd 15Mar46.

United States Army Forces, Pacific Ocean Areas, G–2 Study of Okinawa Gunto, n. d.

United States Army Forces, Middle Pacific, History of the G–5 Section, 7Dec41–2Sept45, n. d. (OCMH).

Commander Amphibious Forces, Pacific, Amphibious Gunnery Bulletin No 2, Assault on Okinawa, dtd 24May45.

Headquarters, Aircraft, Fleet Marine Force, Pacific, Air Support Reports of Units Participating in the Okinawa Operation, dtd 28Aug45.

Engineer Section, Fleet Marine Force, Pacific, Engineer Intelligence Information, Okinawa Gunto, n. d.

Amphibious Reconnaissance Battalion, Fleet Marine Force, Pacific, Action Report, Phase I, Nansei Shoto Operation, dtd 10May45; Action Report, Phase II, Nansei Shoto Operation, n. d.; Action Report, Assault and Occupation of Kume Shima, dtd 15Aug45.

Commander Fifth Fleet Action Report, 1Apr–27May 45, Ryukyus Operation, dtd 10Jul45.

Commander Fifth Fleet Operation Plan No 1–45, dtd 11Jan45.

Commander Task Force 51 Operation Report, FORAGER, dtd 25Aug45.

Commander Task Force 51 General Action Report, Capture of Okinawa Gunto, Phases I and II, 17Feb–17May45, dtd 25Jul45.

Commander Task Force 51 Operation Plan A1–45, dtd 16Feb45.

Commander Task Force 52 Action Report, Okinawa Gunto, 21Mar–20Apr45, dtd 1May45.

Commander Task Force 52 Operation Plan No A106–45, dtd 5Mar45.

Commander Task Force 53 Report of Participation in the Capture of Okinawa Gunto—Phases I and II, dtd 20Jul45.

Commander Task Force 55 Report of the Capture of Okinawa Gunto, Phase I and II, 14Mar–9Jun45, dtd 31Jul45.

Commander Fifth Amphibious Force Action Report, Capture of Okinawa Gunto, Phases I and II, 17May–21Jun45, dtd 4Jul45.

Commander Task Group 51.1 Action Report, Capture of Okinawa Gunto, Phases 1 and 2, 9Mar–2Apr45, dtd 26May45.

Tenth Army Action Report, Ryukyus Campaign, 26Mar–30Jun45, dtd 3Sept45.

Tenth Army Tentative Operation Plan 1–45, dtd 6Jan45.

Tenth Army G–2 Intelligence Monograph, 5 Parts, August 1945. (TAGO)

Tenth Army G–2 Weekly Summaries Nos 1–5, 19May–21Jun45.

Tenth Army G–2 Prisoner of War Interrogation Summaries Nos 1–19, July–August 1945. (OCMH)

Tenth Army G–2 Reports Nos 9–97, 4Apr–1Jul45.

Tenth Army G–2 Counterintelligence Collecting Agency Subsection Translations Nos 4–308, 17Apr–11Jul45. (TAGO)

Tenth Army G–2 Interrogation Reports Nos 10–28, 23Dec44–6Aug45. (TAGO)

Tenth Army G–3 Journal and File, July–September 1945. (TAGO)

Tactical Air Force, Tenth Army Action Report, Phase I, Nansei Shoto, 8Dec44–30Jun45, dtd 12Jul45.

III Amphibious Corps Action Report, Ryukyus Operation, Phases I and II, dtd 1Jul45.

III Amphibious Corps Operation Orders and G–3 Periodic Reports, Ryukyus Operation, Phases I and II, dtd 1Jul45.

III Amphibious Corps Operation Plan 1–45, dtd 1Feb45.

III Amphibious Corps Administrative Plan No 1–45, dtd 22Feb45.

III Amphibious Corps G–2 Periodic Reports Nos 1–92, 2Apr–2Jul45.

III Amphibious Corps Artillery Action Report, Phase I, Nansei Shoto, 1Apr–30Jun45, dtd 25Jul45, including Action Reports from the following units:

  2d Provisional Field Artillery Group
  Henderson Group
  1st 155mm Howitzer Battalion
  3d 155mm Howitzer Battalion
  6th 155mm Howitzer Battalion
  7th 155mm Gun Battalion
  8th 155mm Gun Battalion
  9th 155mm Gun Battalion

Air Delivery Section, Headquarters and Service Battalion, III Amphibious Corps Action Report, ICEBERG Operation, dtd 24Jun45.

1st Marine Division Special Action Report, Nansei Shoto Operation, 1Apr–30Jun45, dtd 10Jul45.

1st Marine Division Operation Plan 1–45, dtd 10Feb45.

1st Marine Division G–2 Journal, 1Apr–18Jul45.

1st Marine Division G–2 Periodic Reports Nos 1–105, 2Apr–16Jul45.

1st Marine Division G–3 Journal, 28Feb–14Jul45.

1st Marines Special Action Report, Nansei Shoto Operation, dtd 25Jul45.

1st Battalion, 1st Marines Special Action Report, 23Feb–21Jun45, n. d.

2d Battalion, 1st Marines Narrative Report—ICEBERG, 23Feb–22Jun45, n. d.

3d Battalion, 1st Marines Special Action Report, Phase I & II of the Nansei Shoto Operation, dtd 10Jul45.

5th Marines Special Action Report, 22Apr–23Jun45, n. d.

5th Marines S–3 Journal, 15Jan–26Jul45.

1st Battalion, 5th Marines Special Action Report, Phase I and II, dtd 29Apr45; Phase III, dtd 9Jul45.

2d Battalion, 5th Marines Special Action Report, Okinawa, 1Apr–22Jun45, n. d.

3d Battalion, 5th Marines Special Action Report, 1–21Apr45, dtd 30Apr45; 22Apr–22Jun45, dtd 10Jul45.

7th Marines Special Action Report, Phase I and II, dtd 1May45; Phase III, dtd 11Jul45.

1st Battalion, 7th Marines Special Action Report, 22Apr–22Jun45, dtd 29Jun45.

2d Battalion, 7th Marines Special Action Report, 2May–22Jun45, dtd 2Jul45.

3d Battalion, 7th Marines Special Action Report, Phase III, dtd 1Jul45.

11th Marines Special Action Report, Message File, and Unit Journal, n. d.

11th Marines S–3 Reports, 2Apr–21Jun45.

1st Reconnaissance Company Journal, 25Aug44–12Aug45.

1st Engineer Battalion Reconnaissance and Intelligence Reports Nos 1–74, 4Apr–24Jun45.

1st Tank Battalion Summaries of Tank Action, 15Apr–23Jun45.

3d Armored Amphibian Battalion Special Action Report, Nansei Shoto Operation, dtd 1Jul45.

6th Marine Division Special Action Report, Phases I and II, Okinawa Operation, dtd 30Apr45, including as annexes the Special Action Reports of the following units:
> 4th Marines (each battalion)
> 22d Marines (each battalion)
> 29th Marines (each battalion)
> 15th Marines (each battalion)
> 6th Tank Battalion
> 6th Engineer Battalion
> Division Shore Party
> 6th Medical Battalion
> 1st Armored Amphibian Battalion
> 4th Amphibian Tractor Battalion
> 9th Amphibian Tractor Battalion

6th Marine Division Operation Plan No 1–45, dtd 10Feb45.

6th Marine Division Unit Journal, Okinawa Operation, Phase I and II, 1–22Apr45.

6th Marine Division Special Action Report, Okinawa Operation, Phase III, dtd 30Jun45, including as annexes the Special Action Reports of the following units:
> 4th Marines (each battalion)
> 22d Marines (each battalion)
> 29th Marines (each battalion)
> 15th Marines (each battalion)
> 6th Tank Battalion
> 6th Engineer Battalion
> Division Shore Party
> 6th Medical Battalion
> 1st Armored Amphibian Battalion
> 4th Amphibian Tractor Battalion
> 9th Amphibian Tractor Battalion

6th Marine Division Unit Journal, Okinawa Operation, Phase III, 23Apr–30Jun45.

6th Marine Division G–2 Summary, Okinawa Shima, dtd 1Aug45.

6th Marine Division G–2 Periodic Reports Nos 27–60, 28Apr–31May45.

2d Marine Division Action Report, Phase I, Nansei Shoto, dtd 15Apr45.

Combat Team 8, 2d Marine Division Action Report, Iheya and Aguni Operations, n. d.

Combat Team 8 Action Report, Okinawa Operation, 11–22Jun45, n. d.

XXIV Corps Action Report, Ryukyus, 1Apr–30Jun45, n. d.

XXIV Corps Field Order 45, ICEBERG, dtd 8Feb45.

XXIV Corps Administrative Order No 10, ICEBERG, dtd 10Feb45.

XXIV Corps G–3 Journal and File, 1Apr–30Jun45. (TAGO)

XXIV Corps Artillery Action Report, 31Mar–30Jun45, n. d.

7th Infantry Division Action Report, Ryukyus Campaign, dtd 30Jul45.

27th Infantry Division Operation Report, Phase I, Nansei Shoto, 1Jan–30Jun45, dtd 19Jul45.

27th Infantry Division G–2 Periodic Reports Nos 5–23, 14Apr–2May45.

77th Infantry Division Operation Report, Phase I, (in 3 parts; Kerama Retto; Ie Shima; Okinawa), n. d. (TAGO)

96th Infantry Division Action Report, Ryukyus Campaign, dtd 28Jul45. (TAGO)

Island Command Action Report, Okinawa, 13Dec44–30Jun45, dtd 30Jun45.

Island Command Operation Plan No 1, dtd 15Feb45.

Military Government Section, Island Command, Histories of Military Government Operations on Okinawa, April–August 1945, n. d. (TAGO)

53d Antiaircraft Brigade After-Action Report, dtd 21Jun45.

1st Information and Historical Service, Documents Relating to the Surrender of Japanese Garrison in the Ryukyus and the Occupation of that Area by Elements of the Tenth Army, September-October 1945, dtd 9Dec45. (TAGO)

WAR DIARIES

Monthly war diaries for the appropriate periods from October 1944 through September 1945 have been consulted for all of the following organizations; these are listed overall rather than separately for purposes of convenience and simplicity.
> Pacific Fleet
> Tactical Air Force, Tenth Army
> III Amphibious Corps
> 1st Marine Division
> 6th Marine Division
> 2d Marine Air Wing
> Air Defense Command, Okinawa
> Marine Air Defense Command–2
> Marine Air Group–14
> Marine Air Group–22
> Marine Air Group–31
> Marine Air Group–33
> Marine Air Group–43
> VMF(CV)–112

BOOKS, PAMPHLETS, PERIODICALS

Appleman, Roy E., *et al, Okinawa: The Last Battle*, U. S. Army in World War II. Washington: Government Printing Office, 1948.

Bartley, LtCol Whitman S., *Iwo Jima: Amphibious Epic*, Marine Corps Historical Monograph. Washington: Government Printing Office, 1954.

Bergren, Maj Orville V., "School Solutions on Motobu," *Marine Corps Gazette*, December 1945.

Boggs, Maj Charles W., Jr., *Marine Aviation in the Philippines*, Marine Corps Historical Monograph. Washington: Government Printing Office, 1951.

Cannon, M. Hamlin and Smith, Robert R., *Triumph in the Philippines*, U. S. Army in World War II. To be published by the Government Printing Office in 1955.

Carleton, Maj Philips D., *The Conquest of Okinawa; An Account of the Sixth Marine Division*. Washington: Historical Division, USMC, 1947.

Carter, RAdm Worrall R., *Beans, Bullets, and Black Oil*. Washington: Government Printing Office, 1953.

Cass, Bevan (ed.), *History of the Sixth Marine Division*. Washington: Infantry Journal Press, 1948.

Crown, LtCol John A. and Heinl, LtCol Robert D., *The Marshalls: Increasing the Tempo*, Marine Corps Historical Monograph. Washington: Government Printing Office, 1954.

Davidson, Orlando R., *et al*, *The Deadeyes: The Story of the 96th Infantry Division*. Washington: Infantry Journal Press, 1947.

del Valle, MajGen Pedro A., "Old Glory on Shuri," *Marine Corps Gazette*, August 1945.

del Valle, MajGen Pedro A., "Southward from Shuri," *Marine Corps Gazette*, October 1945.

Fuller, MajGen J. F. C., *The Second World War*. New York: Sloan and Pearce, 1949.

Halsey, FAdm William F. and Bryan, LCdr J., III, *Admiral Halsey's Story*. New York: McGraw-Hill Book Company, 1947.

Hawks, Francis L., *United States Japan Expedition by Com M. C. Perry*, 3 vols. Washington: A. O. P. Nicholson, 1856.

Hoffman, Maj Carl W., *Saipan: The Beginning of the End*, Marine Corps Historical Monograph. Washington: Government Printing Office, 1950.

Hough, Maj Frank O., *The Assault on Peleliu*, Marine Corps Historical Monograph. Washington: Government Printing Office, 1950.

Hough, LtCol Frank O. and Crown, Maj John A., *The Campaign on New Britain*, Marine Corps Historical Monograph. Washington: Government Printing Office, 1953.

Isely, Jeter A. and Crowl, Philip A., *The U. S. Marines and Amphibious War*. Princeton: Princeton University Press, 1951.

Johnston, Richard W., *Follow Me: The Story of the Second Marine Division in World War II*. New York: Random House, 1948.

King, FAdm Ernest J. and Whitehill, Cdr Walter M., *Fleet Admiral King: A Naval Record*. New York: W. W. Norton & Company, 1952.

Leahy, FAdm William D., *I Was There*. New York: Whittlesby House, 1950.

Liggett, MajGen Hunter, *A. E. F.: Ten Years Ago In France*. New York: Dodd, Mead & Company, 1928.

Lodge, Maj O. R., *The Recapture of Guam*, Marine Corps Historical Monograph. Washington: Government Printing Office, 1954.

Love, Capt Edmund G., *The 27th Infantry Division in World War II*. Washington, Infantry Journal Press, 1949.

Matsumoto, Capt Kitaro and Chihaya, Cdr Matsataka, "Design and Construction of the *Yamato* and *Musashi*," *United States Naval Institute Proceedings*, October 1953.

McMillan, George J., *The Old Breed: A History of the First Marine Division In World War II*. Washington: Infantry Journal Press, 1949.

Military Intelligence Division, War Department, Order of Battle for the Japanese Armed Forces, dtd 1Mar45, with amendments through 11Jul45.

Myers, LtCol Max (ed.), *Ours To Hold It High: The History of the 77th Infantry Division in World War II*. Washington: Infantry Journal Press, 1947.

Shepherd, MajGen Lemuel C., Jr., "Battle for Motobu Peninsula," *Marine Corps Gazette*, August 1945.

Sherrod, Robert, *History of Marine Corps Aviation In World War II*. Washington: Combat Forces Press, 1952.

Spruance, Adm Raymond A., "The Victory in the Pacific," *United Service Institution Journal*, November 1946.

Smith, Robert R., *The Approach to the Philippines*, U. S. Army in World War II. Washington: Government Printing Office, 1953.

Stockman, Capt James R., *The First Marine Division on Okinawa*. Washington: Historical Division, USMC, 1946.

United States Strategic Bombing Survey (Pacific), Naval Analysis Division, *The Campaigns of the Pacific War*. Washington: Government Printing Office, 1946.

United States Strategic Bombing Survey (Pacific), Naval Analysis Division, *Interrogations of Japanese Officials*, 2 vols. Washington: Government Printing Office, 1946.

Vogel, Bertram, "Who Were the *Kamikaze?*," *United States Naval Institute Proceedings*, July 1947.

War Department Technical Manual E–30–480, *Handbook on Japanese Military Forces*. Washington: Government Printing Office, 1944.

The War Reports of General of the Army George C. Marshall, General of the Army H. H. Arnold, and Fleet Admiral Ernest J. King. Philadelphia and New York: J. B. Lippincott Company, 1947.

Yanaga, Chitoshi, *Japan Since Perry*. New York: McGraw-Hill Book Company, 1949.

Yokoi, RAdm Toshiyuki, "*Kamikazes* and the Okinawa Campaign," *United States Naval Institute Proceedings*, May 1954.

Zimmerman, Maj John L., *The Guadalcanal Campaign*, Marine Corps Historical Monograph. Washington: Government Printing Office, 1949.

MISCELLANEOUS

Carleton, Maj Philips D., Notes for *Conquest of Okinawa: An Account of the Sixth Marine Division*, n. d.

Combat Records Review, Office of the Chief of Naval Operations, Index of Action Reports, War Diaries, Operation Plans and Orders and British Reports of the Okinawa Operation, dtd 1Oct47.

File of Comments on *The Conquest of Okinawa: An Account of the Sixth Marine Division*, 2 vols.

File of Comments on *The First Marine Division on Okinawa*, 2 vols.

"A History of the 7th Marines on Okinawa," Enclosure A to Col Edward W. Snedeker Letter to Commandant of the Marine Corps, 27Mar47.

Jenks, Maj Almet, Notes, Outlines, and Comments on a proposed Okinawa monograph, n. d.

Ludwig, Capt Verle E., Memorandum for the Historical Branch, G–3, dtd 28Oct54.

Office of the Chief of Military History, Department of the Army, Japanese Monograph No 53, Okinawa Operation Record of the Thirty-second Army, August 1946. (OCMH)

Office of the Chief of Military History, Department of the Army, Japanese Monograph No 135, Okinawa Operations Record of the Thirty-second Army, 24th Division, and 8th Air Division, Revised Edition, November 1949. (OCMH)

Shutts, Sgt Kenneth A. and Trilling, Sgt. Paul, 1st Marine Division Company Interviews and Action Overlays, n. d.

Stockman, Capt James R., Notes, Outlines, and Drafts of a proposed Okinawa monograph, n. d.

APPENDIX II

Chronology

1944

2 January_____ U. S. Army troops land at Saidor, New Guinea.

31 January–
7 February_____ U. S. forces assault and capture Kwajelein and Majuro Atolls in the Marshalls.

16–17 February_____ Task Force 58 strikes Truk, revealing weakness of that base.

17–22 February_____ U. S. forces assault and capture Eniwetok Atoll in the Marshalls.

29 February–
28 March_____ U. S. forces assault and capture the main islands of the Admiralties.

6 March_____ 1st Marine Division lands near Talasea on New Britain in the Bismarks.

22 April_____ U. S. Army troops land at Aitape and Hollandia in northern New Guinea, beginning drive up the coast.

6 June_____ Allied troops invade the continent of Europe in Normandy.

15 June–9 July_____ U. S. forces assault and capture Saipan in the Marianas.

19–20 June_____ Battle of the Philippine Sea. Japanese naval air arm suffers decisive defeat.

21 July–
10 August_____ U. S. forces assault and capture Guam in the Marianas.

24 July–
1 August_____ V Marine Amphibious Corps assaults and captures Tinian in the Marianas.

30 July_____ Westward drive reaches end of New Guinea at Sansapor Point.

15 September_____ U. S. Army troops assault and capture Moratai, Netherlands East Indies.

15–30 September_____ U. S. forces assault and capture Peleliu and Anguar in the Palaus.

23 September_____ U. S. Army troops seize Ulithi Atoll in the Western Carolines.

10 October_____ First carrier raid on Okinawa.

20 October_____ U. S. Army troops land on Leyte in the Philippines.

23–26 October_____ Battle of Leyte Gulf. Elimination of the Japanese surface fleet as a major threat.

25 October_____ CinCPOA issues Joint Staff Study outlining plans for the Okinawa operation (ICEBERG).

24 November_____ Saipan-based B–29's bomb Tokyo in the first attack on the enemy capitol by land-based planes.

15 December_____ U. S. Army troops invade Mindoro in the Philippines.

25 December_____ Leyte declared secure.

1945

6 January_____ Tenth Army issues Tentative Operation Plan 1–45 for ICEBERG.

9 January_____ U. S. Army troops land on Luzon in the Philippines.

25 January_____ First support mission flown by Marine dive bombers in the Philippines.

19 February–
16 March_____ V Marine Amphibious Corps assaults and captures Iwo Jima in the Volcano-Bonins.

11 March	General Buckner puts Tenth Army Operation Plan 1–45 into effect by dispatch.
21 March	Western Islands Attack Group carrying assault troops of the 77th Infantry Division sorties from Leyte Gulf for the opening phase of ICEBERG.
24 March	Southern Tractor Flotilla carrying assault troops of the XXIV Corps sorties from Leyte Gulf for ICEBERG.
	Planes and battleships of Task Force 58 open the preliminary bombardment of Okinawa.
25 March	Northern Tractor Flotilla carrying assault troops of the III Amphibious Corps sorties from Ulithi for ICEBERG.
26–31 March	77th Infantry Division assaults and captures Kerama Retto and Keise Shima.
27 March	Transport and covering forces of the Joint Expeditionary Force sortie from Leyte Gulf and Ulithi for ICEBERG.
	Demonstration Group carrying troops of the 2d Marine Division leaves Saipan.
1 April	Tenth Army makes an unopposed landing on the Hagushi beaches of Okinawa.
2 April	Forward elements of the 7th Infantry Division reach the eastern coast of Okinawa, severing the island.
6–7 April	First of ten major *Kamikaze* attacks on ships in Okinawan waters.
7 April	Planes of Task Force 58 sink the Japanese super-battleship *Yamato*, a cruiser, and four destroyers, ending all chance of a sea attack on Okinawa.
9–10 April	3/105 of the 27th Infantry Division assaults and captures Tsugen Shima, the only defended position in the Eastern Islands.
10 April	27th Infantry Division lands on Okinawa to reinforce the XXIV Corps.
16–21 April	77th Infantry Division assaults and captures Ie Shima.
19 April	XXIV Corps makes an all-out attack against the outer ring of Shuri defenses.
20 April	The end of organized resistance on Motobu Peninsula in the 6th Marine Division zone of action.
30 April	77th Infantry Division relieves the 96th Infantry Division in southern Okinawa.
1 May	1st Marine Division relieves the 27th Infantry Division in southern Okinawa.
4 May	27th Infantry Division relieves 6th Marine Division in northern Okinawa.
4–6 May	XXIV Corps repulses major Japanese counterattack.
7 May	IIIAC takes over the western sector of the Tenth Army front in southern Okinawa.
8 May	First elements of the 6th Marine Division enter the lines on the southern front.
9–10 May	96th Infantry Division replaces the 7th Infantry Division on the eastern coast.
11 May	Tenth Army all-out attack on the inner Shuri defenses.
17 May	Admiral Turner relieved by Admiral Hill as Commander Task Force 51. General Buckner now directly responsible to Admiral Spruance for operations of Tenth Army.
21 May	7th Infantry Division recommitted on the east coast to encircle Shuri.
27 May	Third Fleet relieves Fifth Fleet and General Buckner now directly responsible to CinCPOA for operations of Tenth Army.
30 May–4 June	Bulk of the Japanese Thirty-second Army withdraws under cover of rain from the Shuri bastion to new positions in the Kiyamu Peninsula.
31 May	5th Marines capture Shuri Castle.
3–4 June	8th Marine Combat Team secures Iheya Shima.
4 June	6th Marine Division assaults Oroku Peninsula.
9 June	8th Marine Combat Team secures Aguni Shima.
18 June	General Buckner killed watching progress of 8th Marines' first attack on Okinawa; General Geiger assumes temporary command of Tenth Army.
21 June	End of organized resistance on Okinawa.
22 June	Official flag-raising at Tenth Army Headquarters marking capture of Okinawa.
23 June	General Stilwell assumes command of Tenth Army.

24–30 June _____ FMF Reconnaissance Battalion secures Kume Shima.

30 June _____ Completion of the mop-up sweep of southern Okinawa.

1 July _____ Task Force 31 dissolved by CinCPOA: General Stilwell assumes responsibility for defense and development of Okinawa Gunto.

5 July _____ Philippines campaign declared ended.

4 August _____ 27th Infantry Division reaches Hedo Misaki ending three and a half month mopping-up action in northern Okinawa.

6 August _____ First atomic bomb dropped on Hiroshima.

9 August _____ Second atomic bomb dropped on Nagasaki.

10 August _____ Japan sues for peace.

14 August _____ End of war in the Pacific.

2 September _____ Formal surrender of the Japanese Empire on board the *Missouri* in Tokyo harbor.

7 September _____ General Stilwell accepts the surrender of Japanese Ryukyus garrisons signifying the beginning of American political hegemony in Okinawa.

Command and Staff List of Marine Units on Okinawa

APPENDIX III

1 APRIL–22 JUNE 1945 [1]

Amphibious Reconnaissance Battalion, FMFPac

CO	Maj James L. Jones
ExO	Maj Earl R. Marquardt
S–3	1stLt Leo B. Shinn
HqCo	1stLt James R. Bentley
A Co	Capt Merwin H. Silverthorn, Jr.
B Co	1stLt Russell E. Corey

III AMPHIBIOUS CORPS
III Amphibious Corps Headquarters

CG	LtGen Roy S. Geiger
CofS	BrigGen Merwin H. Silverthorn
G–1	Col Gale T. Cummings
G–2	Col Charles C. Brown
G–3	Col Walter A. Wachtler
G–4	Col Francis B. Loomis, Jr.
G–5	Col Elmer H. Salzman

III Amphibious Corps Troops

CO	Col Edward G. Hagen (CO,Rear-Ech)
ExO	LtCol William F. Whitaker
S–3	Maj Julius H. Flagstad

III Amphibious Corps Headquarters and Service Battalion

CO	LtCol Harry A. Traffert, Jr.
ExO	Maj Harold C. Howard (To 6J)
	Maj Robert J. Kennedy (From 7J)
S–3	Capt Andrew Dura
HqCo	Capt Andrew Dura (FwdEch)

[1] Compiled from unit muster rolls available at Headquarters Marine Corps. Only those offcers who are officially listed as having held the indicated command and staff positions are included. Ranks shown are those held on 22Jun45.

MP Co	Capt Thomas G. Barry, Jr.
SerCo	1stLt Worthen Brooks
1st BomDispCo	Capt Donald J. Merriman
1st SepTopoCo	Capt Byrl W. Munger (FwdEch)

III Amphibious Corps Medical Battalion

CO	LCdr Maurice A. Diehr, (MC) (To 29A)
	LCdr Donovan C. Blanchard, (MC) (29A–18J)
	Cdr Robert Mazet, Jr. (MC) (From 19J)
ExO	Lt William H. Hanna, (MC) (From 1J)
S–3	(Not shown)
H&S Co	(Not shown)
A Co	Lt William H. Hanna, (MC)
B Co	Lt Thomas A. Glass, (MC)
C Co	Lt Albert W. Diddle (MC)

III Amphibious Corps Signal Battalion

CO	Col Robert L. Peterson
ExO	LtCol Alan Sutter
S–3	Capt. Carlton E. Tripp
HqCo	Capt Herbert D. Raymond, Jr.
A Co	1stLt Lloyd "E" Watson
B Co	Capt Edmund J. Anderson
C Co	Capt Roscoe E. Cole

1st Military Police Battalion

CO	LtCol Alfred H. Marks
ExO	Capt Ralph L. Robinson
S–3	1stLt Russell M. Roberts (To 30A)
	1stLt Harold B. Moe (From 1M)
HqCo	Capt Paul B. Doster (To 14M)
	Capt Kenneth J. Becker (From 15M)

A Co_____ Capt Kenneth J. Becker (To
14M)
1stLt Walter S. Metzger (From
15M)
B Co_____ 1stLt Thomas J. Donoghue (To
25M)
1stLt Arthur L. Seay, III
(From 26M)
C Co_____ 1stLt Joseph F. Carney
D Co_____ 1stLt Horace E. Curtis

1st Separate Engineer Battalion

CO_____ LtCol Alonzo D. Gorman
ExO_____ Maj William C. Mikell
S-3_____ Capt George S. Sinnicks
H&S Co_____ Capt John E. Bibby (To 26M)
Capt Edward A. Menuez (From
27M)
A Co_____ Capt Morgan P. Hammer
B Co_____ Capt Robert J. Bobber (To
26M)
Capt John E. Bibby (From
27M)
C Co_____ Capt Franklin J. Blythe, Jr.

11th Motor Transport Battalion

CO_____ Lt Col Franklin A. Hayner
ExO_____ Maj Kenneth E. Murphy
S-3_____ 1stLt Thomas H. Prestridge
HqCo_____ Capt Bowen Asserson, Sr.
A Co_____ Capt John H. L'Estrange
B Co_____ 1stLt Hugh F. Ferguson
C Co_____ 1stLt Richard P. Jones
Corps TransCo_____ 1stLt John Bookhout

7th Service Regiment

CO_____ Col Harold E. Rosecrans
ExO_____ LtCol Edwin D. Partridge
S-3_____ (Not shown)
CO, HqBn_____ LtCol Kenneth L. Moses
ExO, HqBn_____ Maj Ben F. Dixon, III
S-3, HqBn_____ (Not shown)
HqCo_____ Capt William M. Milne, Jr.
EngCo_____ Maj Clarence M. Thomas
GenSupCo_____ Capt Adrian F. Pilliod, Jr.
MP Co_____ Capt Lester J. Putney
OrdCo_____ Capt Arthur P. Bretherick, Jr.
(To 9J)
Maj George G. Pafford (From
10J)
SigCo_____ Capt Albert N. Hunt
TransCo_____ Capt Frederick P. Traill, Jr.
1st MarAmmoCo_____ Capt Price R. Ashton
3d MarAmmoCo_____ Capt Louis P. Shine
12th MarAmmoCo___ Capt Albert Shapiro (To 5J)
1stLt Kenneth E. Moyer (6–9J)
Capt Arthur P. Bretherick, Jr.
(From 10J)
5th MarDepCo_____ 1stLt Edmond C. Forehand
18th MarDepCo_____ Capt William M. Barr
19th MarDepCo_____ Capt Orville A. LaMotte

20th MarDepCo_____ Capt William C. Adams
37th MarDepCo_____ 1stLt William A. Hodrick
38th MarDepCo_____ 1stLt John W. O'Donoghue

III AMPHIBIOUS CORPS ARTILLERY
III Amphibious Corps Artillery Headquarters

CG_____ BrigGen David R. Nimmer
CofS_____ Col John A. Bemis
G–1_____ LtCol Frederick W. Miller
G–2_____ Maj Paul O. Engelder
G–3_____ LtCol Frederick P. Henderson
(To 15M)
LtCol Ernest P. Foley (From
16M)
G–4_____ LtCol Llewellyn Powell, Jr.
HqBtry_____ 1stLt Walter T. Anderson

1st Provisional Antiaircraft Artillery Group

CO_____ Col Kenneth W. Benner
ExO_____ LtCol Willard C. Fiske
S–3_____ LtCol John F. Dunlap (To 11J)
LtCol Jack H. Brown (From
11J)
HqBtry_____ 1stLt Leon H. Huttner (To 11)
1stLt William D. Rummans, Jr.
(From 11J)

2d Antiaircraft Artillery Battalion

CO_____ LtCol Max C. Chapman
ExO_____ LtCol Charles W. May (To 5J)
LtCol Norman E. Sparling
(From 6J)
S–3_____ Maj Walter L. Eddy, Jr. (To 4M)
Maj John W. Graves (From 5M)
H&S Btry_____ Capt Carl E. Fulton
HAA Grp_____ LtCol Charles T. Hodges
LAA Grp_____ Maj Emile P. Moses, Jr.
S/L Btry_____ Capt Lewis A. Huddle (To 8J)
Capt John L. Buckley (From
9J)

5th Antiaircraft Artillery Battalion

CO_____ LtCol Harry O. Smith, Jr.
ExO_____ LtCol Charles J. Siebert, II
S–3_____ Capt Ralph W. Nicholson (To
21J)
Maj Monson J. McCarty (From
22J)
H&S Btry_____ Maj Monson J. McCarty (To
21J)
Capt Herbert B. Gross (From
22J)
HAA Grp_____ Maj Donald T. Regan (To 20A)
Maj Robert M. White, II (Actg
21A–4M)
Maj Donald T. Regan (5M–14J)
Maj Robert M. White, II (From
15J)
LAA Grp_____ LtCol Arthur B. Hammond, Jr.
S/L Btry_____ Capt Sylvan J. Naughtrip, Jr.

8th Antiaircraft Artillery Battalion

CO	LtCol James S. O'Halloran
ExO	LtCol Robert F. Scott
S–3	Maj Howard S. Nelson (To 8J)
	Maj Arthur J. Bachhuber (From 9J)
H&S Btry	Capt Robert J. Granger
HAA Grp	LtCol William R. Dorr, Jr. (To 8J)
	Maj Raymond F. Aton (From 9J)
LAA Grp	LtCol John D. Mattox (To 7J)
	Maj John W. Graham (From 14J)
S/L Btry	Capt Paul N. Ierardi

16th Antiaircraft Artillery Battalion

CO	LtCol August F. Penzold, Jr. (To 18J)
	LtCol Charles T. Tingle (From 19J)
ExO	LtCol Edward N. Rydalch
S–3	Maj Robert A. Merchant, Jr.
H&S Btry	Capt Robert H. Twisdale (To 13M)
	Capt John J. Dyer (From 14M)
HAA Grp	Maj Robert G. Baumann
LAA Grp	Maj Edward H. Gartside (To 20M)
	Capt John D. Briggs (21M–8J)
	LtCol John D. Mattox (From 8J)
S/L Btry	Capt George Anderson (To 13J)
	1stLt Claude R. Laplant (From 14J)

2d Provisional Field Artillery Group

CO	LtCol Custis Burton, Jr.
ExO	LtCol John S. Twitchell (To 10M)
	Maj Alfred L. Owens (11M–20J)
	LtCol John S. Twitchell (From 21J)
S–3	LtCol Ernest P. Foley (To 20A)
	LtCol John S. Twitchell (21A–7M)
	Maj Alfred L. Owens (From 8M)
HqBtry	Capt Jacob J. Fortunato

1st 155mm Howitzer Battalion

CO	LtCol George H. Ford
ExO	Maj William H. Atkinson
S–3	Capt Eugene C. Swift
H&S Btry	Capt Michael T. Harbrook
A Btry	1stLt Roy E. Moffett
B Btry	Capt Grant E. Rose
C Btry	Capt Owen H. Blexrud

3d 155mm Howitzer Battalion

CO	LtCol Robert C. Hiatt
ExO	Maj James H. Tatsch

S–3	Capt David L. Moberly
H&S Btry	Capt Elwyn D. Siefert
A Btry	Capt William W. Wander, Jr.
B Btry	Capt Robert W. Besch
C Btry	Capt Alexander B. Sharpe

6th 155mm Howitzer Battalion

CO	LtCol Lewis A. Jones
ExO	Maj Alfred L. Owens (To 7M)
	Capt John V. Downs (Actg From 7M)
S–3	1stLt Charles H. Berkmeyer
H&S Btry	1stLt Samuel M. Rogers
A Btry	1stLt Ira E. Steele
B Btry	1stLt Cornelius J. Kelleher, Jr. (To 13A)
	Capt Matthew J. Lynott, Jr. (From 14A)
C Btry	1stLt George H. Goldsborough (To 13A)
	Capt John V. Downs (14A–6M)
	1stLt George H. Goldsborough (Actg From 7M)

7th 155mm Gun Battalion

CO	LtCol Guido F. Verbeck, Jr.
ExO	LtCol Francis W. Benson
S–3	Capt Philip Ahwesh (To 20A)
	1stLt George N. Parks, Jr (21A–21J)
	Maj William N. Taft (From 22J)
H&S Btry	Capt Warren R. Loney (To 20A)
	Capt Philip Ahwesh (From 21A)
A Btry	Capt Richard H. Pearson (To 9M)
	1stLt James V. Gurge (From 10M)
B Btry	Capt Gilbert N. Powell
C Btry	Capt Andrew W. Bisset (To 8M)
	1st Lt Edward L. Fossum (From 9M)

8th 155mm Gun Battalion

CO	LtCol George V. Hanna, Jr.
ExO	Maj Robert F. Meldrum
S–3	Maj Richard A. Vanderhoof
H&S Btry	Capt Richard A. Schaefer
A Btry	Capt Harry "E" Dickinson
B Btry	1stLt Herbert H. Johnson
C Btry	1stLt James W. McJunkin

9th 155mm Gun Battalion

CO	LtCol Merritt Adelman
ExO	Maj Raymond D. Wright
S–3	1stLt Howard W. Lull
H&S Btry	Capt James D. Owens (To 2M)
	Capt Gilbert J. Geiser (From 3M)
A Btry	1stLt Albert E. Leonard
B Btry	Capt Harry E. Kipp
C Btry	Capt Thomas L. Weyandt

FIRST MARINE DIVISION (REINFORCED)

1st Marine Division Headquarters

CG	MajGen Pedro A. del Valle
ADC	BrigGenLouis R. Jones
CofS	Col Robert O. Bare
G–1	LtCol Harold O. Deakin
G–2	LtCol John W. Scott, Jr.
G–3	LtCol Russell E. Honsowetz
G–4	LtCol Harvey C. Tschirgi

1st Marine Division Headquarters Battalion

CO	LtCol James S. Monahan (To 20M)
	Col Kenneth B. Chappell (24–31M)
ExO	Maj Lewis M. Andrews
S–3	2dLt William G. Porter
HqCo	Capt John E. Williams
1st MP Co	1stLt Lawrence E. Kindred
ReconCo	1stLt Robert J. Powell, Jr.
1st SigCo	Capt Thomas J. Flynn, Jr.
1st ASCO	LtCol John E. Morris
3d AmphTruckCo	Capt Grammer G. Edwards

1st Engineer Battalion

CO	Maj Theodore E. Drummond
ExO	Maj William A. Swinerton
S–3	Capt Robert C. Snyder
H&S Co	Capt William H. Owens, Jr. (To 2M)
	Capt John N. Rathwell (From 3M)
A Co	Capt Daniel J. McLellan
B Co	Capt Charles A. Hamilton
C Co	Capt John G. Aldworth

1st Medical Battalion

CO	LCdr Francis Giuffrida, (MC)
ExO	(Not shown)
S–3	(Not shown)
H&S Co	Lt Roger Stevenson, (MC)
A Co	Lt Charles E. Schoff, (MC) (To 1J)
	Lt Lloyd F. Sherman, (MC) (From 1J)
B Co	Lt Rupert B. Turnbull, (MC)
C Co	Lt David S. Slossberg, (MC)
D Co	LCdr Joseph C. Fremont, (MC)
E Co	LCdr Edwin B. Murchison, (MC)

1st Motor Transport Battalion

CO	LtCol Marion A. Fawcett (To 15A)
	LtCol Calvin C. Gaines (From 18A)
ExO	Maj Henry D. Shields
S–3	1stLt Walter M. Greenspan
H&S Co	1stLt Edwin J. Sehl
A Co	Capt Ben Sutts

B Co	Capt Francis I. Ford, Jr.
C Co	1stLt Wayne "W" Miller

1st Pioneer Battalion

CO	LtCol Robert G. Ballance
ExO	Maj Warren S. Sivertsen
S–3	1stLt William J. Selfridge, Jr.
H&S Co	Capt Benjamin T. Cocke (To 1J)
	1stLt Darrell A. Watson (From 1J)
A Co	Capt Stanley W. Slowakiewicz
B Co	Capt John M. Kennedy
C Co	1stLt John H. Heussner

1st Service Battalion

CO	LtCol Calvin C. Gaines (To 17A)
	Col John Kaluf (WIA 6A,* From 18A)
ExO	Capt Edwin B. Glass (To 14M)
	Maj William F. Belcher (15–17M)
	Capt Alton C. Bennett (From 20M)
S–3	(Not shown)
HqCo	1stLt Harry L. Tovani
OrdCo	Capt Edward P. Faulkner
S&S Co	1stLt Herbert R. Peterson

1st Tank Battalion

CO	LtCol Arthur J. Stuart (WIA 13J)
ExO	Capt Richard A. Munger (To 18J)
	Maj Robert M. Neiman (From 19J)
S–3	1stLt Lester T. Chase
H&S Co	Capt John K. Gaieski
A Co	1stLt Howard R. Taylor, Jr.
B Co	Capt Jack R. Munday
C Co	1stLt George E. Jerue

3d Armored Amphibian Battalion (Provisional)

CO	Lt Col John I. Williamson, Jr. (To 7M)
	Maj Arthur M. Parker, Jr. (From 8M)
ExO	Maj Arthur M. Parker, Jr. (To 7M)
	Capt Wilfred S. LeFrancois (From 8M)
S–3	Capt Marvin E. Mitchell (To 19J)
H&S Co	Capt. Whitley A. Cummings, Jr. (From 22A, FwdEch)
A Co	1stLt Norman C. Bray, Jr.
B Co	1stLt Harold A. Ipson
C Co	Capt Wilfred S. LeFrancois (To 7M)
D Co	1stLt Hillard "D" Thorpe

* WIA, Records show returned to duty.

1st Amphibian Tractor Battalion

CO ———————————— LtCol Maynard M. Nohrden
ExO ———————————— Maj Victor J. Harwick
S–3 ———————————— 1stLt Harold F. Harman
H&S Co ————————— Capt John A. Lockwood, Jr.
A Co ———————————— 1stLt Paul Phillips
B Co ———————————— 1stLt William H. Blatti
C Co ———————————— 1stLt Harry O. Lee

8th Amphibian Tractor Battalion

CO ———————————— LtCol Charles B. Nerren (To 13A)
Maj Bedford Williams (14–17A)
LtCol Charles B. Nerren (From 18A)
ExO ———————————— Maj Bedford Williams (To 13A)
Maj Bedford Williams (From 18A)
S–3 ———————————— 1stLt John R. Tull
H&S Co ————————— 1stLt Robert W. Caveney
A Co ———————————— Capt Robert P. Rapp
B Co ———————————— Capt William D. Evans
C Co ———————————— 1stLt Norman Haweeli

Headquarters, 1st Marines

CO ———————————— Col Kenneth B. Chappell (To 5M)
Col Arthur T. Mason (From 6M)
ExO ———————————— LtCol Richard P. Ross, Jr. (To 20M)
LtCol James S. Monahan (From 21M)
S–3 ———————————— Maj Bernard T. Kelly (WIA 5A,* To 21A)
Maj Jonas M. Platt (From 22A)
H&S Co ————————— 1stLt Walton M. Rock (To 21A)
1stLt Eustace C. M. Waller (22A–1J)
Capt Wayne B. Davis (From 1J)
WpnsCo ————————— Capt Lawrence K. Hennessy (To 21A)
Maj Robert W. Burnette (From 22A, WIA 3J)
Capt Francis D. Rineer (From 19J)

1st Battalion, 1st Marines

CO ———————————— LtCol James C. Murray, Jr. (WIA 9M)
LtCol Richard P. Ross, Jr. (10–12M)
LtCol Austin C. Shofner (From 13M)
ExO ———————————— Maj Jonas M. Platt (To 22A)
Maj Henry G. Baron (23A–14M)
Capt Thomas K. Greer (14M–10J)
Maj Franklin B. Nihart (From 11J)
S–3 ———————————— 1stLt Fendall W. Yerxa (To 18J)
Maj Leon Goldberg (From 19J)

HqCo ———————————— Maj William F. Belcher (To 14M)
1stLt Richard M. Highsmith, Jr. (14–20M)
1stLt Marion G. Truesdale (From 21M)
A Co ———————————— 1stLt Paul E. Burke (WIA 6J)
1stLt James R. Currier (From 6J)
B Co ———————————— Capt Francis D. Rineer (WIA 30A,* To 29M)
Capt Richard A. Poe (29M–6J)
Capt Francis D. Rineer (7–18J)
1stLt Fendall W. Yerxa (From 19J)
C Co ———————————— 1stLt Weldon M. Longbotham (WIA 14M)
Capt Richard A. Poe (15–28M, WIA 24M*)
1stLt Francis T. Burke (29M–3J)
Capt Richard A. Poe (From 7J, WIA 11J)
Capt Thomas K. Greer (From 11J)

2d Battalion, 1st Marines

CO ———————————— LtCol James C. Magee, Jr.
ExO ———————————— Maj Raymond C. Portillo (To 21A)
Maj Bernard T. Kelly (From 22A)
S–3 ———————————— Maj Robert W. Burnette (To 21A)
Maj Raymond C. Portillo (From 22A)
HqCo ———————————— Capt George L. Dacy (To 14M)
1stLt William K. Hunt (From 16M)
E Co ———————————— 1stLt Robert W. Schmitt (WIA 7M)
1stLt Richard B. Watkins (From 7M, WIA 13M*)
F Co ———————————— Capt Edward R. Tiscornia (KIA 2M)
1stLt Walter E. Burke (From 3M)
G Co ———————————— 1stLt Fay K. Koiner, Jr. (WIA 14M)
1stLt Jim "J" Paulos (15–17M)
1stLt John J. Cavanaugh (17M–1J)
1stLt Marcus H. Jaffe (From 2J)

3d Battalion, 1st Marines

CO ———————————— LtCol Stephen V. Sabol (To 20M)
LtCol Richard P. Ross, Jr. (From 21M)
ExO ———————————— Maj Frederick W. Lindlaw (To 18M)

Capt Wayne B. Davis (19–25M)
Maj Leon Goldberg (26M–6J)
Maj John V. Kelsey (7–18J)
Maj Frederick W. Lindlaw (From 19J)

S–3 _____ Capt Wayne B. Davis (To 21A)
Capt James M. Marshall (22A–18J)
Maj John V. Kelsey (From 19J)

HqCo _____ 1stLt Eustace C. M. Waller (To 21A)
Capt Wayne B. Davis (22A–1J)
1stLt James D. Currie (1–18J)
1stLt Charles J. Kohler, Jr. (From 19J)

I Co _____ 1stLt William A. Young, Jr. (To 21A)
Capt Lawrence K. Hennessy (From 22A, KIA 21M)
1stLt Elmer L. Cochran (21M–1J)
1stLt William A. Young, Jr. (From 2J)

K Co _____ 1stLt William O. Sellers
L Co _____ Capt Alton C. Bennett (To 13M)
1stLt James J. Haggerty (13–15M)
1stLt Harry L. Ziegler (From 16M, WIA 4J)
1stLt Eustace C. M. Waller (From 4J)

Headquarters, 5th Marines

CO _____ Col John H. Griebel
ExO _____ LtCol John D. Muncie
S–3 _____ Maj James H. Flagg
H&S Co _____ Capt Nicholas R. Goche
WpnsCo _____ Capt Carl H. Lockard

1st Battalion, 5th Marines

CO _____ LtCol Charles W. Shelburne
ExO _____ Maj. Frank W. Poland, Jr. (To 16M)
Maj Reed F. Taylor (From 17M)
S–3 _____ Capt Lloyd E. Howell
HqCo _____ 2dLt Lewis J. Schott (1–30A)
A Co _____ Capt Julian D. Dusenbury (WIA 10M,* 18J)
B Co _____ 1stLt Walter R. Wilson
C Co _____ 1stLt Walter E. Lange

2d Battalion, 5th Marines

CO _____ LtCol William E. Benedict (To 20J)
Maj Richard T. Washburn From 21J)
ExO _____ Maj Richard T. Washburn (To 20J)
1stLt Martin F. Fritz (From 21J)
S–3 _____ Maj John R. Hogan (WIA 4M)

1stLt Ward M. Wilcox (From 1J)
HqCo _____ 2dLt Richard F. Simpson (To 30A)
1stLt Martin F. Fritz (From 1M)
E Co _____ 1stLt Michael D. Benda (WIA 29M)
Capt Franklin D. Sills (From 29M, WIA 13J*)
F Co _____ 1stLt William A. Taylor (WIA 3M)
1stLt Joseph H. Bowling (From 4M, WIA 10M)
1stLt Robert F. Fry (From 11M, WIA 17M)
1stLt William A. Brougher (From 17M)
G Co _____ 1stLt Richard R. Breen (WIA 7M*)

3d Battalion, 5th Marines

CO _____ Maj John H. Gustafson (WIA 1A)
LtCol John C. Miller, Jr. (4A–16M)
Maj Frank W. Poland, Jr. (17M–8J)
LtCol Robert E. Hill (From 9J)
ExO _____ Maj Martin C. Roth
S–3 _____ Capt George S. Sharp (WIA 14M)
Capt Edwin B. Glass (From 15M)
HqCo _____ Capt William Flynn
I Co _____ Capt James P. O'Laughlin (WIA 7M,* WIA 24M)
1stLt John A. Fredenberger (From 24M, WIA 28M)
1stLt Carrol R. Wilson (From 28M, KIA 2J)
1stLt Richard H. Sengewald (From 3J)
K Co _____ 1stLt Thomas J. Stanley (To 24M)
1stLt George B. Loveday (From 25M)
L Co _____ Capt Robert P. Smith (To 8J)
1stLt Robert D. Metzger (From 9J)

Headquarters, 7th Marines

CO _____ Col Edward W. Snedeker
ExO _____ LtCol James M. Masters, Sr.
S–3 _____ Maj Walter Holomon (To 22M)
LtCol Stephen V. Sabol (23M–19J)
H&S Co _____ Maj John W. Arnold (To 4A)
1stLt Maurice J. Cavanaugh, Jr. (From 5A)
WpnsCo _____ Capt Welton H. Bunger, Jr.

1st Battalion, 7th Marines

CO	LtCol John J. Gormley
ExO	Maj Hector R. Migneault (WIA 14M)
	Capt Don P. Wyckoff (14–17M)
	Maj Henry G. Baron, Jr. (18M–9J)
	Maj Harold C. Howard (From 10J)
S–3	Capt Don P. Wyckoff
HqCo	Capt Robert L. Gibson (To 31M)
	1stLt Russell R. Feazell (From 1J)
A Co	1stLt Robert Romo (KIA 14M)
	1stLt Ernest McCall (From 15M)
B Co	1stLt Roger A. Golden (To 18M)
	Capt Leonard R. Heller (19M–11J)
	Capt Lee W. Langham (From 12J)
C Co	Capt Richard E. Rohrer (To 17J)

2d Battalion, 7th Marines

CO	LtCol Spencer S. Berger
ExO	Maj Louis G. Ditta
S–3	1stLt Harry E. Wheeler (To 18J)
	Maj James M. Robinson (From 19J)
HqCo	Capt Lee W. Langham (To 10M)
	1stLt Joseph W. Kensik, Jr. (From 11M)
E Co	Capt Paul C. Beardslee, Jr. (KIA 1A)
	1stLt William G. Hudson, Jr. (1–15A)
	Capt Robert J. Noonan (From 16A, WIA 2J)
	1stLt William G. Hudson, Jr. (From 2J, WIA 11J)
	1stLt Franklin W. Myers (From 12J)
F Co	Capt Harold E. Grasse (DOW 12M)
	Capt Lee W. Langham (11M–11J)
	1stLt John W. Huff (From 12J)
G Co	Capt Kirt W. Norton

3d Battalion, 7th Marines

CO	LtCol Edward H. Hurst (WIA 19J)
	LtCol Stephen V. Sabol (From 19J)
ExO	Maj John F. Corbett (To 18M)
	Maj William F. Belcher (19–22M)
	Maj Walter Holomon (From 23M)
S–3	Maj James E. Kirk, Jr. (To 15M)
	Capt Henry J. Guinivan, Jr. (From 19M)
HqCo	Capt James G. Triebel (To 28A)
	Capt Henry J. Guinivan, Jr. (30A–15M)
	1stLt Arlus C. Henderson (16–17M)
	Maj William F. Belcher (From 18M, KIA 14J)
	Maj Alexander W. Chilton (From 14J)
I Co	Capt Robert I. Owen (To 30A)
	1stLt Peter I. McDonnell (From 1M, KIA 18M)
	Maj John F. Corbett (From 18M, WIA 19M)
	2dLt Emory A. Bauer (19M)
	1stLt Charles E. Crow (20M–20J)
	Capt Robert I. Owen (From 21J)
K Co	1stLt Robert B. Morton (1–18A)
	1stLt Charles R. Hickox (19–20A)
	1stLt Robert B. Morton (21–23A)
	1stLt Robert W. Dalrymple (From 24A, WIA 16M)
	Maj James E. Kirk, Jr. (From 16M)
L Co	Capt Roland H. Collins (WIA 9M,* 16M)
	Capt Henry J. Guinivan, Jr. (16–18M)
	Capt Roland H. Collins (From 19M)

Headquarters, 11th Marines

CO	Col Wilburt S. Brown
ExO	LtCol Edson L. Lyman
S–3	Maj Charles D. Harris
H&S Btry	1stLt Joseph Ermenc

1st Battalion, 11th Marines

CO	LtCol Richard W. Wallace
Exo	LtCol George M. Lhamon
S–3	Maj Ernest E. Schott
H&S Btry	Capt Glenn E. Morris
A Btry	Capt Neal C. Newell
B Btry	Capt Maurice L. Cater
C Btry	Maj Lawrence A. Tomlinson, Jr.

2d Battalion, 11th Marines

CO	LtCol James H. Moffatt, Jr.
Exo	Maj John L. Donnell
S–3	Maj William C. Givens
H&S Btry	1stLt Martin R. Bock, Jr.
D Btry	Capt James T. Pearce
E Btry	Capt Lorenzo G. Cutlip (WIA 22J)

Capt Fritz Stampeli (From 22J)
F Btry_____ Capt Robert S. Preston

3d Battalion, 11th Marines

CO_____ LtCol Thomas G. Roe
ExO_____ LtCol Samuel S. Wooster
S–3_____ Capt Benjamin H. Brown (To 6J)
                        Maj Robert E. Collier (From 7J)
H&S Btry_____ 2dLt Charles E. Edwards (WIA 12A)
                        Maj Everett W. Smith (12–26A)
                        Capt Edward T. Haislip (From 27A)
G Btry_____ Capt Charles W. Fowler
H Btry_____ Capt William R. Miller
I Btry_____ 1stLt John L. McDonald, Jr. (WIA 4A*)

4th Battalion, 11th Marines

CO_____ LtCol Leonard F. Chapman, Jr.
ExO_____ Maj Andre D. Gomez
S–3_____ Capt James A. Crotinger (To 12J)
                        Maj Lewis D. Baughman (From 13J)
H&S Btry_____ Capt Randall L. Mitchell (To 30A)
                        Capt Thomas F. Moran (1–31M)
                        1stLt Gordon C. Petersen (From 1J)
K Btry_____ Maj Lewis F. Treleaven (WIA 28A*)
L Btry_____ Capt Richard M. Moordale
M Btry_____ Capt George S. Nixon

8TH COMBAT TEAM, 2D MARINE DIVISION (1–22 JUNE)

Headquarters, 8th Combat Team

CO_____ Col Clarence R. Wallace
ExO_____ LtCol Martin S. Rahiser
S–3_____ Maj William C. Chamberlin (WIA 18J)
H&S Co_____ Capt Bob S. Griffin
WpnsCo_____ Maj David V. Van Evera
ReconCo, 2d MarDiv. Maj John R. Nelson
C Co, 2d EngBn_____ Capt Osman B. Latrobe
E Co, 2d MedBn_____ Lt Richard L. French, (MC)
B Co, 2d MT Bn_____ 1stLt Paul A. Schott
A Co, 2d PionBn____ Capt James B. Finley
A Co, 2d TkBn_____ Capt Edward L. Bale, Jr.
2d AmphTruckCo____ Capt James L. George

1st Battalion, 8th Marines

CO_____ LtCol Richard W. Hayward
ExO_____ Maj Robert L. Holderness
S–3_____ Capt William H. Pickett (WIA 22J)
HqCo_____ Capt August W. Berning
A Co_____ Capt Joseph F. Haley, Jr.
B Co_____ Capt John C. Lundrigan

C Co_____ Capt Harry P. Anderson

2d Battalion, 8th Marines

Co_____ LtCol Harry A. Waldorf
ExO_____ Maj William H. Junghans, Jr.
S–3_____ Capt Martin F. Barrett (To 18J)
HqCo_____ (Not shown)
E Co_____ Capt Robert H. Rogers
F Co_____ Capt Donald L. Walls
G Co_____ 1stLt Thurman L. Perkins

3d Battalion, 8th Marines

CO_____ LtCol Paul E. Wallace
ExO_____ Maj Byron V. Thornton
S–3_____ Maj John I. Warner, Jr.
HqCo_____ Capt Paul Cook (To 19J)
                        1stLt Winfield S. Wallace, Jr. (From 19J)
I Co_____ Capt George S. Skinner
K Co_____ Capt John Adrian, Jr. (WIA 3J)
                        1stLt David V. Carter (Actg From 4J)
L Co_____ Capt Joseph A. Zielinski (WIA 20J)

2d Battalion, 10th Marines

CO_____ LtCol Richard G. Weede
ExO_____ Maj Kenneth C. Houston
S–3_____ Capt William M. Spencer, III
H&S Btry_____ Capt Richard M. H. Harper, Jr.
D Btry_____ Capt Robert W. Anderson
E Btry_____ Capt Ralph E. Myer
F Btry_____ Capt Robert H. Hensel

2d Amphibian Tractor Battalion

CO_____ Maj Fenlon A. Durand
ExO_____ Capt Eugene A. Siegel
S–3_____ Capt William H. Houseman, Jr.
H&S Co_____ Capt Wilfred A. Ronck
A Co_____ Capt James F. Perry
B Co_____ Capt Philip T. Chaffee
C Co_____ Capt Wallace E. Nygren

6TH MARINE DIVISION (REINFORCED)

Headquarters, 6th Marine Division

CG_____ MajGen Lemuel C. Shepherd, Jr. (WIA 16M*)
ADC_____ BrigGen William T. Clement
CofS_____ Col John C. McQueen
G–1_____ Maj Addison B. Overstreet
G–2_____ LtCol Thomas E. Williams
G–3_____ LtCol Victor A. Krulak
G–4_____ LtCol August Larson (To 16M)
                        LtCol Wayne H. Adams (From 17M)

Headquarters Battalion, 6th Marine Division

CO_____ LtCol Floyd A. Stephenson
ExO_____ Maj Ralph W. Bohne

S-3_____ Maj Ralph W. Bohne
HqCo_____ Capt Donald J. McCaffrey (To 5A)
                    Maj John M. Downey (From 6A)
ReconCo_____ Maj Anthony Walker (To 14J)
                    1st Lt William J. Christie (From 15J)
6th ASCO_____ Capt Alfred C. Griffin
6th MP Co_____ Maj John M. Downey (To 5A)
                    Capt Donald J. McCaffrey (From 6A)
6th SigCo_____ Maj George W. Carr (To 4J)
                    LtCol William C. Moore (From 4J)
6th AmphTruckCo____ 1stLt David Astor (To 30M)
                    1stLt Murrel S. Hansen (From 31M)

6th Engineer Battalion

CO_____ Maj Paul F. Sackett
ExO_____ Maj Robert S. Mayo
S-3_____ Capt James H. Cooper
H&S Co_____ 1stLt William M. Graham, Jr.
A Co_____ Capt John W. McCuiston
B Co_____ Capt Noel E. Benger
C Co_____ Capt Burt A. Lewis, Jr.

6th Medical Battalion

CO_____ Cdr John S. Cowan, (MC)
ExO_____ Lt Joseph M. Shelton, (MC)
S-3_____ (Not shown)
H&S Co_____ (Not shown)
A Co_____ LCdr Owen W. E. Nowlin, (MC)
B Co_____ LCdr Gerald Flaum, (MC) (To 27A)
                    Lt Burton V. Scheib, (MC) (From 27A)
C Co_____ LCdr Aaron A. Topcik, (MC) (To 27A)
                    LCdr Robert J. Crawley, (MC) (27A–17M)
                    Lt John C. Wilson, (MC) (18M–9J)
                    LCdr Robert J. Crawley, (MC) (From 10J)
D Co_____ LCdr Horace B. McSwain, (MC) (To 18M)
                    LCdr Gerald Flaum, (MC) (19M–3J)
                    Lt Michael T. Michael, (MC) (From 4J)
E Co_____ Lt Charles M. Ihle, (MC)

6th Motor Transport Battalion

CO_____ LtCol Ernest H. Gould
ExO_____ Maj Robert E. McCook
S-3_____ 1stLt Robert E. Wagoner
H&S Co_____ Capt Albert Hartman
A Co_____ Capt Hershel J. Hall
B Co_____ Capt William F. A. Trax
C Co_____ Capt Willis M. Williams

6th Pioneer Battalion

CO_____ LtCol Samuel R. Shaw (To 10M)
                    Maj John G. Dibble (Actg 11M–8J)
                    LtCol Samuel R. Shaw (9–18J)
                    Maj John G. Dibble (From 19J)
ExO_____ Maj Olin L. Beall (To 23A)
                    Maj John C. Dibble (24A–19J)
                    Capt Harry B. Smith (From 19J)
S-3_____ 1stLt Harold L. Manley
H&S Co_____ 1stLt John G. Wintersohle
A Co_____ Maj John C. Dibble (To 23A)
                    1stLt Charles T. Robertson, III (From 24A)
B Co_____ Capt Harry B. Smith (To 18J)
                    Capt Richard J. Morrisey (From 19J)
C Co_____ Capt Russell J. Lutz

6th Service Battalion

CO_____ LtCol George B. Bell (To 25A)
                    LtCol Alexander N. Entringer (From 26A)
ExO_____ (Not shown)
S-3_____ 1stLt William F. Ragan (To 9M)
                    Capt Charles A. Harper, Jr. (From 12M)
HqCo_____ 2dLt Warren A. Lee (To 26A)
                    Capt Ira E. Hamer (From 27A)
OrdCo_____ Capt Oscar C. Miller
S&S Co_____ Capt William L. Batchelor

6th Tank Battalion

CO_____ LtCol Robert L. Denig, Jr.
ExO_____ Maj Harry T. Milne
S-3_____ Maj Henry Calcutt (WIA 18M*)
H&S Co_____ 2dLt Robert E. Wren (To 23A)
                    1stLt James C. Vail (From 24A)
A Co_____ Capt Philip C. Morell
B Co_____ Capt Robert Hall (WIA 10M)
                    Capt James R. Williams, Jr. (From 10M, WIA 21M*)
C Co_____ Capt Hugh Corrigan (WIA 15M)
                    Capt John H. Clifford (From 16M)

1st Armored Amphibian Battalion

CO_____ LtCol Louis Metzger (To 21J)
                    Maj Richard G. Warga (From 22J)
ExO_____ Maj Richard G. Warga (To 21J)
                    Capt William L. Eubank (From 22J)

S–3	1stLt Thomas M. Crosby
H&S Co	1stLt Clyde E. Browers
A Co	Capt Thomas J. Garfield
B Co	Capt Edgar S. Carlson
C Co	Capt William L. Eubank (To 21J)
	Capt Theodore A. Burge (From 22J)
D Co	Capt Robert E. McDowell, Jr.

4th Amphibian Tractor Battalion

CO	LtCol Clovis C. Coffman
ExO	Maj Arnold S. Dane
S–3	Capt Ralph J. Parker, Jr.
H&S Co	Maj Harold L. Oppenheimer
A Co	1stLt Frank Dayes
B Co	1stLt Theodore M. Garhart
C Co	Capt David E. Skipper

9th Amphibian Tractor Battalion

CO	Maj Theodore E. Watson
ExO	Maj Francis J. Farias
S–3	1stLt Clair C. Edmondson
H&S Co	WO Glenn M. Matthieu
A Co	Capt Robert H. Lage
B Co	Capt Ellwood P. Varner
C Co	1stLt Gerald G. Palaia

Headquarters, 4th Marines

CO	Col Alan Shapley
ExO	LtCol Fred D. Beans (To 14A)
	LtCol Fred D. Beans (From 1M)
S–3	Maj Orville V. Bergren
H&S Co	Capt Robert B. Corey (To 26A)
	1stLt Russell A. Thompson (From 27A)
WpnsCo	Capt Raymond L. Luckel

1st Battalion, 4th Marines

CO	Maj Bernard W. Green (KIA 15A)
	LtCol Fred D. Beans (15A–1M)
	LtCol George B. Bell (From 1M, WIA 4J*)
ExO	Maj Robert V. Allen
S–3	Capt Frank A. Kemp (To 22M)
	Maj John R. Kerman (From 22M)
HqCo	1stLt George Proechel, Jr. (To 5J)
	2dLt John M. Keeley (From 6J)
A Co	Capt Clinton B. Eastment (WIA 8J)
	1stLt David N. Schreiner (From 8J, DOW 21J)
	1stLt Joseph I. Deal (From 21J)
B Co	1stLt Thad N. Dodds (KIA 2A)
	1stLt Charles E. James (From 2A)
C Co	1stLt James G. Washburn (WIA 15A)

	1stLt William H. Carlson (From 15A, WIA 23M,* 27M,* KIA 5J)
	1stLt Lawrence S. Bangser (From 5J)

2d Battalion, 4th Marines

CO	LtCol Reynolds H. Hayden (To 26M)
	Maj Edgar F. Carney, Jr. (From 27M)
ExO	Maj Roy C. Batterton (WIA 15A)
	Maj Edgar F. Carney, Jr. (15A–26M)
	Maj Lincoln N. Holdzcom (From 27M)
S–3	Maj Lincoln N. Holdzcom (To 26M)
	Capt Wayne L. Edwards (27M–6J)
	1stLt James E. Brown (7–19J)
	Capt Wayne L. Edwards (From 20J)
HqCo	Maj Edgar F. Carney, Jr. (To 14A)
	2dLt Ernest L. Tongate, Jr. (1–7M)
	2dLt Gerald Fitzgerald (8–17M)
	Capt Wayne L. Edwards (18–26M)
	1stLt Merrill F. McLane (From 27M)
E Co	Capt. Leonard W. Alford (To 24M)
	1stLt Robert J. Herwig (25–29M)
	Capt Leonard W. Alford (30M–11J, DOW 17J)
	1st Lt Robert J. Herwig (From 11J, WIA 21J)
	1stLt Lester J. Markusen (From 21J)
F Co	Capt Eric S. Holmgrain
G Co	Capt Archie B. Norford (KIA 15A)
	1stLt Leo J. Gottsponer (From 15A)

3rd Battalion, 4th Marines

CO	LtCol Bruno A. Hochmuth
ExO	Maj Thomas E. Beeman (To 16A)
	Maj Carl E. Conron, Jr. (From 16A, KIA 20M)
	Maj Wilson E. Hunt (From 20M)
S–3	Maj Carl E. Conron, Jr. (To 15A)
	Maj Rade Enich (From 20A, WIA 23M)

	Capt Martin J. Sexton (1–14J)
	Maj Clay A. Bond (From 15J)
HqCo	Capt Robert B. Corey (27A–14J)
I Co	Capt Robert G. McMaster (WIA 21J)
K Co	Capt Martin J. Sexton (To 1J)
	Capt Vernon Burtman (1–13J)
	Capt Martin J. Sexton (From 15J)
L Co	Capt Nelson C. Dale, Jr. (WIA 2A)
	1stLt Marvin D. Perskie (From 2A)

Headquarters, 22d Marines

CO	Col Merlin F. Schneider (To 16M)
	Col Harold C. Roberts (From 17M, KIA 18J)
	LtCol August Larson (From 18J)
ExO	Col Karl K. Louther (To 16M)
	LtCol August Larson (17M–17J)
	LtCol John B. Baker (18–20J)
	LtCol Samuel R. Shaw (From 21J)
S–3	LtCol John B. Baker (To 17J)
	LtCol Walter H. Stephens (18–20J)
	LtCol John B. Baker (From 21J)
H&S Co	Capt David E. Cruikshank
WpnsCo	Maj George B. Kantner (To 2M)
	LtCol Gavin C. Humphrey (4–16J)
	Capt Francis D. Blizard, Jr. (From 17J)

1st Battalion, 22d Marines

CO	Maj Thomas J. Myers (KIA 15M)
	Maj Earl J. Cook (From 15M, WIA 17J)
	LtCol Gavin C. Humphrey (From 17J)
ExO	Maj Earl J. Cook (To 14M)
	Maj Edward G. Kurdziel (15M–15J)
	Maj Norman R. Sherman (From 16J)
S–3	Maj Edward G. Kurdziel
HqCo	Capt Charles P. DeLong (To 20A)
	Capt Eldon W. Autry (23A–19M)
	Capt Alfred H. Benjamin (From 20M)

A Co	Capt Walter G. Moeling, III (WIA 15M)
	1stLt Thomas J. Bohannon (From 15M, WIA 31M)
	1stLt Leland J. Gulligan (1–3J)
	2dLt Ralph R. Desso (From 4J, WIA 9J)
	2dLt Robert T. Johnson (9–15J)
	1stLt Evan L. Wolcott (From 16J)
B Co	1stLt Ernest George (1–9A)
	1stLt Thomas Parran, Jr. (Actg 10–20A)
	Capt Charles P. DeLong (From 21A, WIA 15M)
	1stLt Thomas Parran, Jr. (From 15M)
C Co	Capt Warren F. Lloyd (To 17M)

2d Battalion, 22d Marines

CO	LtCol Horatio C. Woodhouse, Jr. (KIA 30M)
	LtCol John G. Johnson (From 31M)
ExO	Maj Henry A. Courtney, Jr. (WIA 9M,* KIA 14M)
S–3	Maj Glenn E. Martin (To 21J)
	Capt Charles S. Robertson (From 22J)
HqCo	Capt John C. Deal, Jr.
E Co	1stLt Frank E. Gunter
F Co	Capt Maurice F. Ahearn, Jr. (WIA 13M)
	Capt William L. Sims (From 1J, WIA 9J)
	1stLt Robert O. Hutchings (From 9J)
G Co	Capt Owen T. Stebbins (WIA 12M)
	1stLt Hugh T. Crane (From 12M)

3d Battalion, 22d Marines

CO	LtCol Malcolm "O" Donohoo (WIA 16M)
	Maj George B. Kantner (16–19M)
	LtCol Clair W. Shisler (From 20M)
ExO	Maj Paul H. Bird (KIA 11A)
	Maj George B. Kantner (2–15M)
	Maj Roy D. Miller (16–19M)
	Maj George B. Kantner (From 20M)
S–3	Maj Roy D. Miller
HqCo	Capt Frank H. Haigler, Jr. (To 15M)
	1stLt Buenos A. W. Young (16M–21J)
	2dLt Leo M. Humphrey (From 22J)

I Co	1stLt Arthur E. Cofer (To 20A)
	Capt John Marston, Jr. (From 21A)
K Co	Capt Joseph P. Dockery (WIA 10M)
	1stLt Reginald Fincke, Jr. (From 11M, KIA 15M)
	1stLt James D. Roe (From 16M)
L Co	Capt John P. Lanigan (WIA 16M)
	Capt Frank H. Haigler, Jr. (From 16M)

Headquarters, 29th Marines

CO	Col Victor F. Bleasdale (To 14A)
	Col William J. Whaling (From 15A)
ExO	LtCol Orin K. Pressley
S-3	LtCol Angus M. Fraser (To 14J)
	LtCol George W. Killen (From 14J)
H&S Co	1stLt Robert E. Stinson
WpnsCo	Capt James G. Petrie

1st Battalion, 29th Marines

CO	LtCol Jean W. Moreau (WIA 16M)
	Maj Robert P. Neuffer (16–25M)
	LtCol Samuel S. Yeaton (26M–14J)
	LtCol Leroy P. Hunt, Jr. (From 15J)
ExO	Maj Robert J. Littin (To 21A)
	Maj James H. Brock (24A–26M)
	Maj Robert P. Neuffer (From 26M)
S-3	Maj James H. Brock (To 23A)
	Capt Ernest P. Freeman, Jr. (24A–27M)
	Maj James H. Brock (From 28M)
HqCo	Capt Ernest P. Freeman, Jr. (To 23A)
	1stLt Elliot L. Walzer (24A–15M)
	Capt Ernest P. Freeman, Jr. (From 1J)
A Co	1stLt Raymond J. Kautz (To 21A)
	Capt Jason B. Baker (24A–15J)
	1stLt Warren B. Watson (From 16J)
B Co	Capt Lyle E. Specht (WIA 17M)
	1stLt Charles P. Gallagher (18–22M)
	1stLt Griffith E. Thomas (From 24M, WIA 28M)
	1stLt Robert H. Neef (From 1J)
C Co	Capt Edwin H. Rodgers (WIA 8A)

	Capt George Heiden (From 10A, WIA 15M)
	Capt Jack F. Ramsey (From 16M, WIA 28M)
	1stLt Eugene T. Lawless (From 28M, WIA 15J*)

2d Battalion, 29th Marines

CO	LtCol William G. Robb (WIA 19A*)
ExO	Maj Thomas J. Cross
S-3	Maj Robert P. Neuffer (To 16M)
	Capt Robert B. Fowler (From 16M, KIA 12J)
	Maj Wallace G. Fleissner (From 14J)
HqCo	Capt Billie Musick (To 21A)
	Capt Martin J. Harrington (22A–22M)
	Capt Ralph D. Porch, II (23M–18J)
D Co	Capt Howard L. Mabie (WIA 16A*)
E Co	Capt Alan Meissner
F Co	Capt Robert B. Fowler (WIA 15A*, To 15M)
	1stLt George S. Thompson (From 15M, WIA 8J)
	1stLt Robert J. Sherer (From 8J)

3d Battalion, 29th Marines

CO	LtCol Erma A. Wright (To 14J)
	LtCol Angus N. Fraser (From 15J)
ExO	Maj Crawford B. Lawton (WIA 9A)
	Maj Everett W. Whipple (9–21A)
	Capt Walter E. Jorgensen (From 24A, WIA 16M)
	Capt Thomas P. Tomasello (17–22M)
	Capt Walter E. Jorgensen (1–13J)
	Maj Anthony Walker (From 15J)
S-3	Maj Everett W. Whipple (To 8A)
	Capt James R. Stockman (9A–6J)
	Capt Richard M. Haynes (6–13J)
	Maj Merlin Olsen (From 14J)
HqCo	Capt James R. Stockman (To 8A)
	1stLt Leroy W. Noyes, Jr. (9A–13J)
	Capt Walter E. Jorgensen (From 14J)

G Co_____ Capt Thomas J. Blanchet (To 17M)
1stLt John J. Keating (17–22M)
Capt William P. Tomasello (From 23M, WIA 9J)
1stLt Robert M. Hontz (From 10J)

H Co_____ Capt William P. Tomasello (To 16M)
Capt William A. Gamble (From 17M, WIA 5J*)

I Co_____ Capt Walter E. Jorgensen (To 23A)
Capt Philip J. Mylod (From 24A, WIA 14M)
1stLt Harvey F. Brooks (From 14M, WIA 15M)
1stLt John P. Stone (From 15M)

Headquarters, 15th Marines

CO_____ Col Robert B. Luckey
ExO_____ LtCol James H. Brower
S–3_____ Maj William H. Hirst
H&S Btry_____ 1stLt Lawrence I. Miller

1st Battalion, 15th Marines

CO_____ Maj Robert H. Armstrong
ExO_____ Maj William T. Box
S–3_____ 1stLt William N. Larson, Jr.
H&S Btry_____ 1stLt Paul K. Lynde
A Btry_____ 1stLt Benjamin S. Read (To 19A)
1stLt John J. O'Connor (From 20A)
B Btry_____ 1stLt James H. Boyd
C Btry_____ Capt Herbert T. Fitch

2d Battalion, 15th Marines

CO_____ Maj Nat M. Pace
ExO_____ Maj Edward O. Stephany (To 13A)
Maj William C. Roberts (From 14A)
S–3_____ Maj Robert P. Yeomans
H&S Btry_____ 2dLt Henry H. Lawler (Rear Ech)
D Btry_____ 1stLt Henry C. Schlosser
E Btry_____ Capt McCuthen G. Atkinson (WIA 13A)
1stLt Joseph A. Edwards (Actg From 13A)
F Btry_____ Capt John L. Noonan

3d Battalion, 15th Marines

CO_____ LtCol Joe C. McHaney
ExO_____ Maj Benedict V. Schneider, Jr.
S–3_____ Maj Hugh C. Becker
H&S Btry_____ Capt Edward C. O'Donnell
G Btry_____ Capt Harris H. Barnes, Jr.
H Btry_____ 1stLt Charles F. Petet, Jr.
I Btry_____ Capt Louis D. Abney, Jr.

4th Battalion, 15th Marines

CO_____ LtCol Bruce T. Hemphill
ExO_____ Maj Francis F. Parry
S–3_____ Capt Benjamin F. Spencer
H&S Btry_____ Capt Robert D. Lackland
K Btry_____ 1stLt Robert T. Patterson
L Btry_____ Capt John "T" Haynes, Jr.
M Btry_____ Maj Robert F. Irving

2D MARINE AIRCRAFT WING

CG_____ MajGen Francis P. Mulcahy (To 10J)
MajGen Louis E. Woods (From 11J)
CofS_____ Col Hayne D. Boyden
G–1_____ Capt Robert E. Coddington
G–2_____ Maj David B. Decker
G–3_____ Col Perry O. Parmelee
G–4_____ LtCol Charles T. Young, III (WIA 20A)
Capt William L. Woodruff (From 11J)
HqSq–2_____ Capt Richard F. Hyland
VMO–3_____ Capt Wallace J. Slappey, Jr.
VMO–6_____ Capt. Donald R. Garrett
VMO–7_____ Capt William A. Seward

Air Defense Command

CG_____ BrigGen William J. Wallace
CofS_____ Col Ford O. Rogers
G–3_____ Col Boeker C. Batterton

Marine Aircraft Group 14 (1–22 June)

CO_____ Col Edward A. Montgomery
ExO_____ LtCol Curtis E. Smith, Jr.
S–3_____ LtCol Robert H. Richard
HqSq–14_____ Capt Robert M. Crooks
SMS–14_____ Maj Francis H. Smythe (To 7J)
Maj Julius W. Ireland (From 8J)
VMF–212_____ Maj John P. McMahon
VMF–222_____ Maj Harold A. Harwood
VMF–223_____ Maj Howard E. King

Marine Aircraft Group 22 (1–22 June)

CO_____ Col Daniel W. Torrey, Jr.
ExO_____ LtCol Elmer A. Wrenn
S–3_____ Maj Thomas C. Colt, Jr.
HqSq–22_____ Capt Linsay K. Dickey
SMS–22_____ Maj Bruce Prosser
VMF–113_____ Maj Hensley Williams
VMF–314_____ Maj Robert C. Cameron
VMF–422_____ Maj Elkin S. Dew
VMF(N)–533_____ LtCol Marion M. Magruder
VMTB–131_____ Maj Douglas H. Bangert

Marine Aircraft Group 31

CO_____ Col John C. Munn
ExO_____ LtCol Gordon E. Hendricks (To 20J)
LtCol Kirk Armistead (From 22J)

S-3 _____ LtCol Kirk Armistead (To 21J)
Maj Charles M. Kunz (From 22J)

HqSq–31 _____ Maj Leon A. Danco (To 14M)
1stLt Frederick L. Donnelly (From 14M)

SMS–31 _____ Maj Archibald M. Smith (To 28A)
Maj Paul T. Johnston (29A–1J)
Maj Joseph A. Gray (From 2J)

VMF–224 _____ Maj James W. Poindexter (To 30M)
Maj Robert C. Hammond, Jr. (31M–14J)
Maj Allan T. Barnum (From 15J)

VMF–311 _____ Maj Perry L. Shuman (To 15J)
Maj Michael R. Yunck (From 15J)

VMF–441 _____ Maj Robert O. White (To 19J)
Maj Paul T. Johnston (From 20J)

VMF(N)–542 _____ Maj William C. Kellum (To 22M)
Maj Robert B. Porter (From 24M)

Marine Aircraft Group 33

CO _____ Col Ward E. Dickey
ExO _____ LtCol James L. Beam
S–3 _____ LtCol Eschol M. Mallory

HqSq–33 _____ Capt Richard Kilbourne
SMS–33 _____ Maj Hugh P. Calahan
VMF–312 _____ Maj Richard M. Day (MIA 14M)
Maj Hugh I. Russell (14–24M)
Maj Frank "J" Cole (From 25M)

VMF–322 _____ Maj Frederick M. Rauschenbach (To 30M)
Maj Walter E. Lischeid (From (31 F)

VMF–323 _____ Maj George C. Axtell, Jr. (To 14J)
Maj Martin E. W. Olerich (From 16J)

VMF(N)–543 _____ Maj Clair "C" Chamerlin (To 17J)
Maj James B. Maguire, Jr. (From 18J)

VMTB–232 _____ Maj Allen L. Feldmeier

Marine Aircraft Group 43

CO _____ LtCol Robert O. Bisson
ExO _____ (Not shown)
S–3 _____ LtCol Radford C. West
HqSq–43 _____ Maj William F. Feasley
AWS–1 _____ Capt Edward R. Stainback
AWS–6 _____ Capt Clarence C. Gordon
AWS–7 _____ Capt Paul E. Bardet
AWS–8 _____ Maj Frank B. Freese
AWS–11 _____ Capt John L. Carnegie

III Amphibious Corps Task Organization[1]

III AMPHIBIOUS CORPS . . . MajGen Roy S. Geiger
I. *Corps Troops* . . . . . . LtCol William F. Whitaker
  Headquarters and Service Battalion
  Signal Battalion
    3d Separate Radio Intelligence Platoon, Mobile Communication Unit 43D, Detachment, Air Warning Squadron
  1st Military Police Battalion, FMFPac (less Company D)
  Company A, 1st Provisional Military Police Battalion (USA)
  Landing Force Air Support Control Unit No 1
  Medical Battalion
  Corps Evacuation Hospital No 2
  Corps Evacuation Hospital No 3
  Corps Engineer Group
    44th Naval Construction Regiment (less 58th Naval Construction Battalion, 130th Naval Construction Battalion, 145th Naval Construction Battalion, and 11th Special Naval Construction Battalion, reinforced)
    71st Naval Construction Battalion
    1st Separate Engineer Battalion
    802d Aviation Engineer Battalion (USA)
  Corps Service Group
    Headquarters, Service Group
    Headquarters, Shore Party
    Company D, 1st Military Police Battalion, FMFPac
    11th Motor Transport Battalion, FMFPac
    7th Field Depot, reinforced
  1st Bomb Disposal Company (less 2d and 3d Platoons)

  1st Laundry Company (less 1st, 2d, and 3d Platoons)
  Detachment B–8, Military Government
  Detachment C–1, Military Government
  G–10 Dispensary No 12
  G–6 Hospital No 1
II. *Corps Artillery* . . . . . . BrigGen David R. Nimmer
  Headquarters Battery, Corps Artillery
    6th 155mm Howitzer Battalion
    8th 155mm Gun Battalion
    9th 155mm Gun Battalion
  Headquarters Battery, 2d Provisional Field Artillery Group
    1st 155mm Howitzer Battalion
    3d 155mm Howitzer Battalion
    7th 155mm Gun Battalion
  456th Amphibian Truck Company (USA)
  Marine Observation Squadron 7
III. *Corps Antiaircraft Artillery* . . . Col Kenneth W. Benner
  Headquarters, 1st Provisional Antiaircraft Artillery Group
    2d Antiaircraft Artillery Battalion
    5th Antiaircraft Artillery Battalion
    8th Antiaircraft Artillery Battalion
    16th Antiaircraft Artillery Battalion
IV. *Corps Reserve* . . . . Col Victor F. Bleasdale
  29th Marines
  Company A, 6th Tank Battalion
  Company C, 6th Engineer Battalion
  Company C, 6th Pioneer Battalion
  Company C, 6th Motor Transport Battalion
  Company C, 6th Medical Battalion
  3d Platoon, 6th Military Police Company
  3d Platoon, Ordnance Company, 6th Service Battalion
  3d Platoon, Service and Supply Company, 6th Service Battalion (less Post Exchange Section)

[1] IIIAC OpPlan No 1–45, 1Feb45, 1–3; 1st MarDiv OpPlan 1–45, 10Feb45, 1–3; 6th MarDiv OpPlan No 1–45, 10Feb45, 1–3; *29th Mar SAR, Ph I&II*, Chap II, 1–2.

3d Band Section

Detachment, 6th Amphibian Truck Company

Detachment, 11th Special Naval Construction Battalion

Detachment, 26th Replacement Draft

Detachment, 33d Replacement Draft

3d Shore Fire Control Party, 6th Joint Assault Signal Company

3d Air-Ground Liaison Party, 6th Joint Assault Signal Company

3d Shore Party Communication Team, 6th Joint Assault Signal Company

1st War Dog Platoon

V. *1st Marine Division (Reinforced)* . . MajGen Pedro A. del Valle

Division Troops

Headquarters Battalion (less 1st Military Police Company)

1st Medical Battalion (less Companies A, B, and C)

4th Joint Assault Signal Company (less detachments)

454th Amphibian Truck Company (USA) (less detachments)

Detachment A–1, Military Government

Detachment B–1, Military Government

G–10 Dispensary No 17

G–10 Dispensary No 18

Assault Air Warning Teams

4th Provisional Rocket Detachment

4th War Dog Platoon

Combat Team 1

1st Marines

Company A, 1st Engineer Battalion

Company A, 1st Pioneer Battalion

Company A, 1st Medical Battalion

Company A, 1st Motor Transport Battalion

Detachment, Ordnance Company, 1st Service Battalion (Attached: 2d Platoon, 1st Bomb Disposal Company, less 2d and 3d Squads)

Detachment, Service and Supply Company, 1st Service Battalion

1st Platoon, 1st Military Police Company

Detachment, 4th Joint Assault Signal Company

Detachment, 454th Amphibian Truck Company (USA)

Combat Team 5

5th Marines

Co B, 1st Engineer Battalion

Co B, 1st Pioneer Battalion

Co B, 1st Medical Battalion

Co B, 1st Motor Transport Battalion

1st Amphibian Tractor Battalion (less detachments)

Detachment, Ordnance Company, 1st Service Battalion

(Attached: 3d Squad, 2d Platoon 1st Bomb Disposal Company)

Detachment, Service and Supply Company, 1st Service Battalion

2d Platoon, 1st Military Police Company

Detachment, 454th Amphibian Truck Company (USA)

Detachment, 4th Joint Assault Signal Company

Combat Team 7

7th Marines

Co C, 1st Engineer Battalion

Co C, 1st Pioneer Battalion

Co C, 1st Medical Battalion

Co C, 1st Motor Transport Battalion

8th Amphibian Tractor Battalion (less detachments)

Detachment, Ordnance Company, 1st Service Battalion (Attached: 2d Squad, 2d Platoon, 1st Bomb Disposal Company)

Detachment, Service and Supply Company, 1st Service Battalion

3d Platoon, 1st Military Police Company

Detachment, 454th Amphibian Truck Company (USA)

Detachment, 4th Joint Assault Signal Company

Artillery Group

11th Marines

3d Amphibian Truck Company

Detachment, 454th Amphibian Truck Company (USA)

Marine Observation Squadron 3

Detachment, 1st Amphibian Tractor Battalion

Detachment, 8th Amphibian Tractor Battalion

Armored Amphibian Tractor Group

3d Armored Amphibian Tractor Battalion (Provisional)

Tank Group

1st Tank Battalion

Detachment, 1st Amphibian Tractor Battalion

Detachment, 8th Amphibian Tractor Battalion

Tank Maintenance Platoon, Ordnance Company, 1st Service Battalion

Engineer Group

1st Engineer Battalion (less Companies A, B, and C)

145th Naval Construction Battalion (less detachments)

Shore Party Group

1st Pioneer Battalion (less Companies A, B, and C)

One-half, 11th Special Naval Construction Battalion

Detachment, 145th Naval Construction Battalion

Detachment, 4th Joint Assault Signal Company

Replacement Group

Service Group

1st Service Battalion (less detachments)

1st Motor Transport Battalion (less Companies A, B, and C)

2d Platoon, 1st Laundry Company

Military Police Group

1st Military Police Company (less 1st, 2d, and 3d Platoons)

Company B, 1st Provisional Military Police Battalion (USA)

VI. *6th Marine Division* (*Reinforced*) . . . MajGen Lemuel C. Shepherd, Jr.

Division Troops
 Headquarters Battalion (less detachments)
 Company C, 1st Provisional Military Police Battalion (USA)
 6th Joint Assault Signal Company (less detachments)
 6th Amphibian Truck Company (less detachments)
 Detachment A–3, Military Government
 Detachment B–3, Military Government
 Corps Artillery Liaison Teams
 Early Air Warning Team

Combat Team 4
 4th Marines (less 2d Battalion (less Company E))
 Company A, 6th Engineer Battalion (less 2d Platoon)
 Company A, 6th Pioneer Battalion (less 2d Platoon)
 Company A, 6th Motor Transport Battalion (less 2d Platoon)
 Company A, 6th Medical Battalion (less one collecting section)
 Detachment, 26th Replacement Draft
 Detachment, 33d Replacement Draft
 1st Platoon, 6th Military Police Company (less detachment)
 1st Platoon, Ordnance Company, 6th Service Battalion (less detachment)
 1st Platoon, Service and Supply Company, 6th Service Battalion (less Post Exchange Section and detachment)
 Detachment, 58th Naval Construction Battalion
 Detachment, 11th Special Naval Construction Battalion
 Detachment, 6th Amphibian Truck Company
 1st Band Section (less detachment)
 1st Shore Fire Control Party, 6th Joint Assault Signal Company (less detachment)
 1st Air-Ground Liaison Party, 6th Joint Assault Signal Company (less detachment)
 1st Shore Party Communication Team, 6th Joint Assault Signal Company (less detachment)
 1st Section, 3d Platoon, 1st Bomb Disposal Company

Combat Team 22
 22d Marines
 Company B, 6th Engineer Battalion
 Company B, 6th Pioneer Battalion
 Company B, 6th Motor Transport Battalion
 Company B, 6th Medical Battalion
 Detachment, 26th Replacement Draft
 Detachment, 33d Replacement Draft
 2d Platoon, 6th Military Police Company
 2d Platoon, Ordnance Company, 6th Service Battalion

 2d Platoon, Service and Supply Company, 6th Service Battalion (less Post Exchange Section)
 Detachment, 58th Naval Construction Battalion
 Detachment, 11th Special Naval Construction Battalion
 Detachment, 814th Amphibian Truck Company (USA)
 5th Provisional Rocket Detachment
 2d Band Section
 3d Platoon, 1st Bomb Disposal Company (less 1st Section)
 2d Shore Fire Control Party, 6th Joint Assault Signal Company
 2d Air-Ground Liaison Party, 6th Joint Assault Signal Company
 2d Shore Party Communication Team, 6th Joint Assault Signal Company

Division Artillery Group
 15th Marines
 Detachment, 6th Amphibian Truck Company
 Detachment, 814th Amphibian Truck Company (USA)
 Marine Observation Squadron 6

Armored Amphibian Group
 1st Armored Amphibian Battalion
 3–9–A Unit

Tank Group
 6th Tank Battalion (less Company A)
 Tank Maintainance Platoon, Ordnance Company, 6th Service Battalion

1st Amphibian Tractor Group
 9th Amphibian Tractor Battalion

2d Amphibian Tractor Group
 4th Amphibian Tractor Battalion

Engineer Group
 6th Engineer Battalion (less detachments)
 58th Naval Construction Battalion (less detachments)

Shore Party Group
 6th Pioneer Battalion (less detachments)
 26th Replacement Draft (less detachments)
 33d Replacement Draft (less detachments)
 Detachment, 6th Joint Assault Signal Company
 814th Amphibian Truck Company (less detachments)
 One-half, 11th Special Naval Construction Battalion (less detachments)

Service Group
 6th Service Battalion (less detachments)
 6th Motor Transport Battalion (less detachments)
 6th Medical Battalion (less detachments)
 (Attached: G–10 and G–11 Dispensary Units)

Division Reserve
 2d Battalion, 4th Marines (less Company E)
 2d Platoon, Weapons Company, 4th Marines
 2d Platoon, Company A, 6th Engineer Battalion
 2d Platoon, Company A, 6th Pioneer Battalion

2d Platoon, Company A, 6th Motor Transport Battalion

Detachment, Collection Section, Company A, 6th Medical Battalion

Detachment, 26th Replacement Draft

Detachment, 33d Replacement Draft

Detachment, 11th Special Naval Construction Battalion

Detachment, 1st Band Section

Detachment, 1st Platoon, 6th Military Police Company

Detachment, 1st Platoon, Ordnance Company, 6th Service Battalion

Detachment, 1st Platoon, Service and Supply Company, 6th Service Battalion

Detachment, 1st Shore Fire Control Party, 6th Joint Assault Signal Company

Detachment, 1st Air-Ground Liaison Party, 6th Joint Assault Signal Company

Detachment, Shore Party Communication Team, 6th Joint Assault Signal Company

APPENDIX V

Japanese Order of Battle[1]

ARMY UNITS

Unit	Strength
Thirty-second Army Troops	
Headquarters	1,070
Ordnance Depot	1,498
Ordnance Duty Unit	150
Field Freight Depot	1,167
36th Signal Regiment	1,912
Okinawa Army Hospital	204
27th Field Water Purification Unit	244
Well Digging Unit	34
Defense Construction Unit	108
7th Fortress Construction Duty Company	322
2d Field Construction Duty Company	366
24th Infantry Division	
Headquarters	267
22d Infantry Regiment	2,796
32d Infantry Regiment	2,870
89th Infantry Regiment	2,809
42d Field Artillery Regiment	2,321
24th Reconnaissance Regiment	346
24th Engineer Regiment	777
24th Transport Regiment	1,158
Signal Unit	275
Decontamination Training Unit	77
Ordnance Repair Unit	57
Veterinary Hospital	11
Water Supply and Purification Unit	241

[1] The order of battle is based on a listing compiled by Tenth Army G–2 contained in *IntelMono*, Part I, Sect B, Chap II, 3. Obvious discrepancies in this list have been corrected with the aid of *POW InterrSum* Nos 1–19 and *CICAS Trans* No 212, Extracts from 32d Army Order of Battle, mid-March 1945. Units are listed by their original designation with the strengths they are believed to have had just prior to the American landings.

Unit	Strength
1st Field Hospital	174
2d Field Hospital	181
62d Infantry Division	
Headquarters	65
63d Brigade Headquarters	129
11th Independent Infantry Battalion	1,091
12th Independent Infantry Battalion	1,085
13th Independent Infantry Battalion	1,058
14th Independent Infantry Battalion	1,085
273d Independent Infantry Battalion	683
64th Brigade Headquarters	121
15th Independent Infantry Battalion	1,076
21st Independent Infantry Battalion	1,080
22d Independent Infantry Battalion	1,071
23d Independent Infantry Battalion	1,089
272d Independent Infantry Battalion	683
Engineer Unit	255
Signal Unit	359
Transport Unit	300
Field Hospital	371
Veterinary Hospital	22
44th Independent Mixed Brigade	
Headquarters	63
2d Infantry Unit	2,046
15th Independent Mixed Regiment	1,885
Artillery Unit	330
Engineer Unit	161
5th Artillery Command	
Headquarters	147
1st Medium Artillery Regiment (−)	856
23d Medium Artillery Regiment	1,143
7th Heavy Artillery Regiment	526
100th Independent Heavy Artillery Battalion	565
1st Independent Artillery Mortar Regiment (−)	613
1st Light Mortar Battalion	633
2d Light Mortar Battalion	615

Unit	Strength
21st Antiaircraft Artillery Command	
Headquarters	71
27th Independent Antiaircraft Artillery Bn	505
79th Field Antiaircraft Artillery Battalion	513
80th Field Antiaircraft Artillery Battalion	517
81st Field Antiaircraft Artillery Battalion	514
103d Independent Machine Cannon Battalion	336
104th Independent Machine Cannon Battalion	338
105th Independent Machine Cannon Battalion	337
Machine Gun Units	
3d Independent Machine Gun Battalion	340
4th Independent Machine Gun Battalion	344
14th Independent Machine Gun Battalion	334
17th Independent Machine Gun Battalion	331
Antitank Units	
3d Independent Antitank Battalion	363
7th Independent Antitank Battalion	353
22d Independent Antitank Battalion	402
32d Independent Antitank Company	144
11th Shipping Group	
Headquarters	100
7th Shipping Engineer Branch Depot	600
23d Shipping Engineer Regiment (−)	850
26th Shipping Engineer Regiment (−)	550
5th Sea Raiding Base Headquarters	42
1st Sea Raiding Squadron	104
2d Sea Raiding Squadron	104
3d Sea Raiding Squadron	104
26th Sea Raiding Squadron	104
27th Sea Raiding Squadron	104
28th Sea Raiding Squadron	104
29th Sea Raiding Squadron	104
1st Sea Raiding Base Battalion	886
2d Sea Raiding Base Battalion	874
3d Sea Raiding Base Battalion	877
26th Sea Raiding Base Battalion	908
27th Sea Raiding Base Battalion	897
28th Sea Raiding Base Battalion	900
29th Sea Raiding Base Battalion	900
49th Line of Communication Sector	
Headquarters	202
72d Land Duty Company	508
83d Land Duty Company	496
103d Sea Duty Company	711
104th Sea Duty Company	724
215th Independent Motor Transport Company	181
259th Independent Motor Transport Company	182
Engineer Units	
66th Independent Engineer Battalion	865
14th Field Well Drilling Company	110
20th Field Well Drilling Company	110
19th Air Sector Command	
Headquarters	41
29th Field Airfield Construction Battalion	750
44th Airfield Battalion	377
50th Airfield Battalion	360
56th Airfield Battalion	380

Unit	Strength
3d Independent Maintenance Unit	120
Makoto 1st Maintenance Company	90
118th Independent Maintenance Unit	100
6th Fortress Construction Duty Company	330
Detachment, 20th Air Regiment	27
10th Field Meteorological Unit	80
26th Air-Ground Radio Unit	117
46th Independent Air Company	132
1st Branch Depot, 5th Field Air Repair Depot	130
21st Air Signal Unit	310
Okinawa Branch, Army Air Route Department	359
223d Specially Established Garrison Company	200
224th Specially Established Garrison Company	200
225th Specially Established Garrison Company	200
27th Tank Regiment	750
Army Unit Total	[2] 66,636

NAVY UNITS

Unit	Strength
Okinawa Base Force (Headquarters, Coast Defense, and Antiaircraft Personnel)	3,400
27th Motor Torpedo Boat Squadron	200
33d Midget Submarine Unit	130
37th Torpedo Maintenance Unit	140
Torpedo Working Unit	130
81mm Mortar Battery	150
Oroku Transmitting Station	30
Naha Branch, Sasebo Naval Stores Department	136
Naha Branch, Sasebo Transportation Department	136
Naha Navy Yard, Sasebo Naval Base	53
Oroku Detachment, 951st Air Group	600
Nansei Shoto Air Group	2,000
226th Construction Unit	1,420
3210th Construction Unit	300
Navy Unit Total	[3] 8,825

OKINAWAN

Unit	Strength
502d Special Guard Engineer Unit	900
503d Special Guard Engineer Unit	700
504th Special Guard Engineer Unit	700
Blood-and-Iron-For-The-Emperor-Duty-Unit	750
Boeitai Assigned to the Army	16,600
Boeitai Assigned to the Navy	1,100

[2] This figure represents the total Japanese strength. Included in it, however, are an estimated 5,000 Okinawans, mostly regular conscripts, who were integrated into Japanese units.

[3] This total represents both regular naval ratings and the Japanese, Korean, and Okinawan military civilians who were utilized in the naval land combat organization.

Unit	Strength
Students	600
Regular Conscripts Not Included Under Army Units	2,000
Okinawan Total	23,350
Grand Total (Rounded Out)	
Army Units	67,000
Navy Units	9,000

Unit	Strength
Okinawans	24,000
Japanese Strength On Okinawa	[4] 100,000

[4] Final figures have been rounded out to avoid the appearance of exactness. Thirty-second Army's peak combat strength may have been anywhere between 95,000 and 105,000.

APPENDIX VI

Marine Casualties

1 APRIL–22 JUNE 1945 [1]

MARINE CASUALTIES	KIA		DOW		WIA		MIAPD		CF		TOTAL	
	Officer	Enlisted	Officer	Enlisted	Officer	Enlisted	Officer	Enlisted	Officer	Enlisted	Officer	Enlisted
ReconBn, FMFPac		3			2	10				3	2	16
IIIAC Troops												
H&S Bn		7	1	2	11	36				4	12	49
MedBn						4				6		10
SigBn		4			1	25			1		2	29
1st MP Bn		5				21				2		28
1st SepEngBn		1		1		22			1	12	1	36
11th MT Bn				1		12				2		15
7th ServRegt		1			2	28				8	2	37
IIIAC Artillery												
HqBtry	1	1	1	1	2	9					4	11
HqBtry, 1st ProvAAAGrp		1		1		3						5
2d AAA Bn					1	11				4	1	15
5th AAA Bn		1			1	10				1	1	12
8th AAA Bn				1	2	8					2	9
16th AAA Bn		2		2		32				2		38
HqBtry, 2d ProvFAGrp						2				1		3
1st 155mm HowBn		1		1		27		1		1		31
3d 155mm HowBn		2		2	3	16	1			3	4	23
6th 155mm HowBn		1		2	1	25				1	1	29
7th 155mm GunBn				1		2						3
8th 155mm GunBn						9				4		13
9th 155mm GunBn		1			1	10				1		12
1st Marine Division												
HqBn	2	22		3	11	117			1	10	14	152
1st EngBn	1	11		5	6	119			1	5	8	140
1st MedBn					2	12					2	12
1st MT Bn		1				25			1	1	1	27
1st PionBn		1		2	1	28				4	1	35
1st ServBn		2			1	39				6	1	47
1st TkBn	2	12	1	1	15	135				3	18	151
3d LVT(A) Bn		1		1	3	43				3	3	48

See footnote at end of table.

MARINE CASUALTIES	KIA		DOW		WIA		MIAPD		CF		TOTAL	
	Officer	Enlisted	Officer	Enlisted	Officer	Enlisted	Officer	Enlisted	Officer	Enlisted	Officer	Enlisted
1st Marine Division—Continued												
1st LVT Bn	-----	1	----	1	5	24	----	----	----	4	5	30
8th LVT Bn	-----	3	----	------	2	22	----	----	----	------	2	25
1st MarRegt												
H&S and WpnsCos	-----	8	----	------	3	53	----	----	----	3	3	64
1stBn	11	109	----	10	25	635	----	----	----	108	36	862
2dBn	5	126	----	15	22	630	----	----	1	76	28	847
3dBn	3	89	----	15	25	673	----	----	----	77	28	854
5th MarRegt												
H&S and WpnsCos	-----	8	1	------	1	52	----	----	----	3	2	63
1st Bn	2	117	1	14	28	572	----	----	----	30	31	733
2d Bn	5	113	2	14	27	540	----	----	----	34	34	701
3d Bn	4	79	1	12	21	405	----	----	----	43	26	539
7th MarRegt												
H&S and WpnsCos	2	17	----	2	7	105	----	1	----	4	9	129
1st Bn	5	91	2	9	28	557	----	----	----	42	35	699
2d Bn	4	125	2	21	27	608	----	1	----	29	33	784
3d Bn	6	83	1	14	26	475	----	----	----	34	33	606
11th MarRegt												
H&S Btry	-----	1	----	1	3	10	----	----	----	1	3	13
1st Bn	1	3	1	1	2	47	----	1	----	------	4	52
2d Bn	----	5	----	5	6	52	----	----	----	------	6	62
3d Bn	----	3	1	2	9	64	----	----	----	1	10	70
4th Bn	3	5	----	1	5	52	----	----	----	1	8	59
8th CT												
H&S and WpnsCos	-----	1	----	2	2	15	----	----	----	1	2	19
1st Bn	1	3	----	------	1	50	----	----	----	1	2	54
2d Bn	-----	13	----	3	1	115	----	----	----	12	1	143
3d Bn	-----	16	----	4	4	99	----	----	----	7	4	126
Reinforcing Units	-----	3	----	2	3	38	----	----	1	7	4	50
6th Marine Division												
HqBn	1	25	1	3	22	165	----	----	1	64	25	257
6thEngBn	----	10	----	6	10	146	----	----	----	15	10	177
6th MedBn	-----	------	----	------	-----	8	----	----	----	1	------	9
6th MT Bn	-----	------	----	1	7	17	----	----	----	1	7	19
6th PionBn	-----	4	----	------	3	50	----	----	----	9	3	63
6th ServBn	-----	9	----	------	----	32	----	----	----	5	------	46
6th TkBn	1	7	----	2	19	105	----	----	----	2	20	116
1st LVT(A) Bn	-----	2	----	1	-----	39	----	1	----	4	------	47
4th LVT Bn	-----	1	----	1	2	26	----	----	----	3	2	31
9th LVT Bn	-----	3	----	1	----	48	----	----	----	2	------	54
4th MarRegt												
H&S and WpnsCos	-----	16	1	6	6	101	----	----	1	5	8	128
1st Bn	13	113	4	28	38	699	----	3	----	42	55	885
2d Bn	7	120	2	32	30	799	----	1	1	45	40	997
3d Bn	3	128	2	25	33	735	----	----	----	67	38	955
22d MarRegt												
H&S and WpnsCos	1	7	----	9	5	71	----	----	1	13	7	100
1st Bn	9	143	----	21	38	582	----	----	1	158	48	904
2d Bn	6	127	3	26	31	555	----	----	2	190	42	898
3d Bn	3	101	----	33	34	659	----	----	1	141	38	934

See footnote at end of table.

MARINE CASUALTIES	KIA		DOW		WIA		MIAPD		CF		TOTAL	
	Officer	Enlisted	Officer	Enlisted	Officer	Enlisted	Officer	Enlisted	Officer	Enlisted	Officer	Enlisted
6th Marine Division—Continued												
29th MarRegt												
H&S and WpnsCo		14			4	71			1	6	5	91
1st Bn	9	133	1	31	40	679		1	1	47	51	891
2d Bn	10	129		16	20	583		4		52	30	784
3d Bn	3	175	3	27	26	676			2	57	34	935
15th MarRegt												
H&S Btry						6				2		8
1st Bn	2	9	1	1	7	55				5	10	70
2d Bn	1	9		1	6	66	1		1	5	9	81
3d Bn		3			5	29					5	32
4th Bn	2	5		3	2	39				3	4	50
2d Marine Air Wing												
HqSqn	1	1			8	11			2		11	12
VMO-3					2	1	1				3	1
VMO-6	1	1			1		1				3	1
VMO-7					1						1	
MAG-14												
HqSqn-14										1		1
SMS-14						1						1
VMF-212	2					1	3				5	1
VMF-222					1		1				2	
VMF-223					2		2			1	4	1
MAG-22												
HqSqn-22					1	1				1	1	2
SMS-22		6		1	5	24	1			1	6	32
VMF-113					2		1		1		4	
VMF-314	1				1	3					2	3
VMF-422	1										1	
VMF(N)-533					1						1	
VMTB-131		1				1	1	2		1	1	5
MAG-31												
HqSqn-31					1	18				1	1	19
SMS-31					2						2	
VMF-224	1				1	8	1				3	8
VMF-311	4	1			2	4				1	6	6
VMF-441	3				3	1	5				11	1
VMF(N)-542						9	2				2	9
MAG-33												
HqSqn-33						2						2
SMS-33		1		2		9			1		1	12
VMF-312	2	1			5	1	2		2	1	11	3
VMF-322	2				2	8	2			1	6	9
VMF-323	2				2	3	2			1	6	4
VMF(N)-543	3				2	4	2				7	4
VMTB-232	1	3			3	20	1	1			5	24
MAG-43												
HqSqn-43		4		2	1	13				2	1	21
AWS-1						1						1
AWS-6						3						3
AWS-7		2		3	1	8					1	13
AWS-8				1	1	7					1	8

See footnote at end of table.

MARINE CASUALTIES	KIA		DOW		WIA		MIAPD		CF		TOTAL	
	Officer	Enlisted	Officer	Enlisted	Officer	Enlisted	Officer	Enlisted	Officer	Enlisted	Officer	Enlisted
Replacement Drafts [2]	1	157	1	28	9	735	----	1	1	34	12	955
Miscellaneous Air [3]	4	------	1	------	9	11	4	----	----	------	18	11
Miscellaneous Ground [4]	----	16	----	8	----	117	----	----	3	14	3	155
Total Casualties	158	2,590	[5]35	[5]494	806	14,799	34	18	29	1,609	1,062	19,510
Marine Ship Detachments	1	47	----	1	8	97	----	10	----	5	9	160
Marine Carrier Air Detachments	10	40	----	------	7	6	2	----	1	1	20	47
GRAND TOTAL, MARINE CASUALTIES	169	2,677	35	495	821	14,902	36	28	30	1,615	1,091	19,717
Naval Medical Personnel Attached to Marine Units [6]	1	108	----	9	12	430	----	----	----	----	13	547

[1] These final casualty figures for World War II were compiled from records furnished by Statistics Unit, Personnel Accounting Section, Personnel Department, Headquarters Marine Corps. They are audited to include 26Aug52. The key to the abbreviations used at the head of columns in the table follows: KIA, Killed in Action; DOW, Diew of Wounds; WIA, Wounded in Action; MIAPD, Missing in Action, Presumed Dead; CF, Combat Fatigue.

[2] Most members of replacement drafts who became casualties did so as members of regular combat units. In many instances, these men were hit before official notice of their transfer reached Headquarters Marine Corps, and therefore, they are carried on the casualty rolls as members of the various drafts.

[3] Included in the miscellaneous categories are those men whose personnel records still showed them as members of units not part of Tenth Army when the report of their becoming a casualty reached Headquarters Marine Corps.

[4] This category includes the casualties suffered by the 2dMarDiv while it was in the Okinawa area.

[5] Because of the method of reporting casualties used during World War II a substantial number of DOW figures are also included in the WIA Total.

[6] Compiled from NavMed P–5021, *The History of The Medical Department of the Navy in World War II*, vol 2, (Washington, 1953). Personnel MIAPD are included in the KIA total; no breakdown of combat fatigue cases is provided.

Marine and Naval Corpsmen Medal of Honor Winners

APPENDIX VII

CORPORAL RICHARD E. BUSH, 1st Battalion, 4th Marines. Severely wounded while leading the first squad to penetrate the Mt. Yae Take inner defenses, he was evacuated to a nearby aid station. When an enemy grenade landed in the midst of the wounded men, he unhesitatingly pulled it to his body to protect his comrades from serious injury or death. (16 April 1945)

HOSPITAL APPRENTICE FIRST CLASS ROBERT E. BUSH, 2d Battalion, 5th Marines. He was administering plasma to a wounded officer on an exposed ridgeline when the enemy attacked. He fought off the charging enemy with his pistol and a carbine, killing six despite his own serious wounds. He calmly ignored his critical condition until his patient was evacuated. (2 May 1945)

*Indicates posthumous award.

MAJOR HENRY A. COURTNEY, JR., 2d Battalion, 22d Marines. Gallantly leading by personal example, he inspired a small group of men from his unit to assault and capture the crest of Sugar Loaf Hill. He continued to lead attacks against the superior enemy defending forces until killed by a hostile mortar burst. (14–15 May 1945)*

CORPORAL JOHN P. FARDY, 1st Battalion, 1st Marines. When heavy enemy small-arms fire drove his squad to cover in a narrow drainage ditch and an enemy grenade fell among the men, he smothered the lethal explosion with his own body to protect his comrades' lives. (6 May 1945)*

PRIVATE FIRST CLASS WILLIAM A. FOSTER, 3d Battalion, 1st Marines. Dug in with another Marine on the point of a perimeter defense during a fierce close-in battle with the enemy, he threw himself on a grenade that landed out of reach in his foxhole to protect the life of his comrade with his own. (2 May 1945)*

PRIVATE FIRST CLASS HAROLD GONSALVES, 4th Battalion, 15th Marines. After repeatedly braving terrific enemy bombardment to aid his forward observation team, he dived on an enemy grenade which landed in its midst, sacrificing his own chances of survival to protect his fellow Marines. (15 April 1945)

PHARMACIST MATE SECOND CLASS WILLIAM D. HALYBURTON, JR., 2d Battalion, 5th Marines. When his assault unit suffered severe casualties he unhesitatingly went to the aid of the wounded man closest to the enemy positions. He interposed his own body as a shield in the line of fire and continued his ministrations until he was killed. (19 May 1945)*

PRIVATE DALE M. HANSEN, 2d Battalion, 1st Marines. Using a rocket launcher, a rifle, and grenades, he seized the initiative at a critical point in the battle action and in a one-man assault destroyed a pillbox, a mortar, and twelve of the enemy, materially aiding the accomplishment of his company's mission. (7 May 1945)*

CORPORAL LOUIS J. HAUGE, JR., 1st Battalion, 1st Marines. Making a determined one-man assault on a pair of enemy machine-gun positions holding up his company's advance, he wiped out one with grenades and, although painfully wounded, continued his attack and succeeded in destroying the second. (14 May 1945)*

SERGEANT ELBERT L. KINSER, 3d Battalion, 1st Marines. During an enemy counterattack when a grenade fell in the midst of his men, he threw himself on the deadly missile and absorbed the full force of the shattering explosion with his own body. (4 May 1945)*

311

HOSPITAL APPRENTICE FIRST CLASS FRED F. LESTER, 1st Battalion, 22d Marines. He was hit while going to the aid of a wounded man. Although he was again wounded dragging his patient to safety, he directed the administration of proper medical treatment to several men, steadfastly refusing aid for his own wounds which he realized were fatal. (8 June 1945)*

PRIVATE ROBERT M. McTUREOUS, JR., 3d Battalion, 29th Marines. When machine-gun fire suddenly assailed stretcher bearers evacuating his unit's wounded, he made two one-man grenade assaults on the enemy gun positions. Although seriously wounded, he stoically crawled 200 yards to shelter before calling for aid. (7 June 1945)*

PRIVATE FIRST CLASS ALBERT E. SCHWAB, 1st Battalion, 5th Marines. Attacking alone up a high ridge, he used his flame thrower to burn out an enemy machine gun that had pinned down his unit. When a second machine gun opened up, he attacked directly into its fire, silencing it as he fell fatally wounded. (7 May 1945)*

APPENDIX VIII Navy Unit Commendations

The Secretary of the Navy takes pleasure in commending the

AMPHIBIOUS RECONNAISSANCE BATTALION
FLEET MARINE FORCE, PACIFIC

for service as follows:

"For outstanding heroism in action against enemy Japanese forces in the Gilbert Islands, from November 19 to 26, 1943; the Marshall Islands, from January 30 to February 23, 1944; Marianas Islands, from June 15 to August 4, 1944; and Ryukyu Islands, from March 26 to July 24, 1945. The only unit of its kind in the Fleet Marine Force, Pacific, the Amphibious Reconnaissance Battalion rendered unique service in executing secret reconnaissance missions on enemy-held islands. Frequently landing at night from submarines and other vessels prior to the assault, the small unit entered areas where friendly aircraft, Naval gunfire and other forms of support were unavailable and, under cover of darkness, moved about in hostile territory virtually in the presence of enemy troops. Despite hazards incident to passage through dark and unfamiliar hostile waters, often through heavy surf onto rocky shores, the Battalion persevered in its mission to reconnoiter enemy islands and obtain information vital to our assault forces and, on several occasions, succeeded in overcoming all enemy resistance without the aid of regular troops. Carrying out its difficult tasks with courage and determination, the Amphibious Reconnaissance Battalion contributed materially to the success of our offensive operations throughout four major campaigns and achieved a gallant record of service which reflects the highest credit upon its officers and men and the United States Naval Service."

All personnel attached to and serving with the Amphibious Reconnaisse Battalion during one or more of the above-mentioned periods are authorized to wear the NAVY UNIT COMMENDATION Ribbon.

James Forrestal

JAMES FORRESTAL

Secretary of the Navy.

The Secretary of the Navy takes pleasure in commending the

FIRST SEPARATE ENGINEER BATTALION

for service as follows:

"For exceptionally meritorious service in support of military operations on Guadalcanal, December 10, 1942, to February 27, 1943; Tinian from August 20, 1944, to March 24, 1945; and Okinawa from April 14 to September 2, 1945. Faced with numerous and difficult problems in engineering throughout two major campaigns, the First Separate Engineer Battalion initiated new techniques and procedures in construction, repair and maintenance, executing its missions under adverse conditions of weather and terrain and in spite of Japanese shellings, artillery fire, bombing raids, sickness and tropical storms. Technically skilled, aggressive and unmindful of great personal danger, the officers and men of this gallant Battalion constructed, developed and maintained vital routes of communication, airfields and camp facilities; they served as combat engineer units in performing demolitions, mine detection and disposal and bomb disposal tasks in support of various units of the Fleet Marine Force; and they built bridges and repaired air-bombed air strips toward the uninterrupted operations of Allied ground and aerial forces. Undeterred by both mechanical and natural limitations, the First Separate Engineer Battalion completed with dispatch and effectiveness assigned and unanticipated duties which contributed immeasurably to the ultimate defeat of Japan and upheld the highest traditions of the United States Naval Service."

All personnel attached to the First Separate Engineer Battalion during any of the above mentioned periods are hereby authorized to wear the NAVY UNIT COMMENDATION Ribbon.

JAMES FORRESTAL
Secretary of the Navy.

The Secretary of the Navy takes pleasure in commending the

III AMPHIBIOUS CORPS SIGNAL BATTALION

for service as set forth in the following

CITATION:

"For extremely meritorious service in support of military operations, while attached to the I Marines Amphibious Corps during the amphibious assault on Bougainville, and attached to the III Amphibious Corps during operations at Guam, Palau and Okinawa, during the period from November 1, 1943 to June 21, 1945. The first American Signal Battalion to engage in amphibious landings in the Pacific Ocean Areas, the III Amphibious Corps Signal Battalion pioneered and developed techniques and procedures without benefit of established precedent, operating with limited and inadequate equipment, particularly in the earlier phase of these offensive actions, and providing its own security while participating in jungle fighting, atoll invasions and occupation of large island masses. Becoming rapidly experienced in guerrilla warfare and the handling of swiftly changing situations, this valiant group of men successfully surmounted the most difficult conditions of terrain and weather as well as unfamiliar technical problems and, working tirelessly without consideration for safety, comfort or convenience, provided the Corps with uninterrupted ship-shore and bivouac communication service continuously throughout this period. This splendid record of achievement, made possible only by the combined efforts, loyalty and courageous devotion to duty of each individual, was a decisive factor in the success of the hazardous Bougainville, Guam, Palau and Okinawa Campaigns and reflects the highest credit upon the III Amphibious Corps Signal Battalion and the United States Naval Service."

All personnel attached to the III Amphibious Corps Signal Battalion who actually participated in one or more of the Bougainville, Guam, Palau and Okinawa operations are hereby authorized to wear the NAVY UNIT COMMENDATION Ribbon.

James Forrestal

JAMES FORRESTAL

Secretary of the Navy.

Index

Admiralty Islands, 1
Advance fleet base, 27
Aguni Shima, 6, 243
Aha, 108
Ainu aborigines, 9n
Air attacks
  American, 20, 23, 37, 111, 126, 164. *See also* Air
    support.
  Japanese, 23, 55, 63, 68, 76, 83, 122, 135, 147, 160, 200.
    See also Kamikaze.
Air bases
  American, 16, 25, 27, 38, 80, 267, 266
  Japanese, 25, 46
Aircraft
  American
    aerial observation, 46, 93, 112, 202
    aerial photographs, 265
    aerial reconnaissance, 108
    air base development, 28, 267
    air defense score card, 262
    air operations, 15, 23, 84, 90–91, 97, 104, 124–125,
      145, 147, 149–150, 152–153, 156, 162, 177, 186,
      202, 204, 209, 217, 228, 232, 239, 243, 248, 273
    air warning, 243, 261
    carrier air, 20, 37, 46, 119, 122, 263
    combat air patrol, 44, 83, 114, 200, 203, 258, 262–264
    types
      B–29's, 2, 15, 20, 23n, 37, 261, 274
      bombers, 41, 115
      carrier, 20, 41, 86, 90, 264
      Corsairs, 262, 266
      fighters, 76, 83–84, 115
      liaison, 236
      night fighters, 145
      P–47, 262
      observation, 32, 72, 76, 155, 167–168, 202
      search, 86
      seaplane, 37–38, 43, 86
      torpedo bombers, 265
      transports, 73, 85n
      very long-range (VLR) bombers, 14–15, 37, 111

Aircraft—Continued
  Japanese, 82, 262
    pilots, 83, 111, 123, 130, 135, 145
    reconnaissance, 120
    suicide tactics, 45, 60, 84, 111, 130. *See also Kami-*
      kaze.
    types
      bombers, 45, 84, 144, 145, 203
      general, 83–85, 114, 123, 130, 135, 145, 200, 232
      reconnaissance, 36, 83, 85
      suicide, 41, 43–45, 85, 123, 145, 203. *See also*
        Kamikaze.
Airfields. *See* Air bases.
Air Liaison Parties, 264–265, 270
Air support, 18, 26–27, 33–34, 42, 63, 69, 71, 86, 96,
  98–99, 120, 123, 134, 136, 138, 160, 186, 200, 221,
  245, 262, 264. *See also* Air attacks, American.
  air drops, 198, 210–212, 215, 217, 229, 232, 238, 265,
    270
  air lift, 85n
  control, 46, 85, 127, 264
Air units
  American
    Aircraft, Fleet Marine Force, Pacific, 200n
    Far Eastern Air Force, 266, 274
    7th Air Force, 275
    Tactical Air Force, 18, 27, 35, 125, 145, 160, 202,
      210, 259, 261–266
    Air Defense Command, 261–262, 266. *See also*
      Air attacks, American; Air support.
    Bomber Command, 266
    2d Marine Aircraft Wing, 18, 262, 266
    301st Fighter Wing, 262, 266
    MAG–14, 262
    MAG–22, 262
    MAG–31, 36n, 262, 266
    MAG–33, 262
    MAG–43, 261
    318th Fighter Group, 262
    28th Photo Reconnaissance Squadron, 265
    VMF–311, 262
    VMO–2, 72
    VMO–6, 76

Air units—Continued
  American—Continued
    VMO-7, 32
    VMTB-131, 238, 265
    VMTB-232, 238, 265–266
  Japanese
    5th Air Fleet, 83, 86
    6th Air Force, 83
    8th Air Division, 37n, 44–45
    19th Air Sector Command, 52, 58, 60
    32d Makoto Special Attack Unit, 45n
    aircraft maintenance units, 51–52, 57–58, 71, 112
Aitape, 2
Aka Shima, 38, 40–41, 41n, 42
Amami Gunto, 6
Amami-O-Shima, 11, 14, 84
Amamiya, ItGen Tatsumi, 50, 149, 194, 208, 255
American Far Eastern relations, 3
Amike, 160
Ammunition
  American. See also Weapons.
    ammunition ships, 85, 85n, 135, 172
    dumps, 96, 102, 106, 174
    expenditure restrictions, 125
    reserves, 72, 125
    shortages, 108, 121, 164, 180, 211, 224, 229, 254
    supply and resupply, 46, 82n, 102, 168, 172, 193
    types
      bombs, 86, 99, 125, 147, 180, 221
      81mm, 85n
      .50-caliber, 125
      howitzer, 172
      napalm, 99, 115, 138, 187, 190, 247, 249
      155mm, 172
      75mm, 154n, 187
      16-inch, 43
      small arms, 173
      star shells, 147
      .30-caliber, 187
      20mm, 125
      unit of fire, 29n
  Japanese, 103
    shortages, 244
    types
      bombs, 45, 84, 115, 160
      47mm, 88
      smoke, 201
      mortar, 116, 138, 139
      75mm, 88
      6-inch, 88
      white phosphorus, 182
Amoy, 14, 16–17
Amphibian tractor. See Amphibian vehicles.
Amphibian vehicles
  DUKW's, 41, 64, 66, 68, 80
  LVT's, 40–42, 63–64, 68, 69n, 72, 80, 88, 96, 114, 116, 159, 174, 198, 200, 215–218, 220, 232–233
  LVT(A)'s, 41, 63–64, 66, 88, 90, 95, 108, 115, 145–147, 154n, 167, 194, 216–218, 232–233, 271
  weasels, 72

Amphibious corps. See Marine units.
Amphibious Forces, Pacific Fleet, 18–19
Amphibious Support Force, 18, 18n, 40, 44. See also Task forces.
Amuro Shima, 42
Andre, Maj. D. C., 37n
Antitank artillery
  American, 32, 83, 275. See also Marine units.
  Japanese, 49, 52
Aoyanagi, LtCol Tokio, 47, 71
Appleman, R. E., 63n
Aragachi, 249, 251–252, 255, 259
Aragusuku, 213, 244–245
Arakachi, 119
Ara Saki, 244, 253–255
Armor. See Tactics; Weapons.
Army Air Force. See Air units, American.
Army units.
  First Army, 273
  Sixth Army, 273
  Tenth Army, 18–21, 25–28, 30, 30n, 31n, 33–36, 46, 49, 69, 79, 80, 82–83, 85n, 87–88, 93, 110–112, 120, 122, 124–126, 129n, 133–135, 143–145, 150, 154–155, 157, 160, 165, 167, 172, 172n, 173–176, 197–199, 201, 206, 209–210, 212–213, 215–216, 222, 228, 236, 245, 249–252, 257, 259–260, 264–268, 270–273, 275
  Headquarters, Ryukyus Area, 260
  XXIV Corps, 18, 21, 25–26, 28–31, 34–36, 38, 63–64, 69, 69n, 79–80, 82, 84, 88, 90, 93n, 110n, 111, 114, 118–127, 127n, 128–136, 141–145, 147–148, 150–152, 152n, 154, 172, 173, 192, 195–196, 196n, 199, 203, 209, 212–213, 216–217, 240, 244–245, 249, 250n, 254–255, 257, 259, 264, 272–273, 275
  7th Infantry Division, 25, 34, 66, 69, 71, 73, 74n, 79–80, 119–123, 125, 127–129, 131–134, 136, 137n, 143–145, 147, 149–151, 154, 157, 196–199, 201–203, 207–210, 213, 215–216, 244–246, 246n, 247–249, 251, 254, 259–260, 275
  27th Infantry Division, 18, 25, 31–34, 87n, 88, 90, 122–123, 125–126, 128, 128n, 129–137, 137n, 152, 152n, 154, 260–269, 272, 275
  77th Infantry Division, 18, 25, 31n, 34, 36, 36n, 38, 40, 42, 42n, 43, 111–112, 116, 117n, 118, 133–134, 136–138, 143–145, 148–151, 154, 157, 164, 167–178, 189, 191–195, 197–199, 202–203, 206–207, 210, 212–213, 255, 260, 273
  81st Infantry Division, 18, 25
  96th Infantry Division, 25, 31, 34, 79–80, 119–125, 127–131, 133–134, 136, 136n, 137, 137n 143n, 154, 157, 176, 192, 194–199, 201, 203, 207, 210, 212–213, 216–217, 224, 229, 229n, 230, 235, 240, 244–246, 246n, 247–249, 251–252, 255, 259–260, 273
  53d Special Engineer Brigade, 82
  419th Field Artillery Group, 120
  420th Field Artillery Group, 43, 64
  17th Infantry Regiment, 123, 131, 133–134, 136, 138, 141, 149, 154, 157, 213, 215–216, 245–249, 255
  32d Infantry Regiment, 79, 120, 122–123, 126–127, 129–131, 133–134, 136, 198–199, 201, 203, 210, 213, 216, 244–246, 248–249, 251–252, 255, 257–258

Army units—Continued

105th Infantry Regiment, 5, 88, 122, 125, 128, 130–134, 137, 269

106th Infantry Regiment, 122–123, 125, 128–133, 136–137, 269

165th Infantry Regiment, 122–123, 125, 130, 131, 133–134, 243, 269

184th Infantry Regiment, 79, 119–120, 122–123, 126–127, 129–131, 136, 141, 154, 157, 196, 198–199, 202–203, 210, 213, 215–216, 244–245, 249, 252

305th Infantry Regiment, 41–42, 111, 114, 116–118, 154, 157, 164, 167–168, 189, 192–195, 212, 217, 255

306th Infantry Regiment, 114–117, 117n, 118, 136, 138, 141, 149, 151, 157, 164, 167–168, 192, 194–195, 210–211

307th Infantry Regiment, 114, 116–117, 134, 136–141, 148, 151–152, 154, 168, 192–195, 210, 259

381st Infantry Regiment, 79, 121–123, 125–126, 128, 130–131, 133–134, 194, 196, 213, 215–216, 244, 247–249, 251–252, 255, 259

382d Infantry Regiment, 79, 119, 122, 125–127, 130, 157, 167, 168, 192–195, 210, 249, 252, 255

383d Infantry Regiment, 79, 119, 121–123, 125, 130–131, 133–134, 157, 164, 167–168, 192, 194–196, 213, 216–217, 229, 231, 244, 246, 249

780th Amphibious Tank Battalion, 88

534th Amphibious Tractor Battalion, 88

713th Armored Flamethrower Battalion, 272

102d Engineer Combat Battalion, 126

104th Field Artillery Battalion, 152n

145th Field Artillery Battalion, 152n

249th Field Artillery Battalion, 137n, 152n

304th Field Artillery Battalion, 114

305th Field Artillery Battalion, 114

306th Field Artillery Battalion, 114

749th Field Artillery Battalion, 120

902d Field Artillery Battalion, 114

Infantry Battalions

1/17, 128, 131, 133, 141, 148, 246–247

1/32, 136, 245–247, 254

1/105, 128–129, 131

1/106, 128–129, 269

1/165, 129, 131, 136, 269

1/184, 119, 136, 138, 203, 216, 251, 254–255

1/305, 41–42, 116, 118, 164, 193, 195, 256–257

1/306, 41–43, 115, 117, 136, 148, 164

1/307, 116, 126, 134, 141, 195

1/381, 122–123, 128–130, 133, 210, 212, 244, 246–248, 251

1/382, 79, 120–122, 128–129, 164, 167–168, 192–193, 195, 249

1/383, 120, 122, 164, 168, 193–196, 244, 246, 248–249

2/17, 133, 138, 149, 247

2/32, 127, 129, 198, 210, 246–247, 254

2/105, 128–129

2/106, 123, 126, 128–129

2/165, 129–131, 133, 136

2/184, 129, 196, 198, 203, 255

2/305, 40n, 42, 114, 154, 213

2/306, 41–43, 164, 167, 195

Army units—Continued

Infantry Battalions—Continued

2/307, 40, 40n, 41–42, 116–118, 141, 164, 192–194

2/381, 122–123, 125, 129–130, 168, 192, 194, 248, 251

2/382, 79, 119, 122, 128–131, 193–196, 210, 249

2/383 79, 119, 122, 130, 133, 136, 164, 167–168, 193–196, 215, 230, 244, 247–249

3/17, 130, 138, 141, 148, 246–247

3/32, 129, 198, 255

3/105, 128–129

3/106, 125, 128–130

3/165, 131, 133–134

3/184, 119–120, 129, 138, 196, 198, 251, 255

3/305, 40–42, 87n, 88, 90, 116, 117, 117n, 118, 151, 157, 193–194, 256–257, 259

3/306, 40–42, 115, 136, 148, 164, 194–195, 204

3/307, 134, 148, 150–151, 192–193, 195

3/381, 121–123, 128–131, 194–196, 244, 246–247

3/382, 122, 128–130, 164, 167–168, 192–195, 249, 251

3/383, 79, 121–122, 130–131, 133–134, 136, 212, 215. 244, 246, 248–249

193d Tank Battalion, 128n

711th Tank Battalion, 246

763d Tank Battalion, 134

105th Infantry Cannon Company, 131

7th Reconnaissance Troop, 147, 207

27th Reconnaissance Troop, 123, 126, 130

Counterintelligence Corps Detachments, 72

Arnold, Maj Gen A. V., 25, 79, 119, 136, 157, 215–216, 245, 247

Artillery

American, 21, 23, 25–26, 32, 68–69, 79, 95, 97–99, 102, 104, 109, 116–117, 120, 122–125, 127–128, 136–137, 145, 147, 149–156, 159–160, 162, 165–167, 170, 177, 179–180, 183–184, 186, 188, 190, 192, 194, 200–204, 211–213, 217–218, 220–221, 225–226, 228–229, 232, 235–237, 239–240, 242, 245–246, 248–249, 272–273. See also Antiaircraft artillery.

Japanese, 49–52, 59–60, 64, 79, 94–99, 102–103, 119, 122–123, 129, 133–134, 136, 138–140, 143, 145, 147, 149–151, 159–160, 162, 164–165, 168, 170–171, 176–178, 180, 182, 184, 186–188, 190, 196, 198–200, 202, 204, 207–208, 211–212, 220–221, 229, 232, 234–235, 238, 250, 255

Asa, 150–151, 160, 177

Asa Kawa, 138, 140, 143, 148, 150–152, 154–155, 157–160, 165–167, 171, 177, 185

Asato Gawa, 165, 170, 177, 182, 184, 197–198, 200–201, 204

Atomic bomb, 274

Atsutabaru, 77

Attaniya, 79

Awa, 92, 92n, 95–98, 100, 103, 107n, 129, 137, 140–141, 149–151, 153, 157, 159

Awacha Draw, 156, 159

Awacha Pocket, 140, 151–152, 154, 157, 163

Aware Shima, 42

Bailey Bridge. See Engineer operations.

Banzai, 102

Barry, USS, 258
Bartley, LtCol W. S., 45*n*
Base development activities. *See* Planning.
Bates, USS, 199
Battalions. *See* Army units; Japanese units; Marine units.
Battleships. *See* Ships.
Beans, LtCol F. D., 98, 102, 184*n*
Beaches, 23–28, 63, 88, 114. *See also* Hagushi beaches; Minatoga beaches.
  Blue, 64
  Green, 66, 68, 70, 114–115
  Orange, 82, 88
  Purple, 82
  Red, 66, 82, 114, 116
Bell, LtCol G. B., 184, 184*n*, 198n, 218, 224, 253
Bemis, Col J. A., 26*n*
Bemis Group, 26*n*
Benedict, LtCol W. E., 74*n*, 137, 153, 159, 217, 229, 229*n*, 239, 252, 254–255, 255*n*, 256
Berger, LtCol S. S., 68, 146, 151, 215, 233, 238*n*
Bergren, Maj O. V., 96*n*, 97*n*, 105
Besena Misaki, 93
Biak, 53
Bibliography, 276–280
Biddle, Como J., 4*n*
Biloxi, USS, 45*n*
Bimbo Tai, 50*n*
Birmingham, USS, 145
Bise Saki, 95
Bishi Gawa, 64, 68
Bismarck Archipelago, 1
Blakelock, BrigGen D. H., 24*n*, 172*n*
Blandy, RAdm W. H. P., 18, 18*n*, 40, 46, 87–88, 126
Bleasdale, Col V. F., 96, 99
Block Island, USS, 263
Bloody Ridge, 116–118
Boggs, Maj C. W., 265*n*
Bonins, 14
Bradford, BrigGen W. B., 130
Bradford Task Force, 131
Bradley, MajGen J. L., 25, 136, 157, 210, 215–216, 229*n*, 255
Bridges, 91, 94*n*, 108, 140, 165, 198, 215, 220, 230. *See also* Engineer operations.
Brigades. *See* Army units; Japanese units; Marine units.
British Carrier Force, 1, 18*n*, 45, 260
Brown, Col W. S., 122*n;* MajGen, 32*n*, 122*n*
Bruce, MajGen A. D., 18, 34, 40, 42, 111–112, 114, 116, 117*n*, 133, 136, 154, 195
Bryan, LCdr J., III, 2*n*
Buckner, LtGen S. B., Jr., 16–19, 23, 26, 30, 30*n*, 34, 76, 80, 88, 96*n*, 120, 133, 142, 151, 174, 202–203, 215, 236, 236*n*, 243–244, 250, 267
Buckner Bay, 273
Burton, LtCol C., Jr., 26*n*
Bush, USS, 85
Bushido, 83

Cairo Conference, 1
Calhoun, USS, 85
Canada Victory, SS, 135, 172
Cannon, M. L., 52*n*
Cape Esperance, 34
Carleton, Maj P. D., 178*n*, 219*n*
Carney, Maj E. F., 201*n*, 222, 224, 253
Carolines, 2
Carriers. *See* Ships.
Carter, RAdm W. R., 43*n*, 273*n*
Cass, B., 96*n*
Casualties
  American
    Marine, 260, 305–308
    Navy, 260
    Army, 260
  Japanese, 260
CAUSEWAY, 15–17, 81–82
Caves, 99, 101–105, 108, 112, 116–117, 127, 139, 141, 149, 151–155, 159–160, 163, 165, 167, 178, 180–181, 186, 190, 193, 196, 206–207, 217, 220, 222, 224–225, 227, 232, 235, 239–240, 242, 246, 251, 254–255, 257, 269. *See also* Japanese defenses.
Central Pacific, 1–2, 11–12, 12*n*, 15, 17, 18*n*, 19, 50, 172
Central Pacific Task Forces, 63
Chan, 199, 208–209, 213, 215, 229–230
Chapman, LtCol L. F., Jr., 32*n*
Chappell, Col K. B., 68, 139–140, 146, 152*n*
Chatan, 54, 69, 123
Chibana, 134, 151, 154
Chihaya, Cdr M., 85*n*
Chimu, 26, 77, 110
Chimu Wan, 25, 60, 87, 173, 273
China, 1, 3–4, 6, 9*n*, 11*n*, 12–15, 15*n*, 16, 25, 30, 37, 49, 275
China Sea, 37, 43
Chinen Peninsula, 54–55, 60, 88, 143, 196, 199, 202, 210, 213, 215–216, 244
Chinese, 4, 9, 9*n*, 13, 16
Chiwa, 224–225
Chiyuna, 79
Cho, LtGen Isamu, 49, 55–56, 143, 150, 236*n*, 258
Chronology, 281–283
Chuda, 77, 91, 105, 107
Chungking, 13
Churchill, Prime Minister. 1
Cobb, RAdm C. H., 261
Colorado, USS, 147, 186
Combined Chiefs of Staff, 13–14.
Comfort, USS, 135
Command and Staff List of Marine Units on Okinawa, 284–297
Commander Air Support Control Units, 263–264. *See also* Air support.
Commander in Chief, U. S. Fleet (Cominch), 17
Commander in Chief, Pacific Fleet (CinCPac), 12*n*, 17, 261
Commander in Chief, Pacific Ocean Areas (CinCPOA), 12, 12*n*, 17–19, 24*n*, 111, 203, 266
Commander in Chief, South West Pacific (CinCSWPA), 12, 12*n*

Commanding General, Army Air Forces Pacific Ocean Area (CGAAFPOA), 19
Commanding General, Army Forces Pacific Ocean Area (CGAFPOA), 16
Command relationships, 17–19
Communications
difficulties, 229, 231
direct ground-air, 265, 270
fighter director, 44, 96n, 243
fire direction center, 69. *See also* Artillery, American.
Japanese, 103, 147
loud speakers, 71, 211, 227, 251, 254
radar, 69, 82, 95, 114, 243, 258–259
radio, 230
shore party, 270
wire, 110, 219
Conscription, Japanese, 53, 53n
Cook, Maj E. J., 177, 205, 242n
Coolidge, LtCol J. B., 111, 116
Corbett, Maj J. F., 191n
CORONET, 273
Corregidor, 275
Courtney, Maj H. A., Jr., 171, 176–177
Coxswains, 81
Crist, BrigGen W. E., 268
Crowl, P. A., 265n
Crown, Maj J. A., 33n; LtCol, 33n
Cruisers. *See* Ships.
Curtis, USS, 258

Dakeshi, 137, 140, 151–152, 157, 159, 163–165, 167–168, 170, 186, 188–189, 192
Dakeshi Ridge, 158–159, 161–165, 167, 186
Dakeshi road, 159
Dakiton, 232, 239
Davidson, O. R., 136n
DeGroff, Maj C., 88, 90, 90n
del Valle, MajGen P. A., 25, 73–74, 133, 136, 153, 202, 204n, 206, 211, 215, 222, 228n, 230, 232, 237, 250, 250n, 265, 272; LtGen, 73n, 250n
Demonstration beaches. *See* Minatoga beaches.
Denig, LtCol R. L., 76
Destroyers. *See* Ships.
Deyo, RAdm M. L., 18, 18n, 43–44
Dickerson, USS, 83, 111
Divisions. *See* Army units; Japanese units; Marine units.
Doma Cove, 34
Donohoo, LtCol M. "O", 67, 159–161, 178–179
Drexler, USS, 203
Durgin, RAdm C. C., 264

Easley, BrigGen C. M., 136n, 252
East China Sea, 2–3, 6, 229
Eastern Islands, 6, 25–26, 87–88, 90, 259
Eastern Islands Attack and Fire Support Group, 87–88
See also Task groups.
Emmons, USS, 85
Empire of Japan 3, 17, 23

Emperor, 11
Engineer operations. *See also* Shore Party.
aviation, 80, 262
Bailey bridge, 126, 160, 199–200, 219
bridging material, 155
construction, 23, 27–28, 134, 232, 253
demolitions, 45, 101, 154, 164, 180, 183–184, 188, 194, 222, 224, 227, 249
footbridges, 126, 155, 159, 199, 201, 205
infantry-engineer teams, 31, 136
mine-removal, 72, 190
personnel, 6n, 22, 28, 64, 72, 80, 101n, 155, 159–160, 180, 188, 198, 201, 205, 221–222, 266
pontoon bridges 126, 219–220
water supply, 106, 110, 232
Eniwetok, 24n, 27
Enterprise, USS, 38
Equipment. *See* Supply; Weapons.
Espiritu Santo, 27, 31, 34
Essex, USS, 86
Estes, USS, 46, 88
Europe, victory in, 154
Evans, USS, 160
Expeditionary Troops, 18–19, 25, 28, 30, 33, 35–36, 43.
See also Army units; Marine units.

Fast Carrier Force, 18n, 37, 83. *See also* Task forces.
Feldmeier, Maj A. L., 265.
Flag raising, 211, 255
"flycatcher" duty, 145
Foley, LtCol E. P., 152n
Foreign Office, Japanese, 4
Formosa, 1–2, 12–14, 14n, 15–17, 17n, 23, 30, 37, 44, 48, 60, 62, 83, 144, 257
Franklin, USS, 38
Frogmen, 40. *See also* Navy units.
Fujioka, LtGen Takeo, 50, 208
Fuller, MajGen J. F. C., 15n
Futema, 54–60, 79, 123, 143, 148

Gagusuku, 94
Gaja, 132, 142, 151, 157
Gaja Ridge, 138, 154, 168, 196
Geiger, MajGen R. S., 18, 35, 76–77, 80, 104, 107, 110, 133, 151–152, 182, 199, 213, 215, 217, 222, 228, 250, 255, 257, 259, 263n, 266, 269, 271–272
Genka, 109
Geruma Shim, 38, 40–41, 41n
Gilbert Islands, USS, 263
Gilberts, 48
Gilliam, LtCol W. M., 202n
Ginowan, 79, 119, 128, 192, 194
Ginowan road, 149
Gisushi, 217, 238
Gormley, LtCol J. J., 156, 159, 163, 186, 233
Government House, 116–118
Green, Maj B. W., 98
Griebel, Col J. H., 68, 74n, 137, 149, 153, 157, 185, 217, 252

Griner, MajGen G. W., Jr., 18, 34, 88, 122, 125–126 136
Ground Defense Forces, 266
Guadalcanal, 27, 29, 32–33, 33n, 34–35.
Guam, 7n, 17, 21, 33, 35, 36n, 37, 73, 73n, 111, 135
Gunfire and Covering Force, 18, 18n,. *See also* Task forces.
Gunto, 6n
Gushi, 222–223, 225
Guishi Ridge, 223
Gushichan, 208–209, 245–246
Gushichan-Nakaza Valley, 245
Gushikawa, 74
Gustafson, Maj J. A., 68, 68n
Gusuku Ridge, 259
Gusukuma, 129–131, 137, 140, 143, 156

Hackleback, USS, 86
Hadley, USS, 160
Hagushi, 23, 25, 60, 80–82, 82n, 116, 144, 160
Hagushi anchorage, 82, 84, 114, 145, 243
Hagushi beaches, 23, 27, 34, 38, 45, 47, 55–60, 63, 173
Halazone, 233
Hall, RAdm J. L., Jr., 18, 34–35, 174, 174n
Halsey, Adm W. F., 2, 13, 17, 37, 203; FAdm, 2n, 13, 17, 37
Hamahika Shima, 88
Hamilton, Col S. S., 116
Hanagusuku, 208, 246, 248
Hancock, USS, 85
Hanja, 231–232
Hanlon, Capt B. H., USN, 40n
Hanza, 68–69, 71
Harmon, LtGen M. F., 14–16
Hawaiian area, 27, 96
Hawks, F. L., 3n
Hayden, LtCol R. H., 68, 183
Hayward, LtCol R. W., 243
Heanza Shima, 88
Hedo Misaki, 96, 108–109, 243, 269
Heinl, LtCol R. D., 33n
Hemphill, Col. B. T., 184n
Henderson, LtCol F. P., 120
Henrico, USS, 111
Hentona, 109
Hideoshi's Korean Campaigns, 4
Hills
    Chocolate Drop, 192–194
    Conical, 126, 138, 141, 151, 154, 157, 164, 167–168, 176, 193–194, 196, 199, 201, 203, 224
    Dick, 164, 167–168, 192–195
    Easy, 227
    Flat Top, 192–195
    Half Moon, 176–184, 190–191, 197
    Hill 28, 224–226
    Hill 39, 224
    Hill 53, 222, 226–227
    Hill 55, 185, 187–188, 190–192, 204, 206, 224, 226
    Hill 55(1), 224–226
    Hill 55(2), 225–226

Hills—Continued
    Hill 57, 220
    Hill 58, 226
    Hill 60, 152, 155–156
    Hill 62, 226
    Hill 63, 226
    Hill 69, 234–235, 237
    Hill 72, 253, 255
    Hill 75, 232
    Hill 79, 250–252, 254–257
    Hill 80, 253
    Hill 81, 250, 252, 254–256
    Hill 85, 254, 257, 259
    Hill 89, 209, 248–250, 252, 254, 257–259
    Hill 95, 245–248
    Hill 103, 222, 232
    Hill 107, 229
    Hill 108, 229, 232
    Hill 115, 248–249
    Hill 138, 134, 136, 141
    Hill 153, 244–245, 248–249, 257
    Hill 165, 70n, 79
    Hill 200, 99
    Hill 210, 99–100, 104
    Hill 220, 55
    Horseshoe, 176, 178, 180–184
    Little Sugar Loaf, 221–222
    Love, 192–196
    Oboe, 167, 192
    110 Meter, 189–191, 193–195, 204, 207
    150 Meter, 193
    Ozato hill mass, 196, 199, 203
    Sugar, 192, 194–196
    Sugar Loaf, 171–172, 176–184
Hill, VAdm H. W. 174, 258, 261, 263
Hill, LtCol R. E., 239, 239n, 256
Hindenburg, 49
Hinsdale, USS, 63
Hinunangan Bay, 34
Hiroshima, 274
Hiruyama, Capt, 96
Hitler Youth Organization, 57
Hiza, 68
Hizaonna, 74, 74n, 76, 78
Hobbs Victory, SS, 85
Hochmuth, LtCol B. A. 183–184, 184n, 253
Hodge, MajGen J. R., 18, 36, 88, 120–122, 125, 130, 132, 137, 141, 152, 196, 210, 217, 232, 245, 248, 272
Hoffman, Maj C. W., 12n
Hogback Ridge, 192, 194–196
Hokaji Shima, 40–41, 41n, 42
Hollandia, 2, 12
Holomon, Maj W., 191; LtCol, 230n
Home Minister, Japanese, 6, 8–9
Honan Province, 50
Honshu, 11, 15, 38, 56n, 86, 275
Honsowetz, Col R. E., 69n
Hopping, USS, 88
Hough, Maj F. O., 33n; LtCol, 33n
Hudson, Maj J. S., 236n

Humphrey, LtCol G. C., 242n
Hunt, BrigGen L. P., 243
Hurst, LtCol E. H., 68, 76, 78, 188; Col. 74n
Hydrographic Survey, 266

Ibaru Ridge, 252
ICEBERG, 17, 19, 26, 30–32, 34, 38, 44, 46, 112, 172, 174, 203, 260, 262, 266, 268–269, 273
Ichi, 109
Ie, 112, 114–117
Ie airfield, 111–112, 114–115
Iegusugu Yama, 111–112, 114–117, 117n, 118
Ie Shima, 6, 19n, 23, 25–26, 34, 52, 54, 60, 96, 111–112, 114, 116, 117n, 118, 126, 133, 154, 160, 262
Ie Shima Attack Group, 111, 114. See also Task groups.
Igawa, Maj Masashi, 112, 114, 118
Iheya Retto, 6
Iheya Shima, 243
Ike Shima, 87
Imadomari, 95
Imperial General Headquarters, 11, 49, 53, 251. See also Japanese units.
Imperial Rescript, 275
Inasomi, 203, 216
Index, 316–332
India, 37
Indianapolis, USS, 17, 45
Indo-China, 38
Intelligence
    American, 19, 96, 112, 123, 227, 260, 265, 270
        agencies, 20
        air photos, 19–21, 46, 93, 112
        estimate, 21
        language personnel, 71, 83, 211, 227
        maps, 20
        order of battle, 49
    Japanese
        documents, 11, 124
        maps, 124
        personnel, 62
        propaganda, 185
Intrepid, USS, 38, 114n
Isa, 79, 147
Isely, J. A., 265n
Ishado, 79
Ishikawa, 76–78, 91, 91n, 105
Ishikawa Isthmus, 6–7, 26, 54, 76, 91, 107, 108, 111, 269
Ishikawa Take, 105–106
Ishimine, 74n
Ishimmi, 143, 192–194, 210
Ishimmi Ridge, 192, 193, 195
Ishin, 126
Island Command, 19, 19n, 30, 35, 82, 133–134, 174, 243, 251, 259, 266–269
Item Pocket, 129–131, 133–134, 136
Itokazu, 213, 216
Itoman, 8, 208–209, 224–225, 229, 232–233, 235–236, 244, 246
Itomi, 94–96, 98–99, 99n, 102–104, 107

Iwa, 216, 229–231, 244–246
Iwo Jima, 2, 14–17, 17n, 23, 25–28, 36–37, 42n, 45n, 52–53, 83, 87n, 185
Iwa-Shindawaku Ridge 230

Japan, 1–4, 6, 11, 13–15, 17, 23, 37–38, 48–49, 52, 57, 83, 86, 144, 251 266 273–275
Japanese defenses, 26, 48, 55, 59, 91, 122, 127
    barbed wire, 119
    booby traps, 91
    bunkers, 102, 112, 152
    cave system, 121, 168, 194, 228. See also Caves.
    demolished bridges, 77, 91, 155
    emplacements, 102, 134, 160, 163, 178, 181, 186, 190, 192, 194, 196, 198, 235, 238–240
    fortification activities, 54, 80, 103, 117
    fortified tombs, 116, 211–212, 235–236
    observation points, 192
    pillboxes, 99, 108, 117–118, 121, 134, 138, 141, 149, 151, 155, 159–160, 163, 168, 187, 190, 251
    road blocks, 77, 91, 94
    spider holes, 112
    strong points, 76, 79, 87, 90n, 94, 100–102, 108, 119, 157, 164, 168, 171, 193, 195, 210, 221, 254
    tank trap, 74, 94n, 104, 119, 122
    trenches, 88, 104, 112, 180, 186, 196
    tunnel systems, 112, 125, 228
Japanese Diet, 6
Japanese Order of Battle, 302–304
Japanese units. See also Air units, Japanese.
    Army
        Chinese Expeditionary Army, 50
        Kwantung Army, 50
        Southern Army, 49
        Thirty-second Army, 11, 40, 43, 45n, 46, 48, 49n, 50–55, 55n, 56, 56n, 57–60, 60n, 61–62, 85, 120, 122–126, 130, 134, 137, 142–145, 147, 149–150, 153n, 155, 178, 182, 182n, 191, 196, 198–199, 203, 207–213, 217, 236n, 237, 244, 247, 249–251, 254, 257–259, 261, 267, 271, 275
        2d Armored Division, 51
        9th Infantry Division, 49, 54, 56–57, 60
        24th Infantry Division, 37n, 50–51, 54, 58, 60, 123–124, 126–127, 130, 142–144, 147–150, 157, 207–209, 244, 246, 250, 252, 255, 259
        62d Infantry Division, 50, 54, 58, 60, 69n, 119, 123–124, 126, 130–131, 137, 142–144, 148–151, 153n, 154, 157–158, 185, 202–203, 208–210, 213, 215, 244, 248–249
        85th Infantry Division, 56n
        1st Air Raiding Brigade, 200
        1st Specially Established Brigade, 58, 178
        2d Specially Established Brigade, 58
        5th Artillery Command, 43, 51–52, 60, 123, 142, 144, 147, 150, 208, 244
        44th Independent Mixed Brigade, 49–50, 52, 54, 57, 60, 96, 142–143, 148, 157, 182, 208–209, 211–212, 244, 246–249
        63d Infantry Brigade, 50, 132, 138
        64th Infantry Brigade, 50, 126, 167, 185, 192

Japanese units—Continued
  Army—Continued
    1st Independent Artillery Mortar Regiment, 52
    1st Medium Artillery Regiment, 52
    1st Specially Established Regiment, 58, 71
    1st Infantry Unit, 50
    2d Infantry Unit, 50, 50n, 54, 60
    7th Heavy Artillery Regiment, 51, 88, 209, 213
    15th Independent Mixed Regiment, 50, 149, 157, 178, 185, 247
    22d Infantry Regiment, 50, 123, 126, 142–143, 147, 157, 194, 243, 255
    23d Medium Artillery Regiment, 52
    23d Shipping Engineer Regiment, 144, 147, 209–210, 212–213, 243, 255
    24th Reconnaissance Regiment, 50, 248
    24th Transport Regiment, 208
    26th Shipping Engineer Regiment, 144, 147, 157
    27th Tank Regiment, 51, 51n, 52, 143, 157
    32d Infantry Regiment, 50, 132, 138, 143–144, 148–149, 157, 192, 194, 209
    42d Field Artilley Regiment, 51
    89th Infantry Regiment, 50, 132, 143, 147, 157, 193, 195, 246, 248–249, 255
    1st Base Battalion, 38
    1st Independent Battalion, 57, 57n, 157
    1st Light Mortar Battalion, 124
    1st Sea Raiding Squadron, 38, 42
    1st Battalion, 1st Medium Artillery, 52
    1st Battalion, 2d Infantry Unit, 112
    1st Battalion, 22d Regiment, 123, 132
    1st Battalion, 32d Regiment, 132, 149, 194
    2d Base Battalion, 38
    2d Independent Battalion, 57, 157
    2d Sea Raiding Squadron, 38, 42
    2d Battalion, 22d Regiment, 124, 132
    2d Battalion, 32d Regiment, 149
    3d Base Battalion, 38
    3d Independent Battalion, 57
    3d Sea Raiding Squadron, 38, 42
    3d Battalion, 2d Infantry Unit, 153n, 157
    3d Battalion, 22d Regiment, 124
    3d Battalion, 32d Regiment, 149
    3d Battalion, 89th Regiment, 126
    7th Independent Antitank Battalion, 157
    11th Independent Infantry Battalion, 50, 126, 129
    12th Independent Infantry Battalion, 50, 71, 119, 124, 126
    13th Independent Infantry Battalion, 50, 121, 124, 126, 248
    14th Independent Infantry Battalion, 50, 124, 126
    14th Independent Machine Gun Battalion, 152, 185
    15th Independent Infantry Battalion, 50, 126
    21st Independent Infantry Battalion, 50, 126, 131
    22d Independent Infantry Battalion, 50, 191, 208–209, 212
    23d Independent Infantry Battalion, 50, 123, 126. 152, 185
    26th Independent Battalion, 57
    26th Sea Raiding Squadron, 144

Japanese units—Continued
  Army—Continued
    27th Independent Battalion, 57
    27th Sea Raiding Squadron, 144
    28th Independent Battalion, 57
    28th Sea Raiding Squadron, 144
    29th Independent Battalion, 57, 57n
    29th Sea Raiding Squadron, 144
    50th Airfield Battalion, 112
    50th Specially Established Infantry Battalion, 112
    81st Field Antiaircraft Artillery Battalion, 185
    100th Independent Heavy Artillery Battalion, 52
    272d Independent Infantry Battalion, 50, 123–124
    273d Independent Infantry Battalion, 50, 123–124, 126, 185
    Miscellaneous
      antitank units, 49, 50, 52
      automatic weapons units, 49–50, 52, 59, 96
      Blood-and-Iron-for-the-Emperor-Duty-Units, 57
      Boeitai, 53, 57, 59, 68, 71, 78, 87n, 106, 110, 157, 244, 251, 255, 275
      11th Shipping Group Headquarters, 58
      engineer units, 50–52, 58, 143, 147, 247, 255
      49th Line of Communication Sector Headquarters, 58
      Intendence Service, 54n
      Kunigami Detachment, 60, 112
      mortar units, 49–50, 52
      Nakagusuku Wan Fortress Artillery Unit, 51
      103d Sea Duty Company, 38
      sea raiding units, 52, 157, 247
      service units, 56, 58, 68, 124, 143, 157, 182, 247, 255
      transport units, 50, 58
      Udo Force, 96, 99n, 109
  Navy
    Combined Fleet, 83
    Okinawa Base Force, 11, 53, 53n, 58, 60, 60n, 144, 157, 182, 208, 227, 232
    Special Naval Landing Force, 53
    Iwao Force, 182n
    Miscellaneous, 59, 94, 124, 182, 184, 209, 212
      coast defense battery, 53
      construction troops, 52, 58, 112
      81mm mortar battery, 53
      midget submarine unit, 53, 94
      13mm AAA battery, 59
      torpedo boat squadron, 53, 60, 60n, 94
      25mm AAA battery, 59
Jichaku, 138–140, 148
Jima, 6n
Johnson, Maj J. G., 211; LtCol, 226
Johnston, R. W., 250n
Joint Assault Signal Companies (JASCO's), 264, 270
Joint Chiefs of Staff, 2, 12, 14, 17, 17n, 268
Joint Communication Activities, 266
Joint Expeditionary Force, 18–19, 34, 80, 174. See also Task forces.
Joint Staff planners, 14
Jones, Maj J. L., 42, 87, 108, 112, 260

Kadena, 8, 71, 82, 88, 262
Kadena airfield, 23, 52, 54–55, 58, 60, 69, 80, 144, 200
Kakazu, 120–122, 126, 128–131
Kakazu Ridge, 121–122, 128–131, 136, 272
Kakazu West, 122–123, 125–126
Kakibana, 216
Kamikaze, 38, 44, 47, 63, 83–86, 111, 114, 114n, 120, 122–123, 130, 135, 144–145, 160, 172, 174, 199, 203, 258–259, 261–262, 270. *See also* Air attacks, Japanese; Air units, Japanese.
Kamizato, 215–216
Kaniku, 120–122, 126–128
Kanoya, 83
Kanter, Maj G. B., 179, 200n
Karadera, 208–209, 213, 215
Kashukai, 133
Katchin Peninsula, 6, 25n, 74, 78, 87–88, 90n, 106, 110
Kawada, 95n, 107–110
Kawada Wan, 95
Keise Shima, 25, 38, 42–43, 45, 64, 82n
Kerama Retto, 6, 23–25, 34, 36, 38, 40, 40n, 41–46, 52, 58, 60, 83, 88, 90, 111, 154, 258, 269–270, 273
Kerman, Maj J. R., 218n
Kibara, 154
Kikai Shima, 23n, 266
Kiland, RAdm I. N., 18, 34, 40n, 41, 41n
Kimberly, USS, 44–45
King, FAdm E. J., 2, 12, 12n, 13, 16–17, 17n, 62, 263, 263n, 273
Kitagawa, MajGen Kiyom, 49n
Kiyamu-Gusuku, 253–255
Kiyamu Peninsula, 207–209, 215–217, 232, 244, 246, 252, 259, 271
Kiyamu Ridge, 255, 259
Kobakura, 8, 182
Kobe, 37
Kochi, 131–134, 141, 143, 148, 154, 167, 192
Kochi Ridge, 133–134, 136, 138, 141, 157
Kokuba, 8, 199, 204–206, 210, 212, 215, 229
Kokuba estuary, 203, 211, 226
Kokuba Gawa, 182, 201, 208, 211, 213, 215, 217, 220, 224, 227, 229, 231
Komesu, 208, 237, 249, 252, 254, 259
Komesu Ridge, 254
Korea, 38, 275
Korean laborers, 42
Kouri Shima, 108
Krulak, LtCol V. A., 205
Kuba, 79
Kuba Saki, 26
Kuba Shima, 40, 42
Kuhazu, 131–132, 134, 136, 138
Kumamoto, 49–50, 56n
Kume Shima, 6, 23n, 243, 259
Kunigami Gun, 54
Kunishi, 208, 236–240, 242, 244, 275
Kunishi Ridge, 234–240, 242–243, 247, 250–252, 254
Kurdzeil, LtCol E. G., 205n
Kuro Shima, 42
Kutaka Shima, 88

Kuman, 134–135, 145–146
Kuwanga, 242, 250–251
Kuwanga Ridge, 242, 251, 253
Kyushu, 2, 6, 11, 14–15, 23, 38, 44–45, 50, 56n, 83–84, 86, 144, 261–262, 273

Landing craft. *See* Ships.
Landing ships. *See* Ships.
Landing vehicles. *See* Amphibian vehicles.
Larson, LtCol A., 182n, 251
Laws, USS, 88
LCS 15, 130
LCS 33, 123
LCS 88, 160
Leahy, FAdm W. D., 14n
L-Day, 22, 24–25, 29, 38, 40, 42n, 45–46, 60, 63, 66, 69, 71–72, 78, 82, 90, 111–112, 124–126, 144, 203, 207, 255, 265
Landing Force Air Support Control Units (LAFAS-CU's), 264–265, 270. *See also* Marine units.
Leper Colony, 108
Lew Chew, 4. *See also* Ryukyus.
Leyte, 2, 14, 15, 15n, 27, 28, 31, 36, 83, 111
Leyte Gulf, 34–35, 83
Leyte Gulf, USS, 40n
Liggett, MajGen H., 49n
Lingayen Gulf, 83
Little, USS, 144
Lodge, Maj O. R., 33n, 255n, 263n
Logan Victory, SS, 85
Logistics, 27–30, 38, 55, 80–82, 92, 172–175, 233, 273. *See also* Planning.
Loochoo, 4n. *See also* Ryukyus.
Louther, Col K. K., 182n
LSM 59, 258
LSM 135, 199
LSM 195, 144
LST 447, 85
LST 557, 90
LST 884, 63
LST 990, 36n
Luce, USS, 145
Ludendorf, 49
Ludwig, Capt V. E., 105n, 146n, 233n
Luzon, 1–2, 12, 14, 14n, 15, 15n, 16–17, 17n, 28, 31, 31n, 37, 49

Mabuni, 209, 248–252, 254–255, 257, 259, 275
MacArthur, Gen Douglas, 1–2, 12, 12n, 14, 17, 37, 49, 275
Machinato, 125–126, 275
Machinato airfield, 133–137, 140, 143, 145
Machinato estuary, 126
Machisi, 198, 200–201
Madaira, 105, 107
Maeda, 131–134, 136, 141–143, 157
Maeda Escarpment, 133–134
Mae Shima, 42
Magee, LtCol J. C., Jr., 69, 150, 152–153, 162, 165, 190, 204, 239

Magee, Col V. E., 264–265

Majiya, 98, 101, 104, 107–108

Makabe, 208, 237, 242–243, 249–250, 252, 254, 256

Makabe Ridge, 254–256

Malaya, 15, 15n

Manchu, 9n

Manchuria, 49–52

Manila, 14

Manna, 95–96, 104

Marianas, 1–2, 12–15, 17, 23, 27, 31, 35–36, 36n, 37, 48, 81, 172, 273

Marine and Naval Corpsmen Medal of Honor Winners, 309–312

Marine units
  Fleet Marine Force, Pacific, (FMFPac), 30, 36n
  III Amphibious Corps, 18, 20–22, 24–28, 33–35, 63–64, 66–70, 72, 76, 78, 80, 82, 82n, 93, 93n, 104–105, 108, 110, 133–134, 141–152, 152n, 157–158, 161, 167–168, 172, 174, 174n 182, 189n, 202n, 204, 209, 213, 231, 244, 251, 254–256, 264, 271–273, 275
  V Amphibious Corps, 37, 42n, 87n, 174
  1st Provisional Marine Brigade, 33
  2d Field Service Command, 29
  1st Marine Division, 20, 25, 25n, 26, 26n, 29, 32–35, 64, 66–69, 69n, 71–74, 76, 76n, 78–79, 81, 105–106, 111, 122, 133–135, 137, 140, 143–144, 146, 148–152, 152n, 154–155, 157–158, 161, 165–167, 176, 185, 189, 189n, 192, 197–199, 202, 204, 206, 212, 215, 217, 222, 228–229, 231–233, 237, 243–246, 250, 250n, 251–252, 254, 259–260, 265, 269, 273, 275
  2d Marine Division, 18, 25, 25n, 28, 31, 33–34, 36, 63–64, 69, 243, 273
  3d Marine Division, 273
  4th Marine Division, 273
  5th Marine Division, 273
  6th Marine Division, 20, 20n, 25–26, 26n, 29, 33, 35, 46n, 66–71, 76–78, 82, 90, 91n, 92–93, 95–96, 100, 104–105, 107–108, 109n, 111, 134, 151, 154–155, 158–159, 160n, 161, 165–167, 170, 176–178, 182, 197–198, 200–201, 203, 207, 211–213, 215, 217, 219–220, 222, 228–229, 231–232, 240, 242, 252–255, 259–260, 265, 269–270, 273, 275
  1st Marines, 26, 34, 68–69, 73–74, 78, 135–136, 140, 145, 148, 151–152, 154n, 157, 159, 165, 170, 185, 188–189, 189n, 190, 191n, 195, 202, 204, 204n, 212, 229–235, 237–239, 259
  4th Marines, 26, 33, 66–70 70n, 71, 76–77, 91, 93–95, 95n, 96–104, 108, 167, 182–184, 184n, 190, 197–201, 203–204, 215, 217–222, 224–227, 229, 251–254, 275
  5th Marines, 26, 68, 68n, 69, 74, 78, 105, 137, 139–140, 148–152, 154n, 155–156, 156n, 157, 159, 165, 170, 177, 183, 185–190, 192, 199, 202, 206, 211–213, 215, 217, 229–230, 238, 242, 250, 252, 255
  7th Marines 26, 66–70, 70n, 74, 74n, 78, 90, 105, 107–108, 110, 140, 146, 151, 156n, 157, 159, 162, 167, 170, 174, 186–188, 191, 191n, 215, 220, 222, 229–233, 235–240, 243, 247, 254–255
  8th Marines, 189n, 243, 250, 250n, 252–255
  11th Marines, 32n, 33n, 68–69, 72, 121, 137, 137n, 152n, 235

Marine units—Continued
  15th Marines, 33, 68–69, 92, 100, 102, 152n, 220
  22d Marines, 26, 33, 66–70, 76–77, 91–94, 106–107, 109, 154–155, 160–161, 165–166, 171, 177, 179, 182, 182n, 183–184, 201, 204–206, 211–213, 215, 217, 222, 224, 226–227, 231–232, 240, 242, 251, 255n
  29th Marines, 26, 33–34, 67, 69–70, 77–78, 91–100, 102, 104, 107–108, 167, 171, 177–180, 182, 203–205, 211–213, 215–216, 219–222, 225–227, 247, 253–255
  1st Provisional Antiaircraft Artillery Group, 200
  2d Provisional Field Artillery Group, 26n, 32, 92, 93n, 132n
  III Corps artillery, 26, 26n, 32, 33n, 69, 72, 105, 120, 137n, 152, 152n
  III Corps Service Gorup, 82
  7th Field Depot, 36n
  Amphibious Reconnaissance Battalion, 42, 42n, 87–88, 90, 108, 112, 259
  Antiaircraft Artillery Battalions
    2d, 36n
    16th, 36n
  Armored Amphibian Battalions
    1st, 92–93, 100, 160
    3d, 146
  Artillery Battalions
    1st 155mm Howitzer, 26n, 120, 152n
    1/11, 72, 122, 136, 154, 154n
    1/15, 106, 109
    2/11, 122, 152n, 154n
    2/15, 96–97
    3d 155mm Howitzer, 32, 26n, 120, 152n
    3/11, 32n, 122, 154n
    3/15, 218
    4/11, 32n, 122
    4/15, 108–109, 184n
    6th 155mm Howitzer, 26n, 32, 120, 152n
    7th 155mm Gun, 26n, 93n, 100, 152n
    8th 155mm Gun, 26n, 32, 120, 152n
    9th 155mm Gun, 26n, 120, 152n
  Engineer Battalions
    1st, 185
    1st Separate, 36n
    6th, 72, 76, 91, 102, 155, 160, 216, 218
  Headquarters Battalion, 1st Marine Division, 191n
  Infantry Battalions
    1/1, 69, 73–74, 136, 138–140, 145–146, 148, 150–151, 155–156, 156n, 159, 161, 168, 170, 191, 206–207, 211, 229–231, 233, 235, 239, 247–248
    1/4, 70, 77, 91–92, 97–99, 101–104, 108, 183–184, 184n, 197–198, 201, 203–204, 216–218, 220–227, 253
    1/5, 66n, 68–69, 74, 140, 148–150, 152–154, 156, 158–159, 164, 190–191, 204, 206, 212, 215, 217, 239n, 250–252, 254–255
    1/7, 70n, 78, 105, 140, 156, 156n, 157, 159, 163–165, 167–168, 170, 170n, 186, 188, 231, 233, 235–240, 242, 250, 259, 260
    1/8, 243, 250
    1/22, 67, 76–77, 95, 100–104, 107n, 108–110, 155, 159–161, 165–166, 170–171, 177–179, 181–182, 198, 205, 211, 213, 220, 224–226, 242–243, 251

Marine units—Continued
Infantry Battalions—Continued
1/29, 68–70, 76, 76n, 77, 94–96, 99, 103, 171, 177–178, 180–181, 201, 204–205, 205n, 206, 211–212, 219, 222, 227, 227n, 228, 253, 255
2/1, 69, 73–74, 108, 140, 146, 148, 150–152, 155–156, 161–162, 165, 167, 170, 189, 189n, 190–191, 204, 206–207, 211, 230–235, 237–239, 239n
2/4, 26, 68, 77, 91–92, 97–99, 101–104, 108, 177, 182–184, 197, 199–201, 201n, 203–204, 216–219, 221–222, 224–227, 253, 255
2/5, 74, 137–141, 148–150, 152–153, 156, 159, 163, 185–190, 211–212, 217, 229–230, 238–240, 242, 251–252, 254–256
2/7, 68, 70n, 78, 105–106, 140, 146, 146n, 151, 154, 159, 163–165, 168, 170, 188, 215, 231–233, 235–240, 242
2/8, 243, 250, 252
2/22, 67, 76–77, 95, 108, 109n, 154–155, 160–162, 165–166, 171, 171n, 172, 176–177, 201, 203, 205, 211–212, 224–227, 242, 251, 255
2/29, 94–95, 98–99, 103–104, 177, 180–182, 219–222, 227, 227n, 253
3/1, 69n, 73, 78, 107–108, 139–140, 148–152, 154n, 155, 159, 162, 162n, 165, 167, 170, 188, 190–191, 204, 206, 207, 211, 229, 233, 239
3/2, 63
3/4, 66, 70, 91–92, 95–98, 100–104, 108–110, 182–184, 184n, 197–198, 200, 200n, 203–204, 218–227, 251, 253, 254n, 255
3/5, 68–69, 73–74, 88, 106, 137, 139–140, 146n, 149–150, 152–153, 156–157, 159, 185, 199, 204, 204n, 206, 212, 215, 217, 239n, 240, 242, 251–252, 254, 256
3/7, 68, 74, 74n, 78, 105, 107, 149, 153, 156, 156n, 157, 159, 163, 167, 186, 188, 188n, 191n, 215, 217, 230, 230n, 231–233, 240, 242–243, 250, 252
3/8, 243, 250, 252
3/22, 67, 76–77, 95–98, 108–110, 154–155, 159–161, 165–166, 170–171, 177–179, 200, 200n, 201, 203, 211–212, 222, 224–226, 242, 251
3/29, 94–101, 103–104, 166–167, 171–172, 177–182, 204–206, 219–222, 227, 227n
6th Motor Transport Battalion, 205n
1st Pioneer Battalion, 110
1st Provisional Military Police Battalion, 36n
Tank Battalions
1st, 66, 135, 138, 185, 237, 239
2d, 250
6th, 66, 76, 95, 160–161, 218, 218n, 219–221
46th Replacement Draft, 189n
Division Reconnaissance Companies
1st, 74, 74n, 78, 217, 231
6th, 70, 76–77, 91–92, 92n, 95, 108, 177, 198, 201–202, 205, 213, 216, 218, 228
LAFASCU–1, 36n, 264
LAFASCU–2, 264
LAFASCU–3, 264

Marine units—Continued
Regimental Weapons Companies
4th, 92, 97–98, 101, 218, 253n
7th, 105
22d, 217
III Corps Air Delivery Section, 265, 270
III Corps Evacuation Hospitals
No. 2, 36n
No. 3, 145
Marshalls, 1, 36, 48
Mashiki, 79–80
Mason, Col A. T., 152, 152n, 155, 162n, 188, 190–191, 204, 204n, 206, 211, 230
Masuya, 70
Matsumoto, Capt K., 85n
McCain, VAdm J. S., 37
McDonnell, 1stLt P. I., 191n
McMillan, G. J., 33n
Measurement ton, 82, 82n
Medeera, 208, 249–252, 254–255, 259
Medical. See also Casualties
evacuation, 28, 73, 102, 109, 162, 165, 184, 217, 220, 231–232, 238, 240
hospitals, 110
surgery wards, 145
wound classification, 28
Meka, 213, 245
Mezado, 208, 236, 240, 242–244, 251
Mezado Ridge, 236, 238–139, 242, 250–251
Mikado, 4
Military government, 243, 266, 268–269
Miller, Col F. D., 42n
Miller, LtCol J. C., Jr., 68n, 146n, 204n
Milliken, 1stLt F. A., 73n
Minami, 120
Minami-Uebaru, 143
Minatoga, 60, 63, 114, 244–245
Minatoga beaches, 25, 44–45, 60, 64, 69, 69n, 126, 142
Mindanao, 2, 12, 14–15, 15n
Mines. See Weapons, Japanese.
Ming Dynasty, 4
Minister for Foreign Affairs, Japanese, 6
Minna Shima, 112, 116
Missouri, USS, 275
Mitscher, VAdm M. A., 37–38, 43, 85, 126
Miyagusuku, 134–135, 138–140
Miyako Jima, 23n, 49, 51n, 266
M. L. Abele, USS, 123
Momobaru, 110
Monahan, LtCol J. S., 191n
Moore, MajGen J. T., 200n
Moreau, LtCol J. W., 68, 178
Morotai, 2
Morrison, USS, 4n, 145
Motobu Peninsula, 6, 26, 53–54, 60, 78, 92–94, 94n, 95–97, 104–105, 107n, 108–112, 268–269
Motor transport. See Supply; Vehicles.
Mt Yae Take, 96–97, 99, 99n, 101–102, 104, 106
Mueller, MajGen P., 18
Mukue Gawa, 233

Mulcahy, MajGen F. P., 18, 27, 200n, 261–262
Murray, LtCol J. C., Jr., 69, 135, 138–140, 148, 155–156
Myers, Maj T. J., 67, 177, 177n

Nagahama, 70
Nagasaki, 274
Nago, 8, 55, 82, 92, 94, 94n, 108, 275
Nago Wan, 93, 96, 106
Nagoya, 37
Nagusuku, 208
Naha, 7–8, 27, 37, 40, 48, 53–55, 57–58, 142–144, 161,
    165–166, 168, 178, 182, 190, 196–199, 201–205, 207,
    210–211, 213, 215–217, 219, 229, 259
Naha airfield, 219, 221, 223
Naha canal, 204–205
Naha harbor, 219, 222, 227
Nakadomari, 76–77, 91, 91n, 92, 105
Nakagasuku Wan, 21, 27, 60, 74, 76, 87–88, 90, 173, 196
Nakama, 129, 132
Nakanishi, 135, 139
Nakaoshi, 92–94, 106, 108
Nakaza, 245, 248
Nansei Shoto, 2, 6, 11, 48–49, 62, 275
Narashido, 94
Naval aviation. See Aircraft; Air support.
Naval Construction Battalion. See Engineer opera-
    tions; Naval units; Seabees.
Naval Gunfire, 23–24, 26–27, 32n, 33–34, 41, 43–45, 45n,
    46, 56, 63–64, 71, 90, 93, 97–99, 102, 103n, 104, 111–
    112, 114, 117, 122–125, 136, 145, 147, 149–152, 156,
    160–161, 170, 177, 186, 202, 204, 209, 217, 228, 232,
    237, 239, 243, 245–246, 248–249, 270, 273
Naval Units. See also Naval gunfire; Ships; Task
    forces; Task groups.
    Pacific Fleet, 1, 12n, 37, 260
    Third Fleet, 203
    Fifth Fleet, 17, 19, 25, 37, 63n, 86, 203
    Naval Forces, Ryukyus, 261
    Service Squadron Ten, 174
    Transron 12, 35
    Transron 15, 36, 36n
    Transron 18, 35
    Mine Group One, 43
    Transport Division 50, 111
    58th Naval Construction Battalion (NCB), 176
    11th Special Naval Construction Battalion, 174n
    Underwater Demolition Group Able, 40n, 44–45
    Underwater Demolition Group Baker, 45
    Underwater Demolition Team 7, 88.
Navy Unit Commendations, 313–315
Neuffer, Maj. R. P., 178, 180, 201, 205n
Nevada, USS, 45n
New Caledonia, 27
New Guinea, 1–2, 48
New Hebrides, 31
New Orleans, USS, 202
New York, USS, 120, 147, 202
Nimitz, Adm C. W., 1–2, 12, 12n, 13–14, 16–17, 17n, 18–
    19, 37, 62, 203, 261, 268
Nimmer, BrigGen D. R., 26n, 32, 152n

Nippa, RAdm Teizo, 53n
Nishibaru, 121–122, 126, 128–131
Nishibaru Ridge, 126, 129, 131
Nishikoku beaches, 215, 217
Nodake, 79
North China, 275
Northern Attack Force, 18, 26, 28, 34–35, 47, 103n, 111.
    See also Task forces.
Northern Tractor Flotilla, 36
North Pacific, 2–3, 12n

Oahu, 27, 30, 35, 172
Okinawa, 2–4, 6, 6n, 7, 7n, 8, 9n, 11, 11n, 14–17, 19, 19n,
    20–21, 21n, 23, 24n, 25–28, 31–32, 34–38, 43–46, 48–
    55, 56n, 58, 60, 62–63, 69, 72, 73n, 74, 76n, 78, 80–84,
    85n, 86, 88, 90, 95, 97, 99, 105–108, 110–111, 118, 123,
    130, 133–135, 139, 142, 144, 150, 154, 172–175, 179,
    185, 199–200, 207, 210, 216, 229, 233, 235, 243–245,
    250–251, 256–259, 261–262, 264, 266, 268–275
    government, 6, 8–9, 71
    history, 3–6, 9n, 71
    population, 4, 6, 8–9, 9n, 50, 56–57, 59, 71–72, 74, 78,
        87–88, 93–94, 96, 105–108, 109n, 112, 118, 182, 234,
        240, 243, 251–252, 254–255, 257, 267–268, 275
    railroads, 8, 140, 159, 161–162, 180, 187–188 210, 246
    road network, 7–8, 68, 72, 76–77, 79–80, 91, 97, 105–106,
        138, 157, 192, 198, 202, 207, 213, 220, 245, 267
    terrain, 6–9, 11, 26, 31, 66, 77, 91–94 96–99, 101–103,
        105, 109–112, 120, 134, 138, 151, 154–157, 159–160,
        164–166, 180, 182, 184, 186, 191, 194, 197–198, 205,
        225, 227–228, 235, 246, 248
    vegetation, 6–8, 68, 98, 106, 121, 242
    weather, 20, 82, 90, 122–123, 133, 138, 154, 184–185,
        191–192, 196–197, 199, 201–202, 205, 209–211, 215–
        216, 218–220, 228–230, 254, 272
Okinawa Gunto, 6, 11, 20–21, 23n, 44, 46, 52, 114, 243,
    259, 265–266, 275
Okinawa Ken, 56n
Okino Daito, 23n
Oldendorf, VAdm J. B., 18n
OLYMPIC, 273–274
Onaga, 131–134, 143, 148
100-fathom curve, 43
Onna, 77–78, 105
Onna Take, 269
Ono Yama, 216, 218–220
Ora, 92–94, 95n, 108
Oroku, 220, 224, 226–227
Oroku airfield, 60, 213, 215, 220
Oroku-Mura, 220–221
Oroku Peninsula, 60, 143, 182, 209, 213, 215, 217–222,
    225, 229, 232, 244, 247, 253, 275
Osaka, 37
Osumi Gunto, 6
Ota, RAdm Minoru, 53, 53n, 60n, 143–144, 182, 209, 227,
    229
Ouki, 120, 122, 126–127
Oyashi, 70
Oyama, 143–145
Ozato, 54, 198, 233–234, 237, 248–249

Pacific Northwest, 3
Pacific Ocean Areas, 12n, 19
Palaus, 12–13, 15, 37. *See also* Peleliu.
Patrols. *See* Tactics.
Paul Hamilton, USS, 88
Pavuvu, 32n, 33
Pearl Harbor, 14, 17, 114n, 261
Peiping, 275
Peleliu, 2, 32, 32n, 53
Pensacola, USS, 88
Perry, Como M. C., 3–4
Pescadores, 16
Philippines, 1–2, 12–14, 14n, 15, 17, 37, 48–49, 52, 60, 83, 273, 275
Picket screen, 82–83, 85, 114, 145, 199, 243, 258. *See also* Ships, American.
Pinckney, USS, 135
"The Pinnacle", 240
Pitt, USS, 36n, 40n
Planning
    air, 27
    base development, 27–28, 30, 266, 274
    concept, 23
    logistical, 15, 25n, 27–29, 172
    naval, 27, 46
    tactical, 22–28
Poland, Maj F. W., Jr., 204, 204n, 212
Post, MajGen E. D., 17n
Potsdam Declaration, 274
Powell, 1stLt R. J., 74
Preston, USS, 95
Prince of Satsuma, 4
Pringle, USS, 114n
Prisoners of war, 90, 211, 252, 253n, 254
Psychological warfare teams, 251
Pyle, Ernie, 117n

Radar. *See* Communications.
Rabaul, 2
Radio Tokyo, 69
Randle, BrigGen E. H., 116, 118
Rawlings, VAdm Sir B., 45
Razorback Ridge, 167
Rehearsals, 30–34
Reifsnider, RAdm L. F., 18, 34–35, 103n, 111, 114, 143
Reorganization of Marine divisions, 94n
Replacements
    American, 32, 82n, 125, 159, 171, 204, 212, 260, 272–273
    Japanese, 124, 141, 209
Richardson, LtGen R. C., Jr., 16
Rineer, Capt F. D. 156
Roads. *See* Okinawa.
Robb, LtCol W. G., 180–181
Roberts, Col H. C., 182, 182n, 251
Rocky Crags, 127–131
Roi, 36, 36n
Roosevelt, President, 1, 14
Ross, LtCol R. P., Jr., 156, 156n, 191, 204, 206, 211, 229–230

Roth, Maj M. C., 68n, 139n
Russells, 27, 29, 32–33, 35
Russo-Japanese War, 49
Rutland, USS, 88
Ryukyus, 4, 6, 8, 14–17, 19–20, 23, 23n, 37, 48–49, 203, 261, 263, 266, 268, 275

Sabol, LtCol S. V., 135, 138–139, 148, 151, 162n, 191, 191n
Saidor, 1
Saipan, 13, 16, 27–28, 31–33, 35–36, 36n, 124, 172
Sakishima Gunto, 6, 44–45, 60n, 83, 264
Samar, 2
Samuel Chase, USS, 36n, 40n
San Francisco, 13, 17
Sangamon, USS, 145
Sarasota, USS, 111
Sasebo Naval Barracks, 53n
Satsumas, 4
Scaling ladders, 136
Schmidt, MajGen H., 263n
Schneider, Col M. F., 67, 77, 110, 160, 177, 179, 182n
Schofield Barracks, 30
Scott, LtCol J. W., Jr., 202
Seabees, 6n, 28, 80. *See also* Naval units.
Secretary of the Navy, 273
Senaga Shima, 221, 228
Senior Officer Present Afloat (SOPA), 18, 18n
Sesoko Shima, 108
Shana Wan, 95
Shansi Province, 50
Shanghai, 13, 53n
Shapley, Col A., 67, 70, 91, 97, 104, 109, 183, 201, 215, 218, 221–222, 251, 255
Shea, USS, 145
Sheetz, BrigGen J. R., 25, 120, 122n, 127n
Shelburne, LtCol C. W., 140, 149, 153, 158, 206, 250, 252, 254
Shepherd, MajGen L. C., Jr., 25, 33, 46, 67, 69, 77, 95–96, 96n, 103n, 107, 154, 161, 167, 177n, 178, 182, 184, 198, 201, 203, 213, 215, 222, 228, 251, 253, 255, 271; Gen, 20n, 92n
Sherman, Capt F. P., 17
Sherman, Maj N. R., 242n
Sherrod, R., 261n
Shichina, 199, 203, 212–213
Shikoku Island, 38
Shima, 6n
Shimabuku, 123
Shimajiri, 38
Shinazato, 203
Shindawaku, 229–230, 233, 245
Shipping. *See* Planning, logistical.
Ships
    American
        barges, 81–82, 174
        battleships, 41, 45–46, 64, 83, 114, 123, 125–127, 145, 160, 202, 218, 238, 270–271
        cargo vessels, 28, 36, 43, 72, 82–83, 114n, 160
        control vessels, 34, 64, 80–81, 88

Ships—Continued
  American—Continued
    cruisers, 41, 45–46, 64, 88, 125–127, 145, 160, 202, 218, 270
    destroyers, 41, 44–45, 64, 82–83, 85, 88, 114, 114n, 123, 125–127, 130, 135, 144–145, 160, 199, 203, 218
    destroyer escorts, 85, 114n, 123, 258
    escort carriers, 27, 35, 83, 145, 262–265
    fast carriers, 1, 27, 60, 83–85, 261
    gunboats, 41n, 44–45, 64, 114, 145
    hospital ships, 28, 28n, 135
    landing craft, 25, 40, 40n, 41n, 45, 45n, 63, 66, 80–81, 82n, 83, 114n, 123, 126, 135, 144–145, 251
    landing ships, 28, 36, 40–41, 63–64, 66, 80–82, 82n, 88, 90, 116, 123, 145, 172, 243, 258
    mine vessels, 40, 43–46, 83, 85, 87, 114n, 144–145
    mortar gunboats, 41n, 88, 114
    reconnaissance boats, 87, 108, 215
    repair vessels, 43, 45
    rocket craft, 41n, 237
    seaplane tender, 258
    submarines, 2, 37, 50, 86
    support craft, 41, 64, 82, 145, 147, 166, 177, 221, 270
    transports, 28, 34, 36, 44, 63, 72, 82–83, 84n, 87–88, 111, 114, 116, 172
  Japanese, 42n, 45, 58, 60, 85–86, 144–146, 166
Shisler, LtCol C. W., 200, 200n, 211, 226, 242
Shofner, LtCol A. C., 156n, 230, 230n, 235
Shore party, 80, 82, 82n, 172, 174, 273
Shoto, 6n
Shukan, 4n
Shuri, 7–8, 11n, 38, 54–60, 90, 118–119, 125–126, 128, 132, 134, 140–143, 147, 149, 151, 155, 157, 160, 164–165, 167–168, 170–174, 176, 180, 182–185, 189–199, 202–204, 206–210, 212–213, 228–230, 245, 271–272
Shuri Castle, 143, 190, 206–207, 209, 211
Shuri Ridge, 190–191, 204, 206
Shutts, Sgt K. A., 76n
Sino-Japanese War of 1894, 6
Skyline Ridge, 127–131
Smith, Col A. D., 115–117
Smith, LtGen H. M., 263n
Smith, R. R., 52n, 53n
Snedeker, Col E. W., 68, 74, 74n, 140, 157, 165, 188, 215, 217, 236; BrigGen, 36n, 105n
Sobe, 68, 145
Solomons, 1, 31–32, 35, 48
South China Coast, 37, 48
South China Sea, 15n
Southern Attack Force, 18, 28, 34, 47. See also Task forces.
South Pacific, 12n, 31
Southern Tractor Flotilla, 36
Southwest Pacific, 2, 11, 12n, 15
Spruance, Adm R. A., 2, 2n, 16–17, 17n, 18n, 19, 37, 45, 174, 203
Staging area, 36
Stilwell, Gen J. W., 259–261, 275
Stockman, Capt. J. R., 230n
Straits of Tsushima, 3

Strategy, 1–2, 12–13, 15–17
Supply
  American, 133, 184, 188, 220, 238, 267
    aerial delivery. See Air support.
    dumps, 80, 82, 106–107, 110, 172, 174, 185, 198, 211, 217, 232–233, 273–274
    movement of supplies, 69, 72, 80, 102, 106, 196, 198, 201–202, 211, 215, 217, 229, 267
    problems, 74, 76–77, 91, 99, 102–104, 172, 197, 199, 216, 230–232
    resupply, 27, 65, 85n, 111, 172–173
    unloading, 80–82
  Japanese, 94, 103, 127, 143, 182
Support Air Direction Net. See Communications.
Supreme Allied Commander, 275
Suzuki, MajGen Shigeru, 208
Sunabe, 54
Support Craft Flotilla, 41n. See also Ships, American.
Suriago, 14
Swallow, USS, 130

Tactics
  American
    armor, 76–77, 91, 191
    counterbattery, 25, 98. See also Artillery, American.
    flame thrower, 154, 194
    liaison, 46n, 186
    mopping up activities, 118, 139, 194, 210–212, 229, 238–240, 242, 252, 254–255, 259, 273
    original scheme of maneuver, 22–23
    patrolling, 31, 71, 73–74, 74n, 77–79, 91–92, 95–100, 102, 104–106, 108, 125, 131, 133, 137–139, 149, 154–155, 159, 166, 185–186, 193–194, 197–199, 202–203, 211–213, 224–225, 229, 231, 233, 237–239, 247, 260
    reconnaissance, 31, 45, 73, 76–78, 87, 92–93, 108–109, 112, 134, 138, 198, 213, 230, 236, 261
    reinforcements, 146, 159, 236
    ridge-hopping, 102
    screening smoke, 64, 84–85, 114, 138–139, 152, 158–159, 167, 178, 186, 223, 233, 233, 238, 240, 246, 250
  Japanese
    ambushes, 73, 94, 108n
    counterattacks, 42, 94, 101, 108, 120, 122–124, 127, 129, 134, 136, 141, 143–144, 149–153, 158, 164–165, 167, 170–171, 177–178, 180, 182, 184, 194, 196, 201, 204, 226, 234–235, 239, 242–243, 246, 248
    counterlandings, 146, 166
    demolitions, 94, 94n, 106, 144, 159, 187, 200
    doctrine, 21
    guerrilla operations, 57, 99, 104–109, 109n, 110, 251
    infiltration, 57, 73, 116, 128, 134, 139, 158, 167, 170, 182, 185, 201, 204, 219, 227, 235, 248, 251, 253
    reinforcements, 37, 153, 157, 178, 199
    screening smoke, 238
    sniping, 68, 70, 95, 106, 118, 165, 167, 201, 211–212, 217, 219, 240, 251–252, 254
    withdrawal, 202, 207–209

Taira, 106–107, 109–110
Takabanare Shima, 88
Takamotoji, 178.
Takanyuta, 231
Talaud, 14
Tamikamiya, 224
Tanabaru, 126–131, 143, 149
Tanabaru Ridge, 131
Tanzola, Col V. J., 111
Tarawa, 60
Target Information Center, 270
Task forces
  TF 31, 203, 259, 261
  TF 34, 270
  TF 38, 37
  TF 51, 18, 26, 83, 84n, 85, 114n, 123, 125, 130, 145, 160, 174–175, 203
  TF 52, 40n, 43–46, 60
  TF 53, 18, 36, 103n, 111
  TF 54, 18, 43, 46, 60, 270
  TF 55, 18
  TF 56, 18
  TF 57, 18n, 45, 83
  TF 58, 18n, 36–38, 40n, 43–44, 83–86, 114n, 126–127, 160
  TF 59, 43
Task groups
  TG 51.1, 41, 87
  TG 51.19, 88
  TG 51.2, 33
  TG, 51.21, 111, 114
Task Organization, III Amphibious Corps, 298–301
Tengan, 74
Tennessee, USS, 103
Tera, 215–216, 229, 233–236
Terrain. See Caves; Japanese defenses; Okinawa.
Teton, USS, 34
Threadfin, USS, 86
Tientsin, 275
Tinian, 17, 35, 36n
Tiscornia, Capt E. R., 140n
Tjisdane, SS, 160
Toan, 50
Toguchi, 94–97, 99, 102–104, 107
Tokara Gunto, 6
Tokashiki Shima, 38, 41–42, 44
Tokuno Shima, 23n
Tokuyama, 86
Tokyo, 2, 6, 14, 37, 48, 50, 56, 273
Toma, 220
Tolman, USS, 60, 60n
Tombs, 127, 149, 165, 167, 188, 206. See also Okinawa, terrain.
Tombstone Ridge, 127–129
Tomigusuku, 53, 226, 227
Tomui, 213, 245–246
Tomusu, 209, 229, 231
Tori Shima, 243
Toyama, 216
Toyama Maru, 50, 50n

Toyoda, Adm Soemu, 83, 85n, 86, 130
Training, 30–34
Transport Quartermasters, 36
Transports. See Ships.
Trilling, Sgt P., 76n
Truk, 2
Tsingtao, 275
T–6 flotation devices, 64, 64n, 66
Tsugen, 87–88, 90
Tsugen Shima, 87, 90, 90n, 125
Tsukasan, 54, 208, 212–213, 215, 217, 230
Tsuwa, 144
Turner, VAdm R. K., 16, 18, 23, 24n, 25, 27, 34, 63, 69, 80–82, 85, 87, 95, 111, 126–127, 174–175, 243, 263

Uchima, 138, 140, 155
Uchitomari, 79–80, 121–123, 125, 140
Udo, Col Takehiko, 60, 96, 99, 104, 112, 254, 255
Uebaru, 120
Uibaru, 225
Ulithi, 2, 18, 24n, 27, 35–38, 43
Unaha, 133
Underwater demolitions, 40, 43, 45, 45n, 46, 46n, 88, 114. See also Naval units.
United Nations, 275
Unten-Ko, 53, 60, 94, 96
Urasoe-Mura Escarpment, 125–126, 128–131, 133, 136, 142, 144, 148, 151
Ushijima, LtGen Mitsuru, 49, 52, 54, 69n, 142–143, 149–150, 208–209, 227, 236, 236n, 244, 248, 251–252, 258

Vehicles
  American, 72, 80, 91. See also Amphibian vehicles.
    armored bulldozers, 77, 91, 122, 165, 168, 183, 221, 225, 237, 241, 253–254
    bulldozers, 198
    jeeps, 72, 91, 110
    trailers, 72, 105
    trucks, 72, 77, 80, 97, 110, 202, 208, 210, 154n, 166
  Japanese, 94, 105, 108, 115, 202

Wachtler, Col W. A., 110
Wada, MajGen Kosuke, 51, 144, 208
Waldorf, LtCol H. A., 250
Walker, Maj A., 70, 77, 92, 201, 205, 213, 215, 228
Wallace, MajGen F. C., 82, 174, 243, 250, 266, 268–269
Wallace, LtCol P. E., 252
Wallace, BrigGen W. J., 261–262
Wana, 161, 165, 168, 170, 185, 188, 190
Wana Draw, 165, 167, 176, 185–191, 204, 206, 211, 212
Wana Ridge, 162, 165, 168, 170, 185–192, 207
War Department, 268
War dogs, 94n, 106, 108
War Ministry, Japanese, 53
Washburn, Maj R. T., 256
Washington, D. C., 62
Wasp, USS, 38
Watanabe, LtGen Hasao, 49n
Watson, MajGen T. E., 18, 36

Western Islands Attack Group, 18, 28, 34, 40. *See also* Task groups.

Weapons

  American

    antiaircraft guns, 63, 83, 144–145, 200, 203, 258, 271

    armored flame throwers, 134, 138, 150, 152, 159, 161, 164, 188, 190, 193, 238, 240, 246–248, 254–257, 272

    assault guns (M–7's), 105, 116, 128, 130, 134, 139, 151, 152, 154n, 155, 167, 185, 188, 190, 205, 217–218, 221–222, 225–226, 271

    bazookas, 167, 206

    bayonets, 118

    depth charges, 44

    8-inch howitzers, 127, 147, 180, 271

    81mm mortars, 95–96, 140, 159, 166, 186, 226, 233, 238–239, 272

    explosive charges, 138, 161

    5-inch guns, 41, 44, 46, 174, 270

    flame throwers, 117, 161, 163, 183–184, 188, 227

    4.2-inch mortars, 64, 129, 167, 186, 217, 256, 272

    14-inch guns, 120, 147

    grenades, 101, 117, 118, 124, 163, 171, 176, 190, 201, 217

    machine guns, 170, 232, 256

    mortars, 42, 123, 138, 146–147, 152, 156, 170, 188, 190, 201, 202, 211, 232, 238–240, 242–243, 256–257

    105mm howitzers, 41, 66, 96

    155mm guns, 43, 82n, 147, 271

    155mm howitzers, 130, 147, 271

    recoilless rifles, 246

    rockets, 41, 125, 147, 153, 166, 190, 211, 217, 237, 239–240, 249, 255

    75mm howitzers, 66, 127, 154, 160, 170, 271

    16-inch guns, 174, 180

    60mm mortars, 101

    small arms, 123–124, 167, 238

    supporting weapons, 117, 120, 122, 148, 151, 172, 186, 193–194, 197, 204, 225, 232, 235, 247

    tanks, 57, 63–64, 64n, 66, 70, 77, 79–80, 91, 116–117, 120, 122, 128, 128n, 130–131, 133–134, 137–138, 150–155, 158–163, 165–168, 170–171, 177–180, 183–191, 193–194, 198, 201, 205, 208–209, 212, 217, 220–223, 225, 228, 234–240, 242, 245–252, 254–256, 272–273

    37mm AT guns, 167, 189, 217, 220, 222, 225–226

    torpedoes, 86

    20mm cannon, 44, 147

    240mm howitzers, 271

  Japanese

    antiaircraft guns, 15, 46, 52, 86, 128, 244

    antitank guns, 50, 59, 80, 115, 120, 126, 138, 152, 161, 180, 186, 235, 238, 250

    automatic weapons, 166, 171, 178, 182, 185, 219–222, 224

    baka bombs, 123, 145

    coast-defense guns, 11, 24, 26, 45n, 55, 103

    8-inch rockets, 219

Weapons—Continued

  Japanese—Continued

    18-inch rifles, 85n

    81mm mortars, 50, 52, 59, 88

    47mm antitank guns, 50–52, 88, 137, 151, 171, 186, 211, 240

    grenades, 101, 106, 110, 117, 123–124, 128, 138, 144, 167, 171, 181, 184, 188, 198, 200, 227, 238, 244, 246

    "Idiot-sticks", 110, 110n, 112

    machine cannon, 52–53, 71, 74, 94, 102, 138, 217, 219, 221

    machine-guns, 87–88, 94–95, 97–99, 102, 105, 115–116, 117n, 119, 121–123, 127–130, 133, 138–141, 158–161, 164–168, 170–176, 178–179, 186, 188, 190–195, 198, 202, 204–206, 211–212, 215, 217–220, 222–223, 225, 230, 232, 238, 244, 246, 248, 250, 252–256

    mines, 45, 91, 94, 104, 106, 112, 115–120, 128, 135, 140, 159, 166, 179–180, 183, 187, 200, 212, 218–219, 221, 224, 240, 248

    mortars, 42, 52, 59, 64, 66, 74, 79, 88, 90, 94, 97–99, 101–102, 105–106, 108, 115–116, 119–123, 127–128, 133–134, 136, 138, 140, 144, 147, 149, 151, 158–159, 162, 164–168, 170–171, 176, 178–188, 190–191, 193–195, 198, 200–202, 204, 206, 211–212, 217, 219–220, 222–225, 230, 234–236, 238, 240, 244–245, 247–248, 250, 253–254

    90mm guns, 157

    90mm mortars, 52n, 124, 238

    150mm guns, 43, 52, 224

    150mm howitzers, 52, 177, 244

    120mm guns, 53, 220

    rifles, 71, 88, 94, 98, 105, 114, 123, 127, 136, 160, 166–167, 178, 185, 188, 204–205, 212, 215, 220, 223, 230, 233–234, 238, 246, 250, 256

    satchel charges, 117, 120, 128, 166, 253

    70mm howitzers, 50, 124

    75mm guns, 11, 50–52, 88, 99, 101, 112, 124, 225

    6-inch guns, 88, 220

    small arms, 66, 70, 74, 101–102, 133–134, 141, 159, 165–166, 178, 186–187, 190, 194, 201, 204, 206, 211, 238–240, 254

    tanks, 51, 149, 157, 202

    3-inch guns, 220

    320mm spigot mortars, 52, 122

    torpedoes, 84

Weather. *See* Okinawa.

Western Pacific, 13, 37

Whaling, Col W. J., 99, 99n, 180, 212, 219, 253

Whitehead, Capt R. F., USN, 127

Whitehill, Cdr W. M., 12n

Window, 145

Winn, Col W. S., 88

Woodhouse, LtCol H. F. Jr., 67, 161, 166, 171, 176–177, 203, 211

Woods, MajGen L. E., 262, 266

Wright, LtCol E. A., 178, 222

Wright, RAdm J., 18

Wycoff, Maj D. P., 170n

Yabuchi Shima, 78
Yaeju Dake, 207–208, 245–249
Yaeju Dake-Yuza Dake Escarpment, 244, 249, 259
Yafusu, 133–134, 148
Yagachi Shima, 94, 108
Yahara, Col Hiromichi, 54, 55n, 123–124, 143–144, 150, 236n, 251
Yaka, 91
Yakabi Shima, 40, 40n, 41–46
Yakada, 77, 91
Yakamaru, Maj, 55n
Yamadadobaru, 94
Yamato, 85, 85n, 86
Yanaga, C., 4n
Yap, 2
Yeaton, LtCol S. S., 205n
Yellow Sea, 3
Yofuke, 96–97
Yokoi, RAdm T., 83n

Yokosuka Naval Base, 275
Yonabaru, 8, 25, 54–55, 58, 126, 142–143, 192–196, 198–199, 202–203, 207–208, 210, 213, 215, 229, 259
Yonabaru airfield, 120, 133, 147
Yonawa, 198–199
Yontan airfield, 23, 25–26, 52, 54–55, 58, 60, 64, 67, 70n, 71–72, 76, 76n, 77–78, 80, 82, 144, 200, 262, 266–267
Yorktown, USS, 38
Yoron Shima, 6
Yunagusuku, 208–209
Yuza, 232–235, 246–249
Yuza Dake, 207–208, 235–236, 245–249, 255
Yuza Hill, 235, 239

Zamami Shima, 38, 40–41, 41n, 42–43
Zampa-Misaki, 60n, 69, 70, 76n
Zawa, 232–233
Zimmerman, Maj J. L., 33n

U. S. GOVERNMENT PRINTING OFFICE: 1955